PASSING LINES
SEXUALITY AND IMMIGRATION

D1637187

Brad Epps, Keja Valens, & Bill Johnson González

Published by Harvard University
David Rockefeller Center for Latin American Studies

Distributed by Harvard University Press
Cambridge, Massachusetts
London, England
2005

Library of Congress Cataloging-in-Publication Data

Passing lines : sexuality and immigration / [edited by] Brad Epps, Keja

Valens, and Bill Johnson González.
    p. cm.
  Includes bibliographical references and index.
  ISBN-13: 978-0-674-01885-3
  ISBN-10: 0-674-01885-0
  1. Gays—Government policy—United States. 2.
Immigrants—Government policy—United States. 3.
Immigrants—United States—Sexual behavior. 4.
Emigration and immigration law—United States.
5. United States—Emigration and
immigration—Government policy. 6. Latin America—Emigration and
immigration. I. Epps, Bradley S. II. Valens, Keja, 1972– III. Johnson
González, Bill, 1970–
    HQ76.3.U5P37 2005
    304.8'086'640973--dc22
                        2005018971

For David, Blanca, and Clelia

Contents

Kathleen M. Coll
Stanford University; Feminist Studies

Norma Mogrovejo
Universidad de la Ciudad de México; Centro de Documentación
y Archivo Histórico Lésbico de México "Nancy Cárdenas"

Heloisa Maria Galvão
Brazilian Women's Group; Community Field
Coordinator, Boston Public Schools

ACKNOWLEDGMENTS

We would like to thank John H. Coatsworth, director of the David Rockefeller Center for Latin American Studies at Harvard University, for his backing of the initial conference, Passing Lines, that was the seed for this book, and for his continued support for this project.

We would also like to thank June Carolyn Erlick for her unwavering support, intelligence, and good humor. This project would not have been possible without her.

ABOUT THE CONTRIBUTORS

Laura Aguilar is a self-taught photographer. She was born in California, where she continues to live and work. Aguilar's photographs have won numerous awards, including the Anonymous Was a Woman Award in 2000, the California Community Foundation's J. Paul Getty Grant for the Visual Arts in 1998, and the California Arts Council Artist in Residence Grant 1991–1994. Aguilar's work has been on exhibit in solo shows at Susanne Vielmetter Los Angeles Projects in Los Angeles, California, at ArtPace in San Antonio, Texas, and at the Fundació "la Caixa" in Barcelona, Spain. Aguilar's work has also been exhibited in numerous group shows, including "Only Skin Deep: Changing Visions of the American Self" curated by Brian Wallis and Coco Fusco at the International Center of Photography, "Fat Attitudes: An Exploration of an American Subculture and the Representation of the Female Body" at Columbia University, and "Fusion: A Los Angeles LGBT People of Color Film Festival" in Los Angeles, California.

Deborah Anker has been practicing, writing, and teaching in the fields of immigration and refugee law for over twenty years. She now is Jeremiah Smith, Jr. Lecturer on Law, and Director of the Immigration and Refugee Clinical Program at Harvard Law School. Anker has litigated refugee cases before asylum adjudicators at all administrative levels in the federal courts, and has filed amicus curiae briefs in the U.S. Supreme Court in many of the major refugee cases heard by the Court over the last fifteen years. She has developed training programs for immigration judges and asylum officers on U.S. asylum law and authored the leading treatise in the field, *The Law of Asylum in the United States*, which is now in its third, most comprehensive edition. She has directed ground-breaking empirical studies of the asylum and refugee determination processes and received numerous awards for her work, including, along with her colleagues, the Founders Award of the American Immigration Lawyers Association for the work of the Women Refugees Project. The Project drafted the historic U.S. Gender Asylum guidelines, spearheading the development of gender asylum law in the United States, and greatly advancing its development internationally.

Angélica Cházaro is a J.D. candidate at Columbia Law School. She graduated from Harvard College in 2001 with an A.B. in Women's Studies. Prior to pursuing a law degree, she worked at a crisis shelter run by Sanctuary for Families, a domestic violence service agency in New York City, primarily focusing her advocacy efforts on the needs of undocumented Latin American women. She subsequently spent time in Ghana with a legal aid organization that provides services to poor women and children.

Kathleen Coll is a cultural anthropologist and lecturer in Feminist Studies at Stanford University. Previously she taught Women, Gender, and Sexuality Studies at Harvard University and Anthropology and Women's Studies at the City College of San Francisco. Her ethnographic research in California and Massachusetts focuses on issues of gender, immigration, and cultural citizenship in the context of local political participation. Her work has received support from the Stanford Department of Anthropology, the Radcliffe Institute for Advanced Study, the Social Science Research Council, and the David Rockefeller Center for Latin American Studies.

Brad Epps Brad Epps is Professor of Romance Languages and Literatures at Harvard University. He has published over fifty articles on modern literature, film, art, and architecture from Spain, Latin America, Catalonia, and France as well as on immigration, sexuality, AIDS, and critical theory. The author of *Significant Violence: Oppression and Resistance in the Narratives of Juan Goytisolo* (Oxford University Press), he is currently preparing two books: *Daring to Write*, on gay and lesbian issues in Latin America, Spain, and Latino/a cultures in the United States, and *Barcelona and Beyond*, on modern Catalan culture. He is also co-editing a collection of essays on Spanish literary history with Luis Fernández Cifuentes, *Spain Beyond Spain: Modernity, Literary History, and National Identity*.

Bill Fairbairn is a project coordinator at the Centre for Research on Latin America and the Caribbean (CERLAC) at York University in Toronto, Canada. Between 1983 and 2001 he worked as South America coordinator with the Inter-Church Committee on Human Rights in Latin America (ICCHRLA), a national ecumenical coalition formed by the Canadian churches in response to the September 11, 1973 coup d'état led by General Pinochet in Chile. For more than two decades, Fairbairn has traveled widely throughout Latin America, working closely with Latin American organizations in documenting human rights abuses and developing appropriate solidarity responses. He has presented these findings on repeated occasions to senior Canadian government officials, Latin American heads of state, and international bodies, including the United Nations and the Inter-American Commissions on Human Rights. Mr. Fairbairn was the driving force behind and author of a report produced in 1996 by the Canadian Churches entitled *Violence Unveiled: Repression Against Lesbians and Gay Men in Latin America.* He has appeared as an expert witness before Canada's Immigration and Refugee Board in numerous cases involving asylum seekers from Latin America including those facing persecution because of their sexual orientation.

Paul Farmer, co-founder of the nonprofit Partners In Health, is a physician-anthropologist whose work draws primarily on active clinical practice: he divides his clinical time between the Brigham and Women's Hospital in Boston, Massachusetts (where he is chief of the Division of Social Medicine and Health Inequalities) and the Clinique Bon Sauveur, a charity hospital in rural Haiti. The Program in Infectious Disease and Social Change, which Farmer runs along with his colleagues in Harvard Medical School's Department of Social Medicine, has pioneered novel, community-based treatment strategies for AIDS, tuberculosis, and other diseases that disproportionately affect the poor. Harvard Medical School's Presley Professor of Medical Anthropology, Farmer received his M.D. from Harvard Medical School, and his Ph.D. from the Harvard University Department of Anthropology in 1990. Farmer is the author of over 100 scholarly articles and books, most recently *Pathologies of Power: Health, Human Rights, and the New War on the Poor* (University of California Press).

Heloisa Maria Galvão (formerly Heloisa Souza) is the president of the Brazilian Women's Group, a grassroots organization, and a Community Field Coordinator for Boston Public Schools. She is a journalist with more than 30 years of experience reporting for Brazilian newspapers and frequently freelances for the *Diário de Natal* and *O POTI* published in Natal, Rio Grande do Norte, Brazil. Ms. Galvão holds a M.S. in Print Journalism and in Broadcast Journalism from Boston

University. A community activist and advocate, she has written and presented extensively on the subject of immigration rights, community organizing, education, and women's issues. Her latest publications are "Language Loss and Language Gain in the Brazilian Community: The Role of Schools and Families," in *Lifting Every Voice: Pedagogy and Politics of Bilingualism* (Edited by Zeynep F. Beykont, Harvard Education Publishing Group) and *As Viajantes do Século Vinte: Uma história oral de mulheres brasileiras imigrantes na área de Boston* (2005). Ms. Galvão has received numerous awards for her work with the Brazilian community, including the "Ordem do Rio Branco" awarded by the President of Brazil to Brazilians living overseas and the 1997 Massachusetts Alliance of Portuguese Speakers Community Service Award.

Nicole Gastineau is a research assistant at Partners In Health, and received her A.B. from Harvard University in 2001. She is currently a Master of Science degree candidate in Health Policy and Management at the Harvard School of Public Health in Boston, Massachusetts.

Bill Johnson González teaches Latino/a literature at Wesleyan University and is a doctoral candidate in the Department of Comparative Literature at Harvard University, where he is writing a dissertation on psychoanalysis and "race" that examines the roles of narcissism and whiteness in the works of Richard Rodriguez and James Baldwin. He has received Mellon and Ford Graduate Fellowships and has also been a Tutor in Harvard's Literature Concentration, where he has taught in the areas of U.S. and Latin American Studies as well as critical theory.

Lawrence La Fountain-Stokes is Assistant Professor of Latino/Latina Studies and Spanish at the University of Michigan, Ann Arbor. He received his Ph.D. in Spanish from Columbia University in 1999, where he wrote about cultural representations of the Puerto Rican Queer Diaspora. His essays and short stories have appeared in *Chicano/Latino Homoerotic Identities* (1999), *Sissies and Tomboys: Gender Nonconformity and Homosexual Childhood* (1999), *Bésame Mucho: New Gay Latino Fiction* (1999), *Tomás Carrasquilla: Nuevas aproximaciones críticas* (2000), *Queer Globalizations: Citizenship and the Afterlife of Colonialism* (2002), *Tortilleras: Hispanic and U.S. Latina Lesbian Expression* (2003), and in journals such as *Centro* and *GLQ*.

Roger N. Lancaster is Professor of Anthropology and Director of the Cultural Studies Ph.D. Program at George Mason University. He has published widely on gender, sexuality, and politics in the United States and Latin America, with a particular focus on Nicaragua. Lancaster's previous books include *Life is Hard: Machismo, Danger, and the Intimacy of Power in Nicaragua* (California 1992), which won the C. Wright Mills Award and the Ruth Benedict Prize, and *The Gender/ Sexuality Reader* (Routledge 1997) (edited with Micaela di Leonardo). His most recent book is *The Trouble with Nature: Sex in Science and Popular Culture* (California 2003). He is presently completing a book tentatively titled *Sex, Play, and Terror*.

Eithne Luibhéid is the Director of LGBT Studies and an Associate Professor of Women's Studies at the University of Arizona. Her book, *Entry Denied: Controlling Sexuality at the Border*, was published by the University of Minnesota Press in 2002. She is also the co-editor of a special issue of *Women's Studies International Forum* on "Migrant Women Transforming Ireland and the E.U." with Ronit Lentin (Oct-November 2004); and the co-editor of *Queer Migrations: Sexuality, U.S. Citizenship and Border Crossings* (University of Minnesota Press, 2005) with Lionel Cantú. She has published articles in *GLQ*, the *Journal of Commonwealth and Postcolonial Studies*, and the *Journal of the History of Sexuality* as well as in numerous edited volumes. Her research interests include post-1965 immigration to the United States; the intersections of sexuality, racialization, and immigration control regimes; asylum seekers in the European Union; and immigrant, refugee, and transnational women.

Alice M. Miller is an Assistant Professor of Clinical Population & Family Health at the Mailman School of Public Health (MSPH) at Columbia University and an adjunct Professor at the School of International and Public Affairs. Her work focuses on gender, sexuality, health and human rights, and humanitarian issues, putting scholarly work in service to human rights activism in the United States and globally. In 1998–1999, Ms. Miller was a Rockefeller Fellow in the Program for the Study of Sexuality, Gender, Health, and Human Rights at MSPH. Prior to joining Columbia, she directed the Women's Rights Advocacy Project at the International Human Rights Law Group, and AIUSA's

Campaign to Abolish the Death Penalty. Ms. Miller graduated from Radcliffe College, Harvard University in 1979; and received her J.D. from the University of Washington School of Law in 1985. She writes regularly for legal, sexuality, health, and rights-oriented publications.

Norma Mogrovejo Aquise is an activist, a sociologist, and a historian who has dedicated her time to documenting the lives and struggles of lesbians and gays in Mexico. She works at the Universidad de la Ciudad de México and maintains the Centro de Documentación y Archivo Histórico Lésbico de México "Nancy Cárdenas." She holds degrees both in the law and Social Sciences, and received her Ph.D. in Latin American Studies from the National University of Mexico, D.F., in 1988. She has served as Co-Director of Social Projects for Women and Children for the local government of Mexico City, and since 1999 has been the Coordinator of the Integral Help for Women Center in the Venustiano Carranza Delegation in Mexico City. She has published *El amor es bxh/2: Una propuesta de análisis histórico-metodológico del movimiento lésbico, feminista y homosexual en América Latina* (Archivo Histórico Lésbico de México, 1996); *Un amor que se atrevió a decir su nombre: La lucha de las lesbianas y su relación con los movimientos feminista y homosexual en América Latina* (Plaza y Valdez, México, 2000); *Lestimonios: Voces de mujeres lesbianas 1950–2000* (Plaza y Valdez, México, 2001, as well as various essays in edited volumes. She is currently working on questions of (self)-exile, migration, and sexual dissent.

Matthew E. Price holds a Ph.D. in Political Science from Harvard University and is a J.D. candidate at Harvard Law School. He writes on the ethics of asylum policy, and the political theory of immigration policy and citizenship more broadly. Currently, he is completing a book, tentatively titled *Wielding Asylum: Persecution, Politics, and Refugee Policy*, that addresses the historical origins and normative justification for limiting asylum to persecuted people. Prior to pursuing graduate studies, he lived in Jerusalem, where he worked for the Palestinian Human Rights Monitoring Group, investigating human rights violations committed by the Palestinian Authority; and the U.S. State Department, monitoring settlement activity in the West Bank.

Alberto Sandoval-Sánchez is Professor of Spanish at Mount Holyoke College. He is both a cultural critic and a creative writer, and he has published numerous articles in books and journals on U.S. Latino/a theater, Latin American colonial theater and colonial identity formation, Puerto Rican migration, images of Latinos/as in film and Broadway, and Latino/a theater on AIDS. He is the author of *José Can You See?: Latinos On and Off Broadway* (1999), coeditor of *Puro Teatro: A Latina Anthology* (2000, in collaboration with Nancy S. Sternbach), and *Stages of Life: Transcultural Performance and Identity in Latina Theatre* (2001, also in collaboration with Sternbach).

Marcelo Suárez-Orozco is the Courtney Sale Ross University Professor of Globalization and Education and the Co-Director of Immigration Studies at New York University. A leading expert in the field of immigration studies, professor Suárez-Orozco's recent publications include *Latinos: Remaking America* (co-edited with Mariela Paez, UC Press, 2002); the six volume *Interdisciplinary Perspectives on the New Immigration* (co-edited with Carola Suárez-Orozco and Desiree Qin-Hilliard, Routledge, 2001); *Globalization: Culture and Education in the New Millennium* (co-edited with Desiree Qin-Hilliard, UC Press and Ross Institute, 2004); and the forthcoming *The New Immigration: An Interdisciplinary Reader* (co-edited with Carola Suárez-Orozco, and Desiree Qin-Hilliard, Routledge).

Keja Valens is Assistant Professor of English at Salem State College. She received her Ph.D. in Comparative Literature from Harvard University in 2004 with a dissertation on desire between women in Caribbean literatures. Ms. Valens writes on Caribbean literatures and cultures, literatures of the Americas, literatures of the African Diaspora, and queer theory. She has published articles on Jamaica Kincaid in *Frontiers: A Journal of Women Studies* and on Maryse Condé in the *Journal of Commonwealth and Postcolonial Studies*. She has an article on José Martí forthcoming in *Changing Currents: Anglophone, Francophone, and Hispanophone Literary and Cultural Criticism* and an article on Audre Lorde and Paule Marshall forthcoming in *La Torre*. She is also working on a new project that examines inheritance, legacy, and the expression of cultural affiliations and individual hungers in Caribbean food writing from the colonial period to the present.

PART

I

INTRODUCTION

Introduction

Brad Epps, Keja Valens, and Bill Johnson González

> "In the modern world everyone can, should, will 'have'
> a nationality, as he or she 'has' a gender."
> —Benedict Anderson, *Imagined Communities*

> "One achieves full citizenship in the nation-state
> by becoming a blank slate."
> —Renato Rosaldo, *Culture and Truth*

To Those Who Have Tried, But Not Been Able

Border crossings, a daily reality throughout the world, have become a dominant trope in understanding transnational migration. But border crossings can be recast, we submit, as *passing lines*, so as to bring to the fore more than geopolitical boundaries and physical movement.[1] Lines, as the dictionary reminds us, are not just marks drawn or engraved on a surface; they are also queues, furrows, or seams; a unit of writing, such as a short letter; a marked tendency, a policy or trend; the words of an actor's part; and, more colloquially, a glib or superficially attractive mode of address or behavior, plausible talk.[2] To pass a line is thus not only to traverse a boundary, but also to tell a story, a tale, even a whopper, which if done successfully passes as truth itself; it is to play a part or to act in a way that strives to convince, persuade, or "move" another; and it is to convey a tendency or a trend, a mode of behavior, a way of being. Inasmuch as immigrants must typically tell a story or make a verbal case for themselves if they are to enter and/or remain in a country, border crossings necessarily entail passing lines. "To pass" is, of course, a phrase rich in its own right and can mean to go unnoticed; to fit in; to be the blank slate that Renato Rosaldo, in a remark that serves as one of our epigraphs, presents as a requisite for full cultural citizenship. In this sense, passing is the other side of showing one's cards, or of dropping all pretense, or of throwing caution to the wind, or even of coming out—though, in a recent development in asylum practice, "coming out" (as a persecuted gay, as a battered wife) may actually help one gain asylum in the United States, the country

3

that will be at the fractured center of the present volume. The phrase "passing lines" is, then, a play on words that signals the quite serious play of people as they move—or attempt to move—across geopolitical borders, as well as the discursive and bodily acts by which one person "relates" to another *not* as an *other* but as fundamentally the same or, perhaps more accurately, as "almost the same, but not quite" (Bhabha 86). Mimicry, which cultural critic Homi Bhabha has so suggestively studied in relation to post-Enlightenment British colonialism, holds for the post-colonial realities of global (im)migration and nationalization as well, ensnaring subjects here and there, "native" and "foreign," "legal" and "illegal" in a terribly uneven game of mirrors in which the newcomer tries to assume (convincingly) the prevailing values of U.S. society. Rife with mimicry, passing lines are, in short, the performative acts by which a person passes, or strives to pass, as conforming to certain norms of identity and behavior.

What one says and does; how one says and does it, when, where, and to whom, give a general measure of these lines. The goal of passing lines may be entry into, or escape from, a country, but it may also be admission into, or exclusion from, a social group; it may be privilege, power, and profit, peace of mind, a better life, or just plain survival. Within the context of U.S. immigration, there have been attempts, for example, on the part of the sick to pass as healthy (significantly, but by no means exclusively, in relation to HIV/AIDS); of political activists to pass as docile and apolitical; of battered women to pass as powerless victims in need of state support; and of gays, lesbians, bisexuals, and others to pass as straight and even as happily married (and lately, amid the twists of asylum practice, of men who desire men and women who desire women to pass as visibly and even stereotypically gay or lesbian). Needless to say, the attempts are not always successful, and their felicities are shadowed by their failings: a cough, a telltale blotch, a revealing tattoo, a look of defiance, a sigh of frustration, a slip of the tongue, or (before recent changes regarding the status of sexual orientation) a simple, little lisp.[3] Passing lines are thus also shibboleths of identity, shibboleths not just in the sense of slogans and catchwords, but also in the sense of distinctive markers—gestural and corporeal as well as linguistic—that do not admit of easy control: mimicry, by which a subject conforms or appears to conform to existing standards, and hence passes as acceptable, must contend with the often unruly turns of language and visibility.[4]

Linda Schlossberg, one of the editors of a book on passing, recognizes that "passing can be experienced as a source of radical pleasure or intense danger; it can function as a badge of shame or a source of pride. Passing as practice questions the assumption that visibility is necessarily positive, pleasurable, even desirable" (3). Long considered critical to the history of race and racism, ethno-racial passing—by which a "person of color" seeks to escape racial stigmatization by "erasing" color and approximating a white racial norm—is the subject of powerful works of literature by James Weldon Johnson, Nella Larsen, Langston Hughes, Michelle Cliff, and other African American and Afro-Caribbean writers (as well as by a white who passed as black, John Howard Griffin), and can indeed be far from positive, pleasurable, or desirable. U.S. Latino/a and Asian American writers have also tackled the pressures to pass as "American," pressures that may be most intense at the border but that persist over time and across places, effectively embroiling ethnically marked, non-white subjects, regardless of their actual citizenship status, in a peculiar coming out and/or passing game of their own. The immigrant's attempts to go unchecked and unnoticed, to be seen as not particularly worthy of being seen or, alternatively, as worthy of being seen *only* as a proper citizen or potential citizen, is the counterpart of governmentally supported attempts to monitor, question, identify, and "know" those who enter, or would enter, and stay, or would stay, in the country. Passport controls, border checks, interviews, interdiction, detainment, "secondary inspection,"[5] profiling, and other tactics have served to establish or determine identities, to draw out "confessions" of who one is. Such controls, checks, and interviews are crucial, it seems, not only to the maintenance of national borders and to the often dubious turns of national security but also to the plays of identity that are mobilized by, through, and as immigration.

As Nella Larsen's novel *Passing* (1929) illustrates, the act of passing can implicitly question not only the solidity of ethno-racial lines but of sexual lines as well. According to Judith Butler, Deborah McDowell, Barbara Johnson, and others, Larsen's is a tale in which two married African American women, who may desire each other, pass, or can pass, as white *and* as heterosexual in order to advance in various social contexts. Different as it is from *Passing*, Richard Rodriguez's controversial autobiography, *Hunger of Memory* (1982), likewise engages questions of race and sexuality in the context of national belonging. For Rodriguez, becoming a "public man" in the United States partly serves as a way of escaping the repressive norms of Mexican *machismo*. The relatively more freely expressed array of racial and sexual identities in the United States appears to motivate some individuals' desire to immigrate to it—even though they face new challenges once they arrive. Taken together, these two otherwise disparate texts and authors signal the myriad ways in which citizenship and immigration are not only ongoing daily practices reminiscent of Ernest Renan's "daily plebiscite" (55) but also verbal and corporeal negotiations of preexisting acts and identities. These negotiations, configured here as passing lines, are at the heart of the present volume: to wit, the increasingly significant, if still relatively little studied, interplays of race, ethnicity, gender, sex, and sexuality in migratory movements and national formations. Aware of the immensity of such a project, we focus in the following essays on immigration to the United States (though also to Canada and, more elliptically, to Mexico) from Latin America and the Caribbean, the regions that have become the greatest "exporters" of people to the United States in the past decades.[6]

Of course, the very idea of a focus of any sort is vexed. After all, many of the nations of the Western Hemisphere—which is historically the first area of the globe to come under the explicit tutelage or neo-imperial domination of the United States (although many Caribbean islands remain in situations of neo-colonial affiliation with their initial European colonizers)—are freighted and fissured by regional tensions, indigenous movements, and alternative national projects. Still others, such as Puerto Rico, are nations without a state or territories without full statehood (depending on one's perspective) that remain under the sway of other more powerful nation states in manners that complicate the legal and experiential realities of migration (technically, the Jones Act of 1917 granted Puerto Ricans United States citizenship, but that does not mean that they do not experience their movement from the island to the mainland, and back, as a mode of immigration). For that matter, the nation state itself is an increasingly embattled formation, as the extraordinarily imbalanced forces of multinational capitalism, along with war, poverty, and other forms of violence and inequality, propel massive global migrations that alter, often quite profoundly, national contours and contents. Faced with the complex magnitude of migration on a global scale, and with the arbitrariness of any delimitation or focus, we can only consider a sampling even of Latin America and the Caribbean, whose populations, as already intimated, can be as diverse racially, ethnically, economically, linguistically, and socially as they are in terms of gender and sexuality. Accordingly, while Haiti, Guatemala, Mexico, Puerto Rico, Peru, Trinidad and Tobago, the Bahamas, Nicaragua, Cuba, and Brazil, or rather aspects of them, figure in the present collection, Argentina, Jamaica, Venezuela, Dominica, Colombia, Guadeloupe, Bolivia, and Surinam, to name but a few, do not. Far from being exhaustive, totalizing, or definitive, the present collection opens—or, more accurately, further opens—the variegated subject of immigration and sexuality.

Despite the persistent imperiousness of binary logic (male/female; heterosexual/homosexual; natural/perverse), sexuality is arguably no less vast and complex than race, ethnicity, and nationality; consequently, the collection makes no pretense at being exhaustive or definitive on this score either. If we set our sights more concertedly on non-heteronormative sexualities, it is, however, because U.S. immigration law and practice have historically considered queer people as *problems* and have made our sexualities, desires, and "lifestyles" into objects of interrogation, debate, censure, control, and exclusion. By "queer people" we mean, as a rule of thumb, anyone who does not conform, or who is understood as not conforming, to conventional sexual mores.[7] William N. Eskridge, Jr. and Nan Hunter, authors of an important casebook titled *Sexuality, Gender, and the Law*, give a roster of people that we might restyle, somewhat daringly, as queer. They include "women desiring contraceptives or abortions, sodomites and homosexuals, prostitutes and other people soliciting sex, unmarried pregnant women, cross-dressers and transvestites, pornographers and purveyors of indecent materials, people who love those of another race or the same sex, polygamists, and so on" (xi). Thus, even though queerness is, as in the present book, most tightly tied to homosexuality and often functions as a virtual synonym for it (arising, as it does, as part of an effort by gay men, lesbians, bisexuals, and transgendered people to redeploy a pejorative epithet and to stress the commonalities of their resistance), it does not perforce designate a specific sexual orientation, preference, aim, or object. It can therefore serve, with variable political efficacy, as something of a portmanteau word to designate anyone who is at odds with the sexual *status quo*, that is to say, with heteronormativity. The heteronormative *status quo*, which tends to come into being by way of contraventions of it, is not immutable—despite the desires and efforts of many—and some of those included in the previous roster have clearly fared better than others. What is certain is that, under whatever name, people who fit or are made to fit into the aforementioned categories have been, as Eskridge and Hunter remark, particularly vulnerable to the "deprivation of life, liberty, and property without 'due process of law'" (xl). The categories are themselves far from neutral, and may even constitute "suspect classifications" to the degree that they prejudicially construct and not merely designate groups of people based on preexisting morally charged concepts.[8]

Although Eskridge and Hunter make only a passing reference to race in their overview of sexually contested categories, there can be little doubt that race and ethnicity have played a momentous role in U.S. legal and cultural history in ways that implicate yet outstrip nationally inflected concerns about miscegenation. As women's studies scholar M. Jacqui Alexander points out, "colonial rule simultaneously involved racializing and sexualizing the population" in such a way that the sexuality of people of color came to the fore as deviant and dangerous against the naturalized and hence often only implicit backdrop of white heterosexuality (11–12). For all the advances in civil rights, the legacy of colonial racial and sexual prejudice endures in the present. Caribbean and Latin American immigrants, for instance, have generally had to face far more legal obstacles than their European counterparts. It will come as no surprise, then, that of the mid-20th century cases involving homosexuality that legal scholar Margot Cannaday has studied, those in which the immigrant came from Latin America and the Caribbean resulted in deportation, while those in which the immigrant came from Western Europe at times resulted in admittance. Queerness, however ample a concept and however resistant a corrective to more punitive juridical and medical understandings of homosexuality, is inextricably implicated in racial and ethnic categories—and vice versa. This does not mean that queer people are free from racial prejudice and people of color from homophobia, far from it. But it does mean that queer people of color shoulder a particularly heavy burden in the struggle for full legal and cultural citizenship. The intersections of race, sexuality, and immigration, even when delimited to the Western Hemisphere and to non-heteronormative relations, or to such protracted and varied "disruptions" of heteronormative relations as domestic violence, abortion, and even women's rights, are, in sum, so diverse in their contingencies and conceptualizations that no study can address them in their entirety.

The preceding clarification—which is also evidently a justification—is important because of the ways in which theorization at once relies on generalization and disparages it as an avatar of universalist idealization. To write about immigration, nationality, race, gender, sexuality, and so forth, thus presupposes the general validity of such terms and concepts, but, if it is done critically, it questions rather than merely reasserts their validity by way of more localized and historically specific forms of analysis—which are themselves, in turn, opened to questioning. It is not that the specific "corrects" the general, any more than the general "accounts for" the specific, but rather that they are both simultaneously in play, reinforcing, modifying, troubling, and even contradicting one another. Shifted slightly, the question also comes to be about the relations between collectivity and individuality, impersonality and personality, and bears on the obvious but frequently overlooked fact that for all of the general rules and regulations regarding immigration, for all the statistics and standards, individual immigrants can have widely divergent experiences (indeed, divergence is embedded in legal history in the form of quotas, special categories, grounds for exclusion, and even amnesties). Language is hardly incidental to all of this, for immigrants are, *in general*, repeatedly enjoined by immigration agents, border patrol guards, lawyers, prospective employers, and others to make a *specific* case for themselves, to articulate their lives in ways that at once conform to established codes and that stand out as deserving of attention and acceptance. The burden of proof is on the immigrant, needless to say, with self-presentation folding in and out of preexisting, if often confusingly regulated, conceptions of the self, *the proper self*. Although self-presentation assumes many guises, from skin color to gesture to clothing, some of which are obviously less manipulable than others, verbal expression plays a decisive role, at least in any situation that goes beyond sheer coercion. What American cultural critic and immigration scholar Eithne Luibhéid, following the work of French intellectual historian Michel Foucault, calls the "inducement to speak"(88), which is the requirement that individuals recount their "case histories" to a variety of official (and often unofficial) representatives of the law and government, is critical to the act of passing lines.

The geopolitical dimensions of passing lines are further complicated by the passage of time. Many of the essays that follow were originally delivered at a conference held at Harvard University in April 2001, when *Bowers v. Hardwick* was still the law of the land—and terrorism still largely a "foreign" phenomenon. Since that time, the essays have been modified to account for changes that have occurred in the wake of the calamitous events of September 11, 2001 and in the wake of the June 2003 *Lawrence v. Texas* decision which effectively declared null and void the remaining sodomy statutes in the United

States (save those that, in the guise of the Clinton administration's "Don't Ask, Don't Tell" policy, still hold in the military). The *Lawrence* decision, which Brad Epps examines in his essay, has understandably been hailed as a victory for queer people, but it does not keep the government entirely out of the bedroom, let alone from other less "private" places that have come under new, intensified scrutiny as part of the much-touted "war on terrorism." Although no amount of modification can fully keep pace with all of the changes, which include but are not limited to changes in elected (or court appointed) administrations, the present collection of essays nonetheless strives to engage in the debates current at the moment of its production and to give a sense, as noted earlier, of the larger theoretical questions that have persisted over time. One of our guiding concerns has been official immigration's reliance on uneven, politically charged, and often arbitrarily wrought categories of exclusion and admission. To that end, and in contrast with the rigid, essentialized, and timeless definitions of gender and sexual identity typically deployed in governmentally sanctioned exclusions or admissions, the essays that follow contextualize and historicize race, gender, and sexuality—suffused as they are with the ideologies of the natural—largely as effects or constructs of human society and its laws and rights.

For example, several of the essays address the dialectical relations between human rights and asylum work,[9] and contend that the nationally specific, politically oriented work of asylum, argued on a case by case basis, should supplement the international sweep and theoretical abstractions of human rights work. In a complementary move, they also propose, whether explicitly or implicitly, that human rights workers engage critical theory on gender and sexuality in order to broaden the possibilities for the successful presentation of specific asylum claims. Alice Miller is on this subject as emphatic as she is well-grounded: the law, specifically immigration law, recognizes a limited number of sexual identities, sacrificing diversity to conformity (including conformity to governmentally intelligible forms of homosexuality) and forfeiting the realities of change to the illusions of permanence. Another question that runs through many of the essays involves the insistent if inconsistent manner in which "women's issues" are intertwined with "queer issues," and both, in turn, with "immigrant issues." As if that were not enough, a fourth set of "issues" bears on the family and emerges in such phenomena as "family-sponsored immigration" and "family reunification" as well as in global and local attempts to define or redefine marriage. In keeping with the interconnected nature of these and other issues, the essays that we bring together examine, to varying degrees and from various disciplinary perspectives, the intersections of national affiliation, family formation, sexual attachment, and morality. They attend, more precisely, to the national and international implications of homosexuality, homophobia, heteronormativity, *machismo*, and masculinism; HIV/AIDS and public heath; sexual exile or "sexile"; domestic violence, "victimization," activism, and women's autonomy. Many of the essays, straddling the aforementioned issues, also examine the ways in which the heteronormative home has been, and continues to be, erected, monitored, and maintained as fundamental to the nation, so much so that both asylum and human rights workers must repeatedly engage the home even when they would get beyond it or expand its contours.

Questions of individual liberty, due process, and equal protection are also at the center of debates on sexuality and nationality (understood, as noted, largely in terms of citizenship, immigration, and naturalization), but so too is the much-debated right of privacy, which such Supreme Court Justices as Antonin Scalia and Clarence Thomas deem to be *too* penumbral to be constitutionally legitimate.[10] Pleasure contends with pain, and the violence of legal intrusion into a domain of domesticity (as in *Bowers*) is countered by—or, better yet, attempts to counter—the violence of domesticity itself. If the legal argument for the right to "consensual sodomy" in the United States entails, as in the *Lawrence* decision, the anxious reaffirmation and protection of an "enduringly private" space, domestic violence, whose deep history renders the term something of a redundancy,[11] punctures the right of privacy and brings certain subjects—typically, but not exclusively, women and children—into the public light as "victims" in need of state-sponsored intervention, protection, and, in the case of non-citizens, asylum. Legally defined limits to the right of privacy and the primacy of the domestic sphere are enacted in the name of a higher right (to wit, the protection of the individual) and have been codified most significantly in the various versions of the Violence Against Women Act (VAWA). Domestic as the purview of the VAWA is, immigration policy is also implicated; indeed, the interrelations between the domestic as home and as nation (as in the phrase "domestic policy") are such that a shift in scale from the national to the international ups the ante and casts entire national regimes as more or less peaceful and accommodating, more or less violent and intolerant.

It is not, obviously, that there are no differences between national regimes, but that the differences can be—and have been—instrumentalized in the service of politically interested projects of patriotic reaffirmation and economic and military expansion, as in the George W. Bush administration's violent imposition of "democracy" onto so-called terrorist or rogue states. If migratory movements carry a symbolic charge that says "something" about the places of departure and of arrival (and perhaps all points in between), it is typically of an economic or personal nature: employment opportunities, family ties, cultural offerings, or even, as Alberto Sandoval and Lawrence La Fountain-Stokes note, affective and erotic possibilities (the previously mentioned "sexile"). Asylum and refuge, however, constitute more extreme and dramatic instances of immigration in which violence, whether actual or potential, is prominent and in which the vagaries of international relations loom large.[12] For instance, asylum cases that center on battered or persecuted women hurtle the confines of a Guatemalan house—to allude to the case of Rodi Alvarado Peña studied by Matthew Price and Angélica Cházaro—into the United States legal system and, through it, the nation's political and cultural imaginary. But the very same cases also fan out, in their precedent-setting effects, to encompass, as Cházaro notes, forced prostitution, honor killings, gang rapes, and other atrocities (such as gay bashing) of a more obvious public nature. Privacy goes public—and the public, private—in a manner that complicates discrete domestic bounds and national boundaries and that shuttles between pain and pleasure, individual and collective formations, and localities and globalities.

The aforementioned tensions between individuals, families, homes, and governments are part and parcel of the history of immigration to the United States, which has been punctuated by moments of national and international crisis. A brief review of history will give a measure of what we mean. The Alien and Sedition Acts of 1798, enacted scarcely two decades after the United States declared independence, came in the wake of the French Revolution. The Naturalization Act of 1802, a major piece of legislation modified in 1855 to grant citizenship to alien wives of United States citizens, was further modified in 1870, in the wake of the Civil War, when the naturalization process was opened to people of African descent. Other regulations arise with the Russian Revolution, World War I, World War II, and the Korean Conflict, but also at times of economic depression and political fervor. And so, after the "paupers and convicts" that the thirteen original colonies sought to exclude, one finds "criminals and prostitutes" in 1875; "insane persons, beggars . . . and anarchists" in 1903; "feeble-minded persons," "persons afflicted with tuberculosis," and persons with "a mental or physical defect" in 1907; the illiterate in 1917; "ex-Nazis, war criminals, members of totalitarian parties and those who worked for collaborationist governments in Nazi-occupied areas" in 1948; communists and people with a "psychopathic personality, epilepsy or a mental defect," implicitly including homosexuals, in 1952; people infected with HIV in 1990 and, more explicitly, 1993.[13] Along with the sick, criminal, deviant, and "social charges," entire national and racial groups were also implicated: Irish and German Catholics in the 1830s; the Chinese and other Asians in the 1870s and 80s; Italians, Slavs, and Jews in the early 1900s; Haitians and, more subtly, Black Africans in the early 1990s.[14] Of these exclusions, few were more brutally forthright than the so-called Chinese Exclusion Act of 1882, an unabashedly racist piece of legislation that remained in effect until 1943.[15] Legislation aimed at excluding other Asians, including Japanese, Filipinos, Indians, and Indo-Chinese, was also enacted. As was often the case, waves of immigrants willing to perform hard work for low wages in times of economic prosperity and expansion (the building of the transcontinental railroad, for example) were followed by waves of xenophobic protectionism once projects were completed and prosperity waned.

More recently, nervousness—when not worse—about the growth of Latino/a, Asian, and Arab communities in the United States has incited a variety of nativist and anti-immigrant anxieties and legally binding initiatives, including attempts to make English the official language of the nation (indeed, such provisions have already been advanced in more than twenty states). In addition, contemporary popular fears about the U.S. "homeland's" vulnerability to terrorist infiltration and attack have merely added momentum, and a sense of patriotic urgency, to anti-immigrant sentiments. The upshot of so much anxiety and inflammatory rhetoric has been a series of proposals at both the national and state levels to increase security and regulate movement more effectively across borders by restricting civil rights, creating new requirements for legal documentation, and extending the investigatory powers of local authorities. Other effects include limiting legal recourses and protections for immigrants, and imposing new burdens of proof on immigrants fleeing persecution. Thus, the California Propositions of the 1990s (such as Proposition 187, mentioned in this volume by Kathleen Coll) appear as precursors to powerful federal measures such as the "Clear Law Enforcement for Criminal Alien Removal Act of 2003" (CLEAR Act) and the "Homeland Security Enhancement Act" (HSEA), each of which seeks to recruit state and local authorities (in the case of the CLEAR Act, police officers) to enforce federal immigration laws and to determine the legal status of persons. Under the CLEAR Act (which is still pending at the time we are writing) states would receive federal financial rewards for enforcement and risk substantial penalties for failing to enforce the law. According to a statement issued by the National Council of La Raza (NCLR), a non-profit organization that advocates on behalf of Hispanic Americans, such legislation is bound to have a "negative impact on Latino communities" and to "erode the relationship between immigrant communities and law enforcement" ("State/Local"). Furthermore, according to the NCLR, these policies are "in direct conflict with long-standing legal tradition [and] will inevitably result in higher levels of racial profiling, police misconduct, and other civil rights violations," as local and state police attempt to manage the complexities of legality, immigration status, and civil rights" ("State/Local").

Another example of increased anti-immigrant surveillance is Arizona's tellingly named initiative, Protect Arizona Now (PAN—which, ironically, means "bread" in Spanish) or Proposition 200, which was approved by voters in November 2004 (and has been subsequently challenged in court). PAN explicitly aims to "prevent illegal aliens in the United States from receiving state and local public benefits or services" that are "not federally mandated," but it remains vague as to what counts as a benefit, although education and health care certainly seem to be in question.[16] Such initiatives appear to ignore the U.S. Supreme Court's 1982 decision in *Plyler vs. Doe*, which ruled that undocumented immigrants may *not* be denied state services, including public education, under the Equal Protection clause of the Federal Constitution. Even more broadly than the CLEAR Act, PAN requires state employees to verify the immigration status of any applicant for services and "to make a written report to federal immigration authorities" if s/he discovers "any violation of federal immigration laws by any applicant for benefits," or face severe penalties for failing to do so. Thus, "Proposition 200 would make librarians, doctors, and teachers into immigration agents" ("NCLR Talking Points on PAN"). Sweeping as PAN may be, the "REAL ID Act" (House Resolution 418), which passed the U.S. House of Representatives on February 10, 2005, provides yet more strategies for the documentation, identification, and regulation of illegal immigrants.[17] The "REAL ID Act" also intensifies the burden of proof for asylum applicants with respect to the "central motive" of their persecutors. According to an NCLR pamphlet, the Act requires applicants "to prove not only the existence of some motive in their persecutors' mind, but to distinguish among multiple motives and prove the primacy of one motive above others. Under such an unrealistic burden of proof, a Mexican journalist investigating corruption who was raped and robbed by drunken soldiers will have difficulty showing that her persecutors attacked her because of her political opinion and profession rather than her money or their drunkenness" ("NCLR REAL ID Act Talking Points"). The Act additionally allows for the deportation of persons, including asylum seekers, "*before* the conclusion of their federal court cases," provides for the suspension of the writ of Habeas Corpus, and prevents "federal courts from reviewing virtually all discretionary actions of the Department of Homeland Security in the immigration arena."

In such a legal climate, then, it is hardly surprising that the headline for a recent article by Donna Leinwand in *USA Today* read, "Illegals Going Back by the Planeload." The article details U.S. Immigration and Customs Enforcement (ICE) efforts to "crack down on violators of immigration laws," and reports that deportations have increased at an "unprecedented pace," up 45 percent from 2001 to 2004, keeping the ICE "busy all the time." While many of the measures avoid singling out specific racial or ethnic groups in the text of their initiatives, it is easy to demonstrate the differential impact of such legislation on immigrant populations who are also racially marked. Despite the devastating pall of suspicion that currently attends Muslims in the United States, Leinwand notes that more than 70 percent of those recently deported were returned to Mexico and that a significant number of others were returned to Central or South America and the Dominican Republic. Latinos/as, Latin Americans, and Muslims may well be at the center of ongoing immigration controversies, but African Americans, whose history is in many respects less one of immigration than of outright enslavement, are also implicated in special ways in immigration policy. Bill Ong Hing, who has studied the role of race in United States legal history, notes how American immigration policy sends subtle, and not so subtle, messages of exclusion to African Americans. As a case in point, he refers to the internment of around 270 HIV-positive Haitians at the U.S. Naval Base at Guantánamo Bay in 1993, when the fear of AIDS was wedded, he argues, to the fear of blackness. Legal scholar

Creola Johnson, studying the same case, shows how the United States violated international law even as it maintained the rhetoric of civil liberties and human rights.[18] Even the most cursory comparison of the ways in which Haitians and Cubans were received indicates how medicine could function as a devastating red herring in immigration determinations: for while Haitians were routinely screened for HIV/AIDS (when they were not simply returned), Cubans underwent more flexible medical screenings. The Clinton administration's policy towards Haitians, like that of previous administrations, included perfunctory refusals of admission, interdiction at sea (by which the borders of the United States were effectively extended to the Haitian coast), and immediate deportation.

Under the presidency of George W. Bush, Guantánamo is again in the news, but not because of Haitian immigrants and AIDS. The "enemy combatants" captured in Afghanistan and elsewhere and imprisoned in the U.S. military base on Cuba cast an especially long shadow on Muslim immigrants, residents, visitors, and citizens, embroiling them, as already intimated, in the hype and hysteria that accompany the current "war on terrorism." Indeed, the climate of fear is so great that, as part of a major reshuffling of governmental agencies that occurred after 9/11, the Immigration and Naturalization Service (INS) was reconfigured as the Bureau of U.S. Citizenship and Immigration Services (USCIS) and placed within the newly created Department of Homeland Security.[19] In this nation of immigrants, many treat immigration as nothing less than a threat to national security. No cold rehearsal of historical facts and trends, however, can begin to account for the intensely emotional, psycho-symbolically fraught realities of migration, the countless ways in which immigration history, law, and practice bleed into consciousness (and the unconscious), parceling people who might otherwise be considered the same: immigrants. One of the Haitian "boat people" in Edwidge Danticat's short story, "Children of the Sea," makes the perception of unequal treatment poignantly clear. Noting how his companions in the boat "are showing their first charcoal layer of sunburn," Danticat's character rather wistfully remarks: "'Now we will never be mistaken for Cubans,'" even though, as the narrator interjects, "some of the Cubans are black too" (8). Danticat's fictional story serves as a chilling preface to the very real story of her own uncle, the Reverend Joseph Dantica [sic], who died in Homeland Security Custody in Miami while awaiting an asylum hearing in November 2004. David Adams, in his *St. Petersburg Times* article reporting Dantica's death, remarks that at the very same time a group of Cuban entertainers applying for asylum in Las Vegas was not detained by any government agency.

Origins, accents, and appearances all matter, prompting Renato Rosaldo to assert that we "must consider categories that are visibly inscribed on the body, such as gender and race, and their consequences for full democratic participation" ("Cultural Citizenship" 29). Right as Rosaldo is, he overestimates, understandably, the visibility of race and even gender, losing sight of so-called limit cases in which even race and gender may be in question: bi- or multi-racial individuals, gender-benders, cross-dressers, surgically altered subjects, transgendered and intersexual people, and so on. He points, nonetheless, to the guiding principle of the present volume: to wit, the importance of reflecting on the function of discernible and non-discernible signs of identity—especially as learned, mimicked, rehearsed, and performed—in the phenomenon of immigration, of passing lines. Among the relatively less discernible signs, those of sexuality and sexual orientation (let alone the more voluntaristic "sexual preference") are especially challenging, for the exclusion of sexually non-normative immigrants has been articulated in a far from straightforward manner. As Epps notes in his essay, homosexuality, in keeping with what immigration lawyer Robert Foss has described as the "*crimen innominatum* mentality" (445), was rarely mentioned explicitly. Instead it was adumbrated in such concepts and categories as "constitutional psychopathic inferiority" (1917), "psychopathic personality" or "mental defect" (1952), "sexual deviation" (1965), and, most importantly, "good moral character" (1940). Little wonder, then, that the American Psychiatric Association's decision to drop homosexuality as a disorder in 1973 was not without repercussions for the INS, for the decision effectively left it without scientific ground. And yet, without scientific ground, the INS did not change its position but instead, as Cannaday points out, "refused psychiatric opinion that differentiated psychopaths from homosexuals by arguing that these terms connoted legal-political rather than medicalized identity categories" (353). In so doing, the INS revealed a paradox: science, understood as objective reason, is both necessary and unnecessary to political policy.

Without a presumably rational object set by the medical community, the agents of the government ran the risk of an irrational subjectivity, one that threatened to expose the seamy side of American liberty (exclusion is justified no longer by appealing to, but by rejecting, scientific reason) and that also threatened to bring homosexuality a little too close to home: after all, it was now up to the INS investigating agent, in his or her capacity as a solicitor of stories, to fish out the homos. As Foss puts it, "absent some statement from the alien, no decision was possible. The examining INS official also had no objective nonmedical criteria to follow, except the official's own 'feelings' or perception" (456).[20] Eithne Luibhéid, in her book *Entry Denied*, writes about how "looking like a lesbian," though wildly indeterminate, was sufficient to set in motion a variety of techniques aimed at keeping the "lesbian-looking" person out of the country. Reviewing the case of a Mexican woman with permanent U.S. residency, Luibhéid observes that the "Immigration service techniques, which involved atomizing and evaluating [the woman's] appearance, documents, and speech, also echoed and extended the historical processes whereby Latina bodies became racialized and sexualized in the context of imposing the U.S.-Mexico border" (84). Foss' and Luibhéid's arguments find unexpected corroboration in a participant observation study by George Weissinger, a former criminal investigator, or special agent, for the (former) INS. According to Weissinger, "agents develop a *feel* for the kinds of people they encounter in the field," a "feel" that is both a cause and an effect of "typification" (14). Whether out in the field or in the confines of the interview, a *feeling* is *typically* at issue. Weissinger is not referring here specifically to homosexuality, but he nonetheless acknowledges the slippery, yet entrenched, role of subjectivity in official INS business. With respect to sexuality, the play of subjectivity could take some particularly "odd" turns: the examiner, bereft of scientific ground and medical backing and relying on personal perceptions and "feelings," strived to "get into" the other's mind, but, in so doing, ran the risk of staying "there" or, even more, of having already been "there." The risk could be summarized in common parlance: it takes one to know one.[21] And yet, the determination of homosexuality (and hence of exclusion) more obviously took an agent who felt, or wanted to demonstrate, that he or she was not at all like the interviewee and that he or she could make explicit what had been only implicit (the *real* sexual orientation of the interviewee) and could castigate, by way of detention and/or exclusion, the other *as* other.

In its current incarnation, the Immigration and Nationality Act, which refers explicitly to sexuality only in the form of prostitution and polygamy, continues to leave a great deal of discretion to individual agents.[22] Not only do agents determine the "health-related grounds" by which anyone with "a physical or mental disorder and behavior associated with the disorder" may be excluded, but they also determine the "criminal and related grounds" by which entry can be denied to any person convicted of "a crime involving moral turpitude." Tellingly, the meaning of "moral turpitude" and of the "purely political offense" with which it is contrasted is left undefined. Be that as it may, these morally (and sexually) charged grounds for exclusion differ only slightly from their embodiments in the McCarran-Walter Act, the 1952 Immigration and Nationality Act written in the full spirit of McCarthyism.[23] Against the unwieldy forces of subjectivity, the pretense to objectivity nonetheless continues to hold sway. The pretense to objectivity is often as not bound to principles of decency, discretion, and propriety, as if such morally charged principles had a verifiable, rational basis in objective reality. George Mosse makes a related observation in his groundbreaking *Nationalism and Sexuality*, interrogating the ways that national allegiance and sexual morality involve the idealities and realities, the objectivities and subjectivities, of country and body alike.[24] Mosse, like others, underscores the historicity of ideals, noting that "[i]deals that we may regard as immutable were novel some two hundred years ago, and just as modern nationalism emerged in the eighteenth century, so the ideal of respectability and its definition of sexuality fell into place at the same time" (1). One of the characteristics of the intertwined emergence of nationalism and sexual respectability is the paradoxical disavowal of their modernity, paradoxical because even as progress, order, and development are zealously invoked, they are monumentalized as immemorial. A good example of the complicity between ideologies of national identity and the enforcement of sexual norms is the way in which standards for proper sexual conduct can be tied to universal or timeless values believed to be intrinsic to a particular national identity. The *Lawrence v. Texas* decision is one of the most important recent cases in point, inasmuch as it legitimates homosexuality by articulating a right of privacy in terms of "enduring bonds" and "personal dignity." As a result, sexual stability is again cast as a matter of political stability and, indeed, domestic security. Differences of opinion within the *Lawrence* Court are thus more of degree than of kind, for the not so simple reason that both the majority and the minority endorse a principle of sexual decency. The result is a publicly enforced set of norms that assimilates "homosexuality" to the national order, but only as a privatized identity and set of practices (described, much to Scalia's displeasure, within terms that recall the institutions of marriage) that remain, despite it all, fundamentally heteronormative.

Even a document as ostensibly progressive as the International Covenant on Civil and Political Rights (ICCPR), a resolution of the General Assembly of the United Nations approved in 1966, links national security, public safety, and public order with public health or morals (Articles 20 and 22). Inasmuch as public health and morals have repeatedly been invoked to bolster a conception of society in which homosexuality and other non-heteronormative sexualities are out of place (and even against nature), advances in sexual equality must contend with an all too familiar counterweight: an emotionally charged, institutionally defended family structure. Article 23 of the ICCPR, which employs the rhetoric of nature, is on this score illustrative: "[t]he family is the natural and fundamental group unit of society and is entitled to promotion by society and the State" (quoted in Eskridge 749, emphasis ours).[25] What exactly is meant by "family"— and, for that matter, "natural" and "fundamental"—is a subject of debate, and bears on such well-established components of immigration law and practice as family reunification and the rights and privileges that hold for the lawfully married (bi-national) couple. Furthermore, whatever victories are won—usually piecemeal—for gays, lesbians, and others in the arena of asylum and refuge are largely a function of incremental legal precedent, not of broad-based legislative action or democratic support.[26] The idea of immigrating to the United States in search of sexual freedom continues to be somewhat ironic. Homosexuals, even when ostensibly embraced by the Supreme Court as fully protected citizens, thus continue to be far from unproblematic figures.[27] Such a statement is bland in its very obviousness: current initiatives to amend state and even the national constitutions in order to "protect" marriage as the exclusive right of a man and a woman are only the latest instances that the problem is alive and well.

The problem is commonly decked out as a danger, and the danger as one of war. The "culture wars" that Scalia expressly mentions in his dissent to *Lawrence* (18) and that he had previously invoked in its more imposing German form—*Kulturkampf*—in his dissent to *Romer v. Evans*,[28] exist alongside other bellicose formations, from "border wars" to, as we have already repeatedly noted, the "war on terrorism." Against public security, safety, and order, culturally inflected and globally driven "wars" hulk menacingly on the horizon. Immigration scholars Norman and Naomi Zucker, in a critical depiction of U.S. asylum and refugee policy in their book *Desperate Crossings*, note that "[t]he enemies now [after the fall of communism] face off from north to south, and the threat is not annihilation, but invasion, invasion of the countries of the north by armies of migrants from the south" (3). Although the compass has lately turned from the south to the extended Middle East (sweeping all the way to Indonesia), these latest "invading enemy immigrants" are also viewed as belonging to powerful cultural blocks that, as in the case of Latinos/as (a category that comes into being *beyond* Latin America), supposedly threaten the very integrity of the country. Whatever the case, the fear of persecution that characterizes the refugee and asylum seeker's narrative of self-presentation in official discourse, and that can inflect the immigrant's fear of poverty and disenfranchisement, is reiterated, altered, and shifted by the state and the media into yet another version of a generalized fear of invasion and war.

The often deliberately provocative and cavalier use of bellicose metaphors must therefore be measured against the reality of police power and militarization, as activist journalist Debbie Nathan, who has studied "the look" of legality among immigrants, so justly observes (34). It is, admittedly, a quasi-militarized state of affairs that is rationalized by appealing not just to terrorism, but also, and less spectacularly, to crime, drug trafficking, disease, linguistic incoherence (the specter of Babel), and economic hardship. By marshalling hackneyed if politically powerful images (immigrants spirit jobs away from citizens, encumber public services, exacerbate the crime rate, and jeopardize freedom itself), public officials, media manipulators, and other self-appointed guardians of a restricted "American way" keep the level of tension high. Frosty Woolridge's *Immigration's Unarmed Invasion: Deadly Consequences* and Jon Dougherty's *Illegals: The Imminent Threat Posed by Our Unsecured U.S.-Mexican Border* are among the latest voices in a chorus of catastrophic tonalities. In this all too effective rhetoric, the invasion, destruction, and disappearance of the United States acquire the force of reality. The rhetoric is as lively as it is ubiquitous, at once marking and marring global, multinational business endeavors and trade agreements with the ever so menacing reality of poverty, inequality, and violence the world over. What is more, for all the patriotic posturing, the rhetoric of global culture wars puts the brakes on high-sounding pronouncements of a *new world order* (which has been called, obviously from a decidedly different perspective, "codified international piracy"[29]) in which the United States would be the bearer of peace, democracy, and prosperity to other nations.

A critical take on the rhetoric of war and peace, on the plays of freedom and justice, on the turns of history, on the slippages and blockages of people, identities, and rationales, and on the tensions between passing and not passing (or being stopped, interdicted, turned away, interned, interrogated, deported, and so forth) run through many, if not most, of the essays assembled here. The essays draw on legal decisions, demographic reports, medical analysis, cultural criticism, social activism, fieldwork, and other protocols in order to raise questions about community, dialogue, representation, and participation in the aforementioned "nation of immigrants." But they all also, and more persistently, draw on the act and art of storytelling, by which a subject presents him or herself as acceptable, even desirable, to a given national collectivity. It is here that passing lines most come to resemble narrative endeavors that nonetheless outstrip the putatively discrete confines of literature—the primary disciplinary provenance, by the way, of the editors of this volume—and that spill into any number of other disciplinary formations. Such interdisciplinary resonances are not without precedent, for as legal scholar Kristen Walker notes, "'[n]arrative legal scholarship' or 'storytelling' is a technique increasingly used in what might broadly be termed 'progressive' legal scholarship" (568). Narrative and storytelling are also at work in medical and psychological studies or case histories, in anthropological and ethnographic research, and obviously in oral testimonies, all of which figure in the present volume. Knowing how difficult interdisciplinarity can be, how closed the Academy, we have included essays by activists as well, though virtually all of the essays are positioned as liberal or progressive, and all of the activist interventions raise theoretical questions. Finally, the recourse to narrative forms in many of the essays in this volume acknowledges immigrants as subjects of experience, agency, and creativity and not merely as objects of governmental regulation, depersonalized statistical inquiry, and legal abstraction.

As gender and sexuality appear more fully and more concertedly on the proverbial world stage, as theories, histories, and stories proliferate and travel, the world as "we" know it is transformed. "Sexuality is not only not essence, not timeless, it is also not fixed in space," write critics Cindy Patton and Benigno Sánchez-Eppler, who recognize that "sexuality is on the move" (2). The movement is not, as Patton and

Sánchez-Eppler know, only spatial, for immigration—and the sexual identities of immigrants—are also profoundly temporal phenomena in which the history of an individual, bound up in the histories of national collectivities, is entwined with a future-oriented present of hopes, expectations, and dreams. Immigration is also profoundly temporal in a more mundane, if still crucial sense: immigration law, that most powerful instance of an unquestionably more general phenomenon, is notoriously intricate, and a good part of its intricacy is the effect of its changeable nature. Even as we write this, President George W. Bush, who has hardly been characterized by his sensitivity to other cultures, has called for a broadened guest-worker program and for reducing obstacles to allow millions of undocumented immigrants, primarily Mexican, to receive legal status. Although the political benefits of such a move (in election years, the Hispanic vote matters) feed legitimate suspicions as to the motivations behind it, there can be no doubt that immigration changes and that its changes implicate geography and history, the places and times of the nation.

For many immigrants, often unfamiliar (like their citizen counterparts) with the letter of the law and often unable to keep up with the changes in it (particularly if they are poor and/or do not have access to legal counsel), hearsay and urban or border legend inevitably inflect proclamations and promises of amnesty. Confronted by so much uncertainty, it is little wonder that many would attempt to make the places and times of the body, with all its pleasure and pain, stand in for those of the nation. To quote Patton and Sánchez-Eppler once more, it thus becomes increasingly imperative to examine "the valences of the body-in-place and [to] consider the transformations in sexuality that move between—indeed may have been produced at—the interstices of specific geopolitical territories. Translocation itself, movement itself, now enter the picture as theoretically significant factors in the discussion of sexuality" (2). And in the discussion of so much more: for it is in the light of translocations and, if you will, transtemporalities (the coming together of different peoples with different histories and different conceptions of history) that the presumably simple act of moving, of crossing borders, of passing lines, is endowed with such ethically and politically charged significance. It is with this significance in mind that we now turn to an overview of the specific essays here assembled, essays which move, as it were, from the social and the legal to the theoretical and the poetic to the testimonial and the activist.

* * *

In "Everything You Ever Wanted To Know About Immigration but Were Afraid To Ask," **Marcelo Suárez-Orozco**, a leading authority on the subject, provides a historical overview of migratory movements to the United States as well as an assessment of the global reality of population shifts in the twentieth and twenty-first centuries. Noting that scholarship on immigration has focused on the *homo economicus* and the *homo socialis,* he recognizes the importance of attending to the *homo sexualis,* to the sexed and gendered realities of human beings in massive, yet individually marked, demographic displacements. "Where capital flows, immigrants follow," Suárez-Orozco remarks, though he clearly understands that other flows are at play, not just those of work, but of love as well. As critical as freedom from persecution undoubtedly is, "love and work drive immigration" (in contradistinction to refuge and asylum, which are by official definition driven by fear), and to such a degree that family reunification and marriage, or rather marriage fraud, remain principal concerns of the Bureau of Citizenship and Immigration Service.[30] Although Suárez-Orozco does not delve into the changing conceptions of marriage and the family by which hierarchical, heterosexual arrangements are challenged, he nonetheless signals the variegated ties by which individuals, or groups of individuals, can gain legal entry into, and/or justify staying in, the United States. "Lifestyle," as conventional discourse (including that of the Supreme Court of the United States) would have it, is thus likewise at play, especially as ideas and images of alternative formations circulate with increasing speed throughout the world. Choices, chances, and convictions, like preferences and orientations, inflect migratory movements, and do so in temporally sensitive ways. If "temporality defines immigration" for large numbers of sojourners who follow seasonal cycles in search of work, it also defines immigration for others who find opportunities for refuge, asylum, and immigration in changing attitudes towards gender and sexuality.

The changing, temporally sensitive processes of immigration often serve, however, not as an opportunity for immigrants to find, let alone to benefit from, shifting conceptions of the family and sexuality, but rather as an opportunity for the state to implement a series of measures that it hopes will seal what it sees as cracks in the national family structure. It is with this in mind that **Eithne Luibhéid** analyzes how neo-liberal U.S. legislation encodes the heteronormative family as the site of the "responsible" citizen. The tactic is certainly not new, and is of a piece with a wide array of immigration policies that home in on immigrants' racial, ethnic, and sexual differences even as they channel them towards an implicit but forceful "American Dream" that still has not shaken the image of white-starched mothers keeping house for their dutiful husbands and docile children. Luibhéid demonstrates how the implementation of heteronormative domestic and immigration policies targets not only—and not even primarily—queers, but also economically underprivileged women of color as "irresponsible" and "unwanted" drains on the public and private good. Through a careful analysis of the Defense of Marriage Act, the Personal Responsibility and Work Opportunity Reconciliation Act (which reformed welfare in the 1990s), and the Illegal Immigration Reform and Immigrant Responsibility Act, Luibhéid exposes how legal immigrants, along with other "dependent" populations, are forced into heteronormative family groupings or are precluded from accessing welfare or the most "efficient" form of legal immigration: family reunification. Luibhéid shows how preclusion takes the place of exclusion in contemporary immigration law, so that lawmakers can sidestep the blatant racism and homophobia of certain past laws even as they continue to stop "unwanted" populations such as Latinos/as and queers from entering the United States.

Of course, not all immigration passes, or can pass, through family reunification or sponsorship; instead, a good deal of it engages a loosely defined but often acutely felt "pursuit of happiness," which is not at all disconnected from fear. Home, after all, can be hell, anything but a sweet refuge from the trials and tribulations of public life, and there is thus more than one way that immigration, asylum, and refuge can entail the search for a new "home." Refuge and fear, then, are forged in and out of the home, though legal systems have their own ways of understanding both—and of imagining home and hell in the process. The International Refugee Convention, drafted in 1951 and subsequently ratified by some 138 countries, granted legal protection on the basis of fear of persecution for one of the following five reasons: race, religion, nationality, membership in a particular social group, and political opinion. So far, the most productive avenue for securing refugee status for women who have experienced, or been threatened with, sexual violence, including domestic abuse and genital mutilation (often misleadingly figured as "female circumcision"), has been to argue for "membership in a particular social group," which has also been invoked to grant asylum to gays and lesbians (or to those who identify as such for purposes of legal intelligibility) fleeing physical violence or the real possibility of it. Interestingly, in the United States, some judges have taken "sexual preference," despite its voluntaristic ring, and not just "sexual orientation," to be an "immutable characteristic." Whatever the understandings of immutability, belonging, and group formation, refugee and asylum are considered humanitarian remedies aimed at providing surrogate state protection for people from countries that are determined not to have provided adequate protection.

Deborah Anker, working at the intersections of immigration, gender studies, and legal practice, examines the mutually reinforcing regimes of asylum/refugee law and international human rights law. Although the human rights paradigm has become progressively more international and independent of national domestic legal systems, it is precisely such independence that has made many human rights workers cautious about becoming involved in particular refugee and asylum claims, of moving from theory to practice. And yet, refugee law, which in Anker's formulation often functions as the "poor cousin" of human rights, supplements human rights law by working within a specific national regime to provide protection to those who have fled abuse. The formally non-intrusive nature of refugee law (it does not attempt to intervene in the state of origin) may actually allow it to confront issues involving gender and sexuality that have proved problematic for, and been marginalized by, international law. Sensitive to the complexities of theoretically informed critique, advocacy, litigation, and adjudication, Anker focuses on three interrelated issues: rape and sexual violence, family violence, and female genital surgery (FGS), arguably the most culturally contentious of the three. According to Anker, accusations of cultural relativism concerning FGS have stymied debate within international human rights law, but not so with asylum claims, since asylum exists to protect an individual who wants to dissociate herself from a State's norms, or who has a reasonable fear of persecution if she were to be returned to that State. Although asylum law's solutions, which are largely palliative, cannot be enjoined upon the state of origin, they nevertheless *can* generate opportunities for communities to mobilize and contest injustice. One drawback to asylum and refugee law is, as Anker indicates, its vulnerability to national political backlash and its entrenched relation to domestic legal regimes: hence the reliance on *international* human rights standards. On the other hand, asylum and refugee law may be more sensitive to the multifaceted and contingent nature of socially constructed identities inasmuch as it grapples with individual cases. Despite the differences and tensions between them, asylum law and human rights are tied together in ways that could enable fruitful cooperation, though scholars and activists must pay attention to the interplays of theory, tactics, and strategy.[31]

Working, like Anker, within a legal framework, **Alice Miller** offers a different, albeit complementary, view. For Miller, whose disciplinary field involves family health, the daily effort to win claims for individual asylum seekers must be pursued along with a critical understanding of how the laws of asylum "limit and divide" humanity. Preferring the plural "sexualities" to a seemingly more stable and singular "sexuality," Miller questions how legal knowledge—including expert witness testimony and documentation—bears on the production and regulation of sexuality as immutable, transcultural, and bounded by binary divisions. She contends that asylum advocacy and human rights work, tensely interconnected, must become more cognizant of contemporary theorizations of sexuality as historically and culturally contingent in order to challenge the law's tendency to congeal sexual conduct, behavior, or acts into a delimited set of identities. Miller recognizes that, in arguments for asylum, identities are built in accordance with acceptable norms for the narration of persecution or abuse and, moreover, in accordance with a *recognizable gay transnational identity*. Successful claims fulfill the previously mentioned requirement for group membership by presenting sexuality as innate, fundamental, and unchanging, but often at the price of obscuring or discounting other sexual modalities. As a result, Miller, like Anker, calls for increased human rights documentation, necessary not only to validate individual claims of persecution, but also to *broaden* the understanding of the nature of harm and its manifestations. Human rights organizations can become moral entrepreneurs, Miller suggests, by going beyond the very real need to document abuses to thinking about sexuality and its expression as a right. Examining three asylum cases whose subjects range from the "flamboyant" to the "discreet," the "out" to the "closeted," Miller brings to the fore a number of contradictions to argue that while asylum can recognize violations and grant *individuals* protection, human rights, if adequately reconfigured, can lay the conditions for a more thriving sense of sexuality and for a more supple and permeable practice of nationality in an international frame.

Looking at the law from outside a professional legal framework, **Brad Epps** grapples with the ways in which legality unevenly implicates us all. He does so by bringing to bear interpretative protocols generally associated with the "law-as-literature movement" onto *Lawrence v. Texas*, the landmark 2003 U.S. Supreme Court decision that overturned *Bowers v. Hardwick* and effectively decriminalized homosexuality (understood by the Court in terms of same-sex sodomy). Arguing that *Lawrence* is more than a domestic legal decision concerning U.S. citizens, Epps teases out the international underpinnings and ramifications of the changes in the legal status of "homosexuals" and reads the debates about privacy that the decision reignites against a post-9/11 backdrop of embattled civil liberties, governmental surveillance, and increased anxiety about immigration. The international dimension is figured explicitly in the *Lawrence* Court's reliance on cases and decisions from other Western nations, Canada and Britain chief among them, and in its repudiation of *Bowers'* ahistorical reliance on "Judeo-Christian moral and ethical standards" (*Bowers*, Burger, concurring in judgment). Yet the international dimension is also figured, acutely if implicitly, in the history of the role of sexuality, and particularly homosexuality, in U.S. immigration policy and in long-standing concerns about "national security" (evident, for instance, in the continued ban on gays in the military). The criminalization of homosexual citizens—who, as such, were not "full citizens"—is of a piece, that is, with the exclusion of foreign homosexuals, who, like their American-born counterparts, were, and in many respects still are, deemed to be "undesirable" by virtue of their desires and practices. Although *Lawrence* constitutes a major rebuff to the age-old stigmatization of homosexuals, it does not come without a hitch. For *Lawrence* decriminalizes homosexuality by presenting it in terms of enduring personal bonds, privacy, and dignity, the very terms that have buttressed heteronormativity, focused at its most conservative on "natural," uninterrupted procreation and at its most liberal on private, "recreational" pleasure. Epps, following others, argues that a regime of "national heterosexuality," at once naturalized and disavowed as the very ground of legal reasoning itself, remains firmly in place and allows the Justices to keep their own sexuality discreetly out of consideration. Attending to the chains of equivalence between immigrants, queers, women, and people of color, Epps calls not just for continued vigilance after *Lawrence* but also for a *mise en question* of the identity categories by which groups are constructed, regulated, and controlled.

The *Lawrence* Court's reliance on foreign jurisprudence, which conservative Justice Antonin Scalia roundly lambastes, is only one indication of the ways in which U.S. domestic decisions can have important implications for immigration. Though considerably more progressive than the United States in social matters, Canada is often collapsed—especially by Spanish-speakers—into a general "North America" that effectively excises Mexico and inflates the United States. And yet, for all the differences between Canada and the United States, (including the status of same-sex marriage), gay and lesbian asylum seekers in Canada face many of the same problems as their counterparts in the U.S. Individuals may petition to be granted asylum in Canada based on persecution in their countries of origin, but documenting persecution can be difficult. **Bill Fairbairn**, who has been involved in human rights work and asylum cases in Canada and Latin America for over ten years, articulates some of these difficulties in "Gay Rights Are Human Rights." Detailing several cases on which he has worked, he recounts the efforts of the Inter-Church Committee on Human Rights in Latin America (ICCHRLA), with which he was long affiliated, to remedy the problems faced by asylum seekers in the Canadian legal system. Unlike the other contributors to this volume, whose perspective is rigorously secular, Fairbairn, who also authored a report titled *Violence Unveiled: Repression Against Lesbians and Gay Men in Latin America*, links the struggle for human dignity to faith in God—a proposition that is hardly free from controversy on both the right and the left. Given the importance of religiously based advocacy groups and, more famously, liberation theology in Latin America, Fairbairn's perspective is important, and serves to supplement perspectives in which spirituality figures little if at all. Motivated by a critical version of religion, Fairbairn and his associates criticize the deep-seated homophobia of many Christian organizations and strive to contribute, from within a more tolerant Christian framework, to the realization of a just civil society.

Fairbairn's work in Latin America is productively supplemented by many of our other contributors. **Roger Lancaster** concentrates not on legal or religious systems and their activist critics, but rather on Latin American sexual cultures and on the ways in which the successes of the international gay, lesbian, bisexual, and transgendered movement can issue in devastating local failures. Silence may equal death, but visibility can breed violence: such is the troublesome lesson that Lancaster extracts from his survey of recent developments in Latin America. Rejecting totalizing theories of sexuality that overlook variations not only between nations, or between the urban and the rural, but also *within* a given city or town, Lancaster deploys "traditional culture" and "machismo" in order to sound out, and complicate, their significance. He contends that traditional sexual cultures in Latin America, operating under the sign of *machismo*, are not *uniformly* oppressive and violent and that they have historically enabled, even produced, a certain tolerance whose price is measured in sneers, jeers, catcalls, pinches, pokes, and winks—but not physical violence. In keeping with Herbert Marcuse's notion of repressive tolerance, "a certain tolerance" is more accurately a "tolerant intolerance," a deliberately paradoxical formulation which does not designate so much a new, alluring form of liberty in consumer societies as an old, leering form of survival in traditional societies (it is not by accident that Lancaster focuses on Nicaragua and not, say, on Buenos Aires or Rio de Janeiro, where some of the same problems nonetheless obtain). Examining tradition, Lancaster also examines new social movements and contends that anti-gay violence is *not* predicated only on *machismo*, but derives as well from an international homosexual movement in which "passive" and "active," or as the anthropologists prefer "insertive" and "receptive," are thrown into question, troubling the longstanding notion throughout much of Latin America that the "active" participant in a same-sex act escapes social stigma and shame. The aim is not to cast blame on a gay international, but rather to address some of the unfortunate effects that it has inadvertently generated. In a culture that operates according to homologies, sexual practice is homogenized with gendered sexual identity (hence the gay man is the man who has sex with men), but in a heterologic sexual culture, such as those of Central America, sexual identity is predicated, for example, on what *position* one occupies in having sex. In sum, the international movement of people and ideas is changing the reality of same-sex communities in Latin America, the intolerance faced by gays, lesbians, and other sexual minorities in Latin America, and the places where they can seek truly tolerant refuge and negotiate nationally inflected tensions between sexual identity and practice.

If Lancaster attends to the clashes between traditional and alternative modes of sexuality from an anthropological perspective, **Lawrence La Fountain-Stokes** attends to cultural representations of (homo)sexuality in literature and the arts. In so doing, he explores the twists and turns of Puerto Rican identity, in which the status of the national is particularly fraught. Indeed, the status of the national is here so fraught that the meaning of immigration and emigration is wrenched away from exclusively legal protocols: Puerto Ricans, as holders of U.S. passports, do not, strictly speaking, immigrate to the

United States—and yet they do immigrate, experientially and culturally, to the United States. Writer Manuel Ramos Otero, filmmaker Frances Negrón-Muntaner, and performance artist Erika López are at the center of La Fountain-Stokes' reflections and allow him to tackle differences in genre along with differences in geography and generation. Yet, despite their differences, all three artists grapple with verbal expression and, more precisely, with the highly politicized, culturally laden tensions between Spanish and English. How sexuality is articulated, how it is spoken, written, and named, can vary between and within a given language, as is evident in Ramos Otero's "opening towards linguistic plurality" from within Spanish or in López's performative shifts from English to Spanish. Concerned with aesthetics, La Fountain-Stokes also pays considerable attention to health (primarily through HIV/AIDS), education, family formations, income, and, as noted, language. He therefore understands that sex and sexuality are caught in highly charged webs of representation and that the varieties of cultural production can play critical roles in the construction, and deconstruction, of sexual acts and identities, which La Fountain-Stokes presents as plural and always in process. The dispersion in which a sense of identity still insists, no less than the dispersion that is itself a sense of identity, is critical to the conceptualization of a Puerto Rican diaspora, which La Fountain-Stokes nuances by linking it to the "queer diasporas" that Cindy Patton and Benigno Sánchez-Eppler have also studied.[32] The strings and strains that mark relations between Puerto Ricans who remain in Puerto Rico and Puerto Ricans who emigrate, let alone those that mark relations between Puerto Ricans, (other) U.S. citizens,) Latinos/as, and Latin Americans, obtain in different ways for first-generation migrants and second- or third-generation migrants.[33] The long-dominant perception in Puerto Rico that homosexuality was a "foreign import," a "vice" characteristic of cultures such as the North American where the institution of the family is supposedly less solid, has lately undergone serious revisions, as queer Puerto Rican activists, artists, critics, and others move back and forth and question the very limits of the nation.

Alberto Sandoval-Sánchez, cited by La Fountain-Stokes as a Puerto Rican writer who refuses to desire *the* place of his birth as the place to which he must return to die, offers a moving, autobiographic account of his struggle with AIDS and Latino/a cultural identity. Mixing languages in a manner that engages the bicultural and bilingual movements that unevenly characterize Puerto Rican society, Sandoval also mixes testimony and elegy, poetry and prose, creation and critique, the self and others. Sandoval's writing is a restive, resistant exercise in mourning and melancholy, in letting go and holding on, which bears within it not only a shadow of death but also a pledge of freedom. Unlike the celebrated Cuban writer Reinaldo Arenas, who fled Cuba and committed suicide while in exile in the United States, Sandoval does not long to return to his "native land"; much less does he blame his HIV/AIDS on his exile. Then again, Sandoval does not speak merely of exile, but rather of "sexile," in which exile provides the occasion for sexual pleasure: the land of freedom is, quite queerly, a land of delectation. Sandoval thus courts an audacious division that others understandably contest: the United States as libidinally accommodating and Latin America, shadowed forth shakily through Puerto Rico, as libidinally fettered (interestingly, such divisions underpin arguments for asylum and refuge in the United States). Sandoval holds that in combining gay and Latino/a positions he has had to reinvent the concept of "home" with respect not only to heteronormative and heterosexist family structures but also to configurations of the homeland and the nation. In the process, he reinvents nostalgia itself, that longing for (a) home that is one of the most effective, and affective, props of nationalism. For Sandoval, the expected longing for his Puerto Rican home—and a Puerto Rican nation—is frustrated, fruitfully he suggests, by an ambivalent adherence to his home in the United States but not, for all that, to a dominant conception of U.S. nationalism. He claims, in short, that "to stay in charge of [his] illness, [his] career, [su] vida y [su] cuerpo" he has had to lay claim to a different "familia" and to another country that is not simply the dominant Anglo version of the United States. The between-and-betwixt status of Puerto Rico, combined with the between-and-betwixt status of HIV/AIDS (mortal and/or "manageable") can contribute, Sandoval suggests, to a heightened appreciation of the interstices and precariousness of national and sexual identity in general.

Sandoval's intimate perspective on AIDS at once complements and contrasts with **Paul Farmer** and **Nicole Gastineau's** medically informed study of "structural violence," which outstrips individual agency and implicates entire political and economic systems. Focusing on HIV/AIDS in Haiti, they recognize that domestic violence is also structural, but they argue that poverty and disease tend to be more readily naturalized into an intractable order that tends to understand them as *other* than violations of human rights.[34] Farmer and Gastineau move well beyond personal narratives (on which they nonetheless draw) as they contest complacent, capitalist renditions of human rights and contend that, "the flow of capital can provide some logic to the flow of microbes." HIV/AIDS is, in other words, a transnational pandemic connected to large-scale forces, including those of capital, which implicate the nations of the world in highly irregular ways. Cognizant of the heavy-handed representations of Haiti, HIV/AIDS, and homosexuality in the media (which popularized a dubious "4-H club" of Haitians, Homosexuals, Hemophiliacs, and Habitual Drug Users), Farmer and Gastineau present a nuanced account in which personal testimony and statistical analysis mutually reinforce each other. Refusing to lose sight of either the individual human beings affected by HIV/AIDS or the larger structural forces that exacerbate the spread of the syndrome, they perform a "balancing act" that allows them to attend to the overlaps and contradictions that characterize the realities and the representations of HIV/AIDS. Sensitive to the homophobic manipulations of the syndrome, yet refusing to idealize, in some misguided compensatory move, homosexuality itself, they acknowledge sexual tourism involving U.S. gay men to the island as part, but only as part, of a broader and deeper problem: poverty. It is poverty that impels many Haitians into prostitution, and it is poverty that impels many into relations that "call into question facile notions of 'consensual sex'" and of marriage itself.[35] Such large-scale social phenomena as hunger, forced dislocation, political violence, and lack of housing, services, and education enable the spread of HIV/AIDS and place constraints on how to provide medical aid. The laws controlling the entry of people with HIV/AIDS, unevenly enforced, contribute to a climate of suspicion and to the continued stratification of sexual and national identities, with Haitians occupying an especially vulnerable position.

While it is only recently becoming common knowledge that poor women are most likely to be infected with HIV in Haiti, it has long been understood that women across the globe are the most common victims of domestic abuse. Nonetheless, cases of asylum for women who suffer domestic abuse are relatively rare—and statistics on the role that domestic abuse may play in women's immigration proper are rarer still. The problem here lies in the difficulty in establishing abused women as a persecuted group. **Matthew Price** and **Angelica Cházaro** both examine the recent asylum case of Rodi Alvarado Peña, a Guatemalan woman who suffered severe physical and sexual abuse at the hands of her husband in her home country. An immigration judge granted her claim for asylum, but the Board of Immigration Appeals (BIA) overturned the ruling, prompting former Attorney General Janet Reno to vacate the BIA's decision and to remand the case for reconsideration. Although the BIA agreed that Alvarado Peña had suffered persecution that would likely continue if she were forced to return to Guatemala, it also found that she had *not* been persecuted for any of the reasons covered under the United Nations Convention Relating to the Status of Refugees. Since Alvarado Peña's race, religion, and nationality were not at issue, it was up to the BIA to decide how, or if, a woman battered by her husband could qualify for membership in a social group or could be said to have a political opinion. The Board justified its decision to deny Alvarado asylum by limiting its interpretation of the Convention's reasons. Alvarado Peña, having gone public about her private life, was thus left in a sort of legal no-woman's land, "at home" neither in Guatemala nor the United States.

Matthew Price, working in political science and the law, takes on the logic behind the BIA decisions in the Alvarado Peña case, which he studies in the light of international agreements on human rights. As others in this volume also indicate, human rights, despite (or perhaps because of) their humanist trappings, have not always accommodated sexual minorities or women, at least as legitimate "groups." Most refugee advocates and academic commentators support, according to Price, an approach to asylum that tends "to offer surrogate protection to those who are exposed to violations of human rights and are unable to receive protection from their own state." The status of the state, and not just of the individual applicant or the group to which he or she belongs (or is said to belong), is at the center of the distinctions that Price studies, and leads him to advocate an approach that privileges political membership (and a renewed, refined appreciation of politics) over a victim-prone conception of human rights. And yet, both approaches, as he reminds us, are problematic inasmuch as they construct arbitrary distinctions between similarly imperiled applicants. The theoretical and practical problems that States face in the elaboration and implementation of asylum policy bear on the legitimacy, power, and (self)-perception of the States themselves. Angélica Cházaro, focusing on the language of the BIA decision to deny asylum, supplements Price's focus on logic. A student of law and literature, Cházaro analyzes the language used by the United Nations Convention Relating to the Status of Refugees, by the BIA, and by Alvarado Peña and her lawyers. Revisiting the definitions of "refugee," "well-founded fear," "persecution," and

"social group," Cházaro examines how these terms are molded, modified, and understood in immigration courts. Through a careful analysis of the rhetorical and legal structures that Alvarado Peña encounters in the process of filing her claim, Cházaro exposes the paradoxical positions of citizen and refugee, individual and group member, victim and survivor that the (potential) refugee must inhabit. Cházaro argues that the BIA's refusal to grant Alvarado Peña asylum issues from the inability to fit her experiences into current legal language, all of which prompts her to suggest, like Miller and others, that the language of the law ought to be expanded to address the needs of women who have to pass State-lines in order to escape domestic violence.

Although the courts often fail immigrant women, battered or otherwise, many of these women find ways to form communities of mutual assistance and empowerment once they come to reside, whether with or without legal documentation, in the United States. **Kathleen Coll** discusses her work with *Mujeres Unidas y Activas*, a grassroots Latina immigrant group in San Francisco that provides women emotional support, practical information, and the opportunity for political organization. Combining feminist theories of performativity and cultural citizenship, Coll argues that the women of *Mujeres Unidas* resist hegemonic ideas about subjectivity, political participation, and immigrant rights through their daily practices. Grassroots organizing, which has been particularly important in the context of anti-immigrant legislation such as California's Proposition 187, has helped to combat the social isolation and vulnerability that many immigrants experience by providing a space for peer counseling, education, and mobilization and by resituating personal experiences not as individualistic and apolitical, but as fundamental to a more accurate and compelling understanding of group rights. While many of the women involved in *Mujeres Unidas* may uphold norms of gendered behavior, the maintenance of certain norms can constitute, according to Coll, an unexpected form of resistance: through their everyday, normative performances, the women of *Mujeres Unidas y Activas* give the lie to media images of immigrants as unproductive and prone to criminality. Coll thus contends that community-based organizing and an appreciation of quotidian practices can contribute to a renewed theorization of citizenship and systems of power.

Women's organizing of a different sort is at the center of attention of historian and activist **Norma Mogrovejo**, who documents the evolution of Latin American lesbian and gay organizing, which both

Lancaster and Fairbairn, albeit from markedly dissimilar perspectives, also examine. In her own version of "sexile," Mogrovejo, a Peruvian who immigrated to Mexico in order to live more openly and actively as a lesbian, signals important differences and divisions *within* Latin America as well as within its migratory movements: at the most basic level, Mogrovejo reminds us that people do not merely emigrate from Mexico, as a dominant image would lead us to believe, but that they also immigrate to it. That said, Mexico, unlike Canada and the United States, does not consider sexual orientation as a basis for asylum, and offers minimal legal protection for gays and lesbians living in the country, whether Mexican citizens or not. And yet, it is just this situation, among others, that Mogrovejo and her fellow activists propose to remedy. After all, Mexico boasts one of the more vibrant and organized queer communities in Latin America and thus offers people relatively more opportunities to combat violence against lesbians, gays, transvestites, transsexuals, and other sexual minorities. Combining personal reflection, political action, and scholarly inquiry, Mogrovejo details some of the difficulties that people in search of greater freedom of sexual identity and expression face upon immigrating to Mexico. Inasmuch as Mogrovejo promotes national and international grassroots and academic cooperation from within Mexico, her work complements Coll's U.S.-based work. Taken together, Mogrovejo's and Coll's essays point to the importance of less border-bound initiatives to increase and improve the rights for lesbian and gay immigrants (including a more expansive understanding of family and a critical take on the privileges of marriage) throughout the Americas and to change the conditions that contribute to such sexually oriented immigration in the first place. A viable lesbian movement in Arequipa, Peru, for instance, would have to wrestle with the meaning of "lesbian" as defined, debated, and deconstructed in the United States and elsewhere, while attending to questions of poverty, policy, language (particularly important in countries with large indigenous populations), and collective organization in more nationally diverse and regionally located ways.

Of course, as we have been insisting, many lesbians, gays, and other queer people leave their home countries in search for the same things as straight people: education, employment, and the promise of a better life for themselves and their families (a promise which is no less real for being often deceptive). Thus, the stories of lesbian immigrants belong as much—if not indeed more—to the annals of women immigrants

as they do to those of asylum seekers and refugees. Such is the case of Maria Angelica, who figures as only one among many women in **Heloisa Maria Galvão**'s project on oral, experiential-based histories of Brazilian women immigrants in the Boston area. Attending to concrete, personal narratives, to "passing lines" far removed from the abstract theoretical propositions of many academics and legal experts, Galvão considers the changes in family structure, gender roles, sexual self-understanding, and political engagement that Brazilian women undergo through the double-edged process of emigration and immigration; her work joins studies such as Nancy López's "Transnational Changing Gender Roles: Second-Generation Dominicans in New York City" to begin to account for the long-term effects of "passing lines" on gender and sexuality both "here" and "there." Galvão writes for both Brazilian and U.S. newspapers and journals, works in bilingual education, and also acts as a community organizer; the findings that she presents here, and that are part of a much larger project to document the history of the Brazilian immigrant community in Massachusetts, are thus in the spirit of Coll's and Mogrovejo's "hands-on" appreciation of the critical complexities of agency and representation (who speaks for whom). Among other things, Galvão interrogates the sense of freedom from larger family and community pressures that the mere fact of distance can enable and examines how Brazilian women encounter new sexual possibilities and problems, pursue new careers (both rewarding and frustrating), and shape new neighborhoods. At the same time, even as they engage new and different forms of freedom in and through the United States, the women recount how they miss the family and community ties that were familiar to them in Brazil. Rather than returning to Brazil, however, many women immigrants, grappling with entrenched patriarchal formations, work to reform family and community groups around their activities and interests.

The essays assembled here move between academic inquiry and activist involvement; between statistical analysis and personal testimony; between the law, medicine, history, and literature; between theoretically informed reflection and experientially oriented engagement. The geographic sweep among the activists—from San Francisco, New York, Boston, Canada, and Mexico—attempts to give a measure of the complexities of location, while the range of academic disciplines strives to give a partial account of the complexities of intellectual production. Much remains to be thought, imagined, and done, but *Passing Lines*, we hope, productively throws into relief multiple intersections of im-

migration and sexuality that should inflect any serious consideration of nationality, identity, gendered and sexual practice, and movement in the much-ballyhooed, and much-criticized age of globalization. The nation, as a supposedly natural construct that relies on reproduction, has enshrined a delimited conception of the family that maintains the ascendancy of men over women and of the straight over the queer, an ascendancy that reinforces, in a variety of complex and not so complex ways, that of the "native insider" over the "alien outsider" and of the conformist over the dissident. *Passing Lines* pushes at the shrine of national heteronormativity, and proposes, in the process, a more supple, assertive, and just appreciation of the intricacies of humanity and democracy that might pass beyond, without disavowing or ignoring, the petty lines of patriotism and of gendered and sexual embodiment.

Works Cited

Adams, David. "Haitian Pastor Dies on U.S. Doorstep." *St. Petersburg Times* November 19, 2004. http://www.sptimes.com/2004/11/19/Worldandnation/ Haitian_pastor_dies_o.shtml (accessed January 1, 2005).

Alexander, M. Jacqui. "Not Just (Any) Body Can Be A Citizen: The Politics of Law, Sexuality, and Postcoloniality in Trinidad and Tobago and the Bahamas." *Feminist Review* 48 (1994): 5–23.

Althusser, Louis. "Marxism and Humanism." *For Marx.* By Louis Althusser. Trans. Ben Brewster. London: NLB, 1977.

Bhabha, Homi. "Of Mimicry and Man: The Ambivalence of Cultural Discourse." *The Location of Culture.* London: Routledge, 1994. 85–92.

Bowers v. Hardwick. Supreme Court of the United States. 478 U.S. 186 (1986).

Butler, Judith. "Passing, Queering: Nella Larsen's Psychoanalytic Challenge." *Female Subjects in Black and White: Race, Psychoanalysis, Feminism.* Ed. Elizabeth Abel, Barbara Christian, Helen Moglen. Berkeley: University of California Press, 1997.

California Proposition 187. http://wikisource.org/wiki/California_Proposition _187_ (1994).

Cannaday, Margot. "'Who is a Homosexual?': The Consolidation of Sexual Identities in Mid-twentieth-century American Immigration Law." *Law and Social Inquiry* 28.2 (2003): 351–387.

Chomsky, Noam. *World Orders Old and New.* New York: Columbia University Press, 1994, 1996.

Cliff, Michelle. *No Telephone to Heaven.* New York: Dutton, 1987.

Danticat, Edwidge. *Krik? Krak!* New York: Random House, 1996.

Dougherty, Jon. *Illegals: The Imminent Threat Posed by Our Unsecured U.S.-Mexico Border.* Nashville: WND Books, 2004.

Epps, Brad. "Passing Lines: Immigration and the Performance of American Identity." *Passing: Identity and Interpretation in Sexuality, Race, and Religion.* Ed. María Carla Sánchez and Linda Schlossberg. New York: New York University Press, 2001. 92–134.

Griffin, John Howard. *Black Like Me.* Boston: Houghton Mifflin, 1976.

Griswold v. Connecticut. Supreme Court of the United States. 381 U.S. 479 (1965).

Hing, Bill Ong. "Immigration Policies: Messages of Exclusion to African Americans." *Howard Law Journal* 37.2 (1994): 237–282.

Hughes, Langston. *The Ways of White Folks.* New York: Vintage Books, 1990.

Immigration and Nationality Act. http://uscis.gov/graphics/lawsregs/INA.htm (accessed January 1, 2005).

Johnson, Barbara. "Lesbian Spectacles: Reading *Sula, Passing, Thelma and Louise,* and *The Accused.*" *Media Spectacles.* Ed. Marjorie Garber, Jann Matlock, and Rebecca Walkowitz. New York: Routledge, 1993. 160–166.

Johnson, Creola. "Quarantining HIV-Infected Haitians: United States' Violations of International Law at Guantánamo Bay." *Howard Law Journal* 37.2 (1994): 305–331.

Joseph, May. *Nomadic Identities: The Performance of Citizenship.* Minneapolis: University of Minnesota Press, 1999.

Larsen, Nella. *Quicksand and Passing.* Ed. Deborah E. McDowell. New Brunswick: Rutgers University Press, 1986.

Lawrence v. Texas. Supreme Court of the United States. 539 U.S. 558 (2003).

Leich, Marian Nash. "Contemporary Practice of the United States Relating to International Law." *American Journal of International Law* 85.2 (1991).

Leinwand, Donna. "Illegals Going Back by the Planeload." *USA Today,* February 17, 2005: B1.

Levenson, Michael. "Romney Links Gay Marriage, U.S. Prestige." *The Boston Globe,* February 26, 2005.

López, Nancy. "Transnational Changing Gender Roles: Second-Generation Dominicans in New York City." *Dominican Migrations: Transnational Perspectives.* Ed. Ernesto Sagá and Sintia E. Molina. Gainesville: Florida University Press, 2004.

Luibhéid, Eithne. *Entry Denied: Controlling Sexuality at the Border.* Minneapolis: University of Minnesota Press, 2002.

McDowell, Deborah E. "Introduction." *Quicksand and Passing.* By Nella Larsen. Ed. Deborah E. McDowell New Brunswick: Rutgers University Press, 1986.

Mosse, George L. *Nationalism and Sexuality: Middle-Class Morality and Sexual Norms in Modern Europe.* Madison: University of Wisconsin Press, 1985.

Nathan, Debbie. *Women and Other Aliens: Essays from the U.S.-Mexico Border.* El Paso: Cinco Puntos Press, 1991.

"NCLR REAL ID Act Talking Points." http://www.nclr.org/content/resources/detail/30066/.

"NCLR Talking Points on PAN." http://www.nclr.org/content/resources/detail/26633/.

The New Shorter Oxford English Dictionary on Historical Principles. Ed. Lesley Brown. Oxford: Clarendon Press, 1993.

Parker, Andrew; Mary Russo, Doris Sommer, and Patricia Yaeger, eds. *Nationalisms and Sexualities.* New York: Routledge, 1992.

Patton, Cindy and Benigno Sánchez-Eppler, eds. *Queer Diasporas.* Durham, N.C.: Duke University Press, 2000.

Phelan, Shane. *Sexual Strangers: Gays, Lesbians, and Dilemmas of Citizenship.* Philadelphia: Temple University Press, 2001.

Qureshi, Sarah N. "Global Ostracism of HIV-Positive Aliens: International Restrictions Barring HIV-Positive Aliens." *Maryland Journal of International Law and Trade* 19.1 (1995): 81–120.

Renan, Ernest. *Qu'est-ce qu'une nation? et autres essais politiques.* Paris: Pocket, 1992.

Rodriguez, Richard. *Hunger of Memory.* Boston: D. R. Godine, 1982.

Romer v. Evans. Supreme Court of the United States. 517 U.S. 620 (1996).

Rosaldo, Renato. "Cultural Citizenship, Inequality, and Multiculturalism." *Latino Cultural Citizenship: Claiming Identity, Space, and Rights.* Ed. William Flores and Rina Benmayor. Boston: Beacon Press, 1997. 27–38.

_____. *Culture and Truth: The Remaking of Social Analysis.* Boston: Beacon Press, 1989.

Schlossberg, Linda. "Introduction: Rites of Passing." *Passing: Identity and Interpretation in Sexuality, Race, and Religion.* Ed. María Carla Sánchez and Linda Schlossberg. New York: New York University Press, 2001. 1–12.

"State/Local Police Enforcement of Immigration Laws (CLEAR Act)." National Council of La Raza: nclr.org. http://www.nclr.org/content/policy/detail/1063/.

Takaki, Ronald. *A Different Mirror: A History of Multicultural America.* Boston: Little, Brown and Company, 1993.

Walker, Kristen. "The Importance of Being Out: Sexuality and Refugee Status." *Sydney Law Review* 18 (1996): 568–597.

West, Robin. *Narrative, Authority, and Law.* Ann Arbor: University of Michigan Press, 1993.

Weissinger, George. *Law Enforcement and the INS: A Participant Observation Study of Control Agents.* Lanham, Maryland: University Press of America, 1996.

Woolridge, Frosty. *Immigration's Unarmed Invasion: Deadly Consequences.* Bloomington: Authorhouse, 2004.

Zucker, Norman L. and Naomi Flink Zucker. *Desperate Crossings: Seeking Refuge in America.* Armonk, New York: M. E. Sharpe, 1996.

Notes

1 Limited sections of this introduction are based on Brad Epps' previously published essay, "Passing Lines."

2 The definitions are culled from *The New Shorter Oxford English Dictionary.*

3 Our emphasis on the everyday performances that secure or disrupt a migrant subject's participation in public life is in concert with May Joseph's call for detailed analyses of the "expressive enactments of citizenship" in an era of transnationalism. For Joseph, it is "in the way one holds one's body, the music one consumes, or the kind of theatre one produces" that the agency of those who strive to "reinvent themselves according to prevalent notions of authentic citizenship, either popularly or officially defined" can be found (4).

4 According to Homi Bhabha, "the visibility of mimicry is always produced at the site of interdiction. It is a form of colonial discourse that is uttered inter dicta: a discourse at the crossroads of what is known and permissible and that which though known must be kept concealed; a discourse uttered between the lines and as such both against the rules and within them" (89). The ambivalent and unpredictable effects of visibility in gay and lesbian attempts to secure increased human rights and participation as citizens in national regimes are also recognized by Shane Phelan in her book *Sexual Strangers*: "Assertions that visibility is essential to gay and lesbian citizenship [...] introduce further questions: Who among these diverse groups is to be visible? Is all visibility good? [...] Visibility is no guarantee of either citizenship or equality" (6). Particularly in the area of transnational negotiations concerning human rights, as Miller's chapter in this anthology demonstrates, the increased visibility of some groups can produce the invisibility of others, or inadvertently work to narrow the available definitions of sexual identity.

5   For more on secondary inspection and related means of "eliciting sexual confessions," see Luibhéid's *Entry Denied* (88).

6   According to Marcelo Suárez-Orozco, since 1990, about a million new immigrants have come to the U.S. yearly. There are now about thirty million immigrants in the United States, the largest number in the country's history; it is estimated that some seven million are "undocumented." Many of these undocumented immigrants come from Latin American countries, and the Hispanic population within the U.S. has risen from 3 percent in 1945 to 10 percent in 1995 to an estimated 25 percent by 2050. Over 52 percent of the total documented immigrant population in the U.S. was born in Latin America, a designation that includes the Caribbean nations of Cuba and the Dominican Republic. Within such parameters, the immigrant population in the U.S. is still remarkably diverse: some immigrants are among the most educated and affluent; others have little, if any, education and are poor; still others, finding it difficult to parlay their expertise into gainful employment, are educated and poor. And Latin American immigrants are certainly not alone, as evidenced in the more than 100 languages now spoken in New York Public Schools, and the over 90 in Los Angeles. Nearly 80 percent of immigrants are classified as "people of color." Statistics proliferate, generated, compiled, and deployed for often vastly different purposes.

7   Although the very word "queer" remains so charged as to be offensive to some, especially those who remember all too well its once exclusively derogatory thrust, its recent transvalued vindication and promotion as a malleable, resistant way of designating a wide but still stigmatized variety of people makes it not only all but unavoidable but also conceptually valuable.

8   In her discussion of *Bowers v. Hardwick*, Robin West argues that, "the Court could have held that Georgia's anti-sodomy statute violated the equal protection clause of the Fourteenth Amendment had it found that because homosexuals are a hated and irrationally maligned minority, anti-homosexuality legislation is analogous to legislation based on a 'suspect classification' and therefore should be struck unless it serves a compelling state need" (302). West refers to *Regents of University of California v. Bakke*, 438 U.S. 265, 290–291 (1978) for a discussion of the meaning of "suspect classification."

9   A number of organizations work at the intersections of human rights, asylum, and immigration. For example, 1993 saw the formation of the Lesbian and Gay Immigration Rights Task Force (LGIRTF), an organization that assisted in writing and promoting the Permanent Partners' Immigration Act, which would extend to same-sex bi-national couples the immigration rights and responsibilities already enjoyed by heterosexual

married couples. LGIRTF, which has recently been reconfigured as Immigration Equality, also helps gay and lesbian asylum seekers bring their cases to court in the United States.

10 In *Griswold v. Connecticut*, Justice Douglas writes: "specific guarantees in the Bill of Rights have penumbras, formed by emanations of those guarantees that help give them life and substance" (*Griswold*, 484). Scalia makes explicit, and derisive, reference to the penumbral nature of the right of privacy in *Lawrence v. Texas* (*Lawrence*, dissent, 11). For more on privacy and penumbras, see Epps' contribution to the present volume.

11 Although domesticity is commonly conceived in terms of refuge and respite, its history is hardly gentle. Bound to and by patriarchy, domesticity has been purchased by way of a *taming* whose violence has been largely forgotten or disavowed and which "returns" as a traumatic exception, or aberration, to a regime of happiness, peace, and tranquility. Those so tamed have been primarily women and children, but also people of color, who have served as servants to the master or lord, "head of the house" or "king of the castle."

12 Norman and Naomi Zucker provide a good summation of the history of immigration, refuge, and asylum in the United States: "United States' immigration policy from colonial times to the beginning of World War II was relatively uncomplicated. To both public and policy makers all migrants were "immigrants" to be admitted or denied entrance. But the Russian Revolution and the rise of militant fascism in Germany and Italy rudely thrust the forced migrant onto the world's consciousness. These migrants, who had been driven out of their homelands, were refugees; they were, in a crucial sense, different from would-be immigrants seeking opportunity in new homelands. This critical difference—the difference between those who are *forced* to migrate and those who *choose* to migrate—was not then recognized" (24). We would add, however, that the v ery concept of "choice" is problematic when poverty is the reason that people "choose" to migrate.

13 See Foss (444–448); Leich (334–335); Qureshi (96), and Luibhéid.

14 For more on the more subtle exclusion of Black Africans (and the symbolic implications for the African American community), see Creola Johnson and Bill Ong Hing.

15 For more on Chinese immigration and the Western expansion, or "manifest destiny," of the United States, see Takaki (191–221).

16 Noting the existence of falsely manufactured documents, the text of Proposition 187 stipulated more vigilant verification of the legal status of immigrants by "questioning the person regarding his or her date and place of birth, and entry into the United States, and demanding documentation."

Failing to address exactly how "legal" immigrants will be spared harass-ment, or "questioning," the proposition effectively placed *all* immigrants, indeed any person who *appeared* to be an immigrant, into this question-able category. It also failed to address how its own enactment would not contribute to the even greater manufacture of false documents and hence to even greater measures of verification, that is to say, "questioning." As a result of these and other problems, Proposition 187 was ruled unconsti-tutional by California's Supreme Court. Arizona's Proposition 200, passed in November 2004, has been deemed legal by the U.S. District Court in Tucson and has gone into effect pending the ruling on a challenge filed with the 9th U.S. Circuit Court of Appeals.

17 The "REAL ID Act" introduces a three-tiered system for drivers' licenses, such that one's citizenship or immigration status (for example, perma-nent resident, asylee, refugee, temporary visa, or undocumented) would be identified on the license itself. Furthermore, only passports would be accepted as proof of identity in order to obtain a license.

18 The INS did so by appealing to science, by attempting to ground itself in supposedly objective, rational, and verifiable health concerns. As Johnson notes, "[u]nlike the Jews [themselves denied entry at the height of Nazi persecution], the Haitians were the object of discriminatory treatment arguably because of their medical condition, not their ethnic and racial composition" (328).

19 On November 25, 2002, President George W. Bush signed the Homeland Security Act. The law moved the INS, which was formally abolished as of March 2003, to the new Department of Homeland Security (DHS). As the official website to the DHS clarifies, "Immigration enforcement functions were placed within the Directorate of Border and Transportation Security (BTS), either directly, or under Customs and Border Protection (CBP) (which includes the Border Patrol and INS Inspections) or Immigration and Customs Enforcement (ICE) (which includes the enforcement and investigation components of INS such as Investigations, Intelligence, De-tention and Removals)."

20 Foss writes that the Public Health Service (PHS) "did not want diagnostic responsibility, and the Senators did not want any mention of homosexual-ity" (452).

21 These and other subjective determinations—backed, as we have seen, by dubious objective appeals—targeted homosexuals, who have nonetheless passed, as Alice Miller studies, from being excluded to being eligible for asylum.

22 For a full and regularly updated list of those persons currently excluded from both temporary and permanent entry into the United States, see the

most current version of the Immigration and Nationality Act (INA) as it is maintained on the U.S. Citizenship and Immigration Services website (http://uscis.gov/graphics/lawsregs/INA.htm). The INA is also a part of the United States Code.

23 Margot Cannaday provides an excellent and detailed analysis of the drafting and implementation of bans on homosexual immigration in the Mc-Carran-Walter Act.

24 The contributors to *Nationalisms and Sexualities*, openly indebted to George Mosse's study, expand the field of inquiry to consider a wide variety of nationalities, nationalisms, and sexualities.

25 There seems to be no end to the use of natural metaphors as an instrument both to ground the position of the United States vis-à-vis other nations and to determine the "correct" social order within its borders. In February 2005, Massachusetts governor Mitt Romney, speaking before an audience of Republicans, linked "family values" to the exceptionality of American culture and to the "logic" of its domestic and foreign policies: "America's culture is [. . .] defined by the fact that we are a religious people," Romney said. Michael Levenson, in a *Boston Globe* article reporting Romney's comments further noted that the governor "drew a link between America's prestige around the world and the legalization of same-sex marriages in Massachusetts. 'America cannot continue to lead the family of nations around the world if we suffer the collapse of the family here at home,' Romney said, calling the Supreme Judicial Court's legalization of same-sex marriage in Massachusetts 'a blow to the family.'"

26 As important as the judicial system and, more pointedly, the Supreme Court, are in any consideration of immigration and sexuality, the executive and legislative branches are also profoundly implicated. George W. Bush, for instance, continues to stigmatize homosexuality as inimical to basic U.S. mores, marriage and the militarism chief among them. He opposes gay marriage, for instance, by referring to the vagaries of sin (if we are all sinners, some of us are apparently more so than others) and calls for further codification of heterosexual rights and privileges, especially as they pertain to property, privacy, and public service. Legislative action, dialectically tied to executive action, takes the form of a so-called Defense of Marriage Act, approved under Clinton (1996), that is bound up in a military policy which is still in place after *Lawrence* and which effectively institutionalizes invisibility and silence.

27 Proper conduct—including but outstripping proper sexual conduct—remains a concern of immigration officials. Ronald Takaki describes how, in earlier parts of the century, "[r]acial etiquette defined proper demeanor and behavior for Mexicans. In the presence of Anglos, they were expected to assume 'a deferential body posture and respectful voice tone'" (326).

Virtually the same holds for sexual etiquette, which was as intensely codified as racial etiquette, if not indeed more so. The combinatory modes of such "etiquette," as when race and gender and sexuality are all simultaneously at play, merely heighten the sense of propriety—and perhaps of property—and fuel a system of values and habits that has specific national, and nationalist, vectors.

28 *Romer v. Evans* is the 1996 Supreme Court decision which ruled that Colorado's Amendment 2 banning non-discrimination ordinances based on sexual orientation violated the Equal Protection Clause. Scalia, joined by Thomas and Chief Justice Rehnquist, vigorously dissented.

29 The phrase, "codified international piracy," cited by Chomsky (5), is cited before by David Horst in the *Guardian* of London (March, 1992).

30 We do not mean to suggest, by any means, that love is the basis of marriage or even of the family, but we do mean to say that governmental agencies and agents deploy the concept, in its most heteronormatively limited sense, in their assessment of the legitimacy of claims.

31 We are thinking of Louis Althusser's contention "that there can be no tactics that do not depend on strategy—and no strategy that does not depend on theory" (241).

32 Although "diaspora" originally designated the "scattering" of the Jews in the wake of Babylonian exile, the term itself has been scattered and now designates any people or "social group" that, for various economic, political, and ideological reasons, is no longer bound to a particular geographic location. The scattering, far from disabling identity, can enable new forms of identity, at times condensed and closed but also at times open, fluid, and hybrid. Spanglish is surely an important hybrid formation, related to yet other hybrid formations: the Nuyorican, an uneven combination— varying from person to person—of the Puerto Rican and the New Yorker or indeed the "Diasporican."

33 According to La Fountain-Stokes, second- and third-generation Puerto Rican migrants, many but by no means all of whom are Nuyoricans (there are important communities in Philadelphia, Chicago, and elsewhere), tend to have more fluid connections to English and tighter connections with African Americans and other minority groups than do their first-generation counterparts.

34 According to Norman and Naomi Zucker, "it is not poverty alone but the presence of poverty together with the denial of human rights that causes large-scale refugee displacements. Human rights and economic development must be linked" (134). Linked, indeed, but perhaps a bit differently: for the Zuckers, concerned as they are with securing the rights of refugees, present poverty, as do so many others, as if it were not in and of itself a

problem, even a denial, of human rights. What is thereby purchased is the illusory integrity of the capitalist system, where private property undergirds, and vitiates, human rights.

35 Farmer and Gastineau quote a U.N. Development Programme publication, *Young Women: Silence, Susceptibility, and the HIV Epidemic,* that declares that "for most women, the major risk factor for HIV is being married."

Part

II

TRENDS IN IMMIGRATION

1

Everything You Ever Wanted To Know About Immigration But Were Afraid To Ask

Marcelo Suárez-Orozco

Immigration, like sexuality, is first and foremost about the structuring of desire. Immigration as a libidinal economy of desire is at the very center of the new impulses of globalization. Yet the scholarly study of immigration has long been dominated by the *homo economicus* and the *homo socialis* paradigms—in which men and women are said to migrate because of powerful economic and sociocultural forces that structure choices, generate opportunities, and set constraints. This volume, however, frames immigration within a *homo sexualis* paradigm, foregrounding the roles of sexuality and sexual orientation on recent patterns of Latin American and Caribbean immigration to the United States. In an original contribution to immigration studies, it brings together scholars of sexuality and immigration working on "both sides of the border," thus generating a broader scholarly perspective by introducing the voices and insights of researchers based in Latin America, the Caribbean, Canada, and the United States.

At the turn of the millennium, an estimated 175 million transnational immigrants and refugees are living beyond their homelands (M. Suárez-Orozco, C. Suárez-Orozco, and Qin-Hilliard). Hundreds of millions more are internal migrants within the confines of ever-changing nation states. Gender and sexuality, as the essays in this volume suggest, are powerfully implicated in these global human flows.

Globalization has increased immigration in a variety of ways. First, transnational capital flows and economic development tend to stimulate migration. Where capital flows, immigrants follow (Sassen; Massey, Durand, and Malone). Second, globalization's new information, communication, and media technologies stimulate migration because they generate new desires, tastes, consumption practices, and "lifestyle choices" (M. Suárez-Orozco, C. Suárez-Orozco, and Qin-Hilliard). In addition, they stimulate transnational conversations regarding the meanings of sexual identity and its cultural expressions. Would-be immigrants imagine better lives elsewhere and mobilize to achieve them. Third, deeply globalized economies are increasingly structured around a voracious appetite for foreign workers—both in the highly remunerated knowledge-intensive sector and in the least desirable economic sectors (Cornelius, "From Sojourners to Settlers"; Saxenian). Fourth, the affordability of mass transportation has put the option of migration within the reach of millions who previously could not find the financial means to travel. In the year 2000 alone, about 1.5 billion airline tickets were sold worldwide. Fifth, globalization has stimulated new migration because it has produced uneven results. In short, globalization structures the new migratory flows by increasingly coordinating markets, economies, social practices and cultural models. What had been less clear up to now is how increasingly de-territorialized discourses, social practices and cultural models, regarding sexual orientation, domestic violence, culturally enforced gender norms, and changing definitions of family, are implicated in the new immigration momentum.

"Passing Lines": Lives beyond National Boundaries

During the last decades of the 20th century, most major nation-states saw the topic of immigration emerge as a significant issue with public opinion, policy, and research implications. Indeed, perhaps for the first time in history, nearly all nation-states have become either countries of immigration, emigration or transit countries. Migration, from the Latin *migrare*, meaning to "change residence," has been a defining feature in the making of humanity from our very emergence as a species in the African savanna. Social scientists have traditionally defined *migration* as the more or less permanent movement of people across space (Petersen). In the language of the social sciences, people "emigrate" out of one location and become "immigrants" in a new setting.

The idea of migration as the permanent movement of people across space raises several important concerns. First is the relative permanence of immigrants in a new setting. For many (perhaps most), immigration represents a permanent move. However, for others, it is a temporary state before eventually returning "home." A central feature of the great transatlantic immigration that took place between Europe and the Americas from the 1890s until the 1910s was the high proportion of people who returned to Europe. By some accounts, more than a third of the Europeans who came to both North and South America went back (Moya). Sojourners represent another pattern of labor flow, in which temporality defines immigration. They are the many immigrants who move for well-defined periods of time, often following a seasonal cycle, and who eventually return home. Large numbers of migrant workers have followed this pattern—from Africans in the Sub-Saharan region to Mexicans in California (Cornelius, "From Sojourners to Settlers"). A third type of non-permanence encompasses the many new immigrants worldwide who constantly shuttle back and forth between countries.

In recent years, some immigration scholars have argued that new transnational and global forces structure the journeys of immigrants in more complex ways than previously seen. Anthropologists have been at the forefront of this conceptual and empirical work (for example, Basch, Glick Schiller, and Blanc). This research suggests that many immigrants remain substantially engaged economically, politically, and culturally in both their newly adopted lands and their communities of origin, moving "back and forth" in ways not often seen in previous eras of large-scale immigration (Suárez-Orozco, *Crossings*).

The idea of immigration as movement across space also requires elaboration. Immigration viewed anthropologically involves a change in residency and a change in community. Over the years, scholars have concentrated on two major types of large-scale migration: *internal migration*, within the confines of a nation-state, and *international migration*, across international borders. The differences between these two broad types of migration are often quite blurred, although many scholars would contend that the large-scale movement of people within a nation-state is a phenomenon of a separate order from the large-scale movement of people across international borders.

While much attention has focused on international migration, internal migrants frequently share many characteristics with international migrants. Many move from rural villages to urban centers; many experience linguistic and cultural discontinuities, and many face the same bureaucratic and legal restrictions and discriminations confronted by international migrants. Indeed, the majority of migrants today are internal migrants who stay within the confines of their nation-states, such as in the huge movements of people within the borders of China, Egypt, and Brazil. Despite the widely held impression that the majority of international migrants is heading to the developed world—Europe and North America—most of today's immigration is an intra-continental phenomenon—within Asia, within Africa. China alone has an estimated 150 million internal migrants who, in many ways, experience circumstances similar to those faced by transnational migrants (Eckholm 10). Some of the most important social science contributions to the study of immigration have focused on internal migration (for example, Brandes; Colson; Morgan and Colson; Scudder and Colson; Kemper).

"Love and Work": *Homo Economicus, Homo Socialis,* and *Homo Sexualis* on the Move

Scholars of immigration have generally theorized patterns of migration flows in terms of economic forces, social processes, and cultural practices—the *homo economicus* and *homo socialis* paradigms (M. Suárez-Orozco, C. Suárez-Orozco, and Qin-Hilliard Vol 1.). Social scientists who place emphasis on the economic aspects of immigration have examined how variables such as unemployment, underemployment, lack of access to credit, and, especially, wage differentials are implicated in labor migration (M. Suárez-Orozco, C. Suárez-Orozco, and Qin-Hilliard Vol. 2; Dussel). Douglas Massey, working with an interdisciplinary team of colleagues, has argued that international migration emerges as a risk management and diversifying strategy deployed by families and communities hoping to place their eggs in various territorial baskets (Massey, Durand, and Malone).

Changing cultural models about social standards and economic expectations (Moya), as well as changing opinions in many national contexts regarding sexual identity and human rights (the result of the emergence of a recognizable, transnational "gay" or "queer" identity, as examined in some essays in this volume), have also been implicated in why people migrate. In many cases, people migrate to actualize new consumption and lifestyle standards, as well as to escape sexually intolerant or repressive regimes. This is a different, yet still crucially important, sense of the "risk management" in which immigrants engage. A critical lens on immigration that takes *homo sexualis* seriously can supplement and further illuminate the information that the *homo economicus* and *homo socialis* models already make available.

In terms of the political economy of desire, the preponderance of evidence suggests that immigrants *are* wanted, even if ambivalently. Indeed, in nearly all advanced, post-industrial economies, bifurcated labor markets have worked as a powerful gravitational field, attracting many immigrants to work in the low-wage, low-status, and low-skilled secondary sector. T. Tsuda has noted that in Japan immigrant workers are sometimes called "3k workers," where *3k* stands for the Japanese words meaning "dirty, demanding, and dangerous" (Tsuda). When certain sectors of the opportunity structure are culturally coded as "immigrant jobs," they become stigmatized, and native workers tend to shun them almost regardless of wage dynamics. What would it take, in terms of wages, to make backbreaking work such as strawberry picking in California *not* an immigrant occupation? Other recent research relevant to social science scholarship engages the theoretical debate over the role of immigrant workers in the global, post-industrial economy. In the context of the increasingly advanced, knowledge-intensive economies of today, are low-skilled immigrant workers anachronistic? Are immigrant workers a leftover from an earlier era of production?

The comparative research of T. Tsuda and Wayne Cornelius on the use of immigrant labor in two paradigmatic, post-industrial economic settings—San Diego County, California, U.S., and Hamamatzu, Japan—suggests a remarkable convergence in patterns of growing reliance on immigrant labor, in spite of marked differences in national context (Cornelius, "Structural Embeddedness"). These data reveal an enduring, indeed voracious, post-industrial demand for immigrant labor. Cornelius concludes, "As immigrants become a preferred labor force, employers do more to retain them, even in a recessionary economy" (128).

These and other data suggest that immigrant workers become desirable to a wide variety of employers for three basic reasons. First, immigrants are willing to do low-pay work with little or no prospects for upward mobility—work that is boring, dirty, or dangerous but critical, even in firms involving highly advanced technologies. Second, employers perceive immigrant workers quite favorably, as reliable, flexible, punctual, and willing to work overtime. Often, employers prefer them to native-born workers. Third, immigrant transnational labor-recruiting networks are a powerful method for "delivering eager new recruits to the employer's doorstep with little or no effort on his part" (Cornelius, "Structural Embeddedness" 128).

Scholars working within the *homo socialis* paradigm have long maintained that cultural and social practices can generate—and sustain—substantial migratory flows. In many regions of the world, such as Ireland and Mexico, migration has been an adulthood-defining rite of passage (Durand; Massey, Durand, and Malone). In some cases, people migrate because others—relatives, friends, and friends of friends—migrated before them. The best predictor of who will migrate is who migrated before. Transnational family reunification continues to be a critical vector in immigration today. In the year 1996, 915,900 immigrants were formally admitted in the United States. Among them, 594,604 were family-sponsored immigrants (Suárez-Orozco, "Latin American Immigration"). Since the early 1970s, family reunification has been one of the few formal ways to migrate into Europe (Suárez-Orozco, "Anxious Neighbors"). Patterns of kinship, family, and social organization (recurring themes in the essays of this volume), are thus of paramount importance in structuring worldwide migratory waves. Furthermore, various states recognize "family" bonds, typically heter-onormative, as part of the formal criteria for legal immigration, which raises questions regarding the recognition of queerly constituted fami-lies. Some nations, such as Australia and Canada, already have immi-gration policies that grant the foreign-born partners of gay or lesbian citizens equal citizenship, but this is clearly far from being universal practice. Nevertheless, the success of movements to legalize gay mar-riage in parts of the United States and elsewhere means that such issues will play an increasingly important role in international immigration policies in the near future.

A number of studies have examined how transnational migratory social and sexual chains, once established, can generate a powerful mo-mentum of their own. As Patricia Pessar has argued, gender is deeply implicated in the making of these chains. After all, many immigrants are women, and the children born to them in the United States, as well as in many other countries, can claim citizenship. Established immi-grants lower the costs of subsequent immigration because they ease the transition of new arrivals by sharing crucial economic, linguistic, and cultural knowledge—about job openings, good wages, fair bosses, and dignified working conditions (Waldinger).

We thus have a reasonable understanding of how "love and work" drive immigration. On the other hand, the role of war and its rela-tions to large-scale migratory flows has been generally neglected. Yet, throughout history, war and international migration have been closely linked. The threat of labor shortages during World War II led to temporary labor-recruiting efforts to attract much needed immi-grant workers to the United States (Calavita). The resultant "bracero" program became a powerful force in building—via family reunifica-tion—a Mexican migration momentum that eventually turned into the largest and most powerful immigration flow into the United States in the 20th century (Suárez-Orozco, *Crossings*).

In the aftermath of World War II, many of the major northwestern European democracies, such as Germany and Belgium, developed "guest worker programs" to recruit foreign workers, initially in southern Europe and subsequently in the Maghreb region of North Africa and in Turkey (Suárez-Orozco, "Anxious Neighbors"). Although these programs ended in the early 1970s, family-reunification and chain migration continued to bring immigrants from North Africa into Europe for years.

The Cold War deterred immigration because of strict Iron Curtain controls, yet at the same time it generated large population displacements. The robust Cuban diaspora in the United States can be traced more or less directly to the Cold War (Molyneux). The low-intensity warfare in Central America during the 1980s generated the largest wave of emigration in the region's history. As a result, more than a million Central American immigrants now live in the United States (Suárez-Orozco, *Central American Refugees*). In the 1990s, the ongoing conflicts in Zimbabwe and Angola generated large-scale migratory flows, especially into South Africa. The recent war in Afghanistan resulted in population displacements of nearly two million Afghans. There are over 2 million people displaced in the Congo, and about 500,000 people displaced in the Côte d'Ivoire.

Natural disasters have also displaced populations and started new migratory flows. The 1999 hurricanes which devastated much of Central America spurred significant flows of emigrants into North America. Likewise, the devastating Indian Ocean Tsunami displaced over 1 million people, most of them in Sri Lanka and Indonesia.

Global Flows and the State

The apparatus of the nation-state is decidedly implicated in migratory processes: both by what the state does and by what it cannot do. States are in the business of regulating the movement of people, internally and internationally. The right to leave a country, to emigrate, is a relatively recent phenomenon (Moya).

Nation-states regulate, monitor, and police the inflow of international immigrants across borders. Large-scale international immigration is, in significant ways, the product of nation building. Argentina, Australia, Israel, and the United States come to mind as archetypal examples. Likewise, the reconfigurations of national boundaries have historically and contemporaneously generated large-scale migratory flows. The partition of British India into Pakistan and India stimulated one of the "largest migrations in human history" (Petersen 290). More recently, the disintegration of the former Yugoslavia led to massive, mostly involuntary, migratory movements.

In the area of international migration, nation-states generate policies designed to establish who is a legal or illegal immigrant, who is an asylum seeker, a refugee, and a temporary guest worker. Sex and gender often have critical relevance to the making of these policies, as theorized in a number of contributions in this volume. States regulate how many immigrants are legally admitted every year. The United States, for example, has admitted an average of nearly a million legal immigrants annually since 1990. On the other hand, legal immigration into northwestern Europe was greatly curbed following the oil crisis of the early 1970s (Cornelius, Martin, and Hollifield).

States also regulate the flows of asylum seekers, those escaping a country because of a well-founded fear of persecution. Agents of the state also decide who is formally admitted as a refugee or asylum seeker. In the post-Cold War era, the number of people seeking asylum worldwide has exploded. For example, some 369,000 foreigners requested asylum in Europe during the year 1998. Only a small portion of those seeking asylum are eventually granted formal asylum status. Several essays in this volume address the complicated questions involved in sexual orientation-based asylum claims, including the need for increased international documentation of human rights abuses with respect to sexuality and sexual identity. The essays also address thorny issues involved in the articulation of sexual identities across cultural regimes in ways that will successfully fulfill the often legally narrow requirements of asylum. At the same time, they recognize that asylum may be an effective remedy for individual claimants, but can do little to address the repressive conditions of national regimes that impel people to seek refuge in a different state in the first place.

In recent years, many post-industrial democracies—including the United States and northwestern Europe—have developed new strategies to deal with increasing numbers of asylum seekers (Suárez-Orozco, "Anxious Neighbors"). For example, the 13,000 Kosovars who arrived in Germany in mid-1999 were given a three-month, renewable Temporary Protective Status on the condition that they not apply for refugee status, in effect, forfeiting all the rights and entitlements that come with formal refugee status. Similar arrangements were made for asylum seekers from Bosnia. In the face of growing numbers of asylum seekers and a widespread public concern that many of them are economic refugees in search of a better life in wealthier countries, various countries have put into place new formal and informal strategies. The increase in the numbers of people seeking asylum, and the varying state responses to this increase, are connected to problems of nationalist extremism, ethnic cleansing, religious intolerance, and the lack of freedom to express identity, including gender and sexuality identity. Many of these new strategies seem to be designed to prevent asylum seekers from accessing safe countries, where, under Geneva Convention agreements, they would have the right to a fair hearing.

The high-seas interdiction program put into effect in the United States in the early 1990s is an example. The strategy was conceived to prevent large numbers of Caribbean (especially Haitian) asylum seekers from arriving in U.S. territory, or even within its territorial waters, where they could establish certain legal protections. If asylum seekers are apprehended in international waters, they are returned to Haiti, leaving them with little practical recourse under international law. A panic over HIV/AIDS figured prominently in curtailing the rights of would-be Haitian asylum seekers, who were subjected with greater rigor to mandatory screenings for the disease than other immigrant groups. In Europe, a similar strategy has been to deem certain areas in international airports not part of the national territory. For example, parts of the Zaventem airport are not technically Belgian territory but are considered to be international territory. Asylum seekers entering such airports have been turned back because they are said to remain in international territory and, hence, do not come under the jurisprudence of the Geneva Convention (Suárez-Orozco, "Anxious Neighbors"). Although advanced post-industrial democracies are likely to continue facing significant numbers of asylum seekers, the majority of displaced peoples seeking refuge are nevertheless in the developing world—including Asia and Africa.

The state does wield substantial power regarding internal and international migration, but in certain areas it faces strict limitations in the management of human migratory flows. Nowhere are these limitations more obvious than in the state's inability to control illegal immigration. In many parts of the world, undocumented or illegal immigration has become a permanent challenge that periodically emerges as an unsettling political issue. In the United States, for example, it is estimated that there are more than 10 million illegal immigrants. In Europe, the number of illegal immigrants is a more carefully guarded secret because of its dangerous political connotations. Most hard-core, right-wing political parties in Europe, including France's National Front, Belgium's Vlans Balans, and Austria's Freedom Party, revolve around anti (illegal) immigration platforms. In the 1990s, these once-marginal parties made substantial gains with electorates quite concerned with the problem of undocumented immigration.

The enduring concern over undocumented immigration in many parts of the world suggests that immigration is now structured by powerful global economic factors, social forces, and cultural practices that seem impervious to state actions such as controls of international borders (Cornelius, Martin, and Hollifield; Andreas). Transnational labor-recruiting networks, enduring wage differentials between nation-states, changing standards of consumption, the globalization of new identities and increased transnational conversations regarding sexual identity, family reunification, political persecution, and war generate a powerful migratory momentum not easily curbed by unilateral, or even multilateral, state interventions.

The Varieties of the Immigrant Experience

When settled in a new country, how do immigrants fare? As the ur-country of immigration, the United States provides an interesting case study. It is the only advanced, post-industrial democracy in which immigration is at once history and destiny. The intensification of globalization in the past decade—arguably responsible for the greatest peacetime expansion of the U.S. economy—coincided with the largest number of immigrants in history (U.S. Bureau of the Census). By the year 2000, the foreign-stock (the foreign-born plus the U.S.-born second generation) population of the United States was nearly 55 million people (Portes and Rumbaut). By 2005 more than 34 million were foreign-born. Two dominant features characterize this most recent wave of immigration: its intensity (the immigrant population grew by more than 30 percent in the 1990s) and the radical shift in the sources of new immigration. Until 1950, roughly 80 percent of all immigrants were Europeans or Canadians. Today, more than 52 percent of all immigrants are from Latin America, and more than 25 percent are from Asia—from regions of the world where globalization has generated especially uneven results (see fig. 1).

Immigrants to the United States today are a heterogeneous population defying easy generalizations (M. Suárez-Orozco and C. Suárez-

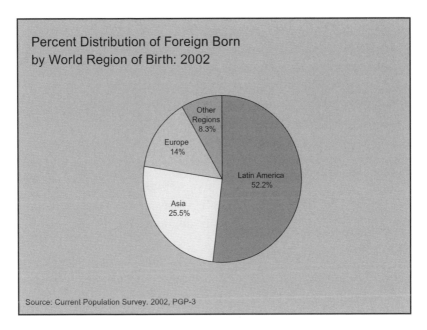

Figure 1.1

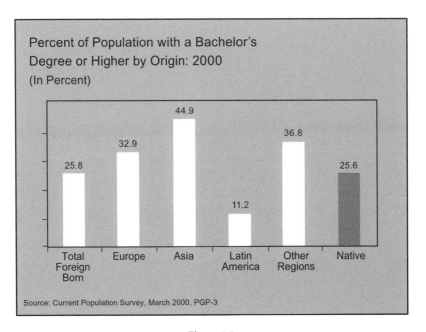

Figure 1.2

Orozco). They include highly educated, highly skilled individuals drawn by the explosive growth in the knowledge-intensive sectors of the economy. They are more likely to have advanced degrees than the native-born population (see fig. 2).

These new arrivals thrive when they come to the United States. These immigrants, especially those originating in Asia, are among the best-educated and skilled folk in the United States. They are over-represented in the category of people with doctorates. Fully half of all entering physics graduate students in 1998 were foreign-born. In California's Silicon Valley, 32 percent of all the scientists and engineers are immigrants (Saxenian). Roughly a third of all Nobel Prize winners in the United States have been immigrants. And, in 1999, *all* (100 percent!) U.S. winners of the Nobel Prize were immigrants. With the possible exception of the highly educated immigrants and refugees escaping Nazi Europe, immigrants in the past tended to be poorly educated and more unskilled than today's immigrants (Borjas). Never in the history of U.S. immigration have so many immigrants done so well so fast. Within a generation, these immigrants are bypassing the traditional transgenerational modes of status mobility and establishing themselves in the well-remunerated sectors of the U.S. economy.

At the same time, the new immigration group contains large numbers of poorly schooled, semi-skilled or unskilled workers, many of them in the United States without proper documentation (illegal immigrants). In the year 2000, more than 22 percent of all immigrants in the United States had less than a ninth-grade education (see fig. 3).

These workers, many of them from Latin America, are attracted to the service sector of the U.S. economy, with its seemingly insatiable appetite for foreign help. They typically end up in poorly paid jobs, often lacking insurance and basic job safety. Unlike the low-skilled factory jobs of yesterday, the kinds of jobs usually available to low-skilled immigrants today do not offer much realistic promise for upward mobility (Portes, *New Second Generation*, 1–15). These immigrants tend to settle in areas of deep poverty and racial segregation (Orfield). Concentrated poverty is associated with the "disappearance of meaningful work opportunities" (Wilson). When poverty is combined with racial segregation, the outcomes can be dim (Massey and Denton 3).

Large-scale immigration is both the cause and consequence of important cultural transformations. Immigration inevitably leads to cultural changes and accommodations among both new arrivals and native citizens (Ainslie). Immigration can be said to be the consequence

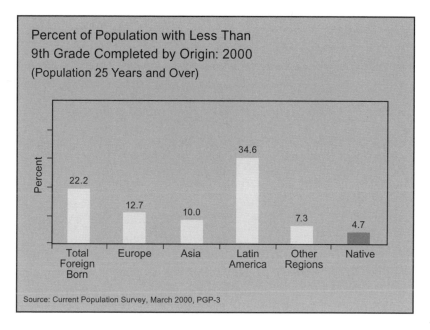

Figure 1.3

of cultural change since new cultural tastes and changing cultural conceptions of what is an acceptable standard of living have been implicated in large-scale migratory flows (Sassen). Culturally, immigrants not only significantly reshape the ethos of their new communities (Ainslie, Gutierrez) but are also responsible for significant cultural transformations "back home" (Durand). As certain immigration researchers (for example, Levitt) have argued, in many settings, immigrant "social remittances" profoundly affect the values, cultural models, and social practices of those left behind. Undoubtedly, the flows of information and people between nation states, and the cultural cross-fertilization that such immigrant flows have engendered, have contributed to new kinds of identities. They have also led to increased social visibility for sexual minorities in their new homes as well as in their countries of origin. Mass transportation and new communication technologies have caused immigration to no longer be structured around the "sharp break" with the country of origin (Ainslie). Although the transoceanic experience was never quite as sharp as imagined because of return-flow migration, immigrants today are more likely to be at once "here" and "there," bridging increasingly unbounded national spaces (Basch, Glick Schiller, and Blanc). In the process, they are transforming both home and host countries. (See La Fountain-Stokes and Sandoval in this volume for a discussion of the vexed questions of transnational queer identity in Puerto Rico and the U.S.)

Increasingly, transnational immigration will need to be framed in the context of powerful—and, as of yet, little understood—global formations. New patterns of capital flows, new information technologies, new patterns of communication, changing cultural expectations, gender, sexuality and sexual orientation, and the ease and affordability of mass transportation are generating dynamics that transverse the traditional boundaries of the nation-state as never before. Global capitalism is increasingly characterized by "borderless" economies predicated on transnational capital flows, newly opened markets, and immigrant-dependent economic niches. All these factors would suggest that immigration is certain to remain a vital social phenomenon in the new millennium. Scholars of sexuality and sexual orientation must add their voices to the chorus of social science and culture studies researchers examining this global vector of change.

Works Cited

Ainslie, Ricardo. "Cultural Mourning, Immigration, and Engagement: Vignettes from the Mexican Experience." *Crossings: Mexican Immigration in Interdisciplinary Perspectives.* Ed. Marcelo Suárez-Orozco. Cambridge, Mass.: David Rockefeller Center for Latin American Studies and Harvard University Press, 1998. 283–306.

Andreas, Peter. *Border Games: Policing the U.S.-Mexico Divide.* Ithaca, N.Y.: Cornell University Press, 2000.

Basch, Linda, Nina Glick Schiller, and Cristina S. Blanc. *Nations Unbound: Transnational Projects, Postcolonial Predicaments and Deterritorialized Nation-States.* Basel, Switzerland: Gordon and Breach Science Publishers, 1994.

Borjas, George. *Heaven's Door: Immigration and the American Economy.* Princeton: Princeton University Press, 1999.

Brandes, Stanley. *Migration, Kinship, and Community: Tradition and Transition in a Spanish Village.* New York: Academic Press, 1975.

Calavita, Kitty. *Inside the State: The Bracero Program, Immigration, and the INS.* New York: Routledge, 1992.

Colson, Elizabeth. *The Social Consequences of Resettlement.* Manchester: Manchester University Press, 1971.

Cornelius, Wayne. "From Sojourners to Settlers: The Changing Profile of Mexican Immigration in the United States." *U.S.-Mexico Relations: Labor Market Interdependence.* Ed. Jorge A. Bustamante, Clark W. Reynolds, and Raúl Hinojosa Ojeda. Stanford, Calif.: Stanford University Press, 1992.

_____. "The Structural Embeddedness of Demand for Mexican Immigrant Labor: New Evidence from California." *Crossings: Mexican Immigration in Interdisciplinary Perspectives.* Ed. Marcelo Suárez-Orozco. Cambridge, Mass.: David Rockefeller Center for Latin American Studies and Harvard University Press, 1998. 113–156.

Cornelius, Wayne, Philip L. Martin, and James F. Hollifield, eds. *Controlling Immigration: A Global Perspective.* Stanford, Calif.: Stanford University Press, 1994.

Durand, Jorge. "Migration and Integration." *Crossings: Mexican Immigration in Interdisciplinary Perspectives.* Ed. Marcelo Suárez-Orozco. Cambridge, Mass.: David Rockefeller Center for Latin American Studies and Harvard University Press, 1998. 207–224.

Dussel, Enrique P. *Polarizing Mexico: The Impact of Liberalization.* New York: Lynne Rienner, 2000.

Eckholm, Erik. "District in Beijing to Shut Schools for Migrants." *New York Times,* October 31, 2001: 10.

Gutierrez, David. "Ethnic Mexicans and the Transformation of 'American' Social Space: Reflections on Recent History." *Crossings: Mexican Immigration in Interdisciplinary Perspectives.* Ed. Marcelo Suárez-Orozco. Cambridge, Mass.: David Rockefeller Center for Latin American Studies and Harvard University Press, 1998. 307–340.

Kemper, Robert. *Migration and Adaptation: Tzintzuntzan Peasants in Mexico City.* Beverly Hills, Calif.: Sage, 1977.

Levitt, Peggy. *The Transnational Villagers.* Berkeley and Los Angeles: University of California Press, 2001.

Massey, Douglas S., and Nancy A. Denton. *American Apartheid.* Cambridge, Mass.: Harvard University Press, 1993.

Massey, Douglas, Jorge Durand, and Nolan Malone. *Beyond Smoke and Mirrors: Mexican Immigration in an Era of Economic Integration.* New York: Russell Sage Foundation, 2002.

Molyneux, Maxine. "The Politics of the Cuban Diaspora in the United States." *The United States and Latin America: The New Agenda.* Ed. Victor Bulmer-Thomas and James Dunkerley. Cambridge, Mass: David Rockefeller Center for Latin American Studies and Harvard University Press, 1999. 287–310.

Morgan, Scott, and Elizabeth Colson, eds. *People in Upheaval.* New York: Center for Migration Studies, 1987.

Moya, Jose. *Cousins and Strangers: Spanish Immigrants in Buenos Aires, 1850–1930.* Berkeley: University of California Press, 1998.

Orfield, Gary. "Commentary." *Latinos: Remaking America.* Ed. Marcelo Suárez-Orozco and Mariela Páez. Berkeley and London: University of California Press, 2002. 389–397.

Pessar, Patricia R. "Anthropology and the Engendering of Migration Studies." *American Arrivals: Anthropology Engages the New Immigration.* Ed. Nancy Fonner. Santa Fe: School of American Research Press, 2003.

Petersen, W. "Migration." *International Encyclopedia of the Social Sciences.* New York: Macmillan, 1968.

Portes, Alejandro. *The New Second Generation.* New York: Russell Sage Foundation, 1996.

Portes, Alejandro, and Rubén Rumbaut. *Legacies: The Story of the Immigrant Second Generation.* Berkeley and London: University of California Press, 2001.

Sassen, Saskia. *The Mobility of Labor and Capital: A Study in International Investment and Labor Flow.* New York: Cambridge University Press, 1988.

Saxenian, AnnaLee. *Silicon Valley's New Immigrant Entrepreneurs.* San Francisco: Public Policy Institute of California, 1999.

Scudder, Thayer, and Elizabeth Colson. "From Welfare to Development." *Involuntary Migration and Resettlement: Problems and Responses of Dislocated People*. Ed. Art Hansen and Anthony Oliver-Smith. Boulder, Col.: Westview, 1982. 267–287.

Suárez-Orozco, Marcelo. *Central American Refugees and U.S. High Schools: A Psychosocial Study of Motivation and Achievement*. Stanford, Calif.: Stanford University Press, 1989.

_____. "Anxious Neighbors: Belgium and Its Immigrant Minorities." *Controlling Immigration: A Global Perspective*. Ed. Wayne Cornelius, Philip L. Martin, and James F. Hollifield. Stanford, Calif.: Stanford University Press, 1994. 237–268.

_____, ed. *Crossings: Mexican Immigration in Interdisciplinary Perspectives*. Cambridge, Mass.: David Rockefeller Center for Latin American Studies and Harvard University Press, 1998.

_____. "Latin American Immigration to the United States." *The United States and Latin America: The New Agenda*. Ed. Victor Bulmer-Thomas and James Dunkerley. Cambridge, Mass.: David Rockefeller Center for Latin American Studies, Harvard University Press, 1999. 227–246.

Suárez-Orozco, Marcelo, and Carola Suárez-Orozco. *Children of Immigration*. Cambridge, Mass.: Harvard University Press, 2001.

Suárez-Orozco, Marcelo, Carola Suárez-Orozco, and Desirée Qin-Hilliard, eds. *Interdisciplinary Perspectives on the New Immigration*. 6 vols. New York: Routledge, 2001.

Tsuda, Takeyuki. *Strangers in the Ethnic Homeland*. Diss. University of California at Berkeley, 1996.

U.S. Bureau of the Census. *Foreign-Born Population of the United States-March 2004*. Washington, D.C.: Current Population Survey, 2005.

Waldinger, Roger. "Social Capital or Social Closures? Immigrant Networks in the Labor Market." Working Paper Series 26, August 1997. Los Angeles: Lewis Center for Regional Policy Studies, University of California, 1997. http://lewis.sppsr.ucla.edu/research/index.cfm.

Wilson, William J. *When Work Disappears: The World of the New Urban Poor*. New York: Vintage Books, 1997.

2

Heteronormativity, Responsibility, and Neo-liberal Governance in U.S. Immigration Control

Eithne Luibhéid

In recent decades, both the Republican and Democratic parties in the United States have implemented a marked shift toward neo-liberal modes of governance.[1] A construct of "personal responsibility," which subjects of the state are expected to cultivate, has comprised the centerpiece of a wide array of neo-liberal programs. "Responsibility," however, is not a self-evident, empirically verifiable condition, but rather a continually shifting set of discourses and practices that are imbued with relations of power. Following Mitchell Dean, it is important to scrutinize "the political programmes and social imaginaries" that draw inspiration from and deploy "responsibility" as their organizing logic (178). This paper examines one such program—the implementation of legally binding affidavits of support between immigrants and their sponsors—as a means to interrogate how neo-liberalism reconfigures the governance of legal immigrants in a manner that operates through a heteronormalizing regime that links together economic and cultural domains.[2]

Sexuality has long been a concern to the framers of U.S. immigration law and policy, and it has consistently comprised an important axis for the regulation of newcomers. Careful scholarship notes the distinctions between the terms through which the U.S. government has attempted to regulate immigrants' sexual acts and identities, and immigrants' *own* constructions and enactments of sexuality, which may exist in positions of alterity or excess to dominant terms. Moreover, the same scholarship recognizes the extent to which governance of and through sexuality is not a one-time event, but instead structures immigrants' possibilities for admission to—and for life within—the United States in an ongoing way. Such analyses therefore point away from dehistoricized or essentialized constructions of sexuality, or strictly cross-cultural comparisons, to inquire instead into the historical, social, political, and economic conditions under which particular actions and identities become available, thinkable, livable, and desirable—and, conversely, unthinkable, unlivable, and undesirable. A focus on normativity—in this instance, heteronormativity—further draws attention to governmental strategies for disciplining immigrant subjects with regard to sexuality and, concomitantly, with regard to race, gender, class, and nationality, which are integrally connected to, and articulated through, sexuality. As David Eng and Alice Hom write:

> We are not delineating an additive model of social inequality whereby queerness is augmented by supplemental notions of difference. On the contrary, our analysis means to underscore that our very epistemological conception of what it is to be queer cannot be understood without a serious consideration of how social differences such as race constitute our cognitive perceptions of a queer world, how sexual and racial difference come into existence only in relation to one another. (12)

The analysis of heteronormativity thus requires attention to the existence of multiple fields of power, inequality, and contestation that continually structure immigrants' experiences.

This chapter brings these concerns together by discussing how programs for cultivating personal responsibility in immigrants operate through heterosexualizing logics that link economic and cultural domains. The chapter first describes how the ideal of the "responsible" subject has historically animated liberal—and now neo-liberal—regimes of governance, and how this ideal connects to economic and cultural domains. Next, I discuss state efforts to cultivate "responsibility" through the promotion of heterosexuality, as reflected in the Defense of Marriage Act of 1996 (DOMA). This Act is linked to two other key pieces of legislation that were also passed in 1996: the Personal Responsibility and Work Opportunity Reconciliation Act and the Illegal Immigration Reform and Immigrant Responsibility Act. Taken together, these laws importantly reconstructed the regulation of contemporary legal immigration. I focus in particular on a new immigration management technology that has emerged through these laws: the use of legally binding affidavits of support that tie immigrants to their sponsors. The affidavit system came into effect in December 1997 and will likely remain in effect for the foreseeable future.

I focus on the affidavit system, rather than on more spectacular examples of immigration control such as the militarization of the borders, precisely because it is so commonplace that it often escapes scrutiny. Nonetheless, the affidavit system is an absolutely central instrument in the forms of neo-liberal governance that are transforming immigration control. Therefore, analyzing this system makes visible the operation of neo-liberal norms and logics of governance. My analysis also participates in the critique of narrow, individualized, elitist constructions of "responsibility," so characteristic of neo-liberal programs, which are reflected in the affidavit system. By addressing these issues, this chapter brings critical scholarship about immigration, sexuality, and governmentality into dialogue, in order to diagnose how immigration control is shifting, as well as to question the resulting consequences.

Responsibility and the Culture/Economy Link

According to Foucauldian scholars of governmentality, liberalism and neo-liberalism are particular styles of government, and a critical task is to identify the problematics that organize them as well as the shifting assemblages of knowledge, expertise, and power that they marshal. Key concerns for both liberal and neo-liberal governance have been how to produce self-governing individuals, and how to ensure that self-governing relationships are directed towards ends that the state deems appropriate. These self-governing individuals have been deemed "responsible"—although the meaning of responsibility has shifted over time and place. For example, in the nineteenth century, "one pervasive objectification of the subject of government was as an impulsive, passionate, and desiring creature, who was civilized and made amenable to moral order by the actions of the will and the inculcation of conscious self-control and habits of responsible self-management" (Rose 43–44). The imperative to become "responsible" therefore reveals "the despotism of the self at the heart of liberalism" (Rose 43). This is crucial, because liberal forms of rule depend precisely on citizens' ability to subjugate themselves to dominant norms—a point examined further below.

In much nineteenth-century European thought, the ability to become self-governing, resulting in responsible and moral conduct (understood normatively), was important to constructs of national culture. In the words of Nikolas Rose, "[n]ations were now seen as populations of individuals with particular characteristics, integrated through a certain moral order" (101). Thus, interventions designed to shape the moral character and conscience of the population, and hence to generate "responsible" action, proliferated. In the context of widespread imperial projects and the rise of forms of knowledge that included scientific racism and sexology, allegedly varied abilities to develop moral character and responsible conduct constituted a means to presume, express, and institutionalize hierarchies of race, gender, class, and colonial status, among others (see Stoler). As Rose puts it, moral character and responsible conduct were "used to differentiate—the child from the adult, the man from the woman, the normal person from the lunatic, the civilized man from the primitive" (44). Rose further suggests that we can trace a series of figures from this nineteenth century formation to the present-day responsible subject of neo-liberal governance (although the series is not strictly linear or unified). I would add that these figures have remained entangled in shifting, contested hierarchies of culture, race, gender, class, colonization, and sexuality, including in present-day neo-liberalism. Such shifts have been associated with changes in forms of knowledge and expertise, in modes of intervention, and in assemblages of individuals, experts, and governmental programs.[3]

The "responsible" subject of today's neo-liberalism is a somewhat different figure than that of the nineteenth century. This is not surprising, since what characterizes neo-liberalism is its valorization and essentialization of the market (Dean 159; see also Rose 139) and its efforts to extend market rules and principles to a growing number of spheres, including those that bear on the conduct of one's life. These efforts have gone hand-in-hand with a view, shared by neo-liberals and neo-conservatives alike, that the citizenry has lost its sense of virtue to such a degree that it must be guided to become virtuous and responsible again (Dean 163; Rose 182).[4] Consequently, neo-liberals and neo-conservatives have both engaged in aggressive culture wars that, as Dean indicates, are not just calculated power plays, but also reach to the heart of what each perceives as a crisis in the governance of so-called liberal democracies: "how to govern through the autonomy of the governed when they were no longer virtuous" (162?) The "responsible" subject that neo-liberals seek to cultivate is, as some critics have noted, an entrepreneurial subject of choice engaged in a quest for self-realization (Rose 142; see also Dean 158–159).[5] By cultivating this subject, the government has sought to "remoralize the United States, and recreate the responsible autonomy and civic virtue upon which Republican government must rely" (Rose 186).

In as much as sexual politics constitutes an arena in which people express and contest questions of responsibility and morality, it is not surprising that sexuality has become a key domain in which these cultural struggles are fought out. In the process, neo-liberals have at once invoked and disavowed sexuality, along with gender, class, and race, as nothing more than a "personal" attribute that can be accommodated as long as the "marked" groups subscribe to the dominant ethos (a sort of conservative multiculturalism), or alternatively, as emblematic of a "deviant culture" that needs to be changed. As we shall see, the cultural project of producing a virtuous and responsible citizenry implicates the domain of sexuality in decisive ways, linking it to various economic programs that cut welfare and other social benefits, privatize the costs of social reproduction, and legitimize the upward redistribution of resources and the growing gaps in wealth and income (Duggan 14). Whereas the welfare state had been supposed to guarantee minimal subsistence and protection against the vicissitudes of life under capitalism, and at stages of the lifecycle when one is dependent, under neo-liberalism these provisions came to apply no longer.[6] Instead, the state now enjoins individuals to take upon themselves "the responsibility for their own security and that of their families" (Rose 159). Individuals are expected to anticipate a range of possible risks and to insure against them within the privatized marketplace.

The logic of risk management also shapes neo-liberal strategies for controlling populations deemed to be troublesome, often on the grounds of their sexuality and their immigrant status. Important features of control under neo-liberalism involve the use of actuarial models to predict which individuals are likely to become self-actualizing, responsible, entrepreneurial subjects, and which are at risk for not doing so. Such models depend on logics that are anticipatory, probabilistic, and pre-emptive, rather than organized around cure or rehabilitation. They often do not target groups defined according to historic racial, ethnic, gender, sexual or class categories, but rather, individuals showing a combination of factors associated with risk (Rose 236). It is notable, however, that such statuses as race, gender, sexuality, class, and nationality significantly shape who is likely to be deemed "at risk" or "risky." As we shall see, these strategies have reconfigured how immigrant inclusion and exclusion operate in the United States.

Heteronormativity and Responsibility: The Defense of Marriage Act

The active production and promotion of heteronormativity has provided a keystone for neo-liberal efforts to cultivate personal responsibility among subjects and to manage risks in ways that conjoin the cultural and the economic. The Defense of Marriage Act (DOMA), which passed in 1996 and which applies not only to U.S. citizens and to residents but also to immigrants, illustrates some of the ways that these linkages have come to be forged. It is here that the concept of heteronormativity is useful, for it moves us away from a strict homo/hetero binary and from the idea that sexual identities are natural, obvious, or pre-given, and instead situates all sexual identities in the terrain of society, history, power, and its contestations. Sexual identities include not just lesbian, gay, bisexual, and transgender ones, but also heterosexual identities, which Jonathan Katz has carefully historicized in his book *The Invention of Heterosexuality*. With respect to the United States, Katz ties heterosexuality to shifts in the economy, the emergence of commodity culture, and the changing role of medical and "psy" experts during the twentieth century. Heteronormativity, of course, refers not only to the emergence of heterosexuality as an identity, but also to the emergence of a range of normalizing discourses and practices that presume that heterosexuality is natural and ahistorical, and that it is, moreover, "the elemental form of human association, . . . the very model of intergender relations, . . . the indivisible basis of all community, and . . . the means of reproduction without which society wouldn't exist" (Warner xxi). For these reasons, Warner argues that challenging heteronormativity requires "a thorough resistance to regimes of the normal" (xxvi). Queer of color scholarship makes clear that resistance entails addressing how sexual regimes and exclusions are implicated in the production not only of sexual, but also of gender, racial, and economic regimes, hierarchies, exclusions, and forms of violence (see Ferguson; Muñoz). Another significant strand of scholarship ties heteronormativity to state- and nation-making projects (see Alexander; Anthias and Yuval Davis; McClintock; Stoler; Yang).

Today, heteronormativity—involving not only the promotion of heterosexual "identity" but also state-sanctioned marriage—has become an important component of neo-liberal programs and strategies for cultivating personal responsibility. DOMA reflects these heteronormalizing strategies and their ties to an array of neo-liberalizing programs of governance. According to Nancy Cott, DOMA's major provisions were the following: "First, it explicitly defined the words 'marriage' and 'spouse' in federal law as involving one man and one woman. Second . . . it provided that no state would be required to give effect to a same-sex marriage contracted in another state, despite the constitutional rule that each state should give 'full faith and credit' to the public acts of others" (218). An accompanying U. S. House of Representatives Report explained that DOMA, like many neo-liberal laws and programs, was a pre-emptive strike that was passed in anticipation of same-sex marriage becoming legalized in Hawaii and thereby opening the door to same-sex marriage in other states. Describing why DOMA was considered necessary, the report suggested that if even one state allowed and recognized same-sex marriage, state laws in general would fall into such "disarray" that "upholding traditional morality, encouraging procreation in the context of families, encouraging heterosexuality, . . . and other legitimate purposes of government would be undermined."[7] Most interesting here is that the report makes a distinction—which is at the same time a link—between heterosexuality and the procreative family. Heterosexuality is a form of sexuality that the state seeks to "encourage" and to channel into procreative families, even though these are not necessarily the same thing.

In regard to encouraging heterosexuality, the report explains, "there is good reason to think that a very substantial number of people are born with the potential to live either gay or straight lives," but the state nonetheless has a compelling interest in encouraging a heterosexual "choice." Thus, the report not only encodes the modern idea that sexuality is something that each of us "has," but also names the promotion of heterosexual "orientation" as an explicit and important state objective. The next step in the report's argument is that heterosexual orientation alone is not sufficient; rather, heterosexuality must be channeled into marriage and directed toward procreation.[8] In striking language, the report explains that marriage is not simply the recognition of "love" between two people of the "opposite sex," but rather that: "the love of marriage is directed to a different end, or it is woven into a different meaning, rooted in the character and ends of marriage." The idea of the "ends of marriage" echoes Foucault's analysis of government as "the right disposition of things, arranged so as to lead to a convenient end" (93). Foucault extends his argument to suggest that "this implies a plurality of specific aims . . . a whole series of specific finalities," which necessitate "a range of multiform tactics" (95). For the Congressional authors of the DOMA report, heterosexual marriage does indeed reflect the right disposition of things in terms of plural aims.

First, according to the report, heterosexual marriage reflects the right disposition of sexuality, directed towards begetting a child within the marital context. Thus, the authors write:

> To discover the 'ends of marriage,' we need only reflect on this central, unimpeachable lesson of human nature: we are, each of us, born a man or a woman. The committee needs no testimony from expert witness to decode this point: our engendered existence, as men and women, offers the most unmistakable, natural signs of the meaning and purpose of sexuality. And that is the function and purpose of begetting. At its core, it is hard to detach marriage from what may be called 'the natural teleology of the body': namely the fact that only two people, not three, only a man and a woman, can beget a child.

Second, for the authors, marriage reflects a proper disposition of social, moral, and civilizational responsibility, because bearing a child within marriage provides a mechanism whereby the members of the marriage supposedly overcome their individual needs and desires to consider the larger good. Marriage, in this line of thinking, also provides the child with the best environment for growing up, and the greatest possibilities for becoming a moral and productive member of society. As the report summarizes, marriage is "the keystone of the arch of civilization." Moreover, it is also:

> an affair of the heart that has enormous economic and political and social implications for America, but, most importantly, has moral implications because families are ordained by God as a way of giving children and their parents the chance to live up to the fullest of their God-given capacities. And when we save them and strengthen them, we overcome the notion that self-gratification is more important than our obligations to others; we overcome the notion that is so prevalent in our culture that life is just a series of responses to impulses, and instead is a whole pattern, with a fabric that should be pleasing to God.

In this way, childbearing within marriage constitutes a technology for the improvement of society and civilization itself; it is presumed to be "the sure foundation of all that is stable and noble in our civilization; the best guaranty of that reverent morality which is the source of all beneficent progress in social and political improvement."

According to the authors of the DOMA report, marriage has been "devalued" by "the sexual revolution, no-fault divorce, and out-of wedlock births." Same-sex marriage also allegedly devalues and weakens the functions of marriage, and, as a result, cannot be countenanced. Moreover, in an era when public benefits are at issue, the report notes, quite frankly, that extending marriage to same-sex couples would make them eligible for a wide range of social recognitions and benefits. Thus, as Anna Marie Smith points out, restricting marriage is a way to keep social spending down ("Politicization of Marriage" 316). At the same time, as discussed below, heterosexual marriage under neo-liberalism has generally become an important mechanism in the privatization of many of the costs of social reproduction and human dependency, "shifting costs from state agencies to individuals and households" (Duggan 14). The rationale for DOMA, therefore, reflects the centrality of the cultural domain to neo-liberal politics and policies. More specifically, it underscores how crucial sexual politics are to neo-liberalism, and delineates some of the more important terms and terrains on which sexual politics—which are connected, but not fully reducible, to economics—are being fought out.

DOMA also demonstrates how policies that target "domestic" populations are deeply intertwined with policies that target immigrants (see Chang; Honig; Lowe; Nevins), including in regard to sexuality (see Luibhéid xviii–xxi). For DOMA, as already mentioned, applies not only to U.S. citizens and to legal residents, but also figures in the selection of who is eligible for legal immigration. DOMA's definition of a spouse and a marriage as applying only to a man and a woman means that same-sex bi-national couples cannot use their relationships as a basis for legal immigration. Moreover, immigration officials interpret DOMA in a manner that sanctions transgender discrimination. "In an interoffice memorandum, William R. Yates, Associate Director for Operations of the U.S. Citizenship and Immigration Services (CIS) announced that in its adjudication of spousal and fiancé petitions, the agency would not recognize a marriage or intended marriage where either party claims to be a transsexual" ("CIS Announces Policy").

Two other major pieces of legislation that passed in 1996 further reinforce the regulation of the sexualities and family forms of citizens and legal immigrants: the Personal Responsibility and Work Opportunity Reconciliation Act (PRWORA) and the Illegal Immigration Reform and Immigrant Responsibility Act (IIRIRA). Both laws conspicuously include "responsibility" in their titles. The PRWORA represents the most significant overhaul of welfare in many decades. In line with neo-liberal strategies for privatizing risk, it "drastically reduced American citizens' social rights by canceling their entitlement to welfare assistance" after a five-year lifetime limit, regardless of how dire their need (Smith, "Politicization of Marriage" 306). The law replaces Aid to Families with Dependent Children (AFDC) with Temporary Assistance to Needy Families (TANF), again with a five-year lifetime limit; it introduces stiff new work requirements for recipients (without adequately funding supports such as childcare); and it seeks to compel a particular set of sexual and family arrangements from welfare mothers and other (potentially) "risky" populations.[9]

In shifting from a logic of entitlement to one of responsibility, Anna Marie Smith suggests that the PRWORA effectively "places most of the blame for poverty—and indeed, for the entire reproduction of poverty—on what it regards as sexually irresponsible women" ("Politicization of Marriage" 315), especially poor women who have children outside of marriage, stereotypically coded as African American. Numerous scholars have analyzed how discourses of "culture"—including the "culture of poverty thesis"—generate such blaming and rearticulate, even as they deny, racist, sexist, classist, and colonialist ideologies. For example, Abramovitz and Winthorn discuss how the culture of poverty thesis maintains "that the poor transmit so-called dependency and anti-social behavior from one generation to the next (in homes headed by women)" (160). Laura Briggs' analysis of the Puerto Rican experience describes how "the culture of poverty thesis shifted the terrain of debate about poverty and colonialism from the economy to sex" (182), especially to the allegedly inappropriate gender roles and sexual behaviors of working class Puerto Rican (and African American) women. She also underscores that such scholarship has made available to popular, academic, and policy-making audiences "the notion of the culture of poverty as wedded to a sexualized, dark-skinned woman" who needs to be disciplined for her own good (188; see also Roberts). Consequently, politicians and others often do not consider it necessary to address systemic and enduring inequalities; rather, they aim to reform the allegedly "deficient" characters, cultures, and morals of poor women of color. The PRWORA strongly advocated the promotion of heterosexual marriage as a strategy for the reform of poor women. The law characterized heterosexual marriage not only as the most desirable state of being,[10] but also as a state into which poor women should be adduced to enter, through a mixture of coercive and calculated incentives, as an important strategy to alleviate their poverty.[11] Of course, the claim that heterosexual marriage is a reasonable route out of poverty for women has been widely disputed in scholarly literature (e.g., see Roberts; Smith, "Sexual Regulation"). Heterosexual marriage as a patriarchal institution has also been widely problematized. Yet, none of these considerations deterred the architects of the PRWORA. Thus, Smith concludes that under the law, "a poor single mother is explicitly expected to marry her way out of poverty, both for her own sake and for that of her children. In this manner, patriarchal heterosexual marriage is more than a moral category; it is an institution that is supposed to replace the state's obligations towards the poor. The promotion of heterosexual marriage—especially among the poor—is therefore integral to the post-welfare state regime" ("Politicization of Marriage" 315).[12]

The specter of the welfare mother in need of discipline had its counterpart in the anti-immigrant image, deployed during California's 1994 Proposition 187 campaign, which presented undocumented women as cynically giving birth to numerous children on U.S. soil. These children, who are U.S. citizens by right of birth, allegedly drained the health, welfare, and education systems (see Hondagneu-Sotelo; Luibhéid). Thus, immigrants' cost to state and federal governments, through their own and their children's use of public benefits, as well as a desire to drive these costs down, featured prominently in discussions preceding the PRWORA (and subsequently, IIRIRA).[13] In addition, some expressed concern that the availability of welfare might serve as a "magnet" for supposedly freeloading foreigners in general—and fecund foreign women in particular.

While the matter of immigrants' costs versus their contributions proved to be undecidable, Congress agreed on a number of principles that involved and applied the construct of the "responsible" individual to immigrants.[14] Consequently, the PRWORA not only hardened the exclusion of undocumented immigrants from public benefits but also greatly reduced even legal immigrants' eligibility for a wide range of public benefits, in a manner that significantly sharpened the significance of the citizen/legal resident distinction. Secondly, the PRWORA required that those sponsoring someone for immigration had to have an income of at least 125 percent of the federal poverty level and, furthermore, that they had to sign a legally binding affidavit of support that would remain in effect until the immigrant naturalized, accrued 40 qualifying quarters of work, permanently departed the United States, or died. Sponsors could be required to reimburse the federal government for any benefits used during this period. IIRIRA, which passed into law just one month after the PRWORA, reiterated and strengthened the requirements imposed on sponsors through legally binding affidavits of support.

Currently, the requirements involving the legally binding affidavits apply to immigrants who enter the country through family reunification preferences, or to work in a relative's business, or to work in a business of which a relative owns 5 percent or more of the total value. We should remember that family-based immigration accounts for approximately three quarters of all legal immigration to the U.S. each year.[15] Of these immigrants, U.S. citizens bringing "opposite sex" spouses have accounted for the largest category of family immigrants for many years (Constable 185; Zimmerman and Fix 64).[16] As has already been described, immigration law (and DOMA) defines "spouse" in a very specific manner, involving biologically born male and female couples only. The affidavits signed by the sponsors of spousal or family migrants are not voided by divorce, although in cases of abuse or battery of children or spouses, some requirements may be waived for twelve months (Congressional Research Service 5). They may also be waived for the same amount of time if the subject would be indigent as a result.

Logics and Rationalities of the Affidavits

In her excellent article on IIRIRA, Kathleen Moore suggests that sponsors were the main targets of the affidavits of support, and that congressional discourse constructed them as equivalent to "deadbeat dads" whose failure to provide financial support pushed immigrants onto the welfare rolls. Moore cites Representative Lamar Smith's telling remark that, "just as we require deadbeat dads to provide for the children they bring into the world, we should require deadbeat sponsors to provide for the immigrants they bring into the country" (138).[17] The U.S. Commission on Immigration Reform, which in 1994 had recommended the use of legally binding affidavits of support, also affirmed that sponsors were the targets. The Commission's report states: "it is likely that making the affidavit of support legally binding will serve primarily as an effective deterrent to sponsors" (133). But the Commissioners extended the language of responsibility as imagined through heterosexual kinship, by analogizing immigrants' sponsors not just to fathers who assume (or not) financial responsibility for their children, but also to heterosexual spouses who assume responsibility for one another (132, 133, 134). In addition, the affidavit was tellingly described as a "deterrent" to sponsors, a means to making them think carefully before "bringing" someone to live in the United States. The terminology echoes not only key dominant discourses of sexual morality (encouraging "responsible" sexuality, which includes thinking ahead to consequences before engaging in sexual activity), but also discourses concerning the United States' strategy for controlling undocumented immigration, which since the 1990s has also focused on deterrence (Andreas; Nevins). In the case of undocumented migration, this has meant pre-empting the entry of undocumented migrants rather than dealing with them once they are within the territory, and it has given rise to new, heavily militarized immigration control technologies which combine with the increasing criminalization of the act of undocumented migration itself.[18] Since September 11, 2001, efforts to pre-empt the entry of undocumented or "undesirable" immigrants, and the proliferation of technologies for criminalizing even those who have entered legally, have reached a new intensity. Thus, the language of "deterrence" conjoins discourses of "responsible" sexuality (coded under DOMA and PRWORA as heterosexual and as confined, ideally, to marriage) to those of undocumented migration and national security, constructing sexual "deviants," the undocumented, "bad" sponsors, and national security threats as in many ways interchangeable, and indeed, as potentially giving rise to one another.[19]

In their written dissent to elements of IIRIRA, Senators Ted Kennedy, Patrick Leahy, and the late Paul Simon provided another telling commentary about affidavits. While they disputed, for example, the requirement that sponsors had to have earnings/assets of at least 125 percent of the poverty level, they did not dispute the system of sponsorship or the idea of making affidavits legally binding. To the contrary, they claimed that such a system "disciplines sponsors, protects immigrants, and safeguards taxpayers" (Senate Report 104–249, 49). Here again, the affidavit functions as a technology that aims to produce responsible sponsors. "Protecting immigrants" is, however, a more ambiguous objective. Congressional debates about IIRIRA suggest that protection may include ensuring that sponsors actually assist immigrants when they arrive and guarding against situations in which sponsors bring in immigrants who are then forced onto welfare, which some sponsors then use for themselves. This last concern mirrors some of the anxieties that animated the PRWORA, including allegations that poor women were deliberately having babies as a way to generate or augment their income.[20] Additionally, through installing a system of responsible sponsorship, the immigrant would be instructed in "American" norms of responsibility and would learn to avoid welfare. For welfare, according to a House Report, "destroys the recipient's work incentives, encourages the breakdown of the family, and transmits dependency across the generations. Furthermore, it keeps immigrants from being productive participants in society" (House Report 104–469, 144). The similarity of the preceding language to that of the PRWORA—and DOMA—is striking; according to the PRWORA, parents who use welfare supposedly teach their children to be dependent and ruin them as future productive members of society.

Finally, the senators described the legally binding affidavits as a means of "safeguarding taxpayers," a description that is consistent with neo-liberal logic in several important respects. According to Lisa Duggan, many taxpayers:

> began to see themselves as consumers of government, expecting the best return for price paid in taxes, rather than as citizens supporting an expansive array of broadly accessible public agencies and institutions. And this consumer citizenship was economically and racially differentiated—according to housing patterns—with racial difference dominating shifting conceptions of taxpayers vs. taxeaters, those who paid the bill, and those who siphoned off the funds of suburban property taxes to support inner city services. (38)

Constructing themselves as consumers who demand control over how their tax dollars are spent, taxpayers have contributed to privatizing the domain of the social, in the process denying the extent to which the "haves" have historically and cumulatively profited from systemic discrimination as well as from state programs that subsidize whiteness (Lipsitz), middle class domesticity, and heteronormativity. Moreover, they have recast social inequalities such as racism, sexism, and poverty as problems to be resolved by developing individual "character" rather than by attending to larger structural factors, and they have constructed the government as accountable to taxpayers (consumers) rather than to all members of the polity. Contending that the legally binding affidavits of support would "safeguard taxpayers," the senators participated in this logic, to such a degree that taxpayers, rather than any other group, emerged as the subjects that the government had to "safeguard" against the alleged costs of immigrants.

Legally Binding Affidavits as Neo-liberal Technologies of Governance

The affidavit system emerged from a longer history of efforts to bar immigration by the poor. Since 1882, immigrants whom the government considered "likely to become public charges" have been excluded from admission to the United States. Beginning in 1917, immigrants who became public charges within five years of admission could be deported. Nonetheless, according to Sheridan, both the 1917 law and subsequent revisions allowed for immigrants who were likely to become public charges to be admitted as long as the immigrant, or someone on his or her behalf, posted a bond. The Department of State and the Immigration and Naturalization Service (which, in 2003, was reconfigured into three separate branches under the Department of Homeland Security) also accepted written affidavits of support. But the courts found that these affidavits imposed only a "moral obligation" rather than a binding financial obligation, and consequently that states could not sue to recover costs associated with immigrants who became public charges (Sheridan 743–44). The legally binding affidavit system was intended to address these difficulties. The Congressional Research Service explains what is new about the legally binding affidavit system:

> There are four major differences . . . (1) all family immigrants must have sponsors who sign the new affidavit of support, whereas previously the affidavit of support was [only] one option [among various] for meeting the public charge requirement; (2) sponsors must satisfy income and other mandatory requirements that did not exist before; (3) the new affidavit of support is a legally binding contract between the sponsor and the U.S. government, which the previous affidavit was not; and (4) the new affidavits are in effect until the immigrant either naturalizes or meets the 40 quarter work test. . . . Under prior

law, the sponsor's responsibilities usually lasted for 3 years after the immigrant entered the U.S. (2)

Affidavits have emerged as distinct technologies of control within their
own right. This is consistent with a general trend within neo-liberalism, where contracts and contract-style agreements have provided
the means for the governance of a wide range of populations who are
deemed to be "problematic."[21]

For one thing, the affidavits serve as important tools in risk management. Whereas certain groups (including employers) need immigrants,
others deem them to be a risky population on grounds including racial, economic, cultural, medical, law-and-order, and security concerns. Affidavits try to mediate between such views by using actuarial
logic to, on one hand, exclude those who are deemed most risky, and
on the other hand, to allow for the admission of other, less risky immigrants, but to situate them within normalizing structures that will
exhort them to become responsible subjects and future citizens.

Specifically, the affidavits exclude families with lower incomes and
fewer assets, even when they are heteropatriarchal; and on the other
hand, they clearly lay out the consequences for legally admitted immigrants and their sponsors if any of the risks associated with immigration do come to pass. Legally admitted immigrants must submit to
externally defined norms, rules, and codes of conduct, including those
embedded in the affidavits, if they are to become eligible for citizenship
in the future. Should legal immigrants break any of the rules, however,
they may become ineligible for citizenship or may even become subject to deportation. This underscores the point that being admitted as
a legal immigrant is not a one-time event, but rather, a process that
situates immigrants within long-lasting, normalizing and disciplinary
relationships, which are expected to instruct them in the proper norms
of American citizenship, teach them their "proper" racial/ethnic, gender, and class location within U.S. society, and condition their subjectivity (see Luibhéid; Ong, *Buddha is Hiding*). The affidavits have been
implemented as a technology for further accomplishing these long-
term goals.

What is quite novel here is that not only are *immigrants* to be made
accountable through the affidavit system—so also are their *sponsors*.
Indeed, the affidavit system implants responsibility for managing the
risks associated with immigration in the hearts, minds, and daily practices of the many U.S. citizens/legal residents who are sponsors, and

holds them accountable, too. The result is an effort to actualize *and partly privatize* immigration control by way of a partnership between individual citizens/legal residents, their immigrant relatives, and various branches and levels of government. Such public/private partnerships are characteristic of neo-liberal governance.[22] Importantly, this public/private partnership is modeled after and depends upon the heteropatriarchal family.

Overall, the affidavit of support organizes the flow of "responsibility" into a particular configuration that ties immigrants, sponsors, communities, and resources into new, ongoing relationships that are contractual,[23] subject to law, and shaped by a heteropatriarchal imaginary. It installs an elite, U.S. government-generated model of "responsibility," which is defined primarily in reference to income and assets that reach at least 125 percent of the federal poverty threshold, and that can be measured and tracked by external others, in place of alternative forms of support and obligation. Effectively, the affidavit attempts to reconfigure the ways that support and obligations are generated, circulated, and fulfilled (or not) in immigrant circles, families, and communities.[24] One might therefore argue that it strongly attempts to alter how families, communities, and social ties are materialized, and how subjectivity is produced and lived.[25] This seems especially clear when we remember that the affidavits are not voided even when a divorce occurs. At the same time the affidavit system leaves immigrants vulnerable not only to the vicissitudes of capitalism and particular stages of the life cycle, but also to the jeopardy that attends immigrant status itself, which is increasingly a grounds for the loss of entitlements, the risk of deportation, and arbitrary detention. How individual immigrants, their circles, families, and communities, negotiate these new technologies of responsibility, in tandem with their growing jeopardy, remains to be examined—especially through forms of knowledge (such as participant ethnography) that are not bound by governmental categories, and that critically scrutinize the grounds of their own possibility.

Exclusions and Neo-Liberalism

The affidavits not only redefine the terms for immigrant inclusion, but also the terms for exclusion and preclusion. Exclusion applies to categories of people who are explicitly barred from legally immigrating to the United States. Preclusion refers to people who are not explicitly barred from entry, but who, because they are unable to conform to aspects of law or procedure, nonetheless find themselves barred. Precluded people, however, garner little political attention or support. Family preference in immigration law has always been embedded in a matrix of exclusions and preclusions. As I argued elsewhere, family preference in U.S. immigration law historically constructed women as dependent wives following pioneering migrant husbands, implemented a sexual double standard, generated classes of women deemed excludable because they were alleged to threaten marital stability, barred married women whose childbearing was feared to result in the birth of "too many" poor children and/or children of color, and generated explicit racial, ethnic, and class exclusions that helped to consolidate the "immigrant family" as necessarily of European (preferably Northern or Western) origin, heteropatriarchal, and of some means (Luibhéid 3–8).

In 1965, Congress enacted significant revisions of immigration law, eliminating explicit racial and ethnic preferences and hierarchies. The revised laws substantially reallocated immigration preferences, so that family reunification came overwhelmingly to predominate in immigration flows. According to David Reimers, Congress fully expected that Europeans (especially Southern and Eastern Europeans whose admission had been sharply curtailed in 1924) and Euro-Americans would be the primary beneficiaries of family reunification laws. Conversely, Asians and Africans, who have had to contend with a lengthy history of race-based exclusion, were not expected to be able to avail themselves of these family preferences as codified. Latin Americans, as "Western Hemisphere" immigrants, were not subjected to the preference system until after 1976 (Reimers 85–87, 132). However, Congress's predictions concerning families turned out to be wrong. In recent decades, Asians and Latin Americans have comprised the majority of legal immigrants to the U.S., including under family preference categories. This is not terribly surprising because extensive and enduring U.S. military, economic, and cultural interventions in Asia and Latin America have effectively created "bridges for migration" (Sassen 14–15). The important point, however, is that the 1965 revisions were *expected* to benefit Europeans and European-American families, even though the law carefully avoided saying so, and such expectations were consistent with the larger history of discrimination and exclusion of families of color (see Reimers 73).

Even as Congress prioritized "family" in the 1965 revisions, in a manner that was expected to maintain white racial hegemony, it reiterated a ban on lesbian and gay immigrants, this time through language barring the entry of "sexual deviates." But despite this effort to shore up the heterosexuality of the immigrant population, concern mounted that heterosexual marriage might be cynically used as a means to acquire immigration rights. To pre-empt this possibility, Congress passed the Immigration Marriage Fraud Amendments (IMFA) in 1986. Under the IMFA, immigrant spouses receive a two year conditional residency, after which time they may file for permanent residency (i.e., regular immigrant status). Both spouses have to carry out the filing. As a consequence of the legislation, immigrant wives (who comprise the majority of those who enter under the "spouse" category) frequently found themselves bound to batterers on whom they were dependent for legal immigration status. Although Congress has tried on several occasions to address the complex intersections of domestic violence and immigration status, it remains a serious problem (see Anderson; Orloff and Kaguyutan; Volpp). In addition, the IMFA signaled more generally that heterosexual marriages in which at least one partner was an immigrant would be under scrutiny, subject to inspection and evaluation by the state in accordance with normative criteria. The upshot is an expansion of state technologies aimed at producing, inspecting, and normalizing specific heterosexual marital forms among the foreign born.

Revisions to immigration law in 1990 lifted the ban on lesbian and gay immigrants, but they did not make lesbians and gays eligible for family reunification through their intimate relationships with U.S. citizens and legal residents. As previously indicated, DOMA further specified that spousal reunification provisions could not include same-sex couples or married couples in which one person was transsexual. Thus, although lesbians and gays are no longer directly banned, bi-national lesbian, gay, and transsexual couples find themselves in the very difficult position of splitting up, shuttling between countries, arranging a fraudulent marriage, or dealing with the fact that one of them will be undocumented. All of these choices entail enormous costs and place great burdens on relationships.

The affidavit of support requirement, introduced by IIRIRA in 1996, further redefined the matrix of inclusions, exclusions, and preclusions. As a result, a not insignificant number of people still find themselves unable to sponsor family members because they have insufficient income or assets.[26] For example, the Congressional Research Service reported that "a draft study sponsored by the INS of immigrants entering in 1994 showed that roughly half of [the] immigrants from Mexico and El Salvador, one-third of Dominicans and Koreans, and one-quarter of Chinese and Jamaicans, could not have met the new income requirements for sponsoring family members" (6).[27] Similarly, Zimmerman and Fix report that "[a] high proportion of mixed families [i.e., including citizens, legal immigrants, and/or undocumented people] is not likely to meet the new income threshold: one-third of all mixed families have incomes under 125 percent of the Federal poverty level. An even larger share (45 percent) of mixed families where there are no citizen parents will be unable to meet the threshold" (72–73).

It is not that family ties do not exist in these cases. They do exist within the domain recognized by immigration law as validly constituting a "family." But when the family's income is not sufficient to meet the 125 percent threshold, this is taken as probabilistic evidence that the immigrant will become a public charge and/or the kind of person who lacks the "responsibility" that Congress hopes to cultivate. The calculation involved is predictive and probabilistic, as is typical with actuarial models. The result, of course, is exclusion from the United States on class grounds. And yet, class-based exclusion is justified by recoding poverty as a matter of individual "responsibility" and "entrepreneurship" (as defined by elites), shorn of all reference to the structural inequalities of capitalism. This exclusion articulates other exclusions in the history of immigration law. For example, as the Congressional Research Service has noted, Mexican and Salvadoran immigrants are disproportionately likely to be poor, which means that they are disproportionately likely to be affected by these rules. Or, keeping in mind that increasing numbers of women enter the U.S. as immigrant workers who support families left behind, and that women as a whole—and Latina and Black women in particular—generally earn less than men, it is not difficult to predict that the affidavit rules have, and will have, a distinctly gendered effect.[28] For example, it may become more difficult for women to sponsor men than vice versa. Lesbian, gay, and transsexual couples, as mentioned, are not even eligible to participate in this system.

Since the affidavit of support system does not exclude *all* Latin American immigrants or *all* women (even though it explicitly restates class exclusions), however, it operates differently than historic practices of excluding entire racial, ethnic, or sexual status groups.[29] It is not that race, ethnicity, gender, and sexuality have been rendered unimportant in shaping life possibilities—far from it. Rather, it is that such shaping occurs in a different manner. In the case of affidavits of support, certain status combinations render an individual, or family, as more or less likely to be excluded or precluded from legal entry—even while *all* members of a particular status group will not necessarily be excluded or precluded.[30] Such a situation is consistent with the logic of actuarial systems, which, according to Janet Halley, disavow status by recoding it as unconnected to systemic inequalities—even as they rely on status to assess so-called risks. Consequently, Halley suggests, the actuarial model "works to disable rights rhetoric, to avoid scrutiny for fairness, and generally to evade moral evaluation" (61). The important question that Halley raises is how to challenge the exclusions and preclusions that reinstall status but allow "deniability" to those in power.

In sum, heteronormative logics and processes—involving multiple forms of systemic inequality that converge without being reducible to one another—continue to shape immigration access. The resulting matrix of exclusions, preclusions, and inclusions are important not just to specific immigrants, families, and communities, but also more generally. This is because immigration control provides the means to materialize the nation-state within very particular, restrictive parameters, and to re-articulate exclusionary constructions of "the people," "the citizenry," and the nation (Berlant; Honig; Lowe).

Conclusion

While this chapter has critically examined "personal responsibility," my intention is not to suggest that responsibility is inevitably negative or undesirable. Instead, while recognizing that responsibility may often be commendable, I have drawn attention to the ways that the term "responsibility" has been deployed in discourses, sites, and practices that are integral to contemporary neo-liberal regimes of governance. I have suggested that we must critically scrutinize the social imaginaries that such a concept generates, the knowledge regimes to which it is tied, the forms of accountability that it generates, and the programs for inculcating "personal responsibility" into the citizenry (and citizenry-to-be) that it has spawned.

This chapter further explores how "responsibility" has become linked to heteronormalizing state projects. Some (though not all) of these projects differentiate heterosexuality from family and/or marriage, but they nonetheless suggest that heterosexuality is best channeled into marital, reproductive family formations, and that this can be accomplished through aggressive, multi-form state initiatives. Such projects not only reanimate the heterosexual norm to which all people are expected to aspire, but they also generate categories of "problem subjects," including immigrants, who then need to be controlled, disciplined, or excluded. These developments underscore that heteronormativity is continually shifting, rather than monolithic or universal, such that even "dominant" groups experience anxiety and the necessity for continual self-monitoring. Yet, these anxious effects are not of the same order as those experienced by groups that are actively subordinated and dispossessed by such normalizing regimes.

Immigrants, while very diverse, remain vulnerable to heteronormalizing regimes. This is because immigration, according to nationalist logics and laws, is a "privilege," not a right, which can be refused or withdrawn at any time. According to this logic, the ability to immigrate legally depends not only on occupying a privileged position in society, but also on continually adhering to rules—including those organized through shifting forms of heteronormativity—that are presently associated with the logics of personal responsibility that traverse economic and cultural domains. Those who refuse to participate in such dynamics may be precluded from immigrating or deported after entry. Since 1986, the IMFA has made heterosexual marriage subject to inspection and evaluation by the state; now, the requirement for an affidavit of support—which remains in effect until the immigrant naturalizes, dies, permanently departs the United States, or accrues 40 qualifying quarters—ensures that married heterosexual couples in which at least one person is an immigrant find themselves bound to marriage in an entirely new way.

These developments are part of a longer historical process in which U.S. immigration laws and procedures have diversely constructed and materialized the immigrant "family" within a matrix of sexual, gender, racial, ethnic, and class hierarchies. Yet, given that neo-liberal governance operates in accordance with actuarial categories that are predictive, probabilistic, and pre-emptive (rather than openly relying on traditional status groupings), it often splits historically excluded groups into more or less preferred subgroups—even as the importance of status groupings remains. Thus, contemporary immigration control, while it perpetuates a long history of exclusion and discrimination, is not simply "the same old thing," but a changing regime for inclusion, exclusion, and preclusion. On the one hand, it provides a great amount of "deniability" to government agencies, officials, and bureaucracies, and, on the other, it renders necessary new strategies for scholarship and activism.

The extent to which law and procedure actively mediate who can count as "family" for purposes of immigration tends to be rendered invisible in dominant discourses, which persist in debating the degree to which immigrant families are "backward" and "traditional" (which then makes it easy to construct North Americans as "modern" and "progressive"; see Lutz), or alternatively, which present immigrant families as the source of "authentic" family values that mainstream America needs to recoup (e.g., Fukuyama). In either case, what is ignored is the extent to which immigrant families are *produced* and *governed* in specific ways, which at present link heteronormativity, responsibility, economic privatization, and cultural logics whose racism, hetero-sexism, classism, and ethnocentrism are disavowed. (This is not to suggest that immigrants do not develop their own strategies for negotiating these circumstances; they do, as Manalansan and others describe). In turn, the production and governance of immigrant families at once draws on and enables ongoing heteronormative state-making and citizenship practices, policies, and ideologies.

These multiple connections underscore the importance of ensuring that critical scholarship on immigration, sexuality, and governmentality remain in dialogue, since each raises important questions about power, inequality, suffering, injustice, and resistance, in terms that recognize the inextricable linkage of economic and cultural domains, but that are not immediately recuperable within dominant neo-liberal logics.

Works Cited

Abramovitz, Mimi and Ann Winthorn. "Playing by the Rules: Welfare Reform and the New Authoritarian State." *Without Justice for All*. Ed. Adolph Reed, Jr. Boulder, Colo.: Westview Press, 1999. 151–173.

Alexander, M. Jacqui. "Erotic Autonomy as a Politics of Decolonization." *Feminist Genealogies, Colonial Legacies, Democratic Futures*. Ed. Chandra Talpade Mohanty and M. Jacqui Alexander. New York: Routledge, 1997. 63–100.

Anderson, Michelle J. "A License to Abuse: The Impact of Conditional Status on Female Immigrants." *Yale Law Journal* 102 (1993): 1401–1430.

Andreas, Peter. "Borderless Economy, Barricaded Border." *NACLA Report on the Americas* xxxii.3 (November/December 1999): 14–21.

Anthias, Floya and Nira Yuval-Davis. "Introduction." *Woman-Nation-State.* Ed. Nira Yuval-Davis and Floya Anthias. New York: St. Martin's Press, 1989. 1–15.

Berlant, Lauren. *The Queen of America Goes To Washington City.* Durham, N.C.: Duke University Press, 1997.

Briggs, Laura. *Reproducing Empire. Race, Sex, Science and U.S. Imperialism in Puerto Rico.* Berkeley: University of California Press, 2002.

Chang, Robert. *Disoriented. Asian American, Law, and the Nation State.* New York: New York University Press, 1999.

"CIS Announces Policy on Transsexual Applicants." http://www.visalaw.com /04aug2/11aug204.html (accessed August 11, 2004).

Congressional Research Service. "Immigration: The New Affidavit of Support—Questions, Answers and Issues." December 15, 1997. http://www .house.gov/judiciary/crs.htm (accessed July 11, 2004).

Constable, Nicole. *Romance on a Global Stage.* Berkeley: University of California Press, 2003.

Cott, Nancy. *Public Vows. A History of Marriage and the Family.* Cambridge, Mass.: Harvard University Press, 2000.

Dean, Mitchell. *Governmentality. Power and Rule in Modern Societies.* London and Thousand Oaks, California: Sage, 1999.

Donzelot, Jacques. *L'invention du social.* Paris: Vrin, 1985.

Duggan, Lisa. *The Twilight of Equality? Neoliberalism, Cultural Politics, and the Attack on Democracy.* Boston: Beacon Press, 2003.

Eng, David L. and Alice Y. Hom. "Introduction. Notes on a Queer Asian America." *Q&A: Queer in Asian America.* Ed. David L. Eng and Alice Y. Hom. Philadelphia: Temple University Press. 1–21.

Ferguson, Roderick. *Aberrations in Black. Toward A Queer of Color Critique.* Minneapolis: University of Minnesota Press, 2004.

Foucault, Michel. "Governmentality." *The Foucault Effect. Studies in Governmentality.* Ed. Graham Burchell, Colin Gordon, and Peter Miller. Chicago: University of Chicago Press, 1991. 87–104.

Fragomen Jr., Austin T. "The Illegal Immigration Reform and Immigrant Responsibility Act of 1996: An Overview." *International Migration Review* 31.2 (Summer 1997): 438–460.

Fredriksson, John. "Bridging the Gap Between Rights and Responsibilities: Policy Changes Affecting Refugees and Immigrants in the United States

Since 1996." *Georgetown Immigration Law Journal* 14 (Spring 2000): 757–778.

Fukuyama, Francis. "Immigrants and Family Values." *The Immigration Reader.* Ed. David Jacobson. Malden, Mass.: Blackwell Publishers, 1998. 388–401.

Gordon, Colin. "Government Rationality: An Introduction." *The Foucault Effect. Studies in Governmentality.* Ed. Graham Burchell, Colin Gordon, and Peter Miller. Chicago: University of Chicago Press, 1991. 1–51.

Halley, Janet. *Don't: A Reader's Guide to the Military's Anti-Gay Policy.* Durham, N.C.: Duke University Press, 1999.

Hondagneu-Sotelo, Pierrette. "Women and Children First: New Directions in Anti-Immigrant Politics." *American Families: A Multicultural Reader.* Ed. Stephanie Coontz, et al. New York: Routledge, 1999. 288–304.

Honig, Bonnie. *Democracy and the Foreigner.* Princeton: Princeton University Press, 2001.

Katz, Jonathan. *The Invention of Heterosexuality.* New York: Dutton, 1995.

Lipsitz, George. *The Possessive Investment in Whiteness. How White People Profit From Identity Politics.* Philadelphia: Temple University Press, 1998.

Lowe, Lisa. *Immigrant Acts. On Asian American Cultural Politics.* Durham, N.C.: Duke University Press, 1996.

Luibhéid, Eithne. *Entry Denied. Controlling Sexuality at the Border.* Minneapolis: University of Minnesota Press, 2002.

Lutz, Helma. "The Limits of European-ness: Immigrant Women in Fortress Europe." *Feminist Review* 57 (Autumn 1997): 93–111.

Lyon, David. *Surveillance After September 11.* Cambridge: Polity, 2003.

McClintock, Anne. *Imperial Leather. Race, Gender and Sexuality in the Colonial Context.* New York: Routledge, 1995.

Manalansan IV, Martin F. *Global Divas.* Durham, N.C.: Duke University Press, 2003.

Migration News. "Welfare Changes Continue." http://migration.ucdavis.edu/mn/comments.php?id=1201_0_2_0.

Moore, Kathleen. "U.S. Immigration Reform and the Meaning of Responsibility." *Studies in Law, Politics and Society* 20 (2000): 125–155.

Muñoz, Jose Esteban. *Disidentifications: Queers of Color and the Performance of Politics.* Minneapolis: University of Minnesota Press, 1999.

National Conference of State Legislatures. "Analysis of the Personal Responsibility and Work Opportunity Act of 1996." http://www.ncsl.org/statefed/hr3734.htm (accessed August 24, 2004).

Nevins, Joseph. *Operation Gatekeeper. The Rise of the 'Illegal Alien' and the Making of the U.S.-Mexico Boundary.* New York: Routledge, 2002.

Ngai, Mae. *Impossible Subjects. Illegal Aliens and the Making of Modern America.* Chicago: University of Chicago Press, 2004.

Ong, Aihwa. *Flexible Citizenship. The Cultural Logic of Transnationality.* Durham, N.C.: Duke University Press, 1999.

_____. *Buddha is Hiding. Refugees, Citizenship, the New America.* Berkeley: University of California Press, 2003.

Orloff, Leslye E. and Janice v. Kaguyutan. "Offering a Helping Hand: Legal Protestations for Battered Immigrant Women: A History of Legislative Responses." *American University Journal of Gender, Social Policy and the Law* 10 (2001): 95–184.

Puar, Jasbir K. and Amit S. Rai. "Monster, Terrorist, Fag: The War on Terrorism and the Production of the Docile Patriot." *Social Text* 72 (Fall 2002): 117–148.

Reimers, David. *Still the Golden Door. The Third World Comes to America.* Columbia: Columbia University Press, 1992.

Roberts, Dorothy. *Killing the Black Body. Race, Reproduction, and the Meaning of Liberty.* New York: Vintage, 1997.

Rose, Nikolas. *Powers of Freedom. Reframing Political Thought.* Cambridge, U.K.: Cambridge University Press, 1999.

Sadowski-Smith, Claudia. "Readings Across Diaspora. Chinese and Mexican Undocumented Immigration Across U.S. Land Borders." *Globalization on the Line. Culture, Capital and Citizenship at U.S. Borders.* Ed. Claudia Sadowski-Smith. New York: Palgrave, 2002. 69–97.

Sassen, Saskia. *Losing Control? Sovereignty in an Age of Globalization.* New York: Columbia University Press, 1996.

Sheridan, Michael J. "The New Affidavit of Support and Other 1996 Amendments to Immigration and Welfare Law Provisions Designed to Prevent Aliens From Becoming Public Charges." *Creighton Law Review* 31: 741–766.

Smith, Anna Marie. "The Politicization of Marriage in Contemporary American Public Policy: The Defense of Marriage Act and the Personal Responsibility Act." *Citizenship Studies* 5.3 (2001): 303–320.

_____. "The Sexual Regulation Dimension of Contemporary Welfare Law: A Fifty State Overview." *Michigan Journal of Gender and Law* 8.2 (2002): 121–218.

Somerville, Siobhan. *Queering the Color Line. Race and the Invention of Homosexuality in American Culture.* Durham, N.C.: Duke University Press, 2000.

Stoler, Ann Laura. *Carnal Knowledge and Imperial Power. Race and the Intimate in Colonial Rule*. Berkeley: University of California Press, 2002.

United States. Commission on Immigration Reform. *U.S. Immigration Policy. Restoring Credibility*. Washington, D.C.: U.S. Government Printing Office, 1994.

United States. Cong. *House Report 104–664, The Defense of Marriage Act*. July 9, 1996. http://web.lexisnexis.com/congcomp/document?_m=68370cd58 35c3550cf016e3cf347c11c&_docnum=1&wchp=dGLbVzz-zSkSA&_md5 =6c1fa00b328a4f917fce47a9c2c14951 (accessed June 28, 2004).

_____. *Report 104–469, Part 1, Immigration in the National Interest Act of 1995. Report of the Committee of the Judiciary of the House of Representative on H.R. 2202*. March 4, 1996. Washington: D.C.: U.S. Government Printing Office.

_____. *Senate Report 104–249, Immigration Control and Financial Responsibility Act of 1995*. April 10, 1996. Washington, D.C.: U.S. Government Printing Office.

_____. Dept. of Health and Human Services, Administration for Children and Families. "Fact Sheet: The Personal Responsibility and Work Opportunity Reconciliation Act of 1996." http://www.acf.dhhs.gov/ programs/opa/facts/prwora96.htm (accessed August 16, 2004).

Vernes, Georges. *Immigrant Women in the U.S. Workforce. Who Struggles? Who Succeeds?* Lanham, Mass.: Lexington Books, 1999.

Volpp, Leti. *Working With Battered Undocumented Women*. San Francisco: The Family Violence Prevention Fund, 1995.

Warner, Michael. "Introduction." *Fear of a Queer Planet. Queer Politics and Social Theory*. Ed. Michael Warner. Minneapolis: University of Minnesota Press, 1993. vii–xxxi.

Welch, Michael. *Detained. Immigration Laws and the Expanding INS Jail Complex*. Philadelphia: Temple University Press, 2002.

White, Stuart. "Social Rights and the Social Contract—Political Theory and the New Welfare Politics." *British Journal of Political Science* 30: 507–532.

Yang, Hyunah. "Re-membering the Korean Military Comfort Women: Nationalism, Sexuality, and Silencing." *Dangerous Women: Gender and Korean Nationalism*. Ed. Elaine Kim and Chungmoo Choi. New York: Routledge, 1998. 123–139.

Yeatman, Anna. "Interpreting Contemporary Contractualism." *Governing Australia. Studies in Contemporary Rationalities of Government*. Ed. Mitchell Dean and Barry Hindess. Cambridge, U.K.: Cambridge University Press, 1998. 227–241.

Zimmerman, Wendy and Michael Fix. "Immigration and welfare reforms in the United States through the lens of mixed-status families." *From Immigration Controls to Welfare Controls*. Ed. Steve Cohen, Beth Humphries, and Ed Mynott. New York: Routledge, 2002. 59–80.

Notes

1   I want to extend warmest thanks to Hai Ren, the volume's editors, the Sexualities and Borders Research Cluster at Bowling Green State University (BGSU), and audiences at BGSU, the University of Arizona, and the University of California, Berkeley for critical feedback on drafts of this article.

2   Neo-liberalism takes a variety of forms, and involves a range of institutions, actors, and programs that are not unified and remain contested. Lisa Duggan notes that it is characteristic of neo-liberalism to link cultural and economic domains (12, 14) without either being determinative of the other. See also Berlant and Ong.

3   Mitchell Dean's analysis of risk, transposed to the question of personal responsibility, suggests that it is necessary to examine the forms of knowledge that make personal responsibility thinkable, as well as the techniques that claim to discover it, the technologies that govern it, and the political rationalities and programs that deploy it (178).

4   Dean notes that neo-liberals and neo-conservatives share a diagnosis that the citizenry has lost its virtue, but they differ in their strategies for re-implanting virtue (163, 172).

5   For Dean, the virtues that people are supposed to cultivate, the responsibilities that they are supposed to accept, are modeled on the market and take the form of "enterprise" and "the consumer" (164).

6   In the words of Rose, the welfare state "was grounded in the presupposition that the gradual betterment of the conditions of all forces and blocs within society [. . .] could be achieved. [. . .] This image of social progress through gradual amelioration of hardship and improvement of conditions of life gradually won out over the image of social revolution on one hand and the image of unfettered competition on the other" (135). For some half a century, that vision of society remained in place, but by the 1970s it was being contested, especially in terms of welfare and other public benefits. We should note, of course, that the U.S. has always had a two-tier welfare system, which somewhat complicates Rose's analysis. As Anna Marie Smith explains, "the United States created an incomplete and differentiated ensemble of programs that is structured according to a single overarching logic, namely the distinction between the universal contributory and non-stigmatizing social security programs (unemployment and old-age insurance) for 'deserving' citizens and stigmatizing pov-

erty assistance programs for the 'undeserving' poor" ("Sexual Regulation" 125). Smith further explains that "whereas the New Deal era of the 1930s represented at least the white American poor as rights-bearing citizens who deserved assistance because they had entered into impoverishment through no fault of their own, neo-conservative risk management discourse transforms the poor into quasi-rational risk-choosers who have independently selected the path that led to their socioeconomic condition. As such, neo-conservatives contend that the poor must be held accountable for their decision to expose themselves to the very 'risk factors' that supposedly determine their condition and that of their children" ("Politicization of Marriage" 307). Echoing other critics, Smith points out some of the limitations of the dominant model of responsibility that has underwritten the slashing of social safety nets: "Within this risk discourse, government ought to merely enhance the effects of market relations such that individuals who 'choose' to engage in 'high-risk lifestyles' are made to pay in a proportionate manner for the 'costs' they impose on society as a whole. Further, that concept of 'social costs' is itself defined from an extremely pro-wealthy/anti-poor perspective, such that the costs of the wealth accumulation and the growing gap between the rich and the poor are concealed. Neo-conservative 'risk management' discourse is therefore specifically skewed towards the location of social accountability exclusively among the poor themselves, and constructs the concept of social cost solely with the respect to the 'dangers' and social costs that are supposedly imposed by the poor onto the rest of society" ("Politicization of Marriage" 307). See also Abramovitz and Winthorn.

7   The four overarching rationales for DOMA given by the report are: "(1) defending and nurturing the institution of traditional, heterosexual marriage; (2) defending traditional notions of morality; (3) protecting state sovereignty and democratic self-government; and (4) preserving scarce government resources."

8   Under the Personal Responsibility and Work Opportunity Reconciliation Act (1996), discussed below, federal funds were provided to states to conduct sexual education programs that promoted total sexual abstinence outside of marriage. According to Anna Marie Smith, the programs are required to teach "that sex outside of marriage is psychologically 'harmful'; that abstaining from sex outside of marriage is 'the only certain way to avoid out-of-wedlock pregnancy, sexually transmitted diseases, and other associated problems;' and that 'a mutually faithful monogamous relationship in the context of marriage is the expected standard of human sexual activity'" ("Sexual Regulation" 196).

9   For more on the terms of the PRWORA, see, for example, Dept. of Health and Human Services, "Fact Sheet," and National Conference of State Legislatures, "Analysis." Ambramovitz and Winthorn summarize the sexual and family provisions of the law as follows: "the law (1) included the child

exclusion, which permitted states to deny aid to children born to a woman receiving welfare; (2) created a $20 million 'illegitimacy' fund to be shared by up to five states that decreased their out-of-wedlock births without increasing abortions; (3) allocated funds for abstinence programs but not sex education; and (4) eliminated almost all direct aid to unmarried teen mothers" (159).

10 "The law begins with a 'Findings' section that extols the virtues of heterosexual patriarchal marriage. In its very first passage, the law states: '(1) Marriage is the foundation of a successful society. (2) Marriage is an essential institution of a successful society which promotes the interests of children. (3) Promotion of responsible fatherhood and motherhood is integral to successful childrearing and the well-being of children'" (Smith, "Politicization of Marriage" 314).

11 Duggan summarizes these technologies: "'family caps' to limit support for newborns, mandatory child support cooperation even in cases of domestic violence, family planning and adoption relinquishment incentives, and sexual abstinence education" (16). See also Roberts.

12 Smith observes that both Republicans and Democrats have embraced the idea that a decrease in out-of-wedlock births will lead to a reduction in poverty, but that "this claim has been widely disputed in the social science literature" ("Sexual Regulation" 137). Nonetheless, according to the logic of the PRWORA, the ideal woman citizen is not just someone who bears and rears children, but also one who does so in a "low-risk manner" (as defined by the state) that reduces costs (Smith, "Politicization of Marriage" 316).

13 Despite the general perception that immigrants were using public benefits, officials could reach no agreement about the best way to calculate and weigh the economic costs against the economic contributions of immigrants, differentiate the costs and contributions of legal immigrants from those of the undocumented, determine the costs and contributions associated with refugees (who are allowed by law to receive substantially more support than legal immigrants) and "mixed status families" (e.g., a citizen child and immigrant parent, or any other such combination), or distinguish local from federal costs and contributions.

14 For example, Senate Report 104–249, which discusses the legislation that eventually became IIRIRA, includes the following: "the committee believes that aliens in this country should be self-sufficient" (5); "In effect, immigrants make a promise to the American people that they will not become a financial burden" (6); and "it should be made clear to immigrants that the taxpayers of this country expect them to be able to make it in this country on their own and with the help of their sponsors" (7).

15 Under immigration law, the words "family" and "relative" designate the immigrant's spouse, parent, child, or adult sibling (Sheridan 755). There

are no quotas limiting the admission of parents, spouses, and unmarried minor children of U.S. citizens, who are technically eligible for immediate immigration—although bureaucratic processing can entail significant delays. Spouses and unmarried children of legal permanent residents, and adult children and adult siblings of citizens, are also given preference, but quotas limit their numbers to such an extent that, for example, eligible siblings from countries that send many immigrants to the U.S. each year may wait a decade or more before the system begins to process them.

16 According to Nicole Constable, "between 1971 and 1997, spouses constituted 20 to 30 percent of all immigrants"; a majority of these were immigrant wives joining U.S. citizen husbands (185). Constable elaborates: "census and immigration department figures show that, during the 1997 fiscal year, out of 796,000 immigrants, over 25 percent were spouses of U.S. citizens (170, 226) or legal permanent residents (31,576). Of these spouses, 66 percent (over 132,000) were women" (185).

17 Smith ("Politicization of Marriage") rightly observes that while it seems reasonable to demand that fathers contribute to their children's support, the PRWORA crossed a line by refusing to recognize legitimate circumstances in which women might decide to sever ties with the father. In a later article, she explains that the bi-partisan approach to welfare "treats child support payments not as one small element within a comprehensive ensemble of anti-poverty policies that would bring about structural economic transformation, job creation, and the redistribution of wealth, but as a 'silver bullet'" ("Sexual Regulation" 140).

18 On the militarization of the border and criminalization of migrants, see Andreas, Nevins, and Welch.

19 In the 1990s, undocumented migration was recoded as an act of lawbreaking that supposedly proved the migrant's "irresponsibility" (Nevins 121). This construction leaves unquestioned the law itself, as well as its tenets, its modes of implementation, and the larger structural factors that give rise to undocumented migration, including globalized inequalities and U.S. demands for undocumented workers (Nevins; also Moore). On connections between sexuality, migration and national security, see Puar and Rai.

20 Smith explains, "it is widely believed in American public policy circles that poor women approach reproductive sex in a purely entrepreneurial manner. It is alleged that they engage in unprotected heterosexual intercourse in the hope that should they become pregnant and bear a newborn child, they would profit handsomely in the form of either public assistance eligibility or—where they already participate in a welfare program—increased cash payments and relief from mandatory work requirements" ("Sexual Regulation" 136). Consequently, many "family cap" laws operate on the unproven and highly questionable assumption that "negative financial in-

centives constitute the best remedies" ("Sexual Regulation" 174) to poor women's alleged sexual entrepreneurship. These and other laws have become very popular, despite the fact that many studies have disputed the existence of a simple, causal connection between poverty and reproductive decisions.

21 On the use of contracts in general as a neo-liberal technology that is especially applied to "problem" populations including immigrants, welfare users, and the unemployed, see Dean, White, and Yeatman.

22 In this situation, "responsibility" is to run along two major axes: not only between the sponsor and the immigrant, but also between the sponsor and the U.S. government, which stands in for the taxpayer. "The sponsor's signing the affidavit creates a contract between the sponsor and the United States government" (Sheridan 761).

23 Yeatman reminds us that the use of contracts for organizing and mediating social relations has a long liberal history, but has tended to depend on the abstract ideal of a subject who *freely chooses* to enter into a contract—when, in fact, a significant portion of the world's population has not been accorded the status of "free subjects." Thus, Yeatman suggests that the neo-liberal utilization of contracts as a technology of governance could be read as a sort of "anti-discriminatory ethos of personhood" (228) that attempts to extend the status of legal individual to all populations, including people of color, women, "sexual minorities," immigrants, and others who were not typically accorded such status. The other, more problematic side of contractualism (as part of an anti-discriminatory ethos of personhood) is its refusal to address the systemic inequalities that still greatly affect people's abilities to enter into contracts, to negotiate them in terms that might benefit them, and to enforce them. Indeed, the affidavits of support illustrate how one-way the process is. David Eng challenges Yeatman's analysis because she fails to account for the process whereby laborers who were hardly "free" have, for centuries, entered into labor migration contracts (personal conversation, Berkeley, Calif., April 9, 2005).

24 Moreover, the circulation of money has acquired greater complexity after 9/11. According to David Lyon, the broad definitions of "terrorist" and "supporting terrorism" that figure in laws like the USA Patriot Act (2001) mean that immigrants have to become much more careful about sending remittances and, in some instances, have ceased sending them altogether, lest they be charged with "supporting terrorism" (see Lyon 51).

25 As Dean describes, contracts such as the affidavit of support "act upon loose forms of identification and obligation to construct certain types of durable entities (e.g., communities, households, regions) which discover themselves as social and political actors in partnership" with a range of other entities (173).

26 There is one possible alternative: the sponsor can try to find someone who will agree to co-sponsor an immigrant (again, under a legally binding contract). The extent to which this represents a viable alternative or simply a replication of the original problem on a different scale remains open to question.

27 The Congressional Research Service continues: "in general, it is argued that immigrants are poor compared to the population as a whole. The Urban Institute reported in a recent study that almost 1 in every 4 of the 4.7 million immigrants who entered between 1980–1985 lived below the poverty level—twice the poverty rate for the U.S. as a whole" (6).

28 According to Georges Vernes's study of immigrant women in the U.S., while some groups earn at or above the U.S. average, Mexican and Central American women "earned only 67 and 64 percent of the earnings of native born women respectively" (123)—and, of course, women as a whole already earn less than men. As Vernes notes, the "gap in labor market outcomes between [Mexican women] and other immigrant women has increased over time" (128).

29 As Claudia Sadowski-Smith describes, "those who share a common national origin or common past in discriminatory immigration legislation may thus no longer have a common future in the contemporary United States" (79).

30 I argue that neo-liberal governance has appropriated the feminist of color concept of "intersectionality" and refashioned it into a tool of dominance through actuarial systems.

Part

III

LEGAL MATTERS

3

Refugee Law, Gender, and the Human Rights Paradigm

Deborah Anker

> Underlying the [Refugee] Convention is the international community's commitment to the assurance of basic human rights without discrimination . . . . Persecution, for example, undefined in the Convention, has been ascribed the meaning of "sustained or systemic violation of basic human rights demonstrative of a failure of state protection."[1]
>
> —*Canada v. Ward,* Supreme Court of Canada, 1993

International refugee law is coming of age.[2] It increasingly refers to, and more explicitly acknowledges its foundations in, an international human rights paradigm, as signaled a decade ago by the Supreme Court of Canada's 1993 landmark *Ward* decision establishing the concept of persecution as a serious human rights abuse.

The refugee regime is generating a serious body of law that elaborates basic human rights norms and has important implications in—and beyond—the refugee context. International human rights law continues, however, to distance itself from refugee law, despite the growing synchronicity and longstanding close connections between the two bodies of law. As a result, refugee law is often treated like a "poor cousin." Many human rights activists remain wary of engagement with refugee advocacy, especially individual claims to refugee status, in part because human rights academics and practitioners are not familiar with the ways in which refugee law has been evolving as international human rights law.

The function of the international human rights regime—in particular the Commission on Human Rights and other specialized human rights bodies—is to judge whether states fulfill their duties under internationally agreed upon human rights norms[3] and to deter, through monitoring and publicizing, future abuse: in short, to change the behavior of states. The norms derive from the international Bill of Rights—the Universal Declaration of Human Rights (UDHR), the International Covenant on Civil and Political Rights (ICCPR), and the International Covenant on Economic, Social and Cultural Rights (IC-ESCR)—and the more specialized instruments related to issues such as race, gender, and children, among others.[4] The regime's institutions are international monitoring bodies without any significant enforcement mechanisms.

Refugee law grants protection to a subset of persons who have fled human rights abuses.[5] Under the International Refugee Convention, a refugee is a person unable or unwilling to avail herself of the protection of her country, "owing to a well-founded fear of being persecuted for reasons of race, religion, nationality, membership of a particular social group or political opinion" (Convention Relating to the Status of Refugees art. 1[A]). Refugee law provides surrogate national protection to individuals when their states have failed to fulfill fundamental obligations, and when that failure has a specified discriminatory impact. As several jurisdictions are recognizing, international human rights standards determine (or should determine) the nature of these obligations, embraced within the refugee definition's concept of persecution.

Refugee law, however, is not aimed at holding states responsible for human rights abuses; it does not seek, that is, *to deter* human rights abuse. Its function is instead remedial. In general, the international community has created two regimes to address human rights abuses: one to monitor and deter abuse, the other to provide protection—including sanctuary, rights[6] and an alternative to state protection—to at least some of those compelled, and able, to flee from abuse by crossing international borders (see Hathaway, *New Directions*).

Human rights lawyers and scholars have often viewed refugee law as too embedded in domestic immigration law and institutions. The great innovation of the international human rights movement of the past half-century was to bring human rights "out of the confines of domestic legal systems" and into the realm of international law and institutions (Sohn 4, see also Steiner and Alston vi). Under the Refugee Convention, the responsibility to provide international protection—a surrogate to the ruptured, national protection—is placed on the states that are parties to the Convention. Thus, in apparent contrast to the international human rights regime, refugee law is implemented by states, to the extent that it is possible, within domestic legal systems. The refugee regime also differs from the international human rights regime in many other respects. For example, there is no regularized monitoring of states' compliance with their obligation to provide surrogate protection, although the United Nations High Commissioner for Refugees (UNHCR) serves an important supervisory function. No international bodies formally part of the refugee regime, furthermore, have been designated to hear inter-state complaints or individual communications.[7]

Yet refugee law *is* international law, grounded in an international treaty. In the case of refugee law, its institutions are both national and international. Over the past decade in particular, refugee law has been claiming its international human rights roots and evolving across national borders. As refugee law matures, judicial bodies are reviewing more refugee cases. In some instances, these cases reach the highest courts of the states, meanwhile some administrative systems display growing sophistication about the issues.[8] The work of scholars and of the UNHCR—which issues non-binding legal interpretations—have become particularly salient,[9] with non-governmental organizations (NGOs) playing a significant role in the articulation of legal principles. For example, governments in some cases have relied on NGO analyses, citing them in major judicial opinions.[10] Furthermore, several states' administrative bodies and courts are in dialogue with one another. By borrowing, adapting, and building on each other's jurisprudence and on such instruments as national guidelines, they are beginning to create a complex and rich body of "transnationalized" international law.[11]

The human rights paradigm has been critical to these developments. It is not only that key criteria of refuge, as formally defined, are being interpreted in light of human rights principles; it is also that international human rights law, in a significant number of instances, provides the theory that binds together, and even unifies, different bodies of national jurisprudence. For example, following the decision in *Ward*, some commentators and jurisdictions have embraced the Canadian Supreme Court's concept of persecution as a serious human rights abuse, that is to say, as a manifestation of injuries reflecting systemic conduct, "demonstrative of a failure of state protection" (*Canada v. Ward* 733.)[12] The British House of Lords in *Shah* solidified this human rights approach by presenting a formal legal construct and analysis of persecution as constituted by two distinct elements: serious harm and a failure of state protection.[13]

This newer, internationalizing direction in refugee law has been limited so far to conversations among only a few states. Cross-fertilization and efforts to ground interpretation in a human rights paradigm—including in those few countries—remain uneven, and examples of inconsistencies and incomplete implementations of the Convention abound.[14] Moreover, the great majority of states that are party to the Convention are not engaged in individual, legalized assessments of claims.[15] However, the UNHCR does play an active role in determining refugee status in these and other cases.[16] Generally, the UNHCR tries to synthesize and advance the best state practices, mediating among different states and protection systems (although no doubt more formalized monitoring mechanisms, suggested by scholars and expert groups, are needed). The UNHCR's non-binding norms influence the standards for protection in both legalized and non-legalized settings. Indeed, a growing number of states—South Africa and countries in East and Central Europe, for example—are specifically incorporating the Convention into domestic law and are developing domestic infrastructures to determine refugee status.[17] They will thus both rely on and help develop other states' interpretations of the refugee definition, especially to the extent that they invoke a common international framework. These states also may enrich refugee law, embedding its interpretations of international human rights norms in a greater diversity of cultural and national traditions.

In many respects, refugee law crosses the threshold of justiciability and enforceability, past which human rights law has found it difficult to proceed. Refugee law provides an enforceable remedy—available under specific circumstances—for an individual facing human rights abuses. Determinations of refugee status entail contextualized, practical applications of human rights norms. Increasingly, refugee law is confronting issues on the forefront of the human rights agenda, especially with respect to questions of gender and women's rights. The discussion that follows offers three examples: rape and sexual violence, female genital surgery (FGS, also often referred to as female genital mutilation),[18] and family violence. In some cases, refugee law applies a human rights paradigm when evaluating instances of violence against women as serious harm within the scope of persecution. In so doing, refugee law has built on the work of the international human rights movement. It has had—or has the potential to have—a substantial impact on human rights law. As these examples illustrate, while conflicts still exist between human rights and refugee lawyers and activists, proven opportunities for partnership and cooperation exist.

The Human Rights Paradigm and Gender-Based Persecution

The development of "gender asylum law"[19] has required a human rights framework. Gender asylum law also has been a catalytic force in itself, a major vehicle for the articulation and acceptance of the human rights paradigm. For example, the 1993 *Ward* decision in Canada (which, while not a gender case, elaborated the human rights paradigm) was issued at the same time as that country's landmark *Guidelines on Women Refugee Claimants Fearing Gender-Related Persecution*.[20] Additionally, the UNHCR and many practitioners, scholars, and activists have consciously constructed gender asylum law on the basis of international women's human rights law and the work of the international women's human rights movement. For reasons that are as much strategic as principled, they have argued that, in order to respond to women's experiences, refugee law needs to evolve and transform in interpretation, rather than simply be amended. The bars to women's eligibility for refugee status lie not in the legal categories per se (i.e., the non-inclusions of gender or sex as one of the five grounds). Rather, women are barred from eligibility because of the incomplete interpretation of refugee law, the failure of decision makers to "acknowledge and respond to the gendering of politics and of women's relationship to the state" (Crawley 2).[21] Simply adding gender or sex to the enumerated grounds of persecution would not solve the problem, nor would it address cases such as those discussed below in which the harm feared—an element of "persecution"—is either unique to or disproportionately affects women.

Accordingly, refugee law, in part, takes an integrative perspective on women's rights. By interpreting forms of violence against women within mainstream human rights norms and definitions of persecution, refugee law avoids some of the problems of marginalizing women's rights in international law.[22] Both the UNHCR and national guidelines, which have served as the foundations for much gender asylum law and have had some surprising normative effects, embrace this "mainstreaming" approach, reinforced in 2001 by the UNHCR's global consultations on the fiftieth anniversary of the Refugee Convention.[23]

Rape/Sexual Violence

Rape was one of the first issues affected by the articulation of the human rights paradigm within refugee law and the increased willingness to consider gender-specific abuses within the scope of persecution.

Despite relatively early Canadian precedent for treating rape as "persecution of the most vile sort,"[24] rape (especially before 1993) was often understood as a private affair, embodying unrestrained—and unrestrainable—male sexual appetite ("exaggerated machismo . . . rampaging lust-hate" in the words of one U.S. jurist in a 1987 case).[25] In short, the public/private distinction, which has so deeply affected international law, was reproduced in refugee law.[26] As a result, even cases that fit the traditional paradigms of refugee law were being dismissed— largely because the physical harm involved was sexual and directed at a woman. For example, when a Salvadoran woman whose family was active in a cooperative movement was raped by death squads while they shouted political slogans and hacked her male relatives to death, she was deemed the victim of private violence.[27] Similarly, a U.S. immigration judge denied asylum to a Haitian woman who was gang-raped because she supported the deposed president.[28] Since these cases were decided, there has been a sea change in the assessment of claims involving rape and other forms of sexual violence. In her 2001 treatise on refugee law and gender, Heaven Crawley suggests that now "[r]efugee law doctrine is unanimous . . . in its opinion that sexual violence, including rape, constitutes an act of serious harm" (44). As a severe form of physical assault, rape should indeed be treated as one of the least controversial forms of serious harm; significantly, it is now described as such in national gender guidelines[29] as well as in the case law of several jurisdictions.[30]

Feminist critics of international law have noted that until recently rape and sexual violence have not been analyzed as core human rights violations, although they have been recognized as violations of international law and even as human rights abuses (see Charlesworth and Chinkin 218–19, 234–35). (Even in the past few years, the analysis has remained largely in the context of international criminal law.) However, some markedly different trends exist in refugee law jurisprudence. New Zealand, Canadian, and Australian authorities have determined that rape and sexual violence violate one's right to security of person as well as the prohibitions against cruel, inhuman, and degrading treatment under the UDHR.[31] Similarly, recent refugee law commentators do not analyze rape as on the margins of traditional human rights law, but at its core (see, e.g., Crawley 44). They understand rape in terms of the prohibition against cruel, inhuman, and degrading treatment and torture, as well as in terms of the right to life and security of person. In the Australian case, all of these core rights are specifically spelled out in their Gender Guidelines.[32] Furthermore, the U.S. Board of Immigration Appeals held in *In re Kuna* that a husband's continual brutal assaults on his wife, including years of rape and sexual violence, constituted torture within the terms of the Convention against Torture.[33] Canadian authorities have found that "matrimonial violence"—for example, a woman imprisoned in her home, raped, and beaten by her husband over a ten-year period—can be the most extreme form of torture because there is no respite.[34]

The work of women activists and jurists in publicizing rape and sexual violence in the context of conflicts in Yugoslavia and Rwanda has been critical to changing opinions and awareness among refugee lawyers. Refugee and human rights lawyers have also worked collaboratively to establish important precedents on rape. Indeed, the first decision of a human rights body recognizing rape as torture—outside of the context of detention or war—arose out of the experience of Haitian women fleeing to the United States after the 1991 coup d'état that overthrew the first democratically elected president of Haiti, Jean Bertrand Aristide. The illegal *de facto* regime that came to power committed a multitude of human rights abuses against the civilian population, creating a climate of terror and destroying democratic movements and civil society. Military and police forces, paramilitary groups, and even civilian auxiliaries used rape and other types of violence as instruments of repression against women. Moreover, women were raped precisely because they had played an important role in the formation of democratic institutions and civil society, because they and/or their male relatives were involved in activities to improve local communities, and/or simply because they were left behind.[35] As the Special Rapporteur on Violence against Women noted: "to rape a woman is to humiliate her community" (Coomarasamy 49,50).[36] In Haiti, several men often gang-raped a woman, usually in her home and in front of her children and/or other family members. In a number of cases, before being raped, the woman was forced to witness the rape and/or murder of her daughter(s) or other family members (See Inter-American Commission on Human Rights, "Report" [OAS Haiti Report] para. 122.).

The earlier flight of Haitian refugees to the United States during the 1970s and 1980s helped precipitate the contemporary refugee rights movement in the United States. A network was established to hear, bear witness, and give further voice to Haitian women who fled violence at the time of the illegal coup. Their stories became the basis for asylum claims and spurred three simultaneous developments. First, scholars and advocates obtained an administrative precedent in the United States that granted asylum to a woman and recognized rape as a serious harm that could constitute persecution (*In re D-V-* 77,79). Second, the United States issued national gender asylum guidelines, which state that "[s]evere sexual abuse does not differ analytically from . . . other forms of physical violence that are commonly held to amount to persecution" (U.S. Gender Guidelines, reproduced in Black et al. 75). The U.S. Guidelines constituted an important development internationally, building on the precedent set by Canada. Third, these same Haitian women brought their stories, duly cast as asylum "affidavits," before the Inter-American Commission of the Organization of American States (OAS), which issued the *Report on the Situation of Human Rights in Haiti,* citing various human rights violations during the illegal regime, including the use of sexual violence against women as a political weapon.

The Inter-American Commission's report also contained a specific legal determination that "rape represents not only inhumane treatment that infringes upon physical and moral integrity under Article 5 of the [Inter-American Convention], but also a form of torture in the sense of Article 5(2) of that instrument" (See Inter-American Commission on Human Rights, "Report" [OAS Haiti Report], ¶¶ 134).[37] This was the first determination by a human rights body that rape, which was here clearly outside the context of detention, constitutes torture, and that it violates specific human rights-based prohibitions against torture.[38] It was not until 1998 that an international body, the International Criminal Tribunal for Rwanda, considered rape outside the context of detention and war as torture under international law.[39] The significance of the earlier Inter-American Commission's *Report on Haiti* has been lost, however, in many human rights and women's international law treatises.[40]

As these cases of rape and sexual violence make clear, refugee law can contribute to the elaboration of human rights norms, deepen understanding, and produce substantive changes—if it is embraced as part of human rights law. Some symbiosis has taken place, most notably between the international women's human rights movement and gender asylum activists, but the commonalties between the two areas of law have been largely lost on the human rights community. In some cases, such as those involving female genital surgery, refugee law addresses issues that remain divisive and unresolved within the international human rights movement. As a result, refugee law can sharpen the focus of human rights discourse by grounding the debate in the circumstances of a real person who seeks refugee law's particular, palliative solution.

Female Genital Surgeries

Female genital surgery (FGS)—also termed female genital mutilation—has been extensively discussed in human rights literature and elsewhere.[41] FGS is a traditional practice that involves removing parts of the female genital organs and, in some cases, stitching the two sides of the vulva together, usually without anesthesia or sterilized instruments.[42] "The range of physical effects resulting from FGS varies with the form of surgery but the physical complications of the most severe forms—clitorectomy and infibulation—can be disabling and life threatening" (Lewis 13). There exists, nevertheless, a complex set of justifications for the continued practice of FGS. "The stated objective is usually the maintenance of some virtue such as chastity, piety and cleanliness rooted in centuries-old social, moral, and religious traditions. It is generally the case that these virtues are thought important to maintain the girl or woman's status as a suitable potential spouse, maintain the social status of her family and thus maintain harmony in the community at large" (Cissé 432). Usually, older women practice FGS on girls or sometimes on young women at the time of their marriage or first pregnancy. FGS is a ritual practice across cultures and religions, although it is especially well documented in the Horn of Africa and in Muslim countries (See Crawley 176; Toubia).

FGS has been identified as a human rights issue in various international fora (Lewis 7), but the feminist analysis of FGS as a human rights violation is complicated because FGS exists at the "intersection of complex cultural, gender, and racial questions in human rights jurisprudence" (Lewis 4). While there is broad-based opposition to FGS, especially among African women, many others have defended it as a ritual that binds together communities, especially communities of women.[43] Many activists and scholars—most prominently Africans and African Americans—have criticized the focus on FGS as obfuscating other issues that are more important to African women. They have also criticized the sensationalized accounts of the practice, the racist and incomplete portrayals of African women, and the involvement of Western feminists, all of which raises questions about who should set the agenda for change and what methods should be used to eradicate the practice (see Tamir). Claims of cultural relativism have acquired renewed force in the 1990s with women's human rights in general and

FGS in particular at the center of many of these debates. As Henkin and others have noted, the cultural-relativist argument "presents a particularly acute challenge in respect to women's human rights since many denials of those rights are justified in terms of social and/or religious custom, sometimes enacted into law" (Henkin et al. 391).

That said, a growing body of law recognizes FGS as the basis for refugee claims. Unlike the international human rights fora, which have identified FGS as a human rights abuse but not necessarily as a violation of core rights (Charlesworth and Chinkin 225–29), several refugee decisions have linked FGS to mainstream human rights violations or have identified it as a form of serious harm within the meaning of persecution. The Immigration and Refugee Board of Canada has found that the return of a woman to Somalia to face involuntary infibulation violated, *inter alia*, numerous provisions of the UDHR and the ICCPR. These provisions included the right to life and the prohibition against cruel, inhuman, or degrading treatment.[44] United Kingdom authorities recognize FGS as a form of torture (U.K. Appellate Gender Guidelines 14 n. 31), and some Australian case law describes it as a serious harm within the meaning of persecution, which includes actions "in disregard of human dignity."[45] In a 1996 U.S. decision, *In re Kasinga*, the U.S. Board of Immigration Appeals found that FGS constituted serious harm "consistent with our past definitions" of persecution and rejected the argument made by immigration authorities that, in cases involving cultural practices, a heightened "shock the conscience" test should be applied.[46] Recent commentators and some prominent refugee decision-makers have taken a strong anti-relativist position, while nonetheless opposing a view of human rights "that precludes flexibility in [its] conceptualization, interpretation and application within and between cultures" (Crawley 184).[47] Bernadette Passade Cissé suggests that reasoned analysis based on human rights principles can and should prevail over sensationalizing reports and culturally-biased judgments (451).

Refugee law offers a different perspective on conflicts between individual and group rights, and between individual autonomy and cultural enfranchisement (the essence of the cultural relativist conundrum), which have been raised in FGS and other cases. Whatever cultural consensus exists, refugee law is concerned with an individual who wishes to dissociate herself from that consensus. The individual who invokes refugee protection asserts that, notwithstanding what her culture may believe, her beliefs are in line with international standards. For example, in the U.S. *Kasinga* case, a 19-year-old woman claimed that she faced an immediate threat of being forced to undergo FGS shortly before being married, against her wishes, to a 45-year-old man (*In re Kasinga* 358). Thus, commentators have argued that a claim against return to face forced FGS goes to the philosophical core of human rights: the protection of individual autonomy and corporal non-interference (Crawley 184). As Cissé points out, "[w]hen an individual challenges societal norms by opposing FGM [female genital mutilation] and his/her basic rights, as articulated in international instruments, are not or cannot be controlled by the *de jure* public authorities, international human rights principles are implicated" (434–5).

Since refugee law does not attempt to set a corrective agenda, to tell another country how to act, or to propose plans for eradicating particular practices, it avoids controversies that have been divisive in debates on FGS and cultural relativism in general. The debates about such matters within the human rights community have at times been almost immobilizing, part and parcel of an unresolved theoretical stand-off. Avoiding such immobility, refugee law addresses an important aspect of the human rights question: whether an international human right is implicated. Indeed, with the cultural relativist conundrum, the continued failure to take women's rights seriously, and the complexity of the state responsibility question, gender asylum law is one of the few areas where the question of FGS as a human rights violation is effectively confronted. As Lewis notes, "[t]he engagement in active conflict on these issues at least removes FGS from the realm of a theoretical debate over whether westerners should ignore an exotic cultural practice and forces us to confront the question of how human rights law and policy could impact the lives of women on a day to day basis" (25). Lewis suggests that African American women should be concerned with how refugee law addresses issues like FGS that affect African women, actively engaging in the determination of the content of gender asylum guidelines and policies "in fulfillment of international human rights obligations" (Lewis 23).

By deploying a human rights paradigm and building on the work of the international human rights community, refugee law has identified such forms of violence against women as rape, sexual assault, and forced FGS as core violations. Making the relationship between refugee law and human rights law explicit creates opportunities for advancement within both fields. With respect to FGS, human rights issues may actually be more clearly identified in refugee law than in the international human rights regime itself, with its broader purposes and emphasis on fundamental change. With respect to other issues, however, such as the scope of state responsibility, refugee law and human rights law may need to struggle together to interpret critical issues common to both.

State Responsibility and Family Violence

The complicated question of state responsibility in the case of non-state actors is a central concern for women in human rights, but will be touched on only briefly here. Some of the most significant and recent case law in gender asylum law addresses just this question. Much of refugee law—and especially gender asylum law—tackles difficult problems of state responsibility. As a matter of doctrine, both human rights law and refugee law recognize state responsibility for human rights violations by non-state actors—although there is a dissenting, minority position in refugee law.[48] Developments in human rights law have supported a long-standing trend in refugee law which grapples with whether "persecution," understood in terms of a failure of state protection, requires direct, indirect, or even any proof of state complicity. The question of locating responsibility is inevitably more difficult when the state in question is in the process of collapsing, or when there is no functioning centralized authority. Although the refugee regime is not concerned with state accountability *per se*, both refugee and human rights law struggle with it. What, for instance, should be the standard for assessing the adequacy or inadequacy of state protection (the "due diligence" standard in human rights law)? Should the state be required to provide some actual reduction in the level of risk?[49] Or should formal and reasonable—however ineffective—actions of the state suffice?[50]

One of the most visible and dynamic areas of refugee case law now emerging is focused on family violence. However, this subject remains on the margins of human rights law, even though family or domestic violence is the most pervasive form of violence against women.[51] In cases of violence by husbands and male domestic partners, questions of state protection are especially complex, since they involve different levels of interweaving responsibility and enabling of the "private" harm by the state. The complexity is paradigmatic of gender-specific violence committed by private actors (Macklin 25). As Wright remarks, "[f]or most women, most of the time, indirect subjection to the State will always be mediated through direct subjection to individual men, or groups of men" (249).

In *Shah*, the House of Lords considered how broader patterns of inequality and discrimination, notably anti-adultery laws, structurally enabled the specific violence that the applicants feared from their husbands (see *Shah*). The case is by no means isolated. In Refugee Appeal No. 71427/99, New Zealand authorities analyzed in detail state patterns that condone family violence and that discriminate against women, even though the state constitution does not *formally* relegate women to second-class status (Refugee Appeal No. 71427/99, 570). The New Zealand authorities thus confronted the "cumulative effect" of various laws, including legal provisions regarding marriage, divorce, custody, and provisions of the criminal code (Refugee Appeal No. 71427/99, 571 para. 78). In *Minister for Immigration and Multicultural Affairs v. Khawar*, the Federal Court of Australia found evidence of state acquiescence in discriminatory enforcement of the law—the deliberate failures of the police to respond to a woman's complaints of her husband's violence (Australia's highest court subsequently upheld the Federal Court's *Khawar* decision).[52] These are some of the issues of structural discrimination that feminist critics of international law have identified as essential to any analysis of state responsibility that truly includes the experiences of women.[53]

The Convention against Torture (CAT or Torture Convention)—which as a human rights instrument extensively addresses prevention of torture—contains a non-return provision.[54] The Torture Convention prohibits states parties from returning a foreign national to a country in which he or she would face torture.[55] The non-return obligation in the Refugee and Torture Conventions is an obvious point of contact between human rights and refugee law. Claims for protection from return to torture often go hand-in-hand with—or follow the denial of—claims for refugee protection and status.[56] Torture is also an extreme example of serious harm within the meaning of persecution. For both these reasons, the human rights corpus defining torture is incorporated into refugee law.

The Convention against Torture includes a requirement of official action, consent, or acquiescence.[57] The Committee against Torture, which monitors compliance with the Torture Convention, has begun exploring the boundaries of the state action requirement, as have some regional human rights bodies (Anker, *Law of Asylum* 500–07). In some limited instances, refugee claimants fleeing family violence have also tested those boundaries. As noted, the U.S. Board of Immigration Appeals in *Kuna* granted a request for protection from return under the CAT to a woman fleeing years of domestic violence by her husband, a man with governmental ties who had previously committed crimes with impunity. As a result, the Board found state acquiescence even where the wife did not seek state protection because she reasonably believed that it would be futile (*In re Kuna*). The Board also found that the international legal definition of torture may include violence within the family under some circumstances (*In re Kuna*). In contrast, the failure of human rights law clearly to designate violence against women as torture (which implicates both a "paradigmatic" right and a norm of *jus cogens*) has been of central concern to feminist critics.[58]

Conclusion

The present chapter touches on just some of the multiple issues of international women's rights that refugee law is now addressing. A growing body of refugee case law considers other forms of violence against women—including forced marriage, forced sterilization, forced abortion, forced prostitution, bride burning, and honor killings—and examines gender in such other contexts as (discriminatory denials of) education, employment, and health care.[59] The inquiry into refugee status is deeply and necessarily contextual. Case law, UNHCR interpretations, and governmental guidelines all emphasize the intensely factual nature of any refugee determination. In the discrimination context, for example, the violations often must be cumulative and of an extreme nature (See Symes 114–16; United Nations High Commissioner for Refugees, *Handbook* ¶¶ 54–55). In all cases, the violation must be sustained or systemic, and the "normal" relationship between state and citizen or resident must be ruptured. The refugee is thus fundamentally marginalized, unable to enjoy basic rights, or vindicate them through change or restructuring from within her society (See Hathaway, *Law of Refugee Status* 135; Shacknove).

The next—or current—stage in refugee law may increasingly implicate economic and social rights.[60] As refugee law continues to mature, it may raise new questions about state responsibility and interact more closely with human rights instruments, not only the Convention against Torture, but other conventions as well.[61] Trafficking refugee cases under the CAT, as well as refugee claims based on the right to health, may portend a shift in focus *away* from the practices of the sending countries, generally of the South, and *to* the practices of the receiving countries, generally of the North.[62] Whatever the case, there can be little doubt that refugee law has been innovative with respect to some human rights issues. Of course, refugee law will only continue to contribute to the elaboration of human rights norms to the extent that it develops within a human rights framework. Explicit and structured application of a human rights paradigm in refugee law is, as I have indicated, new and limited. Indeed, all the developments described in this chapter are nascent, contingent, and fragile. Commentators worry that harmonization of legal measures in Europe may narrow the interpretation of refugee doctrine, or that it may even mean that intra-state bodies, instead of human rights institutions, would have the upper hand in shaping refugee law (Crawley 15). Indeed, the solidification of non-entrée regimes (Hathaway, "Emerging" 40–41) has been closely linked to evolutions in doctrine. Refugee law has many limitations, one of the most salient being its embeddedness in domestic immigration law and structures. As a result, refugee law is vulnerable to political backlash, especially during certain ideologically charged eras such as the Cold War.[63] We appear to be entering another such era, and it will be interesting to see how much of a buffer, if any, the new refugee law, which came of age during the interim years, will provide.

Civil society has become an important force in the refugee field. The case of Haitian women in the United States, discussed earlier in this chapter, is an example of how broad political activism has contributed to the advancement of more inclusive and internationalized interpretations of the law. The Canadian Gender Guidelines were the direct product of the work of NGOs and women in the government (See Gilad 335). The U.S. Guidelines, inspired by the Canadian model, were the product of a continuing political and legal movement for refugee rights that began some twenty years ago. Those efforts have resulted in protection status for tens of thousands, both within and outside the formal terms of the Refugee Convention.[64] The Refugee Women's Legal Group, an NGO founded in part by refugee women living in the United Kingdom, wrote gender guidelines that became the basis for those of the U.K. Immigration Appeals Authority.[65] Critical to all of the political and legal refugee rights movements has been the human rights conceptualization of refugee law, including the call for state parties to meet their international obligations under the Refugee Convention.

The human rights and refugee rights movements are intrinsically connected. Increasingly, contact between the two regimes—and especially between human rights and refugee practitioners—is becoming unavoidable. Refugee lawyers and adjudicators are making extensive use of human rights reports, and human rights monitors are being called upon to give expert testimony and affidavits in refugee cases.[66] Human rights NGOs are focusing more on states' compliance with their obligations under the Convention, such as the treatment and protection of refugees, especially in counties of the North.[67] Tensions between the refugee and human rights movements, however, remain inevitable. Western media have, at times, used refugee cases to sensationalize practices such as FGS, and in cases involving family violence, the media have told caricatured stories of women at war with their cultures.[68] And yet, against such media plays, refugee lawyers can work to guard against cultural judgments and to advocate for their clients with an awareness of the larger human rights context. Refugee and human rights activists can work together on issues such as trafficking, which implicate polices in the North as well as in the South.

The problem of cultural relativism may lie at the heart of the conflicts between the two regimes. While refugee law may be formally non-intrusive and non-judgmental, it does make a determination of a state's willingness and ability to protect a particular citizen or resident, and in so doing it lays claim to *international* human rights standards. The problem, to be sure, is that when the legalized refugee regime consists exclusively of states in the North determining refugee claims from the South, the purportedly international human rights-based judgments can seem one-sided, patronizing, and hypocritical. This discrepancy is especially pronounced in gender persecution cases since violence against women (including intra-family violence) is prevalent throughout the world. Western countries may be unwilling to believe that their own mechanisms of protection are inadequate, for, as Audrey Macklin has commented, "the phenomenon of gender persecution challenges the self-understanding of so-called 'non-refugee producers'" (264).

In a similar vein, Peter Rosenblum has argued that refugee law's human rights claims may send a destructive message to women's rights communities in the South by making judgments that lack nuance and resort to stereotyping, even under cover of an international standard. Then again, at least in this respect, refugee law is not unique. Like all legal regimes, it makes a particularized assessment that tends towards bounded categorizations and incomplete portrayals of individuals, societies, and their circumstances. While refugee law uses limited, legal categories, its factual scope is necessarily broad and complex—more so perhaps than many other areas of the law. As Lord Hoffman commented in *Shah*, "[Refugee law's] adjudication is not a conventional lawyer's . . . exercise of applying a legal litmus test to ascertained facts; it is a global appraisal of an individual's past and prospective situation in a particular cultural, social, political and legal milieu, judged by a test which, though it has legal and linguistic limits, has a broad humanitarian purpose" (*Shah* [Lord Hoffman quoting Sedley] 561). Refugee law does embrace some of the complexities that I have been outlining; for example, it recognizes that identities may be socially constructed and multifaceted. Accordingly, it tends to understand that the definition of refugee does not fix a claimant's individual or group identity; rather, it emphasizes the persecutor's *perception* of the refugee claimant's social status or opinion (See generally, Hathaway, *Law of Refugee Status* Ch. 5). Furthermore, far from obliging a claimant to base her claim on only one of the grounds of persecution, it allows her to make a claim based on any combination of the five grounds (United Nations High Commissioner for Refugees, *Handbook* paras. 66,67).

Refugee law reflects the human rights community's own analyses of human rights conditions in various countries. It also reflects the human rights community's own tensions and dilemmas, as the FGS phenomenon illustrates. Hope Lewis, for one, has commented that "[t]he social, economic, and political conflicts that underlie the conflict over Western feminist involvement on FGS are as deeply rooted as the cultural basis of the practice itself. The discussion must be restructured to expose the conflicts in order for progress to be made on this issue" (21). Refugee law offers a particular structuring that confronts human rights questions, but it does so less contentiously than is possible within the more ambitious framework of the human rights regime. After all, refugee law does not seek to reform states and does not address root causes. Its role is palliative; it represents the interests of the individual who dissociates herself from her community and her state. This is in no way to deny that the broader goals of the human rights community are important, or that refugee law may at times make an indirect contribution to them.[69] Instead, it is to recognize that refugee law may also complicate the work of human rights lawyers and activists, especially when its purposes are misunderstood. Moving forward will require greater clarity about the differences, as well as the similarities, between the two regimes.

Works Cited

Amnesty International. "Lost in the Labyrinth: Detention of Asylum-Seekers: Summary Report." *Amnesty International Online,* September 1, 1999. http://www.amnesty.org (accessed June 8, 2005).

Anker, Deborah E. *The Law of Asylum in the United States.* Managing ed. Paul T. Lufkin. 3rd ed. Boston, Mass.: Refugee Law Center, Inc. 1999 (supp. 2002).

_____. "Refugee Status and Violence Against Women in the 'Domestic' Sphere." *Georgetown Immigration Law Journal* 15 (2000): 391–402.

Australasian Legal Information Institute Online. A joint facility of UTS and UNSW Faculties of Law. http://www.austlii.edu.au (accessed June 8, 2005).

Aydin v. Turkey. 1997-VI Cur. Ct. H.R. 1866, E.H.R.R. 251.

Black, Laura, Mimi Liu, and Elizabeth Da Trinidade-Asher, eds. *Gender Asylum Law in Different Countries.* Boston: Refugee Law Center, Inc., 1999.

Blum, Carolyn P. "License to Kill: Asylum Law and the Principle of Legitimate Governmental Authority to 'Investigate Its Enemies.'" *Willamette Law Review* 28.4 (1992): 719–750.

Brennan, Katherine. "Note: The Influence of Cultural Relativism on International Human Rights Law: Female Circumcision as a Case Study." *Law and Inequality: A Journal of Theory and Practice* 7 (1989): 367–398.

Bunch, Charlotte. *Passionate Politics: Essays, 1968–1986: Feminist Theory in Action.* 1st ed. New York: St. Martin's Press, 1987.

Campos-Guardado v. INS. 809 F.2d. 285 (5th Cir. 1987).

Canada v. Ward. 2 S.C.R. Supreme Ct. of Canada. 1993. 689.

Charlesworth, Hilary, and Christine Chinkin. *The Boundaries of International Law: A Feminist Analysis.* Manchester: Manchester University Press, 2000.

Chen Shi Hai v. Minister for Immigration and Multicultural Affairs [2000] HCA 19; 92000) ALR 553. Available at http://www.austlii.edu.au.

Cissé, Bernadette Passade. "Comment: International Law Sources Applicable to Female Genital Mutilation: A Guide to Adjudicators of Refugee Claims Based on a Fear of Female Genital Mutilation." *Columbia Journal of Transnational Law* 35 (1997): 429–452.

Connors, Jane. "Legal Aspects of Women as a Particular Social Group." Spec. issue of *International Journal of Refugee Law* (1997): 114–128.

Convention Against Torture and Other Cruel, Inhuman or Degrading Treatment or Punishment. S. Treaty Doc. No. 100–20 (1988), 1465 U.N.T.S. 85, art. 3, *opened for signature* Feb. 4, 1985.

Convention Relating to the Status of Refugees. 19 U.S.T. 6259, 189 U.N.T.S. 137, *opened for signature* July 28, 1951.

Cook, Rebecca J. "State Responsibility for Violations of Women's Human Rights." *Harvard Human Rights Journal* 7 (1994): 125–176.

Coomarasamy, Radhika. "Of Kali Born: Women, Violence, and the Law in Sri Lanka." *Freedom from Violence: Women's Strategies from Around the World.* Ed. Margaret Schuler. New York: UNIFEM, 1992. 49–63.

Copelon, Rhonda. "Recognizing the Egregious in the Everyday: Domestic Violence as Torture." *Columbia Human Rights Law Review* 25 (1993–4): 291–368.

Crawley, Heaven. *Refugees and Gender: Law and Process.* Bristol: Jordans, 2001.

Crock, Mary. *Immigration and Refugee Law in Australia.* Sydney: Federation Press, 1998.

D. v. United Kingdom, 24 Eur. H.R. Rep. 423, ¶ 49 (1997) (Eur. Ct. H.R.).

Feller, Erika. "Address to the Conference of the International Association of Refugee Law Judges at Bern, Switzerland." *Georgetown Immigration Law Journal* 15 (1999): 381–391.

Fernando Mejía Egochiago and Raquel Martin de Mejía v. Peru. Case 10.970, Inter_Am. Comm'n H.R. 157, OEA/Ser. L/V/II.91, doc. 7 rev. (1996).

Fitzpatrick, Joan. "Taking Stock: The Refugee Convention at 50." *World Refugee Survey 2001.* New York: U.S. Committee for Refugees, 2001. 22–29.

_____. "Temporary Protection of Refugees: Elements of a Formalized Regime." *American Journal of International Law* 94 (2000):279–306.

Gilad, Lisa. "The Problem of Gender-Related Persecution: A Challenge of International Protection." *Engendering Forced Migration: Theory and Practice.* Ed. Doreen Marie Indra. New York: Berghahn Books, 1999. 334–342.

Gilbert, Lauren. "Family Violence and the Immigration and Nationality Act." *Immigration Briefings* 98–103 (1998): 1–4.

Goldberg, Pamela. "Anyplace but Home: Asylum in the United States for Women Fleeing Intimate Violence." *Cornell International Law Journal* 26 (1993): 565–604.

Goodwin-Gill, Guy S. *The Refugee in International Law.* 2nd ed. New York: Oxford University Press, 1996.

Grahl-Madsen, Atle. *The Status of Refugees in International Law.* 2 vols. Leyden: A. W. Sijthoff, 1972.

Greatbatch, Jacqueline. "The Gender Difference: Feminist Critiques of Refugee Discourse." *International Journal of Refugee Law* 1 (1989): 518–527.

Haines, Rodger. "Gender-Related Persecution." *United Nations High Commissioner for Refugees Online.* Working Paper, Draft August 10, 2001. http://www.unhcr.ch (accessed June 8, 2005).

Hathaway, James C. "The Emerging Politics of Non-Entrée." *Refugees* 91 (1992): 40–43.

_____. *The Law of Refugee Status.* Toronto: Butterworths, 1991.

_____. "New Directions to Avoid Hard Problems: The Distortion of the Palliative Role of Refugee Protection." *Journal of Refugee Studies* 8.3 (1995): 288–294.

_____. "A Reconsideration of the Underlying Premise of Refugee Law." *Harvard International Law Journal* 31.1 (1990): 129–184.

_____. *The Rights of Refugees under International Law.* Cambridge, U.K.: Cambridge University Press, forthcoming 2005.

Hathaway, James C. and Anne K. Cusick. "Refugee Rights Are Not Negotiable." *Georgetown Immigration Law Journal* 14.2 (2000): 481–539.

Helton, Arthur C. "Political Asylum Under the 1980 Refugee Act: An Unfulfilled Promise." *University of Michigan Journal of Law Reform* 17 (1983–4): 243–264.

Henkin, Louis, et al. *International Human Rights.* New York: Foundation Press, 2000.

Horvath v. Secretary of State for the Home Department. [2001] 1 AC 489, [2000] 3 WLR 379 (U.K.).

Human Rights Watch. "Refugee Summit: States Must Reaffirm Commmitments." *Human Rights Watch Online*, December 11, 2001. http://www.hrw.org/ (accessed June 8, 2005).

_____. "Locked Away: Immigration Detainees in Jails in the United States." *Human Rights Watch Online.* Sept 1988. http:www.hrw.org/ (accessed June 8, 2005).

Hungarian Helsinki Committee Online. http://www.helsinki.hu/eng/indexm.html (accessed June 8, 2005).

In re D-V-. 12 I. & N. Dec. 77, 79 (1993).

In re H-. 21 I. & N. Dec. 337 (BIA 1996).

In re Kasinga, 21 I. & N. Dec. 357, 365 (BIA 1996).

In re Kuna. A76491421 (unpublished decision) (BIA Apr. 25, 2000).

In re S-P-. 21 I. & N. Dec. 486 (BIA 1996).

Indra, Doreen. "Gender: A Key Dimension of the Refugee Experience." *Refuge* 6.3 (1987): 3–6.

Inter-American Commission on Human Rights. "Report on the Situation of Human Rights in Haiti." OEA/SER.L/V/II.88, Doc. 10 Rev. (1995).

International Covenant on Civil and Political Rights. *adopted* Dec. 16, 1966, S. Treaty Doc. No. 95–2, 95th Cong., 2d Sess. (1977), 999 U.N.T.S. 171.

International Covenant on Economic, Social, and Cultural Rights. *adopted* Dec. 16, 1966, 993 U.N.T.S. 3, *reprinted in* 6 I.L.M. 360.

Kälin, Walter. "Non-State Agents of Persecution and the Inability of the State to Protect." *Georgetown Immigration Law Journal* 15.3 (2001): 415–431.

_____. "UNHCR's Supervisory Role under Article 35." Unpublished essay, 2000.

Kelly, Nancy. "Gender-related Persecution: Assessing the Asylum Claims of Women." *Cornell International Law Journal* 26 (1993): 625–674.

Koh, Harold H. "Reflections on Refoulement and Haitian Centers Council." *Harvard International Law Journal* 36 (1994): 1–47.

Lambert, Hélène. "Seeking Asylum on Gender Grounds." *International Journal of Discrimination and Law* 1 (1995): 153–178.

Lazo-Majano v. INS. 813 F.2d 1432, 1438 (9th Cir. 1987).

Lewis, Hope. "Between *Irua* and 'Female Genital Mutilation': Feminist Human Rights Discourse and the Cultural Divide." *Harvard Human Rights Journal* 8 (1995): 1–56.

Loescher, Gil, and John A. Scanlan. *Calculated Kindness: Refugees and America's Half-Open Door, 1945 to the Present.* New York: Free Press, 1986.

Macklin, Audrey. "Cross-Border Shopping for Ideas: A Critical Review of United States, Canadian, and Australian Approaches to Gender-Related Asylum Claims." *Georgetown Immigration Law Journal* 13 (1998): 25–71.

Merwine, Maynard H. "How Africa Understands Female Circumcision." Letter. *New York Times*, November 24, 1993, A24.

Minister for Immigration and Multicultural Affairs v. Khawar. (2000) F.C.A. 1130, ¶¶191–93. Available at http://www.austlii.edu.au/; Minister for Immigration and Multicultural Affairs v. Khawar and ORS (S128/2001) (High Court of Australia).

Moore, Jennifer. "From Nation State to Failed State: International Protection From Human Rights Abuses by Non-State Agents." *Columbia Human Rights Law Review* 31 (1999–2000): 81–122.

Newman, Frank C., and David Weissbrodt. *International Human Rights: Law, Policy, and Process.* 2nd ed. Cincinnati: Anderson Pub. Co., 1996.

N.M. v. Swiss Federal Office for Refugees. Asylum Appeals Commission. February 11, 2000. Available online at http://www.refugeecaselaw.org (accessed June 6, 2005).

Pertman, Adam. "I Want to be Treated Like A Human: Rejecting Subservience and Abuse-and Fearing the Price—A Turkish Woman Files What Could Be a Precedent-Setting Asylum Claim." *Boston Globe*, April 15, 2001: D1.

Prosecutor v. Akayesu. Trial Chamber, International Criminal Tribunal for Rwanda [ICTR], 1998, Case No. ICTR-96-4-T. http://www.ictr.org/ (accessed June 2, 2005).

Protocol relating to the Status of Refugees. 19 U.N.T.S. 6223, 606 U.N.T.S. 267, *opened for signature* Jan. 31, 1976.

Refugee Appeal No. 71427/99, [2000] N.Z.A.R. 545. (New Zealand Refugee Status Appeals Authority).

Secretary of State for the Home Department v. Klodiana Kacaj [2001] INLR 354 (U.K.)

Shacknove, Andrew. "Who is a Refugee?" *Ethics* 95 (1985): 274–280.

Shah and Islam. (a.k.a. Regina v. Immigration Appeal Tribunal and Another, *ex parte* Shah), [1999] 2 All E.R. 545 (H.L.) (U.K.).

Sitaropolos, Nicholas. *Judicial Interpretation of Refugee Status: In Search of a Principled Methodology Based on a Critical Comparative Analysis, with Special Reference to Contemporary British, French and German Jurisprudence.* 1st ed. Athens: Ant. N. Sakkoulas, 1999.

Sohn, Louis B. *The Human Rights Movement: From Roosevelt's Four Freedoms to the Interdependence of Peace, Development, and Human Rights.* Cambridge, Mass.: Harvard Law School Human Rights Program, 1995.

Special Rapporteur of the Commission on Human Rights on Violence against Women, Its Causes and Consequences. "1996 Report." Commission Human Rights., U.N. GAOR, 52d Sess., Provisional Agenda Item 9(a) ¶¶ 36, 38, 39, U.N. Doc. E/CN.4/1996/53 (1996).

_____. "Preliminary Report submitted by the Special Rapporteur on Violence against Women, its Causes and Consequences." Ms. Radhika Coomarasamy in accordance with the Commission on Human Rights Resolution 1994/45, November 22, 1994, UN Doc. E/CH.4/1995/42.

Spijkerboer, Thomas. *Gender and Refugee Status.* Burlington, Vermont: Ashgate, 2000.

Steiner, Henry J., and Philip Alston. *International Human Rights in Context: Law, Politics, Morals: Text and Materials.* 2nd ed. New York: Oxford University Press, 2000.

Symes, Mark. *Caselaw on the Refugee Convention.* London: Refugee Legal Centre, 2000.

Tamir, Yael. "Hands off Clitoridectomy." *Boston Review* 21.3 (1996): 21–25.

Toubia, Nahid. *Female Genital Mutilation: A Call for Global Action.* New York: Women, Ink., 1993.

U.K. Immigration Appellate Authority. Asylum Gender Guidelines. *Asylum and Immigration Tribunal Online.* 2000. http://www.iaa.gov.uk/ (accessed June 6, 2005).

United Nations High Commissioner for Refugees (UNHCR). *Handbook on Procedures and Criteria for Determining Refugee Status under the 1951 Convention and the 1967 Protocol Relating to the Status of Refugees.* Rev. ed. Geneva: Office of the United Nations High Commissioner for Refugees, 1988.

_____. *The State of the World's Refugees 2000: Fifty Years of Humanitarian Action.* New York: Oxford University Press, 2000.

Universal Declaration of Human Rights (UDHR). G.A. Res. 217A, U.N. GAOR, 3d Sess., Supp. No. 16, U.N. Doc. A/810 (1948).

The University of Michigan Law School Refugee Caselaw Site. http://www.refugeecaselaw.org/ (accessed June 8, 2005).

Waldron, Sidney. "Anthropologists As 'Expert Witnesses.'" *Engendering Forced Migration: Theory and Practice.* Ed. Doreen Marie Indra. New York: Berghahn Books, 1999. 343–350.

Walker, Kristen. "The Importance of Being Out: Sexuality and Refugee Status." *Sydney Law Review* 18 (1996): 568–97.

Wright, Shelley. "Economic Rights and Social Justice: A Feminist Analysis of Some International Human Rights Conventions." *Australian Year Book of International Law* 12 (1988–89): 241–265.

Zucker, Norman L., and Naomi Flink Zucker. *The Guarded Gate: The Reality of American Refugee Policy.* 1st ed. San Diego: Harcourt Brace Jovanovich, 1987.

Notes

1   *Canada v. Ward* 733; see also Hathaway, *Law of Refugee Status* 108. Further discussion of this case and an earlier elaboration of the arguments in this chapter appear in Volume 15 of the *Harvard Human Rights Journal.*

2   International refugee law is based on the international refugee convention. See, Convention relating to the Status of Refugees, and Protocol relating to the Status of Refugees (together hereinafter "Convention" or "Refugee Convention"). For a general description of the Convention, the Protocol, and their predecessor international instruments, see Hathaway, *Law of Refugee Status* 1–13. States parties to the Convention incorporate the Convention into domestic law (although incorporation is not uniform). Some states also have unique municipal law protections. In addition, there are regional refugee regimes. See generally Goodwin-Gill 20–25. For a treatment of refugee law as part of the corpus of human rights law, see Newman and Weissbrodt.

3   The general applicability of these human rights norms is also supported
    by natural law and universalist theories. See, e.g., Brennan 373 (also ex-
    cerpted in Newman and Weissbrodt 677–78), (discussing the difference
    between positivist and natural law theories).

4   Universal Declaration of Human Rights, G.A. Res. 217A, U.N. GAOR, 3d
    Sess., Supp. No. 16, U.N. Doc. A/810 (1948) (hereinafter UDHR); Inter-
    national Covenant on Civil and Political Rights, *adopted* Dec. 16, 1966, S.
    Treaty Doc. No. 95-2, 95th Cong., 2d Sess. (1977), 999 U.N.T.S. 171 (here-
    inafter ICCPR); International Covenant on Economic, Social, and Cul-
    tural Rights, *adopted* Dec. 16, 1966, 993 U.N.T.S. 3, *reprinted in* 6 I.L.M.
    360 (hereinafter ICESCR). See also Steiner and Alston Part A, B, C (dis-
    cussing various instruments and institutions of the international human
    rights regime).

5   Most importantly for purposes of this discussion, refugee status is limited
    by the requirements of international border crossing and discriminatory
    impact, i.e., for reasons of one of the five grounds. In other words, proof of
    a prospective human rights abuse and failed state protection—"persecu-
    tion"—is not sufficient to establish eligibility as a refugee. The person also
    must have left her country of citizenship or last habitual residence, and
    she must establish that the violation she fears has a discriminatory impact
    based on one of the five grounds. Furthermore, there are other restrict-
    ing elements; for example, a putative refugee must prove a "well-founded
    fear" that he will be subjected to the relevant human rights violation. This
    article focuses only on the meaning of the Convention's criterion of per-
    secution.

6   The Convention's various articles define a range of rights—protection
    from return, basic civil and political rights such as rights of association,
    to education, and access to the courts—that a state party must grant a
    refugee (i.e., a person who meets the definitional requirements of article
    1 of the Convention) over whom it has *de facto* authority. Some of these
    rights attach by virtue of a person's fulfilling the criteria of article 1 and
    being under the authority of the state; others only attach if a refugee is for-
    mally recognized and granted status by the state party; some rights require
    other, or lesser, levels of attachment. See generally, Hathaway, *Rights of
    Refugees;* Hathaway and Cusick, "Refugee Rights" 484; and Grahl-Madsen,
    vol. 2 195–397 (comprehensively describing and analyzing the rights of
    refugees, including under the Convention).

7   See, e.g., Steiner and Alston 592–641 and 705–773 (describing state re-
    porting and optional individual communication procedures under the
    ICCPR). See also Kälin, "UNHCR's Supervisory Role" 1–11 (noting the
    extensive and positive impact of UNHCR's role on the protection of asy-
    lum seekers, contrasting with other human rights treaties). As Kälin sug-
    gests, "Unlike the [Refugee Convention and 1967 Protocol, these treaties

do not have an operational agency with a world-wide presence and 'protection officers' in a large number of countries working to ensure that these instruments are implemented" ("UNHCR's Supervisory Role" 11).

8 This is true in the United States where, especially during the decade of the 1990s, immigration courts and the immigration appellate body, the Board of Immigration Appeals, issued a larger number of reasoned decisions providing better guidance for decision makers. See, e.g, *In re S-P-*, 21 I. & N. Dec. 486 (BIA 1996) (relying extensively on human rights reports of Congress and State Department in finding related to motive of agent of harm, and providing list of criteria for identifying a relevant motive); *In re H-*, 21 I. & N. Dec. 337 (BIA 1996) (explaining meaning of past-persecution standard, and specifying burdens of proof in such cases); see also Blum (discussing some problems in earlier Board jurisprudence). The New Zealand Refugee Status Appeals Authority has a long-standing distinguished reputation (see Symes ii).

9 For one prominent example of the influence of the UNHCR on the development of refugee law, specifically with reference to the protection of women refugees, see Kelly 633; see also Lambert 162–65; Macklin 28–30; and Kälin, "UNHCR'S Supervisory Role" 2–10 (discussing the exceptional role of UNHCR and in particular the authoritative character of its pronouncements and its 1979 *Handbook on Procedures and Criteria for Determining Refugee Status*) (hereinafter UNHCR Handbook). For a general discussion of the current challenges facing UNHCR and the refugee regime, see Fitzpatrick, "Taking Stock" 22.

10 See, e.g., *Shah* [1999] 2 All E.R. 545, 565 (Hoffman, L.) [1999] (citing gender guidelines of the Refugee Women's Group for definition of persecution), and "Memorandum from Phyllis Coven, INS Office of International Affairs, to All INS Asylum Officers and HQASM Coordinators, Considerations For Asylum Officers Adjudicating Asylum Claims From Women" (May 26, 1995) [hereinafter U.S. Gender Guidelines], reproduced in Black, et al. 67 (describing guidelines as "natural . . . outgrowth" of UNHCR, Canadian and draft guidelines of Women Refugees Project, Harvard Law School Immigration and Refugee Clinical Program and Cambridge and Somerville Legal Services).

11 One of the best examples of such transnationalization is the interpretation of the "particular social group" ground to include sex and gender. See Anker, "Refugee Status."

12 The New Zealand authorities, for example, have held that, "Core norms of international human rights law may be relied on to define forms of serious harm within the scope of persecution" (Refugee Appeal No. 71427/99, [2000] N.Z.A.R 545, 562). The New Zealand authorities have included with the International Bill of Rights other instruments such as the Convention on the Elimination of Racial Discrimination and the Convention on the

Elimination of Discrimination against Women (hereinafter CEDAW or Women's Convention), as sources of those norms (Refugee Appeal No. 71427/99, 564). Nicholas Sitaropolos comments, "Case law in the U.K., France and Germany [. . .] has established a close relationship between human rights violations and persecution," emphasizing a requirement of serious human rights violation (245–6).

13 This analysis is important for refugee claims where the direct agent of harm is a non-state actor. See generally Anker, "Refugee Status."

14 See Kälin, "UNHCR's Supervisory Role" 12–15 (highlighting problems of incomplete implementation of the Convention by, and inconsistencies in interpretation among, states parties).

15 This is largely due to the numbers of refugees involved and/or the lack of infrastructures for refugee determinations. See Hathaway, *Law of Refugee Status* (noting the impracticality of individual determinations in cases of large scale refugee movements); Goodwin-Gill (commenting that "[o]nly comparatively few States have instituted procedures for assessing refugee claims" (34)); and United Nations High Commissioner for Refugees, *State of the World's Refugees* 310, Annex 3 (showing, in table of regional distribution of refugees, largest numbers arriving in countries in Asia and Africa).

16 See Goodwin-Gill 33–4 (commenting that many states parties allow UNHCR to participate in status determinations and that certification of status by UNHCR pursuant to its own governing statute is often required, especially in states that have no domestic status determination processes).

17 See 1998 Refugees Act 130 (GG 6779) (S.AFR.). In May 2001, the Hungarian Parliament passed four pieces of legislation affecting the regulation of asylum as well as migration matters. See http://www.helsinki.hu/eng/indexm.html (describing amendments to the 1998 Act on Asylum, including changes to determination procedures).

18 See Lewis 2–4 (describing controversy over terminology, with many referring to the practice as "female genital mutilation").

19 Gender refers to socially contingent divisions of roles between men and women, socially constructed notions of femininity and masculinity and resulting power disparities which implicate women's identities and status within societies (see Charlesworth and Chinkin 3–4). Although this article focuses on women, gender also has implications for men's identities, especially in claims for refugee status and protection by gay men (and lesbians). See, e.g., Crawley 161–63; see generally Walker. Crawley (among others) argues that the term "sex" (as opposed to gender) should be avoided, since the former suggests biological determinacy (6–7). Hilary Charlesworth and Christine Chinkin opine, however, that sex may be used

as well as gender, as sex is also a contestable category, resting on socially defined dichotomies between body and mind, nature and culture (3–4).

20 Canadian Immigration and Refugee Board, Guidelines Issued by the Chairperson Pursuant to Section 65(3) of the Immigration Act: Women Refugee Claimants Fearing Gender-Related Persecution (Mar. 9, 1993) [hereinafter Canadian Gender Guidelines], reproduced in Black, et al. 87. Canada issued a subsequent update; see Canadian Immigration and Refugee Board, Guideline 4: Women Refugee Claimants Fearing Gender-Related Persecution: Update (Nov. 25, 1996) [hereinafter Canadian Gender Guidelines: 1996 Update], reproduced in Black, et al. 106. Other national guidelines include the U.S. Gender Guidelines and those of Australia, Department of Immigration and Multicultural Affairs, Refugee and Humanitarian Visa Applicants: Guidelines on Gender Issues for Decision Makers (July 1996) [hereinafter Australian Gender Guidelines] reproduced in Black, et al. 7; and U.K. Immigration Appellate Authority [hereinafter U.K. Gender Guidelines]. See generally Crawley 12–16; Kelly 633–34; Spijkerboer 1–3 (all describing background to guidelines).

21 See also Greatbatch 526 (reconsidering feminist critiques of refugee law and suggesting a human rights approach which, *inter alia*, addresses the refugee's relationship to her state); Indra 3; and Kelly (suggesting an interpretive framework which, *inter alia*, examines "the political nature of seemingly private acts" (642)). See generally, Spijkerboer. There are equal if not more important problems in asylum procedures and evidentiary rules—as well as with access to those procedures—which have a major impact on women refugees' ability to pursue refugee claims. See, e.g., Kelly 629–30 and Crawley 199–223.

22 See Charlesworth and Chinkin 218–22 (discussing marginalization problem as well as particular weaknesses in enforcement and implementation under the Women's Convention) (see note 12 above).

23 The most notable example of this integrative approach is Rodger Haines, "Gender-Related Persecution," paper submitted for expert roundtables under the "second track" of the Global Consultations on International Refugee Protection (on web). See also U.S. Gender Guidelines, Canadian Gender Guidelines, Australian Gender Guidelines, and U.K. Appellate Gender Guidelines, note 20 above, and in Black et al. See also Feller 381, 382–3 (noting that violence against women is included in the concept of persecution, and advances in human rights law have contributed to a gender-sensitive approach to refugee law).

24 Maria Veronica Rodriguez Salinas Araya, Immigration Appeal Board Decision 76–1127, January 6, 1977, at 8 (quoted in Hathaway, *Law of Refugee Status* 112 n.109).

25 *Lazo-Majano v. INS*, 813 F.2d 1432, 1438 (9th Cir. 1987) (Poole, J. dissenting); see discussion of case in Connors 121.

26 See e.g., generally, Charlesworth and Chinkin. The alternate feminist critique—that the public/private distinction can be overemphasized—also has been made in the refugee context. See, e,g., Greatbatch: "It roots women's oppression in sexuality and private life, thereby disregarding oppression experienced in non-domestic circumstances, and the interconnnections of the public and private spheres" (520).

27 *Campos-Guardado v. INS*, 809 F.2d. 285 (5th Cir. 1987).

28 *In re D-V-*, 12 I. & N. Dec. 77, 79 (1993) (describing immigration judge decision in Board opinion overruling it).

29 See, e.g., Australian Gender Guidelines (Black et al. 16); U.K. Appellate Gender Guidelines (¶¶ 2A.18–2A.21, also in Black et al. 14–16); U.S. Gender Guidelines (Black et al. 9).

30 See Anker, *Law of Asylum* 255–57; Crawley 42–45, 131–33 (providing examples of some of this case law); *Re SDS*, Refugee Appeal No. 2373/95 (1996) (New Zealand Refugee Status Appeals Authority) (Black et al. 634); and *N.M. v. Swiss Federal Office for Refugees* (2000) (Switzerland Asylum Appeals Commission). Available at www.refugeecaselaw.org.

31 See, e.g., U92-06668, Immigration and Refugee Board of Canada (1993), reproduced in Black et al.187; *Re SDS*, Refugee Appeal No. 2373/95 (Refugee Status Appeals Authority of New Zealand), reproduced in Black et al. 634 (stating that "fear of rape amounts to fear of persecution, rape being a violation of the fundamental right to be free from inhuman or degrading treatment . . . [that can] deny human dignity in a key way" [640]); and Australian Gender Guidelines, ¶¶ 4.6–4.7, reproduced in Black et al. 22–23 (stating that rape and sexual violence may violate the prohibitions against torture and cruel, inhuman or degrading treatment, as well as the right to security of person and the right to life).

32 Australian Gender Guidelines 16–17, reproduced in Black et al. 22–23.

33 *In re Kuna*, A76491421 (unpublished decision) (BIA Apr. 25, 2000) (on file with author).

34 See U92-08714 (1993) (Canadian Immigration and Refugee Board) reproduced in Black et al. 221.

35 See Inter-American Commission on Human Rights, "Report," OEA/Ser. L/V/II.88, Doc. 10 rev. 9 (1995), ¶¶ 119–123. [hereinafter OAS Haiti Report].

36 See also, Special Rapporteur of the Commission on Human Rights on Violence against Women, Its Causes and Consequences, "Preliminary Report."

37 See also Inter-American Commission on Human Rights, "Report" (OAS Haiti Report) (finding violations of parallel provisions in other human

rights instruments: "it is clear that in the experience of torture victims, rape and sexual abuse are forms of torture which produce some of the most severe and long-lasting traumatic effects." ¶¶ 135). The Inter-American Commission on Human Rights also found that widespread, open and routine use of rape as a weapon of terror constitutes a crime against humanity under customary international law (see ¶¶ 135).

38 See Henkin et al. 372–84 (discussing treatment of rape by human rights bodies and significance of OAS Commission's Haiti Report). See also *Fernando Mejía Egochiago and Raquel Martin de Mejía v. Peru*, Case 10.970, Inter-Am. Comm'n H.R. 157, OEA/Ser. L/V/II.91, doc. 7 rev. (1996) (further elaborating on rape as torture). See also *Aydin v. Turkey*, 1997–VI Cur. Ct. H.R. 1866, E.H.R.R. 251 (finding that rape committed in state detention constituted torture, under specific torture prohibitions in European Human Rights Convention).

39 See *Prosecutor v. Akayesu*, Trial Chamber, International Criminal Tribunal for Rwanda (ICTR), 1998, Case No. ICTR-96-4-T (finding, in the context of massive violence and repression against an ethnic group in Rwanda, that rape and sexual brutality constituted torture as a crime against humanity). According to earlier (and later) decisions of the International Criminal Tribunal for Yugoslavia (ICTY), sexual assaults of women constituted torture within the meaning of crimes against humanity, but largely in the context of forced detention in camps, and formally limited to situations of armed conflict. See Trial Chamber I, Review of Indictment pursuant to Rule 61, Nikolic case, IT-95-2-R61. See also *Prosecutor v. Zelnil Delali_ et al.*, Case No. IT-96-21-T, Judgment, (Nov. 16, 1998); *Prosecutor v. Anto Furunddija*, Case No. IT-95-17/1-T, Judgment (Dec. 10, 1998). *Cf. Prosecutor v. Dusko Tadic*, ICTY Trial Chamber, 1995, Case No. IT-94-1-T (interlocutory decision of Yugoslavian tribunal including as crimes against humanity acts in context of widespread or systematic attacks on civilian population). See generally, Charlesworth and Chinkin 313–37 (discussing advances as well as problems in emerging international criminal law with respect to recognition of rape as torture and limitations of the armed conflict context for women's rights).

40 But see Henkin 373–74 (discussing the significance of the Haiti Rape Report in recognition of rape as torture).

41 For a sampling, see Steiner and Alston 409–25.

42 See, "A Traditional Practice that Threatens Health—Female Circumcision," excerpted in Steiner and Alston 409–11.

43 For an example of a qualified defense, see Merwine, also excerpted in Steiner and Alston 421–22.

44 See M95-13161 (1997) (Canadian Immigration and Refugee Board), reproduced in Black et al. 419, 425–26.

45 RRT Reference V97/061456 (1997) (Australia), available at http://www .austlii.edu.au.

46 *In re Kasinga*, 21 I. & N. Dec. 357, 365 (BIA 1996).

47 See also Haines, "breaches of human rights cannot be ignored, discounted, or explained away on the basis of culture, tradition, or religion" (29). In addition, see Refugee Appeal No. 71427/99, 565 (¶ 52).

48 See Anker, *Law of Asylum* 191–99; Moore (discussing refugee and human rights law doctrine); and Kälin, "Non-State Agents" (describing changes and reinterpretations in the non-state actor doctrine in Switzerland and other countries).

49 This is, of course, a question that must be addressed in actual refugee cases, where an individual makes a claim for protection based on concrete, specific circumstances.

50 Compare Refugee Appeal No. 71427/99, 568 (¶ 62) (holding that the standard for assessing state protection requires the risk of serious harm to be below that of a "well-founded fear"), with *Horvath v. Secretary of State for the Home Department* (2001) 1 AC 489, (2000) 3 WLR 379 (U.K.) (suggesting that the refugee standard may be met when a state has a formal system of protection in place, irrespective of the applicant's well-founded fear). There is indication that the U.K. authorities may be moving away from a stricter reading of Horvath. See, e.g., *Secretary of State for the Home Department v. Klodiana Kacaj* (2001) INLR 354 (U.K.) (suggesting that the existence of state protection mechanisms, although presumptively adequate, may not be sufficient if the refugee claimant can show that they are practically ineffective and have not eliminated the reality of risk). Thanks to Rodger Haines for bringing *Kacaj* to my attention.

51 See "Report of the Special Rapporteur on Violence Against Women, Its Causes and Consequences," Comm'n Hum. Rts., U.N. GAOR, 52d Sess., Provisional Agenda Item 9(a) ¶¶ 36, 38, 39, U.N. Doc. E/CN.4/1996/53 (1996) (describing family violence as a human rights abuse); see also Charlesworth and Chinkin 12; and Copelon (both discussing the pervasiveness of family violence as a human rights abuse against women and the failure of human rights law to address it seriously). See also Goldberg (discussing family violence basis for asylum claim); Gilbert 2 (discussing asylum and other remedies available to survivors of family violence under U.S. law). For a sampling of the refugee case law on this issue, see Black et al. See also Crock 148–51 (describing Australian asylum case law on family violence).

52 *Minister for Immigration and Multicultural Affairs v. Khawar* (2000) F.C.A. 1130, ¶¶191–93, (available at http://www.austlii.edu.au/); *Minister for Immigration and Multicultural Affairs v. Khawar and ORS* (S128/2001) (High Court of Australia).

53 "[Violence against women] is caused by 'the structural relationships of power, domination and privilege between men and women in society. Violence against women is central to maintaining those political relations at home, at work and in all public spheres.' . . . The maintenance of a legal and social system in which violence or discrimination against women are endemic and where such actions are trivialized or discounted should engage state responsibility to exercise due diligence to ensure the protection of women" (Charlesworth and Chinkin 235, quoting Bunch 491 and also citing Cook 126).

54 Convention Against Torture and Other Cruel, Inhuman or Degrading Treatment or Punishment, *opened for signature* Feb. 4, 1985, S. Treaty Doc. No. 100–20 (1988), 1465 U.N.T.S. 85, art. 3 [hereinafter Torture Convention].

55 See Anker, *Law of Asylum* 469–70 (describing key differences between the two non-return obligations). Some regional human rights instruments contain similar non-return prohibitions (see Anker, *Law of Asylum* 473–76, 477–78).

56 See, e.g., 8 C.F.R. §§ 208.3 (b), 208.16, 208.17 (2001) (providing under U.S. law that an application for asylum filed with the immigration court also will be considered a request for protection under the Convention Against Torture. See generally, Anker, *Law of Asylum* 465–522 (discussing, *inter alia,* some case law under the Convention Against Torture and the European Human Rights Convention, involving rejected asylum claimants seeking non-return protection under the Convention Against Torture).

57 Convention Against Torture, art. 1 (requiring that the relevant acts be "inflicted by or at the instigation of or with the consent or acquiescence of a public official or other person acting in an official capacity").

58 See, e,g., Charlesworth and Chinkin 217–18, 246; see also 234 (arguing that the Convention Against Torture's state action requirement excludes most cases of violence against women; as noted, interpretation of that provision in the refugee context has in some instances embraced intra-family and other forms of violence against women, where the state is the enabler rather than the immediate perpetrator).

59 For some examples, see Anker, *Law of Asylum* 252–66, 365–75, and 388–93; Crawley 107–29, 147–60; Black et al. 155–57, 169–70; and Symes 114–16.

60 See, e.g., *Chen Shi Hai v. Minister for Immigration and Multicultural Affairs* [2000] HCA 19; 92000) ALR 553 at para. 29 (recognizing that denial of access to food, shelter, medical treatment as well as education for children "involve such a significant departure from the standards of the civilised world as to constitute persecution").

61 See, e.g., Kälin, "UNHCR's Supervisory Role" 11–12.

62 In asylum claims based on trafficking, some of the harm the claimant fears

may be from traffickers located in the country of refuge. Similarly, the country that returns a person to face substantial health risks may be the more significant agent of harm, rather than the country of origin, which cannot provide the needed care; the serious harm is constituted in the act of removal itself. For example, the European Court of Human Rights determined that sending a dying AIDS patient back to his home country and depriving him of treatment he was receiving constituted inhuman or degrading treatment or punishment under the European Human Rights Convention. See *D. v. United Kingdom,* 24 Eur. H.R. Rep. 423, ¶ 49 (1997) (Eur. Ct. H.R.).

63 See Hathaway, "Reconsideration" (arguing generally that the political and other interests of Western states dominated in shaping the Refugee Convention); see also Loescher and Scanlon, Zucker and Zucker, and Helton (all describing problems of politicization in U.S. refugee policy, including during the Cold War).

64 In the United States, for example, over 16,000 asylum cases were granted in FY2000. Refugee protection also has generated various forms of subsidiary protection laws (granting either temporary or permanent protection or status, outside the human rights/asylum context). Persons covered include members of groups disproportionately excluded under past asylum policies. See generally Anker, *Law of Asylum* 572–74; Fitzpatrick "Temporary Protection."

65 See U.K. Appellate Gender Guidelines (see note 20 above) at back cover (acknowledging the work of the Refugee Women's Group and the origins of the appellate guidelines in those of the NGO).

66 Academics and medical professionals, among others, are also providing such testimony, involving them in the complex ethical issues surrounding advocacy and human rights. See, e.g., Waldron 343 (describing tensions in providing expert testimony for Somali refugee claimant).

67 See, e.g, Press Release, Human Rights Watch, "Refugee Summit: States Must Reaffirm Commitments" (Dec. 11, 2001) (see http://www.hrw.org); Human Rights Watch, "Locked Away: Immigration Detainees in Jails in the United States" (1998) (see http://www.hrw.org); Amnesty International, "Lost in the Labyrinth: Detention of Asylum Seekers" (1999) (see http://www.amnesty.org).

68 See Pertman D1 (stating, based in part on her lawyer's comments, that the claim is unique because it is against "the very culture" of her country).

69 It could be argued, for example, that the U.S. government's support of the 1993 return of President Aristide to Haiti was motivated in part by concerns regarding refugee arrivals and related publicity and litigation. For background on the treatment of Haitian refugees and this litigation, see Koh.

4

Gay Enough: Some Tensions in Seeking the Grant of Asylum and Protecting Global Sexual Diversity

Alice M. Miller

Asylum functions as a key site of border crossing. However, asylum claims involving sexuality straddle more than national borders. Under a more political gaze, these claims and their legal dispositions reveal connections to historically charged structures and processes in law, rights, evidence, and advocacy that must be critiqued for their potential to limit and divide concepts of human sexuality. At the same time, asylum as a system must be exploited in order to win claims for desperate—and disparate—asylum seekers. In attending to the contemporary forces making meaning for and about sexuality today, this chapter examines some of the rhetoric and practice of asylum law in light of its own discourse and principles, and in relation to the separate but connected rules and rhetoric of human rights.

In part, this chapter explores the constituting power (the potentials and limits) of *success* in legal action—in this case, grants of asylum to "gay" claimants. Yet, the particular kind of identity created, named, and rewarded is one constrained by asylum's historically specific development and role in the modern regulation of the movement of people. Moreover, asylum's role in shaping migrating sexualities is increasingly intertwined with evolving and contested human rights practice and doctrine on sexuality. Given their role in making meaning for contemporary sexuality, both asylum and rights as practices must become more aware of the implications of (and problems posed by) contemporary theories of sexuality. At the same time, a very material reality—the need to broaden, not narrow, the grounds of successful claims by queer/non-heteronormative persons—must inform our critique of asylum advocacy. Thus, while being critical of the legal institutionalization of (simplistic) winning identities and neo-colonial cultural representations, conscientious scholars are challenged to engage with advocates in the production of public sexual identities across borders.

I focus on asylum as one system of law and as a very particular discourse of how one becomes worthy to claim rights. This system and its discourse contribute to an increasingly globalized process of making meaning around sexual identity and difference.[1] To understand how asylum functions in this larger conversation, I consider some specific aspects of the production of knowledge about sexuality in asylum litigation. These include such basic legal functions as the use of expert witness testimony, documentation, and the application of judicial knowledge or folk knowledge (see also Valverde). I analyze three cases that suggest how the fluidity of sexuality, particularly "queer sexuality" (or even more reductively, homosexuality), is frozen in the name of the protection offered by asylum. These cases exemplify the tendency of law, including asylum, to prefer fixed identities, identities that map neatly and recognizably onto conduct (see Halley, "Politics").

To make sense of the contortions and advances arising from the engagement of complex, lived sexuality with the demands of asylum law, the first section of the chapter analyzes general principles of asylum law, and critiques this particular branch of law in light of geo-political conversations concerning sexual identities, citizenship, and national power. The second section spotlights three asylum cases as demonstrations of the mutually constituting processes of legal decision-making and popular understandings of the nature of gayness. These cases provide three very different snapshots, from different jurisdictions: one United States, one Canadian, one Australian. They address, respectively, a gay man (possibly transsexual) from Mexico, a gay man from Argentina, and a lesbian from China. In the United States and Australian cases, I focus on the case in chief; in the Canadian case, the dissent. These cases arise across a decade that has seen many general legal changes in asylum law, as well as specific changes with respect to gender and sexuality. While attempting to be mindful of the limitations of generalizing from three such disparate cases, I think one can still glean some important insights. Each of the cases, for example, implicates the way that folk knowledge—here, judicial common sense on sexuality—informs legal decision-makers (see Valverde).[2] While it is true that legal decision-makers always rely on their own culturally bounded knowledge, in cases concerning sexuality, especially non-normative and culturally "strange" sexuality, reliance on folk knowledge may be more myopic and fearful—with profound effects.

In exploring (homo)sexualities' engagement with asylum law, another intersection becomes clear: the cross-fertilizing movements between asylum strategies and "gay rights as human rights" strategies. Thus, in the second section, I also move toward a more structural examination of the cases, revealing facets of an emerging globalized discourse and practice of queer rights as human rights. Here, I highlight two particular aspects: human rights documentation as a key element in the production of transnational knowledge of sexual harm and sexual behavior, and the dynamics of rights non-governmental organizations (NGOs) as they begin to function as players in the international realm of standard setting—a form of "norm entrepreneurship."

The third section broadens these reflections, looking at some of the complex and often contradictory ways in which rights activism interacts with law. Much scholarship on the construction of identity considers the way that law constitutes homosexual or queer identity through its stigmatizing function (in the form of sodomy statutes, for example).[3] Ironically, in taking on the way that asylum may contribute to constituting a global notion of "the homosexual," we are examining asylum victories, and are in the less well-traveled world of examining how law's *rewards* help produce a popularly recognizable gay identity.[4] However, reward in asylum claims is intimately tied to violation. Therefore, in examining asylum cases involving (homo)sexuality, we are attending to how and where sexuality-oriented violations claims emerge, and how identities are built in relation to the acceptable narration of both violation and responses to violation. This focus on violations can have peculiar impacts on constructions of sexuality, both hetero- and homo-. If queer claimants first turn up on the world stage as rights claimants in the guise of the abjectly persecuted—as the tortured, or in some human rights settings, "first as a corpse"—how then do queers move towards being empowered rights holders alive in political and cultural life?[5]

Shortcuts in representation are produced in a real world work dynamic that favors simplicity over complexity because of its apparently more successful effect on law and policy. This tension between what appears to work vs. what seems to reflect complex reality bedevils many of us, as scholars and advocates. It compels us to evaluate our strategies and our coalition as we move between the law and our various disciplines, including anthropology, history, comparative literature (and all of its modes of criticism), cultural studies, and queer theory. Yet, in this chapter, I hope that the discussion of asylum cases will provide examples of the interaction of scholarly experts with the legal structures of asylum decision-making, encouraging further engagement both in the name of protection for real persons, and as pressure to transform imperfect systems.

Asylees live and act at the intersection of the fundamental need to survive and flawed systems of response to violation. However, through grants of asylum, they are empowered to move into full citizenship in a new country. This is a real benefit. How their claims are recognized marks an important moment in claiming potentially transformative, transnational rights with impacts both in the law and popular understanding, especially in light of the increased attention by media and rights campaigners to grants of asylum as indicative of new rights and new rights-worthy personhood. How harm is told and how identity is constructed therefore matter not only to the claimant and the judge, but also to many larger audiences. However, understanding how narratives of harm succeed also requires understanding how the asylum system relates to other systems of subordination and supremacy within the nation of asylum, between the nation(s) of asylum and nation of origin, and within the nation of origin. Attending to the many operations in the system is critical, since the trap of asylum-as-gate-keeping hinges on its promotion of lines drawn between the few who can enter and the many who cannot. At the same time, I do not mean to invest the law with too much power to make meaning. Rather, my goals here are to recognize the power and limits of the law (bodies are detained or expelled by law, but all understanding is not created by law), and also to recognize the interaction between the law and *other* domains of meaning making, such as scholarship on sexuality.

My simultaneous concern for the limitations and constraints of asylum, while respecting its real benefits, leads to my change in direction in the conclusion. The potentials for causing harm to the diverse expressions of sexuality in the specific contortions of asylum practice compel contemporary rights practitioners to re-examine their theory and practice toward asylum. Rights advocates should ask not only how human rights can better support asylum claims, but also how sexualities' engagement with rights could present a critical moment for "doing rights differently." The conclusion begins to sketch out ways in which opening up to the global array of claims and players in sexual rights may advance a liberatory and more inclusive vision of sexuality as an element of human rights.

Some Additional Cautionary Tales

In all these discussions about asylum and human rights, I remain concerned about the way in which the focus remains on "queer sexuality" as *the* sexuality to be studied. For example, in talking about "gay identity" in asylum as the *only* kind of sexuality to engage asylum, one risks failing to unpack both heterosexuality and homosexuality. Heterosexuality is also simultaneously constrained, and certain forms naturalized, by asylum practice in particular and border crossing in general.[6] How do we understand the diversities of migrating heterosexualities?

Anthropologist Jiemin Bao's recent work on the changes in heterosexuality within ethnic Chinese migrants in Thailand and the United States is a reminder that migrating heterosexualities are remarkably under-theorized and researched. The failure to attend to heterosexualities as sites of claim-making can hinder the work to advance sexual rights as part of indivisible human rights. Experience demonstrates that this gap can result in dangerous disjunctions and even opposing claims within the human rights system (see Saiz). The gender lens also matters: my discussion of specific cases demonstrates that how asylum decision-makers "see" a lesbian may differ from how they know how to "see" a gay man, and that transgender or transsexual claimants may be read as "gay men." Moreover, in assessing the role of asylum cases in the gay rights movement, it is important to note the lower number—and the lower profile of—queer and/or lesbian-identified women as asylum claimants.[7] Women's sexuality more generally, while figuring in relatively fewer asylum cases, nonetheless features significantly in border crossing. Limits of space allow me only to flag the many narratives of racialized and sexualized women crossing borders which arise not as asylum cases, but in the discourse of "trafficking"—often in the guise of morality tales for why girls and women should stay home if they want to avoid harm ("Thai sex slaves found in American brothels").[8] The few grants of asylum to "trafficked women" or to women fighting gendered sexual non-conformity—"rewards" for deviance *and* traveling—do not function the same way for women of any sexual identity as for men.

Finally, even as this chapter relies on and joins with critiques of asylum strategies, I also consider how we must re-evaluate these concerns with reference to the intensified polarities of the post-9/11 world.[9] Border drawings, policing of migrants, and militarizing exclusionary ideologies predominate, not only in the nationalisms of the United

States and the North, but also in the nationalisms of the global South.[10] How do we discuss contradictory (regressive and liberatory) aspects of sexual rights-claiming in order to revise these narrow "successes" in a rapidly shifting and border-closing world? Many countries, including the United States, have already revised their immigration and asylum structures in light of anti-terrorism campaigns.[11] Endeavors critiquing asylum encounter a tense moment, as the direction of law reform in border crossing is toward closure. The concluding section, while presenting no solutions, suggests some possible ways forward with the broadened claim of sexual rights as human rights. As engaged advocates and scholars, we are compelled by our times to do the idealistically impossible and the strategically necessary, together.

(Homo)sexuality and Systems of Asylum: The Origin and Place of Refugee Law in National Systems of Asylum Adjudication

Refugee law is both international and national law.[12] The 1951 UN Convention Relating to the Status of Refugees,[13] responding to the persecution and forced displacement of European peoples during and after World War II (hereafter referred to as "the Convention"), sets the international frame. Its 1967 Protocol[14] extends the Convention's protections to persons fleeing abuse beyond the territories and time period envisioned in 1951.[15] Refugee protection in general, and its incarnation as an individualized national system of asylum adjudication, constitute a back-up or subsidiary form of protection, sometimes called "surrogate,"[16] "remedial," or "last resort" (Anker 135).

Refugee law (including the possibility of asylum) is called into play under specific circumstances: when your own government either attacks you or fails to protect you in a way that shows specific persecutory impact, *and* you have been able to cross a border to claim the surrogate protection afforded by another state. A refugee is a person who has crossed a national border and who has "a well-founded fear of being persecuted for reasons of race, religion, nationality, membership of a particular social group, or political opinion" (Refugee Convention article 9).[17] Asylum is the system of individualized decision-making that allows a permanent refuge: At the moment of the grant of asylum, your "protector" is the country where you have arrived. The failures of your home country are explicitly named as the basis for your individual grant of protection. Your home country's policies, however, are not legally affected by being the object of condemnation.

This secondary help comes after you flee; it is not the same as rights protections in your country of origin. It is limited, though it can be very concrete. However, the right to seek asylum is only a right to *seek*, not a right to *receive*. The moment of implementing the international obligation on national governments to ensure the "right to seek" is the moment marking when refugee law moves from the international sphere to the national (United Nations, Universal Declaration of Human Rights [UDHR article 12]). The specific criteria and processes governing seekers of asylum are *nationally determined,* as national governments bind themselves by ratifying the Refugee Convention and/or its Protocol to institute a system of refugee and asylum determination that meets the standards of the Convention. Refugee law respects yet constrains the sovereignty of states: nations retain the individual power to determine which persons can stay within their borders, but can be criticized according to internationally agreed upon standards for the processes that determine this. National governments look to the Convention, and its authoritative interpretation, the *United Nations High Commissioner for Refugees (UNHCR) Refugee Handbook,* for guidance in forming and interpreting their national asylum systems, but the Convention does not create a body with the power to judge the national system.

The sovereign power to grant entry and to give permission to stay produces a moment of transnational judgment, when the decision-makers of one nation decide not only on the credibility of the individual asylum claimant, but on the errors or strengths of the protection of rights in the country from which the claimant flees. Significantly, this determination is called into play not by the receiving nation, but rather by the agency and voice of the asylee her or himself.[18] This moment of cross-national seeing and speaking that occurs in grants of asylum is explored below for its engagement with claims of persecution and (homo)sexual identity. It is an individualized response, with all the powers and limits that individualistic claims encompass. "Your country has failed you, you are safe here" is the siren song of asylum—but how true, and in what way is it true, for queer asylum seekers? Who does one become, in what image is he or she made and remade in the process?

Asylum is thus conceived by national governments, particularly in the developed industrial and postindustrial states, as a generous grant under highly contingent and scrutinized terms. Kristen Walker has incorporated and amplified the work of Pheng Cheah to suggest that the way to understand this grant is as a "violent gift" (Walker, "Importance" 589–591). Implicated in the "violence" of the gift is the self-serving stance of the receiving nations. As James Hathaway notes, "because international refugee law currently is a means of reconciling the sovereign prerogative of states to control immigration, with the reality of forced migrations of people at risk, it does not challenge the right of states (including Northern states) to engage in behavior which induces flight" (593). That the Northern industrialized world receives most of the high-profile, individualized asylum seekers and resettled refugees ought to be counter-posed with the massive, crushing reality of the actual numbers of refugees carried by the developing world, such as nearly 6 million refugees in Asia and 3.3 million refugees in Africa.[19, 20] Yet this reality—and its meaning for changing subjectivities, as well as new forms of sexual behavior and identity—often falls off our maps of attention, rights, and even aid in the North.

As there is no right to free movement across borders (except the citizen's right to leave and return to her own country), the prerogative of determining who crosses borders, and under what terms, creates a narrow door that reinforces the power and validity of the wall itself (see Bhabha; also Morrison and Crosland). Queer identities, thus, are produced under these conditions, and become part of a self-regarding, nationally-inflected public debate, mostly informed by media-mediated announcements of legal decisions about which asylum seekers are allowed to enter a nation, and why. Gay and lesbian asylum seekers entered U.S. public consciousness and were designated as "new claimants" in the early 1990s, often paired in media reports with (heterosexual?) women fleeing various gender-based abuses. Both sets of stories were framed in the press by the fear-mongering query as to whether these cases were "opening the floodgates." This was also a paradoxical moment for the United States, which accepted as "worthy" for entry queer asylees whose sexuality was metonymically defined by,[21] and factually was, the basis of criminal prosecution in at least fourteen jurisdictions.[22]

The process by which national adjudicators carry out this task of granting asylum must be examined simultaneously for formal legal maneuvers as well as rhetorical alchemy. Articulating "gayness" within the asylum process, bringing queer sexuality into the national consciousness of who is here, or who *should* be here, can be seen as part of a broader engagement with multi-layered legal principles, national prejudices, and struggles for public space involving not only asylum seekers but their advocates, including NGO champions. All are caught up in the process of making meaning for one's national and international audience at the same time as an individual subject seeks refuge.

Key Elements of an Asylum Claim in Relation to Queer Claims

In practice, the criteria required to make a successful claim of asylum, particularly in the emerging area of "gay" asylum, are a mixture of fact and law in two main areas: (1) proving "membership of a particular social group," and (2) demonstrating "persecution."[23] Evidence, such as published human rights documentation and expert opinion, plays a particular role in shaping the legal reasoning and rhetoric of these cases, and therefore requires us to examine the players who produce evidence as well.

In asylum decisions, advocates and adjudicators in receiving countries have applied their own understanding of the relationships between sexual conduct, identity, gender roles, and what makes a group a "group." According to the International Lesbian and Gay Association (ILGA), at least 10 countries accept gay men or lesbians as constituting a particular social group within the terms of the Convention (ILGA Online). The acceptance of other queer categories, such as transgender or transsexual, is less clear (see Queer Resources Directory, also Ramanathan n. 35). Because asylum's purview straddles borders, advocates' understanding of which sexual identities satisfy the condition of "membership in a particular group" engages perceptions of sexuality in the advocates' own countries, as well as notions of group identity in the societies from which the asylees come.

The concept of immutability permeates this discussion. This concept has evolved to refer to characteristics that members of a group cannot change, or should not be required to change, because they are considered to be fundamental to their identity or consciousness.[24] Religion (which is written into the Refugee Convention as a prohibited basis of persecution) is often analogized to "gayness" as something that may not be biologically immutable or located in the body, but is something that one should not be forced to change.[25] Thus, immutability as a concept holds together involuntary and innate characteristics as well as ideals of human dignity and respect for self-definition. Legally, it means more than it might in other contexts, such as biology. And yet, in the popularization of cases in the discourses of receiving countries, the word "immutable" swerves dangerously close to the biologized meaning deployed in disputes over the "gay gene." As news of asylum victories spreads through mainstream and gay presses, the visibility of *some* "gay asylees" could not only function to bolster the "we are everywhere" claims of some gay political strategists, but also to naturalize a sense that "*one* gay is everywhere," or in other words, that cultural difference in sexuality is not so important as a supposedly recognizable transnational "gayness" (See Warner; Halley, "Politics"; Altman).

How immutability—the vesting of a characteristic with sufficient significance to not *have to be* changed—attaches to queer sexualities is a major subject of contention in current critiques of sexuality in asylum law.[26] While social constructionist theories of sexuality do not imply that sexual desires and identities are so fluid as to be easily acquired and put off, they nonetheless challenge the production of any singular template for understanding gay behavior or same-sex orientation, and any unitary identity making, in a given country or across borders. "At a minimum, all social construction approaches adopt the view that physically identical sexual acts may have varying social significance and subjective meaning depending on how they are understood in different cultures and different historical periods" (Vance, "Anthropology" 878). Yet, in order to set out the principles justifying the grants of asylum, asylum decision-makers work within a system that privileges simplified analogies, and they may create rules for "seeing" persecuted gayness that preclude or exclude unrecognizably "gay" persons, or others fleeing abuse for their sexual or gender difference.

The drawing of this legal line of asylum responds to and subsumes many political anxieties: *finitude* (fear of huge numbers of applicants, the proverbial opening of the "floodgates"), *credibility* (how do we know if we are being fooled by this outsider, why should we believe this evidence of harm?), and *acceptability* of the members of the group (not just any "deviant" should be admitted). It is also closely tied to *distinguishability*: how one convincingly distinguishes the applicant from other "unworthy" queer citizens. The latter concern leads to a requirement that the claimant demonstrate suffering *beyond* "just prosecution" for sodomy; indeed the claimant must prove persecution for a social *identity*. While this sub-requirement of distinctiveness is part of the rhetorical alchemy which structures claims, and not formally part of the legal template, many have argued that it plays a critical role in how cases are decided (see Goodman, Ramanathan, and Yoshino). In the end, it reinforces the self-congratulatory posture inherent in the geopolitics of asylum: the northern nations that receive asylum seekers are constituted as good and just, while the nations that send are constituted as failures. The North receives worthy *victims* and presumably represses only unworthy *behaviors*.

In describing the move to distinguish worthy asylum seekers from appropriately penalized persons (here and there), I have begun to examine persecution, the other main area of contention in asylum cases. How the decision-makers define persecution bears on how a group can be constituted. Indeed, some experts advocate a focus on persecution in order to move away from the dangers of "immutability" and the fallacies inhering in the attempt to find definitive characteristics for emerging groups. Guy Goodwin-Gill has argued for a focus on evidence of persecution and discrimination against "homosexuals" in their home countries as a way of proving their existence as a social group (Goodwin-Gill; see also Walker, "Importance" 573; Ramanathan 9–10). This approach, sometimes called the "social context" approach, implicates the fact-finder in another form of knowledge production through searching for evidence of discrimination, but its case- and country-specific gaze generates another conundrum: do homosexuals disappear as a social group if they are not persecuted? Or do they just disappear as valid categories of refugee claiming? Why do we give the persecutor the power to name the group?

The nature of persecution itself is contested. Elements in question include whether the "well-founded fear" contains both subjective and objective components, whether a single act is sufficient to prove persecution or if it is necessary to demonstrate a pattern of harassment, and how much of the fear can be for the future instead of the present or past. The three cases that follow show how issues of persecution engage with sexual difference and reveal confused understandings of gender, cultural difference, and identity formation. They also show how fact-finders grapple with what exactly is/are the important aspect(s) of a queer person that must be protected: how they have sex? With whom they associate? Their right to be "out?" Their right not to be "out?" Is "being out" a global, constitutive aspect of gayness? How much fear do you have to live with?

Other disputed issues in finding "persecution" include the nature of the harm that counts as persecution—what constitutes a "threat to life or freedom." A growing legal literature advocates the use of evolving human rights standards to support an expansive understanding of persecution (see Hathaway). This expansion in rights work includes broadening the nature of the harm (rape as torture, violations of privacy in laws penalizing same sex conduct) and widening the kinds of perpetrators of harm (such as when violence is committed by non-state actors with impunity from prosecution, as in domestic violence or gay bashing) (see Anker). I will return in the conclusion to the question of why asylum law needs rights and what human rights can and should do vis-à-vis sexuality. In discussing the following cases, I focus on how persecution is established (documentation), and how this evidence is understood by the fact-finders (shaped by expert witnesses, or according to their own biases).

While many commentators on asylum ritualistically invoke, as if they were hermetically sealed categories, the various elements of the Convention definition that have to be proved, a more realistic reading of the cases would see that various elements "bleed" into or interact with one another.[27] In the cases presented, this bleeding and interaction between factors to be proved has been troubled ground for queer asylum seekers, since what makes a claim of persecution successful may—or may not—become the conduct that supposedly defines the group.[28]

How Do Adjudicators See? How Are Legal Templates Formed?

The way the cases are decided can be examined from two perspectives: first, according to the internal legal reasoning by which sexualities are made into identities to meet key legal tests, and second, in regards to the interaction between legal reasoning and popular or social norms. In examining how popular awareness connects to legal decision-making, it is important to note that, in the practice of precedent-based law (as in the common law of Anglo-American systems), the courts where the most number of people encounter the law are the least powerful in re-making the content of the law. If judicial decision-making power were portrayed geometrically, it would be as a triangle in which the number of people actually in the pyramid decreases as the capability for norm changes increases.[29] At the top of the judicial pyramid sit the famous appellate cases—they are more rare numerically, without blood and guts (literally, claimants do not appear, and figuratively, their factually complicated stories are boiled down into questions of law). Appellate decisions have the most powerful legal effects, traveling into popular attention through media campaigns that highlight and interpret their meaning, but the lower fact-finding decisions are also arguably places of popular impact, because of the greater numbers of people who find themselves disciplined subjects of the law.[30]

Understanding how legal decisions become part of social knowledge yields complex and even contradictory diagnoses of the reach of legal meaning making into daily lives. In the context of U.S. asylum, the site under investigation here, conscious, concrete steps have been taken to intervene in the interplay between legal knowledge and popular knowledge at the bottom of the pyramid. The U.S. Board of Immigration Appeals (BIA), aware of the connection between legal decisions and litigation strategies, does not regularly publish its decisions. Practitioners rely on their own informal networks of support to get copies of the reasoning in these cases.[31] A BIA adjudicator is reported as saying that the BIA does not seek to publish cases in order to avoid providing a "template" of the lines of reasoning that will most likely be acceptable (Ramanathan n. 2).[32] Such diffuse "not-knowing" at the level of numerically great, local decision-makers suggests that advocates and claimants struggle fiercely in each case to overcome the multiple limits of knowledge of both the advocate and adjudicator.[33] In what follows, after presenting the specific interactions of law and sexual difference, I focus on this struggle in the guise of the production of information through documentation and expert testimony in the framing of the claims as narratives of violation. My analysis draws attention to the continuing need for careful documentation in order to win cases while, if possible, producing more nuanced knowledge of sexual difference.

Domesticating Social Construction Theory: The Role of the Scholar as Expert

In 2000, in a case named *Hernandez-Montiel v. INS*,[34] a U.S. federal court quietly domesticated some of the revolutionary implications of social constructionist theories of sexuality for a laudable purpose: a grant of asylum. The case came to the 9th Circuit after the BIA first denied petitioner Geovanni Hernandez-Montiel his claim for asylum (and for withholding deportation, a related claim in U.S. asylum processes which requires a slightly different standard of proof). The BIA had previously found that Hernandez-Montiel did not meet his burden of showing that the abuse he suffered was on account of his membership in a particular social group. The BIA had determined Hernandez-Montiel's group to be "homosexual males who dress as females," (*Hernandez-Montiel* 5) but also decided that cross-dressing conduct did not fit the requirements for membership in a social group with a specifiable identity. Neither the original hearer of the claim, the

Immigration Judge (IJ), nor the BIA had questioned the credibility of his testimony regarding harassment from his family and authorities, including at least two incidences of rape by Mexican police. Accordingly, the elements of persecution were clear under even a conservative test: serious harm at the hands of state agents in Mexico.[35]

Still, the grounds for denial at the hearing and first review (BIA) level were the claimant's failure to prove membership in an identity group that was cognizable under the Refugee Convention. The case was even heard six years after the U.S. Attorney General had designated another BIA case, *Toboso-Alfonso*,[36] as precedent for the legal claim that "homosexuals" *can* meet the requirement of constituting a particular social group.[37] In *Toboso*, the INS did not contest the notion that "homosexuality" constitutes an "immutable" characteristic (*Toboso-Alfonso* 822), and the decision focused on the "status" of "being a homosexual" as constituting a group. How then could Hernandez-Montiel have failed to prove his category? The answer is that the BIA and IJ narrowed the gateway for "seeing" a persecuted identity, describing Hernandez-Montiel as one of those "homosexual male[s] who *dress as females*," and thus locating his claim as one of mistreatment due to, as one of the adjudicators wrote, the *way he dressed* (as a male prostitute) (*Hernandez-Montiel* 10).

Thus scripted as something like a "cross-dressing tart," Hernandez-Montiel failed to qualify as a worthy homosexual. The various decision-maker's limited capacities of recognition demonstrate the extent to which claimants need to simplify their self-representations to portray immutable identity, as well as to adjust them to fit pre-existing norms and standards of acceptability (cross-dressing is not only not essential to a person's selfhood, doing it to sell sex is also unacceptable). Kristen Walker notes that in Australia, successful queer-themed asylum claims often strive to demonstrate stable relationships in order to resemble worthy heterosexual relationships. The dilemma in all this for asylum seekers consists in providing accurate information regarding the reasons why asylum is being sought, while simultaneously having to avoid a judgment of being found "too much the bad gay" or of having "flaunted" sexual mores. However, the BIA's aside about Hernandez-Montiel's "dressing like a prostitute" compellingly reminds us that only *certain* forms of non-heternormative sexuality have been recognized by the asylum system. Other forms of sexual conduct often seriously penalized by the state, such as sex for money (prostitution), or adultery (absent some greater, disproportionate harm—the facing of the death penalty, for example), have had no success in asylum claims.[38] The implications of how the system understands persecution, stigma, and group formation in the context of these behaviors merits serious thought, as they involve stigmatized sexual behaviors that do not correspond to identity formation strategies employed by gay rights advocates.[39]

In reversing the BIA's original decision regarding Hernandez-Montiel, the 9th Circuit revised its own general test for gaining asylum. It took this case—a queer case from Mexico—to clarify a much-criticized test for group membership, one which had required proof of "the existence of a voluntary associational relationship among the purported members."[40] In its new ruling, the Court set out a new test: evidence of an innate characteristic that is so fundamental to the identities or consciousnesses of its members that they cannot or should not be required to change it. Moreover, in its reversal of the BIA, the 9th Circuit reclassified Hernandez-Montiel's identity: they decry the BIA's determination that he was a "man dressing as a woman." Rather, the Court determines he is a "gay man with a female sexual identity in Mexico." Thus, the Court converts a sexually provocative conduct that can be easily modified (wearing dresses/dressing like a prostitute) into an identity claim, specifically a female sexual identity.

The Court relied extensively on the expert testimony of a historian, a Professor Davies at San Diego State University, an "expert in Latin American history and culture," for authority in undertaking this transformation (*Hernandez-Montiel* 3). The 9th Circuit extensively relied on the professor's testimony, using it to establish that there are at least two kinds of homosexuals in Mexico: those who perform the role of the male (i.e., "active" or "penetrator") and who may marry, and those who are "perceived" to perform the role of the female (i.e., "passive" or "penetrated"), and are ostracized and subject to persecution. Without a copy of Professor Davies' testimony, I cannot assess the content and tenor of his remarks. It appears that the Court used his testimony to establish its conclusion that "female sexual identities" constitute a separate subset of the men who have sex with men, and are "the persecuted homosexual." The Court bolsters its conclusions by reference to selected U.S. federal decisions that address freedom of association and anti-discrimination claims by gay groups seeking the right to organize on college campuses. It also references U.S. sexologists such as Alfred Kinsey. Thus, the Court arrives at its understanding of the recognizable—and persecuted—identity of the "Mexican homosexual" by invoking in part U.S. conceptual frames and research on the relations between behavior, conduct, and the meaning of identity and the person.

In effect, the Court has created a new subject of the U.S. juridical gaze: gay men with female sexual identities. Interestingly, it potentially excludes another subject from asylum consideration: men who may engage in same-sex conduct and still marry—i.e., have *male* sexual identities. My point here is not that gendered social distinctions based on sexual behavior do not exist in Mexico or elsewhere, nor that the subjects here in question do not indeed face varying kinds of social inclusion and exclusion (See Parker, "'Within Four Walls'" and "Sexual Diversity"; see also Lancaster). But the Court has begun a potentially disfiguring and narrowing process of recognition with regard to certain persecuted identities, such that men not wearing women's clothes or taking the "passive" or penetrated role will *not* be seen as fitting the category of "persecuted homosexual." Will differently framed homosexual identities therefore be excluded?

Moreover, what the court reads as "female sexual identity" perhaps more properly ought to be thought of as a gendered/"feminized" sexual role. That is, the Court not only conflates penetration with passivity, but conflates sexual position with social identity and, more precisely, with female sexual identity. For *Hernandez-Montiel* the result is positive, but an important question nonetheless comes to the fore: have we won the claim by reifying a category that will now freeze out other identities? And how will this case move through contemporary global communication, including scholarship and the media? To what effect?

The reasoning of the case resonates with current tensions between some global advocacy work on "gay identity" and modern theoretical, as well as locally contextualized, work on sexuality. It raises questions concerning how courts are able to deal with homosexuality, or even "gayness," when it is not perfectly congruent with a specific, dominant set of pre-established conducts and other attributes. In the *Hernandez-Montiel* case, the 9th Circuit re-shapes a loosely gendered form of conduct (dressing as a woman) into a naturalized identity-related conduct (female sexual behavior), which the court then erects into an immutable (sexual) identity. The Court tugs away at conduct to make it identity, using U.S. legal scholarship on identity for support. Many careful, social constructionist studies of sexuality, cognizant of the importance of location and history, lead us to question whether U.S.

legal reasoning (for U.S. queer complainants) has any recognizable, accurate describing power for asylum seekers from culturally different social and sexual systems? Then again, the judges are, of course, U.S. judges, and the claimant *wins* in a U.S. court, which is of course where s/he wants to win.[41]

At any rate, perverse, diverse sexual conduct will not be easily deserving of asylum protection. It helps if the persecution is horrendous, and seems to work best when adjudicators see the persecution as directed at people who can be made to fit into a distinct category of identity mapped over the meaning they understand as derivable from their sexual behavior. In *Hernandez-Montiel*, a progressive, sophisticated court struggles to figure out how the state might be convinced to push open the narrow door of asylum. The Court at once pushes open the door and yet reinforces the wall, laboring to make the "sexually deviant" into "worthy claimants." As asylum is one alternative to persecution, such efforts are not trivial. Still, it is worth considering how legally successful strategies (ones culminating in a grant of asylum) might be informed by the more complex, culturally specific knowledge about sexuality that is emerging today. Can successful arguments recognize that the meaning of sexual conduct changes over time, that conduct will not *always* be congruent with identity or, more accurately, that conduct will not always be congruent with the identities that asylum judges recognize? How, in short, will advocates with a more nuanced appreciation of sexuality make their arguments and win?

The *Hernandez-Montiel* Court found the testimony of the "expert on Latin America" essential to its legal reformulation of the social group of the petitioner. This extensive reliance on expert testimony merits closer scrutiny. The 9th Circuit Judge positions himself as someone without independent knowledge of sexual orientation and sexual practice in Mexico; the IJ and BIA, however, had applied "common sense" and had used their folk knowledge-based prejudices as interpretive devices. The upshot of these decisions and reversals is that so-called expert testimony functions as a device to counteract the "common sense" interpretation, but may be put to imperfect use as judges search for generalizable principles and rules. Many scholars resist the distortion that comes with this use, and thus, ironically, advocates and legal decision-makers often proceed without sufficiently contextualized information. Anthropologists, particularly in the United States, have been engaged in contentious debates about their roles in rights protection and, more specifically, in legal processes, including asylum.

Some have argued that because ". . . anthropologists have become conventional sources of information to understand the cultural contexts of claims each practicing anthropologist has the responsibility under international law to protect persons from human rights violations" (Gilad 337).[42] Conversely, other experts confess doubts, especially because they may be asked to base their testimony on "minimal, second hand reports." Clearly, the engagement of scholars—anthropologists and others—with asylum cases may reinforce skepticism and reproduce many prejudices on all sides. Yet, since deadly persecutions continue, and legal decision-makers will continue to seek reasons to open or close doors, how can scholars and advocates forge engagements informed by more sophisticated research and principles?

The Incredible True Story of the Gay Man Raped by Macho Cops: *In re Inaudi* and the Power of Documentation

In 1992, Canada made its first grant of asylum on the grounds of persecution because of homosexuality. In *In re Inaudi*, the Canadian Immigration and Refugee Board (IRB) found that the harassment and arrest of the Argentine claimant while at gay bars, his expulsion from his apartment, and his rape at the hands of police were sufficient to prove persecution on account of membership in a social group. According to the Board, inasmuch as homosexuals are, by definition, capable of being united or associated by a common characteristic (their attraction to their own gender), both female and male homosexuals can easily prove membership in a social group. The Board invoked a German decision, citing persecution of homosexuals by the Third Reich as evidence of homosexuals as a "group." The IRB also references *U.S. Department of State Commission on Human Rights Practices* for its documentation of the widespread use of torture by Argentine police (*In re Inaudi*).

Yet it is the dissent that attracts my attention, because in it the judge explains his skepticism that the claimant's testimony "regarding rape, torture, and beatings by the Argentine police [is] credible or plausible" (*In re Inaudi*). While he finds the harassment by non-state actors believable, he states that such harassment amounts only to discrimination. The attacks by the police are essential to the claim of persecution. The dissenting judge bases his disbelief that the rapes occurred in two kinds of knowledge available to him: first, the silence of documented abuse against homosexuals by mainstream human rights groups such as Amnesty International, and second, his folk knowledge of sexuality and masculinity, revealed as incredulity at the idea of male-male police rape in Latin America.

The dissent's argument was deeply troubling in 1992, because Amnesty International had only just agreed in 1991 to view the detention of persons for same sex sexual activity as a rights issue under their mandate. Although the organization's documentation of abuse on the basis of sexual orientation was in the process of being expanded, research on sexual assault against anyone was as yet partial and incoherent, a state common to all the dominant human rights organizations. The specific lacuna of documentation on rape of men (because of or *regardless* of their sexual identity) meant skeptical judges could disregard documentation by less accepted organizations. As this Canadian judge wrote: "most of the documentary evidence is from gay advocacy groups or publications that would understandably highlight and possibly exaggerate the issues of the homosexual community." He went on to say: "[t]heir reporting must be compared with the documentary evidence submitted . . . including human rights reports from the Human Rights World Watch [sic], the Lawyers' Committee for Human Rights, Amnesty International and the U.S. State Department Reports on Human Rights Practices [Exhibit R-1] all of which do not highlight homosexuals as being at a heightened risk of persecution."[43]

The Judge's rejection of documentation by what he termed "self-serving"[44] gay groups is connected to his evaluation of the (un)likelihood of male-male rape, given the silence of dominant human rights organizations regarding the documentation of such practices. When the mainstream NGOs fail to document specific rights abuses, their silence is used to impugn the authority of non-traditional rights groups and nascent rights claims. In asylum decision-making, then, folk knowledge that parallels hegemonic rights knowledge (and its own prejudices) tends to remain unchallenged (see Mutua, "Ideology" and "Human Rights"). In the context of asylum, many gatekeepers operate in overlapping but discrete ways: the rights NGOs whose information is utilized by asylum courts, the litigators who shape the claims, and the legal decision-makers, whose personal "knowledge" of sexuality—in addition to all their other geopolitical, racial, cultural, and gendered assumptions—inflects their decision-making. Of course, the claimant is also a kind of gatekeeper, for he or she assesses which part of his or her life can be told or should be told, but the willingness of claimants to tell painful stories is shaped by their understanding of their usefulness. Here we enter the re-inforcing or transformative feed-back loop of knowledge production and advocacy.

In *In re Inaudi*, the dissenting decision-maker's folk knowledge prevented him from believing that "a police force that allegedly hunts homosexuals would take part in sexual assaults that involve the very activities it finds so disturbing, including homosexual contact" (*In re Inaudi* author numbered page 13). In disbelieving the applicant's claim that he had been raped by Argentine police while in detention,[45] the judge relied on a now-outmoded test for credibility from 1952: "[credible testimony] . . . must be in harmony with the preponderance of the probabilities which a practical and informed person would readily recognize as reasonable in that place and in those conditions."[46] This legal test entrenched folk knowledge on sexuality in the law, including common-sense understandings of rape as lust. The Judge relied on the very same descriptions of the society that Inaudi had fled as were presented by Inaudi's advocates ("homophobic Catholic," "latino-macho," "AIDS loathing security establishment") to bolster his own disbelief. Ironically, these shortcut terms in the pleadings were drawn from various gay presses, struggling to bring abuses against queers to light. But these popular press concepts and terms re-affirmed stereotypical, polarized understandings of homo- and heterosexuality. The absence of countervailing information from "credible" rights organizations left the Judge free to use his own knowledge, historically and culturally shaped by ideologies of heterosexual masculinity. This common sense believes it "knows" that heterosexual men, such as the Argentine police, would never sexually penetrate another man. But careful historical and anthropological research in all societies and cultures demonstrates, of course, that men who occupy public, masculinist, and heterosexual roles can play the penetrator role without compromising their power and masculine image (see Parker and Aggleton). While feminist analyses of male/female rape cannot be shifted without modification to explain the specific politics of male/male rape,[47] these analyses nevertheless do function to remind us in general that powers to subordinate operate through sexual assault. Our question in asylum jurisprudence is whether such abuses count as persecution. Fortunately, in this case, the majority did not fall into this faultline, but the dissent did. One might guess that similar reasoning has prevailed in other cases for which there has been a lack of mainstream human rights documentation on the incidence of male/male rape.

Why no documentation, then? The reasons for lack of research on male-male rape can be linked to the state of conceptual and practical work on sexuality-related abuse in the early 1990s, with reference to all genders of victims and both hetero- and homosexual orientations. In 1991, Amnesty International had only just amended its mandate to allow action calling for the release from detention of persons imprisoned for consensual same sex activity. No other mainstream rights organization, nor the United Nations, had even progressed that far. The International Gay and Lesbian Human Rights Commission (IGLHRC) and International Lesbian and Gay Association (ILGA), as gay-identity focused (not sexual rights) research and campaigning groups, were struggling for credibility. Yet, for mainstream groups, this lack of policy on criminalizing same sex desire should not have foreclosed research on *sexual assault* on men or women as a form of torture or of cruel, inhuman, or degrading treatment in detention. Torture, whether directed at a person because of his or her sexual orientation or identity, or in ignorance of it, was, and is, prohibited.

Yet, at that time, Amnesty International—along with all the other major human rights organizations—demonstrated two kinds of myopia in regard to sexual rape as torture. First, research on the sexual assault of men in detention was inconsistently split, and second, research on the rape of women as torture was close to non-existent. On the one hand, documentation on torture of men in detention often depicted a male detainee who was sexually assaulted in a "traditional" torture scenario (i.e., electrodes to the genitals). These acts were always characterized as torture. On the other hand, male-on-male rape (meaning forcible penetration, particularly, though not exclusively, by a penis) was hardly catalogued at all.[48] Conversely, the rape/sexual penetration (most often reported if vaginal penetration) of women in detention was often noted, but not characterized as torture if the penetration was by a male body, as opposed to electric shocks and other devices that *did* get named as torture (International Human Rights Law Group, *Token Gestures*).

In this brief account, I can only hazard a few reasons for these bifurcated responses. I suggest that they relate not only to the general disregard of women of any sexuality as players in the public life of rights-claiming dominant at the time, but also to the NGO researchers' own understanding of sexuality, and finally to the then-dominant paradigm of torture. In regard to personal bias, one can see various factors operating: a hetero-normative squeamishness, even fear, about revealing males as penetrated in any way, coupled with reluctance on the part of men or women (let alone transgendered persons) who had been abused to come forward. In regard to the legal frame, the then-dominant legal test did not attribute rape to the state and thus did not allow it as torture, because rape was depicted as the product of male lust operating outside of the agency of the state. Rape thus portrayed did not advance the interests of the state, which is what the litmus test for torture (as opposed to an individual criminal act) requires under traditional rights doctrine (Amnesty International, *It's in Our Hands* 75–7). This paradigm kept the rape of women in detention legally invisible, while the rape of men was conceptually unimagined.

The presence or absence of documentation is frequently the linchpin upon which a claim turns, underscoring the interrelationship of rights advances and asylum progress. It also highlights that documentation is not neutral data collection but is dynamically constituted by, and contributes to, the evolution of the conceptual and legal frameworks. Facts are not spontaneously produced, but are generated in response to demands to account for harms often directed at newly emerging claimants.[49] Queer asylum cases are key sites for this dynamic, and yet can generate dangerous effects because of the specificity of asylum law's requirements.

The Discreet Chinese Lesbian Wanna-be

The third case, that of the "discreet Chinese lesbian" (RBT Reference V95/02999)[50] of 1995, reveals some of the traps into which blinkered asylum policies can fall. Documentation on the "invisible lesbian" has been, as the term suggests, notoriously hard to produce for traditional rights groups (Rosenbloom). However, theory and research into how lesbians as women face different forms of persecution in private and public life have begun to change how rights documentation and advocacy are shaped.[51] These analyses are also slowly intersecting with the development of gender-based asylum guidelines, which show some sensitivity to differences in different countries vis-à-vis ethnicity, religion, race, and age.[52]

In this Australian case, the gendered and culture-bound assumptions of the fact-finders resulted in the denial of asylum to the claimant. According to the RR Tribunal, the testimony of the applicant indicated that she had been forced out of her parents' home because she had refused to marry and had told them that "her reason for not marrying was that her sexual preference was to have a relationship with a

woman" (Australian RRT Decision 4). Somewhat obscurely, she is reported to have testified that "she has girl friends but she has not had a
sexual relationship with a woman. She has never tried to have a sexual
relationship with a woman in China" (Australian RRT Decision). The
adjudicator denied her claim on the grounds that she is not a "practicing lesbian," and thus, her sexuality has never been "forcibly repressed."
Even more bizarrely, the Court suggested she did not qualify for asylum because a "homosexual lesbian can avoid the risk of harm by being discreet in her conduct" (Australian RRT Decision 8).

As Walker notes in "The Importance of Being Out," the Australian
decision-makers in this case were skeptical of the claim of persecution,
in part because of their own cultural notions of what being gay means:
being "out" according to a very male—and sexual conduct-specific—
model of gayness. The claimant is not a "practicing lesbian" according
to the RBT: "girlfriends," desire, and erotic imagination do not suffice
to make her a lesbian—only sex does. The adjudicator of this case does
not attend to the particular ways that a person's sense of self, including
her sexuality, operates within and is constrained by family roles, gender
notions, implicit threats of force, as well as by the gender-specific need
of many girls and women to live in the family home for economic survival. Moreover, another barrier arose in her case, the now-discredited
practice of human rights NGO documentation focusing exclusively on
persecution by state agents. Thus, until recently rights advocacy (and
asylum) did not address the violence at the hands of family members
or neighbors.[53]

The "would-be" lesbian also faces another (gendered) trap: the legal dilemma created by Australian asylum jurisprudence on discretion. Australian decisions had made an explicit rule out of a limiting
principle which elsewhere "remains sub-textual or non-existent in the
queer asylum decisions of most other jurisdictions—whether a queer
refugee may be *refouled* [returned] if some degree of 'discretion' would
help him/her avoid persecution" (Ramanathan 35). Notably, in the *In
re Inaudi* case above, the Canadian IRB rejects this theory and specifically affirmed that it is no bar to asylum that the asylum seeker "returns to the very bars where he faced harassment" (*In re Inaudi* author
numbered page 7). The Canadian IRB decision (and as of this year,
by a new rule, the Australian courts) holds that if a right to be free of
persecution is real, it must be a right which is not circumscribed by the
(discriminatory, because sexual orientation-specific) need for discretion (*In re Inaudi*).

But in this case, the then-binding test for discretion by the Australian adjudicators created a compound problem. By using discretion as
a test unique to sexual orientation, they undercut the right to be free
from persecution on that basis. Second, the adjudicators raise the discretion bar by linking it to their own Western gay male identity-based
knowledge of homosexuality or "gayness." Their test is both wrong in
principle and additionally skewed against responsiveness to the gender-specific obstacles that women face in "proving" their sexuality.[54]
The adjudicators construct a circular argument: burdening sexual dissidents with the obligation to be discreet, the adjudicators are then
unable to understand how a woman who has been discreet can be
"gay"—after all, she has not even been sexually "out" or active. The adjudicators implicitly rely on the expressive and associational aspects of
"outness" to find the asylum seeker's identity, and when they do find it,
here, they "sex" it in a particular way to deny that it is gay enough. The
Australian decision-makers see a "non-practicing lesbian" as simply a
woman without a man. While this status alone can expose women to
persecution, it is not the same as a lesbian identity. Thus, the Australian refugee board denies that the claimant is "really gay" *and* asserts
that she therefore has no need of refuge.[55]

Complexity, Simplicity, and Complicity in Strategies for (Homo)sexual Rights

I now turn to a kind of "shadow list" of cautionary tales derived from
my experiences as an advocate and academic working her way through
the divergent interests circulating in rights advocacy and scholarly research (Snitow 35). I focus on strategic "shortcuts" (and their specific
implications for understanding sexuality) that advocates often employ
as they strive to make successful claims. These shortcuts are related to
the issues of documentation and advocacy described above, but they
also move beyond them into the particular problems posed by gay
rights advocacy in asylum, and the particular historical moment when
queer-themed asylum cases were then re-deployed as leverage in the
struggle to gain acceptance of gay rights in human rights.

Some of the shortcuts that I address here are common in the debates between scholars and activists and among activists themselves
(for example, the resonance between successful popular advocacy and
culturally dominant stereotypes); others are specific to sexuality. All
arise in part in the pressures of the moment, often from the need for
quickly identifiable allies.

Simplified arguments, stereotyping, and de-contextualization are all dangerous for rights work in themselves, but they are even more damaging when they arise in the cross-border geo-political conversations, and judgments, that underpin asylum and human rights work. As Uma Narayan writes, the problem with many accounts of violation (here generated as asylum claims) in the first world is the manner in which they raise questions "that have less to do with *exclusion* than with the manner and mode of *inclusion*" (Narayan 45).[56] Asylum is a process of inclusion—thus Narayan's warning directs us to analyze how problematic elements of narratives of sexual and cultural difference have been successful in gaining asylum.

The Peculiar Role of "Gay" Asylum Cases: Perverts and Rights NGOs as Moral/Norm Entrepreneurs

Many commentators struggle to understand the processes by which forms of social knowledge about sexuality and sexual difference become increasingly globalized, cross borders, and have effects in multiple sites simultaneously (see Altman; also McClintock, Mufti, and Shohat). Asylum and human rights are intra-national and inter-national conversations shaping legal norms, and thus also function in cross-border meaning making. At a minimum, the recognition of particular kinds of gay identities *within* a national legal context is then deployed as part of a complicated, international conversation about gayness and gay rights. In discussing the ways that asylum decisions function in the claiming of gay rights, I do not rely on any one framework for how law makes meaning (see Halley, "Reasoning"; Goodman; Yoshino). Nor does this discussion claim that the "gay identity" recognized by a U.S., Canadian, or other national court creates or imposes a particular gay identity on the rest of the world. Rather, it focuses on a particular moment in the early stages of globalizing conversations about rights, abuse, and the need to protect sexually non-conforming people from abuse, in order to bring to the surface some key dynamics and mechanisms at play in rights work.

In the late 1980s through the early 1990s, gay rights groups—sometimes working with, sometimes in critical opposition to, human rights groups—highlighted asylum cases in their campaigning. Through documentation and networking, they worked to affect the outcomes of these cases as well as to advertise the outcomes as part of demonstrating why the human rights framework had to respond to queer claims. "Moral entrepreneur" concepts can play a useful role in understanding the particular forces and mechanisms by which NGOs, particularly the gay rights and human rights NGOs, enlist queer-themed asylum cases in their national and international movement for LGBT human rights. Howard Becker's classic work on "moral entrepreneurs" describes those interest groups that come to public consciousness by generating both the definition of the problem and the proposed solutions. Jenkins highlights how, in highly contested moments, "we should be alive to the possible presence of an enterprising individual or group. Their activities can properly be called 'moral enterprise' for what they are enterprising about is the creation of a new fragment of the moral constitution of society, its code of right and wrong" (Jenkins 6, Becker).[57] In what follows, I consider gay rights and human rights NGOs as moral entrepreneurs or, better yet, as "norm entrepreneurs," inasmuch as they set their sights on norms—here, human rights norms, that relate to the constitution of specific views of sexual rights and wrongs (see also Finnemore, Wheeler).

In regard to the disparate but linked movements seeking to apply human rights to queer people, quite a few elements of "entrepreneurship" are in play. Over the last 20 years, small groups in the North and South, representing despised minorities, sought to get attention and protection, as well as to improve their own group's standing. The language of rights—and the victories of asylum cases—were key tools in this project. These groups' campaigns—especially those based in the North—operated through increasingly globalized media. They used the language of rights as a core part of their claim to civic status and legal protection. Thus, the validation that comes through legal triumph—as in a grant of asylum to a gay petitioner—informs gay rights organizing globally. Asylum cases are visible victories, rare in the human rights world. Insofar as asylum cases are about cross-border looking and judging, advocates can use the cases not only to reach domestic audiences, but also to re-frame the place of the national in the international, as in the local application of an international right, or as in a national commentary on another nation's practice. Advocates based in both the North and South use these strategies, but what follows deals primarily with the issues arising from Northern-based groups engaged in this work in the early 1990s.

I am particularly mindful of these aspects of rights work because of my own role in using asylum cases—and seeing them used around me—during this time, when "gay rights" began to make real inroads outside of Europe as a valid human rights claim. As a member of

Amnesty International USA's (AIUSA's) national staff during the late 1980s and early 1990s, I worked with extraordinary activists inside and outside AI, seeking to move AI to protect the human rights of persons arrested for same sex behavior—sometimes self-identified as lesbians and gay men. Campaigning within and on Amnesty International to change its policies vis-à-vis prisoners of conscience and sexual behavior, including the call for the unconditional release of persons arrested solely for consensual, same sex behavior, began in the late 1970s. However, a much more internationalized, oppositional, and public attention-seeking campaign started after 1990.

During that time, the organization was pressured to change their mandate, internally by staff and volunteers, and externally by nascent gay rights groups such as the newly founded, United States-based International Gay and Lesbian Human Rights Commission (IGLHRC) and the more established European-based ILGA. This was also the period of the first successes in gay-themed asylum petitions (see *In re Inaudi*, above). IGLHRC and ILGA used their campaigning against Amnesty International's silence together with the asylum victories to put their issues on the screens of mainstream media, gay media, and governmental agencies. After 1991, when Amnesty International adopted the new understanding of its mandate, AI activists also reported on these victories in our newsletters and in the mainstream media. (*AIMLGC Newsletter*).[58] Other human rights organizations such as Human Rights Watch (HRW) eventually adopted policy on sexual orientation and began documenting and doing media work on gay rights-related cases. A careful and scholarly accounting of these efforts is yet to be written. Most chronicles have been left at the level of the "narratives of triumph and virtue" that each of the organizations has produced. Also missing is a contextualized assessment of the complicated roles and interests of the various players at all levels, inside and outside the various NGOs. Given the need of rights-oriented NGOs, including gay and traditional human rights organizations, to maintain an appearance of infallibility in the face of attacking governments, such accounting and assessment may not be likely. Yet, as the earlier examination of the cases made clear, the various positions taken or claimed have had serious effects on the determination of these cases and on the globalized construction of "gay identity."

One of the critical insights arising from the Harvard-sponsored "Passing Lines" symposium relates to how complexly queerness migrates, how it is constituted and constitutes itself differently on different sides of borders and in motion across them, in a dynamic that engages nation, family, law, body, and mortality. Asylum as a discourse and as a legal system of claims-making reconstitutes migrating "queerness" yet again, but with a bias favoring advocates who use strategies of simplicity and reductionism which can succeed within the particular lenses of receiving countries' legal regimes.

Short Cuts to Success: The Importance of Extreme Horror and its Dangers in Cross-Border Advocacy

Human rights theorist Jacqueline Bhabha has written on the perils of advocates "hav[ing] to rely on a domestic image" of the client, yet at the same time, "[having] to dispel some of the narrow, culturally limiting assumptions associated with that image to open up space for very different types of [experience and aspirations]" (Bhabha 179–80). The most successful shortcut, one that obliterates the need to present unpleasant or hard-to-read nuances of complex lives, is the representation of extreme horror affecting the lives of claimants in the state of origin. But inherent in this representation is a non-beneficent aspect of asylum: adjudicators in receiving countries proclaim the failures of the state of origin without having to reflect on how the actions of the receiving state might be connected to those very abuses (or on how such representations might reproduce colonial relations of power) (see Hathaway).

In 1998, on a panel at an NYU Law School-sponsored forum, Safed Rahman, a gay-identified asylee from Pakistan living in the United States, said: "The asylum process requires the painting of one's country in extremely racist and colonialist ways in order to show its homophobia" (Wei and Satterthwaite 515). Rahman described the ways that he felt he had to "act queer" so that the hearing examiner would understand he was gay. Rather stunningly, a U.S. asylum adjudicator in the audience stood up to claim that the training and widespread experience of the INS decision-makers in many cross-cultural matters make such subterfuges unnecessary. Yet, the three examples discussed above certainly provide ample evidence of the limited exposure to diverse sexualities and the crabbed reasoning of receiving country decision-makers. As Bhabha writes, "the worse the better" is the central principle guiding the representations advocates create to win. "Are there limits to how—what tropes—an advocate should employ in rendering the horror in the sending country? Advocates often totalize the cultures of the sending countries as 'violent toward women,' 'primitive or tribal in their control of sexuality," etc."; as Bhabha notes, they have no incentive to nuance their representations: "hard-pressed, relatively uninformed immigration and asylum decision-makers may readily consume this shorthand" (Bhabha 162). And their client wants to win. What is the harm of these narratives? Can one minimize the complicity of asylum storytelling with imperial project, while still being successful in ensuring that those who seek to cross borders can still cross?

Bhabha has analyzed dangerous shortcuts—simplifications powered by the search for winning stories—in her evaluation of how refugee, asylum, and migration policies and programs constitute the notion of the "child," and at the same time exclude "bad children" from protection. Bhabha's analysis is suggestive here as well: how might advocates in queer cases contend with the dangers of generating simplified versions of "good" gay or lesbian identities? (Her work also reminds us that sexual claims by young people are among the most fraught in traditional rights work.) I have already demonstrated how legal success tied to one kind of representation (i.e., feminized gayness, as in *Hernandez-Montiel*) can inadvertently work to foreclose remedies for others who may be equally persecuted but not similarly gay.

Asylum decision-makers seek to ensure (in courts of law and in public policy) that they have persuasively distinguished the winning claimant from others, with one of the few rights-worthy claims. With regard to LGBT asylum cases, the asylum decision-maker's quandary is to grapple first with whether there is such a thing as a transnationally recognizable gay identity. Fluid and traveling identities are seeking recognition from a system that seeks to freeze and limit identity formation as part of its gate-keeping function. How do advocates convince decision-makers that what they are looking at is an honest-to-God gayness worthy of consideration under the category of persecuted social group? The fluidity of sexuality causes problems for determinations not only because of its mutable character, but also because of the need to distinguish the worthy identity from the unworthy sexual practice, a recognition made more difficult by being cross-boundary and cross-cultural. Hence, narratives of sexual harm and violation emerge as key strategies for those seeking asylum. Advocacy relies on *embodiment of the harm* in the stories of specific individuals facing abuse. Intra-border and trans-border campaigning thus often deploys easy-to-read representations, such as the idea of "innocent torture victims," which often rely for their impact on connecting with conventions and stereotypes that already resonate in various societies (Narayan).

However, campaigns depicting the "violated innocent" in the context of sexuality face a more difficult struggle because the claimants must define themselves publicly as sexually active and deviant, since recognizable difference forms part of the basis of their claim for persecution. How is a so-called pervert to become visible *and* sympathetic? This is where asylum functions so beautifully in regard to transnational rights-claiming, since here the claimant by definition faces extraordinary abuse—indeed, persecution—which no one, not even a pervert, should be expected to tolerate. Yet, the very spectacular nature of the claim can occlude attention to other pervasive but less spectacular harms—the denial of education or the loss of housing, for example—that arise both in country of origin and country of destination for the asylee. It can allow a judgment of "barbarism" to be fixed on the sending country, almost always Third World, and produce a sense of moral superiority or complacency for the receiving country. The sheer scope of the violence can make it difficult to imagine the person as alive and claiming participation rights as a citizen. Finally, the category of "what a gay victim looks like" becomes frozen in the "violent gift" bestowed by the asylum decision-makers. Representing the sexual in the midst of the asylum conundrum of the need to make the "pervert" rights-worthy through highlighting the egregious violations proves deeply vexing: the gate of asylum will in fact never be made wide and flexible. If we understand asylum reasoning as a cross-border and intra-border reasoning process about protection worthiness (and thus, by extension, the claimant's right *not* to be persecuted, to exist?), then we must understand the discourse on gay asylum to be part of the sovereignty's tendency to favor narratives that widen the door slightly, but leave its own power in place, including the power to make distinctions between entrants. How do we read, and then participate in, this moment of acceptance of persecution for "gayness" for asylum, including the need to convert diverse and diffuse practices into a worthy identity?

Inter-related Dynamics, Separate Rules: Human Rights and Asylum

The three cases examined, the many more asylum stories, won and lost, and the oral histories and ethnographies of persons of diverse sexualities crossing borders highlight the way in which new work on sexuality poses particular challenges to the reified identities that qualify as worthy victims under asylum law.

Moreover, as both the *Hernandez-Montiel* and the "discreet lesbian" case make clear, asylum tends to favor identity as the touchstone of what is essential to protect about the human, and deems only some forms of conduct or behavior as fitting that identity. Asylum law came into being as a global response to genocide: the targeting for destruction of a group of people because of their identity. Thus, the Refugee Convention enumerated "race, religion, nationality, membership in a particular social group, or political opinion" as the bases of protection. The Universal Declaration of Human Rights (UDHR) and the Genocide Convention were both adopted in 1948; the Refugee Convention in 1951.[59] These standards are premised on the notion that a discriminated identity simply "is" and can be found in the body.[60]

Asylum law thus has a double bias: toward believing in identity as "findable," and toward understanding new identities only as analogous to other fixed forms of identity (the biologized reification of race, for example). These biases have a political impact as well: if asylum is a generous grant, strictly scrutinized in the giving, then the notion of only the narrowest, most "tried and true" identity will do for asylum—there can be no invention of new identities to make the floodgates open. This attitude contrasts with that of human rights work, which, at least superficially, has no such floodgate problem to worry about, since the first principle of rights protection is the local enforcement of structures that promote overall rights.

These and many other cases reveal the tensions and contradictions in asylum claiming for queer persons. They join questions arising from the new work on sexuality, work which spotlights the historical specificity of the meanings given to sexual identities and behaviors, including the ideas that sexual conduct and claimed sexual identity can be non-congruent. They constantly return us to the vexed question of how we understand agency and behavior for making identity or resisting it, and its varied meanings and constraints across gender, age, and racial/ethnic identities. In sum, how does asylum respond to the complexities of sexual lives—and to the grim reality, no less complex, of abuse and persecution?

One response to the limitations of asylum as currently figured is to broaden its scope of vision—what the legal process can "see" through the expansion of rights-based documentation of violation. The *Hernandez-Montiel* and *In re Inaudi* cases demonstrate the importance of producing more nuanced sexuality-relevant documentation and expert testimony. Asylum advocates acknowledge—and self-consciously exploit—the inter-relationship between asylum and human rights, working with human rights groups to expand documentation to include broader concepts of persecution. Asylum advocates increasingly promote the evolving rights principle of state accountability for non-state actor abuse. However, although this synergy between a more sensitive understanding of structures of subordination and identity formation and more nuanced rights-based documentation generally suggests a benign, mostly positive inter-relation between the two fields, there are grounds for caution.

Rights advocates should be careful to acknowledge the particularities of asylum: it is a Procrustean bed into which sexuality is forced to fit as an identity for a single person's claim. Human rights campaigners therefore should not unquestioningly accept the identities produced for asylum claims as the template for finding and protecting sexual difference, even as they trumpet the winning of asylum cases as victories for human rights protections for queer asylum seekers. We must self-consciously re-construct the key elements of asylees' stories as they become "human rights narratives," especially if we do not want to replicate the "colonial," nationally driven, ageist, or sexist exclusions of asylum as a gate-keeping mechanism.[61]

Although human rights has its own history of "gate-keeping," I would argue that this failure is not intrinsically related to its practice, in the way that for asylum, gate keeping *is* related to its practice vis-à-vis national sovereignty (see Mutua).[62] However, the fact that human rights has often functioned to reinforce hierarchies or walls suggests that it is not un-problematically available for sexual rights. Yet, I believe the work of many advocates around the world demonstrates that it has liberatory potential for sexuality, even though it has sometimes and still may be a place of danger.

Thus, I close this discussion with some brief thoughts on the dynamic between asylum as a system of recognition of violations and grants of refuge, and human rights as a place which can campaign not only to end abuse, but also as a place where sexualities can potentially thrive. To borrow from a conceit in poetic analysis, one could describe a key element of difference in the two systems of law as the difference between regarding (asylum) and beholding (human rights). The first (asylum) responds, sees, and limits by externalizing and narrowing. It is therefore wary in its remedy. The second system (rights) contains the potential not only to apprehend something—to have human rights is to be human—but also to transform the notion of the human in light of diversity. Moreover, it has the potential to connect to the material and social conditions that are required to produce diversity and humanness. Elsewhere I have written about existing limits in the practice, but here I also signal the potentials of the framework of rights to promote sexual diversity (Miller, "Human Rights"; "Las demandas"; "Sexual"; "Uneasy Promises"). Many scholars and activists are focusing on the human rights framework of "respect, protect, and fulfill" to move the discussion of human rights engagement with sexuality beyond the work to denounce abuses linked to specific identities into the work of altering the structure of society (see Correa and Petchesky).

In asylum work, proof of violations has provided the motor that allowed an individual to breach the wall of a sovereign country and gain entry as an asylee. In human rights worlds, it has been documentation (a form of representation) of egregious rights violations—torture, extra-judicial execution—on the basis of homosexuality that has proved itself the most successful strategy for overcoming the moralistic squeamishness of human rights NGOs, and to some extent, human rights bodies in the UN. Asylum and rights interconnect in being discourses that deploy the story of great abuse in order to build the legal, social, moral, and emotional context for demanding a response "as of right." Human rights work on sexuality, and the conditions that allow diverse sexualities to thrive, will have to knit together the locally driven specificities with the power of claiming universal obligations: we are just on the threshold of this work. Yet it is being done, carefully and creatively and locally around the world.

Still, while we contest "gay" identities and universal meaning-making as strategies that may re-inscribe power in the name of "doing good," the challenge is to go beyond critique. Real harm, real fear is driving movement; real bodies are seeking justice. We expect United States and other Northern-based advocates to win the cases they take on behalf of their queer claimants, and we demand that they do so in ways that do not replicate the structures of power and prejudice of the systems in which they operate. We are thus face-to-face with the classic contradictions between successful delivery of aid (grants of asylum in the United States) and the ways in which remedial assistance reinforces the very structures within systems of oppression. However, human rights can function as more than the (powerful and necessary) system of documentation of abuse that compels the grant of aid. It can also function as the basis of reconstructing the conditions for full participation in one's own society, and this use of rights may be one way forward.

Acknowledging this means something quite demanding in regard to a political strategy of coalition of advocates and scholars around sexuality. As long as bodies, real bodies, with love, desire, hope, and messy lives, are crossing borders and demanding a response with justice in whatever place they find themselves, we must monitor and even join in the production of evidence/knowledge that wins in asylum, while making a claim that adequately reflects complex realities. At the same time, rights work on the complexity of lives can focus on the obligations of states which would promote difference in diverse cultures without an easily scanned common identity. Can lives differently constructed, sexualities multiply layered across ethnicity, class, age, and gender, be represented well, when we speak into another kind of reality, one where all media and advocacy work seems to demand strategies of simplicity?

Acknowledgments

The author wishes to acknowledge that many of the ideas for this piece are drawn from conversations made possible by the Program for the Study of Sexuality, Gender, Health and Human Rights, directed by Carole S. Vance, funded by the Rockefeller Foundation at the Mailman School of Public Health, Columbia University. This chapter expands specific dialogue made possible by the organizers of the David Rockefeller Center for Latin American Studies "Passing Lines: Immigration and (Homo)sexuality" conference. Special thanks for additional comments and thoughtful conversations are due to AnnJannette Rosga, Margaret Satterthwaite, Carole S. Vance, and members of the Columbia University Human Rights Seminar. Particular thanks are due to Brad Epps, Bill Johnson González, and Keja Valens for their support and superb editing. Finally, Christal Stone, Ann Drobnik, and Rana Barar have provided yeoperson research and other support.

Works Cited

Altman, Dennis. *Global Sex.* Chicago: University of Chicago Press, 2001.

American Civil Liberties Union. "Crime and Punishment in America: State-by-State Breakdown of Existing Laws and Repeals." *American Civil Liberties Union Online,* June 9, 2003. http://www.aclu.org/ (accessed October 9, 2002).

Amnesty International. "The Backlash—Human Rights at Risk throughout the World." *Amnesty International Online.* October 4, 2001. http://web.amnesty.org/library/Index/engACT300272001?OpenDocument&of=THEMES%5CDISCRIMINATION (accessed June 2, 2005).

_____. *It's in Our Hands: Stop Violence Against Women.* New York: Amnesty International, 2004.

Amnesty International USA. "Canada Grants Refugee Status to Gay Man." *LesbiGay Newsletter,* (Amnesty International Members for Lesbian and Gay Concerns). Ed. Margaret Satterthwaite. Spring 1992.

Anker, Deborah. "Refugee Law, Gender, and the Human Rights Paradigm." *Harvard Human Rights Journal* 15 (2002): 133–154.

Bao, Jiemin. "Same Bed, Different Dreams: Intersections of Ethnicity, Gender, and Sexuality among Middle- and Upper-Class Chinese Immigrants in Bangkok." *Positions* 6.2 (1998): 475–502.

Becker, Howard S. "Moral Entrepreneurs." *Constructions of Deviance: Social Power, Context, and Interaction.* Ed. Patricia A. Adler and Peter Adler. Upper Saddle River, N.J.: Prentice Hall, 2002. 139–146.

Bhabha, Jacqueline. "Internationalist Gatekeepers?: The Tension Between Asylum Advocacy and Human Rights." *Harvard Human Rights Journal* 15 (2002): 155–182.

Black, Laura, Mimi Liu, and Elizabeth Da Trinidade-Asher, eds. *Gender Asylum Law in Different Countries.* Boston: Refugee Law Center, Inc., 1999.

Canada (A.G.) v. Ward. (1993) 2 S.C.R. 689.

Center for Gender and Refugee Studies. Ed. Stephen Knight. April 4, 2005. http://www.uchastings.edu/cgrs/ (accessed October 7, 2002).

Chanock, Martin. "'Culture' and Human Rights: Orientalising, Occidentalising and Authenticity." *Beyond Rights Talk and Culture Talk: Comparative Essays on the Politics of Rights and Culture.* Ed. Mahmood Mamdani. New York: St. Martin's Press, 2000. 15–36.

Convention Governing the Specific Aspects of Refugee Problems in Africa. 1001 U.N.T.S. 45, entered into force June 20, 1974.

Convention Relating to the Status of Refugees. 189 U.N.T.S. 150, opened for signature July 28, 1951.

Correa, Sonia, and Rosalind Petchesky. "Reproductive and Sexual Rights: A Feminist Perspective." *Population Policies Reconsidered: Health, Empowerment, and Rights.* Ed. Gita Sen, Adrienne Germain, and Lincoln C. Chen. Boston: Harvard University Press, 1994. 107–126.

Crooms, Lisa. "'Everywhere There's War:' A Racial Realist's Reconsideration of Hate Crimes Statutes." *Georgetown Journal of Gender and the Law* Inaugural Issue (1999): 41–66.

Darcy, James. "Human Rights and International Legal Standards: What Do Relief Workers Need to Know?" ODI Network Paper No. 19. *Overseas Development Institute Online.* February 1997. http://www.odi.org.uk/rights/publications.html (accessed June 2, 2005).

Decision of Apr. 26, 1995. Refugee Review Tribunal. No. BN93/01754. Available at http://www.austlii.edu.au.

Dowsett, Gary. Lecture. "Community and Academy: A Critical Collaboration or Just Making Ends Meet?" HIV Center for Clinical and Behavioral Studies, December 12, 2002.

Ensler, Eve. *The Vagina Monologues.* New York: Villard, 2001.

Faryna v. Chorny. 2 D.L.R. 354 (B.C.C.A.).

Finnemore, Martha. "Rules of War and Wars of Rules: The International Red Cross and the Restraint of State Violence." *Constructing World Culture: International Nongovernmental Organizations Since 1875.* Ed. John Boli and George M. Thomas. Stanford, Calif.: Stanford: Stanford University Press, 1999. 149–168.

Foucault, Michel. *The History of Sexuality.* Vol. 1. New York: Pantheon Books, 1978.

Gilad, Lisa. "The Problem of Gender-Related Persecution: A Challenge of International Protection." *Engendering Forced Migration: Theory and Practice.* Ed. Doreen Marie Indra. New York: Berghahn Books, 1999. 334–342.

Goldberg, Pamela, and Nancy Kelly. "Recent Developments: International Human Rights and Violence Against Women." *Harvard Human Rights Journal* 6 (1993): 195–209.

Goldberg, Suzanne. "Give Me Liberty or Give Me Death: Political Asylum and the Global Persecution of Lesbians and Gay Men." *Cornell International Law Journal* 26 (1993): 605–624.

Goodman, Ryan. "Beyond the Enforcement Principle: Sodomy Law, Social Norms, and Social Panoptics." *California Law Review* 89.3 (2001): 643–740.

Goodwin-Gill, Guy S. *The Refugee in International Law.* 2nd ed. New York: Oxford University Press, 1996.

H.L.R. v. France. (Euro. Ct. Hum. Rts. 1997). HUDOC reference #REF00000628.

Halley, Janet E. "The Politics of the Closet: Legal Articulation of Sexual Orientation Identity." *After Identity: A Reader in Law and Culture.* Ed. Dan Danielson and Karen Engle. New York: Routledge, 1995. 24–38.

_____. "Reasoning about Sodomy: Act and Identity in and after *Bowers v. Hardwick.*" *Virginia Law Review* 79 (1993): 1721–1780.

_____. "Sexual Orientation and the Politics of Biology: A Critique of the Argument from Immutability." *Stanford Law Review* 46 (1993–4): 503–568.

Hathaway, James C. "A Reconsideration of the Underlying Premise of Refugee Law." *Harvard International Law Journal* 31 (1990): 129–184.

Helton, Arthur. "Keynote Address: Symposium: Shifting Grounds for Asylum: Female Genital Surgery and Sexual Orientation." Ed. Timothy Wei and Margaret Satterthwaite. *Columbia Human Rights Law Review* 29 (1997–8): 467–475.

Hernandez-Montiel v. INS. 225 F. 3rd 1084; 2000 U.S. App. LEXIS 21403; August 24, 2000 Cal. Daily Op. Service 7112.

Human Rights Watch. *No Escape: Male Rape in U.S. Prisons.* New York: Human Rights Watch, 2001. *Human Rights Watch Online.* 2001. http://www .hrw.org/reports/2001/prison/ (accessed June 2, 2005).

Human Rights Watch. *Owed Justice: Thai Women Trafficked into Debt Bondage in Japan.* New York: Human Rights Watch, 2000. *Human Rights Watch Online.* 2000. http://www.hrw.org/reports/2000/women/ (accessed June 6, 2005).

Hunter, Nan. "Life After Hardwick (1992)." *Sex Wars: Sexual Dissent and Political Culture.* Ed. Lisa Duggan and Nan Hunter. New York: Routledge, 1995. 85–100.

Ignatieff, Michael. "The Attack on Human Rights." *Foreign Affairs* 80 (2001): 102–116.

In re Acosta. 19 I. & N. Dec. 211, 232–33 (B.I.A. 1985).

In re Inaudi. No. T91-04459, Immigration and Refugee Board of Canada, April 9, 1992. (Indexed as N.[L.X.] [Re] Convention Refugee Determination Decisions [1992] C.R.D.D. No. 47 No. T91-04459, faxed copy of decision in file numbered by author pages 1–14).

In re Pitcherskaia. No. A72-143–932 (B.I.A. Nov. 13, 1995) (unpublished opinion).

In re Toboso-Alfonso. 20 I. & N Dec, 819, 820 –23 (BIA 1990).

International Lesbian and Gay Association (ILGA). "On-line Legal Survey." *International Lesbian and Gay Association Online.* http://www.ilga .info/Information/Legal_survey/ (accessed October, 2002).

International Human Rights Law Group. *Token Gestures: Women's Human Rights and UN Reporting.* New York: IHRLG, 1993.

Jenkins, Phillip. *Intimate Enemies: Moral Panics in Contemporary Great Britain.* New York: Aldine de Gruyter, 1992.

Kapur, Ratna. "The Tragedy of Victimization Rhetoric: Resurrecting the 'Native' Subject in International/Post-Colonial Feminist Legal Politics." *Harvard Human Rights Journal* 15 (2002): 1–38.

Lancaster, Roger. *Life is Hard: Machismo, Danger, and the Intimacy of Power in Nicaragua.* Berkeley: University of California Press, 1992.

Macklin, Audrey. "Refugee Women and the Imperative of Categories." *Human Rights Quarterly* 17 (1995): 213–277.

Major, Marie-France. "Sexual-Orientation Hate Propaganda: Time to Regroup." *Canadian Journal of Law & Society* 11 (1996): 221–240.

Malkki, Liisa H. *Purity and Exile: Violence, Memory, and National Cosmology Among Hutu Refugees in Tanzania.* Chicago: University of Chicago Press, 1995.

McClintock, Anne, Aamir Mufti, and Ella Shohat, eds. *Dangerous Liaisons: Gender, Nation, and Postcolonial Perspectives.* Minneapolis: University of Minnesota Press, 1997.

Meron, Theodor. "The Humanization of Humanitarian Law." *American Journal of International Law* 94 (2000): 239–278.

Miller, Alice M. "Human Rights and Sexuality: First Steps Toward Articulating a Rights Framework for Claims to Sexual Rights and Freedoms." *American Society of International Law Proceedings* 93 (2000): 288–303.

_____. "Las demandas por derechos sexuales [Sexual Rights: Evolution, De-volution and Revolution]." *Derechos Sexuales, Derechos Reproductivos, Derechos Humanos.* Ed. Roxana Vasquez Sotelo. Lima: CLADEM, 2002. 121–140.

_____. "Sexual but Not Reproductive: Exploring the Junction and Disjunction of Sexual and Reproductive Rights." *Health and Human Rights: An International Journal* 4.2 (2000): 68–109.

_____. "Uneasy Promises: Sexuality, Health, and Human Rights." *American Journal of Public Health* 91.6 (2001):861–864.

Mutua, Makua wa. "Human Rights International NGOs: A Critical Evaluation." *NGOs and Human Rights: Promise and Performance.* Ed. Claude E. Welch, Jr. Philadelphia: University of Pennsylvania Press, 2001. 151–166.

_____. "The Ideology of Human Rights." *Virginia Journal of International Law* 36 (1995–6): 589–658.

Morrison, John and Beth Crosland. "The Trafficking and Smuggling of Refugees: The End Game in European Asylum Policy?" Working Paper No. 39. *United Nations High Commissioner for Refugees (UNHCR) Online.* April 2001. http://www.unhcr.ch (accessed June 2, 2005).

Narayan, Uma. *Dislocating Cultures: Identities, Traditions, and Third World Feminism.* New York: Routledge, 1997.

Ordoñez, Juan Pablo. *Breaking the Silence: Human Rights Violations Based on Sexual Orientation.* New York: Amnesty International (AIUSA), February 1994.

_____. *No Human Being is Disposable: Social Cleansing, Human Rights, and Sexual Orientation in Colombia.* New York: International Gay and Lesbian Human Rights Commission (IGLHRC), 1994.

Otto, Diane. "Lesbians? Not in My Country: Sexual Orientation at the Beijing World Conference on Women." *Alternative Law Journal* 20 (1995): 288–290.

Parker, Richard, and Peter Aggleton, eds. *Culture, Society and Sexuality: A Reader.* London: UCL Press, 1999.

Parker, Richard. "'Within Four Walls': Brazilian Sexual Culture and HIV/ AIDS." *Culture, Society and Sexuality: A Reader.* Ed. Richard Parker and Peter Aggleton. London: UCL Press, 1999. 253–266.

_____. "Sexual Diversity, Cultural Analysis, and AIDS education in Brazil." *Culture, Society and Sexuality: A Reader.* Ed. Richard Parker and Peter Aggleton. London: UCL Press, 1999. 325–336.

Phillips, Oliver. "Constituting The Global Gay: Issues of Individual Subjectivity and Sexuality in Southern Africa." *Sexuality in the Legal Arena.* Ed. Carl F. Stychin and Didi Herman. London: Athlone Press, 2000. 17–34.

Pitcherskaia v. INS. 118 F.3d 641 (9th Cir. 1997).

Protocol relating to the Status of Refugees. 606 U.N.T.S. 267, opened for signature January 31, 1967.

Queer Resources Directory. "Queer Immigration: Countries that Accept Homosexuals are a Distinct Social Class." *Queer Resources Directory Online.* September 17, 1995. http://www.qrd.org/qrd/www/world/immigration/asylumc.html (accessed June 2, 2005).

Ramanathan, Erik. "Queer Cases: A Comparative Analysis of Global Sexual Orientation-Based Asylum Jurisprudence." *Georgetown Immigration Law Journal* 11.1 (1996): 1–44.

Regina v. Immigration Appeal Tribunal and Another, *ex parte* Shah (U.K. vs. Shaw). 2 All E.R. 545 (H.L.) (U.K.) 1999.

Richards, David A. J. "Sexual Preference as a Suspect (Religious) Classification: An Alternative Perspective on the Unconstitutionality of Anti-Lesbian/Gay Initiatives." *Ohio State Law Journal* 55.3 (1994): 491–554.

Robinson, Mary. Introductory Address. 56th session of the UN Commission on Human Rights, March 20, 2002.

Rosenbloom, Rachel. "Introduction." *Unspoken Rules: Sexual Orientation and Women's Human Rights.* Ed. Rachel Rosenbloom. New York: Cassell, 1996. ix–xxix.

Rosga, AnnJanette. "Ritual Killings: Anti-Gay Violence and Reasonable Justice." *States of Confinement: Policing, Detention & Prisons.* Ed. Joy James. New York: St.Martin's Press, 2000. 172–190.

Saiz, Ignacio. "Bracketing Sexuality: Human Rights and Sexual Orientation— A Decade of Development and Denial at the UN." *Health and Human Rights: An International Quarterly Journal* 7.2 (2004): 48–81.

Snitow, Ann. "Cautionary Tales." *Proceedings of the 93rd Annual Meeting of the*

American Society of International Law, March 24–27, 1999. Washington, D.C.: American Society of International Law, 1999.

Special Rapporteur of the Commission on Human Rights on Violence against Women, Its Causes and Consequences. "Cultural Practices in the Family that are Violent Towards Women." UN Doc E/CN.4/2002/83. 2002. *United Nations High Commissioner for Human Rights (UNHCHR) Online.* http://www.unhchr.ch/Huridocda.nsf/TestFrame/42e719fae543562c1256ba7004e963c?Opendocument (accessed June 2, 2005).

_____. "Violence Against Women in the Family." UN Doc E/CN.4/1999/68. 1999.

Thomas, Kendall. "Beyond the Privacy Principle." *Columbia Law Review* 92 (1992): 1431–1516.

Turner, Simon. "Angry Young Men in Camps: Gender, Age and Class Relations Among Burundian Refugees in Tanzania." Working Paper No.9. *United Nations High Commissioner for Refugees (UNHCR) Online.* June 1999. http://www.unhcr.ch (accessed June 2, 2005).

United Nations. Universal Declaration of Human Rights (UDHR). U.N.Doc A/810. January 10, 1948.

United Nations Commission on Human Rights. Resolution on Extrajudicial, Summary or Arbitrary Executions. UN Doc E/CN.4/RES/2000/31. April 20, 2000.

United Nations High Commissioner for Refugees. *Handbook on Procedures and Criteria for Determining Refugee Status under the 1951 Convention and the 1967 Protocol Relating to the Status of Refugees.* Rev.ed. Geneva: Office of the United Nations High Commissioner for Refugees, 1988.

_____. "Statistical Yearbook 2001: Refugees, Asylum-seekers and Other Persons of Concern—Trends in Displacement, Protection and Solutions." *United Nations High Commission for Refugees (UNHCR) Online.* October 2002. http://www.unhcr.ch/cgi-bin/texis/vtx/home/opendoc.pdf?tbl=STATISTICS&id=3dcb7dba2&page=statistics (accessed June 2, 2005).

_____. "Statistics." *Office of the United Nations High Commissioner for Refugees Online.* 2001–5. http://www.unhcr.ch/cgi-bin/texis/vtx/statistics (accessed October 4, 2002).

United Nations High Commissioner for Human Rights. "Systematic rape, Sexual Slavery and Slavery-like Practices During Armed Conflict, Including Internal Armed Conflict, Sub-Commission Resolution 1998/18." UN Doc E/CN.4/Sub.2/1998/13. Geneva: Office of the United Nations High Commissioner for Human Rights, 1996–2000. *Office of the United Nations High Commissioner for Human Rights Online.* 29th Meeting, August 21, 1998. http://www.ohchr.org/english/ (accessed June 2, 2005).

United States. Cong. Illegal Immigration Reform and Immigrant Responsibility Act of 1996 (IIRIRA). Pub. L. No. 104–208, 110 Stat. 3009. 1997. Washington: Government Printing Office.

_____. Refugee Act of 1980. Pub. L. No. 96–212, 94 Stat. 102(1980). Washington: Government Printing Office.

United States. Cong. House. Homeland Security Act of 2002. HR 5005. January 23, 2002. Washington: Government Printing Office.

_____. Trafficking Victim's Protection Act of 2001. HR 3244. Washington: Government Printing Office.

Valverde, Mariana. *Law's Dream of a Common Knowledge.* Princeton: Princeton University Press, 2003.

Vance, Carole S. "Anthropology Rediscovers Sexuality: A Theoretical Comment." *Social Science & Medicine* 33.8 (1991): 875–884.

_____. Address. "Opening Presentation: Dilemmas and Desires." Sexual Rites, Human Rights: Activists and Academics in Discussion. Harvard Law School, Cambridge, Mass., November 9–10, 2001.

Walker, Kristen. "The Importance of Being Out: Sexuality and Refugee Status." *Sydney Law Review* 18 (1996): 568–97.

_____. "Refugee Law and Sexuality." Unpublished essay, 2005.

Warner, Michael, ed. Fear of a Queer Planet: Queer Politics and Social Theory. Minneapolis: University of Minnesota Press, 1993.

Wei, Timothy, and Meg Satterthwaite, eds. "Shifting Grounds for Asylum: Female Genital Surgery and Sexual Orientation." *Columbia Human Rights Law Review* 29 (1997–8): 467–532.

Wheeler, Nicholas. "Humanitarian Vigilantes or Legal Entrepreneurs: Enforcing Human Rights in International Society." *Human Rights and Global Diversity.* Ed. Simon Caney and Peter Jones. London: Frank Cass Publishers, 2001. 139–162.

Wilets, James. "Conceptualizing Private Violence Against Sexual Minorities as Gendered Violence: An International and Comparative Law Perspective." *Albany Law Review* 60 (1996–7): 989–1050.

Wilson, Richard. "Human Rights, Culture and Context: An Introduction." *Human Rights, Culture & Context: Anthropological Perspectives.* Chicago: Pluto Press, 1997. 1–27.

Yoshino, Kenji. "Suspect Symbols: The Literary Argument for Heightened Scrutiny for Gays." *Columbia Law Review* 96 (1996): 1753–1834.

Notes

1 For more on the role of law as one of many social systems that contribute to the making of new sexual social identities, see Goodman. Also, see Halley ("Reasoning") and Foucault for arguments drawing upon and examining a long history of how law functions to make and enact norms, as well as individual sense of self.

2 As Carole S. Vance notably and frequently says, "common sense on sexuality is almost always wrong" (Vance, "Opening").

3 There is voluminous literature on this, but note especially Thomas, Goodman, and Halley ("Reasoning").

4 Closely related to this is how the inclusion of sexuality/sexual orientation/ transgender status, as one of the enumerated protected statuses under hate crimes legislation, functions to constitute someone as a full "citizen," able to call on the protective wing of the state (see Major). At the same time, because this literature essentially assumes an inherent gay identity (i.e., "a gay basher knows a fag when he sees one"), it often does not mount a critique, such as I am suggesting, directed at the way in which the template of who is identified as a dyke/fag/queer in the eye of the persecutor becomes a gay identity to be protected in the eyes of the law. Two exceptions in this field that I am aware of are AnnJanette Rosga and Lisa Crooms. Both authors also foreground the way that other factors—such as race, gender, and age—interconnect to render someone recognizably "gay" in both the eyes of the law and the persecutor.

5 The first time that a UN Commission on Human Rights resolution (adopted by a unanimous vote of all of the Commission's 53 participating countries) mentioned the term "sexual orientation" was in a condemnation of summary executions or arbitrary killings targeted at persons because of their sexual orientation (United Nations Commission on Human Rights, Resolution.)

6 For example, Kristen Walker has been tracking the extent to which Australian asylum decisions exclude persons claiming persecution on the basis of their *non*-heteronormative, heterosexual behavior, such as persons (men?) seeking asylum on the grounds of state persecution as adulterers ("Importance"). She demonstrates that in asylum work, asylum is denied when the decision-makers cannot/will not convert heterosexual sexual conduct—adulterous acts—into identity, absent additional factors, such as women facing execution or killing by family members. See *Regina v. Immigration Appeal Tribunal and Another, ex parte Shah* (hereinafter *U.K. v. Shah*). As Janet Halley has noted, the need/desire to convert homosexual conduct into identity in the U.S. political and legal context has allowed the subordination of gayness to heterosexuality through a complex of categories ("Politics"). More broadly, examinations of the asymmetrical but

connected dynamics of mapping one set of sexual acts onto one kind of identity reminds us of the need to see sexuality as a complex whole.

7   On lesbians, see Walker, "Importance," and S. Goldberg. On the lower number of women claimants and changes in the law required to accommodate them, see Otto, Anker, P. Goldberg and Kelly, and Macklin.

8   See, e.g., Andrew Drummon, "Flesh Market: More and more Thai women are being tricked into prostitution by global traffickers," *Bangkok Post,* May 23, 1999; "France bids adieu to 40 vice girls," *Bangkok Post,* April 7, 1999; and "Thai sex slaves working in SA," *Bangkok Post,* September 6, 1994, as cited in Human Rights Watch, *Owed Justice* n. 49. This discourse of women crossing borders arises in multiple forms. Examples include the contemporary phenomenon of the now-globalized V-Day campaigns (through which Eve Ensler's *The Vagina Monologues* is taken on tour internationally in the service of anti-"violence against women" campaigns). See also the UN Special Rapporteur's 2002 report on Violence against Women, in which she explores the deployment of violence to regulate cultural norms for women's sexual behavior, or the U.S. Congress's enactment of the "Trafficking Victim's Protection Act" of 2001 [H.R. 3244] (hereafter TVPA), which featured the sensationalized testimony of young "sex slaves" held in bondage, even though its reach also includes debt-bonded domestic workers and exploited sweatshop workers.

9   Key points of reference on this topic include Bhabha; Anker; Walker, "Importance"; and Ramanathan.

10 Without claiming that North and South have equivalent powers to enact their stereotyping discourses, Martin Chanock's cautionary work on the mutually reinforcing claims of orientalizing and occidentalizing bears paying close attention to. See also the work of Ratna Kapur on the discourse of "Hindutva" in India as an example of the ways that ostensibly anti-West discourses of nationalism exclude difference (e.g., Indian Muslims, non-conforming women of all identities), and Oliver Philips' analysis of the President of Zimbabwe's (Robert Mugabe) colonially inflected diatribe against LGBT Zimbabweans as "inauthentic Africans." The concerns of the mainstream human rights world are expressed by Mary Robinson, UN High Commissioner for Human Rights, in her introductory statement to the Commission on Human Rights' 56th session, in which she criticizes the United States for its abuse of human rights in the name of fighting terrorism and notes the extent to which other nations are selectively using the United States' demand for a "war against terrorism" as a cover to deny rights to political and social dissidents (Robinson).

11 *Confer,* for example, the Homeland Security Act of 2002. See also Amnesty International, *Backlash.*

12 For a more thorough description of the formal system of refugee law and

the United States' incomplete and inconsistent incorporation of its obligations under the Refugee Convention and its Protocol into domestic law through the Refugee Act of 1980 and amended by the Illegal Immigration Reform and Immigrant Responsibility Act of 1996 (IIRIRA), see Deborah Anker's chapter in this book. 1996 should be noted as a classic moment of gate-keeper, geo-political, ideologically inspired schizophrenia as the IIRIRA both broadened some grounds for asylum seeking—recognizing a coercive reproductive policy/practice as potential grounds—and narrowed other processes that make asylum a possibility, reducing the time during which one must claim asylum from three years to six months.

13 Convention Relating to the Status of Refugees, opened for signature July 28, 1951, 189 U.N.T.S. 150 (hereinafter the Refugee Convention).

14 Protocol relating to the Status of Refugees, opened for signature January 31, 1967, 606 U.N.T.S. 267 (hereinafter the Refugee Protocol).

15 The Organization of African Unity (now the African Union), where the vast majority of refugees are found, accepts as reasons for fleeing not only the traditionally accepted politicized persecutions, but also economic causes and "events seriously disturbing public order." Convention Governing the Specific Aspects of Refugee Problems in Africa, 1001 U.N.T.S. 45, entered into force June 20, 1974, article 1.

16 The United Nations High Commissioner for Refugees (UNHCR) is the entity charged with overseeing—but not explicitly monitoring—the implementation of the Refugee Convention and its Protocol. For a lively debate on the overall mission of the UNCHR, the dilution of its mission, and its dual mandate of securing protection and seeking "durable" solutions, coupled with its increasing role in providing temporary humanitarian services, see Darcy. For a gender-oriented evaluation of how this palliative system of relief operates, see Hathaway (also cited in Walker, "Importance").

17 For an interesting, accessible reflection on the potentials for changing, reinterpreting, and expanding the definition of a refugee, see Helton.

18 Arguing that asylum is less of a cultural imperialist system than other forms of international judging, Anker stresses that it is the agency of the dissenting asylee that triggers the moment of transnational judging (Anker 138–139, 145).

19 According to the UNHCR, asylum applications in North America and Europe numbered 104,456 and 466,587, respectively, in 2001; grants of asylum numbered 53,200 in North America and 138,100 in Europe during the same period (United Nations High Commissioner for Refugees, "Statistical Yearbook").

20 The UNHCR/Statistics presents information on host countries, including the nine main countries of resettled refugees for 2001. The list includes

the United States (68,400), Canada (12,200), Australia (6,500), Norway (1,300), Sweden (1,100), New Zealand (760), Finland (740), Netherlands (630), and Denmark (530). (See United Nations High Commissioner for Refugees, "Statistics").

21 The extensive literature on the over- and under-inclusive power of sodomy statutes to define U.S. gay identity is well canvassed by Halley ("Reasoning"), Goodman, Thomas, and Hunter.

22 An online report released by the American Civil Liberties Union ("Crime") notes that only four of those jurisdictions penalize only same sex behavior (Kansas, Missouri, Oklahoma and Texas); the others penalize a conduct possible between different or same gender persons, but as Halley ("Reasoning") and others have recounted, this conduct is still reduced in popular imagination to gay sex.

23 These terms are terms of art—they appear in these phrases in the Refugee Convention definition of a Refugee. (See Refugee Convention). As noted by S. Goldberg, Ramanathan, and others, it is possible to argue from "religion" and "political opinion"—some cases have incorporated elements of these approaches—but the predominantly successful approach has been in regard to "social group." This reflects at least two factors: first, *expedience*, as "social group" has been argued by some to be potentially a forward-looking catch-all notion (Helton) or, at a minimum, an intentionally elastic (but not infinitely elastic) category that can be expanded by analogy; second, *identity creation bias*, operating in the minds of both advocates and adjudicators (cf. a later section in this chapter, "Examining the Implications").

24 The United States BIA statement of this test in Matter of Acosta has been the most cited outside the United States, as well as being determinative in the United States. However, various jurisdictions vary on exactly what makes up 'immutability' in practice. *In re Acosta*, 19 I. & N. Dec. 211, 232–33 (B.I.A. 1985).

25 For an international context, see Walker, "Importance." For a United States context, see Richards.

26 Janet Halley's "Sexual Orientation and the Politics of Biology: A Critique of the Argument from Immutability," while aimed at U.S. Constitutionally-defined challenges, does an excellent job of picking through the import of claims from immutability-as-biology in ways that are doubly suggestive of transnational claims for immutability, requiring a recognition of both cross-cultural and migratory impacts on sexual practices and the identity-laden meaning given to them by some gay rights advocates.

27 See Goodman for an example of distinguishing and accepting the "bleeding in" or inter-constituting characteristics of United States constitutional categories.

28 During the drafting of the International Criminal Court (ICC)—another venue in which "persecution" is addressed as an evolving concept in the context of crimes against humanity—some commentators, notably Cherif Bassiouni, took the principled and progressive position that the list of enumerated groups whose persecution under which would be a crime against humanity should be open-ended. They cited the theory that whatever evil could be devised in the future should have a remedy (see United Nations, "Systematic Rape"). Note that the definitions that form the basis of persecution under the ICC's definition of crimes against humanity do include gender. However, the Vatican attempted to limit these definitions by adding language that indicated that they pertained only to men and women (by which they were trying to exclude sexual orientation), and this suggestion was then further modified by Canadian additions to suggest men and women in their roles in society. The final text includes both the Vatican and the Canadian phrases. The specific interrelation of the ICC and refugee law has yet to be played out. In contrast, the influence of gender- and sexuality-oriented litigation in human rights and asylum clearly had an effect on the way that crimes were conceptualized in Rome and in the definitions components of the ICC.

29 As a technical matter, United States asylum decision-making is a diffuse system of non-precedent-setting decisions at the widest base of the pyramid of asylum—at the level of the BIA (the second level of juridical decision, and first appeal, after the on-the-ground decision of the Immigration Judge)—followed by decisions at the federal court of appeals level (precedent for that circuit only, but influential throughout the other circuits), and then United States Supreme Court decisions (precedent throughout the system). By virtue of the Refugee Act of 1980, the Courts are meant to be applying the criteria of the *Refugee Handbook*, an authoritative guide issued by the UNHCR. However, United States asylum decision-makers at all levels appear to have remained obdurately parochial in their incorporation of, or reference to, the decision-making philosophy of other countries on how to give effect to the common standards of the handbook. A review of Australian, Canadian, New Zealand, and U.K. asylum decisions shows that while their courts are most definitely creating their own national jurisprudence, these courts often extensively catalogue the practices of other national courts. See, for example, *U.K. v. Shah*, (note 6 above), where the Law Lords consider in turn the ways of constituting a social group around women, violence, accusations of immorality, and a national system of gender inequality in the law from the United States, Canada, and Australia.

30 See Valverde for a contrary reading of the reach of law in the first instance of litigants.

31 See, for example, the excellent website in the United States from the Hastings College of Law Center for Gender and Refugee Studies (*Center*).

32 Equally vexing is that the decisions rendered at the first level are usually only one to two pages long, with almost no legal reasoning to give clues as to the basis of the decision (though if a case is appealed, the reasoning in the federal appeals courts is a matter of public record).

33 One relevant strategy of rights groups has been to focus on the dissemination of their reports to adjudicators. Rights groups have also sought to be invited to training for adjudicators at all levels (IJ, BIA, especially) on new formations of state accountability, such as the theories developed around non-state actor abuse, and, increasingly, persecution on sexuality.

34 *Hernandez-Montiel v. INS*, 225 F. 3rd 1084; 2000 U.S. App. LEXIS 21403; August 24, 2000 Cal. Daily Op. Service 7112 (hereinafter *Hernandez-Montiel*).

35 In this case, the important question of the role of the state in the persecution—such that the claimant is unable or unwilling to seek help from the state—is settled because of the fact that the police are implicated as persecutors directly. In the related but distinct line of cases where assaults, including sexual assaults, are carried out by non-state actors, such as family, spouse or intimate partner, or community members, the breakthrough issue in asylum law parallels developments in human rights law: under what conditions does the state become accountable (legally responsible) for abuses carried out by another? As human rights law built up its web of accountability for these crimes, asylum decision-makers also began to take cognizance of the states' failure to protect, particularly in relation to a discriminatory motive or impact: certain categories of persons could be assaulted with impunity. Here we see a point of dual overlap: first, in regard to concomitant developments in asylum and human rights law; and second, in the ways that gender- and sexuality-related claims (in both asylum and human rights) display intertwined needs for theories that re-configure the role of the state and private actors, and the state in private life. We need to account for this intertwining carefully, lest we slide too easily between gender and sexuality as inter-related, but not identical, regimes of control. For example, it is clear that potential violence patrols the borders of respectability for both women and men, as well as the borders between normative and non-normative behaviors. However, for many women of whatever sexual orientation or identity, the fact that their economic and social lives are rooted in family life means that the face and form of the violence will manifest differently than the community violence or police violence directed at gay men.

36 *In re Toboso-Alfonso*, 20 I. & N Dec, 819, 820 –23 (BIA 1990) (hereinafter *Toboso-Alfonso*).

37 Attorney General Order No. 1895 (June 19, 1994).

38 The claims by women that they will face assaults or extra-judicial killing

by family members—such as in the U.K. decision creating a social group for women from Pakistan who transgress social mores (the UNHCR category)—and that they cannot look for protection in their state or communities focus on the nature of the harm and the constitution of the group. They have *not* made the freedom to commit adultery or fornication a core part of the claim. See Walker, "Refugee."

39 In a recent talk, Gary Dowsett explored the concepts of situational identities or communities of interest to capture these groupings. See also Altman.

40 This voluntary association criterion made a powerful impact on me at the time of coordinating amicus briefs for AIUSA and the International Human Rights Law Group in the 1995 appeal of a Russian lesbian name Pitcherskaia. We turned somersaults to produce facts that would support her claim that she was a public and "associational"—i.e., that she had joined groups—lesbian. She got her grant of asylum, and the key issue that emerged with regard to the motivation of authorities in "curing her" did not shield a finding that the forced medical treatment still constituted persecution. See, *In re Pitcherskaia*, No. A72-143-932 (B.I.A. Nov. 13, 1995) (unpublished opinion) and *Pitcherskaia v. INS*, 118 F.3d 641 (9th Cir. 1997). At the time, I was struck by the strangeness of the proof problem and worried about lesbians and gay men who did not join groups.

41 Yet, while it remains vitally important to compare across different systems and moments of decision-making, some other obstructions remain. United States articles call for U.S. adjudicators to attend to the decision-making processes of other countries (comparative law) and of global standards (international law). But the flow of reliance on other countries' case law is asymmetrical: the United States seems to rely the least on other nations, even as its own decision-making is given much attention by other courts. See, for example, *U.K. v. Shah* and *Canada (A.G.) v. Ward* [1993] 2 S.C.R. 689. Both of these tremendously important cases that speak to the meaning of "particular social group" also give serious weight to debates and approaches in the United States, even as they fashion a response that becomes a U.K. or Canadian response. U.S. courts have not found this posture comfortable.

42 Of course, the American Association of Anthropologists has been debating anthropologists' relation to rights (as framed by debates over universal human rights claims as ineluctably imperialist, or in calls to use their access to two worlds to protect cultural rights, etc.) for almost 50 years, and I do not mean this brief vignette to claim any more import for these long-standing debates than as another contemporary intervention into them. See Wilson.

43 This reliance on human rights NGOs for information in asylum cases is one of the first ways that asylum and human rights intersect. As a voice

in the global demand for documentation by mainstream groups of previously invisible people or abuses as a way to force the formal human rights system to evolve, I repeat that documentation is driving theory and framework in regard to sexuality and human rights systems' response. See, for example, Wei and Satterththwaite. See also Ordoñez, *No Human Being* and *Breaking the Silence*. For an example of a way to affect asylum decision-makers' findings by affecting U.S. State Department reports, see, more recently, the memo on violations of the rights of gay, lesbian, bisexual and transgendered individuals in various countries worldwide submitted to the Department of States by IGLHRC and AIUSA, December 19, 2000 (on file with author).

44 *In re Inaudi*, No. T91-04459, Immigration and Refugee Board of Canada, April 9, 1992. (Indexed as N.[L.X.] [Re] Convention Refugee Determination Decisions [1992] C.R.D.D. No. 47 No. T91-04459, faxed copy of decision in file numbered by author pages 1–14).

45 In addition to linking the claimant's undeterred gay bar-going to his disbelief, the dissent also questioned whether it was believable that, being so harassed, the claimant would return again and again to the sites of abuse. The dissenting judge completed the circle of his ignorance by adding that the protection issue was further undermined by the claimant's failure to seek the intervention of the international or domestic human rights organizations which "operate freely in the country" (author numbered page 11). While the decision in chief attempted to deal with this issue quite matter-of-factly, invoking article 20 of the Universal Declaration of Human Rights (UDHR) on freedom of association to explain that it was the claimant's right to socialize, this passage also hints at the issue central to the third case I discuss here, which can be framed as: "should discretion in order to avoid harassment be uniquely required of gay claimants?"

46 The dissenting judge was drawing on a 1952 case, *Faryna v. Chorny*, 2 D.L.R. 354 (B.C.C.A.), now outmoded.

47 For an intriguing but ultimately incomplete attempt to use this frame of male violence/female subordination, see Human Rights Watch, *No Escape*.

48 Detention rape is covered by different regimes of law (national law, human rights law) than rape in war time (humanitarian law, some human rights law, now international criminal law), but faces similar documentation barriers. Yet, the rape of men in war time began to surface increasingly in reporting in the early 1990s, first called to my attention in the AI reports on the Iraqi invasion of Kuwait.

49 A 1997 case in the European Court of Human Rights denied the petition of a Colombian, self-confessed, ex-drug-trafficker-turned-informant, who claimed a fear of torture or execution by drug traffickers and sought to remain in France. Here, the Court noted that no documentation on the

extra-judicial killing of snitches by members of drug cartels was presented in the information by AI and HRW on Colombia (which did however, note the extent of the government's abuses, as well as its inability to protect its citizens generally from attacks by para-militaries connected to drug cartels). See *H.L.R. v. France* (Euro. Ct. Hum. Rts. 1997). HUDOC reference #REF00000628. The importance of this case for "gay cases" is the fact that a novel claim—the duty of a European state to protect a non-national from a non-political crime—failed, both in fact and on the basis of the legal theory of accountability, because of human rights NGO's limitations, in their mandates, to the traditionally political. This failure points again to the need to see coalitions of interest groups work together—groups that have a common *interest* in progressive interpretations of "the political," or of state accountability for non-state actors, but not a common *identity*.

50 Decision of Apr. 26, 1995, RRT no. BN93/01754 (Refugee Review Tribunal), available at www.austlii.edu.au (hereinafter Australian RRT Decision). I am indebted to Kristen Walker for bringing this case to my attention.

51 See Special Rapporteur of the Commission on Human Rights on Violence against Women, Its Causes and Consequences, "Violence Against Women," and "Cultural Practices."

52 Refugee/asylum structures in Australia, Canada, and the United States have adopted guidelines for adjudicators that address gendered differences in the nature of persecution and the formation of social groups. For Canada, see Canadian Immigration and Refugee Board Guidelines Issued by the Chairperson Pursuant to Section 65(3) of the Immigration Act: Women Refugee Claimants Fearing Gender-Related Persecution (March 9, 1993) and, subsequent revisions in Canadian Immigration and Refugee Board, Guideline 4: Women Refugee Claimants Fearing Gender-Related Persecution: Update (November 25, 1996) reproduced in Black, *Gender Asylum Law in Different Countries* 67. For Australia, see, Department of Immigration and Multicultural Affairs, *Refugee and Humanitarian Visa Applicants: Guidelines on Gender Issues for Decision Makers* (July 1996), also in *Gender Asylum Law in Different Countries*. For U.S., see also, Memorandum from Phyllis Coven, Immigration and Naturalization Service (INS) Office of International Affairs, to All INS Asylum Officers and HQASM Coordinators, Considerations for Asylum Officers Adjudicating Asylum Claims from Women (May 26, 1995), also reproduced in *Gender Asylum Law in Different Countries*.

53 Preliminary Report submitted by the Special Rapporteur on Violence Against Women, its Causes and Consequences, E/CN.4/1995/42. November 22, 1994.

54 See notes 7 and 8 above.

55 *Appellant S395/2002 v. Minister for Immigration and Multicultural Affairs* and *Appellant S396/2002 v. Minister for Immigration and Multicultural Affairs*, HCA 71, December 9, 2003.

56 Narayan also highlights the ways "in which issues emerge in various national contexts, and the contextual factors that shape the specific issues that are named and addressed, *affect the information that is readily available* for such connection-making and creating these claims and cross-border judgments" (emphasis in original, 86). Because asylum decision-making relies heavily on "information available across borders" this warning, particularly in reference to the racialized and gendered production of information on sexuality, bears heeding.

57 Jenkins is applying the insights of Becker to "moral panics" in his citation to Becker's work, but Becker's caution is also applicable to human rights struggles.

58 See, e.g., *Amnesty International LesbiGay Newsletter* (AIMLGC), "Canada Grants Refugee Status to Gay Man."

59 For an interesting account of the UDHR as the last cry of an appalled Europe looking at its horrors in the mirror, rather than a triumphant narrative of Western virtues, see Ignatieff.

60 However, the notion according to which racial difference is socially constructed through racisms, although a mainstay in critical race theory and Third World studies, has had very little effect on the formal world of anti-discrimination law internationally.

61 For a fascinating pairing of perspectives on the compatibility and incompatibility of human rights and asylum systems through the lens of gender-specific responses to women, see Anker and Bhabha. For another example of the domains that human rights is "colonizing" or expanding into, see Meron.

62 In regard to sexual orientation, see Wilets.

5

Intimate Conduct, Public Practice, and the Bounds of Citizenship: In the Wake of *Lawrence v. Texas*

Brad Epps

For Ashwini Sukthankar, my friend

"Freedom extends beyond spatial bounds." So declares Justice Anthony M. Kennedy in the principal opinion of the Supreme Court of the United States in *Lawrence v. Texas*, the landmark decision of June 2003 that overruled *Bowers v. Hardwick*, the 1986 ruling that had upheld the criminalization of same-sex sodomy. Amid divisive discussions of (homo)sexuality, tradition, morality, and the law, freedom continues to be a guiding principle, an ideal invoked by almost everyone, a hazy yet intense motive and objective. For Kennedy and the Justices who joined him (Stevens, Souter, Ginsburg, and Breyer, with O'Connor, concurring in judgment), freedom's "spatial and more transcendent dimensions" are linked to "an autonomy of self" and bear on "thought, belief, expression, and certain intimate conduct" (1). Yet if freedom in its more transcendent dimensions extends beyond spatial bounds, it certainly does not erase them or set them at naught. Asserting that "[i]n our tradition the State is not omnipresent in the home" (1), the Court presents the home as a privileged site of freedom, but one that is clearly not beyond the State—the State is not *omni*present in the home; freedom obtains only for *certain* intimate conduct. Despite Kennedy's sweeping reference to freedom, his rhetoric, endorsed by the major-ity of the Justices, here reaffirms spatial bounds in intricate ways that dovetail, interestingly enough, both Justice Antonin Scalia's lengthy and impassioned dissent (joined by Chief Justice William Rehnquist and Clarence Thomas) and Justice Thomas's short supplemental dis-sent. The bounds are necessary, after all, to the maintenance of the very notion of private domains, most notably the home, and public domains, but they are also necessary, and quite fundamentally so, to the maintenance of national, foreign, and international domains as well. In what follows, I will be bringing to bear the interplays of space, freedom, and sexuality, articulated in a domestic legal document of the highest order, on something seemingly far afield: immigration. Writing from outside the legal profession, I will be pushing not only at the tendency to leave legal matters to legal experts but also, and no less importantly, at the tendency to see immigration as significant only in those cases that explicitly cite immigration. I will be doing so, moreover, by way of an interrogation of the spatial and transcendent—or physical and metaphysical—dimensions of freedom, the ways in which a claim about sexuality implicates a complex history of immigration, border controls, and international politics.

The hegemony of the United States in matters global clearly does not spell the extension of freedom beyond spatial bounds. Even as the United States extends—and overextends—itself throughout the world, even as it uses "freedom" as the envelope in which it would tuck away its economic and military interests, it braces its borders and reinforces its controls on the migrations and movements of people, things, and ideas. *Lawrence v. Texas*, with its unbounded definition of freedom, explicitly arises in relation to *Bowers v. Hardwick* and other sexually and morally charged cases of a strongly domestic tenor, most notably *Roe v. Wade*. But it also arises in the wake of the cataclysmic events of September 11, 2001 and in the midst of wars that have arguably only heightened worries about immigration, movement, and assembly. The Court's decision is rendered, that is, at a time when civil liberties, including the much-debated right of privacy,[1] have come under attack and when the rules, rights, and responsibilities of citizenship have acquired renewed urgency.[2] These contextual considerations, by which *Lawrence* is set in play with issues that have little if anything ostensibly to do with sexuality, are not proffered lightly, for they go against the anti-contextual and anti-historicist rhetoric of roots, foundations, and origins that characterizes Scalia's dissent to *Lawrence* and conservative legal discourse in general. Less directly, though no less importantly, they also go against the delimited sense of an "emerging awareness" of adult sexual autonomy that marks the principal, liberal decision—delimited because Kennedy qualifies legally protected sexuality not just as "adult" but also as "enduring" and "private" and pays no heed to how a proclamation about freedom extending beyond spatial bounds extends, or not, to transnational movement and immigration. The lack of reference to such other challenges to the spatial and transcendent dimensions of freedom and personal liberty as "terrorism" and the "war on terrorism" thus ensures, somewhat paradoxically, that Scalia's literal-minded foundationalism or "originalism"—the original letter of the law *is* the law—retains a significance that is not dismantled by the majority decision. In other words, the majority decision relies on an implicit delimitation that while certainly not equivalent to Scalia's is nonetheless consistent with established legal specializations and with well-entrenched notions that more extensive and complex contextual-izations are unwieldy or even counterproductive.

Arguing for the importance of more complex if potentially un-wieldy contextualizations (unwieldy precisely *because* emerging and hence subject to speculation), I will first examine the dissents to *Lawrence* and its extensive, emerging, "spatial and more transcendent" conceptualization of freedom and then move to a consideration of the (enduring, personal, private) limits of the majority decision. In the process, I will be sounding out the significance of the "emerging awareness" or coming into consciousness that is critical—dare I say fundamental—to a progressive historical understanding of freedom and justice. When Scalia impugns the majority claim that recent legal decisions reveal "an emerging awareness that liberty gives substantial protection to adult persons in deciding how to conduct their private lives in matters pertaining to sex" (*Lawrence* 11; quoted, Scalia dissent 13), he effectively contests the mutability, and hence the historicity, of constitutional law[3]—the very historicity that the majority Court at once deploys and disables by not acknowledging the implications that a spatially transcendent notion of domestic freedom may have for transnational movement and immigration, especially at a time of war and of a "new" preemptive kind of war at that. Evincing what might be designated as a fixation on form, Scalia, as already noted, attempts to dismiss any reading that goes "beyond" the explicit letter of the law. "Constitutional entitlements [such as a right of privacy or, more point-edly, a right to consensual, private homosexual sodomy] do not spring into existence because some States choose to lessen or eliminate crimi-nal sanctions on certain behavior" (*Lawrence* Scalia dissent 14), Scalia asserts. "Much less," he goes on, "do they spring into existence, as the Court seems to believe, because *foreign nations* decriminalize conduct" (*Lawrence* Scalia dissent 14, emphasis original). With the Constitution and the Bill of Rights conveniently exempt from the suspicion that ap-parently accompanies any formation that "springs into existence" or that "emerges into awareness," Scalia takes pains to deny the legitimacy of historical contextualizations and geopolitical comparisons. After all, comparisons and contextualizations threaten to relativize temporal and spatial coordinates, exposing the here and now as, well, the here and now, and opening them up to something *other* than a foundationally secure and formally engraved national tradition.

For Scalia, the Court's recognition of "foreign views" is not only "meaningless" but also "dangerous" (*Lawrence* Scalia dissent 14), a veritable affront to the integrity and independence of the United States. Emphasizing the relation between his dissent in *Lawrence* and his support of the earlier *Bowers* decision, Scalia declares: "[t]he *Bowers* majority opinion *never* relied on 'values we share with a wider civilization'" (*Lawrence* dissent 14, emphasis original). In the process, he cites a note to *Foster v. Florida* to reassert that the Court "'should not impose foreign moods, fads, or fashions on Americans'" (*Lawrence* Scalia dissent, quoted 14; *Foster* Thomas concurring 1).[4] Under Scalia's pen, the decriminalization of (homosexual) sodomy is a foreign fad, but its criminalization is the sign of national tradition itself. But as Scalia notes, even as the Court cites an "emerging awareness" of private sexual liberty that would seem to emerge from abroad, it ignores "the many countries that have retained criminal prohibitions on sodomy" (*Lawrence* Scalia dissent 14). The many countries that have retained prohibitions are indeed *not* the countries with which the Court has explicitly aligned itself, and so Scalia is right, technically speaking, when he says that the *Bowers* Court never relied on "values we share with a *wider* civilization" (my emphasis). He is right, that is, if "wider" is understood in an absolute sense as "unbounded," as civilization *in general*. For while the *Bowers* Court may not have relied on the values of an absolutely wider civilization, it certainly did rely on the values of a wider *Western* civilization. Chief Justice Burger, concurring with the majority opinion in *Bowers*, is in fact *explicit* about the reliance on Western protocols: "[d]ecisions of individuals relating to homosexual conduct have been subject to state intervention throughout the history of Western civilization. Condemnation of those practices is firmly rooted in Judeao-Christian moral and ethical standards" (*Bowers* Burger concurring 1).

The "wider civilization" on which the Court most definitely does rely in *Bowers* is delimited to the West and, more precisely, to the so-called Judeo-Christian tradition that is hegemonic in the West. As Janet Jakobsen and Ann Pellegrini note, the Judeo-Christian tradition that

Burger adduces ignores tensions between Judaism and Christianity, let alone within Judaism and Christianity, and promotes an *image* of a religious pluralism that is not realized in legal and political practice and that is decidedly more Christian than anything else (31). Pluralism is apparently more easily asserted than practiced, for alternative moral and ethical standards—which Scalia understands in exclusively religious terms—do not figure at all, even if, as with indigenous traditions, they preceded the founding of the United States. And if alternative traditions might count, as in Scalia's vague reference to the Court ignoring the "many countries" that have retained criminal prohibitions on sodomy, it seems to be because they have *not* undergone, or at least not to the same degree, the transformations—most notably, the processes of secularization—that mark, albeit unevenly, Western and Christian traditions in their colonial and neo-colonial march across the globe. In some sense, when it comes to homosexuality, Yemen, not the Netherlands, would appear to be the standard-bearer of the "deeply rooted" moral values that Scalia so zealously champions. But the values of Yemen, deeply rooted though they may be, are obviously not "Judeo-Christian" or Western. Little wonder, then, that Scalia would prefer that *no* foreign nation be invoked, for to do otherwise would be to recognize that the United States is in a circuit that is *neither* absolutely wider *nor* Western.[5] Such contradictions are, however, fairly common fare in the United States. On the one hand conservative Justices, politicians, preachers, and pundits invoke Western civilization and "Judeo-Christian" moral tradition, and on the other hand they disregard or even demonize changes within them as so many fads and fashions, as passing trends, as alien intrusions and foreign perversions. At odds with the passage of time, they also tend to be at odds with the passage of people, the openness of space; they tend to reify the United States as a nation unto itself, one whose freedom requires that it be free from foreign influence—but whose "exemplary influence" on foreign countries they all but take for granted. Clearly, however, "Judeo-Christian" standards, despite their non-American provenance, do not signify as foreign for the conservative Justices, who naturalize the history of the United States as always already "American" and "Judeo-Christian" and who discount, in the process, the history of the nation as largely one of immigrants and conquered peoples.

Yet the ties of the United States to other nations, even when cast as fads and fashions, cannot be denied. Within both *Lawrence* and *Bowers*, focused as they are on a *domestic* issue (sexual relations between

consenting adult citizens of the same sex in the privacy of the home),
something *global* at play, something that implicates the complex phenomenon of immigration and that complicates, in turn, the significance
of an apparently simple if high-sounding utterance such as "freedom
extends beyond spatial bounds." The bounds, and the freedom that
purportedly extends beyond them, are not only those of the home but
also those of the nation. After all, the concept of freedom as extending
beyond—but also *from*—the United States is central to political justifications of any number of U.S. military and economic interventions the
world over. One of the things that *Lawrence* does is bring out, if you
will, the sexual stakes of the bounds and extensions of freedom. After
all, the sexual acts and identities at the center of this and other decisions propel debates not merely on domestic morality, but also, and no
less crucially, on privacy, individual autonomy, equal protection, due
process,[6] *stare decisis,*[7] political participation, states' rights, national
tradition, change, freedom, and, yes, citizenship and immigration.
Time-sensitive in their very appeals to timelessness, *Lawrence, Bowers*, and other legal cases that involve questions of gender and sexuality—*Griswold v. Connecticut* and *Roe v. Wade* chief among them—are
also spatially fraught, gesturing to other places, practices, acts, and
identities. In *Lawrence*, the international dimension of domestic law
comes to the fore in an especially incisive way.[8] Among the many cases
cited in the majority decision of *Lawrence v. Texas* as evidence that the
Bowers decision did not adequately evince an "emerging awareness"
or "emerging recognition" of adult consensual sexuality as a protected
liberty, several fall outside the jurisdiction of the United States, though
not, as already noted, outside the West. The Court adduces decisions
by the British Parliament (specifically the enactment in 1967 of the
recommendations made ten years earlier by the Wolfenden Report on
Homosexual Offenses and Prostitution) and by the European Court of
Human Rights in order to substantiate its correction of Justices White's
and Burger's claims that homosexuality, metonymically linked to sodomy, is incompatible with Western civilization. Enlarging its citational
field to include decisions from a wider, if still delimited, "Western civilization" (the Council of Europe, it notes, is now comprised of 45 nations; *Lawrence* 12), the *Lawrence* Court legitimizes homosexuality, in
part, and as Scalia complains, by internationalizing it.

   The requirement—adumbrated in the early 20th century, strengthened in the mid-20th century, and in force at least until 1990—that
foreigners seeking naturalization as U.S. citizens had to be heterosex-

ual⁹ (of which more, later) stands in contrast with *Lawrence*, which determines, partially by reference to foreign laws, that homosexual U.S. citizens have the same "right to liberty under the Due Process Clause" (*Lawrence* 18) as their heterosexual compatriots. There can be little doubt that "homosexuals," as a legally articulated group, and "homosexuality," as a legally articulated category, have fared better over the past decades, and that *Lawrence* constitutes an important advance, but the point that I want to make for the moment is the following: whether prohibited or protected, homosexuality has been construed as a "problem" and has functioned in the United States legal system in a manner that has implicated other states, other nations, other cultures and traditions. If the international dimension of sexuality, and of homosexuality in particular, is effectively recognized in legal cases affecting citizens (*Bowers, Lawrence*), it is also at play in widely disseminated images of popular culture, transnational capital flows, and the growth and consolidation of gay, lesbian, bisexual, transgendered, and queer organizations, all of which are most powerfully generated in the West and, within it, the United States, and all of which further complicate the question of freedom's bounds and boundlessness.

Foreign legal decisions, though still Western, may have a limited if significant impact on domestic legal decisions in the United States (*Lawrence* is not, on this score, exceptional). However, the impact that a powerful culture industry made in the U.S.A., and made elsewhere under its stamp, has on the rest of the world is indisputable—no matter how that impact is interpreted. Among the masses of people who immigrate to the United States, many come trailing notions of freedom that do seem almost boundless and that feed all sorts of hopes, dreams, and fantasies of fulfillment. In fact, for some, the spatial bounds beyond which freedom extends are none other than those of their home countries (and their homes in their home countries), cast by comparison as "unfree."¹⁰ Put more directly, non-U.S. citizens may find themselves interpellated by the claim that freedom extends beyond spatial bounds and some, heeding the call, may then turn to the United States as if it were the very center of freedom itself: such, at least, is the upshot of a persistent, self-congratulatory rhetoric in which the United States would function as a beacon or source of freedom. The images and rhetoric of freedom are thus not beyond or beside matters of sex; as such, they appeal to many so-called sexual dissidents and, less dramatically, to many who do not fit or do not believe that they fit within the cultural, moral, and/or legal parameters of their countries of origin. Then again, it is now also the case that some people who are in no way "sexual dissidents" and who actually may "fit" or "pass" (usually by way of a limited roster of identities) within the sexual parameters of their own countries, have to argue otherwise upon arriving to the United States, claiming, for instance, that their immigration—recast as asylum—is motivated by a fear of sexual persecution and *not*, as is more common, by a desire for better economic and sexual opportunities.

The impact of the law on the constitution of human subjects and their desires is as undeniable as it is multifarious. While it is certainly true, as cultural critic Lauren Berlant insists, that "legal subjectivity" cannot account for "subjectivity in general" and that "radical counterpolitics needs to contend with notions of personhood and power that do not attain the clarity of state and juridical taxonomy" (125), it is also true that legal subjectivity—which does not always attain the clarity that Berlant suggests—often functions *as if it were* subjectivity in general, particularly for any non-U.S. citizen who, heeding the call of freedom, prosperity, safety, happiness, and opportunity (especially important for those who immigrate in order to be with a loved one), seeks to enter the United States and to stay there and who, in so doing, must fashion him or herself to "fit" or "pass" within established U.S. parameters. The force of legal subjectivity, its ability to implicate and to interpellate, to command and to constrain, relies, however, on a powerful disavowal of its incompleteness (the very incompleteness that keeps it from being subjectivity in general) and, moreover, of its spatial and temporal particulars, its *boundedness*. Scalia's impatience with foreign citations, his repudiation of legal and moral similarities amid geopolitical differences, is of a piece with a bounded, particularist, and eminently nationalist understanding of freedom in which freedom is always and only freedom for some. But Scalia's spatially bounded notion of freedom relies, as I have been arguing, on a commanding elision of history in which time is paradoxically unbound, cast in the mode of an "always already" at odds with *processes* that are understood in terms of an emerging awareness. Again, Scalia does not lack company. As legal scholar Janet Halley observes with respect to *Bowers*, "[i]n his fundamental rights analysis, Justice White (cheered on by Chief Justice Burger) exploited the rhetoric of acts [as opposed to time-sensitive identities] to make plausible his claim that sodomy has been transhistorically and without surcease the object of intense social disapprobation" (1747).[11] Scalia's reiterated defense in *Lawrence* of a nationally specific, spatially bound history of "deeply rooted" traditions in which homosexual sodomy would have *no place that is not criminal and abject* is thus also a defense of transhistoricism, a denial of history in the name of a morality in which timeless acts, promptly spun into timeless identities, signify what they have supposedly always signified.

But time, even amid timelessness, will have its day. Halley, writing in 1993, anticipates with uncanny precision the Court's statement, in 2003, that "the historical grounds relied upon in *Bowers* are more complex than the majority opinion and the concurring opinion by Chief Justice Burger indicate. Their historical premises are not without doubt and, at the very least, are overstated" (*Lawrence* 10). The Justices of the principal opinion of *Lawrence* determine—by way of scholarly works by Jonathan Ned Katz, John D'Emilio, and Estelle Freedman—that the Justices of *Bowers* ignored or forgot that, "far from possessing 'ancient roots,' American laws targeting same-sex couples did not develop until the last third of the 20th century" (*Lawrence* 9). Undeterred, Scalia dismisses the basically modern formation of "homosexuality" (the term does not arise until the late 19th century) and claims that what really matters is that "our Nation has a longstanding history of laws prohibiting *sodomy in general*—regardless of whether it was performed by same-sex or opposite-sex couples" (*Lawrence* Scalia dissent 11, emphasis original). The dismissal is disingenuous, because even as Scalia marshals forth laws from the original thirteen states and from 1868, when the Fourteenth Amendment was ratified, he does *not* entertain the implications of upholding prohibitions of sodomy *in general* (which implicates subjectivity in general as reducible to legal subjectivity). To do so, after all, would mean taking on a heterosexual majority that, whatever its views of a non-heterosexual minority, would not take lightly—and would certainly not ratify by popular referendum or "normal democratic means" (*Lawrence* Scalia dissent 19)—the prohibition of non-procreative sexual behavior, the originary justification, again *in general*, for anti-sodomy laws. It is critical to Scalia's rejection of sodomy, however, that it not be understood as a *general* affront to procreation but, ever so implicitly, as an affront to the anus, and the male anus in particular.

As William Rubenstein notes, although every state in the Union had a sodomy law in 1961, the popular misunderstanding of sodomy as designating primarily—if not exclusively—anal intercourse among men (with sex among women enduring as a sort of splintered juridical afterthought) has ensured that sodomy laws criminalize "not merely homosexual acts but lesbians and gay men themselves" (xxi), that the prohibitions of sodomy *in general* have a *particularly* heavy significance for gay men and, much more implicitly, lesbians. The fact that the sodomitic act in question in *Bowers v. Hardwick* was *not* anal but oral (i.e., fellatio) is, however, a particular with which the Court does not tarry.[12] Generality and neutrality function, therefore, as lures in Scalia's argument: hierarchical conceptions of particular identities (and more unclearly, particular acts, practices or behaviors) remain intensely in place, severing one person from another and ratcheting up the divisions on which gender, sexuality, and nationality hinge. Halley, for her part, offers a reading that is similar to, though subtler than, Rubenstein's. Addressing applications of *Bowers v. Hardwick* on the state level, she writes: "the case is construed to authorize state decision makers to demote gay men, lesbians, and bisexuals socially, and to exclude them from certain public debates, on the grounds that their identity alone gives rise to an irrebuttable presumption that they have committed criminalizable sodomy, and that this inferred conduct [or act] is, in turn, the essential defining feature of their identity" (1736). The reduction of sodomy to (male) same-sex sexual contacts and, in virtually the same sweep, to (male) homosexual identity *per se*, casts an arguably diffuse and scattered throng of people into a presumably discrete and identifiable group. Gathered up in and as a group, homosexuals are functionally separated from their national compatriots whose heterosexuality does not signify *as* sexuality but functions as the unassailable basis of rational jurisprudence *per se*.

In other words, homosexuals were—and despite *Lawrence* in many ways still are—saddled with a stigma that marks them as quasi-criminals and hence as quasi-citizens, as people who, by dint of their desires, their acts, and their identities, do not fully enjoy the rights and privileges of citizenship. Significantly, Justice O'Connor, though not explicitly broaching the subject of citizenship, offers an argument that runs in a similar direction: "the effect of Texas' sodomy law is not just limited to the threat of prosecution or the consequence of conviction. Texas' sodomy law brands all homosexuals as criminals, thereby making it difficult for homosexuals to be treated in the same manner as everyone else" (*Lawrence* concurring in judgment 4). The "everyone else" is, it almost goes without saying, everyone else that is a U.S. citizen. Scalia, not persuaded by either substantive due process or equal protection arguments,[13] does his best to argue for the maintenance of criminality and hence for less than full citizenship. To that end, he deploys identity and act, "homosexual" and "men [who] can violate the law only with other men, and women only with other women" (*Lawrence* Scalia dissent 15), even "principal actor" and "partner," in ways that mime, however unwittingly or parodically, the distinctions used by some of the most sophisticated scholars of gender and sexuality. He does so, it must be said, in a rather perplexing way that nonetheless leaves some things crystal clear: homosexuality, homosexuals, and same-sex acts, actors, and partners are not acceptable in a traditional, religious-based national morality, which Scalia presents, against all reason, as the very basis of rational-basis critique.[14]

For Antonin Scalia, the *Lawrence* decision is momentous. It "la[ys] waste the foundations of our rational-basis jurisprudence" (*Lawrence* Scalia dissent 20). It "effectively decrees the end of all morals legislation" (*Lawrence* Scalia dissent 15). And it "dismantles the structure of constitutional law that has permitted a distinction to be made between heterosexual and homosexual unions, insofar as formal recognition of marriage is concerned" (*Lawrence* Scalia dissent 20–21). Against a Court that "coos"—the term is Scalia's—that "[w]hen sexuality finds overt expression in intimate conduct with another person, the conduct can be but one element in a personal bond that is more enduring" (*Lawrence* 6; quoted, Scalia dissent 21), Scalia retorts with an apocalyptic ponderousness worthy of an Old Testament prophet.[15] The decriminalization of homosexual sodomy calls into question, in Scalia's reading, "laws against bigamy, same-sex marriage, adult incest, prostitution, masturbation, fornication, bestiality, and obscenity" (*Lawrence* dissent 5) as well as "child pornography" (*Lawrence* Scalia dissent 13); it augurs a world without rhyme or reason in which inversion reigns supreme and fear runs rampant: fear of a "judicial imposition of homosexual marriage" (*Lawrence* Scalia dissent 20) and of the Court's inability to put the gay genie back in the bottle once set free.[16]

The idea that there is a slippery slope of immorality is fundamental to Scalia's dissent, a dissent by which he can play the part of the embattled hero of popular, traditional, time-tested (or rather time-proof) American reason. Scalia plays the part with conviction, crying foul in what he presents as a veritable juridical wasteland in which legal professionals, in bed with the queers, are out of step with a "democratic majority" (*Lawrence* Scalia dissent 19) that does not see freedom as extending beyond spatial bounds but rather as its majoritarian province and privilege. In fact, ridiculing the majority Court's claim that lack of enforcement of anti-sodomy laws is a sign of their out-datedness,

Scalia indicates that the problem is one of surveillance and the availability of evidence. "Surely that lack of evidence," he argues, "would not sustain the proposition that consensual sodomy on private premises with the doors closed and windows covered was regarded as a 'fundamental right,' even though all other consensual sodomy was criminalized" (*Lawrence* Scalia dissent 13). Against the image of a spatially unbounded freedom whose generative source is the home and the autonomous, privacy-loving individual (what Katherine Franke calls "domestinormative sexual citizenship," 1416), Scalia imagines a home so hermetically contained as to be a virtual prison, but one which, for that very reason, motivates a fantasy of governmental intrusion and surveillance, the means by which "evidence" of criminal conduct would no longer be lacking and a "deeply rooted" moral tradition would be reaffirmed.

Morality, Security, and Cultural Citizenship (On Perverts and Terrorists)

Yet *Lawrence*, with all of its spatial and temporal implications, is not only about sexual morality, national tradition, foreign "fads," and the tensions between democratic participation and judicial decisions.[17] As I have been arguing, *Lawrence* does not arise in a vacuum but within the context of beleaguered civil liberties, smarmy reconsiderations of the Geneva Conventions as quaint and out-dated (especially ironic inasmuch as torture constitutes grounds for asylum), and increased governmental intrusion in the "private sector" under the USA PATRIOT Act.[18] Within this context, Clarence Thomas's terse two-paragraph dissent, which follows Scalia's, rings in some intriguing ways. Thomas, unlike the other Justices, does not appeal to freedom, whatever its purview, let alone to fashions, fads or an "emerging awareness" in tension with "deep roots." Instead, he appeals to a principle of fiscal responsibility, an economic bottom line: "[p]unishing someone for expressing his sexual preference with another adult does not appear to be a worthy way to expend valuable law enforcement resources" (*Lawrence* Thomas dissent 1). In a vague, overdetermined way, Thomas intimates not that the government should not expend its resources to intrude into the home, and into the bedroom, but that it should not be doing so with an eye to (homo)sexual activity. Sodomy laws in themselves do not seem to be, in fact, the real issue; citing *Griswold v. Connecticut*, the 1965 case that legalized birth control for married people (unmarried couples were extended the same rights in 1972 in *Eisenstadt v. Baird*), Thomas calls the Texas law "'uncommonly silly'" (*Lawrence* Thomas dissent 1).[19] Going even further, Thomas, the Supreme Court Justice, imagines himself a state legislator and declares: "[i]f I were a member of the Texas Legislature, I would vote to repeal [the law before the Court]" (*Lawrence* Thomas dissent 1). Acknowledging that he is not a legislator, and hence that his legislative imagination has juridical limits, Thomas cites his duty to the Constitution and to the laws of the United States and then gives his reasons for refusing to join the majority and to overturn *Bowers*. In Thomas's words: "just like justice Stewart," whose dissent in *Griswold* Thomas approvingly quotes, "I 'can find [neither in the Bill of Rights nor any other part of the Constitution a] general right of privacy' . . . or as the Court terms it today, the 'liberty of the person both in its spatial and more transcendent dimensions'" (*Lawrence* Thomas dissent 1). Questioning both a right of privacy and a spatially transcendent conception of freedom (both of which play a critical role in the Court's reversal of *Bowers*), while referring to worthy and unworthy expenditures, Thomas leaves the door open for governmental intrusions of an apparently more serious—not "silly"—sort. Like Scalia, Thomas dissents, but he supplements and shifts Scalia's dissent to acknowledge, albeit ever so subtly, a problem *other* than sex and morality.

The presence of the State in the home, after *Lawrence* and after 9/11, may be less a question of "the government's interest in promoting morality" (*Lawrence*, O'Connor, concurring in judgment, 4) than in the government's interest in promoting security. Needless to say, the interest in promoting national security is by no means new, nor for that matter is the critique of a right of privacy, but they are both reinvigorated, and extraordinarily so, in the context of a U.S.-dictated war on terrorism. Put somewhat sensationally (but war, in an age of embedded, live-action, round-the-clock reporting can be tremendously sensational), the terrorist comes to the fore as the pervert recedes. Or perhaps more precisely, the terrorist comes to the fore as the newest, most lethal pervert imaginable, one whose "agenda" goes far beyond an expansive refiguration of marriage and morals legislation and dares to touch the face of God. The apocalyptic scenario that Scalia devises, with the foundations of rational-basis jurisprudence laid waste, pales in comparison with apocalyptic scenarios of a more devastatingly material—and symbolic—type. Dirty bombs would seem to trump dirty sex, especially as the United States turns a queer eye to straight guys and sex fades in the frills and folds and shiny surfaces of consumer goods, the most common materializations of freedom in a capitalist regime. Desexed for the commercialized titillation of the prime-time viewing public, these queer subjects' concerns with privacy take the path of a full-fledged investment in private property. Such, at least, is what a current image, custom-made for the global market, would have "the public at large" and the "queer community" see—and what it would have the "public at large" see *as* the "queer community": the queer as a delightfully assimilable creature, one who may not uphold *all* of the values of traditional morality but who certainly upholds the values of consumer capitalism. Taking a place of pride in a reconstituted, more "tolerant" public at large, this newly assimilated homosexual would have no need for political protest or for solidarity with immigrants or anyone else, only for increased protection *from* those who would destroy a newly expansive, though also newly retracted, way of life. When set against the violent extremist, the religious (read: Islamic) fanatic, and the envious, invidious alien bent on the destruction of freedom itself, the erstwhile pervert, corrupter of minors, sexual deviant or queer is naturalized, domesticated, and even celebrated—to a point.

For even if dirty bombs would seem to trump dirty sex, the so-called culture wars (abortion, gay marriage, euthanasia, stem-cell research, "intelligent design" vs. evolutionism, multiculturalism, etc.) have hardly been resolved and indeed, under the administration of George W. Bush, have acquired a particularly bitter force. However much homosexuals—recast as gays and lesbians, and recast further as queers (a more ample and elusive category that does not figure in *Lawrence*)— have *emerged* as "good" capitalist consumers and as "good" citizens, the shadow of evil still holds. Simply put, the pervert and the terrorist do not function always as mutually exclusive categories—far from it. Sensationalist depictions of Mohammed Atta and his 9/11 associates as a band of rabid, radical, hypocritical homosexuals (hypocritical because of Islam's sexual proscriptions) recall sensationalist depictions of homosexuals as Cold War traitors in waiting, as perpetually potential perpetrators of what Guillermo Cabrera Infante has called a crime of "*lèse* authority" (415).[20] They also recall—and it is here that I begin to flesh out more fully the matter of immigration—any number of notes, directives, policies, and laws that have flecked the history of citizenship and immigration in the United States.

Although it does not seem to have been explicitly named (appearing only in congressional reports and whatnot), homosexuality, perceived as a threat to national morality *and* security, was unmistakably couched in such phrases and categories as "constitutional psychopathic inferiority" (1917), later amended to "psychopathic personality" (1952) and "sexual deviation" (1965), that have marked the language of immigration.[21] According to immigration lawyer Robert Foss, "[homosexuality] was not included under the 'moral exclusions' like prostitution, but rather among the medical exclusions" (446), but according to Jin S. Park, who cites amendments to the Immigration and Nationality Act of 1965, "Congress further clarified its intent to exclude homosexuals by adding 'sexual deviation'" to the list of grounds for exclusion (1118–1119). There can be little doubt that "deviation" carries a negative moral charge and hence that even so-called "medical exclusions" can be shot through with moral judgments. William N. Eskridge, Jr. and Nan D. Hunter pay well-deserved attention to the requirement, dating from the Immigration and Nationality Act of 1940, that an individual prove that he or she is of "good moral character" for a statutory period of five years before soliciting citizenship (739). It is worth remembering that "good moral character" did not just presuppose heterosexuality but an apparently *enduring* mode of heterosexuality as monogamous, and, better still, as bolstered by matrimony.[22] The *Lawrence* decision makes much of enduring, private modes of homosexuality, but for the moment I want to stay with the fact that in the history of U.S. immigration and naturalization, moral arguments veer in and out of psycho-medical arguments, providing prejudice with a veneer of objectivity and neutrality (the very qualities, by the way, that Scalia, inattentive or indifferent to the prejudice that lies beneath his own work, accuses the *Lawrence* Court of having sacrificed).

Homosexuality as an implicitly excludable category was supposedly eliminated in the 1990 Immigration Act, prompting Foss to remark that "[i]n this strange way, the exclusion of homosexuals, which had never been explicitly mentioned in the statute, was repealed, again without explicit recognition of what had transpired" (462). For Foss, the change is promising, as indeed it would be for anyone who does not see civilization as relying on the deeply rooted moral opprobrium that attends homosexuality and on the virtually unassailable maintenance of heteronormativity, that more "positive," prescriptive cousin of homophobia. Also promising is the more recent inclusion of a "well-founded fear of persecution" based on sexual orientation among the legitimate grounds for political asylum,[23] itself bound up in the hard-won acceptance of sexual orientation as a legitimate category of protection by Amnesty International and other organizations.[24] Even

more promising is the decision, in *Lawrence*, to include homosexuality, though figured through sodomy, in the roster of legally protected
forms of "thought, belief, expression, and . . . conduct" (*Lawrence* 1)
and to affirm that "adults may choose to enter upon this relationship
in the confines of their homes and their own private lives and still retain their dignity as free persons" (*Lawrence* 6). That homosexuality
should pass from constituting grounds for exclusion to constituting
grounds for asylum, and that it should pass from being a "stigma"
(*Lawrence* 15) to a right (or something approximating it) and even a
matter of "personal dignity and autonomy" (*Lawrence* quoted 13) is
certainly "promising." However, much less promising, at least for pro-
gressives, are other developments, notably among them the confusing
and inconsistent implementation of medical screenings for [25] in order
to exclude people from entering or remaining in the country (at the
very time that homosexuality is supposedly removed as a reason for
exclusion); constitutionally impervious bans of private, consensual
sodomy among members of the military (specifically, Article 125, reaffirmed as recently as August 2004 by the U.S. Military's highest Court
of Criminal Appeals); frantic defenses of marriage as a sacred union
of man and woman (specifically, the Defense of Marriage Act passed
by the second session of the 104th Congress in 1996, but more generally a flurry of constitutional amendments and proposals for amendments at the state and national level); and, as I shall explore in detail
in a later section, what Katherine Franke presents as the domestication
and privatization of liberty in *Lawrence v. Texas* itself. These and other
practices and procedures put the brakes on the (otherwise under-
standable) celebrations that many, both in and out of the gay, lesbian,
bisexual, and transgendered movement, link to the decriminalization
of sodomy. For as Franke so compellingly puts it, "decriminalization
does not necessarily mobilize any particular ethical projects, or for that
matter, any ethics at all. Rather decriminalization [here] merely disables a form of public regulation of private adult activity. Indeed, it
neither sanctions nor suggests any alternative form of legitimization"
(1411). The elimination of never-quite-explicit prohibitions against
homosexuality in the area of immigration and the decriminalization
of sodomy in the area of citizenship do not spell the end of trouble for
non-heteronormative subjects.

   If homosexuals have been cast as criminals, as perverts contrary to
morality and tradition, as sensualists unfit for military service and for
public office, then they have been cast, as I have indicated, as less or

other than citizens, *proper* citizens. It is here that Renato Rosaldo's notion of cultural citizenship, articulated more precisely as Latino/a cultural citizenship, acquires renewed epistemological and ethical force. For Rosaldo (and many others), the concept of citizenship as universal, according to which all "men" are equal before the law, is challenged and even contradicted by historical reality. As a result, Rosaldo asserts that it is necessary "to distinguish the formal level of theoretical universality from the substantive level of exclusionary and marginalizing practices" (27). Despite the putative (but often actually quite spurious) clarity of legal language, citizenship is not an either/or proposition, something that one either has or does not have—though it can certainly function this way. Rather, citizenship is marked by any number of gradations, variations, and imbalances. Far from designating an unassailable equality, citizenship is an uneven, unequal construction whose ideal, shimmering seductively before us, is not realized in daily practice. As Berlant remarks, for many people the ideal itself has changed, fragmenting in ways that have little to do with "traditional liberal notions that organize the social optimism of law around relatively unimpeded individualism, privacy, property, and conventional values" (122). Berlant goes on to say that, "[t]he class, racial, economic, and sexual fragmentation of U.S. society has emerged into the vision of the law and the public not as an exception to a utopian norm but as a new governing rule of the present" (122). This "new governing rule," with which concepts of cultural citizenship and multiculturalism seem to be in concert, is however far from secure—unity through fragmentation rarely is—and still contends with a powerful and presumably deeply rooted "old governing rule" of facially neutral universality that, turning in on itself when attacked, fuses racial, economic, religious, and sexual fragmentation and difference into the very stuff of terror.

The anxious attempts to champion diversity, multiculturalism, and pluralism at the same time that racial profiling, foreign screening (recently replete with fingerprinting and ocular scanning), and knee-jerk patriotic consent to the government are omnipresent indicate the extent to which the new governing rule of which Berlant speaks holds without quite holding. The anxiety and angry confusion that attend the interplays of democratic diversity and national unity are made manifest in a variety of ways. For some, diversity, as both linchpin and sign of secularization, remains and returns as a problem that attends a newly forged unity of fragmented particularisms: a unity, always in process, that is by no means entirely of the fragmented parties' making. One of the most notorious examples of how the fragments and particularities of democratic secularism are made to cohere not in order to support some sort of Rainbow Coalition but in order to support another, ostensibly prior and more proper coalition, was offered by Christian televangelist Jerry Falwell, who, on his colleague Pat Robertson's show, The 700 Club, gave his account of the intersections of queerness, feminism, progressive politics, and terrorism shortly after 9/11. "I really believe," Falwell intoned, "that the pagans, and the abortionists, and the feminists, and the gays and the lesbians who are actively trying to make that an alternative lifestyle, the ACLU, People For the American Way, all of them who have tried to secularize America—I point the finger in their face and say 'you helped this happen.'" Tellingly, Falwell includes the Supreme Court in his rant against secularization, excoriating it, in a manner that recalls Scalia's criticisms of the legal profession,[26] for having succumbed to "organizations [that] have come into court to take the knowledge of God out of the public square of America." Falwell impugns what he presents as a sort of *privatization* of religion, the occlusion of religious freedom not just in the name of secular freedom but also, and more specifically, in the name of a secular freedom that privileges the privacy of the home, where now even certain forms of same-sex sodomy are permitted. But secular freedom, Falwell asserts, is a contradiction in terms: "sin[ning] against Almighty God, at the highest level of our government," the aforementioned secularists have "created an environment which possibly has caused God to lift the veil of protection which has allowed no one to attack America on our soil since 1812" ("Falwell"). A public, politicized preacher, Falwell clearly has no patience for the separation of church and state—a separation that is practically not one—and does his best to ensure that the "new governing rule" fails.[27] He has, to be sure, a great deal of support in the person of president George W. Bush, whose repeated invocations of God tie together his otherwise "unrelated" criticisms of terrorists, gays, and "activist judges" as well as his defense of national security and family values.

Amid the competing claims to represent the *ideal* truth of the land (it is a fragmented, secularized collocation of particular, overlapping groups that emerge into awareness; it is a spiritually informed unity of deep moral roots), certain subject positions continue to be adduced as suspicious and hence as deserving of scrutiny: this is something that *Lawrence v. Texas* has most decidedly *not* put to rest. The historical stigma with which the sodomite *cum* homosexual has been encumbered is thus not lifted with the *Lawrence* decision; at best, it is only lightened. Or rather, it is lightened, appears to be lightened, because it was so absurdly heavy to begin with. Despite the undeniable "advance" in justice that *Lawrence* signifies, it attests not only to the growing acceptance of homosexual—or, more amply, queer—citizenship but also, and no less critically, to its *continuing contentiousness*. If *Bowers* can be overturned in what Scalia presents as the Court's "surprising readiness to reconsider a decision rendered a mere 17 years ago" (*Lawrence* Scalia dissent 2), there is certainly no guarantee that the Court, with a different membership and in a different national climate (one less secure, more fraught with fear and paranoia, more in tune with Falwell's and Bush's sense of morality), would not reconsider its decision yet again. Tentativeness appears to be the extended state of non-heteronormative—and non-white and non-Christian—citizens in the United States. The situation of non-heteronormative immigrants, many of whom aspire to citizenship or to some form of legal recognition, is even more precarious, inasmuch as they are more subject to governmental intrusions into a private sphere not (yet) girded by a nationally consistent conception of marriage or domestic partnership.[28] Though the situation of the single person has been all but eclipsed by the recent hoopla surrounding same-sex marriage,[29] marriage functions in the United States as yet another phenomenon of national fragmentation (or, more nicely, federalism) and bears in particularly decisive ways on so-called bi-national couples, those couples for whom questions of legality and sexuality directly involve questions of citizenship and immigration. Indeed, the patchwork process of state-by-state same-sex marriage (or its prohibition) recalls the patchwork process of anti-sodomy initiatives, now rendered facially obsolete by *Lawrence*,[30] and brings to the light, once again, significant differences among the states of the United States.

The Disunited States: States' Rights and the Rights of Women, Queers, and Immigrants

The situation of immigrants can vary not only depending on their country of origin but also on the state, district or municipality of the United States in which they come to reside—something that holds, of course, for U.S. citizens as well. The "new governing rule" of diversity must contend not only with the old governing rule of liberal inspiration and its reliance, as noted above, on individualism, privacy, property, and conventional values; it must also contend with the old governing rule of "states' rights," according to which some parts of the country are and can be more or less receptive to homosexuality, as act or identity, and to same-sex marriage (and hence to the possibilities that marriage opens, in theory, to the non-citizen partners of queer citizens). Under *Bowers*, the United States was fundamentally disunited for gay people, with some states permitting sodomy and others prohibiting it. Under *Lawrence*, things are undoubtedly more even, though disunity persists in the form of legally sanctioned unions and marriage, on which score Vermont and Massachusetts occupy a vanguard that throws into relief the rearguard—read, the "mainstream." It is the same disunity, masked as liberty for all but still not for some, that punctuates Scalia's topographical rendition of abortion, part and parcel of his appeal to state-by-state legislative (but also judicial) authority in his dissent in *Lawrence* and, before it, in *Romer v. Evans*, a case which centered on a referendum to prohibit "pro-gay" anti-discrimination measures in Colorado. Lest the reference to abortion seem surprising in a decision on sodomy and homosexuality, it should be remembered that, for Scalia, one unacceptable, socially disruptive act entails another. "What a massive disruption of the current social order . . . the overruling of *Bowers* entrails," Scalia bemoans; "[n]ot so the overruling of *Roe*, which would simply have restored the regime that existed for centuries before 1973, in which the permissibility of and restrictions upon abortion were determined legislatively State-by-State" (*Lawrence* dissent 7). In Scalia's version of *Things Fall Apart*, the overruling of *Bowers* and the non-overruling of *Roe* are two sides of the same fraudulent coin: both decisions disrupt the current social order by understanding it *as* current, as flowing beyond deeply rooted Christian (or as Scalia prefers, "Judaeo-Christian") moral and ethical standards. Both decisions, moreover, constitute what Scalia presents as a veritable affront to the right of the individual states of the union to decide what *their* moral and ethical standards, *their* laws, should be.

The problem is as old as the country and has little if any politically definitive content: if states' rights can allow for prejudice to remain uncontested, they can also allow for prejudice to be contested. Scalia, for his part, is hardly oblivious to the rhetorical turns of change and constancy, for he casts the structural "conservation" of *Roe* as historical, if not ideological, conservatism: against "the rock-solid, unamendable disposition of *Roe*" he pits, or deems that the Court has pitted, "the readily overrulable *Bowers*" (*Lawrence* Scalia dissent 4). Amid a welter of sarcastic jabs, Scalia makes clear that the fantasized dissolution of *Roe v. Wade*, and hence the fantasized failure of a mainstay of women's rights, haunts what others deem to be the success of *Lawrence*. As if glimpsing a silver lining to a gay cloud, Scalia does his best to indicate how the very arguments that were employed to overturn *Bowers* could be used to overturn *Roe*, how the decriminalization of private gay sex (and I will have much to say about privacy in the next section) could be used as a blueprint for the recriminalization of abortion and for the curtailment of choice. The conditions that justify the overruling of *Bowers*—to wit, the erosion of the foundations of a decision by subsequent decisions; the subjection of a decision to "substantial and continuing" criticism; and the lack of "individual or societal" reliance—apply to Roe as well (*Lawrence* Scalia dissent 3). Such at least is Scalia's contention, and it is not without considerable significance—the reinvigoration of privacy doctrine under *Lawrence* and various embattled defenses of *Roe* notwithstanding.

According to Scalia's calculations, it is wrong to assume "that the consequence of overruling *Roe* would have been to make abortion unlawful. It would not; it would merely have *permitted* the States to do so. Many States would unquestionably have declined to prohibit abortion. . . . Even for persons in States other than these, the choice would not have been between abortion and childbirth, but between abortion nearby and abortion in a neighboring State" (*Lawrence* Scalia dissent 7, emphasis original). Scalia's vague use of "nearby" and "neighboring" promotes a false vision of the states of the United States as coexisting in a rhythmic structure of peacefully inconsequential alternation. For it is unquestionable that many states *would* have prohibited abortion and, furthermore, it is quite possible that entire regions of the country, most notably the South, would have codified the current dearth of clinics and services into a legally ordered absence. The "choice" would thus not exactly be easy, *even if* every woman in the nation had the same disposable income to make travel so casual and carefree as Scalia depicts it. In his disavowal of history and geography, Scalia would have us forget that the contrast between states with an "emerging awareness" of transformative moralities and ethics and states with a "deeply rooted" sense of traditional morality resonates in any troubling way.[31] He would dissociate a geopolitical history of racial and ethnic inequality—from slavery to miscegenation statutes to Jim Crow laws—from a geopolitical history of gender and sexual inequality.

Interestingly, Scalia's contention that states should be the ultimate arbiters of certain morally charged issues shifts the scale—*but only to a point.* After all, in his dissent to *Romer v. Evans,* Scalia sided with the state of Colorado in its use of a referendum known as Amendment 2 to overturn anti-discrimination ordinances that had been enacted in the cities and/or counties of Aspen, Boulder, and Denver. Claiming that the case hinged on "a modest attempt by seemingly tolerant Colorodans to preserve traditional sexual mores against the efforts of a politically powerful minority to revise those mores through the use of the laws" (*Romer* Scalia dissent 1), Scalia appealed to the authority of the state over and against its municipalities. In so doing, he logically endorsed "higher levels of democratic decisionmaking (i.e., by the state legislature rather than local government, or by the people at large in the state constitution rather than the legislature)" (*Romer* Scalia dissent 4). Scalia's logic was, and remains, demagogic. Invoking an image of popular democratic process that goes to the very heart of the federal system and majority rule, Scalia effectively discounts the concept of minority protection. One of the principal effects of Scalia's position in *Romer,* when read alongside his more recent position in *Lawrence,* is the projected disablement of anti-discriminatory intervention at the most local *and* the most national level—not to mention the international level, which Scalia ridicules, as we have seen, by reference to foreign moods, fads or fashions.[32]

Scalia thus maps out a battle plan in which relatively progressive towns or cities (those with an "emerging awareness," it would seem) might be kept in check in at least some states. Some states, or many states: for if *Roe* were overruled and *Bowers* restored (which is to say, if *Lawrence* were overruled) and all were made "right" in the United States of America again, the patchwork pattern of "choice" that Scalia so blithely invokes would likewise reassert itself and, in so doing, make the nation, at least in relation to abortion and homosexuality, as uneven as the world. Both *Roe* and *Lawrence,* emotionally and morally charged as they are, make the United States more united by eliminating significant legal differences between, say, Vermont and Colorado, Massachusetts and Texas; more colloquially, they level the playing field and simplify issues of residence for immigrants and citizens, homosexuals and women, alike. Scalia's imaginary "map," whose unsavory history he would ennoble by way of a defense of "democratic participation," is not just disunited; his implicit validation of prejudice and discrimination by state-to-state majorities also ensures that migratory movements *to* the United States will recur—as they already do—*within* the United States. Such internal movements are perhaps inevitable, at least insofar as cultural offerings, community formations, and employment opportunities are concerned. They are *not* inevitable, however, where legal protections and civil rights are concerned. San Francisco and New York, with well-deserved reputations for being more receptive and supportive of queer people than other places, will probably not lose their appeal after *Lawrence,* but Texas, Colorado, and Georgia will, *at least on the level of legal subjectivity,* become somewhat less daunting. Less daunting: for legal unity clearly cannot guarantee cultural unity or equal cultural citizenship. The fragmentation and accompanying chains of equivalence among women, people of color, queers, immigrants and others turn, that is, in often less than progressive or radically democratic ways.[33]

Amid the vagaries of states' rights, sexually and gender-specific rights are fragmented even as ostensibly universal categories—woman, homosexual—are deployed. Despite important geopolitical differences both outside and inside the United States (not only, as previously noted, between Yemen and the Netherlands, but also, *toutes proportions gardées,* between Texas and Massachusetts), homosexuality, not unlike other categories of identity, has tended to function in the U.S. legal system as transhistorical and universal: a homosexual there and then has been taken, over and again, as a homosexual here and now. As immigration scholar Eithne Luibhéid remarks, "mainstream institutions, including the INS [reconfigured after 9/11], remain invested in constructing fixed boundaries about what homosexuality 'is'" (78). The question of what homosexuality "is" effects, furthermore, who is and is not understood as "being" a homosexual. For Luibhéid, with whom I agree, the legal force of identity categories can lead to some deceptive suppositions. "We should not imagine," Luibhéid writes, "that coherent, predefined lesbian or gay identities always existed among immigrant applicants, and that the checkpoints simply captured these performed 'queer' subjects" nor should we imagine lesbian and gay identities as "reducible" to these checkpoints (79). Alice Miller makes similar remarks in her work in the present volume, reminding us that the very signs of identity that have ostensibly been mobilized on behalf of greater freedom can have some terribly restrictive ramifications. The question of what is in a name, and of what is in an act and an identity (or a status and a conduct), demands less thought if names, acts, and identities are taken as consistent over time and space. Inasmuch as U.S. jurisprudence tends to brandish "freedom" as if it were the same for everyone everywhere at every time, thereby masking the particular American turns of freedom (freedom functions simultaneously as the same the world over *and* as eminently American), it is not surprising that it tends to brandish "man," "woman," "heterosexual," "homosexual," and so forth in a similarly universalist manner—even as it explicitly engages historiography and recognizes, as in *Lawrence*, an emerging awareness about liberty in matters of adult sexuality.

Caution amid Victory: Dignity, Privacy, Intimacy, and National Heterosexuality

Having attended to Scalia's defense of states' rights, his repudiation of foreign legal decisions, his understanding of "deeply rooted" moral and ethical standards as essential to rational-basis jurisprudence, and his suggestion that *Lawrence* might serve as a blueprint to overturn *Roe*; having sounded out Thomas's concern with law enforcement resources at a time of embattled civil liberties, anxious national security, and the "war on terrorism"; and having grappled with the morally and culturally laden linkages of "perverts" and "terrorists" as well as the universalist and transhistorical implications of such overarching terms and concepts as "homosexual," I am now compelled to advance a critique, not of Scalia's dissent or of Thomas's concurrence in dissent, but of the majority *Lawrence* Court. As should now be evident, it is my contention that, as promising as *Lawrence* may be, progressive people should be "careful," as bisexual transgendered writer and activist Pat [Patrick] Califia observed in 1982, "that a change in the law is not used as an excuse to set up an elaborate bureaucracy to enforce more stringently defined standards for acceptable sexual behavior" (18). British sociologist and gay activist Jeffrey Weeks, on whom Califia draws, signals a "paradox at the heart" of the aforementioned Wolfenden Committee, cited by the *Lawrence* Court: "the legal penalties for public displays of sexuality could be strengthened at the same time as private behavior was decriminalized" (quoted in Califia 17). In a similar vein, Arthur S. Leonard, in a piece written after *Lawrence*, remarks that "[t]he decriminalization of sodomy in Illinois in 1962 did not suddenly liberate the gay people of that state from oppressive state policing of their sex lives" for the not so simple reason that "statutes *other* than sodomy laws have contributed to [the] stigma" that attends gay people (21, emphasis added). The statutes here in question affect a variety of things ranging from the solicitation of "deviate sexual intercourse" (typically, but by no means exclusively, in parks and public restrooms) to ages of consent for same-sex contact (typically higher and with harsher penalties than for heterosexual contact[34]), but they also call forth the history of sexual exclusions that so profoundly, if subtly, mark immigration. "Even in the post-*Lawrence* world," Leonard concludes, "such laws still bedevil gay people" (21). Police forces that ferret out "closeted" politicians who propose and support measures to defend and protect traditional family values and heterosexual marriage, and religiously inspired groups that bristle at the mere thought of anything remotely "favorable" to homosexuals (such as equal protection or due process, let alone anti-discrimination initiatives or full cultural and legal citizenship), all work to keep such laws and statutes in force.

Judges play their part too, obviously enough, and not always in the simple "pro-gay" or "activist" manner that Scalia, a judge himself, asserts. As Leonard notes, "the issue is not [merely] a statute specifically disadvantaging gay people but rather judicial attitudes deployed in the exercise of relatively unsupervised 'discretion' in a system where appellate courts are generally loathe [sic] to second-guess the front-line decision-makers" (22). Juridical attitudes shaped by an extensive culture of homophobia are hard to shake, indeed. The *Lawrence* court attempts to do just that, and in a way that outstrips the "right" of individual states effectively to maintain institutionalized homophobia even while balking at the idea that it even exists. The attempt is promising, but also dodgy, because the *Lawrence* Court manifestly refuses to consider, as Scalia complains, the ramifications and limits of its decision. Then again, dodginess—the best measure of which is the vague and rather incongruous invocation of a spatially transcendent freedom[35]—may be the price that the Court pays, or believes that it must pay, to overturn *Bowers* and to make a public case for the rights of homosexuals as fuller, if still not entirely full, citizens.[36] The Court makes the case, it should be noted, by way of arguments of due process and the right of privacy, both of which have been crucial to protecting those who have been seen as contravening dominant sexual mores. And yet, it is also important to note that the right of privacy (linked to due process[37]) does not necessarily function in the service of those who buck traditional sexual morality, far from it. Indeed, the Court, in its invocation of dignity and enduring personal bonds not so innocently constructs an ideal image of the homosexual that replicates a more implicit ideal image of the heterosexual.[38]

The public case for the decriminalization of sodomy by way of an appeal to dignity and enduring personal bonds follows a well-worn path, one in which privacy is crucial. The distinction between public and private—developed in such cases as *Griswold* and *Stanley v. Georgia*—is very much at play in *Lawrence*, which opens with the claim that "[l]iberty protects the person from unwarranted government intrusions into a dwelling or other private places" (*Lawrence* 1). Even though the Court immediately goes on to recognize that "there are other spheres of our lives, outside the home, where the State should not be a dominant presence" (which then leads to the aforementioned "[f]reedom extends beyond spatial bounds"), it is the home, as the *locus classicus* of privacy, that focalizes—and binds—references to unbounded freedom. In contrast, the "other spheres" *outside* the home remain nebulous, perhaps quite deliberately so, and hence nebulously protected: after all, sex is the subject here in question, and the very notion of publicly protected sex seems to bleed over and again into the potentially more sensationalist notion of public sex (Scalia's aforementioned slippery slope of immorality is a prime example of such sensationalism). "[T]he legal difference between public and private sex is not a simple matter of choosing either the bushes or your bedroom," Califia writes, for there are "many zones in between—a motel room, a bathhouse, a bar, an adult bookstore, a car, a public toilet, a dark and deserted alley—that are contested territory where police battle with perverts for control" (18). These in-between zones resemble what Lauren Berlant and Michael Warner call "queer zones," spaces "estranged from heterosexual culture" and from "more tacit scenes of sexuality like official national culture, which depends on a notion of privacy to cloak its sexualization of national membership" (187). Although there is a risk of determining these "queer zones" as the zones of queerness itself, these "zones" are not as marginal in their ramifications as some might (dominantly) believe. In fact, as Berlant and Warner indicate, the love that dares not speak its name steels, even as it threatens to sunder, something else that dares not speak its name: national heterosexuality. And national heterosexuality is nothing if not dignified, enduring, and ever so publicly private.

"National heterosexuality is," in the words of Berlant and Warner, "the mechanism by which a core national culture can be imagined as a sanitized space of sentimental feeling and immaculate behavior, a space of pure citizenship. A familial mode of society displaces the recognition of structural racism and other systemic inequalities" (189). A massively unquestioned heterosexuality serves, that is, as the degree zero of the American dream and inflects, among so much else, immigration policy, which privileges family reunification, marriage, and an entrenched reproductive ethos (children born in the United States are considered citizens; children who "merely" arrive are not). So pervasive is this hetero-reproductive dream, so "deeply rooted" its psycho-symbolic mechanisms and material props, that when sexuality appears in legal discourse and national debates it is almost always by way of a deviation from, and resistance to, the norm. And the norm, for its part, is meaningful only insofar as it is distinguished from other formations that, whatever *their* normative gestures, do not enjoy the same degree of power and institutional support. Accordingly, while a "fundamental right to sodomy" and, more generally, a right to privacy is hotly debated in and out of the courts, a fundamental right to procreative sex (as opposed to, say, "fornication" or the interruption of procreation by contraception or abortion) is not. The *natus*, or "being born," that is at the etymological root of both "nation" and "nature" has itself been so profoundly naturalized that the very idea of such a debate borders on absurdity—at least for those who take such matters so naturally.

And yet, the fact is that overwhelmingly male Courts, the heterosexuality of whose members is taken for granted, decide, without any appreciable self-reflection, the bounds of homosexuals' rights and of women's rights in a manner that only further legitimizes, *as beyond any legal doubt or reflection*, the status of heterosexuals and of men, and hence of heterosexual men (interestingly, as Luibhéid notes, the status of lesbians is cast in legal shadows of another sort, 80). What Halley writes about *Bowers* thus holds, despite the different outcome, for *Lawrence*: "the Justices occupied the heterosexual posture even though we know nothing about their personal erotic preferences. It is a public posture, a public identity, and a point of vantage in public discourse. Unlike Hardwick's position—fixed, exposed, visible in the klieg lights trained on the homosexual sodomite—the Justices' heterosexual position is fluid, hidden, ever retaining a rhetorical place to hide" (1747).[39] And the most effective rhetorical place to hide is none other than the normal, normative place, the place that *would be* everywhere but that, of course, is not: a national, "natural" heterosexuality.[40]

Although *Lawrence v. Texas* undoubtedly advances the acceptance of homosexuals, it does so in unexamined heteronormative terms. It privileges, as we have seen, relationships among individuals "in the confines of their homes and their own private lives" (*Lawrence* 6), and it casts these relationships as "enduring" (*Lawrence* 6).[41] Inasmuch as an enduring personal relationship is conventionally understood as a monogamous, matrimonial relationship, Scalia's fear that *Lawrence* will pave the way to homosexual marriage is hardly irrational.[42] Quite the contrary, it is eminently rational, and in a way that clearly disturbs the defender of rational-basis jurisprudence (tied, as Scalia insists, to traditional "Judeo-Christian" morality). Given the history of "national heterosexuality," none of this is surprising, neither the Court's recourse to an implicit heteronormativity in its legitimation of homosexuals nor Scalia's fear that in so doing the Court opens the door to same-sex marriage and other rights/rites, rituals, and institutions heretofore the exclusive province of heterosexuals. With so much attention focused on the home, the couple, marriage, and family "values," the conventional distinction between the conventional and the non-conventional fades as convention itself expands and becomes more alluringly accommodating—accommodating, that is, *as long as privacy is maintained.*

The debate over privacy as a constitutional right divides the Justices, but it also links them, for none of the Justices dares to imagine—at least in public—anything remotely like a right to same-sex "relations" *outside* the bounds of the home, or a right to *fleeting* and/or *multiple* encounters, let alone a right to a public "display" of homosexuality. Katherine Franke, in a brilliant reading of *Lawrence* that on this point anticipates mine, describes the liberty that *Lawrence* legitimates as "domesticated," "geographized," "privatized" (1400, 1403), all of which is part and parcel, tellingly enough, of "a pull towards domesticity in current gay and lesbian organizing" (1400). The majority decision of *Lawrence*, with its rhetoric of dignity *as* discretion, is thus curiously consistent with a "don't ask, don't tell" policy in which secrecy, decorum, and seemliness are at a premium, but it is also consistent with the normalizing bent of a good deal of gay and lesbian advocacy that understands political success as an adaptation to, and expansion of, the *status quo* rather than as a radical *mise en question* of its premises and purposes. It might not be necessary for the windows to be covered and the doors to be locked (though closed, certainly) for the State to keep its distance, but the Court, in its very insistence on privacy, reinscribes domesticity *cum* privacy as the site from which freedom can be ever so dubiously unbound. Which is to say, more properly, that the Court uncannily *reinforces* the spatial bounds of freedom by way of a homey, heteronormative rhetoric of privacy that is neither accommodating nor "dignified" for all alike.

Privacy implies intimacy. As Berlant observes in an article published just a year before *Lawrence*: "the romantic banality that sanctions certain forms of intimacy as nationally privileged remains hardwired into the practice of sex privacy law in the United States" (117). The national privilege of intimacy, duly housed in a familiar space (home sweet home), extends its romantic banality to the unbounded freedom that the Court so solemnly champions and gives Scalia further ammunition. Cranky as he may be, Scalia is no stranger to the idiom of romantic love. Oozing ridicule, he lambastes the Court on the basis of "its famed sweet-mystery-of-life passage"(*Lawrence* Scalia dissent 3). The passage, cited by the *Lawrence* Court, is drawn from *Planned Parenthood of Southeastern Pennsylvania v. Casey* (yet another sexually charged case), which affirms "the right to define one's own concept of existence, of meaning, of the universe, and of the mystery of human life" (quoted in *Lawrence* 13). The previously cited reference to "personal dignity and autonomy" is also from the *Planned Parenthood* decision, but it is *Griswold* which constitutes, as the majority Court states, "the most pertinent beginning point" for *Lawrence* (*Lawrence* 3) and which further reinforces the linkage between heteronormatively modeled understandings of privacy, intimacy, dignity, and autonomy or freedom.[43] The linkage is smooth in the grooves of tradition and brings us back to the previously adduced "old governing rule" of liberal universalism. As political philosopher Chantal Mouffe writes, "the public realm of modern citizenship was constructed in a universalistic, and rationalistic manner that precluded the recognition of division and antagonism and that relegated to the private all particularity and difference" (377). The *Lawrence* Court, with its appeals to freedom and its dignified "feel" of progressive tolerance, is more deeply rooted in tradition than Scalia recognizes or wants to admit, for it effectively maintains the public sphere as sexually unmarked, that is to say, as heteronormative, and it keeps sexual practice, ideally, as a private, dignified matter.[44] Indeed, as Franke puts it, "*Lawrence* is a slam-dunk victory for a politics that is exclusively devoted to creating safe zones for homo- and hetero-sex/intimacy, while at the same time rendering all other zones more dangerous for nonnormative sex" (1415).

The persistence of a dominant social script, prescriptive and proscriptive in one fell swoop, cannot be overestimated: *Lawrence*, overturning much, has not overturned *that*. It may be that nothing can fully overturn a social script so deeply "rooted" in a history of racial, class, gender, religious, sexual, and other modes of inequality. This history maintains that particularity and difference, as Mouffe indicates, can only ever fitfully leave their mark on a public space that would yet retain its *fundamentally* unmarked status: as if the race, class, gender, and sexual orientation of the founding fathers[45] had not left *their* mark, an image of authority that queers, women, people of color, and immigrants, among others, must process if they are to pass as acceptable citizens. The fact that certain marks of identity must be redeemed as enduring, private, and even dignified in and by a legal system that does not acknowledge its own particular marks should be sufficient to put the more critically and progressively minded on guard. In academic circles, activist scholar Michael Warner has been at the forefront of such endeavors. Not only has he pushed at the delimitation of freedom by way of words and concepts such as "dignified," "enduring," and "private," but he has also written, freely and unapologetically, of the *indignity* of sex, of freedom *from* "any attempt at respectability and dignity" (34).[46] Warner's freedom to speak so "indignantly" is itself, as he knows, a function of a national political regime and democratic *praxis* (as well as a function of being white, male, and financially and educationally privileged) that does not obtain for the non-citizen, at least not with the same impunity—which is precisely why it is important to consider it.[47] For even as Warner engages in a brilliantly involute, yet at times demandingly direct, critique, he surely knows that many others, born elsewhere, have been enjoined to play the part of the enduringly dignified, properly private subject as the *condition* for legal residence, let alone naturalization, in the United States, the national space from which Warner speaks. Then again, some immigrants, specifically those who seek asylum or refuge, are enjoined to play the part of the properly private subject by laying bare the indignity that *others* would heap on them. The significance of privacy, and of dignity, in the dominant social script can vary considerably according to the subject's citizenship status.

The variability of privacy and dignity is perhaps most evident in asylum cases, in which an asylum applicant's country is figuratively put on trial—often in spite of the best efforts of the framers and practitioners of asylum law—as unable and/or unwilling to protect their citizens.[48] Women who seek asylum by claiming to have suffered domestic violence in their home countries—but also, under the Violence Against Women Act of 1994, spouses and children of U.S. citizens and permanent residents who may "self-petition" to secure lawful permanent residency—conjure forth a very different sense of privacy than do gay men and lesbians who seek asylum by claiming to have suffered various modes of *public* violence.[49] Berlant, who shares Warner's suspicion of the ideal of privacy and its capacity to inculcate shame and to create ostensibly more "tolerable" closets, notes how "the intimate feelings of married sexual partners [which] represent that zone of privacy and personhood beyond the scrutiny of the law" (121) that were codified in *Griswold v. Connecticut* and reaffirmed in *Roe v. Wade*[50] give way, in *Planned Parenthood*, to "[t]he deutopianization of sexual privacy established in *Griswold* and the installation of female citizenship at the juncture of law and suffering" (120). Berlant's critique of the politically interested deployment of the suffering of disenfranchised people, which functions as the prop of a "universally intelligible" (122) subjectivity that would replace the facially neutral universal subjectivity of liberalism, casts a somber light on the slippery turns of autonomy and privacy in U.S. political culture. For while a romantically tinged homosexual practice is legitimized (i.e., enduring love "redeems" sodomy), at least in part, through an affirmation of a right of privacy, a longstanding mode of heterosexual practice—a man's violent ascendancy over a woman—is delegitimized through the negation of a right of privacy as absolute. As Berlant so memorably puts it: "the 'gruesome and tortuous' conditions of marital domesticity in battering households requires the Court *not to protect privacy* for the couple but to keep the couple from becoming the unit of model citizenship where privacy law is concerned" (120, emphasis original). However, in *Lawrence*, with its emphasis on enduring bonds, it is the couple that is most densely figured as the unit of model citizenship; indeed, both the majority decision and the dissent are peppered with references to "married couple," the "same-sex couple," "opposite-sex couple," "homosexual couple," and even, through a work cited, "gay couple." Asylum cases based on domestic violence, not unlike asylum cases based on anti-gay violence, *internationalize* the public-private debate, generating concrete benefits for a few *individuals* but also symbolic benefits for the United States as a nation that succors the suffering, traumatized subjects of other nations and that extends freedom, however piecemeal, to them.[51] How the privilege of the couple in *Lawrence* will bear on such individually structured cases remains, of course, to be seen.

Chains of Equivalence and Inhabited Identities

The ways in which a dominant social script bears, unevenly, on everyone who is in or who comes to the country leads immigration lawyer Robert Foss to make a concise, self-positioned assertion: "[t]he gains we have made as gays and lesbians [in the United States] ought to be defended and at the same time the queer community should more clearly express its solidarity with immigrants." Michael Hardwick, John Geddes Lawrence, and Lawrence's "co-petitioner" Tyron Garner are U.S. citizens, but through them *all* citizens *of* the United States and all non-citizens *in* the United States, or who come to the United States, are variously implicated. This is the crux of my argument. It is, admittedly, a problematic crux because it must contend with both the reification of national borders, their obsessive control and policing (a firm "us" and "them") *and* the dissolution of national borders, their performative refashioning (a diffuse "us" and "them," which is to say, a diffuse "us").[52] It must contend with both the hard negation of any linkage between citizen and non-citizen and the all too easy affirmation of a linkage. Foss's call for solidarity between queers and immigrants might accordingly be understood along the lines of what Chantal Mouffe presents as a "chain of equivalence," an "articulation" of "historical, contingent, and variable links" (372).[53] Where queer people and immigrants are concerned, the chains of equivalence are indeed historical, contingent, and variable. Both "groups" are anything but internally coherent, and even in their overlaps, in the guise of "queer immigrants," they are the effects of social and juridical constructs rather than anything psychologically or physically essential. As Roger Lancaster, Alice Miller, and others in this volume argue, the consolidation of a universal homosexual identity, folded in and out of specific and yet often quite vaguely described sexual acts, runs through national legal systems, some obviously more powerful internationally than others. As important as such identities are to any project of solidarity and resistance, they bear the imprint of dominant heteronormative and nativist formations that render their deployment slippery, when not even counter-productive.

Janet Halley insists, therefore, that, "those of us who inhabit gay and lesbian identity must loosen our grip on these identities, and admit into the field of our self-identification a cross-cutting set of identities founded on acts" (1771). Halley is hardly sanguine about such a loosening, for she recognizes the "double bind" by which gays and lesbians, and more generally queers, are constituted through stigmatization as a group and, as a group, strive to resist, or at least to rework, stigmatization.[54] Too much of a loosening risks disabling a queer counterpolitics—or, for that matter, what Berlant and Warner call "queer counterpublics" and "counterintimacies"—and leaving the dominant social script untouched. Too tight a linkage, in contrast, risks reducing difference and leveling sexual practice in the name of a singular identity. The problems that many immigrants have in "defining" themselves as they attempt to pass into a legal system that has carved out an acceptable homosexual identity snake back on the very activists and scholars who have helped shape legally acceptable identities. Although these problems are especially acute for those who seek asylum, they also hound others who, in their interviews and interactions with immigration agents and other officials, must articulate their experience in preexisting terms that may or not be deployed—duly translated, when possible—in their home countries.[55] Although many immigrants come to the United States with an understanding of homosexuality that, though highly mediated, is more or less consonant with that which is dominant in U.S. legal culture, others do not. As a result, in some cases, the homosexual, gay, or lesbian subject may actually be an *effect* of entry into, and negotiation with, the United States, an identity that the subject must take on or "inhabit" in order to be legally and socially intelligible.

Given the fraught reality of identity and legality internationally, Halley's claim that people *inhabit* identity is felicitous in several ways. First, it recognizes that identity is contingent and contextual and that it *can* be strategic even when it presents itself as, or appears to be, essentialist. Second, it makes identity less a self-contained property of interiority (of inside out) than the effect of exteriority (of outside in); better yet, it promotes a dialectical movement in which the putative interiority of identity, along with its private, intimate force, is modified by, and modifies in turn, the putative exteriority of society, along with its public, "extimate" force. Third, and most importantly, it opens the way to understanding identity, ever so figuratively, as a home or a country, as a *habitus* or *domus*, an inhabitable (though at times inhospitable and hence uninhabitable) site in which nature, custom, and spatial bounds are all at play. To understand identity, sexual and otherwise, as inhabitable is to render the divisions between native and non-native, citizen and alien, domestic and foreign, less rigid without tossing them aside or wishing them away—as if subjectivity in general could bypass, entirely, legal subjectivity. To understand identity as inhabitable is also to participate in a practice of redefinition that throws the home, the individual, the family, and the nation into a potentially radical democratic circuit of negotiations in which the ideal of a freedom that extends beyond spatial bounds might just be realized. For it is not that the *Lawrence* Court simply errs when it invokes the "liberty of the person both in its spatial and more transcendent dimensions" (*Lawrence* 1), but rather that it fails to address the myriad ways in which heteronormativity remains the unacknowledged, and hence unexamined, basis for its nation-wide decriminalization—or, put more positively, legitimation—of homosexuals and homosexuality. Furthermore, the *Lawrence* decision fails to attend to the implications that its reliance on a private, enduring model of human relationality—whose most legally "consacrated" form is the married couple—has on the very freedom that it claims to champion, a freedom whose spatial and more transcendent dimensions necessarily implicate transnational movement and immigration.

So what is to be done? Well, at the very least, progressive critics and activists need to temper their chants of post-*Lawrence* victory with calls for vigilance. Many, aware that *Lawrence* is a decision that cannot be extricated from a wider context of besieged civil liberties, embattled human rights, reinvigorated militarism, and messianic nationalist projects, are doing just that. Then again, conservatives, currently in power in the United States, also temper their chants of victory with calls for vigilance of an increasingly fundamentalist Christian nature. *Lawrence*, for them, simply underscores the need for vigilance and, in fact, for a reassertion of the seriousness of "deeply rooted values" that even a conservative Justice like Clarence Thomas can call "silly." A more difficult task than vigilance is therefore required, one that would involve "broaden[ing] the domain of the exercise of democratic rights beyond the limited traditional field of 'citizenship'" while questioning—not perfunctorily rejecting, but questioning—"the very idea of a natural domain of the 'private'" (Laclau and Mouffe 185).[56] Such a task also involves questioning the very idea of a natural domain of the "national" and broadening the domain of democratic rights beyond the nation-state, a reinvigoration of the United Nations, or something like it, over and above the United States.

Difficult, it is also a utopian task, one that must grapple with a principle of reality (of the here and now) without petrifying that principle into reality *per se* (of the always and forever more). Domestic freedom in a more bounded, familial, publicly private sense calls forth, as its most spatially transcendent mode, freedom in an expansive, perpetually negotiated, multilateral, and international sense. Such an understanding of freedom (which motivates what is here a sort of "normative upshot" that ironically questions normativity) has been the guiding principle of the present article, which has attempted to attend to the imbrication of the domestic, the national, and the international in an age of terribly uneven global capitalism and vast migratory movements. It has attempted to do so, of course, from a position that takes seriously so-called minority politics and the seemingly—that is to say, deceptively—marginal role of sexuality, and more particularly homosexuality, in immigration. If in at least some parts of the United States homosexuality is brought increasingly into the fold of domestic culture and deemed to be as deserving of autonomy and respect as heterosexuality (*Lawrence* 13), if it is styled to sell and sells as style, and if it is increasingly yet unevenly internationalized, it continues to be the object of considerable scorn, derision, prejudice, and violence. The newly "legitimated homosexual," like the "naturalized citizen," the "liberated woman," and the "unassimilated immigrant," still meets with suspicion and rejection, when not something worse, on the part of those who see the nation as a natural, native-born, heterosexual entity and who bridle at the "emerging awareness" of sexual rights as human rights in an international frame. This is the awareness that has yet fully to emerge and that constitutes the trial of justice and freedom before us.

Works Cited

Amnesty International USA. *Breaking the Silence: Human Rights Violations Based on Sexual Orientation.* New York: Amnesty International Publications, 1994.

Anker, Deborah E. *Law of Asylum in the United States.* Boston: Refugee Law Center, 1999.

Berlant, Lauren. "The Subject of True Feeling: Pain, Privacy, and Politics." *Left Legalism/Left Critique.* Ed. Wendy Brown and Janet Halley. Durham, N.C.: Duke University Press, 2002. 105–133.

_____ and Michael Warner. "Sex in Public." *Publics and Counterpublics.* By Michael Warner. New York: Zone Books, 2002. 187–208.

Boutilier v. Immigration and Naturalization Service. Supreme Court of the United States. 387 U.S. 118 (1967).

Bowers v. Hardwick. Supreme Court of the United States. 478 U.S. 186 (1986).

Cabrera Infante, Guillermo. *Mea Cuba.* Trans. Kenneth Hall. New York: Farrar Straus Giroux, 1994.

Califia, Pat. *Public Sex: The Culture of Radical Sex.* San Francisco: Cleis Press, 2000.

Citron, Jo Ann. "*Lawrence v. Texas*: A Victory for Liberty." *The Gay & Lesbian Review* 10.6 (Nov.–Dec. 2003): 18–21.

Edelman, Lee. "Tearooms and Sympathy, or, The Epistemology of the Water Closet." *Nationalisms and Sexualities*. Ed. Andrew Parker, Mary Russo, Doris Sommer, and Patricia Yaeger. New York: Routledge, 1992. 263–284.

Epps, Brad. "The Fetish of Fluidity." *Homosexuality and Psychoanalysis*. Ed. Tim Dean and Christopher Lane. Chicago: University of Chicago Press, 2001. 412–431.

Eskridge, William N., Jr. and Nan D. Hunter. *Sexuality, Gender, and the Law*. Westbury, New York: Foundation Press, 1997.

"Falwell apologizes to gays, feminists, lesbians." CNN. September 14, 2001. http://www.cnn.com/2001/US/09/14/Falwell.apology/.

Foss, Robert J. "The Demise of the Homosexual Exclusion: New Possibilities for Gay and Lesbian Immigration." *Harvard Civil Rights-Civil Liberties Law Review* 29.2 (1994): 439–475.

Foster v. Florida (Charles Kenneth Foster v. Florida, et al.). Supreme Court of the United States. 537 U.S. (2002).

Franke, Katherine M. "The Domesticated Liberty of *Lawrence v. Texas*." *Columbia Law Review* 104 (2004): 1399–1426.

Goldberg, Jonathan. *Sodometries: Renaissance Texts, Modern Sexualities*. Stanford, Calif.: Stanford University Press, 1992.

Goldberg, Suzanne B. "Give Me Liberty or Give Me Death: Political Asylum and the Global Persecution of Lesbians and Gay Men." *Cornell International Law Journal* 26 (1993): 605–623.

Goldstein, Anne B. "History, Homosexuality, and Political Values: Searching for the Hidden Determinants of *Bowers v. Hardwick*." *Yale Law Journal* 97 (1988): 1073–1103.

Griswold v. Connecticut. Supreme Court of the United States. 381 U.S. 479 (1965).

Halley, Janet E. "Reasoning About Sodomy: Act and Identity in and after *Bowers v. Hardwick*." *Virginia Law Review* (1993): 1721–1780.

Hamdi et al. v. Rumsfeld, Secretary of Defense, et al. 124 S. Ct. 2633. 2004. Plurality Opinion.

Jakobsen, Janet R. and Ann Pellegrini. *Love the Sin: Sexual Regulation and the Limits of Religious Tolerance*. Boston: Beacon Press, 2004.

Kirby, David. "Coming to America to be Gay." *The Advocate*, March 27, 2001: 29–32.

Laclau, Ernesto and Chantal Mouffe. *Hegemony and Socialist Strategy: Towards a Radical Democratic Politics*. London: Verso, 1985.

Lawrence v. Texas. Supreme Court of the United States. 539 U.S. 558 (2003).

Leonard, Arthur S. "Legal Challenges after Lawrence." *The Gay & Lesbian Review* 10.6 (November–December 2003): 21–22.

Luibhéid, Eithne. *Entry Denied: Controlling Sexuality at the Border.* Minneapolis: University of Minnesota Press, 2002.

McGoldrick, Brian J. "United States Immigration Policy and Sexual Orientation: Is Asylum for Homosexuals a Possibility?" *Georgetown Immigration Law Journal* 8 (1994): 201–226.

Mouffe, Chantal. "Feminism, Citizenship and Radical Democratic Politics." *Feminists Theorize the Political.* Ed. Judith Butler and Joan W. Scott. New York: Routledge, 1992. 369–384.

Olmstead v. United States. Supreme Court of the United States. 277 U.S. 438 (1928).

Park, Jin S. "Pink Asylum: Political Asylum Eligibility of Gay Men and Lesbians Under U. S. Immigration Policy." *UCLA Law Review* 1069 (1995): 1115–1156.

Planned Parenthood of Southeastern Pa. v. Casey. Supreme Court of the United States. 505 U.S. 833 (1992).

Ramanathan, Erik D. "Queer Cases: A Comparative Analysis of Global Sexual Orientation-Based Asylum Jurisprudence." *Georgetown Immigration Law Journal* 11 (1996): 1–44.

Resnik, Judith. "Categorical Federalism: Jurisdiction, Gender, and the Globe." *The Yale Law Journal* 111.3 (2001): 619–681.

Rasul et al. v. Bush, President of the United States, et al. Supreme Court of the United States. 542 U.S (2004).

Roe v. Wade. Supreme Court of the United States. 410 U.S. 113 (1973).

Romer v. Evans. Supreme Court of the United States. 517 U.S. 620 (1996).

Rumsfeld, Secretary of Defense v. Padilla, et al. 124 S. Ct. 2711 (2004).

Rosaldo, Renato. "Cultural Citizenship, Inequality, and Multiculturalism." *Latino Cultural Citizenship: Claiming Identity, Space, and Rights.* Ed. William Flores and Rina Benmayor. Boston: Beacon Press, 1997. 27–38.

Rubenstein, William B. *Cases and Materials on Sexual Orientation and the Law.* 2nd edition. St. Paul, Minnesota: West Publishing Co., 1997.

Sandel, Michael. "Moral Argument and Liberal Toleration: Abortion and Homosexuality." *California Law Review* 77 (1989); excerpted and reprinted in Eskridge and Hunter, 71–72.

Sosa v. Alvarez-Machain. Supreme Court of the United States. 124 S. Ct. 2739 (2004).

Thomas, Kendall. "*Corpus Juris (Hetero)Sexualis*: Doctrine, Discourse, and

Desire in *Bowers v. Hardwick.*" *A Queer World: The Center for Lesbian and Gay Studies Reader.* Ed. Martin Duberman. New York: New York University Press, 1997. 438–451.

Walker, Kristen. "The Importance of Being Out: Sexuality and Refugee Status." *Sydney Law Review* 18 (1996): 568–597.

Warner, Michael. *The Trouble with Normal: Sex, Politics, and the Ethics of Queer Life.* Cambridge, Mass.: Harvard University Press, 1999.

West, Robin. *Narrative, Authority, and Law.* Ann Arbor: University of Michigan Press, 1993.

Notes

1   Legal historians point to Justice Luis D. Brandeis, in his dissent in *Olmstead v. United States*, as being the first to advocate a "right to be let alone" (Eskridge and Hunter 8). But the so-called "right to privacy" remains contentious. Antonin Scalia, in his dissent to *Lawrence*, openly rejects a constitutional right of privacy, calling it "penumbral to the *specific* guarantees in the Bill of Rights" (11 emphasis original). The penumbral reference harks back to *Griswold v. Connecticut*, in which Justice Douglas wrote that "specific guarantees in the Bill of Rights have penumbras, formed by emanations of those guarantees that help give them life and substance" (*Griswold* 484). As Eskridge and Hunter note, it is *Roe v. Wade* that "authoritatively established the right of privacy in the due process clause and formally abandoned *Griswold*'s experiment in penumbral reasoning" (xliv).

2   Such cases as *Rasul v. Bush*, *Hamdi v. Rumsfeld*, and *Rumsfeld v. Padilla*, all of which involve questions of national and international jurisdiction, sovereignty, and citizenship, and all of which were decided only a year after *Lawrence*, give a measure of what is at stake. José Padilla is a U.S. citizen arrested at Chicago's O'Hare International Airport on charges that he had conspired with the al Qaeda network in the attacks of September 11, 2001. The Court did not decide Padilla's case, claiming that it had been improperly filed. It did decide the case of Yaser Esam Hamdi, a U.S. citizen who had been classified as an "enemy combatant" and was being held at a naval brig in Charleston, South Carolina and that of Shafiq Rasul (a British citizen who was subsequently released from custody after the Court granted certiorari) and two Australian and twelve Kuwaiti citizens who were captured during recent hostilities in Afghanistan and who were imprisoned, without counsel, at the U.S. Naval Base in Guantánamo, Cuba. In the Hamdi case, the Court decided that "although Congress authorized the detention of combatants in the narrow circumstances of this case, due process demands that a citizen held in the United States as an enemy combatant be given a meaningful opportunity to contest the factual basis for that detention before a neutral decisionmaker" (*Hamdi* syllabus 2).

The decisions have been read as a rebuke to the Bush administration, as has—albeit with certain well-founded reservations—the decision in the case of *Sosa v. Alvarez-Machain,* which centers on the U.S. Drug Enforcement Administration's use of Sosa and other Mexican nationals to abduct Alvarez-Machain, also a Mexican national, and to bring him to the United States to stand trial for a DEA agent's torture and murder.

3   "Apart from the fact that such an 'emerging awareness' does not establish a 'fundamental right,' the statement [that there is 'an *emerging awareness* that liberty gives substantial protection to adult persons in deciding how to conduct their private lives in matters pertaining to sex'] is factually false. States continue to prosecute all sorts of crimes by adults 'in matters pertaining to sex': prostitution, adult incest, adultery, obscenity, and child pornography. Sodomy laws, too, have been enforced 'in the past half century,' in which there have been 134 reported cases involving prosecutions for consensual, adult, homosexual sodomy" (Scalia dissent 13–14, emphasis original). Scalia invokes a sense of history as an unfolding process— "States *continue* to prosecute"—only to reassert a putatively unassailable, "factual" ground: "In any event, an 'emerging awareness' is by definition not "deeply rooted in this Nation's history and tradition[s],' as we have said 'fundamental right' status requires" (*Lawrence* Scalia dissent 14).

4   *Foster v. Florida* deals with the death penalty and the delays in its administration, about which the Supreme Court of Canada, as Justice Breyer reminded the U.S. Court, had expressed concern. Justice Thomas is critical of Justice Breyer for having "only added another foreign court to his list while still failing to ground support for his theory in any decision by an American court" (*Foster* Thomas concurring 1, note).

5   The peculiarity of the United States *vis-à-vis* the rest of the West is by no means limited to questions of sexuality. Capital punishment, for instance, places the U.S. in a circuit with China and Iran, not with Great Britain and Germany.

6   Due Process is frequently qualified as "procedural" or "substantive." Jo Ann Citron, in an engaging article on the differing status of "liberty" and "equality" in *Lawrence,* writes that: "lawyers speak tautologically of 'procedural due process' and oxymoronically of 'substantive due process.' In its procedural garb, the Due Process Clause guarantees that the government may not deprive you of life or liberty or property without giving you some kind of procedure whereby you can challenge the threatened deprivation. In its substantive garb, the Due Process Clause guarantees that the government cannot interfere with an individual's fundamental liberty interests. Perhaps as a way of avoiding the 'emanations and penumbras' problem [as articulated in *Griswold*], the *Lawrence* court styled the petitioners' right to privacy as a liberty interest grounded in the Fourteenth Amendment's Due Process Clause" (20). While a reference to the Due Process Clause is

indeed typically to the Fourteenth Amendment, the Court also refers to the Fifth Amendment and hence to "Due Process Clauses" (*Lawrence* 18).

7   *Stare decisis*, a Latin term, means "to stand by that which is decided" and designates the principle of legal precedent.

8   The invocation of foreign laws and traditions with regards to sexuality and morality is by no means unprecedented. The American Law Institute's Model Penal Code, from 1955, distinguishes between private and public morality and makes reference to the Anglican clergy and the British Government (Eskridge and Hunter 745).

9   Eskridge and Hunter engage the question of heterosexuality as a requirement for citizenship by citing the 1981 case of Horst Nemetz, a West German whose petition for naturalization was denied by the INS' inquiry board on the grounds that Nemetz did not demonstrate "good moral character" (742–743). See *Nemetz v. INS*, 647 F.2d 432 (4th Cir. 1981). Arguably more significant is *Boutilier v. Immigration and Naturalization Service*, a case involving a Canadian who was ordered deported on the grounds that, as a homosexual, he was excludable on the basis of "psychopathic personality." As Eskridge and Hunter note, "[b]y the 1970s, the INS did not consider either fornication or adultery to be disqualifying, but it still considered private homosexual conduct disqualifying" (743).

10 An article by David Kirby in the popular gay and lesbian magazine, *The Advocate*, maintains that "coming out often means joining the sexual migration to the U.S." (29). Needless to say, the sexual migration is not always clear-headed. As a member of a queer Latino/a advocacy group called LLEGO reports, sometimes people arrive with the "expectation that as a gay person you can live the life you see on *Will and Grace*—like you get a toaster when you join the club" (29).

11 Although identity is frequently presented, defended, and impugned as transhistorical (i.e., there have been homosexuals throughout history), it has also been presented as eminently historical (i.e., the homosexual is a modern formation). The recourse to acts, most notably "sodomy," though frequently associated with a constructivist method, can serve however to support a transhistorical argument of its own: the names may change, but the acts remain the same and, on the basis of said sameness, identity reasserts itself: a homosexual is a sodomite, and sodomites practice sodomy, and sodomy is such and such an act regardless of time and place. Still, as Anker notes, "[u]nder current U.S. law [before *Lawrence*], "criminalization of homosexual *conduct* is not necessarily unconstitutional, whereas distinctions based on homosexual *orientation* may be" (396 n. 747, emphasis original). Parallels with the religious distinction between the sin and the sinner are unavoidable.

12 "In Hardwick," Halley writes, "the Court refused to specify what it steadfastly termed 'sodomy.' Although it set out to determine whether a right

to commit sodomy was denied at constitutionally significant moments in the past, it failed to ask itself what an act of sodomy is. Throughout Justice White's footnote history of sodomy, and even more sweepingly in Chief Justice Burger's concurring opinion, sodomy is always and only 'sodomy'; 'homosexual sodomy' is treated as its equivalent, and no specification of bodily contacts is offered. By this means the Court can hide—but just barely!—the problem exposed with great care by [Anne B.] Goldstein: that fellatio, the act for which Hardwick was in fact arrested, cannot be shown to have been sodomy in 1791 or 1868" (1760–1761). Justice White's majority opinion does offer a definition of "sodomy," however. It cites the "Georgia Code Ann. 16-6-2 (1984) [that] provides, in pertinent part, as follows: '(a) A person commits the offense of sodomy when he performs or submits to any sexual act involving the sex organs of one person and the mouth or anus of another. . . .' (b) A person convicted of the offense of sodomy shall be punished by imprisonment for not less than one nor more than 20 years" (*Bowers* footnote 1).

13 The Court relies on the substantive component of the Fourteenth Amendment's Due Process Clause and O'Connor on the Fourteenth Amendment's Equal Protection Clause (*Lawrence* O'Connor concurring 1).

14 As if aware of the precariousness of his argument, Scalia goes on to say that "[e]ven if the Texas law *does* deny equal protection to 'homosexuals as a class,' that denial *still* does not need to be justified by anything more than a rational basis, which our cases show is satisfied by the enforcement of traditional notions of sexual morality" (*Lawrence* dissent 17, emphasis original). All of the niceties of argumentation come down to this: homosexuality, as a "lifestyle," is "immoral and destructive" and "the moral opprobrium that has traditionally attached to [it]" (*Lawrence* Scalia dissent 18) should be preserved unchecked. Accusing the Court of having "signed on to the so-called homosexual agenda," Scalia rants against what he presents as the Court's lack of "rational basis" and "neutrality" (*Lawrence* Scalia dissent 18). That his own "rationality" is based on traditional morality, which has hardly functioned rationally, and that his own position is in no way neutral, does not deter Scalia from impugning his colleagues.

15 Scalia's anxious claim that he has "nothing against homosexuals, or any other group, promoting their agendas through normal democratic means," no less than his begrudging recognition that "[s]ocial perceptions of sexual morality change over time" (*Lawrence* Scalia dissent 19), does *not* change the fact that he holds on to a an essentially unchanging understanding of morality, rationality, and constitutional law (after all, he writes of changes in *perceptions* of sexual morality, not in sexual morality itself).

16 Fearing that *Lawrence* contains the seeds for a new understanding of sanctioned relationality, Scalia writes: "[t]his case 'does not involve' the issue of homosexual marriage only if one entertains the belief that principle and logic have nothing to do with the decisions of this Court. Many will hope

that, as the Court comfortingly assures us, this is so" (*Lawrence* Scalia dissent 21). Others who hope otherwise obviously do not signify.

17   One of Scalia's major complaints is that the Court imposes its gay-friendly views "in absence of democratic majority" (*Lawrence* Scalia dissent 19); it is the same complaint that motivated his dissent in *Romer v. Evans*. Scalia's notion that democratic change can only be effected through legislation is historically shaky. As Eskridge and Hunter remind us, Margaret Higgins Singer, an important forerunner in the push for the right of privacy in matters sexual, "decided that birth control reform would come about more quickly by challenging the laws through the judiciary than by seeking legislative change" (4). We can also think of the role of the judicial system in the Civil Rights movement, perhaps most famously in *Brown v. Board of Education*.

18   The USA PATRIOT Act, passed by the 107th Congress in October 2001, stands for "Uniting and Strengthening America by Providing Appropriate Tools Required to Intercept and Obstruct Terrorism."

19   Silliness seems to dog the law. Scalia, in his dissent to *Romer v. Evans* avers that the majority's decision is evidence that "our constitutional jurisprudence has achieved terminal silliness" (*Romer* Scalia dissent 4).

20   Rumors and speculations about Atta's sexuality peppered the popular press and the Internet. The "homosexualization" of the enemies of the United States has a long history. Jonathan Goldberg, for instance, has studied the plays between "Saddam" and "Sodom" in jingoistic depictions of the ousted Iraqi leader (1–2). For more on the Cold War view of homosexuals as potential traitors, see Lee Edelman's excellent article.

21   Justice Clark, delivering the opinion of the Court in *Boutilier*, affirms that "the term 'psychopathic personality,' as used by the Congress . . . was a term of art intended to exclude homosexuals from entry into the United States. It further found that the term was not void for vagueness and was, therefore, not repugnant to the Fifth Amendment's Due Process Clause" (119). For more on nomenclature and exclusion, see Rubenstein (109–111), Foss (446), and Luibhéid (77–79). At any rate, the legacy of the "unmentionable vice" and the "love that dare not speak its name" permeates discussion of sexuality in the Courts. What Halley wrote of *Bowers* still largely holds for *Lawrence*: "When an act is not fit to be named among Christians, a court seeking to find its first prohibition might be expected to have difficulty" (1760).

22   Eskridge and Hunter cite the case of *Marie Posusta v. United States* (U.S. Court of Appeals for the Second Circuit, 1961), in which a Czechoslovakian woman, Marie Posusta, appealed an order that had denied her petition to be naturalized as a U.S. citizen on the basis of her "moral character." The petitioner had been Posusta's lover and was the mother of a child by him while Posusta was married to another woman (740–742).

23 For more on asylum and homosexuality, see Anker (394–398); Suzanne Goldberg; McGoldrick; Ramanathan; Park; and Walker.

24 The status of "homosexuals" and homosexuality in many countries, especially those with laws based on deeply rooted morals, remains obscure. Amnesty International, after its 1991 meeting in Yokohama, Japan, in which it voted to advocate on behalf of people imprisoned, tortured, or otherwise persecuted by the state for their homosexuality, has paid special attention to Iran, where sodomy is punishable by death, but also to Mauritania, Yemen, Saudi Arabia, Pakistan, the Sudan, and Oman (33–34).

25 As Eskridge and Hunter note: "Just as the exclusion of gay people was being polished off, a new exclusion was inserted. Senator Jesse Helms in 1987 sponsored an appropriations rider that directed Health and Human Services (HHS) to list AIDS (later, 'HIV infection') as one of the infectious diseases for which noncitizens could be excluded from entering the United States. [. . .] To the extent that HIV infection is associated with gay and bisexual men, the HIV infection exclusion becomes a partial replacement for the gay exclusion—a striking example of the medicalization of American anxieties about sexuality" (189).

26 Scalia excoriates "the law profession's anti-anti-homosexual culture" as not belonging to the "mainstream" (*Lawrence* Scalia dissent 19). The mainstream, with its traditional morality, is for Scalia the site and sign of neutrality and rationality; prejudice, bigotry, and intolerance simply do not obtain.

27 Strong as the old governing rule is, Falwell's "retraction" in a phone call to CNN is nonetheless indicative of the power of the "new governing rule." After all, he feels compelled by the roar of public response to nuance his position and to reassure the public that he too respects a principle of democratic diversity.

28 Until *Lawrence v. Texas*, the non-heteronormative (or queer) citizen was a logical contradiction, a legal aberration, and a fantasized player in a contestatory, activist-directed *Queer Nation*. And yet, full queer citizenship, as should hopefully be clear by now, is *not* secured with *Lawrence v. Texas*. Moral opprobrium endures and, if Justice Scalia's dissent is any indication, assumes a more heroic, for embattled, tone—a tone in tune with the rhetoric of fear and suspicion that characterizes "America under attack." Restrictions in the military and defenses of marriage likewise endure and even heat up, and a host of prestigious universities, including my own, turn a blind eye to on-campus military recruitment even though the military's policies violate university policies of non-discrimination.

29 The right of homosexuals to marry, or more precisely the right to homosexual marriage, undoubtedly constitutes a commendable opening and expansion of the ideal of equality, but it does not, and cannot, constitute the aim and objective of any politics that seriously invokes said ideal.

Marriage, however expanded (though not, in any remotely realistic way, beyond the couple, the sanctified and sanctioned "two" of Western sexuality), cannot do the work of equality unless the financial and legal privilege that characterizes it is dismantled too. Those who, like Thomas Stoddard or Catharine MacKinnon (see Rubenstein 726), claim that gay marriage might lead to a liberatory destabilization of the institution of marriage as a whole underestimate, I submit, the stabilizing effects that marriage might have on those individuals who enter it.

30 Anti-sodomy laws have been rendered only facially obsolete because, as Nan Hunter notes, "[s]odomy laws have been most frequently enforced indirectly, not directly, by the denial of custody or other parental rights to gay parents or by exclusions from certain jobs . . . even though the litigants had never been convicted of illegal conduct" (unpublished article quoted in Franke 1405).

31 It is tempting, if politically tendentious, to style the difference in terms of permissive or "free" states and prohibitive or "unfree" states. The implicit North-South divide is not, however, historically consistent or neat; Massachusetts and Connecticut (as in *Griswold v. Connecticut*) were, after all, among the last states to prohibit the use of birth control devices. In 1961, in his dissent to *Poe v. Ullman*, Justice Harlan challenged, by way of the due process clause, such prohibitions, but it was not until Griswold, some four years later, that the prohibitions were struck down (Eskridge and Hunter xliii–xliv).

32 Scalia's position, shared by any number of conservative politicians, is consistent with what has been called "categorical federalism," the idea that the category "family," as in "family law," is the province of the states and their particular, popular understanding of morality. Legal scholar Judith Resnik writes of the "not only fictive but harmful" character of categorical federalism in an engaging essay that criticizes the claim that the Violence Against Women Act "impermissibly addressed activities definitional of and reserved to state governance" (619). Sounding out a distinction made by the Chief Justice of the Supreme Court in 2000 between the "truly local" and the "truly national," Resnik argues that the phrases belie considerable anxiety about the international, transnational, and global (620).

33 Lauren Berlant and Chantal Mouffe (also with Ernesto Laclau) discuss fragmentation and "chains of equivalence" respectively: I explore these concepts more fully in the final section.

34 As Franke notes, the tendency to punish those who engage in homosexual activities with a minor much more severely than those who engage in heterosexual activities with a minor (she reports that the length of sentences in Kansas can be thirteen times longer for homosexual acts than for heterosexual acts) has not changed after *Lawrence* (1412).

35 According to Leonard, although *Lawrence* "could have been the vehicle to begin addressing" such questions as parental rights, military service, and marriage, "the way in which Justice Kennedy wrote the Court's opinion falls short of providing a clear roadmap for analyzing the constitutional questions" (22). The effect is as ambiguous as the text, though Leonard opts for a more promising reading: "Perhaps Kennedy concluded, as a strategic matter, that in such an emotionally charged case it was best to 'keep 'em guessing,' and that's just where he has left us" (22). Kennedy himself indicates as much: "Had those who drew and ratified the Due Process Clauses of the Fifth Amendment or the Fourteenth Amendment known the components of liberty in its manifold possibilities, they might have been more specific. They did not presume to have this insight" (*Lawrence* 18).

36 The status of homosexuals as citizens cannot be "full" as long as initiatives to enshrine in the constitution their disenfranchisement (via "protection of marriage" amendments) are so strongly supported. What is more, the discourse of rights is itself not devoid of problems. As Franke writes, "rights, particularly in the form articulated in *Lawrence*, cannot exhaust our political projects. *Lawrence* recognizes, in a manner far more robust than *Romer v. Evans*, that homosexuals are rights-bearing subjects. But the political agenda leveraged by that recognition does not exceed honor of the domesticated private" (1413).

37 The interrelated status of due process and a right of privacy remains charged. According to Scalia, "[t]he Court's description of 'the state of the law' at the time of *Bowers* only confirms that *Bowers* was right. *Ante*, at 5. The Court points to *Griswold v. Connecticut*. . . . But that case *expressly disclaimed* any reliance on the doctrine of 'substantive due process,' and grounded the so-called 'right to privacy' in penumbras of constitutional provisions *other than* the Due Process Clause" (*Lawrence* dissent 10, emphasis original). Scalia is clearly impugning the *Lawrence* Court's invocation of a right to privacy but he is also impugning its reliance, via *Roe v. Wade*, on an argument of due process. In reference to *Roe*, the *Lawrence* Court claims that: "[a]lthough the Court held the *woman's* rights were *not* absolute, her right to elect an abortion did have real and substantial protection as an exercise of her liberty under the Due Process Clause" (*Lawrence* 4, emphasis added). It might be implicit that the Court holds that the *man's* rights are also not absolute, but where more than one Justice insists on the letter of the Law, such plays of the explicit and implicit are not without ramifications. At the very least, references to "woman" and "man," "homosexual" and "heterosexual," implicate the Court itself, the Justices who sit on it.

38 The very notion of structural equality—homosexual equals heterosexual—is troubled by history, for the Court effectively takes the heterosex-

ual, duly idealized, as the unacknowledged model for a fractured, belated, on-going process of "equalization" in which dignity and enduring bonds loom large.

39 "[T]he Justices engage in masking their own status as potential sodomites even if they never stray from the class of heterosexuals. Invisibility is here immunity" (Halley 1770). Kendall Thomas, who ventures an exercise in the "psychoanalysis of juridical discourse" (442) in his reading of *Bowers v. Hardwick*, is even more emphatic: "[a] decision for Hardwick would effectively 'emasculate' the Court by undermining the patriarchal (hetero)sexual ideologies and identities on which American constitutional law ultimately rests" (442).

40 Robin West addresses the Justices' sexuality as well, albeit in a way that foregrounds the solidarity through suffering that Berlant questions: "An expansion of *Griswold* . . . [to encompass *Bowers*] would have required the judge to look behind the differences between himself and his own marriage and Hardwick's relationship, between his desires and Hardwick's, between homosexuality and heterosexuality, to their shared humanity" (342).

41 I can well imagine the protests: I do not mean to say that non-heteronormative, gay and lesbian, or queer relationships cannot be enduring, homey, and private, but simply that enduring, homey, private relationships have long been figured as the privilege and property of heteronormativity; any attempt to vindicate such qualities for non-heterosexuals must contend, like it or not, with the continued drag of said privilege and property.

42 I am in general agreement with Citron that "a legal decision often has a subtext as well as a literal text. *Lawrence* isn't simply about striking down one of the last of the sodomy statutes. If it were, O'Connor's equal protection theory would have sufficed. What the subtext of *Lawrence* is about is marriage" (20). I would simply add that there are often subtexts, in the plural, or indeed subtexts to subtexts, and that abortion rights, women's rights, and immigration rights are also implicated in *Lawrence*.

43 Michael Sandel's contention, in 1989, that the Court had "long since renounced" the "'old-fashioned' reading of *Griswold* as protecting the human good realized in marriage" in favor of "an individualist reading" (quoted in Eskridge and Hunter 71) was clearly premature. Even though the *Lawrence* Court does not specifically endorse gay marriage, it does resort to romantically tinged rhetoric to construct "an analogy between privacy in marriage and privacy in homosexual relations," as Sandel had observed with respect to the appeals court in the Hardwick case (quoted in Eskridge and Hunter 71). As Franke writes, "*Lawrence*'s privatized liberty appears to resuscitate a very early, more limited, and more institutional version of the privacy right" (1404).

44 In the *Bowers* case, the Court had proclaimed that: "[t]he Constitution does not confer a fundamental right upon homosexuals to engage in sodomy. None of the fundamental rights announced in this Court's prior cases involving family relationships, marriage, or procreation bear any resemblance to the right asserted in this case" (*Bowers* 1). *Lawrence* reverses *Bowers*, but it does so by at once *reiterating* and *amplifying* the discourse of family relationships, marriage, and procreation and/or the raising of children; it does so not by affirming difference and particularity as principles of equality but by affirming a *resemblance* that is, more precisely, an enduringly dignified identity.

45 The "founding fathers" function not just as the emblem and incarnation of foundationalism but as subjects whose gender and sexuality are simultaneously avowed (as men who engender, who father) and disavowed (as men whose sexual practice is sublimated into nationalist ideology). The act by which a father founds himself as father, the act of insemination, is ever so properly left unsaid, kept off stage and rendered ob-scene, while a sanitized family structure is stressed amid an obsessive rehearsal of dangers—i.e., homosexuality, female autonomy, abortion, and immigration—*against* which it acquires meaning.

46 "In those circles where queerness has been most cultivated," Warner writes, "the ground rule is that one doesn't pretend to be above the indignity of sex. And although this usually isn't announced as an ethical vision, that what it perversely is. In queer circles, you are likely to be teased until you grasp the idea. Sex is understood as being as various as the people who have it. It is not required to be tidy, normal, uniform, or authorized by the government" (35).

47 Warner, though not focusing on immigration, appears aware of the implications, for he understands that *everyone* in the United States is enjoined to play more or less the same role—more or less, for the variations make the rigidity of the dominant theme seem ever so supple. Far from assuming that, for instance, class and ethnicity do not make a difference in the plays of dignity and shame, Warner sharpens his critical knives against those who, *like himself*, enjoy a certain privilege, notably among them the British critic, Andrew Sullivan.

48 For a careful account of how asylum law takes pains to avoid making international judgments, see Matthew Price's chapter in this volume.

49 "The more people are privatized," claims Warner, "the more vulnerable they are to the unequal effects of shame" (12). Of course, the more people are "publicized," the more vulnerable they are to the unequal effects of shame. Privatization can render people more vulnerable to shame when privatization itself is made vulnerable, when the regime of privacy is threatened with intrusion and exposure—a threat, of course, that may well inhere in the very notion of privacy.

50 West offers a productively different reading. According to her, "*Griswold* and *Roe*, sympathetically read, protect not family rights, but indeed, their very opposite: they represent an endorsement of the intimacy, pleasure, and growth to which decidedly nonfamilial and nonreproductive sexuality is conducive" (341).

51 A comparative consideration of laws designed to protect homosexuals and to protect women, both domestically and internationally, might lead to the following: pleasure is privatized; pain, publicized. Then again, in the United States explicit pleasure has long been consigned to the realm of pornography and explicit violence to the realm of something like everyday life (schools, post offices, airports, streets, subways, and so on, including, of course, an all-pervasive entertainment industry).

52 See my "The Fetish of Fluidity," which offers a critique of a tendency among many queer theorists to abstract arguments from an unexamined U.S. or Western legal regime and to underestimate the force of blockages and borders.

53 For more on the significance of a "chain of equivalence" see Laclau and Mouffe's *Hegemony and Socialist Practice.*

54 The transvaluation of the term "queer" is symptomatic of the reworking of stigmatization: a pejorative term is reclaimed in a way that signals the plays of dignity and indignity, pride and shame.

55 Asylum claims must be based on "the immutable characteristic of [the applicant's] homosexual status," which is, furthermore, extensible to an entire social group (Anker 396). As Park notes, bisexuals and bisexuality do not commonly figure in asylum claims (1116, n. 5). Transsexualism, transgenderism, and even transvestism also constitute "special cases" or "problems."

56 Part of the democratic process, Laclau and Mouffe contend, is the opening of sites traditionally held to be beyond or outside democracy such as the home and, indeed, the body. Lest this democratic opening be taken as absolute, they argue that democracy does not dispense with a certain closure. Accordingly, they set a principle of equivalence, by which all sites are equalized, alongside a principle of autonomy, by which sites remain different, in a mutually limiting way (185).

6

Gay Rights Are Human Rights: Gay Asylum Seekers in Canada

Bill Fairbairn

Proceeding out of a faith-based commitment to the intrinsic value of all human life, Canada's Inter-Church Committee on Human Rights in Latin America (ICCHRLA) has begun the task of breaking the silence surrounding the systematic violations committed against lesbians and gay men in many Latin American countries. Throughout the 1970s and 1980s, a large number of human rights groups emerged in Latin America, often in response to abuses perpetrated under military dictatorships. For the majority of these groups, however, issues of sexual orientation did not, and, sadly, often still do not, register on their cognitive maps. Thus, very few of these groups have documented abuses against lesbians and gay men, and those that have done so have provided only an incomplete assessment of the phenomenon. *Violence Unveiled: Repression Against Lesbians and Gay Men in Latin America* was published by ICCHRLA in 1996 as a modest contribution to help lift the veil of silence in this area of human rights and to provide additional documentation for asylum cases.

ICCHRLA, a broadly based ecumenical coalition, existed from 1977–2001[1] and emerged from an earlier ecumenical project, the Inter-Church Committee on Chile, created by Canadian churches in the days following the 1973 military coup in Chile. ICCHRLA brought together twenty Canadian churches and religious groups and worked closely with churches, human rights associations, and grassroots organizations throughout Latin America. Our work involved regular visits and fact-finding missions to virtually every country in the region. The missions took us to war zones in El Salvador and Colombia, to military barracks and prisons in Peru and Chile (where we accompanied family members of the disappeared looking for their loved ones), and to *maquiladoras* in Mexico and Central America, where human rights are routinely violated.[2] With the information gathered during our visits, ICCHRLA collaborated with Latin American partners to press the Canadian government, as well as corporations and multilateral bodies like the United Nations and the Organization of American States, to implement policies and practices that protect and promote human rights. We also presented our findings to the Canadian Immigration and Refugee Board (IRB), where they have been used as evidence in immigration hearings involving Latin Americans seeking refuge or asylum in Canada. We have occasionally appeared as "expert witnesses" before the IRB in briefings of a general nature, or in individual hearings involving Latin American asylum seekers. In addition to particular information about individual countries and cases, we grappled with the ways in which the status of knowledge—who knows what, and how, and with what amount of eyewitness experience and/or documented research—is critical to any engagement of the complex legalities and realities of immigration.

Asylum Based on Sexual Orientation: The Canadian Model

When a person claims refugee status in Canada, he or she begins what can be a long and daunting process that usually culminates in a formal hearing conducted by the Immigration and Refugee Board. The Canadian Parliament created the IRB in the late 1980s to be an independent, administrative tribunal with quasi-judicial functions. Prior to June 2002, hearings were conducted by a panel of two IRB members and, in most situations, only one member of the panel needed to decide in favour of the claimant in order for him or her to be granted convention refugee status.[3] A Refugee Claims Officer, whose task it was to assist the IRB members before and during the proceedings by ensuring that all relevant evidence was properly presented, normally accompanied the IRB panel. The Immigration and Refugee Protection Act (IRPA), passed by the Canadian Parliament on June 28, 2002, made a number of changes to the procedures, among the most noteworthy and controversial that of reducing the number of decision-makers in the hearing from two to one board member.[4]

Change often comes quickly, and rather confusingly, to immigration law and practice. The first case of a person granted asylum in Canada based on sexual orientation dates only from 1992. The case centered on an Argentine man who testified to being expelled from school, fired from several jobs, repeatedly harassed, and even arrested for being gay.

He charged that during his detention, he had been subjected to beatings and to other forms of torture, including rape. The IRB members were split on their decision,[5] but under the system in place at the time, the one positive vote of an IRB member was enough for the man to be granted asylum.[6] This landmark case motivated others to come forward and tell their stories with the hope that they too might receive formal asylum.

Several immigration lawyers who had solid cases involving persecution based on sexual orientation but who lacked sufficient documentation or witnesses soon approached ICCHRLA. Specifically, they asked for our help in corroborating the stories given by their clients and in providing testimony about the human rights conditions of sexual minorities in Latin America. One of the main obstacles the lawyers identified was that a number of IRB members clearly did not believe that documentation provided by LGBT groups was objective and therefore credible information.

Aware of the importance of narratives of personal experience in the presentation and adjudication of asylum claims, I want to share here, from my perspective as an advocate, two of the cases in which I was personally involved as an expert witness. Both cases involve gay men from Ecuador who had faced repression at the hands of the police. Until 1997, Ecuador's penal code criminalized homosexual activity between consenting adults, with a mandatory prison sentence of four to eight years. Although the penalty was rarely, if ever, enforced, it served as a constant threat, allowing police to harass, abuse, and extort lesbians, gay men, transvestites, and transgendered people.

"Juan's" Case

The story of Juan (a pseudonym) is one of systematic discrimination and persecution. He was arrested for the first time in December 1988 as he was leaving a semi-clandestine gay club with two friends. The three men were held for two days, during which time they were subjected to physical violence, including beatings with police batons. Throughout their detention, the men were repeatedly taunted and insulted by the authorities who called them, among other things, "*maricones*" ("faggots"). Two months after this incident, police raided Juan's house, forcing their way inside, ransacking its contents, and stealing money and jewelry. Juan later went to the police station to file a complaint. The authorities refused to file the report and, instead, insulted him and ordered him to leave the station. Shortly thereafter, Juan began to receive threatening phone calls. The callers said they would kill him and mutilate his body. Juan did not report these threats to the authorities because he suspected that the police themselves were behind them, and he feared that filing a report would only make matters worse.

In September 1989, two armed men attacked Juan as he was leaving his place of work. They called him "*maricón*" and kicked him until he lost consciousness. Despite his serious misgivings, Juan's mother convinced him to report the attack to the police. When he arrived at the police station, Juan recognized a uniformed officer on duty as one of the attackers and immediately left the station. The threatening phone calls increased, prompting Juan to move, under duress, to another Ecuadorian city where he lived with a friend and his family. After a short respite, the calls began again and, in March 1990, three policemen arrived at the house where Juan was staying. They took Juan away and warned the family to keep quiet. Juan was taken to Quito and detained for almost three days during which time he was repeatedly beaten, kicked in the head, and hit with the butt of a gun. A barrage of taunts and insults about his sexual orientation accompanied the attacks. Juan was forced to perform oral sex on each of the guards and was raped by each of them.

Juan was released only after a friend of the family—an army officer—reluctantly intervened on his behalf. Before he was released, one of the guards who had raped Juan threatened him in no uncertain terms: "*Maricón*, you won't be so lucky the next time. You'll be killed and not even God can save you then." Understandably unnerved, Juan fled Ecuador shortly thereafter and came to Canada where he filed a refugee claim in 1992.

I was asked by Juan's lawyer to appear as a witness in his hearing and to testify about the general human rights situation in Ecuador, as well as the overall credibility of Juan's story. Remarkably, many of the questions that the IRB members raised during the hearing echoed the very same misgivings expressed by the dissenting IRB member in the case of the Argentine claimant.[7] I had the distinct impression that the IRB members were trying to find inconsistencies in Juan's story. With regards to the multiple rapes he suffered while in police custody, one of the members asked Juan whether he was trying to insinuate that the police officers who assaulted him were in fact "homosexual." The question itself revealed a lack of appreciation of male-male rape as a crime of violence rather than one of desire. Obviously, for Juan's assailants, there would be no question as to their (hetero)sexual orientation.[8] In her chapter in this book, Deborah Anker describes other accounts of rape described by asylum seekers as being "privatized" and trivialized, stating that "even cases that fit the traditional paradigms of refugee law were being dismissed—largely because the physical harm involved was sexual" (see p. 110).

In addition to questioning the sexual assaults, the IRB members also challenged the supplementary evidence presented by Juan's lawyer, which consisted primarily of reports from the San Francisco-based International Gay and Lesbian Human Rights Commission (IGLHRC). One board member appeared to dispute the credibility of the information, insinuating that the sources were not objective. I challenged the notion that an advocacy group could not gather and distribute credible or objectively verifiable information. Noting that the International Confederation of Free Trade Unions (ICFTU) is not considered biased when it reports on violations against trade unionists, and that the World Council of Churches is not considered biased when it speaks of attacks on religious freedom, I argued that IGLHRC was similarly reliable. After all, the International Gay and Lesbian Human Rights Commission bases its country reports and updates on information provided directly by lesbian and gay activists or organizations in Latin America and other parts of the world. Given the historically entrenched homophobia of many—indeed most—countries, it is entirely reasonable to expect that sexual minorities would feel more readily inclined to share information with groups that they trusted, in most cases, groups comprised of other lesbians and gay men. Therefore, lesbian and gay organizations that provide information about conditions faced by sexual minorities should not be dismissed as unreasonably biased but, rather, should be seen as potentially important, well-placed, and credible sources.

"Camilo's" Case

The second case in which I testified involved another Ecuadorian man, one who, like Juan, had faced arbitrary detention on many occasions and had, during his detentions, been beaten and sexually assaulted by police. In Camilo's (a pseudonym) hearing, the Refugee Claims Officer (RCO) attempted both to discredit the information provided by Camilo's lawyer about conditions in Ecuador, and to limit the scope of expert witness testimony. Before I could give my testimony, the RCO asked me when I had last been to Ecuador. I had returned just weeks earlier from a fact-finding mission to that country. The RCO then asked me whether the purpose of my visit had been to assess the situation of lesbians and gay men in Ecuador. I had to say no: I had been in Ecuador to assess the *overall human rights situation* in that country, which included, but was not limited to, the human rights of lesbians and gay men. At that point, the RCO wanted to know the names and number of groups with which I had met, and the percentage of each meeting that had been devoted to discussing issues of violence against lesbians and gay men.

In the end, the panel ruled that I could be considered an expert witness with respect to general human rights in Ecuador, but that I could *not* be considered an expert witness with respect to the supposedly more specific human rights of lesbians and gay men in Ecuador. All of us were quite surprised by the decision, which effectively separated human rights from gay and lesbian rights. Throughout my years working with ICCHRLA, I had given testimony as an expert witness in dozens of cases involving, among others, trade unionists from Colombia and student leaders from Peru. I found it particularly illustrative that prior to Camilo's case, I had never been challenged as to whether my visits to the region were to determine the situation of any particular group, nor had I ever had to provide details about how much of my time had been devoted to discussing any particular issue. Obviously the rules were different around issues of sexual orientation.

The Need for Credible Information

In spite of the initial concerns, positive decisions were handed down in the cases of both Juan and Camilo; moreover, several countries—including Canada—now interpret the UN Convention Relating to the Status of Refugees as extending to lesbians and gays who have a well-founded fear of persecution based on their sexual orientation. Since the first case of the gay Argentine claimant in 1992, there appears to be a greater appreciation among the IRB of the legitimate nature of asylum cases based on sexual orientation. During the past decade, IRB members have deemed many such cases of asylum seekers from a variety of countries to be credible and have granted the claimants convention refugee status. That said, the manner in which the IRB members dealt with these early cases and in particular the questions they raised about what constituted *credible* information helped convince us that we had a role to play in helping to document and expose violence against sexual minorities. In many ways, the concrete stories of real peoples' lives and life experiences—concretely, gay asylum seekers in Canada—

impressed on us the real need to broaden our own understanding of human rights and to look much more closely at the situation facing sexual minorities in our own fact-finding missions to Latin America and our reporting.

In June 1995, ICCHRLA sent a representative to the 17th World Conference of the International Lesbian and Gay Association (ILGA) in Rio de Janeiro, Brazil. The meeting brought together approximately 300 participants from some 60 countries, including delegates from at least eight Latin American nations, as well as representatives from various human rights organizations, including Amnesty International and IGLHRC.

This meeting, and in particular the testimonies shared by many of the participants, reinforced our belief that as a human rights organization we had both a responsibility and were in many ways well placed to make a positive contribution because of our extensive human rights advocacy and broad range of contacts throughout the Americas. A few months later, the ICCHRLA Board endorsed the proposal to produce a thematic report on violence against lesbians and gay men. In this way, we sought to help lift the veil of invisibility and silence around human rights violations against sexual minorities and to contribute to the pool of credible information that substantiates their legitimate claims for asylum. *Violence Unveiled: Repression Against Lesbians and Gay Men in Latin America* was published by ICCHRLA in 1996.

Challenges in Preparing *Violence Unveiled*

Lesbians and gay men were among the tens of thousands of persons to "disappear" during the Argentine military dictatorship. They have wasted away in Uruguayan prisons and have been tortured by Pinochet's secret police in Chile. They have been killed by death squads in Mexico, Brazil, Colombia, and El Salvador, have sought shelter and protection in Honduran refugee camps, and have been among the hundreds of thousands of internal refugees living in squalid conditions in Peru's *pueblos jóvenes*. At the same time, homosexuals have held, and continue to hold, positions of power in many Latin American countries. They are right-wing politicians and Supreme Court judges, military officials and cabinet ministers. In a few recent cases, it is widely rumoured that they have even occupied the position of president.

If there is a common denominator between these two groups, it is perhaps their *invisibility* as sexual minorities. In Latin America, as elsewhere, the social stigma associated with homosexuality forces the majority of lesbians and gay men to hide their sexual orientation. Furthermore, the rigid socio-economic stratification present in many countries means that those in the upper echelons risk irreversible loss of status and livelihood if their homosexual orientation is revealed. While all sexual minorities experience various degrees of repression, the level and extent of abuse depends largely on the person's degree of "visibility" as a homosexual and on his or her socio-economic position. For lesbians and gay men, many of the most common experiences of persecution are not directly related to state-sponsored acts or omissions but, rather, to the actions of private groups, individuals, and even family members.

The secrecy that surrounds lesbians and gay men, marking the violence perpetrated against them, posed a number of challenges to writing *Violence Unveiled*. Secrecy, silence, and invisibility are themselves contributing factors to the human rights violations suffered by lesbians and gay men in Latin America. In an October 1995 interview, Sister Elsie Monge, president of the Ecumenical Human Rights Commission of Ecuador (CEDHU), told ICCHRLA that abuses occur, "but [that] people are too frightened to come forward and denounce them." A generalized climate of homophobia, constantly reinforced by a variety of social organizations and the media, contributes to distorted, dehumanized views of lesbians and gay men as criminals, objects of ridicule, and/or psychologically impaired subjects. In Ecuador, according to Sister Monge, "Homosexuals are portrayed as abnormal people who are even considered dangerous because people believe they corrupt the youth." Brazilian gay activist Luiz Mott reported that in its coverage of the 7th Brazilian Meeting of Gays and Lesbians, the Rio de Janeiro newspaper *A Notícia* ran a front-page article with the headline "Faggots Want to Be People." The advent of HIV/AIDS and its identification in the media as a "gay disease" led to even more virulent attacks.

As a result, there has been little public sympathy or support when gays are arrested or assaulted. Many lesbians and gay men do not denounce the abuses to which they are subjected because they believe that they have no option but to tolerate them. Widespread impunity for crimes against gay men and lesbians is compounded by the fact that relatives are often too ashamed or embarrassed to push for an investigation. Similarly, the police often refuse to investigate crimes against lesbians and gay men, preferring to blame them on common delinquency or on lover's quarrels. With few exceptions, most of the abuses committed against lesbians and gay men in Latin America remain shrouded in silence, misinformation, and misunderstanding.

The case of Liborio Cruz is illustrative. In the early hours of June 27, 1995, a group of 15 or 20 men wielding iron bars, clubs, stones, and broken bottles hunted down Cruz, a 19-year-old gay man, in Mexico City's Colonia Obrera. Within minutes of the attack, Cruz's broken and lifeless body lay on the road, the Calzada de Tlalpan. In an article published several weeks later in the Mexican newspaper *La Jornada*, columnist Marta Lamas posed the question:

> Why has no one written about this [killing]? If this type of terrifying fascist violence by a death squad had ended the life of a student, a worker, or a woman, wouldn't there have been multiple expressions of indignation? Wouldn't the Attorney General or the Chief of Police have been hounded by reporters and questioned by the media and have been forced to make statements to the press? Wouldn't there have been official interest in clarifying the crime? But [the victim] was merely a transvestite, a "degenerate," someone who is sacrificed by true macho men whose manhood has been offended. Obviously, he looked for it and got what he deserved! (11)

Lamas' article helped expose what many "traditional" human rights groups in the region have not emphasized, nor, until recently, even reported: violence against sexual minorities. The few of these groups that have done so often have an incomplete assessment of the phenomenon. For example, in Colombia, one of the most important human rights organizations has reported killings of "homosexuals" in its quarterly reports, but it refers only to cases in which a man was dressed in a woman's clothing at the time of his murder.

In doing research for *Violence Unveiled*, ICCHRLA learned of a sad case in which a Uruguayan lesbian was arrested in 1977 during a military operation in that country. She was never seen again. The woman's family joined an association of relatives of the disappeared. However, according to Ana Martínez, "[o]nce [the members of the Association] learned of [the woman's] sexual orientation, they began to ignore her and her family. They abandoned all efforts to find her and no longer carried her picture in the marches they organized" (230).

Another important factor in the lack of documentation regarding abuses against sexual minorities is that Latin American lesbians and gay men generally have little faith that the system will protect their rights. The experience of Colombian human rights lawyer and gay rights activist Juan Pablo Ordoñez is, on this score, symptomatic of a more extensive trend. In November 1994, in the course of writing a report on human rights and sexual orientation in Colombia, Ordoñez interviewed Oswaldo Henríquez Linero, the Human Rights Ombudsman for the city of Barranquilla. In the course of the interview, Henríquez Linero stated:

> The moment a faggot begins hanging around my house, [his] human rights are over. . . . I'd rather have a daughter who is a whore than a faggot son. [If I were to have a homosexual child] I would treat him like the family dog, just like any other case from my office. I believe I love my dog more than I'd love a faggot. (65–66)

Although Ordoñez made a formal complaint and presented the National Human Rights Ombudsman, Jaime Córdoba Triviño, with a tape of the interview with Henríquez Linero, no disciplinary action was taken against him, and Henríquez Linero remained in office.

A Theological Option for the Excluded

For a church organization such as ICCHRLA, a key challenge in preparing *Violence Unveiled* was that Christian theology and church doctrines have themselves often been used to promote or legitimize discrimination and violence against lesbians and gay men. It is noteworthy that the report's very first recommendation challenges the Canadian churches themselves to review their policies and statements regarding sexual minorities to ensure that they are not advertently or inadvertently promoting intolerance and violence against lesbians and gay men and that their policies are congruent with international human rights standards.

Homophobia in Latin America, as elsewhere, permeates virtually every sector of society, including, sadly, church institutions and representatives. Many Latin American lesbian and gay Christians have been profoundly disheartened to see that some of their leaders, going against international human rights standards, have been outspoken in their support of colonial-era laws that criminalize homosexual acts. In other cases, Church leaders have worked actively to obstruct lesbian and gay assemblies or to prevent lesbian and gay organizations from obtaining legal status. With few exceptions, Church leaders in Latin America have remained silent in denouncing the ongoing assaults and assassinations of sexual minorities in their countries. Even worse, others, speaking in the name of the church, have made statements that have served to legitimize and incite violence against lesbians and gay men.

The religious roots of homophobia and the all too frequent religious justification of hatred against sexual minorities called us in ICCHRLA to reflect on the less often heard affirmation of God's value and love for all people. From that love, we believe, flow justice and the rejection of all forms of repressive violence and death. In a truly inclusive understanding of faith and justice, the promise of abundant life and freedom embraces lesbians and gay men. Accordingly, in producing *Violence Unveiled*, ICCHRLA followed two interlocking criteria for the defense of the human rights of lesbians and gay men: on the one hand, the theological affirmation of God's option for all who are oppressed, marginalized, and excluded; on the other hand, the political affirmation of the standards and obligations of international human rights laws, declarations, and agreements.

Violence Unveiled and Beyond

Since its publication in 1996, *Violence Unveiled* has served to support asylum claims by lesbians and gay men in Canada and the United States. It has also found its way into other circles, serving, for example, as a resource in a workshop on sexual orientation held at the 1998 General Assembly of the World Council of Churches in Zimbabwe. The Assembly, by the way, aroused great controversy, since Zimbabwean President Mugabe used the occasion to launch frenzied homophobic attacks on lesbian and gay activists.

Despite the intolerant rants of many politicians and religious figures the world over, there is hope of amelioration, particularly in Latin America. In the past few years, associations of gay men and lesbians have gradually emerged throughout Latin America and have begun to press for basic human rights. The process coincides, not surprisingly, with the end of formal military dictatorships throughout the region and with the consolidation of greater spaces for the expression of civil society. In some countries, these nascent groups have made their presence felt among the "traditional" human rights groups founded in the 1970s and 1980s and now work in coalition with these groups on a variety of human rights concerns.[9]

As a result of the growing presence and assertiveness of LGBT groups in Latin America, some of the "traditional" human rights groups in the region have become increasingly aware of attacks against sexual minorities and have sought to expose and combat them. The Colombian Commission of Jurists (CCJ) and the Ecuadorian Ecumenical Human Rights Commission (CEDHU) have both documented cases of arbitrary detention, torture, or killing of sexual minorities in their countries. The Human Rights Office of the Archdiocese of Mexico has denounced the killings of transvestites in the state of Chiapas; the Nicaraguan Center for Human Rights (CENIDH) strongly opposed amendments to the Nicaraguan Penal Code which sought to criminalize homosexual acts. In Uruguay, the highly respected Peace and Justice Service (SERPAJ) has begun to integrate into its annual human rights review information regarding the treatment of sexual minorities and of people living with HIV/AIDS. Indeed, the founder of SERPAJ-Uruguay, Father Luis Pérez Aguirre, frequently spoke of the need to broaden the understanding of human rights. Ana Martínez, in her article in *Unspoken Rules: Sexual Orientation and Women's Human Rights* cites *Si digo derechos humanos . . .* , in which Pérez Aguirre asserts that human rights must incorporate "all those excluded, the marginalized, beggars, prostitutes, street children, homosexuals, the shadows of those who were tortured or disappeared, all those forgotten by the 'human rights' community" (224).

At the international level, various non-governmental human rights organizations such as Amnesty International and Human Rights Watch have now broadened their mandates to attend to violations against lesbians and gay men. Within the United Nations, there has been some slow movement to consider issues related to sexual minorities. In August 1992, the first openly homosexual person addressed a United Nations human rights forum, denouncing the fact that no organization of lesbians and gay men had UN consultative status and that, consequently, questions relating to lesbians and gay men remained unacknowledged and unaddressed by the United Nations. In June 1993, the Australian government echoed this concern at the United Nations World Conference on Human Rights in Vienna, stating:

> One of the remaining areas of discrimination which has yet to receive serious and detailed attention within the United Nations is that of sexual orientation. Australia recognizes that discussion of the issue is bound to be difficult given the diversity of political, cultural and religious traditions which the international community is required to address. Nevertheless,

consideration of this issue is long overdue. (Sanders 67)

In July 1993, the International Lesbian and Gay Association (ILGA) became the first such organization to be accorded UN consultative status.

Despite this progress, much remains to be done. In 2001, ICCHRLA received an urgent action call from Ecuador alerting us that a homophobic group had announced that it would start to kill members of a human rights organization called Quitogay. The anonymous message sent to the group called them "mentally disturbed, faggots, and human rubbish" and warned that they would "exterminate the plague of queers to avoid the risk that their children might follow this cursed example." There was also news from Panama about the struggle of that country's first lesbian and gay organization to apply for legal status. Their requests were denied in 2000 on the grounds that the organization offended "public morals." But they have reapplied and are fighting to get legal recognition.

It is important to ensure that people fleeing persecution based on sexual orientation are given the chance to find safe haven and that the abuses they have faced are recognized as violations of their fundamental human rights. Indeed, as human rights lawyer Deborah Anker points out in her chapter in this volume, "refugee law can contribute to the elaboration of human rights norms, deepen understandings, and produce substantive changes—if it is embraced as part of human rights law" (see p. 112). But it is obviously just as important to do everything we can to help open and defend spaces for lesbian and gay groups to exist in their own countries. Solidarity across national borders is critical.

Works Cited

Dynes, Wayne R., ed. *Encyclopedia of Homosexuality*. New York: Garland, 1990.

Iglesias Prieto, Norma. *Beautiful Flowers of the Maquiladora: Life Histories of Women Workers in Tijuana*. Trans. Michael Stone and Gabrielle Winkle. Austin: University of Texas Press, 1997.

International Lesbian and Gay Association. "Consolidation and Democracy." Press Release. Brussels: n.p., June 26, 1995.

Khosrow, Fatemi, ed. *The Maquiladora Industry: Economic Solution or Problem?* New York: Praeger, 1990.

Lamas, Marta. "Homosexualidad: silencio y derechos humanos." *La Jornada.* [Mexico], July 17, 1995: 11.

Latin American Council of Churches. *Rapidas.* [Quito] September, 1994.

LaViolette, Nicole and Sandra Whitworth. "No Safe Haven: Sexuality as a Universal Human Right and Gay and Lesbian Activism in International Politics." *Millennium: Journal of International Studies* 23 (Winter 1994): 563–88.

Martínez, Ana. "Uruguay." *Unspoken Rules: Sexual Orientation and Women's Human Rights.* Ed. Rachel Rosenbloom. New York: Cassell, 1996. 223–230.

Mott, Luiz. *Violação dos direitos humanos e assassinato de homossexuais no Brasil, 1999.* Salvador: Editora Grupo Gay da Bahia: Associação Brasileira de Gays, Lésbicas e Travestis, 2000.

Ordoñez, Juan Pablo. *No Human Being is Disposable: Social Cleansing, Human Rights and Sexual Orientation in Colombia.* N.p.: Colombia Human Rights Committee, International Gay and Lesbian Human Rights Commission and Proyecto Dignidad por los Derechos Humanos en Colombia, 1995.

Pérez Aguirre, Luis. *Si digo derechos humanos . . .* Montevideo: Servicio Paz y Justicia, 1993.

Sanders, Douglas. "Getting Lesbian and Gay Issues on the International Human Rights Agenda." *Human Rights Quarterly* 18 (February 1996): 67–106.

Wilets, James D. "International Human Rights Law and Sexual Orientation." *Hastings International and Comparative Law Review* 18.1 (1994): 1–120.

Notes

1   In June 2001, ICCHRLA and nine other Canadian ecumenical social justice justice coalitions were disbanded by the sponsoring churches. Some of the work carried out by these former coalitions has been taken on by a new Canadian ecumenical organization called KAIROS.

2   In 1996, Mexico launched its *maquila* program in order to bring industry to the northern border towns. The program allows that *maquila* corporations, or *maquiladoras*, be partly or completely owned by foreign investors. It also allows *maquiladoras* to temporarily import goods duty-free, provided that they will not remain permanently in Mexico; *maquiladoras* are manufacturing plants. The North American Free Trade Agreement (NAFTA) removed almost all taxes and custom fees associated with importing goods from the *maquiladoras* into the United States and Canada. In other words, the *maquila* program provides U.S. and Canadian compa-

nies with a safe Mexican site of operations free of any of the bureaucracy traditionally associated with international operations. *Maquiladoras* employ Mexican laborers, primarily single women, at extremely low wages. Unionization of *maquiladora* workers is limited to the single state-run union. Nonetheless, large numbers of Mexicans migrate to the Northern border regions in order to work at the *maquiladoras* where jobs are, if not well-paid, at least plentiful. For further discussion of the *maquiladoras* from an economic perspective, see Khosrow; for the perspectives of *maquiladora* workers, see Iglesias Prieto.

3   The Convention in question is the United Nations Convention Relating to the Status of Refugees, which will be discussed in more detail below.

4   Canadian non-governmental organizations have criticized the government both for reneging on its commitment to introduce a merit-based appeals mechanism and for reducing the decision-makers from two to one. Canadian refugee rights groups identify the lack of an appeal process in Canada's refugee determination system as one of the most serious flaws in the present system. International organizations such as the United Nations High Commissioner for Refugees (UNHCR) and the Inter-American Commission on Human Rights, have also criticized Canada for failing to fulfill its international obligations to provide refused refugee claimants with a merit-based review.

5   As noted in Alice M. Miller's essay in this volume, the dissenting member of the IRB rejected the documentation provided as it was compiled by gay groups that he qualified as "self serving." He also did not find the claimant's account of male-male rape to be credible. States Miller: "[T]he dissenting decision-maker's folk knowledge [did] not allow him to believe that 'a police force that allegedly hunts homosexuals would take part in sexual assaults that involve the very activities it finds so disturbing, including homosexual contact'" (see p. 251).

6   The successful outcome of this case for the claimant in spite of the split nature of the decision helps illustrate some of the concerns regarding the new system in which a single decision-maker gets to rule on accepting or rejecting the case. Under the present system, refugee claimants often face a "sink or swim" situation as some IRB members reportedly are much more open to believing and ruling favourably on cases based on sexual orientation, while other board members repeatedly reject such cases.

7   See Alice M. Miller's essay in this volume.

8   Reflecting on the Argentine case in her essay, Alice M. Miller notes that historical and anthropological research in all societies and cultures clearly demonstrates that men who occupy heterosexual roles can "play the penetrator role without compromising their power and masculine image" (see p. 251).

9   One example of this is Colombia, where for several years now lesbian and gay organizations sign on to a joint NGO statement—together with dozens of church and human rights organizations, trade unions, indigenous, and Afro-Colombian organizations—delivered each year at the United Nations Commission on Human Rights. The NGO statement gives an overview of the concerns with respect to human rights in Colombia and calls on the United Nations to take specific remedial measures.

PART

IV

SYMBOLIC AND MATERIAL ECONOMIES

7

Tolerance and Intolerance in Sexual Cultures in Latin America

Roger N. Lancaster

Two vignettes vividly illustrate recurring occurrences that contextualize and motivate my remarks in this chapter.[1]

Situation One: Occasionally, I get phone calls or e-mail messages from lawyers working on asylum cases for gays who have fled persecution in El Salvador or for women who have escaped from violent marriages in Nicaragua. After a few minutes on the phone, it usually becomes clear that I am being asked to give expert testimony to the effect that Latin American cultures are, by custom, violently homophobic and misogynist—presumably by comparison to a more enlightened North American culture. Undoubtedly, the nature of legal proceedings tends to favor emphatic statements and reductive pictures. Generally, I resist making broad, declarative statements of a sort that my discipline, anthropology, might judge "ethnocentric." I begin to qualify, to equivocate, and to draw exceptions to the rule. And generally the lawyers with whom I have spoken decide that it would be unwise to put me on the witness stand.

Situation Two: My partner, Samuel, has just been introduced to an educated North American person. Upon learning that Samuel is from Puerto Rico, the person says: "You must be really glad to be here." When Sammy questions his interlocutor on why s/he has this rather presumptuous impression, s/he invariably cites journalistic accounts of homophobia in Latin America or newspaper articles on the precarious position of gays in Puerto Rico. "From what I understand," the enlightened American volunteers, "being gay in Latin America is just about the worst thing imaginable." "Worse," Sammy queries, "than being gay in ——?" And here he usually fills in the blank with his interlocutor's birthplace: "South Carolina," "Virginia," "Cleveland," "Queens."

Many journalistic as well as some scholarly accounts of lesbian and gay immigration give a uniformly bleak picture of sexual intolerance in Latin American cultures—as does the preferred form of expert testimony in asylum cases. A familiar package of ethnocentric presuppositions supports these impressions: it is the opposition between images of dusky-hued savagery versus the image of a liberal, tolerant, enlightened America, respite and safe haven for immigrants from many lands. In this chapter, I seek to challenge the cultural essentialism that I see as prevailing in advocacy circles, in testimonial expertise and in the media. In some small part, what I hope to effect is a shift in the register of public conversations about sex and violence in the hemisphere. But I do worry that my arguments will be misunderstood or misapplied. So let me underscore, from the outset, what I will, and will not, argue.

I do not deny, nor do I wish to mitigate, the existence of informal harassment, state-sponsored violence and even anti-gay death squads in far-removed cities across the Americas. These forms of intimidation and violence are quite real. What I want to suggest is that such levels of violence are unevenly distributed, even within the cultural geography of a single city. And what I claim is that extraordinary levels of anti-gay violence recorded in recent years are not part of the historically normative traditions of cultures of machismo in Latin America. Rather, they characterize a moment of intense contestation, transition and crisis.

The Open and the Closed

Let me set the terms for my analysis with a general description of what I will call, for the moment, "traditional" sexual cultures in Latin America, a generic, catch-all concept critical listeners will immediately recognize—and perhaps denounce—as a Weberian "ideal type."

"Cultures of machismo," as described in numerous ethnographic and historical accounts, tend to classify acts, gestures, and orientations in terms of a stark, binary logic: "masculinized activity" versus "feminized passivity."[2] I use the terms "masculinized" and "feminized" from the outset to denote a process of gendering rather than a state of gender. That is, these classificatory concepts, as they circulate in everyday interactions, are quintessentially "detachable" from persons and bodies. They apply not just to interactions between men and women, but to all manner of relations between men and men, even to relations between people, animals, and things (Lancaster, *Life* 244). Octavio Paz's polemical classic, *The Labyrinth of Solitude*, diagrams the logic of this arrangement and sets the terms for many subsequent arguments about sexual cultures in the Americas. I quote here from his discussion of the meanings that constellate around the vernacular word *chingar* ("to fuck" or "to screw"):

> In Mexico, the word [*chingar*] has innumerable meanings. . . . But in this plurality of meanings the ultimate meaning always contains the idea of aggression. [. . .] The verb denotes violence, an emergence from oneself to penetrate another by force. [. . .] The idea of breaking, of ripping open, appears in a great many of these expressions. The word has sexual connotations but is not a synonym for the sexual act: one may *chingar* a woman without actually possessing her.

Paz describes, in global terms, a dialectic of the open and closed, of phallic agency and wounded abjection: "The person who suffers this action is passive, inert and open, in contrast to the active, aggressive, and closed person who inflicts it" (76–81). Like Catherine MacKinnon's highly reduced depiction of male sexual violence or Lacan's analysis of the role of the phallus in the symbolic, Paz's diagram of the culture of machismo is not a happy picture: the party on the bottom is condemned to being screwed-over, the party on top to keeping up appearances—lest he,[3] too, become one of the used and abused.

A long analytical tradition directly or indirectly indebted to Paz suggests how this gendered binary regulates the political economy of manhood in far-flung settings—that is, how it permeates vernacular sexisms and shapes family relations. Various accounts, including my own ethnographic work in Nicaragua, trace the flow of such ideas and representations in the contest for manhood that structures male interactions in everyday boasting, drinking behavior, and assorted games of one-upmanship. As I argue in *Life is Hard*, machismo is not simply a system for establishing the dominance of adult men over women and children, although that is certainly one of its main effects. In a Foucauldian sense, what is most "productive" about machismo is its disciplinary force over, between, and among men. Men struggle against other men for the pre-given signs of manhood, defined in terms of bravado, risk-taking, and self-assertion. This competition for appropriate manhood engenders dispositions and practices with myriad consequences for women and children (Lancaster, *Life* 235–37).

Applied to sexual relations between men, the logic of phallic activity and wounded abjection has a number of important consequences.

Foremost among them, the culture of machismo is less concerned with sexual objects than with sexual aims. It divides the world, not so much between homosexual and heterosexual as between an active, assertive male sexuality on the one side of the coin, and what symbolic interactionists[4] used to call a "spoiled identity" on the other (Lancaster, *Life* 237–240).

In this mapping of the male body, its extensions and accesses, the "active," insertive, phallic party to homosexual intercourse largely escapes stigma. He is simply performing according to the sexually opportunistic script of manhood. As long as he maintains the gamut of practices otherwise viewed as "manly" (including the pursuit of women), he avoids being labelled "queer." What *is* specifically marked and inescapably stigmatized under the regime of machismo is the "passive" role in sexual intercourse. The so-called "passive"—or better put "receptive"—party is viewed as a feminized object put to someone else's use (Lancaster, *Life* 241–243).

Caveats and Equivocations

I warned the reader that I was going to start with an ideal type—a highly schematic picture, conceptually set off in quotation marks. Left sitting on the page, just-so, the picture I've drawn so far seems just what the newspaper editor or the lawyer ordered: a relatively emphatic and reductive statement on generic sex and implicit violence in Latin America. It would be altogether too easy to deduce current epidemics of violence against gays from this schematic picture. But that deduction, I think, derives from much of what is "ideal" in the ideal type, and not from what is most useful about it.

So let me now make a series of important qualifications, the better to put some flesh on the bones of this generic outline:[5]

1. The picture that I have just drawn is a better reflection of how certain vernacular cultures in Latin America represent manhood and understand male sexual relations than it is of how men actually behave or how sexual relations between men actually transpire. That is, I have described a "discursive formation"—a chunk of ideology—derived from the patter of everyday conversations in field settings. The actual practices of manhood, including sexual relations between men, occur in a context that is largely contextualized by these terms. And many sexual relations *do* in fact proceed according to these terms. But insofar as sexuality is a realm of creativity, invention, and play, sex acts are not

invariably reducible to cultural scripts (the way, for instance, speech acts might be reduced to grammatical structures). People everywhere bend, transgress (or, perhaps, what is even more perverse and playful, fetishize) the rules. And on this point, sexual folklore is emphatic. *Jugar* ("to play") is *the* happy euphemism for sex in many parts of Latin America. A common Brazilian saying noted by Richard Parker gauges the gap between ideal roles and real practices, qualifying the rules of machismo—and, in a sense, positing a different rule: "nobody knows what goes on inside four walls" or, in its more positive version, "within four walls, anything can happen" (*Bodies* 100).

2. It is not quite right to say that homosexual stigma in Latin America is always associated with sexual receptivity and with receptivity alone. As I have tried to suggest in longer reflections on problem, stigma in Latin America, like stigma everywhere, is contagious. This infectious circulation of stigma—and the risk it implies for all men—is precisely what makes it effective at regulating interpersonal relations. Men who fail to maintain an upper hand in their relations with others, boys who lose out at boyhood games and in physical jostling, dogs that don't chase cats, cats who fail to catch mice, pitchers that don't hold water, TVs that don't work: each of these receive daily the vernacular opprobrium: *cochón, maricón, puto, joto*, and so on. So, too, with machos who fail to maintain an appropriate emotional distance between themselves and their queer boyfriends, whose relationships last "too long" to be explained as sexual opportunism, or who otherwise fail to maintain vigorously the signs of appropriate manhood. Anyone and everything is subject to the all-enveloping logic of stigma. Ultimately, no one is impervious to being "queered."

3. The relations that I have sketched, insofar as they are schematic, give a closed and uniform picture of cultures of machismo—a broadly distributed, historically stable phenomenon, impervious to outside ideas and influences. Obviously, this picture requires considerable fine-tuning.[6] In fact, just what sense people make of sex varies considerably from culture to culture, from moment to moment, and from setting to setting. Historically, sexual conventions in colonial Granada, the capital of backwater Nicaragua, were likely not very similar to those that obtained in colonial Oaxaca, in Zapotec Southern Mexico, which, in turn, scarcely seem comparable to those that developed in the fortified Caribbean port of San Juan, with its dense cultural traffic between four continents. And such historical settings hardly seem commensurate with sexual cultures and subcultures that flourish in contempo-

rary Guadalajara (in the big belt-buckle state of Jalisco), which do not quite replicate sexual scenes available in the postmodern megapolis of Mexico City.

But it is not just a matter of mapping out differences between distinct locales, but also of drawing out translocal connections. That is, it is difficult to demarcate even *these* "local" cultures (such as colonial Granada or contemporary Guadalajara) since "outside influences," present from the start, perpetually impinge on changing cultural patterns everywhere. This has always been the case, but it is perhaps especially true in today's globally connected world. In an age of international tourism, transnational migrations, and international mass media images, local sexual cultures never really rest securely within national, regional, or linguistic borders; they are always circulating, in excess of temporary boundaries, and in dialogue with other sexual cultures.[7]

4. Because sexual cultures are open, ambiguous, and subject to myriad contestations, they also "contain" (which is not quite the right word) alternative positions and contending scripts. For instance, the Catholic Church—which views same-sex intercourse in any position and in all contexts as "sinful"—by no means endorses the sexual culture of machismo, as I have drawn it out. (No bishop anywhere exculpates the macho from the sin of Sodom, and might even view the penetrator as the perpetrator of the act, since he is the "active" party). Educated elites—who everywhere take their cues from Europe and North America—tend to understand sexual relations in terms of medical or psychiatric models. That is, they place a stigmatizing—or perhaps liberating—equal sign between both participants in homosexual intercourse. With good reason, since they are differently situated with regard to phallic agency, men do not tend to understand these things in the same terms as women. And since discourse is inherently volatile, subject to contending claims and interpretations, not just discourses but even basic categories—active, passive, masculine, feminine—are subject to dispute or qualification.

5. If the term "cultures of machismo" demands placement inside quotation marks, so do a pair of other conceptual placeholders to which I alluded earlier. I have referred to active/passive roles as "traditional," but Paz's mythic history (and my own early speculations) aside, it is by no means clear that such practices enjoy an uninterrupted continuity with patterns of conquest set in the colonial era, or that they directly derive from similar patterns documented in Iberia

and across the Mediterranean. Today, I would suggest that cultures of machismo are more profitably understood as a highly variegated form of 20th century sexual modernity. Although I have sometimes staged arguments about the culture of machismo as though "it" constituted a single, coherent "system," in view of the number of qualifications and caveats that I have just elaborated, perhaps it might better be understood in terms of "war"—the metaphor that Foucault uses to describe North Atlantic systems of sexual modernity in *The History of Sexuality* (93, 102). As with any ongoing war of positions, North or South, local groups and institutional players attempt to parlay cultural meanings to their own advantage. Among the many tactics at their disposal are evasive maneuvers, power grabs, modernizing agendas, scandalmongering, and calls for moral renovation. Situational discourses draw out alternative schemas, alternative rules, to the generic culture of machismo I have been describing.[8]

Still, for all these caveats, I return to the basic definition of an ideal type: it is a picture that might be subject to myriad qualifications but still does a certain useful work. Properly qualified and historicized, this picture might help us make sense of the subject at hand.

Homology and Heterology

And here, I draw on a contrast with another ideal type. Whereas sexual cultures in the North Atlantic proceed from the principle of homology—"whoever has sex with someone of the same sex is a homosexual"—sexual cultures in Latin America and in many other parts of the world proceed from a principle of heterology: It matters not only with whom, but how, and in what context, one has sex. Writ small, these different principles ground very different conceptions of sexual personhood. Writ large, they imply very different sexual cultures.

Homology, in a word, homogenizes. In fusing aims and objects, it predicates a series of relatively undifferentiated social spaces panoptically overseen by a universal prohibition on homosexual relations and, as Guy Hocquenghem shows in his classic of gay theory, even on homosexual desire. "Homophobia," which signifies the fear of homosexuality but also, literally, "aversion to the same," is a perfectly logical term for describing the resulting field of institutions and relations, each of which enacts the same uniform principle.

Heterology, in separating aims and objects, predicates a series of highly differentiated social spaces. Neither Church, nor law, nor medicine can quite get the upper hand on this variegated and inconsistent terrain. Instead, each institution carves out its own operative fiefdom with local definitions and situational discourses. The overall effect is a quilted patchwork of spaces and contexts where different rules apply.[9] The very singular term, "homophobia," is scarcely adequate for describing the resulting series of situations, whereby some men in some contexts actively seek out homosexual relations without incurring necessary stigma or consistent censure. Contrary to the usual meanings of homophobia, same-sex relations and homosexual desires are neither feared nor prohibited, and it is precisely the "sameness" of *macho* and *maricón* that machismo denies.

The Public Secret, the Taboo on Speaking, and the Tolerant Intolerance

There is, however, one rule that sees to the coexistence of these mutually inconsistent discourses, milieux, and practices. In my "Comment on Arguelles and Rich" from 1986, I used the term "public secret" to describe the uneasy predicament of queers in Nicaragua. Since then, the term has gained a certain currency, much of it derived from Simmel's famous essay on the subject, some of it derived from D.A. Miller's *The Novel and the Police*. My use of the term draws instead on a widely disseminated queer vernacular—which will likely be understood by small-town misfits and *entendidos* everywhere.

How can something be "public" and "secret" at the same time? It is a "secret" that Carlos is queer: a secret known and discussed by everyone. Not quite to Carlos's face, mind you, for then it would not be "secret" anymore. Just what the non-queer men in the neighborhood do with Carlos is also a "secret," subject to similar discussions by everyone—but only in certain contexts. Queers in Nicaragua, and other places, are subject to everyday sneers and taunting, but they are also made available in male gossip as objects of male pleasure. You would not talk about any of this in front of your mother, or your girlfriend, or a schoolteacher, or the priest, but you would talk about it to your peers, your drinking buddies, and men with whom you have joking relationships.

The problem here is more complex, I think, than the usual dialectic of the concealed and revealed conveyed by the North American concept of "the closet"—even if we mean to evoke the perpetual shell-game of shady evasions, substitutions, and deferrals deftly presented in Eve Sedgwick's inspirational books, *Epistemology of the Closet* and *Tendencies*. More to the point is the delicious sense of irony employed by Mexicans when they say that their country's public culture supports a "walk-in closet," that is to say, "a space big enough to hold you and your whole family."[10] In public secrecy, one is neither completely hidden nor, short of catastrophe, completely exposed, but always, it would seem, on the cusp of the two: concealed within what is revealed, and revealed within what is concealed; installed in a liminal space of magical transformations and creative spectacle but also of terror, madness, and paranoia. Indeed, the *locura* of the *loca*—the untranslatable madness of the queen—captures the queer's unstable existential place in the scheme of things, as Marcial Godoy-Anativia argues in an unpublished paper: he is, quite emphatically, a madwoman. The equivocation that circulates along this porous frontier protects both public "propriety" *and* "secret" transgression.

What enables such a secret to sit in full public view, at once tantalizing and terrifying (maddening, really), is a very simple prohibition. The taboo is not against knowing, much less acting, but against speaking. The primary interdiction is: thou shalt not put homosex into discourse. I should be clear here: it is not the universal "thou" who is enjoined from speaking, nor is it generic "homosex" that one is disallowed to speak. It is the queer himself who may not utter the phrase, "I am queer," in any of its myriad vernacular versions, much less in its politicized variant, "I am gay." It is also he, more so than the others, against whom the interdiction on speech about homosex is directed. The result is a zone of perpetual denial: an empty but ever-so densely populated space in the middle of the culture of machismo. As long as these rules hold—and I use the word "rules" advisedly for they are more like the rules of a game or tactics in war than the rule of law—what prevails is a kind of tolerant intolerance.

But how can a culture be tolerant and intolerant at the same time? Radical sceptics of liberal philosophy have often suggested that "tolerance" might function as a ruse. Herbert Marcuse, for instance, imagined that the outcome of sexual liberation in countries of the North Atlantic might be a condition of "repressive tolerance." He worried that variant sexual desires would be "liberated"—but only to the extent that they are subservient to capitalist rationality.[11] I borrow something from Marcuse here, but the paradox I gather under the phrase "tolerant intolerance" denotes a different scene of power struggles from that of Northern consumer societies. It is not that sexuality, once uniformly repressed by a blanket prohibition, is now expressed or tolerated at the service of some other form of domination, but that from the start, and in advance of any new social movements, much is allowed, expressed, and tolerated—in certain tacitly agreed spaces. It is, moreover, that this toleration coexists with marked intolerance in other, more respectable spaces.

Locas vestidas ("drag queens") can saunter down certain streets unharassed. They star in carnival spectacles, and they might even enjoy the amused indulgences of women in the neighborhood. But they cannot go to church in drag, nor can they appear in peace in certain "public" places like the marketplace. Men can cruise the plaza in the *centro*—and everyone knows perfectly well what is going on in full view in the city's most public of spaces—but they cannot take their boyfriends home to meet the folks, and it would be unwise for them to be too visible with their sexual conquests in their own neighborhoods. In cultures of machismo, a man can pretty much do what he pleases; he can even get away with it. He just cannot talk about it. Or rather, he cannot talk about it just any old way. What keeps sex between men "secret" is also what allows it to go on in extraordinarily "public" ways. The irony is that what protects queers from intolerance also protects intolerance from queers, insulates it from public criticism or contestation.

This tolerant intolerance, I think, explains the somewhat schizoid picture conveyed by ethnographic and historical reports on sexual cultures in Latin America: on the one hand, the happy-go-lucky adventurism of carnival transvestism and *zócalo* cruising; on the other, the everyday brutality of inescapable stigma and relentless taunting. Whether one sees expression or repression, tolerance or intolerance, depends on where one looks, on which conversations, and in what settings, one participates. What I want to suggest is that it is not the functioning of this tolerant intolerance but its waning that contextualizes the dramatic upsurge in anti-gay violence in Latin America in the 1980s and '90s.

Sexual Liberation and Sex Panics

This "waning" is implicated in the major social, political, and economic trends of the past thirty years. In the modern world of individual freedoms, in a social milieu reshaped by liberal market economies, and in the aftermath of the global New Left social movements, presumably no one wants to live in stigma and silence any more. And so, by force of the same developments that spurred the proliferation of feminist and indigenous rights groups everywhere in the Americas, visible gay rights organizations have emerged in every major Latin American city, along with a variety of HIV/AIDS outreach and education groups. At the same time, and by dint of the same cultural and economic transformations, sexual demimondes—in which men have sex with men—are increasingly linked to international gay subcultures, which entail a different kind of social space. These demimondes and subcultures have, in short, diversified and changed—a process that Richard Parker maps with exceptional clarity in his book on cultures of desire in Brazil.

Old patterns still remain. One still finds *macho* and *maricón*, closed and open, manly top and queer bottom. One still finds creative subversion of these categories. But new subcultures, new forms of sexual citizenship, and new identities, less beholden to active/passive concepts, have also flourished. The "patchiness" of the quilted patchwork has thus become more pronounced, even as its unifying thread—public secrecy—has unravelled. It would be difficult to say what image from this changing context troubles machismo more: the defiant *loca*, who speaks out on behalf of his own political rights, or the masculine young man who could have once avoided stigma but now claims a gay identity in changing urban spaces.

Things once whispered or left unsaid are now spoken aloud. Unquestionable doxa (that is to say, unstated presuppositions) are now openly politicized. The genie cannot be put back in the bottle. These combined developments, all of which promote queer visibility and gay self-representation, abrogate the injunction against speech—and in so doing, release the violence bound up in tolerant intolerance and public secrecy.

Toward a Typology of Sex Panics

If the analysis that I have just presented is correct, the epidemic violence monitored by the International Gay and Lesbian Human Rights Commission and other human rights groups owes less to the "traditional" attitudes of cultures of machismo than to their breakdown. In saying this, I hope that I am not understood as indulging an unwise nostalgia for an untroubled past. I do not argue that there was no physical violence against queers under the regime of tolerant intolerance. No system of social stratification can exist without periodic violence: that much is axiomatic. Small-scale, individually directed violence in the form of extortion, harassment, and physical abuse were common enough—just ask any middle-aged gay man—as were collective disciplinary acts directed against independent-minded queens or "uppity" queers. What I argue is that this violence was formerly subject to communal checks and that the massive, orchestrated forms of violence fueling human rights concerns and recent asylum cases are relatively new.

If the analysis that I have developed suggests the historicity of recent forms of anti-gay violence in the Americas, it also suggests that specific acts have to be understood in their specific circumstances. Because unevenly developed sexual cultures in transition and crisis are linked to political turbulence and economic uncertainty, outbreaks of violence against gays in Latin America are complex and overdetermined phenomena. For example, when corrupt and scandal-ridden politicians wage highly publicized "moral renovation" campaigns such as those carried out by PRI, Mexico's ruling party in the late 1980s and early 90s, they sometimes crack down on sexual demimondes, gay subcultures, and gay rights activists across the board. Linked to legitimacy crises, this form of repression is often expressly aimed at urban, middle-class sectors and club scenes.

By contrast, murderous "street sweeps" by out-of-uniform police against transvestite prostitutes and homeless children, as happened in various Brazilian cities in the 1980s and 90s, have a different social logic, reflecting elite nervousness about the "dangerous" and "disorderly" classes. This form of repression often leaves urban club-goers and middle-class gay men unscathed. Attacks on professional or publicly visible gay rights activists, as have been reported in El Salvador and other places, express yet another logic: they belong to the genre of political intimidation and selective assassination. Targeted hits against activists do not invariably spill over onto adjacent subcultures and sexual scenes; however, they do embody an attempt at silencing voices of dissent and at halting the ongoing avalanche of changes in sexual cultures.

So far I have touched on political, state, and paramilitary violence against gays. There is also good reason to believe that more diffuse and broadly distributed forms of violence are also on the upswing. The phenomenon recalls the pandemic of queer bashings in U.S. cities in the wake of gay liberation and the development of well-defined gay neighborhoods in the 1970s. That is, it is a function of increased visibility in changing but not yet transformed cultures.

Of course, not all forms of homophobic violence and state repression announce themselves as such, and the opacity of sex panics occludes first efforts to map the emergent terrain or to fully comprehend the situation. A recent case from Tijuana is instructive. A gay activist who owned a gay bed-and-breakfast there was sent to prison, not for being gay or for engaging in political activism, but on unsubstantiated charges of "contributing to the corruption of a minor." A federal appellate court in Mexicali eventually reversed his conviction and freed him—but not before he had spent nearly three and a half years in prison (see "Court Ruling Frees Activist"). The case's eventual outcome, and the international media attention it drew, are both positive signs, but it is only right to point out that other defendants facing trumped-up charges have fewer resources and thus have far less recourse to justice. If sex panics in Latin America follow a trajectory similar to those in the United States, one might logically expect that gay visibility and greater public toleration of homosexuality will be shadowed by an occult backlash: perpetual moral panics over child sexual abuse and expansive social anxieties around the sexuality of adolescents.[12]

Conclusion

My remarks in this chapter have been, of necessity, cursory, even schematic. The picture I've drawn is strongly inflected by travels in Mexico and experiences in Puerto Rico. My analysis will not hold in every instance. The experiences of repression in the fascist dictatorships of the Southern Cone (Argentina, Chile, and Uruguay), where anti-gay violence preceded any local movements for sexual liberation, would seem to pose a strong exception to the rule, as David William Foster has pointed out.[13] I have not directly addressed the question of lesbian visibility—which seems to me very differently situated in changing cultures of machismo than that of gay male visibility. Any adequate discussion of the subject would connect gay visibility and social backlash to wider changes in gender roles and family life—and of course, to social anxieties triggered by the AIDS/HIV epidemic.

Still, I hope my basic arguments are clear: it is not timeless "tradition" that is at work in epidemics of anti-gay violence in Latin America. Each of the above forms of anti-gay violence suggests a local, contingent history—not just of sexual representations and changing cultural categories, but also of class conflicts, political struggles, and institutional contests. Understanding these events means inscribing them in local histories while keeping global political-economic happenings within the frame of reference. In short, when we talk, testify, or write about the indisputable facts of sexual repression in Latin American countries in recent years, we need to apply as critical a logic and as rounded an analysis as we would apply to sex panics in the United States or Northern Europe. Such an approach would have the effect of making sexual asylum arguments more closely resemble other types of arguments for political asylum—and rightly so. Not only would this strategy bring sexual asylum arguments into better alignment with empirical facts; it would also relieve legal and public discourses of their tendency to deploy images of the scary, dark-hued Latino bogeyman as synecdoche for *Latinidad* wherever sexuality is concerned. That is to say, the approach I'm urging would reduce the insidious play of said images in our *own* ongoing sex panics. I thus conclude with two more vignettes that I think begin to capture the sorts of complex transformations now underway in sexual cultures in Latin America—and which I think evoke the thickness of creativity and contradiction in real-world places.

Situation three: Michael Higgins and Tanya Coen describe how, in preparation for the 1996 tourist season, city police in Oaxaca forced transvestite prostitutes off the street by declaring their health books invalid. Although prostitution is neither legal nor illegal in Oaxaca, prostitutes are required to keep a health book that certifies them as being in good health and HIV-negative. Members of the *Grupo Unión*—a gay sex-workers collective formed in the late 1980s, after city police had beaten a transvestite prostitute to death—went on the offensive, staging a march to city hall, where they pressed their case with city officials.

I am struck by the arguments that the drag queens made in protesting police harassment. No one invoked concepts of individual freedom or social tolerance, much less the right to privacy or sexual enjoyment, all of which inform argumentation that one would expect in a North American or Northern European context. They argued, rather, that everyone has the right to make a living, and that this was their livelihood: a matter-of-fact statement deeply grounded in local conceptions of citizenship. As Oaxacans, and as citizens of Mexico, they claimed the same right to benefit from tourism as everyone else—an understanding of right well understood by myriad street-vendors, peddlers, and professional beggars. "Why," they demanded, "are we being harassed for doing our jobs?" The protest, which made use of established procedures for public grievance, was a success. City officials representing PAN, the conservative party then in power in Oaxaca, acknowledged the validity of the sex workers' arguments, and backed their return to the streets that very evening (Higgins and Coen 118—120).

Situation four: Along the boardwalk in Veracruz, young lads stage performances of male derring-do for tourists. "Hey, toss in a coin," they call out to passers-by. And if you toss in a coin, an agile boy will plunge into the stinking, sewage-polluted waters of the Gulf port, to emerge, grinning broadly, with a shiny coin clenched between his teeth. A mere two or three blocks off the *zócalo*, a cramped gay bar hosts throngs of self-identified gay men. The décor, replete with a classic jukebox and giant posters of Marilyn and Elvis, evokes American scenes from the 1950s. But what is perhaps most striking about the design of the bar is its doorway and windows. The windows are covered, painted black, in the style of gay bars in America before the 1990s. The doorway enters into an improvised vestibule, which is situated so that the tough young men who aimlessly circulate on the streets outside cannot catch a glimpse of the patrons inside the bar. "There have been incidents," the bouncer confides, "you know?"

Just outside the bar, on the narrow streets around the *zócalo*, different suppositions, different concepts of sexual agency, prevail. The young toughs who wander the streets—many working as pimps—give the standard come-ons to tourists and visitors. "Hey, you wanna girl? I got a girl. She'll treat you real nice." The inevitable pause. Then, in lowered voice: "And if you don't want a girl—Hey, that's alright. I'll spend some time with you myself."

Works Cited

"Court Ruling Frees Activist After Three Years in Jail." *The Washington Blade*, June 27, 2003.

Almaguer, Tomás. "Chicano Men: A Cartography of Homosexual Identity and Behavior." *The Lesbian and Gay Studies Reader.* Ed. Henry Abelove, Michèle Aina Barale, and David M. Halperin. New York: Routledge, 1993. 255–273.

Alonso, Ana María and María Teresa Koreck. "Silences: 'Hispanics,' AIDS, and Sexual Practices." *The Lesbian and Gay Studies Reader.* Ed. Henry Abelove, Michèle Aina Barale, and David M. Halperin. New York: Routledge, 1993. 110–126.

Altman, Dennis. *Global Sex.* Chicago: University of Chicago Press, 2001.

Brusco, Elizabeth E. *The Reformation of Machismo: Evangelical Conversion and Gender in Colombia.* Austin: University of Texas Press, 1995.

Carrier, J. M. "Cultural Factors Affecting Urban Mexican Male Homosexual Behavior." *Archives of Sexual Behavior* 5.2 (1976): 103–24.

_____. "Family Attitudes and Mexican Male Homosexuality." *Urban Life* 5.3 (1976): 359–75.

_____. "Participants in Urban Mexican Male Homosexual Encounters." *Archives of Sexual Behavior* 1 (1971): 279–91.

Foucault, Michel. *The History of Sexuality, Volume I: An Introduction*. Trans. Robert Hurley. New York: Vintage Books, 1980.

Gledhill, John. *Power and Its Disguises: Anthropological Perspectives on Politics*. Second Edition. London: Pluto Press, 1994.

Godoy-Anativia, Marcial. "The Performance of Parody and the Parody of Performance: Locas, Travestis, and the Production of Sexual Meanings in Contemporary Chile." Unpublished paper. 1994.

Goffman, Erving. *The Presentation of Self in Everyday Life*. Garden City, N.Y.: Doubleday, 1959.

_____. *Stigma: Notes on the Management of Spoiled Identity*. New York: Simon and Schuster, 1963.

Goldwert, Marvin. *Machismo and Conquest: The Case of Mexico*. Lanham, Maryland: University Press of America, 1983.

González-López, Gloria and Matthew C. Gutmann. "Machismo." *New Dictionary in the History of Ideas*. Ed. Maryanne Cline Horowitz. New York: Charles Scribner's Sons, in press.

Gutmann, Matthew C. "The Ethnographic (G)Ambit: Women and the Negotiation of Masculinity in Mexico City." *American Ethnologist* 24.4 (1997): 833–55.

Higgins, Michael James and Tanya L. Coen. *Streets, Bedrooms, and Patios: The Ordinariness of Diversity in Urban Oaxaca*. Austin: University of Texas Press, 2000.

Hocquenghem, Guy. *Homosexual Desire*. Trans. Danielle Dangoor. New York: New York University Press, 1993).

Irwin, Robert McKee. "The Famous 41: The Scandalous Birth of Modern Mexican Homosexuality." *GLQ: A Journal of Lesbian and Gay Studies* 6.3 (2000): 353–376.

Jenkins, Philip. *Moral Panic: Changing Concepts of the Child Molester in Modern America*. New Haven, Connecticut: Yale University Press, 1998.

Kincaid, James R. *Erotic Innocence: The Culture of Child Molesting*. Durham, N.C.: Duke University Press, 1998.

Lacan, Jacques. "The Signification of the Phallus." *Ecrits: A Selection*. Trans. Alan Sheridan. New York: Norton Books, 1977. 282–291.

Lancaster Roger N. "Comment on Arguelles and Rich." *Signs* 12.1: 188—192.

_____. "Guto's Performance: Notes on the Transvestism of Everyday

Life." *The Gender/Sexuality Reader: Culture, History, Political Economy.* Ed. Roger N. Lancaster and Micaela di Leonardo. New York: Routledge, 1997. 559—574.

_____. *Life is Hard: Machismo, Danger, and the Intimacy of Power in Nicaragua.* Berkeley: University of California Press, 1993.

_____. "On Homosexualities in Latin America (and Other Places)." *American Ethnologist* 24.1 (1997): 193–202.

_____. "Sexual Positions: Caveats and Second Thoughts on 'Categories.'" *The Americas* 54.1 (1997): 1–16.

_____. "'That We Should All Turn Queer?' Homosexual Stigma in the Making of Manhood and the Breaking of a Revolution in Nicaragua." *Conceiving Sexuality: Approaches to Sex Research in a Postmodern World.* Ed. Richard G. Parker and John H, Gagnon. New York: Routledge, 1995. 135—156.

_____. *The Trouble with Nature Sex in Science and Popular Culture.* Berkeley: University of California Press, 2003.

Levi, Heather. "Lean Mean Fighting Queens: Drag in the World of Mexican Professional Wrestling." *Sexualities* (Special Issue: Transgender in Latin America) 1.3 (1998): 275–285.

Lumsden, Ian. *Machos, Maricones, and Gays: Cuba and Homosexuality.* Philadelphia: Temple University Press, 1996.

MacKinnon, Catherine A. "Feminism, Marxism, Method, and the State: Toward Feminist Jurisprudence." *Signs* 8.4 (1983): 635–58.

Marcuse, Herbert. *One Dimensional Man: Studies in the Ideology of Advanced Industrial Society.* Boston: Beacon Press, 1964.

_____. "Repressive Tolerance." *Critique of Pure Tolerance.* Ed. Robert Paul Wolff, Barington Moore Jr., and Herbert Marcuse. Boston: Beacon Press, 1969.

Miller, D. A. *The Novel and the Police.* Berkeley: University of California Press, 1989.

Nathan, Debbie and Michael Snedeker. *Satan's Silence: Ritual Abuse and the Making of a Modern American Witch Hunt.* New York: Basic Books, 1995.

Nesvig, Martin. "The Complicated Terrain of Latin American Homosexuality." *Hispanic American Historical Review* 81.3–4 (2001): 689–729.

Ohi, Kevin. "Molestation 101: Child Abuse, Homophobia, and the Boys of St. Vincent." *GLQ: A Journal of Lesbian and Gay Studies* 6 (2) (2000): 195–248.

Parker, Richard G. *Beneath the Equator: Cultures of Desire, Male Homosexuality, and Emerging Gay Communities in Brazil.* New York: Routledge, 1999.

_____. *Bodies, Pleasure, and Passions: Sexual Culture in Contemporary Brazil.* Boston: Beacon Press, 1991.

Paz, Octavio. *The Labyrinth of Solitude (and The Other Mexico, Return to the Labyrinth of Solitude, Mexico and the United States, The Philanthropic Ogre).* Trans. Lysander Kemp, Yara Milos, and Rachel Phillips Belash. New York: Grove Press, 1985.

Rouse, Roger. "Review of Roger N. Lancaster, *Life is Hard: Machismo, Danger, and the Intimacy of Power in Nicaragua.*" *Contemporary Sociology* 23.1 (1994): 57–58.

Sedgwick, Eve Kosofsky. *Epistemology of the Closet.* Berkeley: University of California Press, 1990.

_____. *Tendencies.* Durham, N.C.: Duke University Press, 1993.

Simmel, Georg. "The Secret and the Secret Society." *The Sociology of Georg Simmel.* Trans. Kurt Wolff. New York: The Free Press, 1985. 305—376.

Notes

1   Different versions of this paper were given at three conferences: "Passing Lines: Immigration and (Homo)Sexuality" (Harvard University), "Male Friendship and Homosociality" (Brown University), and "Gender and Sexuality in Latin America" (Ohio University). For helpful criticism and encouragement, special thanks to Luis Aponte-Pares, Samuel Colón, Brad Epps, Ana Mariella Bacigalupo, Alberto Sandoval-Sánchez, Daniel Torres, and Luzma Umpierre.

2   "Cultures of machismo" have been described and analyzed in different Latin American contexts; see, for instance, Goldwert and Brusco. "Active/passive" roles have been examined in an extensive literature, especially studies treating male same-sex relations, dating from J. M. Carrier's early papers on the subject. See also Tomás Almaguer; Ian Lumsden; and Ana María Alonso and María Teresa Koreck. For a critical overview of the origins and uses of the term, "culture of machismo," see Gloria González-López and Matthew C. Gutmann. The point—that twentieth century ideas about "machismo" have played an ethnocentric and racist role in North American narratives about Latin American cultures—is well-taken, and is, of course, the starting point for this paper. Still, certain facts remain. Gay, lesbian, feminist, and other cultural movements in Latin America have appropriated the term "machismo" precisely to gain leverage over certain forms of heteronormative, patriarchal practices and institutions. It thus seems ill advised to dispense with the term altogether.

3   I use "he" here, not because female same-sex relations never correspond to this logic, but because the "active," penetrating party is, in the normative

model, expressly male—and because s/he is effectively "masculinized" in non-normative practices.

4   Symblic interactionism developed a great many of the analytical moves now associated with social constructionism, especially the idea that identity is negotiated in everyday social interactions. See Erving Goffman's *The Presentation of Self in Everyday Life* and *Stigma: Notes on the Management of Spoiled Identity.*

5   I lay out more extensive sets of caveats in "Sexual Positions" and "On Homosexualities in Latin America." I venture a more playful and optimistic assessment of sexual culture in Nicaragua in "Guto's Performance."

6   I am indebted here to suggestions by Roger Rouse and Matthew Gutmann. Martin Nesvig's essay on the "complicated terrain" of homosexuality in Latin America is especially instructive.

7   In *Life is Hard*, I describe a dialogical approach to sexual cultures this way: "No culture has ever been unaware of the other cultures, and this awareness allows its members to both portray themselves as unique and to borrow practices from abroad" (277). On sex and globalization, see Dennis Altman; see also various contributions to the *GLQ* special double issue on travel, sex, and globalization, 8.1–2 (2002).

8   Robert McKee Irwin's traces the circulation of contrary and opposed discourses on homosexual meanings and identity in twentieth-century Mexico.

9   John Gledhill, following Anthony Giddens, uses the term "patchy" to describe the intermittent and inconsistent reach of "traditional" or "underdeveloped" states, as compared to the extensive reach of the "modern," developed, administrative state (15–18).

10 I want to thank Heather Levi for this appropriate image; see also Levi's "Lean Mean Fighting Queens."

11 Marcuse works out the concept "repressive desublimation" in *One Dimensional Man*. See also his "Repressive Tolerance."

12 I have provided a very brief overview of this contradictory dynamic in *The Trouble with Nature Sex* (331–334). The Satanic ritual abuse panics of the 1980s have been discredited, but they left indelible marks on American sexual culture, spawning entire subfields of junk science (e.g., the psychoanalysis of "repressed memories") and consolidating an ever more expansive culture of "child protection," thus expanding the purviews of both official bureaucracies (Child Protection Services) and quasi-official ones ("victim's rights advocates"). All good reason and a growing body of evidence suggest that gay men falsely accused of child abuse face special disadvantages with police investigators, prosecutors, judges, and juries. These difficulties include a public willingness to believe implausible accusations, a propensity to construe as "sexual" things no rational person

would view as sexual, and the application of far lower standards for "prob-able cause" and "burden of proof" when charges are levelled against a gay or putatively gay man. On North American sex panics, see Debbie Nathan and Michael Snedeker; Philip Jenkins; James Kincaid; and Kevin Ohi.

13 Personal Communication.

8

Cultures of the Puerto Rican Queer Diaspora

Lawrence La Fountain-Stokes

Puerto Ricans are a queer bunch: simultaneously Afro-Diasporic, Caribbean, Latin American, Hispanic, Latino/a, and American, at least since 1898; insular, migratory and translocal, with U.S. citizenship and passports since 1917; speaking Spanish or English or sometimes, perhaps rather often, some variation of both; living here and there and sometimes in several places at once. This anomalous, colonial and post-modern predicament has had its negative consequences, at least as far as attracting the attention of scholars of international migration to the United States: for the most part, they have ignored the situation of diasporic Puerto Ricans, focusing more on Puerto Rico as a destination for Cuban and Dominican migration and seeing Puerto Rican migrants as a "native" or colonial minority similar to African Americans.[1] While, in a certain sense, it is correct to recognize Puerto Rican difference and not to lump all migrants together indiscriminately, it is quite unfortunate that the dramatic similarities that link Puerto Ricans to other migrant populations in the United States have not been recognized. Much is lost by this omission, particularly since colonized diasporic Puerto Ricans (as well as colonized Chicanos/as in the U.S. Southwest) have historically anticipated many of the linguistic and cultural experiences that other Spanish-speaking Latin American immigrants have faced.

When Puerto Ricans migrants happen to be queer, that is to say, lesbian, gay, bisexual, or transgender (LGBT), or rather *patos, patas, marimachos, marimachas, mariconas, maricones, bugarrones, dragas, vestidas, travestis, homosexuales, lesbianas, locas, homo thugs, queens, butch dykes, papichulos,* or *on the down low,* as we tend to say in the vernacular, then the similarities to, and differences from, other Latin American migrants are quite relevant. Simply stated, being queer and

Rican has had very particular historical and personal consequences: sometimes provoking migration, but almost always provoking at least some form of social marginality. The particularities of what we will here refer to as "queer Rican migrations" or "queer Boricua diasporas" have been mostly ignored. In fact, sexuality and divergent gender expression and sexual orientation have only recently come to be acknowledged as causal factors in national (internal) and international (cross-border) migration—what the Venezuelan filmmaker Irene Sosa has termed "sexual exile" and the Puerto Rican sociologist Manuel Guzmán calls "sexile"—even though they have long been recognized as important, crucial or even "dangerous" variables affecting immigrant experience, as ethnic studies scholar Eithne Luibhéid lucidly explains in *Entry Denied* and in her chapter in this volume.[2] These physical movements or displacements entail meaningful numbers of people at a global scale, something literary scholars and anthropologists such as David Eng, Gayatri Gopinath, Martin Manalansan, and the contributors and editors of Cindy Patton and Benigno Sánchez-Eppler's volume *Queer Diasporas* have shown. The persecution of individuals on the basis of non-normative sexual practices or identities, and the particular difficulties produced by their localized, autochthonous manifestations or by health-related problems such as HIV/AIDS (an issue which is clearly not limited to the homosexual community), are now documented by international non-governmental organizations such as Amnesty International and the International Gay and Lesbian Human Rights Commission (IGLHRC), which understand them, in general, as joining catastrophic natural and man-made phenomena (war, political persecution, religious intolerance), economic necessity, and personal aspirations as conditions recognized to affect migration.

Insular and diasporic Puerto Ricans and U.S. Latinos/as have been at the forefront of sex/gender migrations, in close contact with (and participating in or affected by) the ways in which hegemonic northern sexual paradigms have extended to other locations. Slowly but surely, sexual orientation has come to be seen as a category relevant to their experience, as well as a constitutive element of metropolitan-colonial relationships and of the diverse transnational, multidirectional flows of sexual paradigms, such as those addressed in Arnaldo Cruz-Malavé and Martin Manalansan's anthology *Queer Globalizations: Citizenship and the Afterlife of Colonialism* and, in the specific case of Puerto Rico, in the work of the geographer Luis Aponte Parés, the sociologist Elizabeth Crespo-Kebler, the literary scholar Rubén Ríos Avila, and the cultural critic Juana María Rodríguez.[3] Literary scholar Brad Epps has further noted how the particularities of homosexual immigration make it similar yet different from other types; he proposes the term "passing lines"—which has been taken up and expanded in the present volume—as a conceptual framework for understanding the performances that non-normative immigrants engage in order to be able to succeed, a topic also explored by Rodríguez in her book *Queer Latinidad* in the context of the INS Tenorio case, which involved a grant of asylum to a Brazilian man on the grounds of sexual orientation (84–113). The field of public health, concerned with the critical situation of the HIV/AIDS pandemic, has aggressively immersed itself in new migrant sexualities, as the research of the epidemiologists Alex Carballo-Diéguez, Curtis Dolezal, Luis López-Nieves, Rafael Díaz and others makes clear for Latino men. At the same time, Latina anthologies such as the groundbreaking 1987 volume *Compañeras: Latina Lesbians*, edited by the Puerto Rican sociologist and lesbian activist Juanita Díaz-Cotto (under the pseudonym Juanita Ramos), explore the specificity of women's experiences in the context of migration. Such individuals as New York City Councilwoman Margarita López or the recently deceased founder of the Latino/a youth-oriented educational program ASPIRA, Antonia Pantoja (who came out publicly as a lesbian at the very end of her life in 2002), remind us of the intersections of multiple struggles for social justice. Finally, historians such as Martin Duberman and Eric Marcus have demonstrated the fundamental contribution of transgender Latinos/as to the modern LGBT liberation movement in the United States, as in the case of the Puerto Rican/Venezuelan Stonewall veteran and trans activist Sylvia Rivera, who passed away in 2002.

While the particular status of Puerto Ricans as U.S. citizens (or colonial subjects, according to one's political perspective) would suggest significant differences from the experience of other Latin American migrants, there are still remarkably numerous parallels. It is well known that Puerto Rican life was profoundly marked during the 20th century (most dramatically from 1945 to 1965) by the massive migration of many of its peoples to the United States, a displacement provoked by the island's colonial situation as an American territory since the end of the Hispanic-Cuban-American-Filipino War in 1898, when Spain ceded control of its former possessions (including Guam) to the United States. Research on the effects of migration on the Puerto Rican diasporic community have often focused on socio-economic mobility, living standards, mental health, rates of intermarriage and degrees of assimilation, always with the assumption of normative heterosexuality. With the exception of AIDS-related public health research, there has been little recognition of how different sexual orientations can make for different immigrant experiences and indeed of how Puerto Ricans' constructions of gender and sexuality can produce different immigrant "homosexualities" from those which are more common in the United States or even in the site of origin. There has also been scant attention paid to how the sexual paradigms of both countries have been affected by the contacts that immigrants have established or the roles that culture plays in documenting and forming such experience.

In the present essay, I will offer some observations about queer Puerto Rican diasporas and then go on to trace some historical and generational shifts that attend queer cultural productions. My observations here condense parts of my forthcoming book *Queer Ricans: Cultures and Sexualities in the Diaspora* (University of Minnesota Press), where these topics are fleshed out in much more detail. I will argue here that cultural productions show how queer migrant experience (or, at the very least, its portrayal or representation) differs or has differed according to such factors as gender, age, race, class, place of birth and historical period. While cultural analysis cannot substitute for historical and ethnographic research, it can show how particular individuals—here artists, filmmakers, and writers—present their experience. Accordingly, I will briefly focus on three figures, Manuel Ramos Otero, Frances Negrón Muntaner, and Erika López, in relation to their peers and to a broader history of queer Boricua migrant culture.

Homosexualities and Society

Social discourses on sexual difference in both Puerto Rico and the United States have traditionally—even after the historic 1969 Stonewall revolt—presented non-normative sexual orientations as forms of deviant behavior against which the national population needs protection. In Puerto Rico, homosexuality has been viewed at different moments during the 20th century as a threat to the national character.[4] As the lawyer Mildred Braulio and the sociologist Elizabeth Crespo-Kebler point out, sodomy was criminalized in 1902, when the Puerto Rican Penal Code was altered to follow North American models more closely. The 1974 reform of the code extended the definition of sodomy, which previously only referred to men, to include sexual acts between women. Only in 2003 was the act decriminalized in Puerto Rico, barely three days before the Supreme Court, with *Lawrence v. Texas*, overturned anti-sodomy laws in the United States.[5] Homosexuality, and especially gay liberation, have at times been seen, by virtue of the island's colonial relationship with the United States, as imported or inflated: modern-day homosexuals, that is, are often seen as foreign or as tinged with something foreign, as a menace from the outside, in short, as other than "Puerto Rican," especially if they are activists.[6] This understanding parallels discourses in other Latin American countries (as Jorge Salessi has shown with respect to Argentina), where homosexuality and other putatively "unsociable" behaviors at the beginning of the 20th century were attributed to immigration.[7]

Often times, social discourse that posits the foreign provenance or "unnaturalness" of homosexuality is accompanied by social measures that seek to confine or expel homosexuals, whether by placing them in institutions of social control or by actually forcing them beyond the national borders. In keeping with the shift in the understanding of homosexuality in the mid- to late 19th century (by which time homosexuality was viewed, as Michel Foucault has studied, as an identity and not as an act or conduct), older forms of homosexual persecution, such as the deadly punishment of sodomites during the Inquisition, were transformed. In their place, incarceration and psychiatric treatment became commonplace. In the United States, immigration laws that prohibited the entrance of people on the basis of ideology, race, behavior or handicaps also technically excluded homosexuals, specifically from 1917 to 1990, under such categories as "moral turpitude." While it is likely that the effects of the law were often more cosmetic than practical, there were documented cases of exclusion.[8] The laws did not apply to Puerto Rican migrants, who received U.S. citizenship in 1917, but they are still indicative of ideas about who should and should not be admitted into the country.[9] That said, U.S. citizenship has allowed Puerto Ricans to partake in recent times of what is referred to as the "air bridge" or "air bus," by which individuals move back and forth from the island to the U.S. mainland; this has been particularly important for those affected with HIV/AIDS, who travel for medical and family reasons. The "air bus," or "*guagua aérea*," as the Puerto Rican writer Luis Rafael Sánchez styles it, facilitates general patterns of circular migration, a constant movement of gays and lesbians who have experienced living both on the island and in the United States and who at different moments may settle in one or the other place. Such is the case of Herminio (Nino) Adorno, one of the most important gay activists on the island.

In the case of Puerto Rico, as well as that of many Latin American countries, displacements have occurred first from rural to urban locations and then, in those countries where there are feasible opportunities for international migration, to other countries such as Brazil, Canada, Mexico, and the United States. The displacements occur in the context of specific social policies and laws, including anti-sodomy statutes, but also as a result of social intolerance, discrimination, poverty and persecution. The "threat" or option of migration affects those who remain on the island as much as those who leave, especially those who have relatives and friends who have already left. Generalized intolerance of homosexuality and increased awareness and organization within the lesbian, gay, bisexual and transgender community in the United States have led, particularly since World War II, to massive geographic displacements, especially towards large urban enclaves on both coasts, particularly San Francisco and New York.[10]

Until recently, general social intolerance of homosexuality in Puerto Rico has had an impact on specific expectations, conventions, and patterns of behavior, at least as far as middle and upper-class individuals are concerned.[11] These patterns of behavior include secrecy or non-disclosure of personal matters in familial, professional, and social environments (homosexuality is "tolerated" as long as it is not discussed in public) as well as, at the opposite end of the spectrum, voluntary, encouraged, or even forced migration. The development of activism on the island since the 1970s has challenged the conventions that attend, or even generate, such behaviors, yet there remains much to be done—just as in the United States. Many Puerto Ricans are still profoundly closeted or engage in complex negotiations of their "open secret," as Lancaster explores in the present volume.

Several points bear consideration: 1) individuals who participate in same-sex relations or have divergent gender expressions may migrate to the United States or to another country for reasons other than those of sexual/gender orientation; 2) not all of the individuals who identify as homosexuals (or LGBT people) or who engage in same-sex relations migrate or leave their countries of origin; 3) the existence of a visible gay community in a country does *not* contradict the perceived or real necessity of specific individuals to migrate. These observations are similar to the preliminary findings that Héctor Carrillo has obtained in his research focusing on male Mexican migration to the United States. Sadly, it has become increasingly apparent that LGBT migration does not necessarily ensure safety, as the tragic murders of Gwen Araujo,

Eddie Garzón, Paola Matos, and Rodney Velásquez remind us—not to mention the deaths of Matthew Sheppard and Brandon Teena.[12]

The experience of first-generation gay and lesbian Puerto Rican immigrants varies according to a number of factors, including the places where they settle; their contact with diasporic Puerto Rican and North American LGBT communities; their race, class, gender, age, self-presentation, educational background, political orientation, command of the English language, mental health, and HIV/AIDS status; the conditions under which they migrated; the degree to which they maintain ties to their families and communities of origin in Puerto Rico; and the ways that they identify sexually. In some cases, apparently quite similar individuals can have very different experiences and perspectives.

Second- and third-generation Puerto Rican LGBT immigrants often have different concerns from those of first-generation individuals, concerns that bear on their degree of acculturation, on their relations to other U.S. ethnic and racial communities, on their loss of Spanish in favor of English and Spanglish, on their uncertainty about their cultural baggage and on their possible rejection by island-born Puerto Ricans. All generations face, however, problems of discrimination. At the same time, the links and shared experiences of second- and third-generation LGBT Puerto Ricans with African Americans (observed most clearly in the investment in African American politics and youth culture) are generally stronger than is the case for first-generation immigrants. The involvement of all of these immigrants in their communities (be it the diasporic Puerto Rican community or the LGBT community or both) can be a source of tension and often requires careful negotiations. Primary and secondary allegiances on the basis of different aspects of identification can strain an individual's energy, but, as the British historian Bob Cant has observed, they can also have creative results.

Cultures of the Queer Diaspora

Cultural studies offer productive ways to understand queer Puerto Rican diasporas. The analysis of a wide variety of cultural materials, in the context of historical and social scientific research, allows us to map a queer diasporic Puerto Rican community that extends from the island, across the sea, to the United States and elsewhere.[13] Puerto Rican, Nuyorican, and diasporic cultural productions grapple with migration, including resistance to it, in diverse ways: most notably, in literature, film, theater, performance, music and cartoons. These productions can be categorized roughly according to the authors' or artists' biographies or according to the portrayals of themselves and others in their works, especially in terms of geographic location, life experience, and generational affiliation. Other parameters for analysis include primary linguistic, cultural, and geographic attachments to the society of origin (Puerto Rico) or the receiving country (principally the United States), as well as primary identifications in terms of such ideologically marked categories as gender and gender politics, most notably feminism or sexual orientation and queer social movements. In this chapter, I will discuss differing depictions of first-hand migration and its diachronic progression over time, paying special attention to the tensions between first- and second-generation productions. It is important to look at the phenomenon of Latino/a queer migration from a long-range, historic perspective rather than as a single occurrence frozen in time.[14]

As Puerto Rican intellectual Juan Flores notes (as well as Jorge Duany, Frances Aparicio, Yolanda Martínez-San Miguel, and Raquel Z. Rivera), Puerto Rican migrants have participated in a wide array of cultural productions, ranging from traditional genres such as literature, film, performance, photography, painting, graphic arts, dance, and music, to more popular or unusual forms such as nostalgic vernacular architecture (as in the case of rural "casitas" or traditional wooden country houses built in abandoned lots in urban environments), clothing (particularly T-shirts), hip-hop, graffiti, jewelry, tattoos, bars, social clubs, dance club culture, customized cars, performance art, and Internet websites. What is more, as Frances Negrón-Muntaner shows in *Boricua Pop*, predominantly white American cultural producers have taken up, or appropriated, Puerto Rican culture and the contributions of individual Puerto Ricans in their own work. All of these forms, in one way or another, contribute to our understanding of immigrant experience and serve different functions in the diasporic communities themselves. Literary works, for instance, have long shown how emigration has served as a regulatory measure, a source of (dis)comfort, and a liberatory strategy in Puerto Rico with regards to non-normative sexualities. As Carlos Gil reminds us, Bernardo Vega, while migrating in 1917, throws his watch overboard as he nears New York City after hearing rumors that he might be considered "effeminate" for wearing it. He later describes arriving in the city only to find out that watches similar to his were extremely popular.[15] At different moments throughout the 20th century, many other Puerto Rican authors, including José

I. de Diego Padró, Pedro Juan Soto, José Luis Vivas Maldonado, Emilio Díaz Valcárcel, and Luis Rafael Sánchez, have all included episodes of sexual marginality linked to emigration in their works. However, it is not until openly, self-identified gays and lesbians begin to document and explore their migration, or sexile, that more insightful, contestatory voices come to the fore, at least among island-born artists. Perhaps the two paradigmatic figures here are Luz María Umpierre, who migrated in 1974, and Manuel Ramos Otero, who migrated in 1968 and died of AIDS in 1990.[16] In their literary works, both explore—albeit in very different ways—the experience of first-generation migrants as they move between traditional Puerto Rican values and foreign realities in the United States. In her poetry, Umpierre does this by freely switching from Spanish to English and by proposing the invention of new tongues; in contrast, Ramos Otero wrote his poetry and narrative almost entirely in Spanish. Umpierre traces a continuum from previous migrant subjects such as Puerto Rico's greatest poet, Julia de Burgos, to the present, inserting, in the process, her own lyrical voice of denunciation in a discourse framed by 1980s U.S. Latina Third World feminism. Umpierre uses strong sexual vocabulary and explicit, even "shocking," images to convey her frustration and courage in the face of widespread social injustice, colonialism, and anti-lesbian prejudice. Umpierre also establishes a literary dialogue with second-generation Nuyorican poets, particularly in her famous exchange with Sandra María Esteves, which entails four poems, two by each poet. Ramos Otero's literary production also invokes Julia de Burgos and documents a series of moments in immigrant experience, which include initial alienation and anonymous wandering, partial integration into the established New York gay world, and, finally, an approximation to the Puerto Rican community of that city and to the wider history of Puerto Rican migration. Literary critics have devoted copious pages to the work of both of these artists, neglecting to some extent that of others who write in Spanish, such as Víctor Fragoso (who died of AIDS in 1982), Nemir Matos Cintrón, Daniel Torres, or Moisés Agosto and Alfredo Villanueva-Collado (both of whom live with HIV/AIDS).

English-language Puerto Rican writers have also received scant attention. A notable exception is the now classic Nuyorican writer, Piri Thomas, one of the subjects of an important article, titled "'What a Tangled Web!'"[17] by Arnaldo Cruz-Malavé, in which the critic points out that Thomas's *Down These Mean Streets*, Pedro Pietri's *The Masses are Asses*, and Miguel Piñero's *Short Eyes*, all include, or are structured by, episodes of male homoeroticism—whether masculine rites of initiation, behavioral acts associated with femininity, or in the context of prison—which tend to function as an unredeemable abject. Alberto Sandoval-Sánchez, in his work included in this volume and elsewhere, has also commented on the back-and-forth nature of Puerto Rican migration, but has clearly resisted participating, as a first-generation immigrant gay man with AIDS, in a nostalgic view of his country of origin as *the* place to which he must return to die. A younger poet, filmmaker, and scholar, Frances Negrón-Muntaner, who is also a first-generation migrant, presents yet another picture: her work benefits from the twenty years of cultural production and activism that separate her from Ramos Otero. Like Luz María Umpierre, Negrón-Muntaner feels equally at home in English and in Spanish, yet unlike earlier artists, she uses a mixture of film and writing to explore questions of migration and sexuality.

As important as literature is, there is a danger in focusing exclusively on it in an attempt to trace a historical—or even generational—model of queer Rican culture; after all, performance and filmmaking actually *antecede* gay liberationist literary portrayals. Appearing in the 1960s and early 1970s, 1.5[18] and second-generation trans performers and activists such as Sylvia Rivera, Holly Woodlawn, and Mario Móntez (née René Rivera), along with the first-generation, island-born underground filmmaker José Rodríguez-Soltero (many of whom engage in what might be called, following José Muñoz, "disidentificatory" political or artistic representations), predate "open" first-generation literary voices, though they are only recently being reclaimed as Puerto Rican. The cases of Woodlawn and Móntez are particularly complex, as Negrón-Muntaner has observed in *Boricua Pop*, because they are more often known for their associations with gay, white, avant-garde artists such as Andy Warhol, Jack Smith, and Charles Ludlam than for their own talent and originality. Negrón-Muntaner does not, however, mention Rodríguez-Soltero, who was an important part of this circle and who can be seen as an *auteur* of a stature at least equal to that of his Anglo colleagues. In his research on the Harlem ball scene of the postwar period, historian George Chauncey has also found that Puerto Rican drag queens were active participants and even won titles as early as the early 1950s. On a different note, Sylvia Rivera, a Stonewall veteran, Gay Liberation Front militant, and trans activist, held political "performances" of quite a different nature from that of individuals in the world of the arts, though she too constructed a public persona that served to advance a collective desire for political rights.

In addition to the new cohorts of first-generation migrants such as writer Angel Lozada (author of *La patografía*), painters Angel Rodríguez Díaz, Rafael Rosario-Laguna and Nayda Collazo-Lloréns, and performers Jorge Merced (from Pregones Theater), Laritza Dumont, or the deceased grande drag diva of *La Escuelita*, Lady Catiria, there are now a healthy number of second-generation gay, lesbian and bisexual Nuyoricans—or, to quote Mariposa (María Fernández), "Diasporicans"—whose work reflects the often dramatically different experience of being born and raised Puerto Rican in the United States. These second-generation Nuyoricans include playwrights Janis Astor del Valle, Milton Díaz, Charles Rice-González, and Edwin Sánchez; dancer/choreographer Arthur Avilés and his first-cousin Elizabeth Marrero; writer and cartoonist Erika López (whom we shall discuss later); writer Aldo Alvarez; L.A.-based performance artist Marcus Kuiland-Nazario; and poets or spoken-word artists like Rane Arroyo, Samantha Martínez, Mariposa, Elliot Torres, and Emanuel Xavier. These "younger" generations can be said to follow in the footsteps of their "elders," but they also depart from the models of earlier 1.5 generation artists such as Holly Woodlawn or bisexual Nuyorican poets such as Miguel Piñero and Miguel Algarín. Some of the more notable features of their work include a pronounced tendency to write or perform in English or Spanglish; significant redefinitions of traditional culture; a greater reliance on Santería and African religious beliefs; and a more intense engagement with the historic diasporic communities of the Bronx, Brooklyn, the Lower East Side (Loisaida), and Spanish Harlem (El Barrio), as well as with Boston, Chicago, Philadelphia, Los Angeles, and San Francisco, as authentic or original sites of Puerto Rican culture. In fact, over and again, the U.S. sites are considered to be principal referents of Puerto Ricanness.

Finally, it is worth mentioning that sexual migration has been addressed not only in diasporic works but also in diverse island-centered cultural productions. Manuel Ramos Otero's short story "Loca la de la locura" (The Queen of Madness) portrays inter-island migration, as the protagonist moves from the small town of Hormigueros to the capital, San Juan. Violent expulsion from a black community, leading to death, marks Luis Rafael Sánchez's poetic short story, "Hum!," which has been carefully studied by Agnes Lugo-Ortiz. Migration to the United

States also figures in Magali García Ramis's *Happy Days, Uncle Sergio*. Resistance to migration is, however, a widespread phenomenon, as obviously not all LGBT individuals migrate or are represented as migrating: such is the case of Antonio Martorell's aunt Consuelo Cardona, as portrayed in his autobiography *La piel de la memoria*, and Lidia, the protagonist of García Ramis's novel.[19]

Manuel Ramos Otero and First Generation Experience: The 1970s and 1980s

The life and writings of Manuel Ramos Otero are profoundly illustrative of the experiences of first-generation gay Puerto Rican migrants to the United States, particularly college-educated, middle class males who left their homeland in the late sixties motivated to a great extent by the persecution, repression, or discomfort they felt in Puerto Rico on account of their sexual orientation. An analysis of a series of Ramos Otero's short stories will allow us to chart some of the different moments of that migratory experience and to reflect on the understanding of departure and distance from Puerto Rico as emancipatory. For Ramos Otero, dislocation was essential to the elaboration of his work and to the representation of his homeland. In New York and, to a lesser extent, New Jersey, Ramos Otero's interaction with gay North American and immigrant Nuyorican communities was particularly important for his writing and for his understanding of Puerto Rican culture.

The short stories of Manuel Ramos Otero, set at first in unspecified geographic spaces, soon become fixed on two principal locations: Puerto Rico and New York. Ramos Otero spent half of his life in the northern metropolis (1968–1990) and produced a body of work that privileges the urban center as both a utopia and dystopia of immigrant Puerto Rican and queer experience. It is no coincidence that New York should have been the destination for the author who, above all other writers of his generation, embodied the confluence of emigration and homosexuality. New York is, after all, the cradle of the modern gay and lesbian liberation movement; it is a huge city, inhabited by hundreds of thousands of Puerto Ricans, where Puerto Rican drag queens such as the recently deceased Sylvia Rivera confronted the police at Stonewall, while others, like Mario Móntez and Holly Woodlawn, graced—and were exploited by—Andy Warhol's famous Factory.

It is this New York, a would-be microcosm of the world, where a good number of Ramos Otero's stories are set. The city figures in, for instance, "Hollywood Memorabilia"; "El cuento de la Mujer del Mar" (The Story of the Woman of the Sea), which is located on Christopher Street, the former center of the gay West Village; "Página en blanco y staccato" (Blank Page and Staccato), where Afro-Puerto Rican-Chinese *Loisaida* detective Sam Fat inhabits a world straight out of 1940s film noir; and "Descuento" (Untelling, or Discount), a deeply personal and philosophic meditation that chronicles the relationship of two exiled (white) gay Puerto Rican men. Approaching the work of Ramos Otero through the optic of his queer poetics of exile allows us to discern a gradual transformation or evolution in relation to the Puerto Rican diaspora. Critic Juan G. Gelpí has astutely pointed to "Hollywood Memorabilia" as one of the most representative stories of Ramos Otero's initial phase of exile in New York.[20] The writings from this period are characterized by the protagonist's loneliness and by first-person narration; Ramos Otero's first book is also marked by the general lack of specificity regarding geographic location and, occasionally, the characters' or narrators' gender.

In "Hollywood Memorabilia" (1971), the narrator/protagonist, having finished his studies in Puerto Rico, has moved to New York City. He is 23 years old, an author, and works as a social science research assistant and film projectionist. He describes his past relationships with three men, with whom he currently has no relationship, although he thinks of them constantly. Not only does he not seem to have any friends, but he also does not seem to know anyone in New York; he is, in short, alone. Against such a backdrop, the protagonist's main relationship is to storytelling and cinema—particularly, to gay camp classics of Hollywood's so-called Golden Age. In contrast to the putative sterility of Puerto Rico, New York becomes the space where the protagonist's nocturnal wanderings lead to sexual encounters. Yet, even here, there is a dichotomy between the physical exchanges and the cerebral meditations on film (that is, the protagonist's fantasies of being a glamorous film character or diva and of reenacting their death scenes). The protagonist's exchanges with men seem rather common or simple: he invites them to his apartment for coffee or tea; has lunch or dinner with them; and, at times, has sex with them. In "Hollywood memorabilia" two spaces are negotiated: the abandoned, dark, desolate streets that lead to sexual encounters and the imaginary, mental space of film predicated on a camp sensibility. These two spaces are resolved, as it were, in narration: the scene of writing allows for constant inter-sections, as the very act of reminiscing conjures forth the memories of men and of film.

Ramos Otero's second collection of short stories, published in 1979, includes a narration that is representative of a second moment of emi-grant, exilic production. "El cuento de la Mujer del Mar" focuses on the relationship between the story's narrator, an unnamed, unemployed homosexual Puerto Rican writer and his Italian-American boyfriend, Angelo, an X-ray technician from New Jersey. Their relationship is sustained by mutual storytelling involving differing versions of the Woman of the Sea: for the Puerto Rican writer, the woman in ques-tion is Palmira Parés, "la Mujer del Mar," inspired by the poet Julia de Burgos; for Angelo, the woman is his grandmother, Vicenza Vitale, "la Donna del Mare."[21] Not only is the story squarely set in New York City and, more specifically, on Christopher Street, but there are also a number of additional locations—Manatí, San Juan, New Jersey, Italy, Montreal—to which the narrator and Angelo travel and where parallel stories take place. The initial resistance to specificity yields to a con-crete effort to map significant locations: a web of loci that the writer, nomad-like, inhabits both in his literary work and in his travels and writing.

Another significant aspect of this second moment in Ramos Otero's work is the opening towards linguistic plurality: while predominantly written in Spanish, the story contains important passages in English and occasional sprinklings of Italian as well as an internal process of translation, as Martínez-San Miguel has observed. The protagonist mentions that his communications with Angelo are in "broken" Eng-lish, indicating that English, or some version thereof, is the language that enables the two immigrants to communicate.[22] English is here a "street" language, a vehicle for colloquial communication, neither eru-dite nor literary. Tellingly, even though the protagonist uses English in his relationship with Angelo, he never uses it in the story to transmit his feelings or ideas; this he does almost exclusively in Spanish.

A third moment of exile/migrant experience in Ramos Otero's work can be found in the stories that comprise *Página en blanco y staccato* (1987). These stories evince a profound engagement with the history of Puerto Rican and other migrations, such as the Black and Caribbean Diasporas, as well as an acute appreciation of the different geographic spaces that Puerto Ricans occupy. The stories are also marked by a common central figure: a gay Puerto Rican writer who lives in New York.

The eponymous short story, "Página en blanco y staccato," is illustrative of the interconnections between homosexuality and migration. The story is marked by its frank treatment of AIDS, which devastated the Latino and gay communities in the 1980s, and by the narrator/protagonist's relationship with a fellow diasporic man. In it, we see how a gay Puerto Rican writer with AIDS named "Manuel Ramos" meets a second-generation Chinese Afro-Puerto Rican private detective called Sam Fat, with whom he has a short but crucial relationship. The initial encounter between these two men occurs at the Aguas Buenas Social Club, a Puerto Rican hangout on Avenue A in Loisaida (the Lower East Side), on December 31, 1983. Loisaida, it should be remembered, is a historically Puerto Rican and Jewish neighborhood in New York, immortalized by Miguel Piñero and other members of the Nuyorican Poets Café. The sexual and affective encounter between the white first-generation and the Afro-Chinese second-generation gay man in Ramos Otero's story allows for a complex negotiation of desire, racial inequality, historical difference, and resentment. At the end of the story, it is suggested that Sam Fat is responsible for the death of Ramos in an act of symbolic vengeance on the part of a descendant of slaves against a "white" Puerto Rican of European descent: the triumph of Santería over Catholicism.

By setting the action in such a neighborhood and, moreover, by making the neighborhood the protagonist of the story, Ramos Otero attempts to integrate questions of homosexuality into a traditional Puerto Rican enclave. As Arnaldo Cruz Malavé has shown in "*'What a Tangled Web!,'*" while other Nuyorican writers have tended to present homosexuality as flatly abject (that is to say, undesirable, suspect, or marginal), Ramos Otero flips the meaning of abjection and shows homosexuality as an integral, constitutive, and profoundly meaningful category: a productive, transformative abjection, as Sandoval-Sánchez posits in the present volume. Such moves, of course, do not free homosexuality from stigma—that is precisely the importance of the representation of AIDS in the story. Ramos Otero is not interested in "sanitizing" homosexuality, but rather in exploiting its subversive potential.

Stories of migration and travel mark the text and leave readers with the image of New York as a place where disparate communities come together, even though many, after seeing it as a temporary stop, end up spending their entire lives there. The African commonality of this mostly Caribbean diaspora is particularly notable, for the narrator of the story traces a map of slave experience which is girded by the survival of Yoruba religious traditions in the often syncretic form of Santería, the same tradition that Sam Fat is reluctant to embrace, even if it defines his maternal family history.[23] Ramos Otero's work thus portrays, in diverse ways, the rich ambiguity, the tensions and celebrations that attend any (new) place. The shifts in Ramos Otero's work point to significant shifts in immigrant experience.

Changing Times: Frances Negrón-Muntaner and Recent First-Generation Migrants

More recently, Frances Negrón-Muntaner's film *Brincando el charco: Portrait of a Puerto Rican* (1994) (Jumping the Puddle: Portrait of a Puerto Rican) allows us to think in a different way of the jump from the island to the mainland, that "other island of Puerto Rico," as Ramos Otero would say. *Brincando el charco* is a hybrid film, one in which the fictional, autobiographical story of a character called Claudia Marín (played by the filmmaker herself and inspired at least in part, by her life) is interspersed with intra- and extra-diegetic sequences of interviews, performances, archival footage, news-like demonstration coverage, and lesbian erotic fantasies. Set principally in Philadelphia, a city with an important Puerto Rican community (see Whalen), the film is situated in the tradition of Puerto Rican documentaries by and about women that Yamila Azize Vargas and Negrón-Muntaner herself have carefully studied. Negrón-Muntaner employs a series of cinematic devices in *Brincando el charco* that at once fragment and order the film. Intertitles appear between segments and are superimposed onto images that are at times frozen, producing the impression that they are slides. Voice-overs and narrations, such as those written and performed by Toni Cade Bambara and Zulma González, contribute to the "feeling" of the film as a multi-voiced essay. *Brincando el charco* is in English and Spanish and switches back and forth from one language to the other. It is, accordingly, a *bilingual* film that attempts to reflect and sound out the experiences of a bilingual and bicultural people.

The last name of the protagonist, Claudia Marín, is the same as that of former Puerto Rican governor Luis Muñoz Marín, a patriarchal figure who in the 1940s and '50s actively encouraged migration to the United States as a strategy for economic development and as a way to alleviate poverty on the island. It was under his stewardship that the "Great Migration" of Puerto Ricans took place, something that Nuyorican poets like Tato Laviera have vociferously decried. Negrón-Muntaner places herself solidly in the framework of the "gran familia puertorriqueña" by adopting Marín as the surname for her allegorical film persona. She also makes clear the stature and importance that she expects her ideas to receive, as the direct, if rebellious, heir of the great patriarch.[24] If Ramos Otero, by way of the abject, tends to deconstruct and delegitimize the master narratives with which Negrón-Muntaner flirts, the filmmaker herself has rather anxiously stated in various essays and interviews that she too is engaging in deconstruction.[25]

Brincando el charco begins with a slow-motion introductory sequence of a Puerto Rican Day parade, full of American and Puerto Rican flags and of faces that we assume are Puerto Rican.[26] The film's Spanish title is superimposed on the images while a voice-over in English posits—in a manner that recalls yet another of Puerto Rico's patriarchal cultural figures, the renowned 1930s intellectual Antonio S. Pedreira—the central question of the film: What is a Puerto Rican? Or rather: How have traditional definitions of Puerto Ricanness excluded numerous types of individuals? In the words of the narrator: "From the moment I learned how to read I have known of Puerto Ricans asking themselves, to the point of despair: Who are we? What is our common destiny? I am an echo of these questions, even as I contest them. That is why I must point my lens elsewhere, to see what escapes the us in nosotros." The voice that we hear is that of the main character, the photographer and filmmaker Claudia Marín. Yet, of course, it is also the voice of the photographer and filmmaker Negrón-Muntaner, who plays the role of Claudia, and who is, in fact, the person responsible for *Brincando el charco*.[27] Just as with Ramos Otero, we see the intersection of autobiography and narrative (and of the authorial persona) in the construction of the diasporic document. Claudia is based on a real lesbian Puerto Rican emigrant filmmaker; hers is not, in other words, some random role that is played by some random heterosexual actress. Her strategy of self-representation is not uncommon among gay and lesbian independent filmmakers, who often include themselves in their productions, as film critics Richard Dyer and Judith Mayne have observed.

The validation of Claudia Marín's character as a "real" subject who goes through a series of events, some of which are akin to the ones in which the filmmaker participates in daily life, operates in tandem with the notion that the individuals interviewed in the film are not fictitious subjects. I am referring not only to the aforementioned performances but also to five "portraits," such as that of Ramón González, who is showed "vogueing" at the beginning of the film. Even though González and the others are not identified when they first appear, the credits at the end of the film reveal who they are. Since several of the people portrayed have relatively public profiles, such as Agnes Lugo-Ortiz, professor of Latin American literature at the University of Chicago, and Moisés Agosto, poet and AIDS activist, the film "speaks" with a certain documentary authority. It is not surprising that Negrón-Muntaner would want to take advantage of the audience's tendency to grant documentary a higher truth-value than fiction. It is also no coincidence that groundbreaking women-of-color feminist and lesbian anthologies such as *This Bridge Called My Back*, *Compañeras: Latina Lesbians*, *Chicana Lesbians: The Girls Our Mothers Warned Us About*, and *Telling to Live: Latina Feminist Testimonios* include many testimonial and oral history pieces in which speaking subjects attempt to validate their assertions by drawing on personal experiences.[28] *Brincando el charco* flirts with testimonial narratives while refusing to be a documentary; and yet, it is nonetheless caught up in documentary discourse all the same.

The problem with flirting with testimony and documentary is, of course, that people tend to believe everything that they see. This is rather notoriously the case with the representation of expulsion from Puerto Rico: a "typically," or "stereotypically," dominant father kicks his daughter out of their home after he finds out that she is a lesbian.[29] While the situation is plausible, the scene itself, according to the director, was inspired by, and styled in the manner of, melodrama—specifically, Latin American *telenovelas* or soap operas. Furthermore, it in no way corresponds to the filmmaker's actual experiences in Puerto Rico; Negrón-Muntaner left the island after finishing college in order to pursue graduate studies in the United States. Critics such as Licia Fiol-Matta have argued that the representation of the family, particularly with its prominent religious iconography, relies on stereotypes of working-class intolerance that are incongruous with the characterization of the protagonist.[30] People nevertheless come up to Negrón-Muntaner all the time and thank her "for showing it the way it really is."

As mentioned earlier, both Negrón-Muntaner and Ramos Otero avail themselves of romantic relationships between island-born and U.S.-born queer individuals to explore different experiences and perceptions of Puerto Ricanness, such as those of Manuel Ramos and Sam Fat in "Página en blanco y staccato" and of Nuyorican lawyer Ana Hernández and Claudia Marín in *Brincando el charco*. As Negrón-Muntaner has observed, these pairings constitute "foundational fictions" in the sense advanced by the literary critic Doris Sommer, yet with an important difference. In traditional 19th-century Latin American novels centered on family romances, the pairings of opposites tended to resolve differences through procreation: the protagonists' children represented the hope for a new society over and against regional, economic, and social distinctions that threatened to pull apart the national whole. Of course, sexual reproduction is by no means a given in queer narratives and, in fact, does not occur in the Puerto Rican texts analyzed so far. What we do see, however, is a gesture towards the construction of a new community based on better understandings of human differences (Negrón-Muntaner) and, quite differently, on revenge and murder (Ramos Otero).

Negrón-Muntaner's film, unlike Ramos Otero's writing, funnels the process of immigration to the United States into two moments: expulsion from Puerto Rico and incorporation into a multicultural community composed of different migrant generations. Tellingly, the film ends with the protagonist boarding a plane to return to Puerto Rico for her father's funeral. It is quite possible that the compression or ellipsis of a longer migratory process corresponds to the chronological difference between Negrón-Muntaner's work, produced between 1989–94, and Ramos Otero's, written roughly between 1967 and 1990. The gay author is an important precedent for the lesbian filmmaker. But what exactly does this heritage entail? Claudia Marín has a Nuyorican girlfriend and Latin American, Spanish, African American, Korean, and Latino/a friends who debate questions of race, ethnicity, and nationality and, more pointedly, of racism, ethnocentrism, and ultranationalism in the United States. Claudia has affirmed bonds with the African American community *and* with the LGBT community. She has friends of many ethnicities; she has a grasp of the history of Puerto Rican immigration, both its causal socio-economic factors and its impoverished, ghettoized results; and she also has friends in Puerto Rico who keep her abreast of the state of queer politics and activism on the island. As mentioned, she eventually returns to Puerto Rico to reconcile with her estranged family, after the death of her "evil" father. In a sense, it appears that she comes to have her cake and to eat it too. But does she really?

Negrón-Muntaner has claimed that the film is a provocation, a means to bring about discussion and generate controversy. She has certainly succeeded in doing just that. I, for one, believe that perhaps the greatest merit of Negrón-Muntaner's project is, quite simply, that it is a film, and, as such, that it partakes of what is arguably the most important genre of our age. As I have claimed elsewhere, the film problematically portrays Americanization in Puerto Rico as a positive step to gay emancipation, a controversial position that coincides with Negrón-Muntaner's more recent defense of "Radical Statehood," which sees annexation as an opportunity for progressive, leftist politics. She also inadvertently misrepresents the predominantly English-speaking Nuyorican transsexual Cristina Hayworth, who originated the Gay Pride Parade on the island, as "una travesti americana" (an American drag queen), a common confusion on the island where language is frequently seen as synonymous with nationality.[31] Such confusions not withstanding, Negrón-Muntaner is one of the most important voices of queer island-born Puerto Rican artists in the United States.

1990s Second Generation Migrants: The Case of Erika López

U.S. born Puerto Ricans often have different life experiences and artistic projects than those of island-born, first-generation migrants such as Ramos Otero and Negrón-Muntaner. This is especially evident with the writer, cartoonist, and performance artist Erika López, in whose work matters of Puerto Ricanness assume a significantly different spin. Her production is characterized by her innovative approach to gender and sexuality (defending bisexuality, for example), her engagement with third-wave feminism, and her reassessment of ethnic and racial identities in the United States.[32] López's genius resides in her ability to use drawings, visual images, words, humor, and her own body to discuss sexuality openly. Drawing on high and low cultural forms such as novels, cartoons, and performance art inspired by stand-up comedy routines, López moves between learned and mass media in a manner reminiscent of Nuyorican dancers and performers like Arthur Avilés and, especially, Elizabeth Marrero,[33] but quite unlike such a second-generation artist like Rane Arroyo, who establishes a poetic dialogue with the high Modernist canon even while addressing working-class, gay Puerto Rican issues in the Midwest. López shares the militant social aspirations of poets such as Miguel Piñero, Pedro Pietri, Luz María Umpierre, and Sandra María Esteves, but she completely reorients their worldview into one that reflects her queer, hip, eccentric, and contemporary San Francisco-based Latina perspective.

If lesbian and feminist discourse in the 1970s and 80s was marked by a passionate and militant stance vis-à-vis women's liberation, the advances and failures of those struggles have led younger Latina women writers in the mid- and late-1990s to adopt a more humorous and less rigid and dogmatic approach. Such is the case with López herself, who began her career as a visual artist and who has published, to date, a book of cartoons and stories titled *Lap Dancing for Mommy: Tender Stories of Disgust, Blame, and Inspiration* (1997) and three illustrated and loosely autobiographical novels which have at their center the exploits of a half-Puerto Rican bisexual Quaker motorcyclist from Philadelphia named Tomato "Mad Dog" Rodríguez. This "Trilogy of Tomatoes," as it is known, is comprised of *Flaming Iguanas: An Illustrated All Girl Road Novel Thing* (1997), *They Call Me Mad Dog!: A Story for Bitter, Lonely People* (1998), and *Hoochie Mama: The Other White Meat* (2001). The first of these works recounts how Tomato crossed the United States on a motorcycle from New Jersey to San Francisco in a journey of self-examination and discovery that culminates with her first fulfilling lesbian sexual relationship with a woman named Hodie, renamed Hooter Mujer. The second describes how Tomato's plans for revenge against the unfaithful Hodie lead Tomato to jail, unfairly accused of murder, where she is raped and engages in lesbianism and comical phone sex. The third work describes Tomato's return to civil society and, more specifically, to a gentrified, over-commercialized, unrecognizable Bay Area overrun by *Latte people* and other Silicon-Valley yuppies. The centrality of California in these texts is key in as much as it addresses the dispersion of Puerto Rican culture across the United States, from sea to shining sea—complementing Ramos Otero's discussion of Puerto Ricans in Hawaii in his story "Vivir del cuento" (1987).

As the literary critic Laura Laffrado has also observed, López's *Lap Dancing for Mommy* includes two pieces on the character Pia Sweden that can be seen as an important antecedent to Tomato Rodríguez: "Pia Sweden: Idle Chatter" and "Pia Sweden Falls in Love with Hooter." Pia's mixed ethnic background is presented as the somewhat funny source of identity problems, specifically in relation to her body and linguistic skills: "Being ½ Puerto Rican + ½ Regular-White-Girl has left Pia Sweden a very hairy woman who doesn't know how to speak Spanish"

(3). She also idolizes Farrah Fawcett as well as "that little blonde girl w/ bangs on 'No More Tears' spray-on conditioner (made by Johnson + Johnson)," in other words, "the queens of the HAIRLESS BLOND PEOPLE" (3). The graphic, illustrated story concludes by describing how Pia, in her "lesbian student mode," attends a talk by Susie Bright, the radical sexual thinker, and goes home and demands that her heretofore sensitive boyfriend have rough sex with her—a feat which he finds almost impossible to perform.

This humorous approach incorporates a challenge to the ways in which mass media and advertising contribute to dominant modes of racialization in the United States and the ways in which non-white children internalize racism and white phenotype models as ideal images of beauty. Humor also posits a different conception of female sexuality, what the literary critic Melissa Solomon has termed "the lesbian bardo," in reference to English professor Eve Sedgwick's theorization of the Buddhist concept for "the space in-between." Solomon brilliantly elucidates the radical nature of Lopez's conception of sexuality, but she misses the ethnic and racial dimensions of the Puerto Rican novelist's work, a blind spot that she shares with film scholar Douglas Crimp, who neglects the Puerto Ricanness of the Warhol drag performer Mario Móntez in his article in the quasi-hagiographic *Regarding Sedgwick*, dedicated to the contributions of one of the key founders of queer theory. Solomon also does not mention third-wave feminism or broader social movements as significant to an explanation of the author's approach to sexuality. In this sense, I clearly side more with Laffrado's critical approach and her close attention to ethnicity and artistic form.

The shift from Pia Sweden to Tomato Rodríguez in these works indicates a conscious choice on the part of the writer to go from a name which indicates whiteness—"Pia," a likely reference to the actress, singer, and scandal-mongering sex symbol Pia Zadora, and "Sweden," a Scandinavian country which stands for white homogeneity, modern design, and cold weather—to one which indicates difference: the equally strange, cartoonish nickname "Tomato"—a fruit often considered to be a vegetable, the key ingredient in Mexican salsa, from the pre-Hispanic Nahuatl "tomatl"—and "Rodríguez," a Spanish surname.[34] In fact, midway through the first novel we learn that Tomato's real name is Jolene Gertrude Rodríguez, names and a surname consistent with the character's mixed ethnic background, which is tellingly disguised by her comical nickname.

López's semi-autobiographical character Tomato Rodríguez is presented as the daughter of a distant and abusive Afro-Puerto Rican
father and a German-American lesbian mother. The early parental separation and subsequent retreat into mostly white suburbia results in a
somewhat artificial link to Puerto Ricanness for the protagonist. While
López never disavows Tomato's Puerto Rican identity, she leads the
reader to understand that it is constructed on the vaguest of referents,
mostly acquired from dominant stereotypes. Scholars of migration
have scarcely considered such identity fashioning except in negative
terms. But it also represents a departure from the central, first-generation characters portrayed by Ramos Otero and Negrón-Muntaner and
comes closer to their depiction of second-generation individuals (Sam
Fat and Ana Hernández). López's work reverses the typical sources of
identity models; she and her characters grow up in lesbian households
and glean an ethnic identity from random sources.

Profusely illustrated with rubber stamp art and cartoons, López's
narratives are further distinguished from other Latina texts by their
explicit sexual descriptions, their presentation of bisexuality as a
valid sexual orientation, and their emphasis on humor (which recalls
standup Latina lesbian comedians and performers such as Marga Gómez, Mónica Palacios, Reno, and Carmelita Tropicana). López's approach differs significantly from that of older, more established Latina
lesbians such as Gloria Anzaldúa, Cherríe Moraga, and Luz María
Umpierre. Even as humorous a play as the Cuban-American Dolores
Prida's 1977 musical *Beautiful Señoritas*, which does not mention lesbianism, seems overly militant if oddly dated in its denunciation of
women's oppression in comparison to the riotous excess of Tomato
Rodríguez's adventures and travails. This is not to say that López's work
eschews social criticism, quite the contrary. Its fundamental marker is
one of tone. While the political exigencies of the 1980s under Reagan
and Bush might have demanded a particular insistence and seriousness, the transformed panorama of the mid-1990s under Clinton allowed for a different type of expression. Needless to say, the situation
under George W. Bush is hardly so supportive. Humor, however, did
not constitute the only means of transcending rigid boundaries. For
example, if it was once inconceivable for a feminist lesbian to interact
sexually with men and to maintain her dignity (a view that tended to
invalidate bisexuality as either "non-committed" or "intermediate"),
nowadays bisexuality has come to be much more accepted. As Tomato
puts it in *Flaming Iguanas*, "I wanted a Bisexual Female Ejaculating

Quaker role model" (251). Tomato has, in short, varied relationships, and struggles to reconceptualize categories in order to find something suitable to her own desires and idiosyncrasies.

Some other outstanding characteristics of López's writing are her link to popular culture, particularly camp and Latino/a kitsch; her interest in lesbian genealogies (that is to say, lesbian daughters and mothers); and her consideration of what it means to be Puerto Rican or Latina, particularly when not raised in a Latino/a environment. Carmen Miranda, the guardian angel Chiquita, and the "Puerto Rican eyebrow" (a reference to particular cosmetic practices and notions of style), in addition to a meditation on "passing" as African American, are some of the main referents of Latinidad in López's work. López's more recent performance piece, first entitled "Grandma López's Country-Mad Medicine Show (A Food Stamp Diatribe-in-Progress)," and now entitled "NOTHING LEFT BUT THE SMELL: A Republican on Welfare," has centered on her critique of classism and racism in U.S. society and on her indictment of the corporate world, particularly of her former publisher, Simon and Schuster, whom she accused of poor treatment and inefficiency.[35] The artist incorporates humor into her harangue and into her exploration of life on the welfare line, where she has become "the Welfare Queen" as she waits for unemployment checks and food coupons. López confronts dominant stereotypes about racialized Latina women like herself, portrayed as oversexed individuals dependent on government support, vis-à-vis the reality of artists who refuse to feed blindly into a capitalist cultural industry. The writer has turned, moreover, to producing her next book by hand, in the belief that this anti-mass market project will enable her to revive a sort of "direct touch" with her craft, responding—indirectly, perhaps—to views such as those expressed by Laffrado, who has questioned López's "marginality." Be that as it may, López also maintains an informative website (www.erikalopez.com) and a subscription e-mail list, regularly bringing her fans up to date about current developments in her life.

Conclusion

As we have seen, LGBT or queer Puerto Rican Diasporic cultural producers have engaged the legacy and experience of migration in widely varying manners. Place of birth, historical moment and even personal idiosyncrasy have all shaped the ways in which an array of individuals portray their different yet intersecting experiences. Whether it be through literature, as with Manuel Ramos Otero; film, as with Negrón-

Muntaner; or cartoons, words, and performance, as with Erika López, Puerto Rican and Nuyorican or Diasporican artists represent, engage, and analyze their richly complex and inevitably particular situations. There is not one homogeneous Puerto Rican queer diasporic experience, even when, as we have seen, many of the artists address similar issues. In English, Spanish, or Spanglish; in Puerto Rico, Manhattan, Philadelphia, New Jersey, or San Francisco; through the written word, celluloid, digital images, cartoons, or live bodies, queer Rican artists have documented and transformed an immigrant experience characterized by racism, poverty, linguistic difficulties, and homophobia (both from the receiving society and the community of origin), but also characterized by personal resiliency and cultural creativity. Puerto Ricans may have U.S. citizenship, but that has not meant that their integration into U.S. society has been easy, particularly for queer or LGBT individuals. Furthermore, the U.S. gay community has not necessarily been any more embracing of Puerto Ricans and other Latin Americans or Latinos/as than society at large. Much remains to be done, but an enormous amount has already been accomplished—at least in the realm of culture and the arts.

Works Cited

Aponte-Parés, Luis. "Outside/In: Crossing Queer and Latino Boundaries." *Mambo Montage: The Latinization of New York.* Ed. Agustín Laó-Montes and Arlene Dávila. New York: Columbia University Press, 2001. 363–85.

_____ and Jorge B. Merced. "Páginas Omitidas: The Gay and Lesbian Presence." *The Puerto Rican Movement: Voices From the Diaspora.* Ed. Andrés Torres and José E. Velázquez. Philadelphia: Temple University Press, 1998. 296–315.

Arroyo, Rane. *Pale Ramón.* Cambridge, Mass.: Zoland Books, 1998.

Azize Vargas, Yamila. "Otro modo de ver: El documental desde la perspectiva feminista." *Hómines* 17.1–2 (1993–94): 224–231.

Baumgardner, Jennifer and Amy Richards. *Manifesta: Young Women, Feminism, and the Future.* New York: Farrar, Straus & Giroux, 2000.

Bell, David and Gill Valentine, eds. *Mapping Desire: Geographies of Sexualities.* London: Routledge, 1995.

Binnie, J. "Invisible Europeans: Sexual Citizenship in the New Europe." *Environment and Planning A* 29 (1997): 237–48.

Braulio, Mildred. "Challenging the Sodomy Law in Puerto Rico." *NACLA Report on the Americas* 31.4 (1998): 33–34.

Bruns, Manfred. "Hopes for Same-Sex Binational Couples. Comments on Two Supreme Court Rulings (Eine Hoffnung fur gleichgeschlechtliche binationale Paare. Zu zwei hochstrichterlichen Entscheidungen)." *Zeitschrift fur Sexualforschung* 10.1 (1997): 48–51.

Cabrera, Lydia. *El monte. Igbo. Finda. Ewe Orisha. Vititi Nfinda. (Notas sobre las religiones, la magia, las supersticiones y el folklore de los negros criollos y el pueblo de Cuba)*. Miami: Ediciones Universal, 1992.

Cant, Bob, ed. *Invented Identities?: Lesbians and Gays Talk About Migration*. London: Cassell, 1997.

Carabine, Jean. "'Constructing Women': Women's Sexuality and Social Policy." *Critical Social Policy* 12.1 (1992): 23–37.

Cela, Camilo José. *Diccionario del erotismo*. Barcelona: Grijalbo, 1982.

Costa, Marithelma. "Entrevista: Manuel Ramos Otero." *Hispamérica* 20.59 (1991): 59–67.

Crespo-Kebler, Elizabeth. "'The Infamous Crime against Nature': Constructions of Heterosexuality and Lesbian Subversion in Puerto Rico." *The Culture of Gender and Sexuality in the Caribbean*. Ed. Linden Lewis. Gainesville: University of Florida Press, 2003. 190–212.

Crimp, Douglas. "Mario Montez, For Shame." *Regarding Sedgwick: Essays on Queer Culture and Critical Theory*. Ed. Stephen M. Barber and David L. Clark. New York: Routledge, 2002. 57–70.

Cruz Malavé, Arnaldo. "Towards an Art of Transvestism: Colonialism and Homosexuality in Puerto Rican Literature." *¿Entiendes? Queer Readings, Hispanic Writings*. Ed. Emilie Bergmann and Paul Julian Smith. Durham, N.C.: Duke University Press, 1995. 137–167.

_____. "'What a Tangled Web!': Masculinity, Abjection, and the Foundation of Puerto Rican Literature in the United States." *Sex and Sexuality in Latin America*. Ed. Daniel Balderston and Donna J. Guy. New York: New York University Press, 1997. 234–49.

_____ and Martin Manalansan. *Queer Globalizations: Citizenship and the Afterlife of Colonialism*. New York: New York University Press, 2002.

Duberman, Martin. *Stonewall*. New York: Plume, 1994.

Dyer, Richard. "Believing in Fairies: The Author and the Homosexual." *Inside/Out: Lesbian Theories, Gay Theories*. Ed. Diana Fuss. New York: Routledge, 1991. 185–201.

Epps, Brad. "Passing Lines: Immigration and the Performance of American Identity." *Passing: Identity and Interpretation in Sexuality, Race, and Reli-*

gion. Ed. María Carla Sánchez and Linda Schlossberg. New York: New York University Press, 2001. 92–134.

Fiol-Matta, Licia. Personal communication, March 1996.

FitzGerald, Frances. "The Castro (I)." *New Yorker* 62, July 21, 1986: 34–8.

Flores, Juan. *Divided Borders: Essays on Puerto Rican Identity.* Houston: Arte Público Press, 1993.

Foss, Robert J. "The Demise of the Homosexual Exclusion: New Possibilities for Gay and Lesbian Immigration." *Harvard Civil Rights—Civil Liberties Law Review* 29.2 (1994): 439–75.

Foucault, Michel. *The History of Sexuality.* Vol. I. Trans. Robert Hurley. New York: Vintage, 1978.

García Ramis, Magali. *Happy Days, Uncle Sergio.* Trans. Carmen C. Esteves. Freedonia, N.Y.: White Pine, 1995.

_____. "La mayor de las muertes (Breve semblanza de Manuel Ramos Otero)." *La ciudad que me habita.* Río Piedras: Huracán, 1993. 121–132.

"Gay Man Who Cited Abuse in Mexico Is Granted Asylum." *New York Times,* March 26, 1994: 5.

Gelpí, Juan G. *Literatura y paternalismo en Puerto Rico.* San Juan: Editorial de la Universidad de Puerto Rico, 1993.

_____. "Manuel Ramos Otero, *Página en blanco y staccato.*" *La torre (NE)* 4.14 (1990): 245–250.

Gil, Carlos. *El orden del tiempo: Ensayos sobre el robo del presente en la utopía puertorriqueña.* San Juan: Editorial Postdata, 1994.

Green, Jesse. "Where the Boys Went. (Migration of Gay Men from Greenwich Village to Chelsea)." *New York Times Magazine,* October 19, 1997: 68–70.

Guzmán, Manuel. "'Pa' La Escuelita Con Mucho Cuida'o y por la Orillita': A Journey through the Constested Terrains of the Nation and Sexual Orientation." In Negrón-Muntaner and Grosfoguel, 209–228.

Hernández, Wilfredo. "Homosexualidad, rebelión sexual y tradición literaria en la poesía de Manuel Ramos Otero." *Sexualidad y nación.* Ed. Daniel Balderston. Pittsburgh: Instituto Internacional de Literatura Iberoamericana, 2000. 225–41.

Heywood, Leslie and Jennifer Drake, eds. *Third Wave Agenda: Being Feminist, Doing Feminism.* Minneapolis: University of Minnesota Press, 1997.

Hart, John. "A Cocktail of Alarm: Same-Sex Couples and Migration to Australia 1985–90." *Modern Homosexualities: Fragments of Lesbian and Gay Experience.* Ed. Ken Plummer. London: Routledge, 1992. 121–133.

Ingram, Gordon Brent, Anne-Marie Bouthillette, and Yolanda Retter, eds.

Queers in Space: Communities, Public Spaces, Sites of Resistance. Seattle: Bay, 1997.

Juhasz, Alexandra. "Frances Negrón-Muntaner." *Women of Vision: Histories in Feminist Film and Video.* Minneapolis: University of Minnesota Press, 2001. 277–289.

La Fountain-Stokes, Lawrence. "1898 and the History of a Queer Puerto Rican Century: Gay Lives, Island Debates, and Diasporic Experiences." *Centro Journal* 11.1 (Fall 1999): 91–109.

_____. *Culture, Representation, and the Puerto Rican Queer Diaspora.* Ph.D. dissertation, Columbia University, 1999.

_____. "Dancing La Vida Loca: The Queer Nuyorican Performances of Arthur Avilés and Elizabeth Marrero." *Queer Globalizations: Citizenship and the Afterlife of Colonialism.* Ed. Arnaldo Cruz Malavé and Martin Manalansan. New York: New York University Press, 2002. 162–175.

_____. "Tomboy Tantrums and Queer Infatuations: Reading Lesbianism in Magali García Ramis's *Felices días, tío Sergio.*" *Tortilleras: Hispanic and U.S. Latina Lesbian Expression.* Ed. Lourdes Torres and Inmaculada Pertusa-Seva. Philadelphia: Temple University Press, 2003. 47–67.

Laffrado, Laura. "Postings from Hoochie Mama: Erika López, Graphic Art, and Female Subjectivity." *Interfaces: Women, Autobiography, Image, Performance.* Ed. Sidonie Smith and Julia Watson. Ann Arbor: University of Michigan Press, 2002. 406–429.

López, Erika. *Flaming Iguanas: An Illustrated All-Girl Road Novel Thing.* New York: Simon and Schuster, 1997.

_____. *Grandma López's Country-Mad Fried Chicken Book.* Limited artist edition, 2003. (Text also available on the web).

_____. *Hoochie Mama: The Other White Meat.* New York: Simon and Schuster, 2001.

_____. *Lap Dancing for Mommy: Tender Stories of Disgust, Blame and Inspiration.* Seattle: Seal Press, 1997.

_____. "Postcards From The Welfare Line: The Rise and Fall of Erika López." *Junction-City/ Progressive America* Internet website. http://www.junction-city.com/content/lopez.asp (accessed March 24, 2002).

_____. *They Call Me Mad Dog!: A Story for Bitter, Lonely People.* New York: Simon and Schuster, 1998.

Lugo-Ortiz, Agnes. "Community at Its Limits: Orality, Law, Silence, and the Homosexual Body in Luis Rafael Sánchez's '¡Jum!'" *¿Entiendes? Queer Readings, Hispanic Writings.* Ed. Emilie Bergmann and Paul Julian Smith. Durham, N.C.: Duke University Press, 1995. 115–136.

Luibhéid, Eithne. *Entry Denied: Controlling Sexuality at the Border.* Minneapolis: University of Minnesota Press, 2002.

_____. "Obvious Homosexuals and Homosexuals Who Cover Up: Lesbian and Gay Exclusion in U.S. Immigration." *Radical America* 26.2 (October 1996): 33–40.

Marcus, Eric. "The Drag Queen: Rey 'Sylvia Lee' Rivera." (Interview) *Making History: The Struggle for Gay and Lesbian Equal Rights, 1945–1990 (An Oral History).* New York: Harper Perennial, 1993. 187–196.

Markowitz, Laura M. "Out in the Burbs." *Utne Reader* (July–August 1995): 22+.

Mariposa. "Ode to the DiaspoRican." *Centro Journal* 12.1 (Fall 2000): 66.

Marqués, René. *El puertorriqueño dócil y otros ensayos 1953–1971.* Río Piedras: Editorial Antillana, 1977.

_____. *La mirada.* Río Piedras: Editorial Antillana, 1976.

Martínez-San Miguel, Yolanda. *Caribe Two-Ways: Culturas de la migración en el Caribe insular hispánico.* San Juan: Editorial Callejón, 2003.

Martorell, Antonio. *La piel de la memoria.* Trujillo Alto, Puerto Rico: Ediciones Envergadura, 1991.

Mayne, Judith. "A Parallax View of Lesbian Authorship." *Inside/Out: Lesbian Theories, Gay Theories.* Ed. Diana Fuss. New York: Routledge, 1991. 173–184.

McCormick, John. "The Gay Refugees: Seeking an AIDS Oasis on the Great Plains." *Newsweek* 111, May 9, 1988: 20+.

Merrett, Jim. "Sister & Brother, Wife & Lover. (Gay Man Marries Lover's Lesbian Sister So She Can Get A Green Card)." *Nation* 259, November 21, 1994: 611–14.

Miles, Sara. "Gimme Shelter: Gay and Lesbian Immigrants Can't Get Citizenship by Marrying Their American Partners, and Now Access to Asylum from Persecution Is Being Restricted." *Out* 42 (1997): 34+.

Mohr, Richard D. "Policy, Ritual, Purity: Gays and Mandatory AIDS Testing." *Law, Medicine and Health Care* 15.4 (1987–88): 178–185.

Muñoz, José Esteban. *Disidentifications: Queers of Color and the Performance of Politics.* Minneapolis: University of Minnesota Press, 1999.

Murray, Stephen O. "Ethnic and Temporal Patterns of Gay Male Migration to San Francisco." American Sociological Association Annual Conference. 1989. *Sociological Abstracts.* Online, August 10, 1998.

Musto, Michael. "Lost in Yonkers. Sylvia Rivera May Be the Rosa Parks of Gay Rights, But on the Streets, She's Just Another Homeless Queen." *Village Voice*, May 30, 1995: 25.

Negrón-Muntaner, Frances, dir. *Brincando el charco: Portrait of a Puerto Rican.* Film. Women Make Movies, 1994.

_____. *Boricua Pop: Puerto Ricans and the Latinization of American Culture.* New York: New York University Press, 2004.

_____. "Echoing Stonewall and Other Dilemmas: The Organizational Beginnings of a Gay and Lesbian Agenda in Puerto Rico, 1972–1977." *Centro Journal* 4.1 (1992): 77–95; 4.2 (1992): 98–115.

_____. "Of Lonesome Stars and Broken Hearts." *New Latin American Cinema, Volume Two: Studies of National Cinemas.* Ed. Michael T. Martin. Detroit: Wayne State University Press, 1997. 233–257.

_____. "When I Was a Puerto Rican Lesbian." *GLQ* 5.4 (1999): 511–526.

Negrón-Muntaner, Frances and Ramón Grosfogel, eds. *Puerto Rican Jam: Essays on Culture and Politics.* Minneapolis: University of Minnesota Press, 1997.

Park, Jin S. "Pink Asylum: Political Asylum Eligibility of Gay Men and Lesbians Under U.S. Immigration Policy." *UCLA Law Review* 42 (April 1995): 1115–56.

Patton, Cindy and Benigno Sánchez-Eppler, eds. *Queer Diasporas.* Durham, N.C.: Duke University Press, 2000.

Pedreira, Antonio S. *Insularismo.* (1934). Río Piedras: Edil, 1969.

Pérez-Firmat, Gustavo. *Life on the Hyphen: The Cuban-American Way.* Austin: University of Texas Press, 1994.

Portes, Alejandro and Rubén Rumbaut. *Immigrant America: A Portrait.* Berkeley: University of California Press, 1996.

_____. *Legacies: The Story of the Second Generation.* Berkeley: University of California Press, 2001.

Puig, Manuel, Manuel Ramos Otero and Olga Nolla. "Escritura y ensoñación. Transcripción de la actividad celebrada el 28 de septiembre de 1988." *Cupey* 5.1–2 (1988): 62–77.

Ramírez, Rafael. *What It Means to Be a Man: Reflections on Puerto Rican Masculinity.* New Brunswick: Rutgers University Press, 1999.

Ramos Otero, Manuel. *Cuentos de buena tinta.* San Juan: Instituto de Cultura Puertorriqueña, 1992.

_____. "Hollywood Memorabilia." *Concierto de metal para un recuerdo y otras orgías de soledad.* San Juan: Editorial Cultural, 1971. 77–85.

_____. *Página en blanco y staccato.* 1987. 2nd ed. Madrid: Playor, 1988.

_____. "El cuento de la Mujer del Mar." *El cuento de la Mujer del Mar.* Río Piedras: Ediciones Huracán, 1979. 87–116.

Ríos Avila, Rubén. "Caribbean Dislocations: Arenas and Ramos Otero in New York." *Hispanisms and Homosexualities.* Ed. Sylvia Molloy and Robert McKee Irwin. Durham, N.C.: Duke University Press, 1998. 101–19.

_____. "Gaiety Burlesque: Homosexual Desire in Puerto Rican Literature." *Piso 13 (Edición Gay)* 2.3 (1993): 8–9. Reprinted in *Polifonía salvaje: Ensayos de cultura y política en la postmodernidad.* Ed. Irma Rivera Nieves and Carlos Gil. San Juan: Editorial Postdata and Universidad de Puerto Rico, 1995. 138–146.

_____. "Migrant Hybridity." *Postdata* (San Juan, P.R.) 13 (1998): 45–47.

_____. *La raza cómica: del sujeto en Puerto Rico.* San Juan: Ediciones Cajellón, 2002.

Rodríguez, Dinah E. "Un cine sospechoso: Conversando con Frances Negrón-Muntaner." *Revista de crítica literaria latinoamericana* 23.45 (1997): 411–420.

Rodríguez, Juana María. "Of Sodomy and Sovereignty: Metaphoric Provocations and Queer Activist Interventions." *None of the Above: Contemporary Puerto Rican Cultures and Politics.* Ed. Frances Negrón-Muntaner. New York: Palgrave Macmillan (forthcoming).

_____. *Queer Latinidad: Identity Practices, Discursive Spaces.* New York: New York University Press, 2003.

Rodríguez Juliá, Edgardo. *Las tribulaciones de Jonás.* Río Piedras: Huracán, 1981.

Rumbaut, Rubén and Alejandro Portes, eds. *Ethnicities: Children of Immigrants in America.* Berkeley: University of California Press, 2001.

Salessi, Jorge. *Médicos maleantes y maricas: higiene, criminología y homosexualidad en la construcción de la nación argentina (Buenos Aires: 1871–1914).* Rosario: Beatriz Viterbo, 1995.

Sánchez, Luis Rafael. "Hum!" Trans. Rose M. Sevillano. *Grand Street* 61: 131–35.

Sandoval-Sánchez, Alberto "Puerto Rican Identity Up in the Air: Air Migration, Its Cultural Representations, and Me 'Cruzando el Charco.'" *Puerto Rican Jam: Essays on Culture and Politics.* Ed. Frances Negrón-Muntaner and Ramón Grosfogel. Minneapolis: University of Minnesota Press, 1997. 189–208.

Schneider, Margaret and Brian O'Neill. "Eligibility of Lesbians and Gay Men for Spousal Benefits: A Social Policy Perspective." *Canadian Journal of Human Sexuality* 2.1 (1993): 23–31.

Sedlak, Eric W. "*Nemetz v. INS*: The Rights of Gay Aliens Under the Constitutional Requirement of Uniformity and Mutable Standards of Moral Turpitude [in Petitions for Naturalization; Issue of Variation in State Laws on Homosexuality]." *New York University Journal of International Law and Politics* 16 (1984): 881–912.

Solomon, Melissa. "Flaming Iguanas, Dalai Pandas, and Other Lesbian Bardos (A Few Perimeter Points)." *Regarding Sedgwick: Essays on Queer Culture and Critical Theory.* Ed. Stephen M. Barber and David L. Clark. New York: Routledge, 2002. 201–216.

"Symposium: Stonewall at 25." *Harvard Civil Rights—Civil Liberties Law Review* 29 (1994): 283–475.

Sommer, Doris. *Foundational Fictions: The National Romances of Latin America.* Berkeley: University of California Press, 1991.

Sosa, Irene, dir. *Sexual Exiles.* Film. 1999.

Tuller, David. "Political Asylum for Gays?" *The Nation* 256, April 19, 1993: 520.

Turner, William B. "Lesbian/Gay Rights and Immigration Policy: Lobbying to End the Medical Model." *Journal of Policy History* 7.2 (1995): 208–225.

Umpierre-Herrera, Luz María. *The Margarita Poems.* Bloomington, Indiana: Third Woman Press, 1987.

Weston, Kath. "Get Thee to a Big City: Sexual Imaginary and the Great Gay Migration." *GLQ* 2.3 (1995): 253–277.

Whalen, Carmen Teresa. *From Puerto Rico to Philadelphia: Puerto Rican Workers and Postwar Economies.* Philadelphia: Temple University Press, 2001.

Woodlawn, Holly and Jeff Copeland. *A Low Life in High Heels: The Holly Woodlawn Story.* New York: Harper Perennial, 1991.

Notes

1   See, for example, Portes and Rumbaut as well as Rumbaut and Portes; Puerto Ricans are scarcely mentioned in any of these books, and queer sexualities are not discussed at all. Yolanda Martínez-San Miguel's landmark *Caribe Two Ways* is notable in its comparison of Cuban, Dominican, and Puerto Rican migration in the Caribbean and to the United States.

2   Manuel Guzmán claims authorship of the term "sexile": "A *sexile* is a neologism of mine that refers to the exile of those who have had to leave their nations of origins on account of their sexual orientation" (227). I first heard Frances Negrón-Muntaner employ the term, and am also familiar with Venezuelan filmmaker Irene Sosa's use. I am not able to ascertain Guzmán's role.

3   See Ríos Avila's essays "Final In*queery*" and "Rambling" in *La raza cómica*

(301–310; 311–318) as well as "Caribbean Dislocations," "Migrant Hybridity," and "Gaiety Burlesque."

4   I view Antonio S. Pedreira's harangue in *Insularismo* against effeminate men and René Marqués's comments regarding Puerto Rican men's "docility" as characterizations of unmanly, i.e., homosexual, behavior. In both, what is at stake is the very integrity of the nation.

5   The Reverend Margarita Sánchez de León was one of the leaders responsible for the elimination of Article 103 of the Puerto Rican Penal Code, which penalized consensual, adult male and female same-sex relations with up to ten years of imprisonment.

6   This is certainly how American gay male migration to Puerto Rico in the 1960s was seen; to this day, most gay-owned businesses on the island belong to non-Puerto Ricans; see Negrón-Muntaner's "Echoing Stonewall" and La Fountain-Stokes's "1898 and the History of a Queer Puerto Rican Century." In René Marqués's novel *La mirada*, a subtext indicates that homosexuality on the island is linked to North American sexual liberation movements and that, as such, they are to blame for its preponderance.

7   Associations of male homosexuality and foreignness also occur in the etymology of the words used to describe male homosexuals. For example, the term "bugarrón," used to refer to the "active" partner in same-sex male intercourse, has its origins in the Latin *bulgarus*, or "Bulgarian"; see Cela.

8   See Luibhéid, for example, for an account of the period here in question. With respect to lesbian and gay immigration to the United States, see Merrett, Miles, Mohr, Park, Sedlak, Tuller, Turner, the articles in "Symposium: Stonewall at 25," and "Gay Man Who Cites Abuse in Mexico Is Granted Asylum." Similar analyses for other countries include Binnie (Netherlands and United Kingdom), Bruns (Germany), Carabine (United Kingdom, with emphasis on women's experience), Hart (Australia) and Schneider and O'Neill (Canada). The San Francisco-based International Gay and Lesbian Human Rights Commission Asylum Project currently documents these immigration issues.

9   The most notable current case of exclusion is that of foreigners who are HIV positive or "have" AIDS. While there is no longer automatic exclusion on the grounds of homosexuality, and while asylum is now a possibility, it is still quite difficult to gain asylum on the basis of persecution due to sexual orientation.

10 See, for example, FitzGerald and Murray on migration to San Francisco and Weston on rural to urban migration. See Markowitz and McCormick for the reverse phenomenon. Green has documented migration from one New York City neighborhood (Greenwich Village) to another (Chelsea). See Ingram et al. and Bell and Valentine for a thorough discussion of lesbian and gay geographies.

11 It is generally recognized that working-class and rural communities have different paradigms and levels of tolerance for gender deviance, particularly for so-called effeminate men, though it remains risky to make generalizations; see Ramírez.

12 Gwen Araujo (born Edgar Araujo) was a 17-year-old transgender teen murdered in Newark, California in 2002; Edgar (Eddie) Garzón was a 35-year-old Colombian immigrant murdered in Jackson Heights, New York in 2001; Paola Matos was a 31-year-old transgender woman murdered in Brooklyn, New York in 2002; Rodney Velásquez was a 26-year-old Puerto Rican gay fashion designer murdered in the Bronx, New York, in 2002; Brandon Teena (born Teena Brandon) was a 21-year-old transgender man murdered in 1993 in Nebraska; Matthew Sheppard was a 21-year-old gay man murdered in Laramie, Wyoming in 1998.

13 The case of the Mexican-Puerto Rican painter Oliverio Hinojosa is exemplary of non-U.S. Puerto Rican queer migration. One can also think of scholar Iris Zavala, who for many years has resided in Spain and Holland.

14 See my dissertation, *Culture, Representation, and the Puerto Rican Queer Diaspora* for a more sustained analysis of these issues.

15 See Carlos Gil in *El orden del tiempo* (55–79).

16 Luz María Umpierre's fundamental text continues to be *The Margarita Poems*. Manuel Ramos Otero's oeuvre was centered on questions of homosexuality.

17 See also Cruz Malavé's "Towards an Art of Transvestism."

18 Gustavo Pérez-Firmat borrows the term "1.5" from sociologist Rubén Rumbaut, which is now in common usage in migration literature. In the words of Pérez-Firmat, "Born in Cuba but made in the USA, they belong to an intermediate immigrant generation whose members spent their childhood or adolescence abroad but grew into adults in America. Because this group falls somewhere in between the first and second immigrant generation, the Cuban sociologist Rubén Rumbaut has labeled it the '1.5' or 'one-and-a-half, generation'" (4).

19 See La Fountain-Stokes, "Tomboy Tantrums," for an analysis of Lidia as a lesbian character.

20 See Gelpí's "Manuel Ramos Otero" as well as his *Literatura y paternalismo en Puerto Rico* (137–54).

21 Martínez-San Miguel discusses the role of this central female character as a structuring fictional construct in her analysis of the story (344–50).

22 Ramos Otero comments profusely on his relation to English in his interview with Costa. Regarding his involvement in the New York gay world, he states: "[E]l mundo homosexual en el que me movía era exclusivamente

en inglés" (the homosexual world in which I moved was entirely in English) (64).

23 The work of Fernando Ortiz and Lydia Cabrera, particularly *El monte,* is useful to understand the presence of African religious traditions in Cuba and the Americas at large.

24 The most notorious analysis of Luis Muñoz Marín as great father is Edgardo Rodríguez Juliá's *Las tribulaciones de Jonás.*

25 See Negrón-Muntaner "When I Was a Puerto Rican Lesbian" and her interview with Alexandra Juhasz.

26 Negrón-Muntaner goes to great lengths to insist that the large American flag that appears in this sequence is *queer,* with fifty-one stars arranged in a circle: an American flag that incorporates the lone Puerto Rican star ("When I Was a Puerto Rican Lesbian," 512).

27 See the interview by Dinah E. Rodríguez.

28 One can also think of films such as Marlon Riggs's *Tongues Untied* or Jennie Livingston's *Paris Is Burning,* although the latter film has been taken to task for appropriating and misrepresenting the subjects on which it focuses—a chronic risk of documentary production.

29 See Negrón-Muntaner's "When I Was a Puerto Rican Lesbian" for an extensive discussion of this scene by the filmmaker (515–16).

30 Personal communication, March 1996.

31 See La Fountain-Stokes's "1898."

32 On third-wave feminism, see Baumgardner and Richards as well as Heywood and Drake.

33 On Avilés and Marrero, see La Fountain-Stokes's "Dancing La Vida Loca."

34 López's reference to a Scandinavian country is reminiscent of Rane Arroyo's poem "Island to Island" in which the poet speaks of his experiences as a Puerto Rican who visited Iceland; see *Pale Ramón,* 55–66

35 See López' website as well as "Postcards from the Welfare Line: The Rise and Fall of Erika Lopez." López's entry into performance art occurred with her show titled "Grandma López's Country-Mad Medicine Show: A Tonic for the Age," subtitled "A Food Stamp Diatribe-in-Progress performed by Erika López" (November 2002, Rutgers University). This show was later advertised as "Erika Lopez's Tiny Fisted Tantrum Co. Presents NOTHING LEFT BUT THE SMELL: A Republican on Welfare," with performances in San Francisco, Denver, and New York City.

9

Politicizing Abjection: Towards the Articulation of a Latino AIDS Queer Identity

Alberto Sandoval-Sánchez

Memories are archipelagos of islands surfacing on the horizon waiting to be revisited.[1] With the AIDS epidemic, my memories are anchored in floating cemeteries in an ocean of pleasure and death, remembrance and oblivion, suspiros y cenizas. Wherever I go I carry mis muertos conmigo, en mis recuerdos, a generation of Latino gay men that in a self imposed s/exile migrated to the United States from the Caribbean and Latin America in search of independence and sex, satisfaction and love. The gay party that started with the Stonewall riots in 1969 was over by 1982 with the intrusion of AIDS. We all witnessed when Thanatos killed Eros with the mirrored disco ball on the dance floor. Gone with it were the beams of light that penetrated every single heart to the beat of Donna Summer's erotic cadence of "love to love you baby." Gone were the dancing bodies covered in sweat, smelling sex, desiring an orgasm that would be a fatal attraction.

Uno tras otro, one after the other, they succumbed to AIDS. Enrique from Cuba, Hernán from Colombia, Conrado from Puerto Rico, Orlando from Venezuela, Manuel from El Salvador, José from Mexico, Luis from Panama.

You name your own dead ones.

Silence is death.

Y ahora aquí, we all carry nuestros muertos in our skin, in our eyes, in our lips, in our tongues, en nuestros culos, en nuestras pingas, en nuestros corazones, en nuestra sangre, in every nook and cranny of our bodies, 'til death do us part. Since 1981, with AIDS, and despite all of the changes in medications and their unequal distribution the world over, vivo immersed in abjection. The undead survived with the fear of contagion, with the horror of pollution, with the agony of memories of living

311

dead young men who either went to their homeland to die or whose dead bodies and ashes were brought home to their families to pay their final respects. How many coffins and secrets remained sealed to hide the disfigured and decaying cadavers? How were their early deaths explained en una sociedad latinoamericana que vive del que dirán, where homosexuality and AIDS are still most often taboos? How many broken hearts and shattered dreams did they leave behind? How many were forced to return in the face of death? I still cry for them.

After my own AIDS diagnosis in 1990, I felt that I had no escape. Either I stayed or surrendered. Instead, I rebelled. In a cry of anger and survival, I openly refused to go back sick or to be buried in my native Puerto Rico. I decided to stay in charge of my illness, my career, mi vida y mi cuerpo. I could not leave my lover behind. Nor could I leave mi familia that I had made from scratch.[2] I could not give up the freedom that migration had provided me, particularly the opportunity to articulate a gay identity shaped by a Latino consciousness. With AIDS, just as with migration, once again I had to reinvent life and my notion of home—this time in the shadow of death, en las entrañas del monstruo.

As a Latino gay man with AIDS and as a scholar, I cannot draw a line between my body and my scholarship. My body always pushes me to the limits; my writing always makes me put into practice the dependency between body and mind. I cannot privilege the mind over the body. Con el SIDA, I must constantly challenge the mind/body dualism that reigns in western civilization. I have a body; I am a body, therefore I am. In spite of constant struggles with health complications caused by a damaged immune system and in spite of endless negotiations with a wasting body, I have always managed to think with my body, through my body. For my survival, I make room for AIDS as I write with my body, and as I write on my body, I make corporeal my scholarship.

Both my body and my scholarship are marked, tattooed, by the rages of illness, surgeries, infections, side effects, pain, trauma, loss, and mourning. AIDS is inscribed in my skin, in my chest where scars are the residue of catheters installed to infuse medication that protected me from almost inevitable blindness from cytomegalovirus. Sometimes when I look at my chest in the mirror all I see are cicatrices of wounds, which seem to have been perpetrated by condors that tear away pieces of flesh, mi carne. Now that my right eye has been removed, my mutilated face comes face to face with the one-eyed monsters that hide behind all mirrors. Peek-a-boo! I guess losing an eye is the price one pays for not dying. Irony is a survival skill. In spite of the ups and downs, of periods of hospitalization and of recovery, my writing keeps me alive. It keeps my body going. Peek-a-boo! I am still here! Todavía existo.

I am fascinated with the abject body: if I were not, how would I be able to keep on living with AIDS? EL SIDA is the ultimate embodiment of abjection. As George Whitmore accurately observed in 1988, AIDS is all "about shit and blood" (24), mierda y sangre. How more abject can you get when you are un Latino maricón con SIDA, all in one package? What does it mean to have the monster under your skin? How can you love your abject body when it betrays you? How do you feel in a society that expels the sick, the Latino, the queer, the migrant, the Other?

Since my AIDS diagnosis I have had to negotiate on a daily basis with a body that houses abjection. In the beginning there was no language. Panic and pain made words insufficient and slippery. As a queer migrant with AIDS, abjection makes me dispensable; once cast away into the realm of the living dead, AIDS incubates my own corpse— "the utmost of abjection," as Kristeva puts it (4), a corpse waiting for its body bag to be disposed. In my s/exile, once death becomes the ultimate exile, abjection rules.

* * *

In the beginning
I just sat there.
I exiled myself
into a labyrinth of fear
and dead ends.
I just sat down, got up, laid down, and tried to sleep.
I couldn't.
Could I just close the door and let death in?
It was not death but the phantom of death
opening a door
making me go around and around
in a revolving door that faced emptiness:
exiled
there is no way back.
Time is not timed
once you await death.

Life is breathless.
Colors are blindness.
Music is deafness.
Exiled beings are a mass of memories without shape.
Words lack sound and meaning.
Reality is but fragments.
Living is chaotic.
There is no order of things. None.
The past is slippery.
Nostalgia is porous.
It is a feeling of terminal loss
for what is left behind.
Life is in ruins. So is the body.
The worse is insomnia and amnesia.
You close your eyes and you can not sleep.
You open your eyes and there is only darkness.
You are in eternal estrangement.
Far, far away into the horizon, you see your body wandering
in a twilight zone: Lost. Lost.
And, you cannot even remember where you are coming from
or where are you heading.
You cannot make up your head.
At that point you are homeless.
You are a wanderer.
Lost in a cemetery without finding a tomb.
From nowhere, the shadow of a vampire
offers a glass of blood.
You are thirsty.
So, you follow the scent.
I wake up. My blood is burning.
I am afraid of the light.
I run to the mirror.
There is no image: my face is gone.
There is no memory of what I looked like.
My flesh is so pale that there is no reflection.
My eyes have no pupils. They are two white balls lost in the
      whiteness of the darkness.
I run away from my body.
But I can not even recognize my body.
Where is it?

Mi cuerpo is not my body anymore.
Mi piel is not my skin any more.
Mi carne is not my flesh anymore.
Mis huesos are not my bones any more.
Mi sangre is not my blood anymore.
I must give it away in bloody samples.
Drop by drop.
Only the vampires can touch it.
They are after me.
Something is growing inside me.
I feel it.
My women friends laugh at me.
I tell them I have nausea, feel dizzy, and weak.
They say "You must be pregnant. "
It feels like it.
Can a man give birth?
I know that something is growing inside me.
I feel it.
It moves like a fetus from my stomach to my lungs.
It swims in my blood trying to be born.
What is inside me? What is it?
Do women ever have a fear of giving birth to a monster?
I incubate it.
I feed it.
I nurse it.
I caress it.
I cherish it.
It doesn't feel good.
Whatever it is. It is growing. Inside me. Slowly. Lentamente,
My chest hurts. It itches. I am short of breath.
I continually cough.
I get constant fevers.
I cannot hold anything in my stomach.
After weeks of sickness,
there is no relief.
Its breath wakes me up in the middle of the night.
All I can think of is horror movies.
I sit on the edge on the bed.
On the wall all I see are all kinds of aliens hatching in my body.
My lungs are on the edge of exploding.

My chest is about to split open.
Some kind of Alien creature must be inside me.
I scream out loud.
I scream to the echoes of my scream.
My deaf screaming wakes me up.
My chest is in pain.
My sweat is a cascade of blood.
My saliva is burning lava.
I am erupting.
I am burning.
I am on fire.
I take my temperature: 104.8 degrees.
I scream: The Alien is inside me.
What's inside me? What is it?[3]

* * *

The above is not merely a narcissistic poetic exercise. Rather, it reflects the abject dark side of narcissism, which, as John Lechte has brilliantly observed, "is precisely what Narcissus would not want to have seen as he gazed into the pool" (160). That reflection of a Latino gay man with AIDS constitutes a system of representation in which the body is the foundation for a theoretical project in which writing, as a critical cultural practice, facilitates a politics of survival immersed in the deep and troubled muddy waters of abjection, an abjection entangled en mi mariconería y en mi Latinidad. And given that I do scholarship with my body, my writing is the umbilical cord to abjection, to my migrancy, to my mariconería, and to my Latinidad. In such terms, abjection is the only way to recover my corporeality from a system of knowledge that always tries to transcend and sublimate the materiality of the body, its biological processes, the experience of suffering, and the reality of mortality.

* * *

Julia Kristeva's definition of abjection in *Powers of Horror* as "what disturbs identity, system, order. What does not respect borders, positions, rules" (4), allows for an examination of the very special dynamics between self and other in the queer male body in given relations of power that fuel the machinery of homophobia, racism, xenophobia, machismo, and fear of AIDS. Abjection is repulsive because it manifests a confusion of boundaries that punctures, fractures, and fragments the assumed unity, stability, and closure of the identity of the hegemonic subject and the body politic of the nation. Although abjection is, as Kristeva notes, "above all about ambiguity" (9), it still has the power to be felt somatically and symbolically; it infects and affects both the material body and the self. Elizabeth Grosz's theorization of the abject helps us visualize its existential dimensions: "[i]t is the underside of a stable subject identity, an abyss at the borders of the subject's existence, a hole into which the subject may fall when its identity is put into question" (72). For this reason, the abject must be kept in check, out of sight, always expurgated to avoid any erosion or traversal of borders.

Threatening to contaminate the symbolic order, undoing cultural taboos around the body, and putting at risk all systems of cultural order and logic, people of color, homosexuals, people living with AIDS, and migrants in the U.S. must be kept at bay and relegated to the margins, just as bodily fluids, secretions, and waste are repelled. Expelled from the national body politic, the unclean and improper other is translated as an alien, as a monster, an excess or lack that provokes anxiety, horror, and disgust.

I propose, however, that the abject subject located at the privileged site of boundaries can empower him or herself by way of a positionality between exclusion and integration. The abject Latino gay subject in this liminal zone of abjection is capable of transgressing borders and hence of making possible a certain subversion and emancipation. In this way, the abject other is dangerous because he or she challenges the fragile limits of the order of things and social hierarchies.

The politics of abjection that I suggest engages the Latino gay body with AIDS—a body marked by race, ethnicity, class, sexuality, and migration, a body that endangers and troubles the cohesion of the social order by destabilizing the borders between normal and deviant, insider and outsider, sameness and difference, health and illness, life and death. This body is the site where abjection operates to validate its difference and alterity. It is through the condition of abjection—that continual struggle between the subject and the abject—that a subjectivity in process is articulated in all its performativity. Centering on how abjection is experienced en carne y hueso allows one to perceive abjection as a performative act, as "a doing and a thing done," (*Performance* 1), as always a becoming that has the potential to disrupt normality. It is through unending acts of performative abjection that the marginalized other can gain a paradoxically powerful agency, can subvert and resist.

I want to inquire specifically into how Latino queer bodies materialize and enact abjection as a strategic performance in which identity is always in the making. In so doing, they manifest difference and display a new "politics of identity" in all its inconsistencies and paradoxes. I am interested in investigating what modalities of abjection operate in Latino/a queer cultural projects, how abjection molds new forms of cultural production, and how, and up to what point, queer Latino/a cultural performances materialize a discursive site of and for abjection that menaces the homogeneity and stability of official hegemonic culture and identity and its anxieties that keep the queer, the AIDS survivor, the Latino/a migrant, the racial and ethnic other locked in place. Since abjection problematizes bodies and identities once boundaries are crossed, what is at stake is the dramatic construction of subjectivities in process and mutational identity formations always at risk of dissolution and further marginalization. By privileging and reclaiming abjection, the other inhabits a liminal and interstitial space that recognizes the provisionality of identity and the processual nature of cultural practices such as transculturation. In the words of Kristeva: "'*Where* am I?' Instead of '*Who* am I?' For the space that engrosses the deject, the excluded, is never *one*, nor *homogeneous*, not *totalizable*, but essentially divisible, foldable, and catastrophic. A deviser of territories, languages, works, the *deject* never stops demarcating his universe whose fluid confines . . . constantly question his solidity and impel him to start afresh" (Powers, 8). Accordingly, to embrace abjection is to undo, in some small part, racism, shame, homophobia, and the fear of death, and to allow for a mode of self-empowerment and a liberating counter-hegemonic force of bodies in revolt that corporalize difference and heterogeneity with the potential, as Kristeva remarks, to never cease "challeng[ing their] master" (2) with a boundary crisis, the instability of meaning, and the disruption of order.

Works Cited

Diamond, Ellin, ed. *Performance & Cultural Politics*. New York: Routledge, 1996.

Groz, Elizabeth. *Sexual Subversions: Three French Feminists*. Sydney: Allen & Unwin, 1989.

Kristeva, Julia. *Powers of Horror: An Essay on Abjection.* Trans. Leon S. Roudiez. New York: Columbia University Press, 1982.

Lechte, John. *Julia Kristeva.* New York: Routledge, 1990.

Moraga, Cherríe. *Giving Up the Ghost.* Los Angeles: West End Press, 1986.

Sandoval-Sánchez, Alberto. *Side Effects.* Manuscript, 1993.

Whitmore, George. *Someone Was Here: Profiles in the AIDS Epidemic.* New York: Nal Books, 1988.

Notes

1   A version of this essay is forthcoming in a special volume of *American Literary History* (17.3) on Race, Ethicity, and Civic Identity in the Americas.

2   I am here echoing Cherríe Moraga in *Giving Up the Ghost* (58).

3   The passage is an excerpt from my play *Side Effects*, staged at Mount Holyoke College Theater Department (October 1993).

10

HIV and the Transnational Movement of People, Money, and Microbes

Paul Farmer and Nicole Gastineau

> "If there are connections everywhere, why do
> we persist in turning dynamic, interconnected
> phenomena into static, disconnected things?"
>
> —Eric Wolf

At about 6 A.M. on June 26, 1982, Solange Eliodor expired in Jackson Memorial Hospital in Miami. When not in the hospital, the 26-year-old Haitian refugee spent her final year in a rickety boat, which reached the shores of Florida the previous July, and then in prison, as the reluctant ward of the U.S. Immigration and Naturalization Service (INS). The Dade County Medical Examiner denied that the young woman showed any signs of tuberculosis—"She didn't have it. Period."—although the INS had initially maintained otherwise. The medical examiner also said that "there was no sign the woman suffered a blow to the head," an allegation raised by the director of the Haitian Refugee Center. Other Haitians interned in the Krome Avenue INS detention facility may have been dealt blows to the head, but Solange Eliodor was not one of them. The verdict was toxoplasmosis of the brain, a parasitic infection that, though common, is usually rendered harmless by immune defenses.

The details of this particular grisly story—the flight from Haiti in a boat, the INS detention, the mistaken accusations of both tuberculosis and a blow to the head—are parts of a complicated narrative that extend far beyond any one personal history. Early in the AIDS pandemic, a number of Haitians—including Solange Eliodor—fell ill with opportunistic infections characteristic of the new syndrome. Some of the ill Haitians lived in urban Haiti; some had emigrated to the United States or Canada. Unlike most other patients meeting the diagnostic criteria for AIDS, the Haitians diagnosed in the United States denied homosexual activity or intravenous drug use. Most had never had a blood transfusion. AIDS among Haitians was, in the words of North American researchers, "a complete mystery."

The ties that bind Haiti to urban North America have a historical basis, and they continue to change.[1] These connections are economic and affective; they are political and personal. Although our main focus will be the study of AIDS in rural Haiti, we will return again and again to urban Haiti and the United States, because the boundaries separating these regions are blurred. The AIDS pandemic serves as a striking reminder that even a remote Haitian village belongs to a network that includes Port-au-Prince and Brooklyn, voodoo and chemotherapy, divination and serology, poverty and plenty. Indeed, the sexual transmission of HIV is as eloquent a testimony as any to the salience—and complicated intimacy—of these links. Often, the links manifest the large-scale forces of history and political economy not readily visible to the ethnographer (or physician) and yet crucial to an understanding of AIDS and social responses to it. It is the task of anthropology to seek to bring into focus these interconnections and the effects of large-scale forces on settings such as rural Haiti.

As we turn now to consider how shifting sexual behaviors are a link between transnational flows of capital and microbes, we will also look at larger structural forces and the role they play in the sexual choices made by individuals. Do microbes or poverty cause AIDS? Is AIDS the product of North American imperialism? Are Haitians a special "AIDS risk group"? Are "boat people" disease-ridden and a threat to the health of U.S. citizens? These questions underscore several of the West Atlantic pandemic's central dynamics—blame, search for accountability, accusation, and racism—that have shaped both responses to AIDS and the epidemiology of a new virus.

Transnational Tourism and the Beginning of the Epidemic

> "Homosexuals in New York take vacations in Haiti, and we suspect that this may be an epidemic Haitian virus that was brought back to the homosexual population in the United States."
>
> —Dr. Bruce Chabner, National Cancer Institute, December 1, 1982

Haiti is the poorest country in the Americas. With a gross national product of about $380 per person per year, all of Haiti is poor (World

Bank). But local history undermines, even as it underlines, the poverty of any place created as a slave colony, and Haiti's Central Plateau is no exception. In the 19th century, after a successful slave revolt made Haiti the first independent republic in Latin America, the former slaves turned their backs on the plantation system to become peasant farmers.[2] By their own accounts, rural Haitians were cash-poor but had enough to eat, because they had land. For the people farming the broad banks of the upper Artibonite River, all this changed in 1956. As part of a "poverty-reduction program," the precursor of the World Bank funded the construction of a modern hydroelectric dam in the Péligre gorge. This dam was signed into existence in Washington, D.C. and was built for the most part by an American engineering firm. As water rose in the once-fertile valley, the peasant farmers were forced into the dry and eroded hills. The local inhabitants blame their current poverty on landlessness.

The origins of the dam can be traced back to the U.S. military occupation of Haiti (1915–1934), when initial plans for it were drawn up. At that time, Haiti's constitution was rewritten to abolish one of its most famous articles: the prohibition of foreign ownership of land in Haiti. In 1949, the Haitian government and the Export-Import Bank signed into existence the *Organisme de Développement de la Vallée de l'Artibonite* (ODVA). The stated goals of the ODVA were as follows:

> To use the waters of the Artibonite to irrigate the 40,000 hect-ares of lands deemed irrigable; to drain those areas needing to be drained in order to combat alkalinity; to protect the plains from the periodic floods that impact unfavorably on the regional economy and impoverish the harvest; to undertake, in all of these areas, a methodical agricultural development plan based on the most modern techniques; to implement a logical re-assembly of certain Valley populations in hopes of raising their standards of living through the continual enjoyment of the profits to be made from the newly cultivated and developed lands; to at last turn the Artibonite into an area of production and trade that will exert its influence throughout the country and help to normalize our commercial balance. (cited in Moral*)*

Most of those living in the then-fertile valley village of Petit-Fond did not move until the day the waters chased them off their lands.[3] Most were not reimbursed for their loss of land and crops, making the transition to the dry, rocky hills all the more difficult.

We mention the dam for two critical reasons. First, neither the dam nor the AIDS epidemic would exist as they do today if Haiti had not been caught in a web of relations that are economic as well as sexual. Second, the direct effect of the dam's construction was dire poverty that led to a migration of people. With this poverty and migration came changes in agency that led to changing sexual behaviors.

Regarding the first point, we can see that the AIDS pandemic is closely correlated with transnational economic relationships—that is, the flow of capital can provide some logic to the flow of microbes. Excluding Puerto Rico, which is not an independent country, the five Caribbean basin nations with the largest number of AIDS cases by 1986 were the Dominican Republic, the Bahamas, Trinidad and Tobago, Mexico, and Haiti. According to export indices, in both 1977 and 1983—the years for which such data are available—the same five countries were most linked to the United States economically (International Monetary Fund). And the country with the highest AIDS burden, Haiti, was also the country most fully dependent on U.S. exports. In all the Caribbean basin, only Puerto Rico is more economically dependent on the United States, and only Puerto Rico had reported more AIDS cases to the Pan American Health Organization by the late 1980s.[4]

The thesis that evolving economic forces run parallel to the lineaments of the American epidemics is confirmed by comparing Haiti with a neighboring island, Cuba, the sole country in the region not enmeshed in the West Atlantic system. In Haiti, several epidemiological studies of asymptomatic city dwellers in the mid to late 1980s revealed that approximately 9 percent were HIV-positive.[5] In 1986 in Cuba, only 0.01 percent of one million persons tested were found to have antibodies to HIV.[6] Had the pandemic begun a few decades earlier, the epidemiology of HIV infection in the Caribbean might well have been different.

Epidemiological studies by the Haitian Study Group on Kaposi's Sarcoma and Opportunistic Infections (GHESKIO), formed in May 1982, provide some insight into the early stages of the epidemic, and we will explore the significance of this data to current patterns of disease. Although the Haitian researchers initially had concluded that "no segment of Haitian society appears to be free of opportunistic infections or Kaposi's sarcoma" (Pape, Liautaud, Thomas, et al., 949). AIDS did not strike randomly. Pape and colleagues found that 74 percent of all men with opportunistic infections lived in greater Port-au-Prince, home to approximately 20 percent of all Haitians. Curiously, 33 percent of all AIDS patients lived in a single suburb, Carrefour. Five of 21 men interviewed by one of the GHESKIO clinicians stated that they were bisexual, as did two patients referred by other Haitian physicians. Of these seven men, all had lived in Carrefour (four) or the United States (three). Three had had sexual contact with North American men in both Haiti and in the United States, and two others had had sexual contact with Haitian men known to have opportunistic infections.[7] Furthermore, fully half of the allegedly heterosexual men had either lived or traveled outside of Haiti. Ten to fifteen percent of these patients had traveled to North America or Europe in the five years preceding the onset of their illness, and several more admitted to sexual contact with tourists.[8]

Similar patterns became apparent on other Caribbean islands. Pape and Johnson noted that for gay men in Jamaica, the Dominican Republic, and Trinidad, "sexual contact with American homosexuals rather than promiscuity per se appeared to be associated with increased risk of infection" ("Epidemiology of AIDS" 36). In summary, Haitians with AIDS were then largely men, though increasing numbers of women reported to the GHESKIO clinic. Carrefour, a center of prostitution bordering the south side of Port-au-Prince, became the epicenter of the Haitian epidemic, and a large percentage of the early cases were linked to homosexual contact, some of it with North Americans.

U.S. tourism to Haiti, when coupled with the island's increasing poverty, brought about institutionalized prostitution. And as Haiti became poorer, both men's and women's bodies became cheaper. Although there have been no quantitative studies of Haitian urban prostitution, it was clear that a substantial sector of the trade catered to tourists, especially North Americans. Some portion of the tourist industry catered specifically to a gay clientele:

> During the past five years Haiti, especially Port-au-Prince, has become a very popular holiday resort for Americans who are homosexual. There are also Haitians who are homosexual, and homosexual prostitution is becoming increasingly common. . . . For the young Haitian male between the ages of fifteen and thirty there is no likelihood of escaping the despair that abounds in Port-au-Prince. As elsewhere, those with money can purchase whatever they want. (Greco, 515–516)

Although obviously not all gay sex was prostitution, the deepening poverty of Haiti ensured that money played an inordinate role even in voluntary same-sex relations.

The existence of tourism, some of it gay, does not prove that such commerce was the cause of the Haitian AIDS epidemic, nor is it our intention to argue that it does. Such commerce does, however, throw into relief the ties between Haiti and nearby North America, ties not mentioned in early discussions of AIDS among Haitians, which often posited "isolated Haiti" as the *source* of the pandemic. And although non-Haitians were important carriers in the early stages of the epidemic, they no longer play a major role in HIV transmission on the island. Today the single greatest risk factor for Haitians is poverty, whether or not that poverty connects them to sexual activity with a North American tourist. And while it is finally recognized that AIDS poses especially great risks to poor women, this wisdom comes too late.

Structural Violence and the Assault on Poor Women

> "For most women, the major risk factor
> for HIV is being married."
> —United Nations Development Programme, *Young Women:*
> *Silence, Susceptibility, and the HIV Epidemic*, 1992

In the late 1980s, members of our group, Partners In Health, found themselves sitting in a new clinic in a small village in Haiti's Central Plateau. What awaited us outside, in the noisy courtyard of Zanmi Lasante (Creole for "Partners In Health"), was not entirely what we had expected. Certainly we anticipated the crowd, since ours was the first facility in the region to declare a special interest in the destitute sick. And we expected that many would be gravely ill by the time they reached our doorstep. But why, we wondered, were so many of these patients young women?

The answer, in two words, is structural violence.[9] Neither nature nor pure individual will is to blame, but instead the historically given (and often economically driven) processes and forces that conspire to constrain individual agency. Structural violence is visited upon all those whose social status denies them access to the fruits of scientific and social advances. If meaningful responses to AIDS are to be presented, the differential political economy of risk must be acknowledged: some people are, from the outset, at high risk of HIV infection, while others are shielded from risk.

The story of Acéphie, an AIDS victim, brings us back to the dam and the movement of people due to poverty. While this is just one woman's story, it will illuminate the large and complicated web of structural violence that constrains individual choices and affects individual lives. Both of Acéphie's parents came from families that had made a decent living by farming fertile tracts of land—their "ancestors' gardens"—and selling much of their produce. Her father tilled the soil and his wife, a tall and wearily elegant woman not nearly as old as she looks, was a "Madame Sarah," a market woman. "If it weren't for the dam," he once said, "we'd be just fine now. Acéphie, too." The Josephs' home was drowned along with most of their belongings, their crops, and the graves of their ancestors.

Displaced by the rising water, the Josephs, now refugees, built a miserable lean-to on a knoll of high land jutting into the new reservoir. They lived there for some years; Acéphie and her twin brother were born there. When asked what had induced them to move up to the village of Kay, to build a house on the hard stone embankment of a dusty road, their father replied, "Our hut was too near the water. I was afraid one of the children would fall into the lake and drown. Their mother had to be away selling; I was trying to make a garden in this terrible soil. There was no one to keep an eye on them."

Acéphie attended primary school in a banana-thatched open shelter in Kay, where children and young adults received the rudiments of literacy. "She was the nicest of the Joseph sisters," recalled one of her classmates. "And she was as pretty as she was nice." Acéphie's beauty—she was tall and fine-featured, with enormous dark eyes—and her vulnerability may have sealed her fate as early as 1984. Though still in primary school, she was already 19 years old; it was time for her to help generate income for her family, which was sinking deeper and deeper into poverty. Acéphie began to help her mother by carrying produce to a local market on Friday mornings. On foot or with a donkey, it takes over an hour and a half to reach the market, and the road leads right through Péligre, site of the dam and a military barracks. The soldiers liked to watch the parade of women on Friday mornings. Sometimes they taxed them, literally, with haphazardly imposed fines; sometimes they levied a toll of flirtatious banter.

Such flirtation is seldom rejected, at least openly. In rural Haiti, entrenched poverty made the soldiers—the region's only salaried men—ever so much more attractive. Hunger was a near-daily condition for the Joseph family; the times were as bad as those that followed the flooding of the valley. And so when Acéphie's good looks caught the eye of Captain Jacques Honorat, a native of Belladère formerly stationed in Port-au-Prince, she returned his gaze.

Acéphie knew, as did everyone in the area, that Honorat had a wife and children. He was known, in fact, to have more than one regular partner. But Acéphie was taken in by his persistence, and when he went to speak to her parents, a long-term liaison became a serious possibility:

> What would you have me do? I could tell that the old people were uncomfortable, worried; but they didn't say no. They didn't tell me to stay away from him. I wish they had, but how could they have known? . . . I knew it was a bad idea then, but I just didn't know why. I never dreamed he would give me a bad illness, never! I looked around and saw how poor we all were, how the old people were finished . . . What would you have me do? It was a way out, that's how I saw it.

Acéphie and Honorat were sexual partners only briefly—for less than a month, according to Acéphie. Shortly thereafter, Honorat fell ill with unexplained fevers and kept to the company of his wife in Péligre. As Acéphie was looking for a *moun prensipal*—a "main man"—she tried to forget about the soldier. Still, it was shocking to hear, a few months after they parted, that he was dead.

Acéphie was at a crucial juncture in her life. Returning to school was out of the question. Eventually, she went to Mirebalais, the nearest town, and began a course in what she euphemistically termed a "cooking school." The school—really just an ambitious woman's courtyard—prepared poor girls like Acéphie for their inevitable turn as servants in the city. Indeed, becoming a maid was fast becoming one of the rare growth industries in Haiti, and as much as Acéphie's proud mother hated to think of her daughter reduced to servitude, she could offer no viable alternative.

And so Acéphie, 22 years old, went off to Port-au-Prince, where she found a job as a housekeeper for a middle-class Haitian woman working for the U.S. embassy. Acéphie's looks and manners kept her out of the backyard, the traditional milieu of Haitian servants. She was designated as the maid who, in addition to cleaning, answered the door and the phone. Although Acéphie was not paid well—she received $30 each month—she recalled the gnawing hunger in her home village and managed to save a bit of money for her parents and siblings.

Still looking for a *moun prensipal*, Acéphie began seeing Blanco Ner-
ette, a young man with origins identical to her own: Blanco's parents
were also "water refugees," and Acéphie had known him when they
were both attending the parochial school in Kay. Blanco had done well
for himself, by Kay standards. While joblessness rates reached 60 percent, Blanco had regular work chauffeuring a small bus between the
Central Plateau and the capital; he commanded considerable respect,
and he turned his attentions to Acéphie. They planned to marry, she
later recalled, and started pooling their resources.

Acéphie remained at the "embassy woman's" house for more than
three years, until she discovered that she was pregnant. As soon as she
told Blanco, he became skittish. Nor was her employer pleased: it is
considered unsightly to have a pregnant servant. And so Acéphie returned to Kay, where she had a difficult pregnancy. Blanco came to see
her once or twice. They had a disagreement, and then she heard nothing more from him. Following the birth of her daughter, Acéphie was
sapped by repeated infections. A regular visitor to the Kay clinic, she
was soon diagnosed with AIDS.

Within months of her daughter's birth, Acéphie's life was consumed
with managing drenching night sweats and debilitating diarrhea while
attempting to care for her first child. "We both need diapers now," she
remarked bitterly, towards the end of her life. As political violence surrounding the fall of the Duvalier dictatorship and subsequent military
junta hampered her doctors' capacity to keep the clinic open, Acéphie
was faced each day not only with diarrhea, but also with a persistent
lassitude. She became more and more gaunt, and some villagers suggested that Acéphie was the victim of sorcery. Others recalled her liaison with the soldier and her work as a servant in the city, by then
widely considered risk factors for AIDS. Acéphie herself knew that she
had AIDS, although she was more apt to refer to herself as suffering
from a disorder brought on by her work as a servant: "All that iron-
ing, and then opening a refrigerator." She died far from refrigerators or
other amenities as her family and caregivers stood by helplessly.

In Haiti, little about Acéphie's story is unique. There is a deadly
monotony to the stories told by rural Haitian women with AIDS. In
a study we conducted at the Clinique Bon Sauveur, where Acéphie
received her care, the majority of new AIDS diagnoses are registered
among women, most of them with trajectories similar to Acéphie's.
The women we interviewed were straightforward about the motivations for their sexual activity: in their opinions, they had been driven

into unfavorable unions by poverty.[10] Among other things, their testimony calls into question facile notions of "consensual sex."

We conducted the study by interviewing the first twenty-five women we diagnosed with symptomatic HIV infection who were residents of Kay or its two neighboring villages. Their responses to questions posed during a series of open-ended interviews were compared with those of twenty-five age-matched, HIV-negative controls (Table 11.1). In both groups, ages ranged from 16 to 44, with a mean age of about 27 years. None of these fifty women had a history of prostitution, and none had used illicit drugs. Only two, both members of the control group, had received blood transfusions. None of the women in either group had had more than five sexual partners; in fact, seven of the afflicted women had had only one. Although women in the study group had on average more sexual partners than the controls, the difference is not striking. Similarly, we found no clear differences between the two groups in the number of intramuscular injections they had received or their years of education.

Table 11.1: Case-Control Study of AIDS in Rural Haitian Women

Group	Patients with AIDS	Control
Patient Characteristics	(N = 25)	(N = 25)
Average number of sexual partners	2.7	2.4
Sexual partner of a truck driver	12	2
Sexual partner of a soldier	9	0
Sexual partner of a peasant only	0	23
Ever lived in Port-au-Prince	20	4
Worked as a servant	18	1
Average number of years of formal schooling	4.5	4.0
Ever received a blood transfusion	0	2
Ever used illicit drugs	0	0
Ever received more than 10 intramuscular injections	17	19

The risk factors in this small cohort proved to be history of residence in Port-au-Prince, history of domestic service, and history of contact with soldiers or truck drivers—all of which reflect a desperate attempt to escape rural poverty and are emblematic of the lot of the rural Haitian poor, perhaps especially of poor women. The chief risk factors seem to reflect not number of sexual partners but rather the professions of those partners. Fully nineteen of the women with HIV disease had histories of sexual contact with soldiers (as did Acéphie) or truck drivers. Of the women diagnosed with AIDS, none had a history of sexual contact exclusively with peasants (although one had as her sole partner a construction worker from Kay). Many had also migrated to Port-au-Prince as young women to escape from the harshest poverty—in what Neptune-Anglade has called a "feminine rural exodus" (150). The women are most commonly employed as servants, but this often fails to provide full economic security.

When women who migrate to the city are forced to rely on relationships with men for financial support, they lose the ability to protect themselves. As Desvarieux and Pape have noted, "effective methods of prevention have a better chance of working if the woman does not have to rely on either the consent or the willingness of her partner" (277). In the sociographically "flat" region around the dam—after all, most area residents share a single socioeconomic status, poverty—conjugal unions with non-peasants (salaried soldiers and truck drivers, who are paid on a daily basis) reflect women's quest for some measure of economic security. In the setting of a worsening economic crisis, the gap between the hungry peasant class and the relatively well-off soldiers and truck drivers became the salient local inequality. In this manner, truck drivers and soldiers serve as the "bridge" from the city to the rural population, just as tourists served as a bridge from North America to the urban Haitian population.

But just as North Americans are no longer important in the transmission of HIV in Haiti, truck drivers and soldiers will soon no longer be necessary components of the rural epidemic. Once introduced into a sexually active population, HIV will work its way to those with no history of residence in the city, no history of domestic service, and no history of contact with soldiers or truck drivers.

The Current State of AIDS in Haiti's Central Plateau

> "Everyone with AIDS should be able to get treatment, since we're all God's children. Science is for everyone."
>
> —St Ker, 41-year-old AIDS patient, Cange, Haiti

Health in Haiti continues to deteriorate as the country becomes poorer. For years, economic pressure resulting largely, though not wholly, from an international embargo on loans and aid has left almost nothing to invest in the health of the destitute sick. The impact of this embargo has been profound, as a report from the heavily implicated Inter-American Development Bank (IDB) notes. In a 2001 report on Haiti, bank officials themselves found that "overall, the major factor behind economic stagnation is the withholding of both foreign grants and loans, associated with the international community's response to the critical political impasse" (Robert and Machado). HIV has become a steady presence in rural Haiti, with a prevalence of 5 percent in the sexually active population. In the early 1990s, more than 25 percent of admissions to Zanmi Lasante were HIV-related; by 1995, some 40 percent of adult admissions were patients with HIV infection.

Although our clinic began modest HIV prevention efforts shortly after the first case of HIV was diagnosed in the Central Plateau in 1986, these efforts have been rendered less effective by the same conditions that have facilitated the spread of the disease. Political violence and the coup d'état of 1991 led to the reverse migration of rural-born people from Port-au-Prince back to their home regions. The bulk of state-sponsored violence was targeted at slum areas, such as Cité Soleil, where seroprevalence of HIV was high. The urban exodus to low-prevalence rural areas is likely to have increased the incidence of new HIV infections in rural regions.[11] Our prevention efforts, tightly linked to education and condom promotion, were also hampered by gender inequality and poverty, which conspire to make the male condom an imperfect preventive measure. Thus, HIV transmission continued in spite of an aggressive prevention campaign.

In 1995 Zanmi Lasante and Partners In Health began modest therapeutic efforts. We initially offered treatment to pregnant women to block mother-to-child transmission; interestingly, more than 90 percent of women offered HIV testing accepted it once medication was provided free of charge. Soon after, in 1997, we incorporated post-exposure prophylaxis for victims of rape and professional injury into the treatment group. Beginning in late 1998, a small number of AIDS patients who no longer responded to syndromic treatment of their opportunistic infections were offered supervised, community-based care and treatment with highly active antiretroviral therapy (HAART). Despite much skepticism that the complicated HAART regimen could be administered successfully in such a poor setting, we registered remarkable outcomes among this initial cohort and subsequent patients.[12] With support from the Global Fund to Fight AIDS, Tuberculosis, and Malaria, Zanmi Lasante has now partnered with the Haitian Ministry of Health and rehabilitated several underfunded public health clinics throughout central Haiti; more than 1,500 patients with advanced HIV are currently receiving HAART.

We call these treatment efforts the "HIV Equity Initiative." It is not enough to throw up our hands and bemoan the complexities of gender inequality, political violence, migration due to poverty, and other social forces that incapacitate public health measures. Instead, with international financial support, the Ministry of Health, and committed local personnel, we have managed to register successes, large and small, in improving the health of the residents of rural central Haiti.

Haiti's 33rd coup d'état on February 29, 2004, makes transnational forces even more salient. A long-standing dearth of funds for health care and other services, coupled with a rising tide of violence and mayhem, has led to the worst humanitarian crisis Haiti has known in decades. A report by the Pan American Health Organization mentions the current "disregard for the health institutions' neutrality and immunity" and notes that:

> Several hospitals were the target of violence. Patients were assaulted in some institutions and the staff providing care is worried about exercising their duties safely. In some health institutions, the staff does not report for work on the day of demonstrations. Some of the patients in need of emergency care do not go to hospitals anymore for fear of violence. The Port-au-Prince University Hospital, one of the main hospitals in the country, has been almost at a standstill for weeks, for lack of personnel.

Clearly, Haiti needs emergency assistance, but tardy and disorganized interventions will not undo decades of misguided aid policies. Robust public health requires a strong ministry of health, which should itself derive legitimacy from a democratically elected government. The strengthening of public health infrastructure is urgently needed to begin countering the inevitable spread of disease that follows shortages, hunger, political violence, and a breakdown of sanitation.

Conclusions: Passing Lines

"Violent deaths are natural deaths here.
He died of his environment."
—Dr. Magiot, in Graham Greene's *The Comedians,* 1966

In the early 1990s, Michael Fumento published *The Myth of Heterosexual AIDS,* in which he made the following assertion: "Among the great wide percentage of the nation the media calls 'the general population,' that section the media and the public health authorities has [sic] tried desperately to terrify, there is no epidemic. AIDS will pick off a person here and there in this group, but the original infected partner will be one of the two groups in which the disease is epidemic. Most heterosexuals will continue to have more to fear from bathtub drowning than from AIDS" (32). More than ten years later, in a new millennium, incidence of bathtub drowning remains low, while AIDS has become the leading infectious cause of adult death in the world. And what was once known primarily as a disease of gay men has come to afflict more women than men in many poor countries with a high burden of HIV. If there is irony in Fumento's words, it is not the easy irony of false predictions. Even as such projections were being written, millions of women—whose partners were neither bisexual nor intravenous drug users—had *already* been "picked off" by HIV. Their voices were absent from the literature because in settings of entrenched elitism, they have been poor. In settings of entrenched racism, they have been women of color. And in settings of entrenched sexism, they have been, of course, women.

When we think of HIV and of how it crosses borders, we might initially picture the flow of microbes between North American tourists and local prostitutes. But the bigger picture shows an increasingly complicated relationship among multiple countries and within national and international power dynamics. We must not forget the history of Haiti, a former slave colony that continues to be exploited, or the effects that a lack of power can have on the spread of pathologies. And while HIV has crossed transnational borders, it has also both passed and stayed within lines of gender and class. HIV now burdens the bottom of society, and will continue to plague the poor until conscious changes are made in the complicated web of transnational relations.

Works Cited

Bastien, Rémy. *Le Paysan Haitien et sa Famille: Vallée de Marbial.* Paris: Éditions Karthala, 1985 [1951].

Central Intelligence Agency. *World Factbook 2002.* http://www.cia.gov/cia/publications/factbook/.

Chabner, Bruce. National Cancer Advisory Board meeting. December 1, 1982.

Desvarieux, Moïse, and Jean W. Pape. "HIV and AIDS in Haiti: Recent Developments." *AIDS Care* 3.3 (1991): 271–279.

FAO and UNAIDS. *Sustainable Agricultural / Rural Development and Vulnerability to the AIDS Epidemic.* Geneva: FAO and UNAIDS, 1999.

Farmer, Paul E. "Culture, Poverty, and the Dynamics of HIV Transmission in Rural Haiti." *Culture and Sexual Risk: Anthropological Perspectives on AIDS.* Ed. Brummelhuis H.T., G. Herdt. Newark, N.J.: Gordon and Breach, 1995. 3–28.

_____. "On Suffering and Structural Violence: A View from Below." *Dædalus* 125.1 (1996.): 261–283.

_____. *Pathologies of Power: Health, Human Rights, and the New War on the Poor.* Berkeley: University of California Press, 2003.

_____. *The Uses of Haiti.* 2nd edition. Monroe, Maine: Common Courage Press, 2003.

_____ and Didi Bertrand. "Hypocrisies of Development and the Health of the Haitian Poor." *Dying for Growth.* Ed. J.Y. Kim, J.V. Millen, A. Irwin, and J. Gershman. Monroe, Maine: Common Courage Press, 2000. 65–89.

_____, Fernet Léandre, Joia Mukherjee, et al. "Community-Based Approaches to HIV Treatment in Resource-Poor Settings." *The Lancet* 358 (2001): 404–409.

_____, Mary Catherine Smith Fawzi and Patrice Nevil. "Unjust Embargo of Aid for Haiti." *Lancet* 361 (2003): 420–423.

Fumento, Michael. *The Myth of Heterosexual AIDS : How a Tragedy Has Been Distorted by the Media and Partisan Politics.* Washington, D.C.: Regnery Gateway, 1993.

Greco, Ralph S. "Haiti and the Stigma of AIDS [letter]." *Lancet* 2 (1983): 515–516.

Greene, Graham. *The Comedians.* London: Bodley Head, 1966.

Guérin, J., R. Malebranche, R. Elie, et al. "Acquired Immune Deficiency Syndrome: Specific Aspects of the Disease in Haiti." *Annals of the New York Academy of Sciences* 437 (1984): 254–261.

International Monetary Fund. "Directions of Trade Statistics." *Yearbook 1984.* Washington, D.C.: IMF, 1984.

Johnson, Warren, and Jean Pape. "AIDS in Haiti." *AIDS: Pathogenesis and Treatment.* Ed. J. Levy. New York: Marcel Dekker, 1989. 65–78.

Liautaud, Bernard, Jean Pape, and Molière Pamphile. "Le Sida dans les Caraibes." *Médecine et Maladies Infectieuses.* December (1988): 687–697.

Mintz, Sidney. "Foreword." *The Haitian People.* By J. Leyburn. New Haven: Yale University Press, 1966.

_____. *Caribbean Transformations.* Baltimore: Johns Hopkins University Press, 1974.

Moral, Paul. *Le Paysan Haitien.* Port-au-Prince: Les Éditions Fardin, 1961.

Neptune-Anglade, Mireille. *L'Autre Moitié du Développement: A Propos du Travail des Femmes en Haïti.* Pétion-Ville, Haiti: Éditions des Alizés, 1986.

Pan American Health Organization. 2004. The Haiti Crisis: Health Risks. Available at http://www.paho.org/English/DD/PED/HaitiHealthImpact .htm.

Pape, Jean, and Warren Johnson. "Perinatal Transmission of Human Immunodeficiency Virus." *Boletín de la Oficina Sanitaria Panamerican* 105.5–6 (1988): 73–89.

_____. "Epidemiology of AIDS in the Caribbean." *Baillière's Clinical Tropical Medicine and Communicable Diseases* 3.1(1988): 31–42.

Pape, Jean, Bernard Liautaud, Franck Thomas, et al. "Characteristics of the Acquired Immunodeficiency Syndrome (AIDS) in Haiti." *The New England Journal of Medicine* 309.16 (1983): 945–950.

Reid, Elizabeth and Michael Bailey. *Young Women: Silence, Susceptibility, and the HIV Epidemic.* United Nations Development Programme, Issues Paper No. 12, 1992.

Robert, D., and Roberto Machado. "Haiti: Economic Situation and Prospects." Inter-American Development Bank, Country Economic Assessment, 2001. http://www.iadb.org/regions/re2/sep/ha-sep.htm (accessed June, 2002).

Smith, Jennie M. *When the Hands Are Many: Community Organization and Social Change in Rural Haiti.* Ithaca: Cornell University Press, 2001.

Trouillot, Michel-Rolph. *Haiti, State Against Nation: The Origins and Legacy of Duvalierism.* New York: Monthly Review Press, 1990.

Wolf, Eric R. *Europe and the People Without History.* Berkeley: University of California Press, 1982.

World Bank. 2004. World Development Indicators database. Available at http://devdata.worldbank.org/data-query/.

Notes

1   For an in-depth discussion of these ties, see Farmer's *The Uses of Haiti.*

2   See the work of Mintz; Bastien; Smith; and Trouillot for histories of the declining fortunes of the rural poor in Haiti.

3   For more ethnographies of those displaced by the dam, see Farmer and Bertrand.

4   In 1999, Haiti had the highest HIV rate in the hemisphere: 210,000 people were estimated to have the virus. Compare this to the numbers in Mexico (150,000), the Dominican Republic (130,000), Trinidad and Tobago (7,800), and the Bahamas (6,900) (Central Intelligence Agency's *World Factbook*).

5   See Pape and Johnson's "Perinatal Transmission."

6   See Liautaud, Pape, and Pamphile.

7   In "Epidemiology of AIDS in the Caribbean," Pape and Johnson state that, "in 1983, the majority of male patients with AIDS were bisexuals who had at least one sexual encounter with visiting North Americans or Haitians residing in North America" (32).

8   See Guérin, Malebranche, Elie, et al. as well as Johnson and Pape.

9   For more on structural violence, see Farmer's *Pathologies of Power* and "On Suffering and Structural Violence."

10 See Farmer's "Culture, Poverty, and the Dynamics of HIV Transmission."

11 See Farmer and Bertrand.

12 For a more in-depth description of this project, see Farmer, Léandre, Mukherjee, et al.

PART

V

WOMEN IMMIGRANTS, WOMEN ACTIVISTS

11

Unwilling or Unable: Asylum and Non-State Agents of Persecution

Matthew E. Price

The threats and assaults began almost immediately after Rodi Alvarado Peña and Francisco Osorio were married in Guatemala.[1] Often Osorio would drink heavily and would hit Alvarado Peña if she left a cantina before him. As the marriage progressed, his violence became more frequent and severe. When her period was fifteen days late, he broke her jaw. When she refused to have an abortion, he kicked her in the spine. He hit her "whenever he felt like it, wherever he happened to be: in the house, on the street, on the bus. As time went on, he hit me for no reason at all." Once he kicked her in the genitalia, causing her to bleed severely for eight days. Another time, he asked for 5,000 *quetzales* (around $600), and when she was unable to give the money to him, he broke windows and a mirror with her head. When he misplaced something, he would grab her head and strike furniture with it. Once he threw a machete toward her hands, barely missing her. He raped her almost daily, forcefully sodomized her, and beat her while raping her. When she complained that he was hurting her, he would reply, "You're my woman, you do what I say." When she asked him why he beat her, he would respond, "I can do it if I want to."

On several occasions Alvarado Peña fled to her brother's house and to her parents' house, but Osorio found her and dragged her home. When he caught her trying to leave, he kicked her and beat her unconscious; when she regained consciousness, he beat her unconscious again. Once, after she had run away with the children for two months and returned because the children asked to see their father, Osorio whipped her with an electric cord and threatened to cut off her limbs with a machete if she ever left again. She called the police for help on a number of occasions. Three times, her husband ignored police summons and no further action was taken. Twice the police ignored her calls. Osorio had served in the military, and told Alvarado Peña that calling the police was therefore useless. Once she appeared before a judge who said that he would not intervene in a domestic affair. After Alvarado Peña fled to the United States, her sister told her that Osorio had left word that he would "hunt her down and kill her if she [came] back to Guatemala."

Upon arriving in the United States, Alvarado Peña applied for asylum. An immigration judge initially granted her claim, but the Immigration and Naturalization Services (INS), as the Bureau of U.S. Citizenship and Immigration Services (USCIS) was then called, appealed the ruling to the Board of Immigration Appeals (BIA). In a rare *en banc* decision, the BIA overturned the decision of the immigration judge by a vote of 10–5, ruled that Alvarado Peña was not eligible for asylum, and ordered her to depart the United States within thirty days. Attorney General Janet Reno subsequently rescinded the BIA's ruling following a storm of criticism from refugee advocates, and the case was remanded to the Board for reconsideration following a proposed rule change that was issued in response to the decision.[2] However, the incoming Bush administration did not adopt the proposed rule, leaving adjudicators without clear guidance in similar cases.[3]

Rodi Alvarado Peña's case reflects a more general challenge confronting international refugee law in recent years. Traditionally, forced migration has been caused by state-sponsored violence. The refugee definition, which requires that applicants possess "a well-founded fear of persecution . . . on account of race, religion, nationality, membership in a particular social group, or political opinion"[4] to be eligible for asylum, was interpreted accordingly. But increasingly, refugees seek protection from violence perpetrated by non-state actors—like "death squads, paramilitary forces, insurgent armies, organized criminal entities, family-based political cliques, clans, [and] sub-clans"—able to pursue their various agendas unhindered by states that are too weak to stop them (Moore, "Nation State" 83). How ought asylum law respond to this reality?

This chapter seeks to begin answering this question by analyzing the theoretical underpinnings of recent pertinent court decisions. The differences in international practice with respect to granting asylum for persons persecuted by non-state actors can be traced to a single basic theoretical cleavage between a "protection approach," according to which victims of persecution by non-state actors are eligible for asylum if their state is *unwilling or unable* to protect them and an "accountability approach," which maintains that state involvement is necessary for persecution to warrant the granting of asylum.

Increasingly, states have adopted the protection approach while the accountability approach—still found in France, Austria, Switzerland, in a limited form in the Netherlands, and until recently, Germany—is increasingly disfavored (Vermeulen). However, application of the protection approach entails expansive consequences for states' liability to asylum seekers. Courts have sought to limit the impact by strictly applying the "nexus requirement"—that is, the requirement for asylum eligibility that persecution be inflicted for reasons of race, religion, nationality, membership in a social group, or political opinion (called "Convention reasons" in reference to the 1951 UN Convention Relating to the Status of Refugees.)[5] But the nexus clause is itself indefensible on the protection approach's logic. Once we adopt the victim's standpoint, there seems to be no good reason for distinguishing between one motivation for harm and another. The resulting tension is especially visible in cases like Alvarado Peña's, involving battered women.

Notwithstanding the trend toward the protection approach, I shall argue that the accountability approach is preferable. It offers greater theoretical coherence than courts' current application of the protection approach; and invests asylum with a political significance that is muted by the protection approach.

The Protection Approach and the Accountability Approach

The "protection approach," favored by refugee advocates and most academic commentators[6] and adopted by the majority of signatories to the UN Convention and Protocol,[7] maintains that persecution refers to any infliction of serious harm; an agent of persecution can thus be a state actor or a non-state actor. Persecution can occur even when no effective authority exists and it can occur even when a state authority is willing, but unable, to offer protection against harm by a non-state agent.[8]

The protection approach follows from a specific view of asylum's purpose: asylum is meant to offer surrogate protection to those who are exposed to violations of human rights and are unable to receive protection from their own state (Hathaway, *Law of Refugee Status* 124). The logic of the protection approach is "result-driven"[9] and appeals to the victim's standpoint: it makes no difference to the victim whether the state is unwilling or unable to prevent violence against her. She experiences the same insecurity in either case, and it is the *fact* of insecurity, not the specific source of it, that creates her need for asylum.[10]

The accountability approach, which is increasingly disfavored, holds that state complicity is a necessary element of persecution because persecution involves a misuse of political authority. The state, as the monopolist of violence, must use its authority to repress private violence of all kinds; it "is equally responsible for the protection of its inhabitants against criminal, as against politically motivated violence" (Goodwin-Gill 73 n.183). To carry out its responsibility in a manner consistent with legitimate authority, the state must "take reasonable steps to prevent [the infliction of serious harm] and to use the means at its disposal to carry out a serious investigation of violations committed within its jurisdiction, to identify those responsible, impose the appropriate punishment, and ensure the victims adequate compensation" (Marx 451). The standard here is one of due diligence—states must set up their institutions in such a way that a good faith effort at providing all citizens with protection is assured.

The accountability approach also follows from a specific view about asylum's purpose: it is meant to shelter people whose equal membership in a political community has been repudiated by an official act of violence.[11] When the state refuses to protect a citizen, even against criminal violence, it treats her well-being as less important than the well-being of others. This constitutes a denial of her standing as an equal member. In withholding its protection, then, the state transforms an act of violence by non-state agents into a state-sanctioned act of persecution.

The accountability approach diverges from the protection approaches in a number of important ways. First, according to the accountability approach persecution cannot occur in the context of state breakdown or anarchy. A finding of persecution "presupposes that there is effective state authority over the territory" that can be held accountable for the persecution (Carlier 271). Thus Germany refused asylum to Afghani and Somali applicants on the grounds that neither Afghanistan nor Somalia were governed by states at the time of persecution (Moore, "Nation State" 108). If there is no state, then there is no political body in which equal membership can be guaranteed, and there is no political body that can officially repudiate the victim's equal standing as a member in it. However, both France and Germany do recognize that non-state actors, such as clans or insurgent groups, can exercise effective authority over a swath of territory, and therefore can be classified as quasi-states for the purposes of establishing persecution.[12]

By contrast, the protection approach would make asylum available to applicants fleeing violent anarchy so long as they face harm for a Convention reason. Thus, for example, the United States awarded asylum to H-, a Somali national and member of the Marehan subclan who claimed to fear persecution by the United Somali Congress on account of his clan membership. The applicant's father was murdered in Mogadishu by members of the Congress and his brother was shot and then murdered in the hospital to which he had been taken for treatment. The applicant himself was detained and beaten along with other clan members (*In Re H-*.)

The immigration judge who first heard the Somali applicant's case had adopted an approach similar to that of the German courts and had denied asylum because "there is no evidence there is a government in Somalia. . . ."(*In Re H-*). However, the BIA held that the immigration judge's decision was in error, arguing that individualized persecution could take place even amidst a background of civil strife, in a failed state with "no functioning judicial system" (*In Re H-*). This decision followed the logic of an earlier Canadian decision in which the court ruled that a "situation of civil war in a given country is not an obstacle to a claim provided the fear felt is not that felt indiscriminately by all citizens as a consequence of the civil war, but that felt by the applicant himself, by a group with which he is associated, or, even, by all citizens on account of a risk of persecution based on one of the reasons stated in the definition" (*Salibian v. Canada* 250, 258).

The second scenario in which the protection approach and the accountability approach diverge concerns the infliction of harm by non-state agents against which a state is *willing*, but due to a lack of capacity, *unable* to offer protection cannot constitute persecution. On the accountability approach, "persecution" requires that state agents facilitate, condone, tolerate, or otherwise be complicit in the persecutory act itself. So, for instance, France has denied asylum to individuals fleeing Islamic extremist violence in Algeria on the grounds that the Algerian state is trying to combat this violence and does not tolerate or condone it.[13] This is because membership is a political concept which cannot be recognized or negated by private agents acting without official sanction. When a government is unable to protect a citizen against private violence despite its good faith efforts to do so, it does not repudiate that citizen's claim to equal membership in the political community. The violence suffered by the victims of non-state action against which the government is unable to provide protection, although regrettable, cannot underwrite an asylum claim.

On the protection approach, by contrast, an applicant is eligible for asylum whether the government is unwilling or simply unable to protect against violence by non-state actors. Thus, for example, a British appeals court quashed an asylum denial in a case concerning a Jamaican who feared retaliation from a criminal gang on which he had been an informant to the police. As Baker, LJ, explained:

> The issue is not ... whether the Jamaican authorities have the willingness to deal with the problem but whether they have shown the ability to do so.... Criminal networks in Jamaica continue to act with almost complete impunity in inflicting reprisals upon persons like the appellant who have offended them.... There is no doubt about willingness to tackle the problem. It is another matter, however, whether effective steps have been taken to achieve the bare minimum required to provide reasonable protection for informers and perceived informers who find themselves in situations such as the appellant.[14]

Whether the government is unwilling or simply unable to provide protection is immaterial from the standpoint of an applicant's need for "surrogate protection." Therefore, on the protection approach, it is immaterial to his eligibility for asylum.

Accountability, Protection, and the Nexus Clause

In both the protection and accountability approaches, in order for an asylum-seeker to be eligible for asylum, she must show that she suffers persecution for reasons of her race, religion, nationality, membership in a social group, or political opinion. In the United States, the "nexus clause" is interpreted as requiring the asylum-seeker to show that her persecutor was motivated to inflict harm upon her because she possesses one of these characteristics.[15]

The nexus requirement is incompatible with the logic of both the accountability approach and the protection approach. For accountability theorists, as I have already discussed, the state has a duty to protect its citizens from harm of all sorts. Its unwillingness to do so constitutes a denial of the victim's equal membership in the political community. The motivations of the non-state actors who take advantage of the state's withdrawal of protection to do violence are irrelevant. Similarly, the state's reasons for withholding its protection are irrelevant; there is no good reason for the state to permit harm to be inflicted when it could be prevented.

For protection theorists, the nexus requirement is equally problematic. If we are ultimately concerned with addressing a victim's need for protection from serious harm, then whether the harm is inflicted for a Convention reason should make no difference to her asylum claim. Once we adopt the victim's standpoint, there seems to be no good theoretical reason for distinguishing between one motivation for harm and another. Along these lines, legal scholar James Hathaway suggests that linking refugee protection with human rights protection would require scrapping the nexus clause: "Under current interpretations, refugee status requires a risk to basic human rights . . . *in addition* to some differential impact based on civil or political status [i.e., the five reasons specified by the nexus clause]. The proposal here is that refugee status becomes the entitlement of all persons whose basic human rights are at risk" (Hathaway, "Reconceiving" 121, emphasis in the original).

The expansive implications of the protection approach greatly concern courts. As we shall see, they rely on the nexus clause to limit their exposure to asylum claims, despite the clause's theoretical incompatibility with the protection approach. As a result, their decisions exhibit an uncomfortable tension.

Battered Women: The American Approach in *In re R-A-*

For cases involving battered women, the effects of this tension are extremely dissatisfying.[16] Good "lawyering" in such cases has been a game of trying to shoehorn women's claims into the categories established by the nexus clause. Two main strategies have been attempted. The first argues that husbands batter their wives on account of their wives' political opinions.[17] The second argues that husbands batter their wives on account of their wives' membership in a particular social group. Both strategies were pursued unsuccessfully in Rodi Alvarado Peña's case. While the Board acknowledged that the abuse suffered by Alvarado Peña was "more than sufficient . . . to constitute 'persecution,'"[18] her asylum claim faltered on the nexus issue.

Political Opinion

Alvarado Peña first claimed that she had been persecuted because of her political opinion. The claim is not easy to make. While a convincing argument can be made that Osorio was motivated by the political opinion that men are dominant over women, or that a wife is the husband's property, in order to satisfy the nexus requirement Alvarado Peña needed to show that Osorio was motivated to persecute her *not* for a political opinion *he* held, but rather for a political opinion that *she* held, or that was imputed to her by him. She argued that her attempts to flee from him and her filing of complaints with the police expressed a political opinion "opposing his male dominance," and, further, that her protests led Osorio to impute this opinion to her.[19]

The majority was unimpressed by this claim, holding that even if Alvarado Peña possessed a political opinion or that Osorio imputed one to her, there was no evidence that his abuse was motivated on account of this political opinion. The Board emphasized Alvarado Peña's express claims that she was frequently beaten "for no reason at all" and "whenever he felt like it"; even acquiescence to him did not spare her. The majority took the seeming pointlessness of the beatings as an indication that Osorio not only had no "understanding of the respondent's perspective," but also that he did not "even care . . . what [that] perspective may have been . . . His senseless actions started at the beginning of their marriage and continued whether or not the respondent acquiesced in his demands. The record reflects that, once having entered into this marriage, there was nothing the respondent could have done or thought that would have spared her from the violence he inflicted."[20] Alvarado Peña herself believed that Osorio abused her "because he had been mistreated when he was in the army and, as he told her, he treated her the way he had been treated."[21] Notably, even the dissent acknowledged that, "[t]he record amply supports the conclusion that the abuse suffered by the respondent was on account of the abuser's belief that, as her husband, he could dominate the respondent"—that is, on account of *his* political opinion rather than *hers.*[22]

In response, the dissent argued that Osorio clearly inferred from Alvarado Peña's resistance the opinion that she should not be subject to his domination. It rejected, as "contrary to fact, law, and logic," the majority's "conten[tion] that the abuser was not, even in part, motivated by the respondent's resistance to his domination, even though he had told her he viewed women as property to be treated brutally in order to sustain his domination."[23] The majority found the dissent's response unpersuasive, however. Such an approach, first, would recognize the mere act of resistance to abuse as a political opinion. This, it claimed, is problematic because "it would seem that virtually any victim of repeated violence who offers some resistance could qualify for asylum," a result that seems to dilute substantially the meaning of "political opinion." Second, "this approach ignores the question of what motivated the abuse at the outset" by presuming that future abuse is motivated by the desire to overcome the political opinion expressed in resistance.[24] According to the majority, originally Osorio must have initiated his abuse for some reason other than the desire to overcome Alvarado Peña's resistance; furthermore, there are no grounds for thinking that this reason would not continue to motivate him, especially since there was no "meaningful evidence that [his] behavior was influenced at all by his perception of [her] opinion."[25]

Membership in a Social Group

In addition to her political opinion claim, Alvarado Peña also tried to meet the nexus requirement by maintaining that she had been persecuted on account of her membership in the social group of "Guatemalan women who have been involved intimately with Guatemalan male companions who believe that women are to live under male domination."[26] The majority objected to the claim on several levels. First, it argued that the group appeared to have been constructed solely for the purposes of the case; it did not seem to have any "relation to the way in which Guatemalans might identify subdivisions in their own society."[27] The logic behind the requirement is straightforward: if a group is defined purely for the sake of the case—if it isn't recognized as a group by people within the society—it could not possibly be the case that members of the group are persecuted *because* they are members of the group.

One might object that *all* groups are constructed. "Race" is no more an objectively real category than "Guatemalan women who have been involved intimately with Guatemalan male companions who believe that women are to live under male domination." Since both categories are social artifacts, why should one be recognized as "real" for the purpose of refugee determinations, but not the other? The objection is simply not convincing because what matters for refugee law is whether the persecution has occurred *on account of* the victim's membership in the group. For this condition to be met, the group must be socially recognized. A group constructed for the purposes of a legal case does not enjoy social recognition; race, religion, and nationality may be constructed as well, but they *do* enjoy social recognition. They may not be more "real" in a primordial sense, but they are more real in a sociological sense.

One response to the problem, as the dissent suggests, would be to define the group simply as "Guatemalan women" or "married Guatemalan women," both groups that certainly have a basis in social reality.[28] But now we reach a second problem flagged by the majority: Alvarado Peña needed to prove that she was abused because she was a member of this group, and on the majority's view, there was no corroborating evidence. It reasoned that if Osorio was indeed motivated to harm Alvarado Peña on account of her membership in the social group of Guatemalan women, then one should expect that other members of this social group would also be at risk from him. But, it found, "[t]he record indicates that he has only targeted the respondent. The respondent's husband has not shown an interest in any member of this group other than the respondent herself. The respondent fails to show how other members of the group may be at risk of harm from him."[29] In short, the Board's position was that Osorio abused Alvarado Peña not because she was a woman, but because she was his wife.[30]

	State **Unwilling** to Protect	State **Unable** to Protect
Nexus between harm inflicted by non-state actor and Convention reason	Box I: ASYLUM GRANTED	Box II: ASYLUM GRANTED (The Somali Case)
No nexus between harm inflicted by non-state actor and Convention reason	Box III: ASYLUM DENIED (Alvarado Peña)	Box IV: ASYLUM DENIED

Figure 11.1: The BIA's Approach to Non-State Actor Cases

Assessing the Decision

From both a theoretical and practical point of view, the BIA's decision in *In re R-A-* is deeply unsatisfying. The majority's fixation on the nexus requirement begs for some theoretical justification. It misses the central point: Alvarado Peña is being tortured (Copelon), never mind why, and needs to flee abroad because her own government is unwilling to do anything about it. And the practical result is horrifying: without the U.S. Attorney General's intervention, Alvarado Peña would have been forced to return to Guatemala and quite likely would have been killed by her husband. The immigration judge's original decision appealed to this central point, as did Alvarado Peña in her brief. If protection really is the underlying purpose of asylum, then indeed, Alvarado Peña should be granted asylum. Taking the protection approach seriously means focusing on the applicant's inability to obtain protection against serious harm; the persecutor's motivations in inflicting that harm are quite beside the point.

The trouble is that once we head down this road, it is hard to stop. Walter Kälin takes the protection approach to its logical conclusion. "The intention of the [Convention]," he writes:

> was ... to protect persons ... [in] situations in which there was a risk of a type of injury that would be inconsistent with the basic duty of protection owed by a state to its own population. *A state fails to fulfill this basic duty* not only where its authorities are unwilling to provide protection against persecution by non-state actors, but *also where it is so disorganized that it is no longer in a position to provide security to some of its citizens against acts of violence by other citizens* ... [T]his idea is deeply rooted in Western political thinking: According to Hobbes, to defend the citizen not only 'from the invasion of foreigners,' but also from 'the injuries of one another,' is the very foundation of the political commonwealth. (Kälin 430, emphasis added.)[31]

It is worth noting that the protection logic is concerned with acts of *violence,* with "the injuries of one another," *regardless* of whether those acts are motivated by a Convention reason, and *regardless* of whether the state is unwilling or is unable to provide protection against them. The implications of this position are breathtaking, for the "injuries of one another" against which one relies on the state for protection include not only racial, religious, and ethnic violence, but also civil war and common crime. In other words, the protection approach demands that asylum be granted not only in cases falling in Boxes I and II in the diagram above, but also in cases falling in Boxes III and IV.

Consider the implications for another battered woman case called *Dolamore.* A New Zealand woman is beaten nearly to death by her husband on repeated occasions. Although she moves out and tries to hide from him, he is able to locate her and makes calls and sends letters in which he threatens to kill her. The police are responsive to her requests for help, but she fears that they will be unable to protect her should her husband decide to act on his threats.[32] Protection logic, taken seriously, would require that asylum be given not only to Alvarado Peña and those like her—where the state is unwilling to protect—but also to those at risk in cases like Dolamore—where a state is unable to protect. It may even demand that individuals be eligible for asylum if they have a well-founded fear of being physically assaulted by common thugs.

	*State **Unwilling** to Protect*	*State **Unable** to Protect*
***Nexus** between harm inflicted by non-state actor and Convention reason*	Box I: ASYLUM GRANTED	Box II: ASYLUM GRANTED (The Somali Case)
***No nexus** between harm inflicted by non-state actor and Convention reason*	Box III: ASYLUM GRANTED (Alvarado Peña)	Box IV: ASYLUM GRANTED (Dolamore)

Figure 11.2: Implications of Following the Protection Approach's Logic

The Board in *In re R-A-* was quick to note these implications and to reject their underlying logic: "[C]onstruing private acts of violence to be qualifying governmental persecution, by virtue of the inadequacy of protection, would obviate, perhaps entirely, the 'on account of' requirement in the statute."[33] The Board was reluctant to take such a step because of its significantly expansive consequences:

> We see no principled basis for restricting such an approach to cases involving violence against women. The absence of adequate governmental protection, it would seem, should equally translate into refugee status for other categories of persons unable to protect themselves. A focus on the adequacy of governmental protection would also shift the analysis in cases of refugee claims arising from civil war, as well as any other cir-

cumstance in which a government lacked the ability effectively to police all segments of society.[34]

The Board had good reason to be cautious: the expansive implications of the protection approach are evident in a New Zealand case involving an Iranian battered woman. Chairperson Rodger Haines of the Refugee Status Appeals Authority found in that case that the applicant would, if she returned to Iran, be exposed to serious harm constituting persecution. Although the Authority found no nexus between the husband's infliction of serious harm and a Convention reason, it did find that Iran condoned the husband's violence for a Convention reason: the applicant's gender.[35] This case, in other words, fits into Box III, alongside Alvarado Peña's. But in a *dictum*, Haines hinted at the logical implications of a protection approach. "[T]he refugee inquiry is not an inquiry into blame," he writes:

> Rather the purpose of refugee law is to identify those who have a well-founded fear of persecution for a Convention reason. If the net result of a state's 'reasonable willingness' to operate a system for the protection of the citizen is that it is incapable of preventing a real chance of persecution of a particular individual, refugee status cannot be denied that individual.[36]

In other words, it seems that even if Iran displayed a "reasonable willingness" to protect the applicant from serious harm, but was not effective in doing so, the applicant would still receive asylum. This is exactly the case involving Dolamore, in Box IV. On protection logic, she has as strong a claim to asylum as Alvarado Peña does. Accordingly, if we are protection theorists, we need to revise our asylum policy to include not only applicants in Boxes II and III, but also those in Box IV. The Board in Alvarado Peña's case relied on the nexus clause to block such a move.

Battered Women: The British Approach

Advocates of the protection approach recognize that such an expansive outcome is politically unacceptable. The challenge is to find a way to grant asylum to applicants in Box III—like Alvarado Peña—while resisting the move to including the cases in Box IV. Can such a way be found? And if so, can it be justified? One attempt toward this goal is apparent in a recent British decision called *ex parte Shah*,[37] involving the conjoined refugee appeals of two Pakistani women who had been falsely accused of adultery by their respective husbands and who could be stoned to death if forced to return to Pakistan.[38] Lord Hoffmann most clearly articulates the novel approach taken by the Lords in that case. He states that the "threat of violence" to the applicants by their respective husbands "is a personal affair, directed against them as individuals" (*Shah*). A nexus cannot be found between their husbands' actions and one of the reasons specified in the "for reasons of" clause.

But the inquiry should not end there. He continues: "there is the inability or unwillingness of the State to do anything to protect them. There is nothing personal about this. The evidence was that the State would not assist them because they were women. It denied them a protection against violence which it would have given to men " (*Shah*). In other words, the motivations of the applicants' husbands in accusing them of adultery are beside the point. The reason the women fear harm is that the state is unwilling to apply its laws impartially; it refuses to give women the same protection as men.

Lord Hoffmann bolsters his argument with an analogy: the Nazi government in the early 1930s had not yet begun "actively [to] organise violence against Jews." Instead, it simply refused to protect Jews against violence inflicted upon them by others. Suppose, then, that an Aryan (or even a Jewish) business competitor were to attack a Jewish shopkeeper. We should judge the shopkeeper to have been persecuted, even though the competitor was "motivated by business rivalry and a desire to settle old personal scores" because the government's unwillingness to protect Jews makes him vulnerable to such attacks (*Shah*). The unwillingness of the government to provide the shopkeeper with protection transforms an act of private violence into an act of persecution. Lord Hoffmann would thus allow the nexus clause to attach *either* to the motivations of the private agent inflicting harm *or* to the motivations of the government in withholding protection against the harm.

	State **Unwilling** to Protect	State **Unable** to Protect
Nexus between harm inflicted by non-state actor and Convention reason	Box I: ASYLUM GRANTED	Box II: ASYLUM GRANTED (The Somali Case)
No nexus between harm inflicted by non-state actor and Convention reason	Box III: ASYLUM GRANTED (Alvarado Peña/ Shah)	Box IV: ASYLUM DENIED (Dolamore)

Figure 11.3: The Lords' Approach to Non-State Actor Cases

In cases where *neither* the non-state actor nor the state is motivated by a Convention reason, an applicant would be denied asylum. Consider, for example, the following hypothetical discussed in *Shah*:

> Assume that during a time of civil unrest, women are particularly vulnerable to attack by marauding men, because the attacks are sexually motivated or because they are thought weaker and less able to defend themselves. The government is unable to protect them, not because of any discrimination but simply because its writ does not run in that part of the country. It is unable to protect men either ... I do not think that they would be regarded as subject to persecution within the meaning of the Convention. The necessary element of discrimination is lacking. (*Shah*)

Fairness: Assessing the Lords' Decision

Refugee advocates widely embraced the decision in *Shah* because it extended asylum to a class of applicants who had previously been excluded (Box III).[39] But Lord Hoffmann was only able to do so—while simultaneously excluding applicants from Box IV—by embracing the nexus clause. This renders his position vulnerable to the same critique leveled against the BIA's decision in Alvarado Peña's case: the result seems unfair. From the standpoint of their need for protection, Shah and the victims of marauding men face identical situations. Yet on the doctrine put forward by the Lords, asylum would be granted only to the former.

How might such an outcome be justified to the latter on the terms of the protection approach? One possible response is that the implications of expanding asylum to include those in Box IV are simply too vast—too many people would become eligible. But, one could reply, a solution might be to place a cap on the number of people who could receive asylum in a given time period and hold a lottery among all qualified applicants. Such a solution would ensure that similarly situated applicants are afforded an equal chance of receiving asylum, while at the same time addressing the fear of "opening the floodgates." The "floodgates" concern alone cannot justify the arbitrary, blanket exclusion of applicants in Box IV.

A second possible justification for excluding applicants from Box IV appeals to judicial role: the Lords' hands were, and are, tied by the nexus clause. There is a nexus between persecution and Convention reasons for Boxes I–III, but not for Box IV. This response resolves the issue as a legal matter, but not at all as a policy matter. If we were truly protection theorists, we would need to revise our asylum policy to include not only applicants in Boxes II and III, but also those in Box IV. This is what fairness dictates. In the meantime, we might acknowledge to those in Box IV that the present policy is indeed unfair and work our hardest to fix it. For their part, judges and administrative agencies should try to water down the nexus clause to the greatest possible extent, through, say, establishing a presumption that all asylum applicants are persecuted for a Convention reason, so that the burden would be on the immigration service to show otherwise.[40]

A third possible response would be that given by an Australian court in a case concerning a Pakistani victim of domestic violence: asylum law recognizes the distinction between governmental unwillingness to protect and governmental inability to do so. Building upon Lord Hoffman's opinion, Chief Judge Gleeson wrote:

> [I]t would not be sufficient for Ms. Khawar to show maladministration, incompetence, or ineptitude, by the local police. That would not convert personally motivated domestic violence into persecution . . . But if she could show state tolerance or condonation of domestic violence, and systematic discriminatory implementation of the law, then it would not be an answer to her case to say that such a state of affairs resulted from entrenched cultural attitudes.[41]

But by distinguishing between state unwillingness and state inability to protect, this response employs the logic of the accountability approach, not the protection approach![42] Applied consistently, it would have negative consequences for cases in Box II, in which the government is similarly unable to protect against harm inflicted by non-state actors.

Conclusion: In Favor of the Accountability Approach

The better response to applicants in Box IV (like Dolamore)—the response implicit in the logic adopted by the *Khawar* and *Shah* courts—is that we are accountability theorists, not protection theorists. The reader will recall that the accountability approach, currently out of favor with scholars and refugee advocates, holds that state complicity is a necessary element of persecution, because persecution involves a misuse of political authority.

The accountability approach reinvests asylum with political significance: asylum adjudication is a forum in which other states' treatment of their citizens is scrutinized, evaluated, and, when appropriate, condemned. Asylum, on the accountability approach, can therefore serve as a low-level sanction against abusive regimes, as well as a warning that more coercive sanctions may be forthcoming. Needy refugees who would not qualify for asylum under an accountability approach could be helped by other refugee assistance regimes, such as temporary protection or *in situ* assistance. By contrast, the protection approach, which looks to a refugee's exposure to harm rather than to the identity of the agent responsible for the harm, relegates asylum to an essentially humanitarian, rather than political, role.

	*State **Unwilling** to Protect*	*State **Unable** to Protect*
Nexus *between harm inflicted by non-state actor and Convention reason*	Box I: ASYLUM GRANTED	Box II: TEMPO- RARY PROTEC- TION GRANTED (The Somali Case)
No nexus *between harm inflicted by non-state actor and Convention reason*	Box III: ASYLUM GRANTED (Alvarado Peña)	Box IV: TEMPO- RARY PROTEC- TION GRANTED (Dolamore)

Figure 11.4: An Accountability Approach to Non-State Actor Cases

Obviously, the distinction between an inability to protect and an unwillingness to protect can be hard to administer. In no society are police resources unlimited; law enforcement necessarily requires priority-setting. In light of this reality, how is a court to determine whether a state's failure to protect stemmed from a legitimate need to devote crime-fighting resources to other priorities, or whether a state's failure to protect stemmed from an unwillingness to take action against certain private conduct? A judgment of this sort will necessarily be highly fact dependent but an assessment of the reasonableness of government action is the kind of judgment that courts are accustomed to making.

The distinction between an inability and an unwillingness to protect is important and valuable. It focuses the court's inquiry on the question that is most relevant for a political conception of asylum: whether the state bears some responsibility for the harm inflicted by a non-state actor. In light of this central question, some facts are more relevant than others. In Rodi Alvarado Peña's case, for example, the most important fact is that her entreaties to the state for help were utterly ignored on six occasions: three times the police declined to respond to her call, twice they declined to enforce a court summons of her husband, and once a judge declined to intervene in what he classified as a domestic dispute.[43] The state's unwillingness to assist Alvarado Peña was not an isolated occurrence; while the state generally was able to maintain law and order, it systematically declined to use its power to protect women in abusive relationships because those in charge viewed such abuse as a "private" matter, beyond the purview of the state. The Immigration Judge found the existence of an "institutional bias" against spousal abuse claims "stem[ming] from a pervasive belief, common in patriarchal societies, that a man should be able to control a wife or female companion by any means he sees fit: including rape, torture, and beatings."[44] For these reasons, responsibility for the violence suffered by Alvarado Peña lies not only with her husband, but with her state as well.

Works Cited

Aleinikoff, T. Alexander. "The Meaning of 'Persecution' in U.S. Asylum Law." *Refugee Policy: Canada and the United States.* Ed. Howard Adelman. Toronto: York Lanes Press, 1991. 292–320.

Anker, Deborah. "Refugee Status and Violence Against Women in the 'Domestic' Sphere." *Georgetown Immigration Law Journal* 15 (2001): 391–402.

Anker, Deborah, Lauren Gilbert, and Nancy Kelly. "Women Whose Governments are Unable or Unwilling to Provide Reasonable Protection from Domestic Violence May Qualify as Refugees Under United States Asylum Law." *Georgetown Immigration Law Journal* 11 (1997): 709–745.

Carlier, Jean-Yves, et al., eds. *Who is a Refugee?* The Hague: Kluwer Law International, 1997.

Copelon, Rhonda. "Recognizing the Egregious in the Everyday: Domestic Violence as Torture." *Columbia Human Rights Law Review* 25 (1994): 291–367.

Donovan, Sharon. "Nowhere to Run . . . Nowhere to Hide." *George Mason University Civil Rights Law Journal* 11 (2001): 301–334.

Edminster, Steven. "Recklessly Risking Lives." www.refugees.org/world/articles/wrs99_agentspersecution.htm (acccessed July 17, 2002).

Goldberg, Pamela. "Anyplace but Home." *Cornell International Law Journal* 26 (1993): 565–604.

Goodwin-Gill, Guy. *The Refugee in International Law.* New York: Oxford University Press, 1996.

Grahl-Madsen, Atle. *The Status of Refugees in International Law.* Vol. 1. Leiden: A.W. Sijthoff, 1966.

Hathaway, James. *Law of Refugee Status.* Toronto: Butterworths, 1991.

_____. "Reconceiving Refugee Law as Human Rights Protection." *Journal of Refugee Studies* 4 (1991): 113–31.

In Re H-, 21 I. & N. Dec. 337 (U.S. BIA, 1996).

In re R-A-, Interim Decision 3403 (BIA 1999), cited in Westlaw as 1999 WL 424364 (BIA).

Kälin, Walter. "Non-State Agents of Persecution and the Inability of the State to Protect." *Georgetown Immigration Law Journal* 15 (2001): 415–31.

Kelly, Nancy. "Gender-Related Persecution: Assessing the Asylum Claims of Women." *Cornell International Law Journal* 26 (1993): 625–74.

Marx, Reinhard. "The Notion of Persecution by Non-State Agents in German Jurisprudence." *Georgetown Immigration Law Journal* 15 (2001): 447–61.

Mertus, Julie. "The State and the Post-Cold War Refugee Regime." *Michigan Journal of International Law* 20 (1998): 59–90.

Moore, Jennifer. "Whither the Accountability Theory." *International Journal of Refugee Law* 13 (2001): 32–50.

_____. "From Nation State to Failed State: International Protection from Human Rights Abuses by Non-State Agents." *Columbia Human Rights Law Review* 31 (1999): 81–121.

Musalo, Karen. "Matter of R-A-: An Analysis of the Decision and Its Implications." *Interpreter Releases* 76.30 (1999): 1177–87.

Musalo, Karen, and Stephen Knight. "Steps Forward and Steps Back," *International Journal of Refugee Law* 13 (2001): 51–70.

Ramanthan, Erik D. "Queer Cases: A Comparative Analysis of Global Sexual Orientation-Based Asylum Jurisprudence," *Georgetown Immigration Law Journal* 11.1 (1996): 1–44.

Salibian v. Canada, (1990) 3 F.C.

Sands, Andrea, and Raquel Exner. "Burn Victim's Refugee Claim Rejected." *Edmonton Sun,* January 15, 2003: 3.

Schaffer, Haley. "Domestic Violence and Asylum in the United States." *Northwestern University Law Review* 95 (2001): 779–809.

Sec'y of State for the Home Dep't ex parte Shah, (1999) 2 A.C. 629.

Swarns, Rachel L. "Ashcroft Weighs Granting of Asylum to Abused Women." *New York Times,* March 11, 2004.

United Nations High Commission on Refugees. *Handbook on Procedures and Criteria for Determining Refugee Status.* Available at www.unhcr.ch (accessed June 25, 2003).

Vermeulen, Ben, et al. "Persecution by Third Parties." Paper commissioned by the Research and Documentation Centre of the Ministry of Justice of the Netherlands. Nijmegen, May, 1998.

Notes

1 *In re R-A-.* The following three paragraphs summarize the facts of the case, as described in Section II.A of the majority opinion (the opinion is not paginated).

2 65 Fed. Reg. 76,588 (proposed December 7, 2000).

3 In March 2004, the Department of Homeland Security proposed a rules change that would grant asylum to victims of severe domestic abuse. After some initial skepticism, Attorney General Ashcroft is reported to be favorably disposed to the change, but as of yet, he has not approved the rules change. See Rachel L. Swarns. On January 19, 2005, Ashcroft remanded Alvarado Peña's case to the Board of Immigration Appeals for another hearing.

4 This is the phrasing found in U.S. law at 8 C.F.R. 208.13(b)(2)(A).

5 Available at www.unchr.ch (accessed June 25, 2003).

6 See, e.g., Goodwin-Gill 70–74; Atle Grahl-Madsen 191; James Hathaway, *Law of Refugee Status* 124ff.; Moore, "Nation State" and "Whither the Ac-

countability Theory"; Julie Mertus; Steven Edminster; Vermeulen; and Kälin.

7   These states include Belgium, the United Kingdom, Canada, the United States, Australia, New Zealand, and Sweden (Moore, "Nation State" 108 n. 70; Vermeulen). The protection view is also endorsed by the UNHCR, which states in its *Handbook*: "Persecution is normally related to action by the authorities of a country. It may also emanate from sections of the population that do not respect the standards established by the laws of the country concerned ... Where serious discriminatory or other offensive acts are committed by the local populace, they can be considered as persecution if they are knowingly tolerated by the authorities, or if the authorities refuse, or prove unable, to offer effective protection" (UNHCR, *Handbook on Procedures and Criteria for Determining Refugee Status*).

8   The seminal case on this is the decision *Canada v. Ward*, [1993] 2 S.C.R. 689.

9   The UNHCR has commented, "Inability is a result-driven determination, i.e., does the protection exist or not. The efforts of the State to provide protection are largely irrelevant. A government may take numerous 'reasonable steps,' indeed it may take 'extraordinary steps,' to protect its nationals ... Yet, if despite these best efforts, its nationals continue to have a well-founded fear of persecution, protection should be afforded" (quoted in Karen Musalo and Stephen Knight 62–3).

10 Reinhard Marx writes, "Perpetrators of serious human rights violations in the context of civil wars and internal strife range from traditional agents of the State to militia, paramilitary groups, war-lords, and alike. However, the victims remain largely the same people. A protection-based approach of the Convention ... follows the assessment of a well-founded fear regardless of where [sic] are the perpetrators" (454).

11 This is rarely, if ever, articulated. Usually, the accountability approach's emphasis on state involvement is presented a historical anachronism (cf. Vermeulen 15), or a quirk of German legal theory (cf. Kälin 421–2).

12 The German Federal Administrative Court for example ruled that Somali "clans and clan-leaders who fight each other over influence do not exercise 'state-like' power in their respective areas of influence" (Moore, "Nation State" 108) while German courts *have* recognized anti-Lebanese actions of the Syrian army in Lebanon as persecution, holding that the Syrian army exercises effective authority in Lebanon (Moore, "Nation State" 107 n. 68; on Germany, see Marx 457ff.; on France, see Vermeulen 29–30).

13 See, for instance, the issue involved in *R v. Secretary of State for the Home Department, ex parte Adan* [2001] 2 A.C. 477). Until 1994, this was Germany's position as well. For example, Germany denied asylum to Sri Lankan Tamils fleeing violence at the hands of the Tamil Tigers (BVerfGE 80, 315,

decision of July 10, 1988), since the Sri Lankan state did not tolerate Tamil violence. A 1994 German Federal Administrative Court decision, however, reversed this position, leaving the German position unclear (see Vermeulen 21).

14 *R. (Atkinson) v. Sec'y of State for the Home Dept.* [2004] EWCA Civ 846, at ¶¶ 33–34, 37.

15 *INS v. Elias-Zacarias,* 502 U.S. 478 (1992).

16 There is a large literature on asylum claims by battered women. Good articles include Deborah Anker, Lauren Gilbert, and Nancy Kelly; Nancy Kelly; and Pamela Goldberg. On *In re R-A-* in particular, see Karen Musalo; Sharon Donovan; and Haley Schaffer.

17 This approach had been successful in the past—see *Lazo-Majano v. INS,* 813 F.2d 1432—but the decision in *Elias-Zacarias* undermined the reasoning used in *Lazo-Majano.*

18 *In re R-A-*, Majority Opinion, Section VI.

19 *In re R-A-*, Dissenting opinion, Section IV.B.

20 *In re R-A-*, Majority opinion, Section VI.A.

21 *In re R-A-*, Majority opinion, Section II.A.

22 *In re R-A-*, Dissenting opinion, Section IV.B.

23 *In re R-A-*, Dissenting opinion, Section IV.B. The "law" the dissent is referring to here is the mixed motivations doctrine, according to which applicants need only show that persecutors were partly motivated by one of the five characteristics in order to meet the nexus requirement. *In Re S-P-* 21 I. & N. Dec. 486 (BIA 1996).

24 *In re R-A-*, Majority opinion, Section VI.A.

25 *In re R-A-*, Majority opinion, Section VI.A.

26 *In re R-A-*, Majority opinion, Section VI.B.1.

27 *In re R-A-*, Majority opinion, Section VI.B.1.

28 *In re R-A-*, Dissenting opinion, Section III.B.

29 *In re R-A-*, Majority opinion, Section VI.B.2.

30 Generally speaking, gays and transgendered individuals have not suffered the same hurdles as battered women in establishing their membership in a particular social group. (Of course, as many of the other essays in this volume demonstrate, they have still faced significant legal challenges.) In *Matter of Toboso-Alfonso,* 20 I. & N. Dec. 819 (BIA 1990), the Board of Immigration Appeals recognized that homosexuals are members of a social group under U.S. law. In *Matter of Tenorio,* Immigr. Ct. San Francisco Jul. 26, 1993, a gay Brazilian who had been stabbed outside a gay nightclub

was granted asylum following a finding by the judge that paramilitary groups hunt down and kill homosexuals. And in *Geovanni Hernandez-Montiel v. I.N.S.*, 225 F.3d 1084 (9th Cir. 2000), the Ninth Circuit Court of Appeals recognized that "gay men with female sexual identities" constituted a social group under U.S. law. See Erik D. Ramanthan. However, one suspects that gays and lesbians fleeing domestic abuse would have even more difficulty qualifying for asylum than battered women. While a social group membership claim is compelling when gays suffer serious harm on account of their sexuality by anti-gay paramilitary groups or by policemen, the claim is much less plausible when the violence is perpetrated by a gay lover who is a member of the same social group as his or her victim. While battered women can at least make the claim that their husbands abuse them because they are women (and thus different from their husbands), persons fleeing same-sex relationships would be unable to point to a similar difference as motivating their partners' abuse.

31   Vermeulen et al. write, "In the protection view, *the only relevant issue is whether the persons involved are not effectively protected* against human rights violations, regardless of the source of these violations" (11, emphasis added). Regardless of the motivation of these violations as well, it would seem to follow.

32   *MCI v. Jessica Robyn Dolamore* (2001 FTC 421). Initially, the Refugee Board granted Dolamore asylum in 2000, but upon appeal, the Federal Trial Court found that the Board had not adequately addressed the issue of whether she was able to receive protection in New Zealand. Upon remand in July 2002, the Board denied Dolamore's asylum application (Andrea Sands and Raquel Exner).

33   *In re R-A-,* Majority opinion, VI.B.2.

34   *In re R-A-,* Majority opinion, VI.B.2.

35   Refugee Appeal No. 71427/99 (decided August 16, 2000), pars. 116–119.

36   Refugee Appeal No. 71427/99 (decided August 16, 2000), pars. 63, 66.

37   *Sec'y of State for the Home Dep't ex parte Shah,* (1999) 2 A.C. 629. Hereafter referred to as *Shah.*

38   *In re R-A-* was decided after *Shah,* and both the majority and the dissent make reference to them. The dissent is eager to adopt the approach the British cases lay out, but the majority argues: "the adoption of such an approach would represent a fundamental change in the analysis of refugee claims . . . Instead of assessing the motivation of the actual persecutor, we might, for example, be focusing on the motivation or justification of the government for not intervening and affording real protection." *In re R-A-,* Majority opinion, VI.B.2.

39   See for example Deborah Anker, "Refugee Status and Violence Against

Women in the 'Domestic' Sphere," 391. The decision in *Shah* is described as "landmark," contributing to "one of the most important breakthroughs" in recent asylum jurisprudence.

40 This approach is suggested by T. Alexander Aleinikoff.

41 *Minister for Immigration and Multicultural Affairs v. Khawar,* (2002) HCA 14.

42 Interestingly, even the dissent in *In re R-A-* seemed to recognize the distinctive wrong of denying someone standing to legal redress. In his opening remarks about the case, Board Member Guendelsberger notes, "The harm to the respondent occurred in the context of egregious governmental acquiescence. When the respondent sought the aid and assistance of government officials and institutions, she was told that they could do nothing for her. This is not a case in which the government tried, but failed, to afford protection. Here the government made no effort and showed no interest in protecting the respondent from her abusive spouse" (*In re R-A-*, Dissenting opinion, Section II—Overview).

43 *In re R-A-*, 909.

44 *In re R-A-*, 930 (dissent).

12

Witnessing Memory and Surviving Domestic Violence: The Case of Rodi Alvarado Peña

Angélica Cházaro

> "In crossing a border (. . . or two) the foreigner has changed
> his discomforts into a base of resistance, a citadel of life."
>
> —Julia Kristeva, *Strangers to Ourselves*

In the text of the court decision which denied asylum to Rodi Alvarado Peña in June 1999, the following appears: "The question before us is whether the respondent qualifies as a 'refugee' as a result of the heinous abuse she suffered and still fears from her husband in Guatemala."[1] Definitions are of paramount importance in asylum law. The outcome of a case can hinge on the interpretation of terms such as "well-founded fear," "persecution," and "social group." Rodi Alvarado Peña arrived in the United States in May 1995, and sought asylum shortly thereafter on the grounds of extreme domestic abuse suffered in her marriage. In the courts, she was responsible for using her testimony to create a reality that fit the United States' classification of what constitutes a persecuted person. She has been waiting for ten years to find out if her story can be accepted, if the laws of the United States will consider her a refugee, worthy of protection. The decision depends on the definition of the very term "refugee."

The vicissitudes of interpretation are therefore critical. In her *Law of Asylum in the United States*, Deborah Anker writes:

> [T]he core of both refugee and asylum status is the definition
> of "refugee" derived from the U.N. Refugee Convention. The
> U.S. statute defines refugee as: [A]ny person who is outside
> any country of such persons' nationality or, in the case of a

person having no nationality, is outside any country in which
such person last habitually resided, and who is unable or unwilling to return to, and is unable or unwilling to avail himself
or herself of the protection of, that country because of persecution or a well-founded fear of persecution on account of
race, religion, nationality, membership in a particular social
group, or political opinion. (4–5)

Because asylum law is adjudicated on a case-by-case basis,[2] the meanings of terms like "well-founded fear" and "persecution" shift constantly. As Anker notes, most courts refer to a ruling that sustains that
persecution involves "the infliction of suffering or harm upon those
who differ in a way that is regarded as offensive" (179). In order for
a well-founded fear standard to be met, "an applicant must present
credible, direct, and specific evidence that she has a reasonable fear of
persecution." Anker goes on to say that the Board of Immigration Appeals "defined fear as 'an emotion characterized by the apprehension
or awareness of danger'" (179). The grounds on which one may seek
asylum—race, religion, nationality, membership in a particular social
group, or political opinion—have also been defined on a case-by-case
basis: "These grounds represent basic civil and political rights and statutes, defined by immutable characteristics or protected beliefs basic to
identity, which mark the refugee as somehow outside of the national
community" (Anker 267). In cases of gender-based persecution, asylum has traditionally been granted under "membership in a particular
social group" or under "political opinion."

   In May 1995, Alvarado Peña received an "Order to Show Cause and
Warrant for Arrest of Alien," in which the Immigration and Naturalization Service (INS—now restructured under the Department of
Homeland Security) alleged that she was not a citizen of the U.S. and
had entered the country illegally. That led to her first interaction with
the immigration courts. After conceding her deportability before the
court, Alvarado Peña submitted an application for asylum before the
Immigration Court.[3] This produced a ruling in her favor, and, in September 1996, she was granted asylum by a San Francisco Immigration
Judge. The judge decided that the definition of "refugee" provided by
the U.S. statute fit the circumstances that had brought Alvarado Peña
to the court, that she indeed possessed a well-founded fear of persecution, based both on social group membership and political opinion.[4]
Attorneys for the INS appealed the ruling, and in a decision from June

11, 1999, the Board of Immigration Appeals (BIA) reversed the 1996 decision. The second decision was published, and it is this document that I will be examining.[5] In the document, the courts take full advantage of the mutability of legal language, manipulating Alvarado Peña's testimony in their decision to deny her claim.

The BIA decision was itself vacated (in effect, annulled) on January 19, 2001 by Attorney General Janet Reno as one of her final acts on her last day in office.[6] She ordered the BIA to reconsider the case under a new set of Department of Justice regulations on the subject of gender asylum. As of this writing, the regulations had not been finalized.[7] In February 2003 Attorney General John Ashcroft took the unusual step of ordering the BIA to send Alvarado Peña's case to his office for a decision (Lardner). In his final days as Attorney General, Ashcroft returned her case to the BIA to await the new regulations, declining to decide himself whether to grant or deny Alvarado Peña asylum (Egelko). According to the San Francisco-based Center for Gender and Refugee Studies, which tracks gender asylum cases nationwide, the 1999 *In re R-A-* decision "led to denials of asylum protection to women fleeing a broad range of serious human rights violations, including forced prostitution, gang rape and honor killing, as well as domestic violence."[8] The BIA readily admitted in 1999 that Alvarado Peña suffered "heinous abuse," but because it found no language within existing asylum law under which to place her claim, it reversed the earlier decision of the immigration judge.

The court's voice in the document *In re R-A-* is, as is conventional, the first person plural "we," the nameless, anonymous face representing the voice of the United States of America. In accordance, I will refer to the authors of the BIA decision as "they" or "the court." Rodi Alvarado Peña is referred to as "the respondent." Upon being named "the respondent" within the text of the decision, Alvarado Peña becomes a part of the U.S. legal system. She pleads with another state—a foreign government—to take responsibility for her, using a court system with which she is unfamiliar, respecting a set of legal rules that immediately transform her into a supplicant.[9] Ironically, "the respondent" is treated *almost as if* she were a citizen of the United States, inasmuch as she is submitted to treatment similar to that which U.S. citizens receive when they seek redress in the courts.

Marvin Aron Eisenberg, in his article "Private Ordering through Negotiation, Dispute Settlement and Rulemaking," explains that involvement in a trial makes each disputant:

by posture a supplicant and by role an inferior. He [sic] must tacitly admit he cannot handle his own affairs. He must appear at times and places that may be decidedly and expensively inconvenient. He must bend his thought and perhaps his very body, in ways that will move the adjudicator. He must show various signs of obeisance—speak only when permitted, be orderly, and act respectfully if not deferentially. (cited in Minow 272)

Alvarado Peña's presence in an U.S. courtroom demonstrates, moreover, her ultimate disrespect for Guatemala's laws, albeit a form of disrespect that stems from her country's alleged inability to provide not just for her well-being but to protect her as a citizen. Her arrival in the United States confirms Alvarado Peña's position as an "escapee." But from the moment that she starts legal proceedings to obtain asylum, she becomes an informant, almost a spy, having to air the faults of her country of origin to a system, that of the United States, that is accordingly cast as vitally superior. In effect, she must reject her country by attempting to prove that in Guatemala the social and cultural norms that foster domestic violence override any laws meant to protect women. Thus, she implicitly demonstrates her trust in U.S. laws over Guatemalan ones. She must display respect for the U.S. courts, even if this new system to which she has submitted herself might betray her at the end of the proceedings by returning her to her country of origin.

When she fled, Alvarado Peña made a choice, born out of necessity, to terminate her links with Guatemala. And yet, clearly, she cannot uphold her choice, her decision, on her own. She needs the recognition and validation of the U.S. legal system, a need that, for all its pressingly real effects, is also profoundly symbolic. Mikhail Bakhtin, writing from a more general philosophical perspective, explains the need for recognition in his book *Art and Answerability*:

I *can* strive in an unmediated way for self-preservation and well-being, defend my life with all the means at my disposal, and even strive for power and the subjection of others, but I can never experience within myself in an unmediated way that which constitutes me as a legal person, because my legal personality is nothing else but my guaranteed certainty in being granted recognition by *other* people—a certainty that I experience as *their* obligation in relation to myself. And, similarly, there is an equally profound difference between my inner experience of my own body and the recognition of its outer value by *other* people—my right to the loving acceptance or recognition of my exterior by *others:* this recognition or acceptance descends upon me from others like a gift. (49)

Alvarado Peña can inhabit no space outside of recognition by a nation. In order to remain safe, she requires that the United States recognize her as a "refugee," worthy of the protection of a nation other than her own. She cannot do this on her own, in an unmediated way, but instead she must rely on her lawyers to *recognize* her as a refugee, and to then help her construct her story so that the courts will *extend recognition* to her in the form of asylum. As an asylum applicant, a subject effectively between nations, she cannot assume with "guaranteed certainty" that she will be recognized. Her lawyers must mediate her desire for recognition, helping to translate her experience in order for the Court to grant her the "gift" of recognition. In certifying the case to himself in 2003, Attorney General John Ashcroft adopted the BIA's role. Thus, Alvarado Peña's fate became subject to one individual's interpretation of her testimony and the legal arguments formulated on her behalf. The "we" of the Board of Immigration Appeals was transformed into the "I" of the head of the Department of Justice, and Alvarado Peña's quest for the "gift of recognition" continued. During his time in office, Ashcroft altered the BIA's structure, reducing it to eleven members, in what critics labeled a purge of its pro-immigrant elements (Alonso-Zaldívar). Before leaving office, Ashcroft returned Alvarado Peña's case to a BIA that now constitutes a more formidable "we," a board in which only one of the five original members who offered a dissent to the 1999 decision remains.[10]

The reasons for Alvarado Peña's original flight are clearly detailed in the text of the 1999 decision. Rodi Alvarado Peña, married at the age of sixteen, was brutally abused by her husband, Francisco Osorio, for ten years, until she escaped to the United States, leaving behind her two children. During those ten years, Osorio raped her almost daily, both anally and vaginally. He kicked her in the spine in an effort to abort their second child, dislocated her jaw when her menstrual cycle was two weeks late, whipped her with an electrical cord, threatened her with a machete, broke windows over her head, and pistol-whipped her. The catalogue of horrors is critical to her necessary choice to flee Guatemala and to seek refuge in the United States. While in Guatemala, she escaped her "lawful home" several times, but each time Osorio found her and brought her back, continuing the brutal abuse. Her pleas to the police went unheeded, and Osorio boasted to her that his status as a former soldier rendered him untouchable by the law. In May 1995, she fled Guatemala, arriving in Brownsville, Texas, two days later.[11] Ten years later, the details of her suffering continue to provide the appalling backdrop against which various legal theories surrounding gender and asylum are tried and tested on her behalf.[12]

The circumstances that led to Alvarado Peña's appearance in the courts have been anything but "orderly," but once enmeshed in the legal system she must take part in its protocols and rituals, disciplining her body and her memories to produce an individual that the courts will designate as "refugee." Jean François Lyotard offers an insightful analysis of what is at stake in such structurally conditioned self-fashioning, or self-articulation, in *The Differend: Phrases in Dispute:*

> The one who says there is something is the plaintiff, it is up to him or her to bring forth a demonstration, by means of well-formed phrases and of procedures for establishing the existence of their referent. Reality is always the plaintiff's responsibility. For the defense, it is sufficient to refute the argumentation and to impugn the proof by a counterexample. (8)

As an asylum applicant, Alvarado Peña is not technically a plaintiff—the protective (rather than compensatory) nature of asylum law does not allow for that possibility. Yet her inability to bring her husband to trial in her own country has led to her appearance in the U.S. courts, and as such, she is still responsible for creating a reality, through her testimony and her very presence in the courtroom, that will "move the adjudicator," as Lyotard puts it. The BIA bases its 1999 decision on the written record created during Alvarado Peña's 1996 case, where she originally testified. This testimony took the form of both a written application and oral testimony. The "well-formed phrases" describing Alvarado Peña's experience, crafted with her lawyers, are crucial in her case, as the language and the narrative strategies that she used to describe her situation will decide its outcome.

The Court demonstrates its authority in its description of the respondent's responsibility for bearing "the burden of proof and persuasion of showing that he or she is a refugee within the meaning of section 101(a) (42) (A) of the Act, 8 U.S.C. § 1101 (a) (42) (A) (1994), to be eligible for asylum under section 208 (a) of the Act" (*In re R-A-* 7). The "burden" which the Court places upon Alvarado Peña includes that of revisiting the very events she escaped. Almost ten years after her arrival in the United States, Alvarado Peña must continue to (re)live, at least legally, the time of her abuse. During the time in which an individual applies for asylum, however prolonged the process, her principal goal is to *recreate the events* that she has physically left behind, events which may be extremely difficult to revisit because of the trauma and, no less importantly, the social stigma connected to them (something like the trauma of trauma).

In the eyes of the Court, Alvarado Peña's record of victimization already places her well within the realm of the persecuted: "We agree with the Immigration Judge . . . that the level of harm experienced by the respondent rises beyond the threshold of that required for 'persecution'" (*In re R-A-* 9). But "moving the adjudicator" is not enough. Her lawyers must help Alvarado Peña prove that her individual experience of persecution is "on account of" her membership in a particular social group or her political opinion. Alvarado Peña's lawyers are therefore assigned with transforming her distressing memories into a strong case. They must link her situation with that of those who have come before her, placing her personal memories in a narrative—and a narrative history. Only by constructing the narrative in a way that involves two of the five grounds for asylum can her case be heard and, hopefully, validated by the judges. If Alvarado Peña's testimony is successful, the judges will take it as the voice of an entire group of suffering women, and she will be granted asylum as a "token" woman who has escaped. Her memories will need to function, that is, as the memories of a group that she has left behind; her story will need to become a *standard* narrative.[13] To win her case, Alvarado Peña must wrestle with the paradox of presenting herself both as an individual and as a part of a pre-existing group of persecuted women. If Alvarado Peña succeeds in so presenting herself, however, she may actually ruin her chances for asylum. As previously suggested, the immigration courts have demonstrated what can only be called a fear of "opening the floodgates" if they grant women asylum on "novel" claims such as domestic abuse. They fear, in short, that all women who suffer similar or related abuse will rush to the United States, although such fears are as yet unsubstantiated.[14] The courts ask refugees to show, on a case-by-case basis, that they belong to a group, that there are others who suffer in the same or similar way but are unable to escape.

In the BIA decision, the Court shifts its focus selectively from Rodi Alvarado Peña as an individual respondent to Rodi Alvarado Peña as an individual *represented* by a team of lawyers. Throughout most of the decision, Alvarado Peña's actions are attributed to her, even those actions in which it is obvious that her lawyers played a central role: "The respondent has submitted numerous articles and reports regarding violence against women in Guatemala and other Latin American countries" (*In re R-A-* 6). Alvarado Peña, like many asylum seekers, is represented by lawyers intimately familiar with U.S. asylum law who can build a case around its requirements, finding the "articles and reports" needed to back up their claims. The Court occasionally chooses to differentiate Alvarado Peña from her lawyers, highlighting the distinction between Alvarado Peña's reasoning and her lawyer's reasoning at key points in the text. "The respondent fits," we are told, "within the proposed group ["Guatemalan women who have been involved intimately with Guatemalan male companions, who believe that women are to live under male domination"]. But the group is defined largely in the abstract" (*In re R-A-* 14). Defined largely in the abstract by whom? The use of passive voice attempts to erase the presence of Alvarado Peña's lawyers, who have argued that the respondent "fits" the proposed group. The BIA's critique of the "abstract" is a rebuke aimed at Alvarado Peña's lawyers for their manipulation of language.

Yet asylum law is based on abstractions, on notions of human rights and nationalities. The idea of "well-founded fear" remains a vague one, no matter how many court decisions have attempted to define it. The act of interpreting the law, which Alvarado Peña's lawyers undertake, is by its very nature abstract. Yet the BIA continues to challenge the work of Alvarado Peña's lawyers: "Here, the respondent has proposed a social group definition that may amount to a legally crafted description of some attributes of her tragic personal circumstances" (*In re R-A-* 16). In this passage, they again highlight the division between Alvarado Peña and her lawyers, positing Alvarado Peña as the one who proposed the social group definition, but then shifting agency to her lawyers in describing it as a "legally crafted definition." Since asylum law is based on a reinterpretation of definitions that can vary depending on the case at hand, the phrase "legally crafted definition" seems redundant. The entire decision is in itself the judge's "legally crafted" response to the fact that they will not recognize Alvarado Peña's persecution as rendering her eligible for refugee status. The judges, however, have chosen to read "legally crafted" as somehow insincere or inessential, pointing in the process to the fact that nationality or political opinion (two of the other categories of asylum) have come to be considered "essential" and therefore beyond the apparently suspicious need to be "legally crafted." The arbitrariness of the distinctions is mainly historical, finding its roots in the past of asylum law.

Until the Refugee Act of 1980, an immigrant "had to depart from a Communist-dominated country or the Middle East" in order to qualify as a refugee in the United States (Schrag 29). Even after 1980, the "vast majority of the refugees who were admitted to the United States from overseas came from only two regions, and those two were sites of Cold War conflict: Southeast Asia (still teeming with those who had fled the war in Vietnam) and the Soviet Union" (Schrag 28). During the Cold War years, foreign policy made asylum decisions relatively clear-cut: while the U.S. supported regimes that many people considered oppressive in El Salvador and Haiti, only 2 percent of Haitians and only 3 percent of Salvadoran applicants were granted asylum, in contrast to 78 percent of Russians applicants (Schrag 29). Those applying for asylum clearly fell into one of two camps: those from governments that the United States supported and those from governments that it did not. For a refugee fleeing a Communist regime, to apply for asylum on the grounds of political opinion was a relatively unencumbered option. But things are different for classes or groups of peoples that are *not* primarily, let alone exclusively, nationally or politically determined. A female applicant adducing gender as part of her claim presents the courts with the challenge of expanding, and indeed of codifying by legal precedent, one of the existing five grounds for asylum and refuge. In Alvarado Peña's case, the Court fails to meet the challenge.

In failing to find a place for domestic violence within the existing grounds for asylum, the Court faults Alvarado Peña's lawyers for "forcing" her persecution to fit into the category of "political opinion" or "membership in a particular social group." The Court thus attempts to create a rift between Alvarado Peña's testimony and her lawyer's arguments:

> At the outset, the respondent never testified that she understood that abuse to be motivated by her political opinion or membership in a group of any description. Her husband never articulated such motivation, and she does not seem to have perceived it independent of the legal arguments now being advanced on her behalf. (*In re R-A-* 24)

Alvarado Peña presents her memories to the Court *through* her lawyers, and the Court, in an effort to discredit said memories (and, by
extension, Alvarado Peña herself), effectively claims that her lawyers
distort reality and that Alvarado Peña's "understanding" of her situation outstrips the "legal arguments now being advanced on her behalf."
Based on the requirements of asylum law itself, the distinction is, however, useless. U.S. asylum law requires that all asylum seekers construct
their claims as fitting within one of the aforementioned categories (religion, race, nationality, membership in a particular social group, or
political opinion) and that they work with their lawyers to construct
their testimonies around working definitions of "refugee" and "persecution." The Court implies that in Alvarado Peña's case the construction is dishonest because it is a construction. Yet the law itself requires
construction, compelling lawyers to mold their client's cases to one of
the five grounds, which are also, of course, constructions.[15]

Although the BIA judges are willing to attribute Alvarado Peña's actions to her alone throughout most of the decision, in the passage cited
above they render her powerless. She is presented as a helpless person
"with legal arguments now being advanced on her behalf." The judges
try to separate Alvarado Peña's abuse, her persecution, from the legal
arguments surrounding it, when it is only *through* these arguments
that she can possibly be granted asylum. Lyotard writes:

> The victim does not have the legal means to bear witness to the
> wrong done to him or her. If he or she or his or her defender
> sees "justice done," this can only be in spite of the law. The law
> reserves the authority to establish the crime, to pronounce the
> verdict and to determine the punishment before the tribunal
> which has heard the two parties expressing themselves in the
> same language, that of the law. The justice which the victim
> calls upon against the justice of the tribunal cannot be uttered
> in the genre of juridical or forensic discourse. But this is the
> genre in which the law is uttered. (30)

Even if the Court were to grant Alvarado Peña asylum, "justice" would
not have been done, at least not entirely so. As hyperbolic as it may
sound, in a profound sense there is no justice for refugees. Their flight,
or exile, has seen to that.[16] They must flee from their native countries
in order to save their lives, leaving behind all that is familiar and many
times relinquishing the ability to return. The best that the Court could

do for Alvarado Peña would be to grant her asylum, or, in the words of the decision, "to provide surrogate international protection" (*In re R-A-* 7). There is nothing the Court can do to redress the wrongs done to her by her husband, nothing it can do to make up for the fact that she has left her two children with her husband's parents in order to save her own life. The justice that Alvarado Peña sought unsuccessfully from the Guatemalan police and courts does not exist—at least not readily—in the language of U.S. asylum law. Yet the law is Alvarado Peña's only recourse. Alvarado Peña and her lawyers play by the rules by engaging the "genre in which the law is uttered" and by constructing her case to fit two of the five grounds under which asylum is granted. Still, her request is denied.

Alvarado Peña's lawyers act as mediators, attempting to translate her account into the legal language that the judges expect. Without her lawyers and their knowledge of the law, Alvarado Peña would have little chance of being granted asylum, especially because in her case— and other cases of domestic violence—the Court continues to make the damaging and outdated distinction between the political as public and the domestic as private.[17] Alvarado Peña's case does not fit neatly into the courts traditional definition of "political opinion," a definition that came from the years during which asylum was granted primarily to those fleeing Communism. With the deck correspondingly stacked, the decision faults Alvarado Peña's lawyers for attempting to bring the definition up to date by arguing that a woman resisting domestic violence is demonstrating, in fact, a political opinion. Together, Alvarado Peña and her lawyers strive to construct a version of reality that the courts will accept.

Presenting a convincing reality may be the "plaintiff's burden," but in order to corroborate this reality, the courts rely on outside, "objective" opinions. As a result, they turn to the U.S. State Department and to a U.S.-based expert witness, Dr. Doris Bersing. In Alvarado Peña's case, outside opinions tend to mean the opinions of U.S. citizens on Guatemalan conditions. While every word of Alvarado Peña's testimony is challenged and eventually redeployed to deny her asylum, the testimony of the outside experts on "country conditions" is taken at face value. The Court weighs its understanding of Alvarado Peña's specific testimony against its own quite general understanding of the situation in Guatemala. The Court's understanding of Guatemala must be, in other words, "translated" by U.S. experts on Guatemalan culture. Yet the focus of the Court is on the *translation* of the Guatemalan experience, ignoring that the translators are themselves outsiders. The experts are trusted to show differences between Guatemalan culture and U.S. culture, but at the same time, the process of translation, the process by which they show the difference, is erased: truth, as truth, is conveyed, apparently without a hitch.

Along with a search for the truth of Rodi Alvarado Peña, a search for the truth of Guatemala—and more spectrally, the United States—is also enabled. Moreover, in the search for the "real" Guatemala, the State Department is constructed as a true "insider," virtually interchangeable with the voice of the Court itself. Dr. Bersing earns the position of a partial insider—not being Guatemalan, she is trusted more than Alvarado Peña, but at the same time she is distanced from the "inside" by *not* being an official representative of the United States (as are the State Department *and* the BIA). Under the section "Country Conditions," the decision notes Dr. Bersing's contribution:

> Dr. Doris Bersing testified that spouse abuse is common in Latin American countries and that she was not aware of social or legal resources for battered women in Guatemala. Women in Guatemala, according to Dr. Bersing, have other problems related to general conditions in that country, and she suggested that such women could leave abusive partners but that they would face other problems such as poverty. Dr. Bersing further testified that the respondent was different from other battered women she had seen in that the respondent possessed an extraordinary fear of her husband and her abuse had been extremely severe. (*In re R-A-* 5)

The furthest that the Court goes to flesh out Dr. Bersing's identity is to give her first name "Doris," which thereafter drops out of the text. Her title, "Dr.," is the only clue given as to her expert status.

Dr. Bersing, as an officially recognized expert, is charged with placing Alvarado Peña's case within the framework of Guatemalan culture, and testifies to Alvarado Peña's uniqueness from other battered women due to her "extraordinary fear." Dr. Bersing's presence in court points to her acceptance as an "American" expert, permitting Bersing to make highly subjective statements on the respondent's emotional state and to compare the Alvarado Peña case to that of other abused victims. Dr. Bersing's voice is trusted, with little anxiety or doubt, as that of an

informant on Guatemala. Her status as an outsider to Guatemalan culture actually strengthens her authority before the U.S. court, and her
job is to corroborate information provided by another "informant,"
Alvarado Peña herself. Yet the language of the decision is careful to
distinguish Dr. Bersing's testimony from the Court's own opinion. Her
statements are introduced by clauses such as "Dr. Bersing noted" or "as
we understand her testimony" (*In re R-A-* 5). These statements highlight Dr. Bersing's status as an outsider to the Court, albeit a *trusted*
outsider. Her testimony does not appear within the quotation marks
that mark off many of Alvarado Peña's quotes and that signal its difference. Bersing is apparently enough of an insider that her statements
can stand without quotes, can be summarized without specific clarification.

A different opinion on the "country conditions" is provided not by
an individual but by an institution: "The Department of State issued
an advisory opinion as to the respondent's asylum request. The opinion stated that the respondent's alleged mistreatment could have occurred given its understanding of country conditions in Guatemala."
The opinion further indicated the following:

> [S]pousal abuse complaints by husbands have increased from
> 30 to 120 a month due to increased nationwide educational
> programs, which have encouraged women to seek assistance.
> Family court judges may issue injunctions against abusive
> spouses, which police are charged with enforcing. The [Hu-
> man Rights Ombudsman] women's rights department and
> various non-governmental organizations provide medical and
> legal assistance. (*In re R-A-* 6)

The State department acts as a second type of expert witness, a quintessentially American voice, which provides presumably reliable information about another country. This is the only point in the decision
in which any source is cited at length. Unlike Dr. Bersing, who "noted"
or "testified," the Department of State "issued" and "states." The verbs
associated with the Department of State are forceful ones, indicating an authority not to be questioned. By quoting their statement at
length, by allowing another voice to temporarily invade its own statements, the Court reinforces the authority of the State Department's
statements. Not surprisingly, the Court establishes a clear hierarchy in

regard to the trustworthiness of its informants. The State Department occupies the top of the list, followed by Dr. Bersing, and in last place, at the greatest possible distance, lies Rodi Alvarado Peña, the primary witness and the interested party.

The weight that the Court places on the words of Dr. Bersing and on those of the State Department reappears in its refusal to grant Alvarado Peña asylum on the basis of its understanding of Guatemalan society:

> The respondent fits within the proposed group ["Guatemalan women who have been involved intimately with Guatemalan male companions, who believe that women are to live under male domination"]. But the group is defined largely in the abstract. It seems to bear little or no relation to the way in which Guatemalans might identify subdivisions within their own society or otherwise might perceive individuals either to possess or to lack an important characteristic or trait. (*In re R-A-* 14)

I have already examined this passage in relation to its problematic use of the word "abstract." Nevertheless, the last sentence also warrants consideration. The Court's impression of how Guatemalans "might identify subdivisions" or "might perceive individuals" hinges on statements made by Dr. Doris Bersing and the U.S. State Department. The BIA thus selectively interprets the testimony of the experts as to the place of domestic violence within Guatemalan society. The Court questions Guatemalans' ability to identify themselves and, in the same blush, empowers an outsider to define said identity. Working from only two sources, the experts on Guatemala and Alvarado Peña, the Court assesses an entire nation on the subject of domestic violence. Going one step further, the Court faults Alvarado Peña for not being able to demonstrate the importance of her very personal suffering on the psyche of an entire nation: "She has not shown . . . that the characteristic of being abused is one that is important within Guatemalan society" (*In re R-A-* 15). In court, Alvarado Peña bears the onus for representing not only her own reality as a battered individual, but also the reality of an entire society—a society that she escaped due to her inability to convince the authorities that "the characteristic of being abused" was one that was "important" enough to warrant her protection.

The emphasis placed on Alvarado Peña's role as the party responsible for creating a convincing reality is countered by the Court's emphasis on the voice of Osorio, her persecutor. By testifying on her own behalf, and by extension, against her husband, Alvarado Peña relinquishes her past, passing it on to both the lawyers who construct her claim, and the judges who interpret it. Alvarado Peña describes the atrocities to which Osorio subjected her and provides, in so doing, the only insight that the Court has into his character:

> The record indicates that the respondent's husband harmed the respondent regardless of what she actually believed or what he thought she believed. The respondent testified that the abuse began "from the moment [they] were married." Even after the respondent "learned through experience" to acquiesce to his demands, he still abused her. The abuse took place before she left him initially, and it continued after she returned to him. In fact, he said he "didn't care" what she did to escape because he would find her. He also hurt her before her first call to the police and after her last plea for help. The respondent's account of what her husband told her may well reflect his own view of women and, in particular, his view of the respondent as his property to do with as he pleased. It does not, however, reflect that he had any understanding of the respondent's perspective or that he even cared what the respondent's perspective may have been. According to the respondent, he told her, "You're my woman, you do what I say." In fact, she stated that "[a]s time went on, he hit me for no reason at all," and that he "would hit or kick me whenever he felt like it." Nowhere in the record does the respondent recount her husband saying anything relating to what he thought her political views to be, or that the violence towards her was attributable to her actual or imputed beliefs. (*In re R-A-* 11)
>
> The respondent's statements regarding her husband's motivations also undercut the nexus claim. . . . He harmed her, when he was drunk and when he was sober, for not getting an abortion . . . and "for no reason at all." Of all these apparent reasons for abuse, none was "on account of" a protected ground, and the arbitrary nature of the attacks further suggests that it was not the respondent's claimed social group characteristics that he sought to overcome. (*In re R-A-* 18)

The Court denies Alvarado Peña asylum, using her own telling of Osorio's words and actions to rule against her. Although Alvarado Peña comes to the United States to escape her husband, he is brought back into her life, not only through her recollections of him, but through the Court's recitation of his words and actions ("In fact, he said he didn't care . . .") in its decision against her. Because there can be no persecuted without a persecutor, he is obviously a key figure in her testimony. Since Alvarado Peña's persecution must be "on account of" one of the protected grounds, the statutory definition of "refugee" requires Osorio's motivations to be considered (this is known as the "nexus" requirement). However, by focusing *exclusively* on Osorio's motivations for the abuse (as narrated by Alvarado Peña), the Court isolates the abuse from the context of willful societal and governmental blindness in which it took place, a context that provides the motivation for persecution that the BIA fails to recognize.[18]

By giving Osorio's presence such weight, the Court further breaks down Alvarado Peña's only tools: her voice and her memory. By the Court's reasoning, Alvarado Peña's fear of death at the hands of her husband is not enough to guarantee her asylum precisely because he beat her indiscriminately. The court surmises from this that he would have abused any wife that he might have had and therefore that Alvarado Peña did not express a political opinion by resisting him. In this move, the Court shifts its focus from the suffering of the respondent to her husband's intentions. He becomes, in the process, the centerpiece of the argument, and his views on women, *not* Alvarado Peña's resistance to them, accordingly come to occupy the primary position in the "political opinion" argument. Likewise, Alvarado Peña's testimony on Osorio's seemingly random beatings undercuts her claim for asylum under the second possible ground for asylum, social group membership.

In her testimony, Alvarado Peña establishes her status as a victim of persecution, yet her very presence in the courtroom shows a courage and resolve that also define her as a survivor, as other than a victim. Stepping into the courtroom, she must reconstruct herself as a victim, concentrating only on the parts of her life that show her completely dominated by her husband. Her hope is that the courts will witness this suffering and grant her the privilege of moving from "victim" to "survivor" by granting her asylum. Instead, by believing her suffering ("We also credit the respondent's testimony in general," *In re R-A-* 10) and yet making Osorio the centerpiece of the adjudication, the Court in effect reinstates Alvarado Peña's status as victim, this time in the sphere of the law. The Court reconstructs Alvarado Peña's memories, reformulating them in a way that fits its at once predetermined and still undetermined ends. Ironically, by giving a detailed testimony, Alvarado Peña provides the Court with the ammunition it needs to deny her asylum claim. The upshot is devastatingly neat: Alvarado Peña is systematically taken apart, and her only tool, her testimony, is stripped from her. In a case with a positive outcome, she would be exchanging her testimony for the privilege of choosing to remember or to forget (or to remember in order to forget), but at this point, she is simply left bare. Her presence in the courtroom already proves that the Guatemalan government did not deem her worthy of protection, and in denying her claim, the U.S. government effectively does the same. For all the national differences, sameness rules the day.

Lyotard is again, on this score, enlightening: "It is the nature of a victim not to be able to prove that one has been done a wrong. A plaintiff is someone who has incurred damages and now disposes of the means to prove it. [...] In general, the plaintiff becomes a victim when no presentation is possible of the wrong he or she says he or she has suffered" (8). The Court turns a blind eye to any problems that do not coincide neatly and readily with one of the five grounds for asylum and demonstrates great difficulty in expanding its understanding of asylum to encompass the full range of women's lives, the full force of matrimonial convention. Only if she is granted asylum can a refugee *then* be allowed to reconstruct her identity in a way that does not force it into the categories of race, religion, nationality, membership in a particular social group, or political opinion. If denied asylum, however, the applicant may be returned to a country and to a legal system with which she has destroyed her link by testifying to its uselessness, even nefariousness, in her life. While the Court encounters little difficulty in denying Alvarado Peña's claims by conjuring her husband's voice, it cannot quite respond to the man's actions or to the phenomenon of domestic violence: "[w]e struggle to describe how deplorable we find the husband's conduct to have been" (*In re R-A-* 5). Alvarado Peña herself must describe what the Court finds indescribable and is subsequently faced with having her descriptions, her efforts to put the indescribable into words, used against her.

The Court's inability to describe domestic violence, apparently at odds with Alvarado Peña's ability to describe it (or rather in keeping with her "inability" to describe it), turns out to be a primary reason for denying asylum:

> For example, the perpetrators and victims of persecution because of race, religion, and political opinion typically understand and can explain the societal hatreds that lead to the harm or feared harm. We find it very difficult to accept the proposition that a persecutor targets person who qualify as refugees for reasons that neither the persecutor nor the victims have been shown to understand as playing any role in the persecution. (*In re R-A-* 24–25)

Incredibly, the Court faults Alvarado Peña for not being able to "understand" or "explain" her husband's actions, even though the Court itself finds these actions difficult, if not impossible, to describe. Yet the Court is willing to infer motives and intentions from Alvarado Peña's account of her husband's actions, and uses these words (which it does not believe that it fully understands) to rule against her, while at the same time faulting her for being unable to sufficiently establish Osorio's motives in harming her.[19] It is the Court that has no mechanisms for understanding Alvarado Peña's plight: it equates explaining with understanding and insists on dismissing Alvarado Peña's claim because she is unable to voice her suffering in a "rational" manner. The BIA denies asylum to Alvarado Peña because the motivations for Osorio's "inarguably atrocious human action" were "undetected by both the abuser and the victim" (*In re R-A-* 24). Alvarado Peña was persecuted not as a religious or racial minority, but rather, as a married Guatemalan woman. The crime of domestic violence *did* go "undetected" in her country of origin, leading to Alvarado Peña's quest for recognition in the U.S. courts after her failure to be granted that recognition in Guatemala. The BIA proves similarly unwilling to recognize her, failing to expand the language of the law to include a case of extreme domestic violence because it cannot easily process it in more or less established racial, religious, or political terms. It claims, quite flatly, that "the solution to the respondent's plight does not lie in our asylum laws as they are currently formulated" *(In re R-A-* 27).

Yet, as noted at the beginning of this chapter, asylum law is adjudicated on a case-by-case basis. The law is therefore *interpreted* on a case-by-case basis. It is within these laws, theoretically at least, to provide protection for Alvarado Peña, but in this decision the Court refuses to take that step, to interpret the letter of the law in a more encompassing manner. As if troubled by the implications, it couches its refusal in seemingly sympathetic rhetoric ("it is impossible not to feel sympathy"; "we struggle to describe how deplorable"), without recognizing that its very words call for the expansion of the law to include cases like Alvarado Peña's. Lyotard, again, offers insight into the problem by examining the concept of "differend":

> The differend is the unstable state and instant of language wherein something which must be able to be put into phrases cannot yet be. This state includes silence, which is a negative phrase, but it also calls upon phrases which are in principle possible. This state is signaled by what one ordinarily calls a feeling: "One cannot find the words," etc. A lot of searching must be done to find new rules for forming and linking phrases that are able to express the differend disclosed by the feeling, unless one wants this differend to be smothered right away in a litigation and for the alarm sounded by the feeling to have been useless. What is at stake in a literature, in a philosophy, in a politics perhaps is to bear witness to differends by finding idioms for them. (13)

The Court's "struggle to describe how deplorable" the situation is, its inability to fit into the letter of the law what has happened to Alvarado Peña, should indicate that "a lot of searching must be done to find new rules," that the interpretation of the law needs to be expanded. [20] The search for new idioms is in itself a political act, one that could save the life of Rodi Alvarado Peña and of countless women at once like and unlike her.

Works Cited

Alonso-Zaldivar, Ricardo and Jonathan Peterson. "5 on Immigration Board Asked to Leave; Critics Call it a Purge." *The Los Angeles Times*, March 12, 2003: A16.

Anker, Deborah E. *Law of Asylum in the United States.* 3rd ed. Boston: Refugee Law Center, Inc., 1999.

Bakhtin, Mikhail Mikhailovich. *Art and Answerability: Early Philosophical Es-*

says. Trans. Vadim Liapunov. Ed. Michael Holquist & Vadim Liapunov. Austin: University of Texas Press, 1990.

Egelko, Bob. "Ashcroft will pass asylum case to successor." *The San Francisco Chronicle*, January 22, 2005: B3.

Eisenberg, Marvin Aron. "Private Ordering Through Negotiation, Dispute Settlement and Rulemaking." *Harvard Law Review 89.637* (1976): 659–60.

Executive Office for Immigration Review. Fact Sheet; Biographical Information on Board Members. October 2003 (Revised). Available at http://www.usdoj.gov/eoir/fs/biabios.htm (accessed February 14, 2005).

Federal Register. "Asylum and Withholding Definitions, Proposed Rules." December 7, 2000. (Volume 65, Number 236): 76588–76598.

Hoffman, Eva. *Lost in Translation: A Life in a New Language.* New York: E.P. Dutton, 1989.

In re R-A-, Interim Dec. 3403 (BIA), 1999.

Kristeva, Julia. *Strangers to Ourselves.* New York: Colombia University Press, 1991.

Lardner, George P. "Ashcroft Reconsiders Asylum Granted to Abused Guatemalan." *The Washington Post*, March 3, 2003: A02.

Linarelli, John. "Violence Against Women and the Asylum Process." *Albany Law Review* 60 (1997): 977–987.

Lyotard, Jean François. *The Differend: Phrases in Dispute.* Trans. Geroges Van Den Abbeele. Minneapolis: University of Minnesota Press, 1988.

Minow, Martha. "Institutions and Emotions." *The Passions of Law.* Ed. Susan A. Bandes. New York: New York University Press, 1999. 265–281.

Musalo, Karen and Stephen Knight. "Unequal Protection." *Bulletin of Atomic Scientists* (November/December 2002): 57–61.

Office of the Attorney General. *Order No. 2379–2001, In re: Matter of Rodi Alvarado Peña,* January 19, 2001.

Pavel, Thomas. "Exile as Romance and as Tragedy." *Exile and Creativity.* Durham, N.C.: Duke University Press, 1996. 25–36.

Schrag, Philip G. *A Well Founded Fear: The Congressional Battle to Save Political Asylum in America.* New York: Routledge, 2000.

Sherman, Mark. "Beaten wife can stay in the U.S." *The Seattle Times*, January 22, 2005: A13.

Notes

1   *In re R-A-,* Int. Dec. 3403 (BIA 1999) 2. All other references to this text

will be included parenthetically as "In re R-A-." The decision can be found in the United States Department of Justice's website at http://www.usdoj .gov/eoir/efoia/bia/Decisions/Revdec/pdfDEC/3403.pdf. Page numbers are taken from this version of the document.

2   "The Board's [Board of Immigration Appeals] approach to its case law is markedly fact-specific; its decisions only infrequently state the kind of general rule or policy that may be clearly applied to the determination of other similar cases" (Anker 8).

3   Decision of the Immigration Judge at 2, *In the Matter of Rodi Adalí Alvarado-Peña* (September 20, 1996).

4   Decision of the Immigration Judge, 9, 12.

5   The publication of the decision is itself important. Anker details: "[The BIA] publishes as precedent a very small portion of its decision and the large majority of its precedent asylum decisions are denials, so there are few precedent examples of what is required to successfully establish a claim" (8).

6   Office of the Attorney General. *Order No. 2379–2001, In re: Matter of Rodi Alvarado Peña,* January 19, 2001.

7   The proposed regulations were written partially in response to the BIA's decision in Alvarado Peña's case and were meant to "aid in the assessment of claims made by applicants who have suffered or fear domestic violence." 65 Fed. Reg. 76,588 (December 7, 2000). Under the proposed regulations as drafted in 2000, Alvarado Peña would most likely be granted asylum. As his first act in office, George W. Bush signed an order placing on hold any regulations that had not yet taken effect, including these. Throughout John Ashcroft's tenure as Attorney General the regulations remained on hold. It remains to be seen whether the Department of Justice under Attorney General Alberto Gonzales will work with the Department of Homeland Security to finalize the regulations.

8   "Domestic Violence R-A-, The Story of Rodi Alvarado Peña" (online: web), updated August 31, 2004. Despite Reno's action overturning the decision, some judges continue to apply the negative precedent it established as justification to deny women asylum (Karen Musalo and Stephen Knight).

9   By speaking in the present tense when referring to *In re R-A-*, I do not mean to deny the historical quality of the document. My goal in speaking in the present tense is twofold; it is a way of marking the document as a literary "text" like any other, to be close-read in the present, and it is a way of indicating that this case is still very much "alive," not just for legal scholars, but for Alvarado Peña, who continues to await a decision on her future, and for others whose asylum claims depend on the ultimate outcome of this precedent setting case.

10 Executive Office for Immigration Review. Fact Sheet; Biographical Information on Board Members. October 2003 (Revised). Available at http://www.usdoj.gov/eoir/fs/biabios.htm (accessed February 14, 2005).

11 *In re R-A-*, 8, 9.

12 Alvarado Peña's case has garnered widespread attention and support. An *amicus brief* submitted to Attorney General Ashcroft in February of 2004 arguing for asylum for Alvarado Peña included the signature of 187 NGOs and law professors. Additionally, numerous members of the House and the Senate sent letters to Ashcroft supporting her case, and both Amnesty International and Human Rights First initiated 'actions' on her behalf. Most recently, during his confirmation hearings, Attorney General Alberto Gonzales was questioned specifically on this case and the pending regulations on which its outcome now depends.

13 As previously noted, in taking the highly unusual step of certifying the case to himself, John Ashcroft became the final arbiter of Alvarado Peña's future legal status (before returning the case to the BIA). In doing so, he promoted Alvarado Peña to the status of the ultimate token, as her story became the test case for gender-based persecution, with Alvarado Peña as the stand-in for all similarly situated victims, present and future.

14 John Linarelli, in his article "Violence against women and the asylum process," confirms: "The argument that recognizing the persecution of women in the asylum law would lead to a massive flight of women to the United States is unfounded. Since Canada promulgated its [gender] guidelines in March of 1993, the number of gender-based asylum claims there has not increased significantly, despite the fact that Canada appears to provide a more hospitable forum for these asylees than does the United States. Similarly, since the promulgation of INS's Gender Guidelines, there has been no real increase in the number of gender-based asylum claims in the United States. Asylees on the whole probably comprise the smallest group of immigrants."

15 After certifying the case of Rodi Alvarado Peña to himself, John Ashcroft issued an order on December 8, 2003 directing the "Department of Homeland Security and the Respondent" to "file briefs . . . on the eligibility of the respondent for relief under the Immigration and Nationality Act" (Office of the Attorney General. *Order No. 2696–2003, In re: Matter of Rodi Alvarado Peña*, December 8, 2003.) He was urged to order briefing due to the legal developments that had transpired in the years since the BIA decision. A brief is a written legal argument stating the legal reasons for the suggested resolution to the matter, based on statutes, regulations, case precedents, legal texts, and reasoning applied to facts in the particular situation. The briefs submitted by the parties provide a further example of the work of legal construction surrounding Alvarado Peña's memories. Until she is granted asylum, her story has and must remain static as the

legal arguments surrounding it shift to accommodate changes in the legal theories on the meaning of 'refugee.'

16 Thomas Pavel explores the meaning(s) of exile: "In its strict definition, exile is a penalty imposed by society . . . In modern times, the term is also applied to those who leave their native land of their own accord, as a precautionary measure against the threat of religious or political persecution ("political" here includes totalitarian persecution in the name of ideology, race, and social class)" (27). Eva Hoffman explores the personal effects of exile in her book *Lost in Translation*: "What has happened to me in this new world? I don't know. I don't see what I've seen, don't comprehend what's in front of me. I'm not filled with language anymore, and I have only a memory of fullness to anguish me with the knowledge that, in this dark and empty state, I don't really exist" (107).

17 At one point the court insists that while in a case involving a military abduction during a civil war "the political aspects of the conflict itself were readily apparent," in this case, it "simply has not been shown that political opinion or group membership can reasonably be understood as the motivation behind the spouse abuse." They cite the husband's other possible causes for abusing his wife, attributing it to everything from "jealousy" to "growing frustration with his own life" to the "inherent meanness of his own personality" (*In re R-A-* 25).

18 In contrast to the BIA decision, *In re R-A-*, the briefs filed with Attorney General John Ashcroft by the Department of Homeland Security, Alvarado Peña's counsel, and two amicus briefs all argue for societal attitudes and legal norms of the country of origin to be taken into account when considering the nexus requirement. *See* Department of Homeland Security's Position on Respondent's Eligibility for Relief *In re R-A-* at 35–36 (A 73 753 922) at 35–36; Brief (for respondent) on Behalf of Rodi Alvarado Peña to the Attorney General of the United States at 18–20 (A73 753 922); Advisory Opinion on International Norms: Gender Related Persecution and Relevance to "Membership of a Particular Social Group" and "Political Opinion" re: *Matter of Rod Alvarado Peña* at 9–11 (A73 753 922); Brief of *Amici Curiae* in Support of Affirmance of Decision of the Immigration Judge *In re R-A-* at 26 (A73 753 922). All four briefs support asylum for Rodi Alvarado Peña. Most notably, after eight years of the government arguing against asylum for Alvarado Peña, the Department of Homeland Security's brief marks a reversal of their position. This reversal continues to impact Alvarado Peña's future; immediately following Ashcroft's decision to return her case to the BIA, a spokesperson for the Department of Homeland Security announced that DHS would not seek Alvarado Peña's removal from the U.S. were she to be denied asylum by the BIA a second time (Sherman). This would only be a partial victory for Alvarado Peña, as she would not be able to bring her children to the U.S. if her status re-

mained uncertain (under current immigration law, if she received asylum, she would then be able to bring her children to the U.S.). DHS' offer to refrain from removing Alvarado Peña may ultimately save her life, but it would not offer her the privileges that come with legal recognition. Their humanitarian gesture still locates Alvarado Peña's plight outside of the realm of the protections afforded by asylum law.

19 "In our judgment, it remains for the respondent to establish an evidentiary record from which we may reasonably infer that a qualifying motive led, at least in part, to the harm she suffered, and this she has failed to do" (*In re R-A-* 26).

20 The Proposed Rule discussed in footnote 7, written in the wake of the BIA decision, served as an expression of the Department of Justice's understanding of the law as it applies to asylum based on domestic violence. This document acknowledges that a successful asylum claim can be based on persecution in the form of domestic violence. As of January 2005, the proposed rule had not yet been finalized, and Alvarado Peña continued awaiting word on her ultimate fate.

13

"Yo no estoy perdida": Immigrant Women (Re)locating Citizenship

Kathleen M. Coll

Substantive first-class citizenship is not simply achieved, even after formal rights are granted by the state. Citizens can be socially, politically, or economically marginalized because of race, immigrant status, gender, sexuality, social class, religion, or disability. For non-citizen immigrants, formal exclusion from citizenship makes claiming belonging and entitlement especially complex, both in regards to their nation of origin and their states of residence. Seen from these positions, citizenship includes, but is not defined by, an exclusive and powerful bundle of legal rights and relationships between individuals, groups, and states. Cultural citizenship becomes a multilayered[1] and multifaceted process of continual assertion and re-articulation of oneself and one's community as full social and political members (Flores, Rosaldo). This process is also usually contested, may be conflict-ridden, and always exists in dynamic relationship with the disciplinary forces of history and state institutions (Lowe, Ngai, Ong).

By insisting on the "cultural" aspect of citizenship and the need to theorize newly recognized collectivities of citizens such as Latinos/as, immigrants, the disabled, and gays and lesbians, scholars—including Rina Benmayor, William Flores, and Renato Rosaldo—redefine the exclusionary categories of citizenship. This understanding of cultural citizenship insists on Latina/os' place(s) in the body politic as well as on the importance, to the articulation of new citizen-subjects, of staking claims on state and society (Flores and Benmayor). Nira Yuval-Davis refers to the convergence of subjectivity, emotion, and citizenship as "the politics of belonging" (Yuval-Davis, "Gendered Citizenship"). Cultural citizenship and the politics of belonging highlight the processes and practices that incorporate dynamics of institutional discipline and individual agency with collective issues of inequality, belonging, and rights.

The dynamic relationships between intimate and collective processes underpinning social change are difficult to identify and articulate if our analysis focuses primarily on formal statist politics and institutions. Understanding citizenship in its many valences entails analyzing how domestic lives and relationships are bound up in our experiences of—and our capacity to participate in—society and politics. Which realms of conflict, contest, and affect figure into people's sense of belonging on the ground in everyday life? Refiguring citizenship requires taking our subjects seriously as analysts of their own situation and attending to their citizenship stories in collective political and historical context (Coll, "Necesidades y problemas").

This chapter draws on ethnographic research to show how members of a group of Latin American immigrant women related developments in their political subjectivity to experiences of transgression. When confronted with disappointment and betrayal, they challenged previously imposed limits in order to participate in the collective processes of a women's community organization, while also contesting roles and relations in their families and households.[2] Women who were quite different in many other ways had strikingly similar stories of deception when, after fulfilling the responsibilities of their traditional roles as good wives, mothers, and in-laws, they still found themselves treated with disrespect, disregard, and in some cases, serious abuse at the hands of intimates. These sentiments paralleled their disappointment when, in spite of their sense of themselves as hard-working, law-abiding, social contributors in the United States, they found themselves caught in the hostility against immigrants in 1990s California.

Narratives highlight the women's ways of making sense of their life stories as more than tales of personal development. These narratives cannot be reduced to mere progress stories of female empowerment after emigration or divorce, or to liberal tales of coming to regard oneself as an autonomous, rights-bearing political subject.[3] Instead, the women I met in the course of this research emphasized the centrality of—and interrelationship between—experiences of transformations in community life, friendship, and family/household relations to their coming to feel a sense of individual and collective belonging in the U.S. These stories tack back and forth, chronicling how transgression and transformation in intimate life and public practices of citizenship fed one another in a dynamic and mutually enabling fashion.

Studying with *Mujeres Unidas y Activas*

From 1996 to 1999, I participated in the meetings and community projects of a grassroots organization of Latin American immigrant women in San Francisco.[4] The majority of the members of *Mujeres Unidas y Activas* (United and Active Women) came from Mexico and Central America, spoke only Spanish, had fewer than eight years of formal education, and struggled economically with very low household incomes in high-tech boom-era San Francisco. The priorities of *Mujeres Unidas* included popular political education and collective action as Latinas, as well as work in coalition with other groups around issues of welfare reform, social service provision, and immigrant political rights. The majority of women had not previously participated in social movements in their countries of origin or in the United States. They also reported that *Mujeres Unidas* provided them with a regular opportunity to get outside of their cramped and crowded apartments, to find a break from daily work and responsibilities, and to learn both from the experiences of women with whom they shared similar backgrounds and concerns and from others whose personal and social histories greatly differed from their own.

In addition to regular peer support and informational/educational meetings on wide-ranging topics, the group organized a home-health-care/domestic work training and referral agency.[5] More importantly, in terms of numbers of members involved at any given time, the organization mobilized both women and men in the community to act collectively on issues of shared concern. Examples of such actions were as diverse as intervening with an elementary school principal on behalf of a member and her child, performing popular political theater pieces about one's rights under "immigration reform," accompanying a newcomer to the police station to file a restraining order or to the public housing office for an application, carrying out door-to-door voter registration and education campaigns in immigrant neighborhoods, and traveling by the busload to the state capital to lobby for public service provision.

The group's weekly meetings and day-to-day operations, furthermore, always emphasized the importance of the emotional and personal issues facing members. One striking feature of the women's stories was how experiences of disappointment and betrayal in the family and household units formed with husbands, children, in-laws, and strangers in San Francisco provoked further transgressions and transformations in their lives. The women whose stories I relate here had very different public personas, economic situations, and immigration statuses, yet in each of their stories, they related that unmet expectations about family life and marriage had in some way led them to the women's group. Each woman explained how her participation in *Mujeres Unidas*, with its emphasis on peer support and dialogue combined with political education, leadership development, and direct community action, had changed the way she saw herself in relationships to not only her family members but the larger community.

The venture across national boundaries as immigrants was one of many kinds of transgressions these women risked in seeking out sources of support and respect, and in finding ways to contribute socially through their own labor. They spoke of the particular importance, in the process, of finding opportunities for understanding and analyzing their situation in the company of other immigrant women. The evocative words of particular women illustrated broader themes that came up in interviews, group discussions, and informal conversations and which likely represent products of collective dialogues and experiences shared by women in this organization over extended periods of time. These themes included betrayal and disaffection with stressful or abusive family roles and dynamics, the importance of peer support in seeking out new relationships, and the value women placed on learning new skills and gaining access to good information on a variety of topics. Images of crossing feared boundaries were prominent, as women sought to maintain certain aspects of their self-image as respectable, virtuous adult women in gendered senses that might seem to preclude the kinds of major and minor changes women actually achieved in their home and work lives, and as engaged community members.

This chapter focuses on women who came to understand themselves as positive social and economic contributors in the United States, deserving and demanding of respect as individuals and collectively as Latina immigrants. This was hardly an uncontested claim for low-income, non-citizen, or non-"legal" immigrants to make at that particular moment. It was also a particularly challenging position for women in very precarious legal and economic situations to take. Their stories marked a major contrast to contemporary media representations and political configurations in California at the time in which immigrants of color were portrayed as politically, culturally, and legally marginal to U.S. society. During the mid-1990s, three statewide ballot initiatives sought to cut public services to the undocumented, to eliminate bilingual education, and to end affirmative action in state institutions.⁶ The Proposition 187 "Save Our State" initiative campaign in 1994 exemplified the intensity of the political conflict in which immigrants found themselves. In one "Letter to the Editor" of *The New York Times*, the campaign media director for the so-called "Save Our State" initiative promoted their agenda on the national stage, declaring California and the United States at risk of a "*reconquista*" from the south:

> Proposition 187 is . . . a logical step toward saving California from economic ruin. Illegal aliens collect welfare payments through post office boxes in San Ysidro, just a 15-minute walk from Mexico. They receive free medical care and flood schools with non-English speaking students. By flooding the state with 2 million illegal aliens to date, and increasing that figure each of the following 10 years, Mexicans in California would number 15 million to 20 million by 2004. During those 10 years about 5 million to 8 million Californians would have emigrated to other states. If these trends continued, a Mexico-controlled California could vote to establish Spanish as the sole language of California, 10 million more English-speaking Californians could flee, and there could be a statewide vote to leave the Union and annex California to Mexico. (Hayes)

After voters approved the measure, Proposition 187 was enjoined by the courts and never took effect. However, it did set the political tone for the rest of the decade and paved the way for the passage of later anti-affirmative action and anti-bilingual education measures. During the same period, national welfare and immigration "reforms" sought further to exclude poor people and immigrants from basic entitlements at the national level. These policies eliminated the entitlement to economic supports for poor parents, which had been in place since the Great Depression, and shifted more than thirty years of emphasis in U.S. immigration policy on family reunification.⁷

It helps to know this context in order to understand the relevance of talking about citizenship with respect to non-citizen immigrants' claims for belonging, for rights, and for a legitimate place in a nation-state that defines them as essentially illegitimate and therefore as non-persons. Immigrants were being attacked semiotically and politically for their physical and cultural presence and their reproductive potential. The impact of such policy and discourse on immigrant lives and subjectivity was profound. In the words of one *Mujeres Unidas* member: "Esta es una guerra psicológica en contra de los inmigrantes" ("This is a psychological war against immigrants"). The intersections between such public assaults and the private conflicts and stressors faced by women and their families highlighted the structural issues underlying subjective experiences. For some women, participating in the women's group and in public acts of resistance to the anti-immigrant movement engendered changes in household dynamics and division of labor. For others, conflicts and change at home provoked them to search out new social supports and tools for understanding and improving their situation.

Community groups like *Mujeres Unidas* were among the few spaces in which many people felt safe speaking out about the political climate. Women's collective claims to belonging emerged from both peer support group discussions and larger collective political acts. In this tense moment for immigrants, women spoke movingly about how they came to claim respect, dignity, and services. They located these processes in their experiences of dialogue and activism with other women, and the resulting analyses that emerged relating to their social position as women, Latinas, immigrants, workers, and mothers. My findings from this research[8] resonated with similar observations made earlier in the 1990s by the *El Barrio Project* in East Harlem about their mainly Puerto Rican women participants, namely that "it was the affirmation of their identity, strength, and sense of entitlement" in community with other immigrant women that formed the basis for women's sense of their own "cultural citizenship" (Benmayor iii).

"I am not lost": Caridad Navarro

When I interviewed Caridad Navarro in 1996, she was 41 and had lived in San Francisco for more than twenty years after immigrating with a teenage friend from their small lakeside village in Jalisco, a western state of Mexico. Before being temporarily disabled by a stress-induced illness, Caridad had been a unionized hotel housekeeper in downtown San Francisco, earning a living wage and receiving health benefits for herself and her four children. In 1994, Caridad had separated from her husband after almost twenty years of marriage. Her eldest daughter was studying and working in Los Angeles, one teenage son was living with his father, and she was sharing with her other two children a room in an apartment whose living room, one other bedroom, and back-porch entryway were occupied by seven other immigrants who also shared the kitchen and bathroom. In early 1996, Caridad began working in a garment factory until it shut down like the majority of large textile manufacturers in San Francisco. She began cleaning houses and providing home-care for elders—intermittent work without benefits or a union salary. However, the hours did allow her to attend weekly women's group meetings and to be home many afternoons with her elementary school-aged daughter.

Caridad, a long-term legal permanent resident, was eligible for citizenship and wanted to naturalize. She even tried to attend a citizenship course with me one day at a neighborhood branch library, but the non-profit group which offered the classes cancelled this session at the last minute without notice. Caridad feared the formal application process and the written and oral naturalization exams, and doubted her ability to memorize the answers to what seemed like hundreds of sample questions provided to applicants. We went over the questions once together, but she became even more discouraged when she realized that I myself knew few of the answers. Caridad had a few years of elementary education in rural Mexico, and spoke minimal work-related English. She remembered that she had wanted to continue her schooling as a child, but that the parish priest had warned her single mother that it was not safe for a girl to walk the long distances to the rural school.

In our interview, Caridad discussed her attitude towards everyday community organizing, and how her own views of women's organizations like *Mujeres* had changed since she began participating in the group a few years earlier. Caridad was not a dynamic, highly visible leader, but a soft-spoken, quiet, constant presence in the group. A solid foundational member, her personal warmth, willing smile, and openness to new people and new ideas drew others to her. Caridad spoke of the multiple levels of resistance she had faced in herself and from her family about her participation in the women's group and traced her eventual arrival at *Mujeres Unidas* to the emotional fallout following her separation from her husband.

When Caridad was 19, she moved with her young husband and his family to the Bay Area because he had found good work in construction. They had four healthy children, but Caridad reported that even after their eldest daughter had entered school and she had more time during the day, her husband blocked her efforts to return to school to study English, much as her mother and priest had done when she was a child. Caridad reported that the family dynamics were even more

strained because they always lived with her husband's family, who criticized and demeaned her while her husband never came to her defense.
She said that she put up with years of verbal mistreatment, but that
ended the day her husband slapped her in the face because of "lies" her
in-laws had told him about her. "I said, okay, I have put up with a lot
of things but I will not put up with being slapped. So I dialed 9-1-1."[9]
Caridad's mother-in-law cried and called Caridad a bad woman as her
son was taken away by the police. Caridad took her four children and
left the next day. She rented the same room she continues to live in today. "It's not a bed of roses, but compared to that place, I am good."[10]

At first, Caridad did not feel so good about leaving. When she filed
the police report, she sobbed so much that she could not speak. The
police officer tried to convince her to speak to a psychologist. "I said,
no, I don't believe in those people!"[11] she recalled, chuckling at her
own resistance. The departmental psychologist gave her the name and
address of *Mujeres Unidas* but she told them, "I don't believe in that."[12]
Eventually, though, a woman friend did bring her to the group, though
she stopped again outside the building, resisting entry. The group
meets in a large women's community center in the overlapping territory between San Francisco's Latino Mission and gay Castro districts.
By the 1990s, a visible community of lesbian households and businesses had developed in this area.

> I told her, I will not go into that building, because they are per-
> verse women. "No," she said. "The third floor belongs to the
> Latinas." "Hmm, well, let's see what it's about," so I came and
> I liked the group. They are not perverse. They are people like
> me, who have suffered, have had experiences. One day I told
> the group, you know why I didn't come? For this reason, and
> that reason, and everyone died of laughter. We all think the
> same thing—that we are degenerates, that we are women who
> do drugs . . . we all have bad thoughts about such women, but
> now I invite a lot of women (to join the group, too).[13]

It is important to note there were openly lesbian members of the
group, one FTM transgender member who still lived as a woman, and
that several important supporters of the group from the umbrella
immigrant rights coalition were lesbians who were held in high es-
teem and treated with great affection. In other words, Caridad alludes
clearly to homophobia as a force preventing women from meeting and

working autonomously, yet she is also challenging the conflation of perversion with lesbian and gay identity. To say, "they are not perverse" or "degenerates" does not mean "we are all straight," in this context. Rather, they are all transgressors who have crossed boundaries of nation, gender, language, and sexuality and in invoking this memory and laughing together with her peers, she challenges the notion that transgression is wrong, undesirable, or unseemly.

In the end, the chance to relax, to release troubles through talk,[14] and to learn new and important things were what kept Caridad coming back. Caridad explained that access to "buena información" ("good information") on topics as wide-ranging as child-rearing, immigration law, and public housing rules kept her returning to group meetings and activities until she became more politically committed to the organization and its work. "Información" became the currency she employed to organize other women she encountered in her day-to-day life, as she engaged them in meaningful exchanges about life, politics, and their rights. In a 1996 interview, Caridad contrasted her current views of herself and the group with the presuppositions about *Mujeres* that she had held before she began participating:

> Well, I always like to inform people, to talk with someone I know when we're riding the bus together, or if someone starts talking to me, to give them information. For example, I like to invite women I meet to *Mujeres*, especially the ones who are mistaken [erradas] like I [was], and are thinking that a lot of people criticize us. It hurts me a lot that they have said this to my face, "No, that's for women with nothing better to do (no home to care for), that's for women whose husbands have left them. That's for women who have lost their way in life."[15]

Though Caridad began her comments with what was apparently a politically neutral introduction about the importance of sharing "information,"[16] she then went on to challenge directly the highly charged forms of social discipline that she and other women experience and exercise over one another, practices and beliefs that actually serve as obstacles to participation in a progressive women's organization. "The woman is in the house, the woman should not be out in the street, and if you are in the street, it's because you are looking for another man. And you have to cook and you have to clean. That is hell. It is hell."[17] Husbands, in-laws, friends, all had offered such running commentaries in those days that had undermined her capacity to go to school, to participate socially and in groups with other women. These arguments were potent with respect to gender and sexuality, respectability, and shame, engendering fear of the social-change potential of autonomous women. "Eso es para mujeres que no tienen qué hacer" literally means "That's for women with nothing better to do" but also "That's for women without housework to do," in other words, for women without even homes in which they can labor as respectable housewives. In the double meaning of "lost"—"Eso es para mujeres dejadas por el marido. Eso es para mujeres que ya andan muy perdidas" ("That is for women abandoned by their husbands, women who've lost their bearings")—these women are both pathetic and threatening, thought to have gone out of control sexually as well as socially.

In response to these discourses of social control and limitations on women's participation, Caridad mobilized her resources for respectability to defend her right to participate in community life and women's organizing, summing up again the negative sanctions as another example of lack of information among women in the community:

> I say, no, I am not lost. Yes, I defend myself. I tell them that they are misinformed. Look, I say to them, "I have my children, and where I live I am in charge of cleaning, I have to cook." People criticize me because they see me in the street but now I say, "What's it to you?" I walk around, I do my duties at home, AND I come to *Mujeres*. It fits my schedule and doesn't cause me any trouble. I still feed my children, clean my house, even if I have to do it at night, or really late at night. I do everything and I can come here. Because I am very hardworking.[18]

Caridad located her legitimacy to carry out a public practice of citizenship in her ability to live up to exactly the traditional gender-role responsibilities that usually preclude women's full social and political participation. She inverted the perspective on who should pity whom, and focuses a sympathetic organizer's eye on those who continue to be "erradas" ("totally mistaken") in their beliefs, reaching out to them with more "information."

Caridad narrated a counter-discourse to the hegemonic anti-immigrant, anti-poor people, and anti-woman public rhetoric of that moment. Her ability to fully practice her citizenship was contingent on transforming the ideas and practices of formal institutions that excluded her and of fellow immigrants who diverted one another from activism through informal negative sanctions. While Caridad's political work with *Mujeres Unidas* has focused on reforming state policies on immigration, welfare, housing, and education, she emphasized the importance of personal experiences and relationships to her eventual willingness to transgress social norms and overcome her own fears about breaking rules and making change. This was not a discourse of individual change as primary or as a necessary precursor to institutional change. Instead, it represents Caridad's attention to the very thorny question of the role of the subjective in shaping one's capacity to engage institutions and make social change. Through unpacking such intimate life experiences and how women process them, we can begin to understand what might distinguish a creative transgressor like Caridad from peers or family members who try to dissuade her from changing or developing skills and capacities.

Understanding cultural citizenship as a dynamic process also means allowing for change and development in families and relationships over time. Few women I interviewed saw their husbands, even when there had been abuse, as incapable of change. For most, a decision to leave meant immediate financial hardship for them and their children, even homelessness, and many had passed through the one women's shelter in the city that focused on serving battered Latinas and their children. Caridad did not identify herself as a survivor of domestic violence, having left the relationship at the first sign of physical abuse. She did maintain her distance from her husband for many years after leaving him, while supporting his ongoing relationship with his children and accepting the financial support he offered with occasional gifts of money passed to her through their children. Several years after I interviewed her, Caridad reconciled with her husband and he and their son came to live in the room Caridad had rented on her own years before. Caridad reported at that time that she was pleased because the nature of their relationship had changed as a result of their years of separation and her own development. She added that life for her and her children was much better with their father in the home.

For the women I interviewed, becoming more independent ("independizarse") was important for forging family and social relationships that supported rather than diminished their sense of belonging and entitlement in the broader society as well as in their own households. For many, like Caridad, separating from partners and kin-based households required relocating and learning where and how to find adequate material support for their children, renting rooms in their own name, and paying bills that they may not have managed previously. Rather than a goal of "independence" for its own sake, women spoke of "independizándose" ("becoming independent") as a foundation for healthier intimate relationships as well as more positive senses of themselves.

"Putting everything in my name": Tomasa Hernández

Caridad was not the only woman to vigorously defend her domesticity in her interview "in spite of" her participation in *Mujeres Unidas*. Other women also located their legitimacy and legibility as political agents in their mastery at fulfilling traditional gender-roles in their households. They cited their facility with domestic labor and duty as the basis for claims for fair treatment by kin, equality in decision-making about children and money, and autonomy for themselves, what I refer to as domestic citizenship. Their tales of domestic citizenship meshed with accounts of engagement in a community organization where supporting and organizing other immigrant Latinas resulted in highly public and political acts. Women participated in collective interventions with public schools on behalf of members' children, developed popular theater pieces for grassroots education on the impact of national immigration reforms, and lobbied local elected officials to mitigate the impact of federal cutbacks in welfare and social services, among other activities. How were the stories proving themselves to be dutiful wives, mothers, and homemakers in the "private" sphere related to these "public" acts of citizenship? It was through the process of collective reflection, dialogue, and analysis in which the women participated in *Mujeres Unidas,* as much as through the public organizing activities, that women came to see the connections between problems and issues in their "private" lives with structural and institutional analyses of their collective situation as immigrants and Latinas in the United States. Tomasa Hernández's story offers one vivid example.

Tomasa Hernández was in her late 30s and had lived in San Francisco for two decades when we first spoke at length about these issues in 1998. She was just sixteen when she migrated, coincidently, from the same region of Jalisco as Caridad. She came without much forethought, almost as an adventure with a childhood friend, with hopes of being able to send money home to her parents and siblings. When I met Tomasa she was known as one of the group's founding members because she had begun attending the women's group even before it was institutionalized as *Mujeres Unidas*. She was among its most vocal leaders, and projected an air of confidence and self-possession. She had six children, one grandson, and a boyfriend she loved very much.

Tomasa did not appear to be preoccupied with social conventions. At the time of our interview she was pregnant and homeless, living with her whole family on the sofas of various friends while she and her boyfriend looked for a room they could afford together. Tomasa was always dressed in hip urban sportswear, ready to dance at a party, lead the cheers at a rally, and was outgoing and friendly on the street and within the women's organization as well. Walking around the neighborhood with her, I noticed how she enthusiastically greeted people she knew, including a flamboyant neighborhood drag queen, with waves, kisses, and questions about their well-being. She was an expert at the Mexican verbal art of the *albur*, or good-natured back and forth sexual humor that culminates in one party cleverly out-joking the other, usually at her or his expense. As the object of many of Tomasa's good-hearted but quite pointed *albures*, I knew her as an intellectually powerful figure who projected confidence with her own sexuality and comfort with others' differences as well. This is why it was something of a revelation to me to hear her narrate her own history with a powerful emphasis on very traditional ideas about gender roles.

Though she had left her first husband several years before I met her, Tomasa emphasized how that relationship was critical to transforming her sense of her own rights and autonomy. As Tomasa talked about her first marriage, she shook her head, marveling at how she'd been so confused by her husband's anger towards her, even though she had done everything she was supposed to do as a good wife and mother. At several points, she returned to this same unresolved contradiction in her mind. How could he have treated her so badly when she was living up to all her responsibilities in the home and with their children? She had been raised to believe that it would be enough to care well for her children, husband, and home; yet no matter how clean her home, how well-groomed her children, or how good her meals, she could not win her husband's affection or regard:

> I would pray to God, asking why I loved him if he was so bad to me? And always, I had always been a clean woman, a cooking woman, a woman who always had her children well groomed, even if their clothes were modest, they were always clean. They always go to school clean, very clean. I've never

wanted to be someone that others tell, "Ma'am, your daughter is dirty, you need to change her." No. They were always clean, always bathed, and fed three times a day. The bathrooms in the apartments where I have lived, I clean those bathrooms daily. They are very clean, because of all the sicknesses that are out there. And also so that everything is sanitary. I always cleaned the bathrooms daily, daily, daily, daily; one has to always be cleaning. The stove was always clean. Everything.[19]

In her stories about that period of her life, she returns to her ritualized role as the good housewife, remembering every detail of her efforts, to remind herself how hard she tried, and how the violence she experienced was not her fault. Tomasa's insistence on hygiene and cleanliness was not only the affirmation of a proper performance by an ideal wife and mother; it was a counter-discourse to the culturally dominant representations of immigrants to the United States and their children as unkempt and unsanitary rather than properly hygienic citizen material. However, the discourse of traditional gender roles and domestic hygiene was a dead-end for her in that it alone did not help her understand the cycle of violence and substance abuse in her marriage.

When a neighbor noticed her struggles with violence at home and reached out to her, Tomasa agreed to accompany her to the precursor group that eventually became *Mujeres Unidas*. She explained that it was through participating in the women's group discussions and organized leadership trainings that she developed a conceptual framework from which to reevaluate and change her situation. The way she came to understand her own feelings and social position was neither individualistic nor apolitical. Rather, she came to see herself in the context of economic and political factors such as the systematic practice of discrimination against Latinos/as and contemporary anti-immigrant sentiment:

And when I took those [leadership] trainings [about immigrant rights] and I saw more women with problems and I saw that I wasn't the only one suffering . . . So I said, "Here I have to change because this doesn't have to continue like this." So it was like that little plant that when you give it some water, when you water it, you are giving it life, you are giving it the opportunity to flower, to grow, like a guide that keeps growing. So that's how I see my life since I started coming here until now. Because now I am a woman who, with all my problems, has moved forward with my six children. Although we have gone through many things, problems, they have given me trouble and many things have happened, but I think that if I weren't here in the group, if I didn't have all the information that I have now, I think I would be a ruined woman.[20]

Knowing Tomasa after she had been through all of these struggles and processed them herself and with her peers, it was difficult for me to imagine her as the wilted flower she described. Indeed, Tomasa cited immigration at an early age and the resulting isolation from her own family and friends as the source of her vulnerability. "I was so scared of being alone, so scared. I had never felt such fear before."[21] She emphasized the importance of the combination of good information combined with collective dialogue, support, and activism in her own story of transformation. Tomasa cited "putting everything in my name" ("poniendo todo a mi nombre") as an important and risky series of steps she took after joining the women's group. Not long after she began attending meetings, she began to allow herself to trust others outside of her home and family, including her welfare caseworker. Tomasa told the social worker of her difficulty in getting her husband to turn over the benefits checks to her to feed and clothe her children: "He would threaten me. Since I didn't know my rights or anything, he'd say to me, 'If you don't give me the money, I'll go to the social worker and tell them to take it from you.' And I said, 'If they take it away from me, what are the children going to eat?'"[22]

Not only did the social worker remove her husband's name from the checks, but when Tomasa went to the next women's group meeting and shared her experience at the welfare office, her peers told her she could also change the telephone and utility bills, and even the apartment, to her name. She then embarked on a whole series of transgressions—crossing over previous boundaries that had seemed mysterious and even frightening:

Oooh. I felt so happy when they told me that! Well, later he got mad. "You think you're something because you have everything in your name!" After, I began training myself to be like the father and mother at the same time. But I did feel I was bearing a very heavy burden. I would say, "Go pay the rent?

Me?" Even just going, because he never let me go anyplace so I didn't know where to go to pay anything. I did know what street it was, but the first time I went to pay rent, I was so scared. Trembling![23]

For Tomasa, her willingness to break her husband's rules and attend the new women's group, as well as her subsequent capacity to risk transgression and trust in peer solidarity, allowed for major change in her life. She shared these developments with peers in the group at the time and in subsequent years to collectivize her experience, to inform, and to prompt further dialogue with other women. It was years later that she finally separated from her husband. Tomasa herself had never been willing to complain to the police because her husband was in the process of applying for legal permanent residency. She was concerned for him and for how it might affect his application for residency. Although she laughed self-consciously at having worried about *him*, she continues to feel sympathy and solidarity with the father of her children.

As did many other women, Tomasa infused her personal narrative with commentary on the legal and economic structures shaping the course of her own, her family's, and other immigrants' lives. Tomasa spoke of the stresses immigration and illegality impose on immigrant men like her husband, who had always thought he would be able to support his children through his own hard work, but to whom economic opportunities were not available as an uneducated, non-English speaking worker of color. Tomasa refused to make excuses for his behavior, but believed that this stress, the discrimination he experienced, and his sense of powerlessness over his own life contributed to his abusive behavior to her. In the course of her interview, she also made reference to the 1994 Violence Against Women Act, which she had once hoped would (but later was told by an attorney would not) allow her to legalize as the common-law wife of a battering legal permanent resident. In addition, she referred to her and many other women's terrible fears of the 245i clause ("La 245") of the 1996 immigration reforms that provides for ten year bans on re-entry to the U.S. for anyone found to have lived illegally in the United States. Tomasa learned about these laws and policies in the women's group, where she also participated in numerous dialogues among members about how different group members experienced such structural forces and discipline in their own lives, as well as in many organizing and outreach efforts aimed at informing other immigrants and working to change such policies and practices.

Personal Transgressions and Social Transformation

Our analyses of politics and contest, legal entitlements and rights, law and culture need to address the ways that subjectivity, intimate relationships, and the affective realm factor into people's relationships to the state as well as to one another. Tomasa and Caridad shared with other members of their community organization a vernacular of citizenship, rights, and entitlement that they improvised and elaborated in individual as well as group narratives. They insisted on the importance of gaining autonomy and influence in the family and household, and the particular importance of issues of language, culture, economics, and gender in their daily lives. They did not emphasize personal transformations in consciousness over and above group political action. Rather, by struggling for voice simultaneously in intimate and public, individual, and collective contexts, their understanding of political agency emphasized claiming legal rights, positively contributing to one's community through service, and necessarily some transformation of household and personal relationships as part of this process.

These women's stories and experiences represent gendered notions of citizenship that extend beyond the stratified and ritualized realm of state-oriented politics, even as they are enacted on the ground tangibly and consequentially in real political contest at home and in the local community. If we take these seriously as both theoretical and practical interventions, what happens to state hegemony over the boundaries of national belonging and political agency? At the very least we expand the range of realms and discourses that are relevant to our analyses of politics, agency, and the transformation of political subjectivity.

Highly personal stories map women's processes of political transformation and development as grassroots community activists. Narrators constitute their social roles and rights in part through the repetitive invocation of identities that make sense in the context of the governing rules about what constitutes a legitimate citizen-subject.[24] I use the self-consciously "impure"[25] shorthand of "domestic citizenship" to call attention to the diverse and distinctly gendered struggles women face and the narratives they construct about their intimate relationships and households as part of their coming to participate in publicly enacted collective claims against the state.

These renditions of citizenship that are produced at the community level highlight, without reinscribing, the public/private, domestic/political realms of contest over personhood and citizenship. They offer opportunities to retheorize citizenship, nationality, and global systems of power and inequality in ways that account for subjective experiences like family relations and personal transformation. As we reconsider what constitutes resistance in the face of the bleak hegemonic ideologies and global forces of today, Caridad Navarro, Tomasa Hernández, and their colleagues offer important analytical interventions and exemplary daily practices of citizenship. It is harder to despair and more reasonable to hope for a reinvigoration of what it means to belong, feel entitled, and contribute to this society when Caridad assures us that she "is not lost" and Tomasa articulates that despite all appearances, she is hardly "a ruined woman." Such complex, resistant discourses of subjectivity are closely tied to women's capacity to act collectively and politically and offer both political and analytical "resources for hope" through a feminist rearticulation of cultural citizenship and a new politics of belonging (Pratt).

Works Cited

Benmayor, Rina, Rosa M. Torruellas, Ana L. Juarbe. *Responses to Poverty Among Puerto Rican Women: Identity, Community, and Cultural Citizenship.* New York: Centro de Estudios Puertorriqueños, Hunter College, 1992.

Butler, Judith. *Gender Trouble: Feminism and the Subversion of Identity.* New York: Routledge, 1990.

_____. *Bodies That Matter: On the Discursive Limits of Sex.* New York: Routledge, 1993.

Coll, Kathleen. *Motherhood and Cultural Citizenship: Organizing Latina Immigrants in San Francisco, California.* Diss., Stanford University, 2000.

_____. "Necesidades y problemas: Immigrant Latina Vernaculars of Belonging, Coalition, & Citizenship in San Francisco, California." *Latino Studies* 2.2 (2004): 186–209.

Cruikshank, Barbara. *The Will to Empower: Democratic Citizens and Other Subjects.* Ithaca, N.Y.: Cornell University Press, 1999.

Flores, William, and Rina Benmayor. *Latino Cultural Citizenship.* Boston: Beacon, 1997.

Hayes, Linda B. Letter. "California's Prop. 187." The *New York Times,* October 15, 1994: A18.

Lowe, Lisa. *Immigrant Acts.* Durham, N.C.: Duke University Press, 1996.

Ngai, Mae M. *Impossible Subjects: Aliens and the Making of Modern America.* Princeton, N.J.: Princeton University Press, 2004.

Ong, Aihwa. "Cultural Citizenship as Subject-Making." *Current Anthropology* 37. 5 (1996): 737–762.

Pratt, Mary Louise. Address. Symposium on Gender and Cultural Citizenship. New York University. October 2002.

Rosaldo, Renato. "Cultural Citizenship in San José, California." *PoLAR: Political and Legal Anthropology Review* 17.2 (1994): 57–63.

Weston, Kath. *Render Me, Gender Me: Lesbians Talk Sex, Class, Color, Nation, Studmuffins.* New York: Columbia University Press, 1996.

Yuval-Davis, Nira. "The 'Multi-Layered Citizen': Citizenship in the Age of Glocalization." *International Feminist Journal of Politics* 1.1 (1999): 119–136.

_____. "Gendered Citizenship and the Politics of Belonging." *Symposium on Gender, Cultural Citizenship, and the Nation.* University of California, Santa Cruz, 2002.

Notes

1   This phrase owes much to, but is also distinct from, Nira Yuval-Davis' formulation of "multilayered citizenship" as involving levels of membership and belonging, from the local to ethnic to national and transnational ("The 'Multilayered Citizen'").

2   I distinguish between family and household relationships because most of the women I encountered in this research shared close living quarters with extended kin, in-laws, friends and/or strangers.

3   For a critical feminist analysis of the concept and strategy of "empowerment" as deployed in late-twentieth century social movements, see Cruikshank.

4   The ethnographic fieldwork on which this essay is based was part of a larger project on cultural citizenship, immigration, and women's grassroots political participation (Coll, *Motherhood and Cultural Citizenship*).

5   The "Manos Cariñosas/Caring Hands" project was open to members with six months or more of participation in the group and participants in this project attend weekly meetings of their own for ongoing support, usually in addition to participating in other group activities. Many women reported to me that they first visited the organization's office in the hopes of finding work, but were surprised to find that they enjoyed general meetings and became more active over time in the social and political life of the group.

6   Propositions 187, 227, and 209, respectively.

7   See also Eithne Luibhéid's chapter in this volume.

8   Reported in Coll, *Motherhood and Cultural Citizenship* and "Necesidades y problemas."

9   "Entonces dije bueno, yo te aguanté muchas cosas pero una cachetada no te la voy a aguantar, entonces marqué 9-1-1." Interview 9/20/96.

10   "No estoy en un lecho de rosas pero comparando con aquel lugar, estoy bien."

11   "Dije no, ¡yo no creo en esas personas!"

12   "Yo no creo en eso."

13   "Le dije no, yo a ese edificio no me meto le dije, porque son puras mujeres perversas. No dijo . . . el tercer piso es de las latinas. Mmm . . . pues vamos a ver de que se trata, y vine y me gustó el grupo, no son perversas, son personas como yo, que han te . . . han sufrido, han pasado experiencias, y un día les dije en el grupo ¿saben por qué no venía? Por esto y por esto otro y todas se morían de risa. Todas pensamos lo mismo: que somos bien degeneradas, somos mujeres que se drogan, o que son mujeres . . . , tenemos una mente muy mal para estas mujeres, pero ahora invito yo a muchas personas."

14   The figurative term women used to describe such dialogue was "desahogarse"—literally, to release or unchoke oneself.

15   "Bueno yo, me gusta a mí siempre si voy en el bus con alguien que conozco, o me hace plática, siempre me gusta informar a la gente. Por ejemplo, cuando veo mujeres así, les invito aquí a Mujeres y todas están como yo [estaba antes], erradas, están pensando que muchos nos critican. A mí me duele mucho que me han dicho en mi cara: no, eso es para las mujeres que no tienen que hacer, eso es para mujeres dejadas del marido, eso es para mujeres que ya andan muy perdidas."

16   Caridad explained to me that most women she meets in everyday life lack the information they need to understand the current social and political context affecting everything from their children's schools to their own access to healthcare and housing. Hers is not a missionary spirit, but rather a democratizing orientation towards the key resource of good information which many immigrants and working people are cut off from. Having access to and sharing good information that people need is part of her everyday practice of citizenship and I met women she had spoken with in this way who came to the group and later began reaching out to others in similar fashion.

17   "La mujer es de la casa, la mujer no tiene que andar en la calle. Y si andas en la calle andas buscando otro y tienes que hacer comida y tienes que limpiar. Ese es un infierno, es un infierno."

18 "Digo, no, yo no estoy perdida. Si, y me defiendo ahora. No le digo, lo que pasa es que . . . que no estás bien informada. Mira, yo les digo ¿verdad? yo tengo mis hijos, yo donde vivo estoy encargada de hacer la limpieza, tengo que hacer de comer. La gente me critica porque me ve en la calle. Ahora yo digo, qué les importa. Ando en la calle, hago mis deberes según yo, vengo a mujeres unidas. Mi horario lo acomodo, a mi nada me perjudica. Tan les tengo comida a mis hijos, como limpio la casa, aunque sea en la tarde, en la noche, en la madrugada. Todo hago y puedo venir aquí. Porque no, no, crea que soy muy trabajadora."

19 "Yo me ponía allí a pedirle a dios que ¿porqué lo quería si el era tan malo conmigo. Y siempre cuando, siempre he sido una mujer limpa, una mujer cocinera, una mujer que siempre traigo a los niños arreglados, aunque esté pobremente, pero bien limpiecitos. Siempre van a la escuela bien limpios, bien limpios. A mí nunca me ha llamado la atención que me digan, 'Señora, su niña la trae sucia, tiene que cambiarla.' No. Siempre bien cambiaditos, bien bañaditos. Y comida, tres veces al día. Los baños del apartamento donde yo he vivido, diario, diario tengo que lavar los baños, bien limpiecitos, porque tantas enfermedades que hay. Y también para una buena higiene. Siempre los baños diarios, diarios, diarios, diarios se tiene que estar lavando. La estufa diario bien lavada. Todo."

20 "Y cuando yo agarré estos entrenamientos y que yo miraba a más mujeres con problemas y que yo miraba que yo no era la única que estaba sufriendo. Entonces, yo dije, 'aquí tengo que cambiar porque esto no tiene que continuar así.' Entonces fue como esa plantita que le hechas agua, que la estás regando, que la estás dando vida, que la estás dando la oportunidad que florezca, que crezca, como una guía que va creciendo. Entonces así es como yo miro a mi vida desde cuando yo entré aquí hasta ahorita. Porque ahorita soy una mujer, que, con problemas y todo, he salido adelante con mis seis niños. Aunque hemos pasado por muchas cosas, problemas, me han dado problemas ellos, muchas cosas han pasado, pero yo pienso que si yo no estaría aquí en este grupo, yo no tuviera toda la información que tengo ahorita, yo pienso que yo fuera una mujer derrotada."

21 "Yo tenía tanto miedo a la soledad, pero mucho miedo. Antes no me daba miedo."

22 "El me amenazaba, como yo no sabía mis derechos ni nada, decía, 'si no me das dinero, me voy a ir con la trabajadora social y decirle que te lo quite.' Y yo decía, 'si me lo quita, y los niños, qué van a comer."

23 "Ooo, yo me sentía tan contenta cuando me dijeron eso! Pues, después se enojaba: 'Te crees mucho porque tienes todo a tu nombre!' Después me fui yo capacitando para yo ser como el padre de familia y madre a la vez. Pero sí se sentía una carga muy pesada. Yo decía '¿ir a pagar la renta?' Nomás de

ir, porque como él no me dejaba a mí salir a ningún lado, entonces yo no sabía donde pagaba nada. Sí sabía cual era la calle, pero la primera vez que yo fui a pagar renta, yo iba bien asustada. ¡Temblando!"

24 See for example Kath Weston as well as Judith Butler's *Gender Trouble* and *Bodies That Matter*. My own fieldwork experience confirms that one's identity as woman was constructed in and through repetition of citational practices of identity, politics, and in this case, resistant subjectivity.

25 "Performativity describes this relation of being implicated in that which one opposes, this turning of power against itself to produce alternative modalities of power, to establish a kind of political contestation that is not a 'pure' opposition, a 'transcendence' of contemporary relations of power, but a difficult labor of forging a future from resources inevitably impure" (Butler, *Bodies that Matter* 241).

14

Immigration, Self-Exile, and Sexual Dissidence

Norma Mogrovejo

I begin with my personal experience. I was born and grew up in Juliaca, a small indigenous town in the Peruvian sierra. My family moved to the city of Arequipa when I was fourteen years old. A few years later, I helped to form, in Arequipa, the first Peruvian feminist group outside of the capital city of Lima. In my work with the feminist movement, I traveled and came into contact with Latin American feminist experience and thought. As a result, I was able to construct an identity different from that which awaited me in the town of my birth. I became aware of how important relationships with other women were to me, and began to seek other lesbians in my city—unsuccessfully. In the early 1980s, Peruvian lesbians outside of Lima saw not even the glimmer of a chance of emerging from our confinement and loneliness.

The First Latin American Lesbian Meeting, held in Mexico, in 1987, opened to me a wondrous new world. The meeting brought together more than ten Mexican lesbian groups, all highly political. Some of those in attendance claimed that more than half of all feminists were lesbians, although not many would admit it publicly. Such statements cut a number of ways: they have functioned as homophobic tactics to "discredit" feminism and to drive a wedge between feminists, but they are also important indicators of a lesbian presence. I found a variety of lesbian spaces at the meeting, a community that made lesbian existence visible and livable. I encountered a history of lesbian and gay struggles for rights and dignity—a world light years away from conservative Arequipa. Returning home with the knowledge of a world in which non-heterosexual identity had a place, I was restless. In my city, it was impossible for me to explore or even to experience my lesbianism, for I had no one with whom to share my feelings, let alone my fantasies. I realized that I had to return to Mexico in order to allow myself a chance as a lesbian.

A scholarship to study for my Master's degree at Mexico's Facultad Latinoamericana de Ciencias Sociales (Latin American Faculty of Social Sciences) made the trip possible. In Mexico, I enjoyed the freedom of living openly as a lesbian. But I also encountered the distress of self-exile. I loved my Peruvian roots and the history of my country—the dream of return still haunts my existence—but I could not be a part of Peru's heterosexual community, from which I felt effectively banished. Although the Peruvian police did not harass me, nor did the government officially expel me, I could not return to an environment in which heterosexuality was the only rule allowed.

Far away from the possible censure of my family and my community, I feel much freer to live, write, and politick as a lesbian. But I cannot say that Mexico is absolutely respectful of diverse identities. It is not so with its ethnic identities, nor with its sexual dissidents.[1] Although homosexuality is not criminalized in Mexico, the Citizens' Commission Against Hate Crimes and Homophobia has reported that homophobic hatred claimed 190 victims (179 men and 11 women), many executed cruelly or tortured to death, according to research based on news articles from 1995 to 1999. In 2001, The International Gay and Lesbian Human Rights Commission (IGHLRC) documented 275 murders related to sexual orientation in Mexico. According to the commission's Latin American coordinator, to get a true idea of homophobia in the country, we should multiply the figure by five "because many people live and die in the closet."[2] In 2003, the same commission documented seven deaths resulting from homophobic violence in Mexico (Herrera). The numbers appear to be diminishing, but documentation remains difficult, and even one case of homophobic violence of any type is one case too many. In February 2003, Mexico's Attorney General announced that, since its opening two years earlier, the "061" phone number, dedicated to receiving complaints concerning discrimination against homosexuals, has provided information in forty cases of homophobic crime. The assistant to the Attorney General recognizes the difficulty of establishing proof in discrimination cases, because "often it is subjective, based on pejorative comments, unwanted attention, or mockery. Nonetheless, we prosecute against public employees when these occur."[3]

Fifteen years after I moved to Mexico, my legal documents still identified me as a "non-immigrant visitor." I was not a Mexican citizen, resident, or even a regular immigrant. My self-exile carried with it the cost of a highly conditioned freedom, of fourth-class citizenship. I had permission to work in Mexico, but was forbidden to undertake any other activity. My access to scholarships and employment was restricted. I was obliged to renew my visa and work permit every year. I was required to comply with onerous reporting requirements for changes in address, job, or even my position within the same job. I had to register every entrance into and exit from the country. And I paid higher taxes than any other kind of immigrant or citizen. In short, I was reminded on a daily basis that I was a foreigner in Mexico. Perhaps most odious to me was that foreigners in Mexico are prohibited, under threat of expulsion, from participating in political activities in Mexico.[4] I calculated my actions carefully, but as much as I tried to avoid crossing the line of politics, I could not fool myself: humans are political beings. And even if Aristotle had not already said so, feminism also teaches us that *the private is political* and, faithful to the dictates of conscience, we activists defend sexual freedom as political freedom. My personal commitment placed me on the edge of legality. The Mexican immigration police several times found me on the wrong side of the line. I paid for it in prison.

You might wonder, then, why I did not immediately seek naturalized citizenship in Mexico. Until 1998, a foreign woman could obtain Mexican nationality by marrying a Mexican man or by bearing children in Mexico. I did not wish to engage in heterosexual matrimony or reproduction. Because I am a woman and because I am a lesbian, my citizenship was incomplete. Why not indulge in the farce of a fictitious marriage with some fellow traveler, as some of my lesbian friends have done, forming perfect couples with not a single domestic conflict in years of marriage? Because I have proudly dared to appear in public as a lesbian activist—not to mention that, if discovered, a fake marriage could bring legal consequences even harsher than those I had already experienced.

Why not return to my country and dare to politick at home? Some people have reproached me with the observation that it is more comfortable to be an activist in a foreign country than at home. But in Latin America, coming out of the closet is not only a personal affair. When one comes out, one's entire surroundings also "come out." A public lesbian also implicates her family, which could mean (depending on where it happens) repression against the entire family, and, consequently, not merely personal risk. Nonetheless, I have attempted to return to my country. But the professional profile I have built up over the years as a "lesbianologist" has caused academic and governmental spaces to turn their backs on me. Who in Peru needs a lesbianologist? In the best of cases, people are astonished or disconcerted.

In 1998, the Ley de la Nacionalidad (Nationality Law) passed in Mexico, granting citizens of other Latin American nations who had resided in Mexico for more than two years the right to apply for naturalization. However, the conferral of naturalization is a highly subjective process. Anecdotal evidence suggests that, along with those who participated in the Zapatista movement, lesbians are particularly out of favor with the powers that be. Furthermore, my previous imprisonment for violations of immigration law made me particularly disqualified as a beneficiary of the new law. So, with a certain resignation, I maintained my status as a non-immigrant visitor in Mexico. And I kept wondering, where *is* my citizenship? I was Peruvian, but I could not reinsert myself into my country. I live in Mexico, but I did not meet the legal requirements even for residency, much less nationality. What does nationality mean in my case, both in strictly juridical and in practical terms? The right to a passport? My passport was a daily reminder that I was from neither here nor there.

Finally, in 2003, I met a lawyer who helped me work with the Secretary of Exterior Relations to make a special case for my application for naturalization under the Nationality Law. Normally, applications are processed within eight months; mine took a year and a half. But, finally, sixteen years after I first came to Mexico, in May 2004, I became a Mexican citizen. I have full access to everything from bank transactions to political rallies. And the travel, studies, and work that paved my long road to full Mexican citizenship provided me with the opportunity to explore and develop my own lesbian identity, and to acquire a profound knowledge of the living history of the group, Latin American lesbians, of which I have long been a full member.

* * *

Fixed categories of identity are the basis upon which oppression is exercised and, simultaneously, the basis upon which political power rests. Given that sexual identities are social and historical products, and not natural or self-contained, lesbians search for collective referents to restructure and redefine our identities; we search for collective spaces of acceptance. Italian sociologist Alberto Melucci and others contend that collective identities are not only necessary for collective action, but are also frequently an end in and of themselves.[5] In this model, collective identity is thought of as a "continual process of recomposition more than a given" and "a dynamic aspect, an emerging of collective action." Do Latin American lesbians have collective identities? What are they? How are they emerging?

Issues of sexuality are increasingly important in examining how power works in contemporary society. The history of sexuality has been a history of control, opposition, and resistance to moral codes, examples of which may be found in subcultures and networks of sexual minorities since the end of the seventeenth century. Networks and groups, as Jeffrey Weeks details in his book *Sexuality*, have played a fundamental role in the rise of modern homosexual identities, expressed explicitly over the past hundred years as oppositional movements organized around sexuality and sexual matters.

The history of the Latin American lesbian movement is intimately linked to the political history of the continent. The origins of both the lesbian movement and of any number of popular political organizations can be found in the enormous Mexican student movement that was tragically smashed on October 2, 1968.[6] The 1970s allowed the growth of a new generation of young people who, influenced by the achievements of the Cuban Revolution, Che Guevara, and European and North American student movements, challenged authority with counter-cultural attitudes.

Latin American homosexual men and women were themselves at the center of Stonewall, the first public protest for homosexual rights in the United States.[7] Aburto Gonzalo, in his article "Abriendo caminos" ("Opening Paths"), reports that one of those arrested during the Stonewall riots was an undocumented Argentine, who threw himself out of the third-floor window of the police station, gouging his neck on a steel rod. He was transported to a hospital where he died (4–5). Victor Hugo Monje also avers, in his article "Revolución Gay-Stonewall 1969," that the police at the Stonewall riots tried forcefully to remove from the bar a Latina lesbian who put up a great fight and did not allow herself to be put into the police wagon.

The new concepts of sexual liberation developing in Europe and the United States took root in Latin America at the beginning of the 1970s. In 1969 a homosexual group, Nuestro Mundo (Our World), began to be organized in Argentina, but never got off the ground. Then in 1971, under the Argentine dictatorship, the Frente de Liberación Homosexual (Homosexual Liberation Front) was founded. In the same year, a group by the same name formed in Mexico, where a "formal democratic" regime was in place.

In September 1971, Mexico's Frente de Liberación Homosexual (FLH) published its first document in which it demanded the end of legal and social discrimination against male and female homosexuals, the implementation of sex education programs in the schools that would present homosexuality through scientific criteria, a shift in the psychiatric classification of homosexuality as an illness, and an end to police persecution and labor discrimination. The FLH document also asked that the press not refer to homosexuality as a perversion, a crime, or an aberration, but rather that the term be accepted according to serious scientific theories that considered it a valid form of sexuality. Finally, the FLH affirmed that the liberation of homosexuals was another form of social liberation. The "homosexuality" of the FLH was not exclusive of women, and although the group was composed mostly of men, its public face was Nancy Cárdenas.

A hallmark in the history of the lesbian movement in Latin America was Nancy Cárdenas' 1973 television appearance on Mexican journalist Jacobo Zabludowski's program "24 horas" ("24 Hours"), at the time the most watched television show in all of Mexico. The show marked the first time that homosexuality was spoken of openly on Mexican television, although Cárdenas did not show her face on the program for fear of reprisals. Zabludowski's invitation came as part of a response to the January 1973 denunciation by a U.S. citizen that the government of his country and the Nixon administration had fired him from a position in the federal bureaucracy because of his homosexuality. The gay movement in the United States staged public protests and called other homosexuals to come out to challenge their employers in court, if need be, and to demonstrate to the administration that you could be sane, homosexual, and a worker. Putting the U.S. denunciation into a Mexican context on the program, Zabludowski and Cárdenas discussed equality, rights, and the legal situation of homosexuals, their persecution and systematic repression in Mexico, and the distortions to which psychoanalysis and psychiatry subjected homosexuality. The interview played a key role in advancing an organized homosexual movement.

Also in the 1970s, the Latin American feminist movement began to build momentum with the institutional support of the United Nations and its development programs that were instituted beginning in 1975. Feminism initiated the public discussion of topics such as women's sexuality and reproduction, allowing transformations in Latin American political thought. The first public and political use of the term "lesbian" in Latin America followed the UN-sponsored conference for the Year of the Woman held in Mexico in 1975. A group of Mexican women, including Cárdenas, published the *Declaración de las lesbianas de México (Declaration of Mexican Lesbians)* in support of an Australian woman who spoke openly about her lesbianism at the conference (and was subsequently attacked by the Mexican press).[8]

Between 1978 and 1984, the homosexual movement grew and expanded, organizing itself around the distribution of new ideas about sexuality and its intertwined relationship with politics, the search for legitimacy and recognition in various sectors of society, the creation of a counter-discourse opposed to the characterizations of the yellow press, traditional psychiatry, psychoanalysis and religious morality, solidarity with other social sectors and the defense of democracy. Beginning in 1981—and at first with difficulty—biennial Latin American and Caribbean Feminist Meetings motivated discussions about lesbianism as a women's issue that the feminist movement had to engage, leading eventually to the generation of autonomous lesbian groups and to the strengthening of feminist discourse within mixed homosexual groups.[9] At the same time, a few political parties in Mexico, primarily those of Trotskyite tendencies, were influenced by this new political force, and provided technical and organizational support to the homosexual movement, incorporating its demands into their own.

The criticisms that feminists levied against the misogyny of homosexuals, combined with the lesbophobia of heterofeminists to change the course of lesbian action, led to the creation of autonomous lesbian groups. In Mexico City in 1977, Lesbos initiated a separatist and autonomous lesbian organization, based on a socialist ideology. A year later, Lesbos split into OIKABETH and Lesbianas socialistas (Lesbian Socialists), which lasted until the mid-1980s, with a final stint as the Seminario Marxista Leninista de lesbianas feministas (Lesbian Feminist Marxist Leninist Seminar). In the early 1980s, a number of other lesbian groups formed in Mexico City, including the feminist ecological group Cuarto Creciente (Growing Room), the lesbian sex education group, Mujeres urgidas de un lesbianismo auténtico (Women Insisting on an Authentic Lesbianism), and the support group Madres Lesbianas (Lesbian Mothers). By the 1990s, the lesbian social club El Closet de Sor Juana (Sor Juana's Closet), the Coordinadora Nacional de Lesbianas (The National Lesbian Coordination), El Centro de Documentación y

Archivo Histórico Lésbico Nancy Cárdenas (the Nancy Cárdenas Lesbian Archive), Musas de metal (Metal Muses), the Lesbianas Zapatistas that later became Lesbianas en colectiva (Lesbian Collective), and the magazine *Lesvoz* had added to the ranks of lesbian organizations.

In the rest of the Mexico, parallel to the lesbian movement's explosion in Mexico City, a few organizational experiences were begun under very different conditions. One of the most important experiments was that of the Comuna de Lesbianas Morelenses in the state of Morelos. Founded in 1980, the Comuna consisted of a group of women who lived together and ran an alternative space for lesbians in Ocotépec, a small town that is now part of Cuernavaca's urban sprawl. The experiment was rural in character, focused on self-sufficiency, and lasted approximately two and a half years.

In Jalisco, one of Mexico's most conservative states, the group Patlatonalli has thrived since 1981. Its first public activity was a three-day lesbian film and discussion series at the University of Guadalajara. This activity became a widespread call to the political participation of lesbians in Guadalajara, Mexico's second largest city.[10] At the time this chapter was written, Patlatonalli has celebrated more than eighteen years of existence during which it has opened a space for the education and prevention of cervical, uterine, and breast cancer for lesbians.

While the autonomous lesbian movement was proliferating in Mexico, it also developed throughout Latin America. At the First Latin American Feminist Meeting, held in Colombia in 1981, lesbian feminists from throughout Latin America expressed their concerns, and discussions on the subjects of rape and lesbianism were organized by the Commission on Sexuality and Daily Life.

At the Second Latin American Feminist Meeting in Peru, in 1983, lesbians made their presence and their importance in the feminist movement felt when they converted the mini-workshop on patriarchy and lesbianism into the main topic of the meeting. Around 350 women of all sexual orientations, and from all over the continent, attended. The public coming out of many feminists was one of the most important events of the meeting. From the workshop, many lesbians returned to their own countries to form lesbian feminist groups: the Grupo de Autoconciencia de Lesbianas Feministas (Lesbian Feminist Self-Awareness Group; GALF) in Peru, Ayuquelen in Chile; Cuarto Creciente in Mexico, and Mitilene in the Dominican Republic.

The themes of lesbianism and of relations between women were integral parts of the program at the Third Feminist Meeting in Brazil in 1985. GALF-Brasil and GALF-Peru held a workshop on "How We Lesbians Can Organize Ourselves" which was attended by lesbians from Ayuquelen, Cuarto Creciente and Puerto Rico's Colectiva Concientización Gay (Gay Consciousness Raising Collective), as well as some independent lesbians. Workshop discussions centered on lesbians' demands to the feminist movement, on criticism of the dominant heterosexual model that denies women's sexuality by focusing it on procreation, and on defending lesbian desire as a desire possible for all women.[11] From this workshop emerged the proposal for a Latin American and Caribbean lesbian movement independent of the annual feminist meetings.

A few days before the meeting in Brazil, the Forum of Non-Governmental Organizations at the end of the "decade of the woman" took place in Nairobi, Kenya. During the forum, the International Lesbian Information Service (ILIS) organized a lesbian tent and the workshop "Lesbians of the Third World," in which the need for information exchange was also raised. In March 1986, nine Latina lesbians were invited by ILIS to participate in its seventh Conference to be held in Geneva. For the first time, ILIS included in its conference countries of the second and third world.[12]

The ILIS conference sought to strengthen the network of communication between lesbian groups in different continents and to serve as a springboard for future groups. At the conference, the Mexican and Latin American lesbians who were becoming leaders in their countries of origin honed their political savvy, and the political definitions that were in vogue in Europe began to be transmitted to Latin America.

The five Latin American lesbian meetings in the thirteen years following the Geneva Conference epitomize the characteristics and dynamic of the lesbian movement in Latin America. During the first meeting in Mexico, a power struggle for leadership in the form of control of the secretariat of ILIS exposed the different ideological positions of lesbians from different Latin American countries and groups. The second meeting in Costa Rica demonstrated the reality of violence in general, and against lesbians specifically, in Latin America (particularly in Peru and Costa Rica). The experience cast a doubt on the existence of Latin American democracy and its possible inclusion of lesbians. In the third meeting in Puerto Rico, a Chicana presence opened up the discussion of Latin American identity, racism, and internalized lesbophobia, and underscored the absence of pan-Latin American representation. The fourth meeting in Argentina also had only limited pan-Latin American representation, but was the first to face no overt repression. At the fifth meeting in Chile, governmental and other institutions began to play a part, signaling a certain official support but also endangering the autonomy of lesbian groups.

The Latin American lesbian meetings have fostered important developments, serving to mobilize lesbian groups throughout Latin America. The meetings have enabled regional communication and pan-Latin American analysis and action, albeit still somewhat limited. They have broadened the Latin American women's movement's understanding of, and attention to, sexuality and have helped them to put into practice many of their theoretical stances on women's differences as well as women's rights. The lesbian meetings have facilitated the growth of a lesbian feminist current in the feminist movement: a topic that had been considered private has entered the public and political discourse. Lesbian concerns have now reached diverse social sectors and have even been integrated by some political parties.

Some limitations of the Latin American lesbian movement have also become apparent in the course of the meetings. The frequent polarization of groups or of leaders demonstrates diverse ideological positions, but also continues to reproduce hierarchized power relations and to perpetuate the retrenchment of identity categories that are built on belonging by way of an emphasis on the "other." Finally, the small number of women at the Latin American lesbian meetings reflects lacunae in organizational strategies, but also evidences the persistence, throughout Latin America, of repression that renders necessary clandestine organizing and life in the closet.

Although the lesbian movement, along with the feminist, homosexual, bisexual, and transsexual movements, has achieved important advances and continues to work to eradicate homophobia and heteronormativity, the guarantee of the human rights of Lesbian, Gay, Bisexual, and Transsexual (LGBT) Latin Americans has yet to be achieved. Contraventions of heteronormativity often incur moral condemnation, ostracism, or violence. Questioning heteronormativity is often considered a menace to social order. Homosexuality is considered in many social spheres to be a sin, a sickness, a sign of social or ideological deviance, or a cultural betrayal. Although many governments prohibit the outright violation of the human rights of homosexuals, throughout Latin America (and beyond) official policy and practice often openly condones and even legislates the repression of LGBT folk in the name of culture, religion, morality, or public health. Discrimination based on sexual orientation is often created, encouraged, and deployed for political ends. At the same time, in as much as gender and sexual identity are constructed and, as Simone de Beauvoir argues, even to a certain degree chosen, those who reinterpret gender and sexual norms and proliferate a variety of bodily styles themselves enter into the realm of the political, at the very least that of politicizing the personal. In other words, those who transgress gender and sexual norms render their own identification a political act; they form a political response to political repression.

Identity boundaries interact with the limits of citizenship and with the geographical borders of a country. Like me, many LGBT folk find themselves forced to leave their countries of origin in search of spaces where they can express their dissident sexual identity with greater liberty both in their daily lives and in their more overtly political activities. Some cities, like New York, San Francisco, Los Angeles, and Miami in the United States, London, Amsterdam, Paris, Madrid, and Barcelona in Europe, and Mexico City, São Paulo, Rio de Janeiro, and Buenos Aires in Latin America, offer urban spaces "de ambiente" ("with [gay] atmosphere") and some even guarantee certain civil rights for LGBT folk. These cities attract many LGBT migrants and immigrants who, looking for a "land of freedom," face as I did the daunting complications of self-exile, what Lawrence La Fountain-Stokes refers to elsewhere in this volume as "sexilio" ("sexile").

Most sexiles will not qualify for asylum or refuge. International law defines as a "refugee" an individual who is prevented from returning to his or her country due to persecution for reasons of race, religion, nationality, or belonging to a particular social or political group.[13] Asylum may also be granted to those persons whose governments are not capable of protecting them from persecution by non-governmental actors (including death squads or armed guerrilla groups). "Persecution" includes such acts as murder, torture, sexual violence, rape, arbitrary arrest, unjustified imprisonment and beatings. These grounds for asylum take into account only documented evidence of physical violence, not daily social discrimination or limits on professional activities that inflict psychological, moral, and economic violence. Migration and immigration due to sexual dissidence, like any other form of political exile, implicate a search for freedom and for full citizenship, in other words for the guarantee of political and human rights, whether these rights are actively denied or only passively precluded.

Sexile constitutes a little-explored topic in spite of the fact that migration has become a matter of concern, particularly to the United States. Although some research affords a broad perspective on the problem, knowledge of sexual dissidence and migration is still scarce. Information about immigration and the spread of HIV and AIDS allows us to penetrate into the mystery, but not to disentangle it altogether.[14] Research into the effects of immigration based on sexual preference, of the sort initiated by this volume, will help us to understand the plight of the sexile.

At the same time, sexile should not be necessary. Our societies constantly reformulate themselves; at the same time, they are morally obligated to reformulate their laws, regulations, and *modus operandi* to offer inclusive possibilities for co-existence in which individual identities are respected and human rights guaranteed. Collectivities and collective spaces should not be the sole guarantees for the possibility of dissidence. That is, sexual dissidence should be possible—and enjoy full guarantees—not only in the great immigrant metropoli such as Mexico City or New York, but also in Arequipa—or indeed in any indigenous village.

Translated by Keja Valens

Works Cited

Antecedentes del Grupo Lésbico de Guadalajara. Guadalajara: Patlatonalli Archive, May 1987.

Bronfman, Mario. "SIDA en México. Migración, adolescencia y género." *Salud, cambio social y política: perspectivas desde América Latina.* Ed. Mario Bronfman, Roberto Castro, Lucille Atkin. Col. del Valle, México: EDAMEX, 1999.

Fisher, Amalia. *Feministas latinoamericanas: las nuevas brujas y sus aquelarres.* Master's Thesis. Mexico: UNAM, 1995.

Gonzalo, Aburto. "Abriendo caminos, nuestra contribución." *Llegó Nuestra Herencia, June 25,* 1994.

Herrera, Catalina. "Reportan 42 muertes por homofobia en América Latina y el Caribe durante el 2003." *OpusGay,* February 7, 2004.

International Gay and Lesbian Human Rights Commission. *2003 Update.*

Laclau, Ernesto. "Los nuevos movimientos socials y la pluraidad de lo social." *Foro* 8.2 (1998).

Melucci, Alberto. *Nomads of the Present: Social Movements and Individual Needs in Contemporary Society.* Ed. John Keane and Paul Mier. Philadelphia: Temple University Press, 1989.

Memorias III Encontro Feminista Latinoamericano e do Caribe. Brasil, 1985.

Mogrovejo, Norma. *Un amor que se atrevió a decir su nombre: La lucha de las lesbianas y su relación con los movimientos homosexual y feminista en América Latina.* Mexico: Plaza y Valdés, 2000.

Monje, Victor Hugo. "Revolución Gay-Stonewall 196." *Confidencial* 1.9 (1991).

Office of the High Commissioner for Refugees. *Handbook on Procedures and Criteria for Determining Refugee Status Under the 1951 Convention and the 1967 Protocol Relating to the Status of Refugees.* U.N. Doc. HCR/IP/4/Eng. Rev. 1 (1988).

Red de Lesbianas Latinas y del Caribe. *Boletina 2.* Peru, August 1989.

Touraine, Alain. "Can We Live Together, Equal and Different?" *European Journal of Social Theory* 1.2(1998): 165–178.

Weeks, Jeffrey. *Sexuality.* New York: Routledge, 2003.

United Nations Convention Relating to the Status of Refugees. 19 U.S.T. 6259, 189 U.N.T.S. 137 (July 28, 1951).

United Nations Protocol Relating to the Status of Refugees. 19 U.S.T. 6223, 606 U.N.T.S. 267 (January 31, 1967).

Notes

1   I understand as sexually dissident all sex-gender identities that refuse to conform to heteronormativity.

2   Reported in *La Jornada*, October 21, 2001.

3   Reported in the International Gay and Lesbian Human Rights Commission *2003 Update.*

4   See Article 33 of the *Constitución política mexicana.*

5   See Melucci's as well as Alain Touraine and Ernesto Laclau.

6   For more on the impact of the events of 1968 on the gay and lesbian movement in Mexico, see my *Un amor que se atrevió a decir su nombre.*

7   In the 1960s and early 1970s, Latin Americans tended to avoid the term "lesbian," whose primary connotation was that of insult. The preferred designation in those years was "homosexual femenino" ("female homosexual). By the Third Latin American Feminist Meeting in Lima in 1983, the term "lesbian" was in regular use by Latin American women.

8   For more detailed consideration of these events, see my *Un amor que se atrevió a decir su nombre*, 65–68 and 140–142.

9   For a detailed discussion of the Latin American Feminist Meetings, see Amalia Fisher.

10 A complete history of Patlatonalli can be found in *Antecedentes del Grupo Lesbico de Guadalajara*.

11 *Memorias III Encontro Feminista Latinoamericano e do Caribe* offers a full account of the Third Latin American Feminist Meeting.

12 The significance of the seventh ILIS conference to Latin America is discussed in more detail in the Red de Lesbianas Latinas y del Caribe's *Boletina 2*.

13 The definition of "refugee" is established in a series of documents including: the United Nations Convention Relating to the Status of Refugees; the United Nations Protocol Relating to the Status of Refugees; the Office of the High Commissioner for Refugees's *Handbook on Procedures and Criteria for Determining Refugee Status Under the 1951 Convention and the 1967 Protocol Relating to the Status of Refugees*.

14 Mario Bronfman provides an excellent study of HIV/AIDS and immigration in Mexico. The World Health Organization and the U.S. Department of Health and Human Services, Centers for Disease Control also compile information on HIV/AIDS and immigration.

15

An Oral History of Brazilian Women Immigrants in the Boston Area

Heloisa Maria Galvão

I arrived in the United States in the summer of 1988. It was a sunny, hazy, and hot Monday morning. I had come from Brazil to enroll in a Master's program at Boston University's College of Communication. By the time I graduated, I did not want to go back to a city where the search for a job would be fruitless. Instead, I started a bilingual community newspaper and became involved with the local Brazilian community through the Boston Public School's bilingual program. The decision to stay in the United States turned my life upside down and changed me forever. Meeting other Brazilian women who went through similar life experiences has helped me to understand my own decision and what it has meant.

During home visits I used to do for Even Start, a program based in Somerville, Massachusetts, I found out that other Brazilian women shared many of my feelings, such as loneliness, fear, low self-esteem, a sense of disconnectedness, and eventually depression.[1] Yet, at the same time, we shared a strong will to "make it" in America. We wanted our children to have better educational options and our families better life chances than they would have had in Brazil. We did not want to be mere observers of this process; we wanted to play a role in it. We were aware of the struggle that we faced, but we were ready to take up the challenge.

The home visits led me to start two projects. The first was the Brazilian Women's Group, an advocacy and activist group that supports Brazilian immigrant women and organizes around issues important to them. The second, "In Black and White," was an oral history project about Brazilian women immigrants in the Boston area, in which the women told their stories in their own words.[2] They talked about their

families, mothers and fathers, sisters and brothers, friends, their homeland and dearest traditions. Why and how did they make the decision
to come to the United States? How has this decision changed their lives
and who they are now? They reflected on their own lives and identities,
and on what their lives might have been had they not made the decision to come to America.

There is Graciani, a woman from the state of Santa Catarina in
southern Brazil, a Catarinense who exchanges secret Santa gifts every Christmas with her family over the phone. "They are so scared
of losing me," Graciani says, "that they include me in the secret Santa
even though I have not been there in years." Graciani's parents even
extended the tradition to her husband Misha, whom they have yet to
meet. There is Maria Angélica from the state of São Paulo, a Paulista
who after a 10-year marriage and two children discovered that she was
gay and that she wanted to do something different with her life. Now
the mother of three, she is a nurse working with an HIV prevention
program at a local health organization. And there is Cristina from the
Federal District of Brasília, a Brasiliense who landed at Boston's Logan
Airport in January 1986, her baggage full of clothes and dreams and
a close friend's promise to provide Cristina and her husband work,
housing, and easy savings. Instead, Cristina found herself jobless and
homeless. Cristina and her husband both shared a passion for music
and dreamed of forming a band in the United States but a few months
later she had to give up her beloved flute too: "someone in the house
had to work and make a living. My husband wasn't going to compro-
mise on his music. I had to."

There is Angela from the state of Minas Gerais and her three-year-
old daughter, Nathalia, who came to the United States in 1992 to join
husband and father Luis Claudio, who had left Brazil three years before. Today, the Coutinho family has another baby girl and a brand
new house in Malden, a suburb of Boston. There is also fifty-nine-year
old Ercilia, from the state of São Paulo, who came in 1993 to help her
pregnant daughter Regina. Ercilia planned to stay a couple of months,
but postponed her return indefinitely when granddaughter Lara was
born. Not everyone stays in the Boston area. Some women who belong to the group return to Brazil. Such was the case of Ana Lúcia
from Recife, in northeastern Brazil, who landed in Boston to pursue
her doctorate in music at Boston University in January 1987. At the
age of forty-five, the mother of six was determined to start a new life

in a new country. Married to a Chilean, she had made up her mind to settle in Boston, but eight years later, the couple packed up dreams and belongings and returned to Recife.

Who are these women? What changes are they experiencing in their own lives, and what transformations are they provoking in gender roles and family structures in the Brazilian immigrant community? I turn to these questions in the context of this book because gender roles, family, and sexuality are key issues in Brazil, a country usually described as both macho and sensual. The experience of immigration is so powerful that roles change, constantly evolving. The stories of Brazilian women immigrants are those of negotiating "home" and "new" ideas about gender, family, and sexuality. Maria Angélica's experience with being gay is inextricably linked to her experience with being an immigrant. Had she stayed in her home country she might have struggled much longer with her sexual preference. As she herself says: "Growing up, homosexuality was inconceivable in my social environment . . . I didn't grow up with the freedom to explore [homosexuality]; I didn't even consider it . . . When I left [my home environment] I found more liberty with less [surveillance] from the community." Far away from family and society pressures some women such as Cátia, a homemaker originally from the state of Espírito Santo, feel liberated and may take on roles never thought of before: "Here I am a new Cátia. Before, I used to find it difficult to do anything; nowadays, I have courage. I face it, regardless of whether [things] will go wrong or right, I face it."

What also stands out from my conversations with these diverse women is their ability to put their strength and skills together to fight and overcome adversity. Brazilian women are taking leadership on issues affecting the community, and they are filling most of the professional positions available to them. Brazilian women tend to learn English faster than Brazilian men.[3] They tend to start networks of friends and contacts (Messias), and they tend to be more aware of their rights, to fight for them, and to climb the social ladder more rapidly than their male counterparts. The fact that women are taking leadership in community issues also has had a tremendous impact on their family values and structures. One of the complaints I hear the most is "ele não me apoia" ("he does not support me"). ESL students have told me that they had to quit classes because their husbands "did not like them getting home late."

For their part, husbands may feel insecure and threatened if they come home and do not find their wives ready with a hot meal. They tend to become angrier when they find out their wives are at meetings, speaking up for immigrant rights, and becoming increasingly active in the community.[4] In Brazil, the men might feel the same way, but they would have the support of their extended families, which would be likely to enforce stereotypical gender roles. In addition, in Brazil our perspectives are different; because we are home, in familiar territory, we are more likely to follow patterns previously established by our society.

The changes are not always easy for Brazilian women either. They also tend to feel lonely, to get depressed, to feel unfairly treated, and to be very much in need of support. Many of these women worked in Brazil but did not earn enough to significantly help with the family expenses, so the men were generally the heads of the household. Here, women quickly learn that they can make as much or more money than their husbands. They work the same number of hours as their husbands, and they have to take care of their own needs because in many cases they only see their husbands during weekends or on their days off. Yet, they are responsible for doing all of the work at home: cooking, washing, and caring for the children. "If I don't live alone why should I do the cleaning alone? It has to be split between the two" (Cátia).

As Brazilian psychologist Sylvia Duarte Dantas DiBiaggi states, gender roles in Brazil have been changing but "women and men are still regarded as responsible for distinct spheres in life" (51). Furthermore, regional and class differences affect behaviors. When studying and analyzing the role of Brazilian immigrant women and of immigrant communities, one must remember that there is great diversity in women's experiences. Depending on where in Brazil the women come from, their family's story, and their parents' own gender role experience, they may either be very independent or very vulnerable to traditional expectations. For instance, my mother was from Minas Gerais, a Mineira, while my father was a *gaúcho* from the southern part of Brazil; I grew up in a family where gender roles were not clear-cut. Both of my parents worked outside of the home full-time and also washed, cooked, and took care of their daughters. My mother has always been a strong woman who taught her daughters not to make marriage their destiny, while my father never told us not to do this or that because we were women. But my family experience was unusual. I believe it has allowed me to perceive things from a broader perspective.

The Stories

Between 1995 and 1996, I interviewed eleven Brazilian women who had immigrated to the Boston area in the mid 1980s and early 1990s. The tape-recorded interviews took place in the interviewees' homes and lasted from one to two hours. Since we knew each other, no introductions were needed. I approached the women and they all agreed to be interviewed.

My main questions were: How did you decide to come to the United States? When did you come? How did the immigrant experience change your life? How are you different as a person now? I let the tape recorder roll and tried not to interrupt or have a dialogue with the women, although it did not take me long to realize that I was part of their stories and could not be impersonal while conducting the project. While incorporating the interviews into this chapter, I had to consider the amount of analysis that I wanted to provide. To analyze the women's words was never my intention; to do so felt like a betrayal of their trust. I simply wanted to share theirs stories and to reflect on them from my own position as a member of that same community of Brazilian immigrant women.

The fact that the interviews were conducted in the family kitchen and *regadas a café forte, salgadinhos e pãezinhos de queijo*—over strong coffee, Brazilian pastries, and tasty cheese bread—made me feel at home and helped the women to speak freely. Many times the women's children were nearby, and sometimes their husbands were in the living room. Neither the children nor the husbands bothered us, reinforcing traits of Brazilian culture, where space and privacy are rare and are given as they can be. The conversations were permeated by memories. Many times all of the family members, objects, and places the women had left in Brazil seemed to be floating in the kitchen with us.

The women came from different regions of Brazil. Two of the women had previously migrated inside Brazil, one from Minas to Goiás, the other from Rio de Janeiro to Brasília. Another one had lived overseas for eleven years. The ages ranged from 26 to 58: the majority (six) were in their 30s, two in their 40s, and one had just turned 50. All of the women had worked in Brazil, the majority occupying professional positions. All but one had completed at least some college; indeed, the majority held a Bachelor's degree.

Nine of the women came to the United States for economic reasons and did not know English. Of the two who came for other reasons, one followed her husband and the other came to study. Of the eleven, only two were single when they arrived; all the others were married and had children. Of the two single women, one had married by the time of the interview (and later had a child); the other became a single mother. The oldest was a grandmother, and the youngest had a son (and later another). Only one has since separated. All of the women learned English and straightened out their legal situations, becoming productive professionals and competing in the job market. All of the women became strong advocates for their families and their communities, both in the United States and in Brazil. At least three of them have become U.S. citizens and vote in elections.

It has been seven years since I first interviewed these women. We are still good friends. Two women have moved back to Brazil, another has moved away from the Boston area. Here I include excerpts of six of the interviews; bracketed ellipses indicate editorial omissions; unbracketed ellipses indicate pauses in the women's speech.

Ana Lúcia

My name is Ana Lúcia Altino García, I am 50 years old and from Recife, Pernambuco [northeastern Brazil]. I am married to a Chilean, Rafael García, 51. I have six children: Rafael, the oldest, is 25, Leonardo, the second, is 23, Marcelo is 20, Grácio is 17, Ana Cristina, 14 and Ricardo Jorge is 12, and we have the dogs, two puppies. Boris is three and Rosa is two.

I came to the United States in 1987. Several reasons made me decide to come to the United States. The first one was that Leonardo, my second son, received a scholarship from the Manhattan School, in New York, winning a contest in 1986, in Rio de Janeiro [Brazil]. He was too young at the time; he was 14 years old, and I was told by several mothers of boys who had come here at 14, 15, that they had lost their children. Therefore, I thought that he should not come alone and I applied for a scholarship to see if I also could come and bring my family. I mean, I had always wanted to come here for my doctoral degree, something like that, but it was not something *that* important in my life. It happened because of that, so Leonardo would not come alone to the United States. Then I really applied and won a scholarship. I was accepted at Boston University for my Ph.D. studies and became excited about it. This was one reason, the first one.

The second reason was that I left [Brazil] with the idea of staying here [in the United States]. This really was my idea when I came here. To come, study, and stay, give my children a better education, open the doors to them, mainly the three oldest who at that time had already decided to be musicians, indeed the two oldest, the third one decided here. I had lived in Paraiba for nine years and done good musical work, important at the national level. As always, due to bad Brazilian politics, there is a moment when you suddenly become the bad apple and get all the kicks in your ass. So I left Paraiba and went back to Recife. This was back in 1986. I stayed there during '86, and half of '87. I felt I was poorly welcomed. I wasn't doing too much but teaching at the university, this was also a reason for me to leave.

And the other reason, which I think gave the last push, was the death of my mother in June of '87. At that point I already had the scholarship but I had not made up my mind. [My husband] Rafael did not want to come. [The] children wanted to but they did not understand what it all meant [. . .] but after my mother's death, I thought that I shouldn't stay in the city. I had nothing to do there at that moment. I came in September [of 1987], Leonardo came in August, and Rafael, finally, with the children in December. When I came, more or less I knew he would come, because I had told him I was coming and bringing the children. "If you do not want [to come], it's your problem, we get divorced." I think he was afraid of divorcing me, and one day he said: "You know what, I am going."

I think that my first years here, the five years that I spent studying, during which I was busy at the university, I felt very good and happy. Everything was new to me, the conditions, and I was studying. I also think that it was the best time for the oldest children. The youngest had more difficulties to adapt, but it was quick also, in one semester practically all of them were well placed. But when I finished my studies and started to realize how hard it was to get a job, I concluded that here it's the same as it is in Brazil, the same politics behind everything. The only difference is that here they value the person, they give importance to what you know. In Brazil, politicians ask for favors and it doesn't matter whether you know or don't. All the tests, applications to get into college, these are all marked cards. I gave up applying for a job, because I was either over qualified, due to my Ph.D. and my administrative experience, or I was under qualified, because I didn't start my professional career here. The answers were always the same. So I played with students or with my children, we promoted summer festivals, Rafael taught, but it came to a moment [. . .], it did not happen overnight, for one year, two years, I thought this over, ripening the idea of going back. [. . .]

Since the very first day, Rafael wanted to go back because he never liked the U.S., he was never crazy about the United States. I think that if we had gone to Europe he probably would stay. He loves Brazil; he is the most Brazilian person that I know. For him, there is no shortage of work. I mean, he does not have a [regular] job, this is another reason that made me decide, you get to a certain age, close to fifty, and you realize that you don't have security, no social security, you don't have anything. I live well, I have money, but if he [Rafael] does not teach, we don't have money, if he is sick, or the student is sick, there is no payment for classes. He does not have vacation time; he does not have a full-time job. He teaches at the New England [Conservatory]. They give him 18 hours but they won't give him 20 hours so it won't be a full-time position. [. . .]

I worry mainly for him, because he works like a horse, and he does not take time off. It's mornings, afternoons, nights, Saturdays, and Sundays. Then you come to a moment when you start thinking. The oldest is going to New York; Leonardo will go to Illinois for his Master's; Marcelo will go to Singapore. Gracio is the only one who is not sure . . . I think I am the same person I was in Brazil [. . .] but in certain things, you always change when you live through an experience. I had a wonderful and peaceful time. I am scared of losing this when I go back, maybe because when I left . . . you know, as I said before, political problems, gossip, and a sick atmosphere. Here you are in charge, you don't live with intrigue everyday, and I think that, from this point of view, I have found peace. I'm scared to death of losing it. I even believe that in terms of strengthening the marriage, the family, I think that it was important that we lived very alone, you know. I am not saying that I don't have friends; we have lots of friends, but without family interference in your business. . . . [. . .]

I wanted to go back now while I still can be productive. I could stay here for ten more years, living just the way I am and go back later, but then you go back in pieces, you don't have courage to do anything. I am a dynamic person and I like to work. Here I am frustrated. I do nothing but house chores, and I am fed up. Think about the change in my life, it was from water to wine, radical. I worked from dawn to dusk. [. . .] I think it was easier for me because I had six children. The more children you have, the less you worry about them. Think about it and look back at each birth. You'll see that with the first one, you woke up with any noise. The second one, less, and by the sixth, you don't wake up anymore, you just leave the bottle by the side. You can see it even by the amount of pictures you take, the picture of the first one and the picture of the last one, you may even not have it . . .

Angela

My name is Angela Coutinho. I am thirty-eight years old. I am from Belo Horizonte [in the state of Minas Gerais]. I came in 1991, in September of '91. I came here because my husband had come first. He had lost his job in Brazil and thought that he could no longer live there with us, with his Brazilian salary. Indeed, our expenses were high, there was a family, children, so he came here to stay for two years and I came afterwards, because he did not go back and the money he sent was never enough to live there, so I packed and came . . . At the beginning, adaptation is very difficult, language, people, but as time goes by you learn how to live here, how to deal with it. I like it here, despite . . . here one has to work hard in order to be able to maintain oneself, otherwise you do not live.

I think women become more independent here. She grows; she does more. I think that it's worth it to live here for a good amount of time, and if you can save—which is very difficult—and go back to Brazil, it's wonderful. Meanwhile, we keep going on with life. [. . .] When I came, I had a three-year-old daughter. It's very difficult because you want to work. It's difficult to reconcile work and children; a child cannot be left alone, and you depend on a babysitter. You have to decide whether you work or stay home with the child or whether you get a job that pays for the babysitter because you spend a lot of money, it's too much money, you don't realize it. But when you do the accounting, weekly, monthly, then you realize it's a lot of money that goes away. It's too expensive. I tried to find a school, something. Here you get schooling only when the child is 4 years old and it's only half a day, only four hours a day. Nathalia went to school only for four hours a day, some schools are only for two hours a day. With a child at three, four, five years of age, you suffer a lot; it's very difficult to reconcile work and children. Today, I have another daughter, who is one. I will face the same problem all over because she is so young, so I changed my working schedule, my husband's and mine.

I would not come without her [my daughter], that was my husband's option. I was supposed to come without her. I said: "No, I am going with my daughter." I was not being stubborn, I think that our children have to be raised by us, educated by us. I grew up without my mother, therefore I didn't want this for my children, not for my daughter. The three years that I spent alone were very difficult, but if we can struggle together, reconcile together, it's possible to help.

Brazilians should not come here. Our mistake is to have come, because you come, you work hard to have money, and you end up having it. What they earn there [in Brazil] in a month, you earn here in a week and much more. Therefore, you become addicted to money, you work but you have to work really hard to make some money. [...] Here it is an illusion, for many Brazilians it's an illusion. Many are lucky. I, myself, have relatives who came here, a young boy who stayed here for three years. He is doing very well in Brazil, but he is single. He did not have anyone depending on him; he lived with his parents; he worked for three years on a roll and today he has his own business; he is fine. It's different for someone who comes with a family, a couple. He was lucky; he came here at a time when it was not as difficult to make a living as it is now. To get a job now is very difficult. As time goes by, it becomes more difficult. Everything is difficult: to get a driver's license, to get a social security number, no one gets it anymore.

Here women do not have to be dependent on their husbands to take children to school, go to the doctor, and go to the supermarket. Because the husband works, you have to take care of yourself, with whatever car, pick up the children. If you wait for your husband [it never happens] because he works like crazy and wants to rest. It's like my husband, he works three jobs. I cannot depend on him for anything. This helps a lot for a woman to become independent. She communicates. She adds a lot of good things to the relationship. It's much better, she improves much more, I think. I thought I was already an independent woman, today I think I am more so.

My option . . . I came to be with my husband and with my family and my daughter because I would not stay in Brazil with him here. I like it here. I could live here the rest of my life. But I like Brazil too. I want to go back, but I don't have . . . a specific date to go back. [...] Ah, if I could be there every Christmas with my family! For me it's very important. I love my family . . . Ah, if I could have gone yesterday, I would be there, I would go and come back. But I cannot. It bothers me a lot because I wanted to be able to go with a round trip ticket . . . [. . .]. [What I miss the most] is life there, the people, parties. I miss the way I lived there. I miss the way people are charismatic. It's better there than here, they celebrate Christmas here, it's important for them, but it doesn't have that thing, that human being feeling the way we have there. This let me down, I miss it; I think this is very important. Trying to adapt is difficult while you are also longing for your beloved relatives.

Foreigners are discriminated against in the U.S.; there are too many cases of discrimination, mainly if you do not speak the language. It's very important to go to school and study [English]. I studied [ESL]. I quit now because it became too difficult, but [studying] is worth it. Thank God, the English that I have now, that I understand, that I know, that I speak, it's thanks to the school I went to. If it weren't for the school, I would be in bad shape, because there is discrimination if you don't speak [English]. They don't listen to you, they even don't want you to repeat yourself, they forget you, they abandon you, so studying has a great value here and when you go back to your country. So, those [who] can study should do it.

I come from a large family. My father married three times; I'm from his second marriage. He had eight children from his first marriage. He was a railroad man. [...] I am my mother's sixth [child]. After me there are three more. My mother was my father's second wife; my father married her when she was 15 years old and he had eight children at home and she had nine more. I remember the oldest was my mother's age when he married her. [My mother] would be 64 years old, if I am not mistaken, I am not sure. When she died she was 30 years old, she died 36 years ago. [...] I was five when my mother died ... It's hard, too hard [to be alone], I don't wish it for anyone. It's horrible. If you have to come, come with the family, because it's terrible, loneliness, you and your daughter and the family around you, in my case it was his family. You don't know what to do, where to go. If you work, during the week it's all right, otherwise it's horrible. I don't wish it on anyone. If one has to come, come together, it's the best thing to do, come together, even if it were to face difficulties. It's better to stay together, come together; I will never go through this experience again. He suffered a lot; he thought it was terrible. He suffered like a condemned man, Luis suffered a lot, and he didn't eat well. But it was his option; he thought here it would be better. Once he went back to Brazil [to visit me], and stayed for forty days, then he came back [to the United States] and I stayed there. He would write me a letter every day, his suffering was a hundred times worse. It was terrible. He would not go through that again. He likes it here very much and I say I will go back, but I don't know if he will stay here by himself and I by myself there too. For now he says he wants to live here, but as I said, in order to live here one has to think a lot on one's and the children's future because it is complicated. I think that here I developed; I grew up. I am a different person here, I notice it and my family told me it, that [coming here] was good for me.

Cátia

We came to America in May of 1989 because our economic situation was bad, we had many debts and [my husband's] brother and his sister lived in Cape Cod and offered to help us. We arrived on May 7; on the following day Wilmer started working in a restaurant in the morning. At the time I did not work because Felipe was a baby, he was one year and five months old; I didn't have anyone to leave him with, therefore, I spent some months without working. Afterwards my sister-in-law got me a job in the hotel where she worked, so I could do the laundry and watch Felipe. It was too difficult because I had to strip one bedroom and at the same time I had to take Felipe with me. After two months here we had paid our debts in Brazil because Wilmer started in the restaurant and fifteen days later he started in another restaurant at night. He practically had two full-time jobs so we were able to pay our debts and save some money.

Well, after one year here we had saved about $10,000. It's a lot of money and we thought that in one more year we would save another $10,000 and go back to Brazil because we thought that $20,000 would be enough to buy a house and start a new business. But in the first winter we spent here I became deeply depressed. I felt lonely, my sister-in-law had gone back to Brazil, and she was the only friend I had. Winter came, it lasted forever, I felt lonely, and I practically didn't have anyone whom to talk to. Wilmer worked mornings to evenings. He would come home around midnight. I didn't know how to drive at the time; I didn't speak English; I stayed home. I depended on him for everything: to shop, to do the laundry. I became sick, on the verge of a nervous breakdown, stressed. Then summer came, a friend came over and kept me company, but at the end of August she went back to Brazil and I started feeling depressed again and wondering if the winter would be as bad as it had been in the previous year. I became sick again. I couldn't help it; I wanted to go back to Brazil; I cried. I talked about it; I wanted to go back because there was our place, and we had enough money. Then, because of me, we went back.

We went back in November of 1990 and we had saved about $15,000. It was nothing. I became so frustrated with Brazil, with people. I think that here I changed, I adapted to something without even realizing it, and when I got there I didn't find a Brazil poor in materials, I found a Brazil poor in spirit; I found people were poor in spirit, people worried more about their appearance than . . . I was like that before. I missed my friends but when I got there I didn't recognize my friends, my friends would talk only about manicures, what the maid broke. I had no patience to talk to those people anymore. I realized that I had changed: I worked; I perceived life from a different angle; I had started worrying less about my appearance. To be myself, I do not need to look like a doll, I have to show who I am inside. We stayed for four months.

Wilmer, indeed, had the intention to come back. He was less a dreamer . . . So we came back and I do not miss Brazil that much anymore . . . I had learned how to drive in Brazil and I didn't depend on Wilmer anymore. [. . .] Here I grew as a woman . . . I am a new Cátia. Before, I used to find it difficult to do anything; nowadays, I have courage. I face it, whether [things] will go wrong or right, I face it. I think that when women get here they notice that they have another life here. Life here is different from their life in Brazil; [here] they have more freedom. I think that Brazil is a macho country; women have always felt they're less than men there, and that they cannot grow like a man . . . Here I think that women go for it; women fight. We struggle with the language, for instance, and we study because we are not going to spend our whole lives depending on somebody else [to interpret for us].

I also think that in Brazil husbands do not help their wives at home. [There] Wilmer helped me when I had the baby . . . But afterwards he helped very little; he would help with small things, if the baby cried or if we needed some pasta . . . I see how it is with his and my sisters too. They work all day long, come home and they have to take care of the children, and fix diner. Their husbands sit and watch television. Here husbands help: men do laundry, they clean the bathroom, they clean the floor, they vacuum, they dust, cook. Wilmer cooks a lot, so I think that men here forget a bit about the Brazilian machismo. Let's say that it's half-and-half. Men change a bit because the majority [of the men] come first, so they get here and they have to do everything on their own, right? They have to cook, they have to get by alone, since the man comes first, if he doesn't do it, he doesn't have clean clothes, doesn't have a home, he has nothing, he does not have food, so I believe that because men come first, it helps them to change. On the other hand, the woman gets here and she has to work hard, she is no longer the secretary she was in Brazil and she has to do the cleaning. It's not the same; to be a secretary in Brazil is tiring but it tires the mind, not the body. Here, you get your mind and your body tired. If I don't live alone why should I do the cleaning alone? It has to be split between the two . . .

Women here are split. Certain couples, they get here and the wife begins to notice that the husband she had in Brazil is not the man she dreamed of. She changes—I changed—and she starts noticing that her husband . . . For instance, certain men never change, they keep their macho mind, and what happens? Separation. Many couples come here and separate, because the husband does not accept certain things and does not collaborate at home. The wife feels overwhelmed; she has to resolve everything, then she starts wondering: "this is not the man I married and the one I dreamed of. He is not a man who shares," and separation happens, the marriage ends. She opens her mind . . . I think that when we get here we notice the difference between American [husbands] and us, Brazilians, our culture. We have a cultural shock. This is why women change so much. She starts noticing that the American woman—I noticed that myself when I first came—doesn't care as much as the Brazilian woman about getting manicured; the American woman is not too concerned about her appearance. I go into a store as sloppily dressed as I am today, and the sales person helps me as if he were serving a millionaire. In Brazil if you go into a store poorly dressed, they will treat you like a beggar. The American people do not dress up to go shopping for an air conditioner, right? So, I think that as a result of this all women change. I changed a lot.

Ercília

My name is Ercília; I am from Taquariting, in the interior of São Paulo. I turned 58 on January 20th. I have been here for three years. I came because my daughter was pregnant with my granddaughter. I came to take care of them. I planned to stay three months. Afterwards I talked with my daughter, asked her if she wanted me to go back with the baby or stay and take care of the child so the baby would be close to her, and that's what happened; she wanted me to stay. I stayed and it changed my life a lot. [In Brazil] I was very lonely, I didn't have anything to do, here I have Lara . . . to take care of, and I do catering, appetizers and cakes, and I have fun. I like it. My daughter is a wonderful daughter, I love her; she is intelligent and hardworking.

My heart gets divided, because I left my children, my grandchildren, and we long for our children and grandchildren. I am divided but not concerned. I am always in a good mood. I want to go back on vacation, not to live there. I prefer to live here; I like it here. We have fun; we go out a lot, mainly during the summer; there are beaches. I adapted pretty well.

If I had stayed in Brazil it would have been bad because I wouldn't have learned anything, I wouldn't have gotten anywhere. My life was very busy because my mother lived with me for 10 years. Then she got sick. She stayed in bed; she could no longer walk and I took care of her. She died a year after I came. [My family] had someone to take care of my mother there, but here, there was no one to take care of my daughter and my granddaughter, so I talked to my sisters and they understood me. We are four siblings, three women and one man, all alive. Not my father, my father died already.

I think that the woman here develops more; she works and makes her own money. In Brazil it is more difficult because she's either a maid or she picks oranges in the fields. Here there are more jobs, more chances than in Brazil. I think that Lara has a better future here, in education. Both my daughter and my granddaughter have a better future here.

I come from a small town. I found it different here, of course; to leave a small town and come here, it's a lot different, but I adapted. It was April, three years ago. I did not find it bad; we dress warmly and go out. What I like best is going out to Boston. I love to stroll in Boston. I find it pretty. I already told Regina that someday we're going to live in Boston.

I am the youngest. I went to school but I did not get a diploma; no one would give [a woman] a diploma at that time. [My] parents did not care about it. I only reached fourth grade, no middle school . . . Many girls went to school to be a teacher. Not me. No one pushed me. I worked since I was ten. We worked in the fields: we planted tomatoes, cotton, rice. My father owned the land; he had a small farm. [What he made] was enough to maintain us. When I was thirteen, I moved to a town. I kept on working the land until I moved to the big city, Taquaritinga, then I started working as a maid. I got married at 19 and had three children . . . then we separated. Ten, twelve years have passed already; it was hard but I got over it.

For me it was very important to have come here: I learned a lot; I communicate better; I talk better; I grew up. I advise. . . . when I talk to my nephews, I tell them to come over: they only have to buy the air ticket because they have a place to stay. Over there, it's more difficult. We get monthly salaries, and it comes late and when the month is over, you have already spent it all.

Graciani

My name is Graciani Silva. I am from Brazil, from the state of Santa Catarina, [the city of] Urussanga, and I am 33. I came to the United States six years ago. The dream of the majority of Brazilians is to come here. I wanted to come here and do something that would change my life financially, something that would make it possible to change my life financially. In Brazil, I worked as a teacher. I taught biology. Although I was working in Brazil at the time, I was not satisfied with the salary I was earning, the kind of school I worked at, and also with the conditions of the city I lived in—it was a small town. Then a group of friends came here. I had graduated and had no goals; I decided to get some experience. Today, I realize that I was also looking for myself as a person. [. . .] I think that I needed to go far away from my country, from my family, and from people I lived with, to be able, in a certain away, to understand better all the things [that were happening to me].

When I arrived, the first thing that I felt was a big deception with this country, a huge deception, politically, how people live, the way [they live]. I had an idea of the American life, of people, of Americans in general. I think that it was the idea that was passed to us by the media. The political posture of Americans to have no commitment frustrated me, the ignorance, the lack of commitment to their own community, the idea that they are superior. I felt very discriminated against several times because I am an immigrant, a woman, because I came from South America. I did not give up, though; I decided to stay. I did not speak English. It was a big barrier because I had to take jobs that really didn't make me feel happy; I felt exploited and I had a lot of difficulties learning the language. I think that up to today it still is a problem. However, I decided to stay and build something for myself in terms of things that I believed in.

I wanted to study; I wanted to know about a new culture. I didn't stay just for the money; money was a part of it because it seemed to me that money was so easy. No way you wouldn't think of coming, although I knew it would be difficult in some aspects because I did not speak the language. It seemed, though, that money would fix it all. I knew I had to learn the language so I would be able to study, but things did not happen this way. The frustration with the financial side of it was big. The difficulties of finding a group of people with whom I had some affinities, mainly Brazilians . . .

. . . I changed a lot, there is no way that a person would leave her country and come back the same person. I don't believe this is possible. I think I changed: I am more mature and I grew up. Being lonely made me learn to live in a different way. I still have the same dreams I used to . . . I think that the Brazilian woman faces loneliness. She has to work hard and perform jobs she was not used to and the lack of possibility of having someone to look over the kids and have someone from the family to count on, the mother, the mother-in-law . . . In Brazil, we are for the family: it's the aunt, the mother, the mother-in-law. People do not have that here. Besides, the husband works eighty hours per week; it's a part-time husband: he will never have the ability to get home and the patience to talk, to make love, to do whatever. This situation stresses the relationship. On the other hand, I think that the Brazilian women [who are] coming to this country are changing the relationship in which she lives in—marriage—because she achieves a certain financial freedom which she did not have before. And I believe that many marriages work in Brazil because the woman has no alternative to leave her husband; she can't work, she is not a qualified worker. If she leaves her husband, how will she pay for rent? How will she maintain a child? And here, she is able to have a certain independence, financial emancipation, which gives her some strength to advocate for changes in the relationship. I believe that these changes make women stronger; they suffer a lot, but they feel they are able to say: "It's enough, I don't need your money anymore. If this relationship does not work I can try on my own." This does not mean it makes their lives easier, but I do think it decreases a bit the chains of slavery, which exist in a relationship based on money.

The language barrier was the major difficulty that I encountered here, and, I think, the question of illegality. I came and I went to work; I worked a lot in two, three places over the six-year-period I have been here. I worked in a company where people valued me in a certain way, not because I am a human being, but because I worked hard. I worked for two, three people. I was extremely organized. Despite that, I didn't speak English, but in a short amount of time I assimilated the job requirements and I produced a lot without talking, I did not even complain; I was the perfect worker. Today, I am conscious that I did the work of two men and that I was not able to complain. Instead, I was grateful to them for giving me a chance. They paid above minimum wage; it was a small company. Today, the majority of the employees are Brazilians, the company has grown and the treatment is very different. When I left the situation was unbearable, today exploitation is at a higher level, people work a lot but . . . they are underpaid, [and] they do not have a chance to do overtime. When I was there, I could put in any amount of hours I wanted and I was paid cash so I thought I was lucky and I was grateful for the situation . . . We end up receiving little because we do not believe we are capable. It's incredible. In Brazil, people are independent but here they do not have alternatives . . .

I think language was my worst problem, my worst enemy in this land. Because of the language barrier, I felt incapable of doing things and, therefore, I was dependent on someone who had been here for a while and could communicate. Today, I am married; it's a stable relationship and I am sure that if things come to an end it would be different, because today I feel I am capable. Today I do not feel as dependent as I felt before, I am able to go out alone. In the beginning, people become very vulnerable, dependent on each other, whoever it is, any stranger is welcome, any person who can translate, make a call . . .

. . . Women are the ones who suffer the most. They have been here for five, six years and they have never had a medical checkup and sometimes I take them to the doctor and after the exam they find out they have serious health problems and they had no idea. Then I refer them to other medical facilities, to places where someone speaks Portuguese and I tell them how to proceed so that next time they know where to go. Usually everybody who I take to the clinic, I refer to group therapy, [to a] psychologist, because people need this; many men are deeply depressed; they come to me, it's not my job, but what can I do? I know people who can help, so I send them to different health areas. Sometimes I think it is strange that men come to me, but sometimes they are in such difficult situations that they come. Women, they don't know where to go, what to do, when they are teenagers, when they are pregnant . . .

I am afraid of not adapting [if I return to Brazil]. I am afraid of the economic situation. I am afraid because I went through another experience and, in a certain way, to go back to Brazil, in many ways, is to step back. There is no way of going back and not stepping back, because you will miss out on many things that you have here. It's scary.

Maria Angélica

My name is Maria Angélica, I was born in São Paulo, and I am 45 years old ... How did I end up here [in the U.S.]? Well, I don't know if I ever had the intention of coming to live in the United States. I was living in Brazil and finishing college. I met a Swiss man and we fell in love. He went back to Switzerland and, a year later, I went to meet him to see whether it was or it wasn't [love]. It was. We got married and Martin decided that he wanted to pursue a career in international development, working with rural populations, poor populations and development. We moved; we traveled a lot.

[...] After five years the marriage was over and I knew that I was gay; I knew that I did not want to be with Martin or any other man. I wanted to be in a place where I could find out who I was in my new sexuality. I couldn't return to Brazil, where the family would suffocate me, nor could I remain in Africa, where I knew that I was unlikely to meet any other openly gay women. I decided that the United States would be the best place. I had friends here ... When I came here in 1988, I knew that I wanted to get divorced [...] and I knew I wanted to stay [in the U.S.] and be a nurse. [...] I had savings from my well-paid job, which I used to buy a house in Vermont and to put myself through nursing school. From the beginning, I knew I wanted to work with HIV and with AIDS. [...] I like to help people, I want them to have a voice and fight for what they believe in. [...] Besides, everybody who had AIDS was gay; everyone who worked with it also was gay. So, for me, it was easy. I entered a field where my being gay was neither too much nor too little; I was like everybody else. It was like black beans and rice ...

That is my experience. I don't know what it would be like to be gay in Brazil. I believe that I have changed a lot. At the same time, I also believe that it is crazy to say this because in my family no one—including my sister, my brother, and me—none of us three are very conformist or very much like everyone else. My sister is a film director and decided to be a single mother at a time when no one would be a single mother. She went to live in Trancoso [in Bahia, Brazil] when Trancoso was just a tiny town. I was the oldest; I was the first. I moved out and went to live in Switzerland. My brother abandoned it all—he was an engineer, had a good position—for a pizza place. I don't know what I would have been in Brazil, but I know I wouldn't have been Dona Maria home-maker, having a hairdo and getting manicured; that does not fit my family tradition. Of course, all of the moving and traveling provided me with more experiences of difference.

My relationship with the children didn't change; I mean it might have changed when I discovered I was gay. I had a relationship with my children, which was like . . . was cool. [. . .] I think that they have accepted [me] because all three bring friends home. It even got to a point where I wanted them to invite fewer friends! They wouldn't openly say "my mother is gay" but after two days in the house, they are teenagers, they figure it out. Not that we kiss or hug or anything but children are not stupid, they notice the relationship, the companionship. If someone asks my children if I am gay, they will say that I am. I believe we have a good relationship; my children are good.

Each day, less and less, I think of going back to Brazil. Before, I thought that I had my whole life ahead of me and that part of my reason for not going back was fear, fear of confronting Brazil. Here, I am a foreigner; no one knows me. Today, I think that there is more to it. Going back to Brazil means facing people who think they have the right to impose their views on me, but who do not know me because I have been away since I was 21. I am 45 now. I have more than half of my life lived outside Brazil. If I go back, I want to have a good job, a job that could earn me a living. Here, I am a nurse. What does it mean to be a nurse in Brazil? Can a nurse make a living? I don't know if I would want to live there, even with the same freedom I enjoy [here], living with Cindy. And go through all of that and end up in São Paulo? No, thank you very much, I am not going back to São Paulo *nem morta* (not even if I drop dead). God willing, I am not going back. I was there last year for vacation, half of it I spent in traffic, I swear to God, my three week vacation, so hard earned, I spent half of it discussing whether we would take the Paulista [Avenue] or Brasil [Avenue]. It's impossible. If I go back to Brazil, when I am an old woman, I want to go to Natal. I have been there only once, but it's there that I want to live.

I was married for seventeen years and I always knew that I was different. I did not know how, but I knew I wasn't normal, in the way I wanted to be . . . I didn't know how, I only knew I wasn't like everybody else. That made me feel sad as a girl because I wanted to be like everybody else: I wanted to be more Brazilian; I wanted my hair to be curlier; I wanted to have smaller breasts and bigger *bunda* (butt). I read more than everybody else; I didn't have a boyfriend and I was dying to have a boyfriend because all the girls had one. One day, when I was eighteen, I caught a boy because I wanted to kiss him; I had never kissed a boy.

When I discovered I was gay, I decided I was going to have an affair with a woman I knew was gay. I got on my motorcycle and went to her house. She was pretty and we began an affair. To my surprise, it wasn't an affair. I got into it with my soul, my heart, everything. And I thought to myself: "Know what? I feel alive, my feelings are much more vibrant now than over all these years." It was a discovery that gave me great happiness. If you can only know how proud I was to find out that there was something that made me feel more comfortable with who I am. I did not change a thing, I was the same person, but I had more inner peace. It was good. I did not create a drama. I wasn't sad. On the contrary, I wanted to tell everyone. I wrote a letter to the ten people I loved the most: "I am gay."

Growing up, homosexuality was inconceivable in my (middle class) social environment. I didn't know anybody [who was gay]. My father became furious when the topic was mentioned. Gay men were mentioned, but women? Unthinkable! When I was 14 years old, I saw two women dressed as men, imitating Roberto Carlos, with X jeans, gloss in the hair, hands in their pockets, and I thought: "My God! They didn't look like women! What an awful sight!" When I married, I started to grow. I came to know myself more, and maybe, being far from home, I had more freedom to explore something else.

I have always been very open in theory, always thought that sex can be good with anyone. I didn't know that the nature of my feelings [for women] would be very different than those I had for a man. I found more of a level that was mine. I see myself more physically, emotionally and intellectually. I feel more comfortable, totally, as a woman. I didn't grow up with the freedom to explore [homosexuality]; I didn't even consider it . . . when I left [my home environment] I found more liberty with less [surveillance] from the community. I discovered less fear. I cared less. I felt fewer expectations from people who are not "my people." Martin and I were indeed going to split . . . our marriage had already ended (it didn't end because of the discovery). There was always something in me, in the way I'd always thought I was different. There were other things, but one of them was homosexuality. I lived with someone I didn't want to live with. Homosexuality for me is much more than the mind, and it's not the sex, it's the interaction that's better with women than with men.

Of course I've been discriminated against. I don't consider myself a masculine type, a biker type, but I have heard people talking, discriminating, shouting in the street. I see it, but at the same time it doesn't affect me much. I experience it in the same way that I experience [being discriminated against because I] am not American, or because I have an accent: it makes me mad, but I have a certain security in who I am.

[Being gay] affects me more in Brazil, precisely because of my family's surveillance. I haven't lived there long enough to open all the doors. I feel I don't give Cindy the position she deserves [as my partner]. This bothers me a lot. I am less coherent with my life [there]. It's a problem. I haven't had a conversation about it with my parents. When I was younger I didn't know who I was. I don't want to blame my parents. I won't return [to Brazil] because my life is here. Sometimes I do feel like it. But I have established myself professionally here; there, I'd start from scratch. Would Cindy go along? So there's a certain ambivalence: If I had the opportunity? If she wanted to. . . .

I am open with everyone [but] I am afraid of hurting [my parents]. None of them [friends, relatives] is more important to me than my relationship with Cindy. My parents are the only ones for whom I care as much as I care for Cindy. I am so scared of hurting him [my father]. I do not live there, and I do not want to drop the bomb and walk out. I consider myself totally normal and accept myself. Because it's not a problem for me, I try to not make it a problem for anyone else.

I think two things are very important: we cannot lose sight of who we [Brazilians] are, but I also think it is important that our vision include the fact that we are living in another country and that we have to accept more the host country. I also think that it is very important that we learn the [English] language. It is very important that we try to understand and to integrate but without forgetting who we are.

Conclusions

The interviews presented here touch on some of the most important recent changes in gender roles and sexuality in Brazilian society both in Brazil and in the United States. Brazilian immigrant women are redefining their sense of self in the face of new values and knowledge. The interviews bring together considerations of what it is to be a Brazilian, a woman and an immigrant in the United States, and how the experiences of Brazilian women immigrants is changing gender roles and cultural values in Brazil.

Sexuality, machismo, and femininity are central to the Brazilian culture. As Gustavo Ribeiro, a Brazilian anthropologist, points out, the Brazilian national identity abroad is reduced to "its most stereotypical expressions": carnival, *feijoada*, *capoeira*, samba, soccer, and g-string bikinis (cited in Beserra). Many of these stereotypes have roots at home. For example, rural Brazilians often stereotype urban Brazilian urban as *livre*, *fácil*, and *gostosa* (free, easy, and good in bed). A friend of mine, who recently relocated from an urban setting to a smaller city in the southern coast of Rio de Janeiro told me how uneasy she feels living by herself. As an urban woman, having been stereotyped this way, she feels vulnerable. She gets a *cantada* (a compliment) from any man she meets, from the manager of the restaurant where she eats lunch to the broker who helped her find her new place. She has been advised not to "publicize" that she lives alone. Instead, she should tell people that she lives with her daughter. "They think we (women) cannot survive without a man in the house and in bed," she concludes angrily.

A country the size of Brazil, with large rural and urban areas, cannot and does not produce one model or one standard social behavior. In much of rural Brazil, marriages are seen as a financial security voucher for the woman, men are expected to be the breadwinner, and their extramarital affairs are accepted, almost expected. But as draught, economic hardship, lack of job opportunities, even the local culture lead to male migration, women in rural Brazil (where there is approximately one man to every thirteen women) often find themselves alone with no models for an alternative to their roles as procreators and men's caretakers. In contrast, in big cities women have more access to information and social behavior is regulated differently. Relationships are likely to be established on the basis of love and men are not seen as the sole breadwinners. Indeed, since women are strong competitors in the job market, their incomes give them a voice and apparent equality. On the other hand, in urban areas extramarital affairs are seen as disrespectful and humiliating to both men and women, and are therefore much less tolerated.

Contrary to their friends, mothers, and sisters in Brazil, who often do not expect equality from their husbands, Brazilian women who immigrate to the United States see in the "land of opportunities," and not in their husbands, the source of their financial security or the promise of a better life. In Brazil the ideal of femininity is associated with weakness, fragility, naivety, and dependency; and cleaning, cooking, and washing are identified as the female domain. In the United States, Brazilian women easily perform such tasks as changing a flat tire or a light bulb or carrying shopping bags, tasks that in Brazil are perceived as "inappropriate behavior" for a woman. At the same time, many women, such as Graciani and Angela, must contend not only with linguistic, ethnic, and racial discrimination, but also with gender discrimination in the United States: "When I arrived," says Graciani, "the first thing that I felt was a big deception with this country, a huge deception, politically, how people live . . . I felt discriminated against because I am an immigrant, a woman, because I came from South America."

As they adapt to the new culture and society, Brazilian women have to confront questions such as "What makes a woman?" "What is my role in the family?" "Who am I?" Depending upon their different backgrounds—whether they lived in an urban area, had a college degree, had experience working outside of the home—immigrant women face different issues. For all of the women interviewed, however, gender roles change with immigration, and the disruption of established gender roles and the belief systems that accompany them creates unexpected conflicts in the family structure. For many women, being away from family interference and social pressure, and having to deal with different social pressures (finding work, learning how to drive, being the head of the household) were eye opening and led them to redefine their idea of who they were. The majority thought over their relationships with their husbands and negotiated new boundaries within their marriage. Some marriages come out fortified: says Ana Lucia, "I am at peace. I even believe that in terms of strengthening the marriage, the family, I think that it was important that we lived very alone . . . without family interference in our business." Others, however, fall apart, as Cátia explains: "Women here are split. Certain couples, they get here and the wife begins to notice that the husband she had in Brazil is not the man she dreamed of. She changes—I changed . . . Certain men never change, they keep their macho mind, and what happens? Separation. Many couples come here and separate, because the husband does not accept certain things and does not collaborate at home."

Immigrant women often perceive men as changing more slowly than they do and having a hard time with the new women that they find in their homes. Women quickly realize that their role in the family is as big or bigger than their husband's, and they want to be treated equally. They want to have the same rights as men to make decisions, to make friends, to get help with household chores. They want their individuality as they start to develop their new identities. As Angela says,

"Women become more independent here. They grow; they do more. [...] Here women do not have to be dependent on their husbands . . . because the husband works, you have to take care of yourself . . . This helps a lot for a woman to become independent. She communicates, she brings out many things. . . . she improves much more."

Frequently, we do not realize the full extent to which we have changed or incorporated U.S. cultural values until we go back to our old environment. A friend of mine who has lived in the United States for more than ten years occasionally spends time in Mexico City on business. She confided to me how uncomfortable she feels doing things by herself in the Mexican capital: "Men are always following me, saying *gracinhas*, expecting me to fall into their arms. I go straight to the hotel after work rather than to a bar, a movie theatre, or restaurant as I usually do in Boston." Would she feel that way had she remained in Brazil? Probably not. In Brazil and in Mexico, *gracinhas* (compliments) addressed to women on the streets are not necessarily perceived as offensive, but rather as an acknowledgment of the woman's beauty and the man's desire for her. Throughout Latin America, it is believed that *cantar* (to comment loudly or publicly on someone's good looks) does not humiliate or diminish a woman as a human being, but instead values her. It is also proof that the woman is desired. It is not that one or the other culture is "better" or even necessarily or absolutely treats women better, but that the codes and customs of gender relations diverge. Once they have adjusted to life in the United States, Brazilian immigrant women also relate differently to life in Brazil.

This chapter also raises questions of homosexuality, which in Brazil remains little discussed in the larger society. Despite important gains, homosexuals are still seen and treated in Brazil as weirdoes, sick people in need of treatment. Although Brazilian society has made advances in accepting homosexuals in the context of family and society, denial remains the rule. Maria Angélica's story is typical: had she remained in Brazil, it is most likely that she would still be struggling with her sexuality. The story of another acquaintance illustrates how hard it is for Brazilians to accept or disclose that they have a lesbian or a gay man in the family. A childhood friend revealed to me that one of her sisters had divorced her husband and started living with a woman. She told the story as if her sister were "going through a phase." When, recently, she asked me if I thought that the word lesbian would apply to her sister, she quickly offered her own response: "I don't think so; she is not a lesbian, she just believes she is; she has been married." My own experience in the United States has also affected my perceptions of sexuality, and I see my friend's difficulty in accepting her sister's lesbianism with sadness.

In conclusion, I want to share with readers my feeling towards the women I interviewed. These women are brave; they are my heroines. Despite adversity, they picked themselves up and moved on. They inspire me. Maria Angélica's openness about her sexuality is remarkably spontaneous, as are other women's openness about their relationships with their husbands and families. As they confront themselves within their new culture and in another language, they explore their roles as women and immigrants, their family values, and their sexuality in creative ways. These women are deeply changing the way Brazilians look at gender roles, family values, and sexuality.

Works Cited

Agosin, Marjorie. "I Invented a Country." *Women in Exile.* Ed. Mahnaz Afkhami. Charlottesville: University Press of Virginia, 1994. 140–149.

Beserra, Bernadete. "Brazilian Immigrants in the United States. Cultural Imperialism and Social Class. LFB Scholarly Publishing LLC, 2003. 214.

Burnett, James. "Global Village: Rio Life." *Boston Magazine* May 2003: 110.

Costa, Albertina de Oliveira, Moraes, Maria Teresa, Marzola, Norma, and Lima, Valentina da Rocha. "Memórias das Mulheres do Exílio." *Paz e Terra* II (1980): 28.

De Jesus, Sonia Melo. *Cleaning Under the Rug: Brazilian Housecleaner Immigrant Women in Boston, 1980–2000,* final project for Master's Degree completion, American Studies Department, University of Massachusetts, Boston, 2003.

DeBiaggi, Sylvia Duarte Dantas. *Changing Gender Roles: Brazilian Immigrant Families in the U.S.* New York: LFB Scholarly Publishing, 2002.

Fleischer, Soraya Resende. *Passando a América a Limpo: O Trabalho de Housecleaners Brasileiras em Boston, Massachusetts.* São Paulo: Annablume, 2002.

Jones-Correa, Michael. "Wanting In: Latin American Immigrant Women and the Turn to Electoral Politics." *Between Two Nations: The Political Predicament of Latinos in New York City.* London: Cornell University Press, 1998. 169–188.

Margolis, Maxine L. *An Invisible Minority: Brazilians in New York City.* Boston: Allyn and Bacon, 1998.

_____. *Little Brazil: An Ethnography of Brazilian Immigrants in New York City.* Princeton: Princeton University Press, 1994.

Martes, Ana Cristina Braga. "Brasileiros nos Estados Unidos: Um estudo sobre imigrantes em Massachusetts." São Paulo: Paz e Terra, 2000.

_____. *The Yankee Group Report. Latin American and Caribbean Communications* 4.5 (1998).

Messias, DeAnne Karen Hilfinge. "Narratives of Transnational Migration, Work, and Health: The Lived Experiences of Brazilian Women in the United States." Diss. University of California, San Francisco, 1997.

Nunes, Vicente. "Contas Externas: Brasileiros no exterior mandam mais dinheiro." *Correio Braziliense* , February 25, 2001: 18.

Paiva, Paulo. "Remessas ajudam nas contas do país: Com dois milhões de brasileiros no exterior, tranferências unilateriais atingiram US$ 1,8 bilhão em 2000." http://www.mre.gov/acs/clipping/arquivos2001/gm0813a.htm.

Sales, Teresa. *Brasilerios Longe de Casa.* São Paulo: Cortes Editora, 1999

Souza, Heloisa. "Brazilian Neighborhoods in Boston." *The Brazilian Monthly* I.8–10 (1992): 1.

_____. "Brazilians in Boston Before and After 9/11." *What About the Other Latinos.* ORCLAS Conference. Cambridge, Mass., April 5, 2002.

_____. "Language Loss and Language Gain in the Brazilian Community: The Role of Schools and Families," "Lifting Every Voice: Pedagogy and Politics of Bilingualism." *Harvard Education Review* 44.1 (2000): 7–20.

Yi, Daniel. "The State; Brazilians Turning to Mexican Smugglers, U.S. Officials say; Security: Authorities believe many are enticed by groups in their native country that collaborate with traffickers south of the U.S. border." *The Los Angeles Times,* August 23, 2002: B10.

Notes

1   In interviews with Brazilian women immigrants in the Bay State area, DeAnne Messias states that "Faced with different social, cultural and physical environments migrants often experience feeling of disconnectedness" (27).

2   In 1997, through a small grant from the Somerville Arts Council and the Massachusetts Cultural Council, I published 30 copies of *Retrato em Branco e Preto: Narrativas de mulheres brasileiras imigrantes na área da grande Boston, 1995–1996* (In Black and White, Brazilian Women Immigrants in the Boston Area, 1995–1996: An Oral History Project). Between 2001 and 2002, through another small grant from the same two agencies,

I tape recorded interviews with five other women. These interviews have not been published.

3 Contrary to Garcia Castro's findings in Michael Jones-Correa, "Wanting In: Latin American Immigrant Women and the Turn to Electoral Politics" (181), many Brazilian women in the Boston area learn English faster than men. One reason for this, the author believes, is the fact that women take leadership to resolve all family matters, such as children's school registration, parents' conferences, meetings, health care, among others.

4 It has been called to my attention that some husbands make fun of their wives' participation in the Brazilian Women's Group by saying that they wanted to be in the group so they can see what "these bunch of women do and talk about." Some have expressed their dislike that their wives spend more time in the group than with them. Others sounded jealous of the time their wives spent with group members.

INDEX

INDEX